PSAT/NMSQT®
Prep
2019

PSAT/NMSQT®
Prep
2019

PUBLISHING

New York

PSAT/NMSQT® is a registered trademark of the College Board and the National Merit Scholarship Corporation, which were not involved in the production of, and do not endorse, this product.

S

PSAT/NMSQT® is a registered trademark of the College Board and the National Merit Scholarship Corporation which were not involved in the production of, and do not endorse, this product.

This publication is designed to provide accurate and authoritative information in regard to the subject matter covered. It is sold with the understanding that the publisher is not engaged in rendering legal, accounting, or other professional service. If legal advice or other expert assistance is required, the services of a competent professional should be sought.

© 2018 by Kaplan, Inc.

Published by Kaplan Publishing, a division of Kaplan, Inc.
750 Third Avenue
New York, NY 10017

Printed in the United States of America

10 9 8 7 6 5 4 3 2 1

ISBN-13: 978-1-5062-3521-9

Kaplan Publishing books are available at special quantity discounts to use for sales promotions, employee premiums, or educational purposes. For more information or to purchase books, please call the Simon & Schuster Special Sales Department at 1-866-506-1949.

Table of Contents

Additional resources available at www.kaptest.com/psatbookresources

Your Road to College

WHAT TO DO WHEN

Kaplan is here to help guide you on your path to college. This timeline will help you navigate college admissions testing with confidence.

Junior Year											Summer	Senior Year		
Oct	Nov	Dec	Jan	Feb	Mar	Apr	May	Jun	Jul	Aug	Sept	Oct	Nov	Dec
Take the PSAT		Take the SAT and/or ACT 1–3 times (depending on your performance and your goal score) Take SAT Subject Tests as needed										Finish testing	Early application deadlines	Finalize regular decision applications

TAKE THE PSAT

Check with your counselor for your testing date. In addition to providing excellent practice for the SAT, taking the PSAT may qualify you for recognition as a National Merit® semifinalist, which is the first step on the journey to a National Merit Scholarship.

TAKE THE SAT AND/OR ACT

Both the SAT and ACT are nationally administered, standardized tests that help colleges evaluate your application and see how prepared you are for college success. Start by taking practice tests to see if you tend to score better on one or the other. Both tests are accepted by all four-year colleges, so you can choose the test that is best for you.

By taking the time to study for these tests, you will improve your chances of achieving your goal score on your first try. That said, many students find it helpful to take each test two or even three times, so be sure to plan accordingly.

TAKE SAT SUBJECT TESTS AS NEEDED

The majority of colleges do not require SAT Subject Tests. However, many of the country's most competitive schools either require students to submit two or more SAT Subject Test scores or strongly recommend that students take SAT Subject Tests. Be sure to research the policies of the colleges you are considering applying to; some may accept ACT test scores as a substitute for SAT Subject Test scores.

FINISH TESTING

It's important to complete all of your college admissions testing in plenty of time to send your scores to schools as part of the application process. If you are not planning to submit early applications, you can continue testing throughout the calendar year, with the December test dates in your senior year as your final options.

EARLY APPLICATION DEADLINES

There are two types of early applications: early decision and early action. Submitting either type of early application is entirely optional. If you have a first-choice college, applying early decision can increase your chances of being accepted. Note, however, that applying early decision constitutes a binding contract: if you are accepted, you will have to attend the college to which you applied. Unlike early decision applications, early action applications do not require you to commit to attending a school upon acceptance and do not necessarily increase your acceptance chances. Both types of early applications are helpful because you will be able to learn sooner if you are accepted.

The most common deadlines for early action and early decision are in November, so don't miss out! You must have taken your final ACT by September and your final SAT by October to have those scores qualify as part of your application.

FINALIZE REGULAR DECISION APPLICATIONS

Most standard applications are due at the very beginning of January of your senior year, so you must finish all testing by December.

Introduction to the PSAT

The first step to achieving PSAT success is to learn about the structure of the test and why it's so important for your future. The PSAT, like any standardized test, is predictable. The more comfortable you are with the test structure, the more confidently you will approach each question type, thus maximizing your score.

PSAT STRUCTURE

The PSAT is 2 hours and 45 minutes long and is made up mostly of multiple-choice questions that test two subject areas: Math and Evidence-Based Reading and Writing. The latter is broken into a Reading Test and a Writing & Language Test.

Test	Allotted Time (Min.)	Question Count
Reading	60	47
Writing & Language	35	44
Math	70	48
Total	165	139

PSAT SCORING

PSAT scoring can be pretty complex. You will receive a score ranging from 10 to 40 on each of the three tests (Reading, Writing & Language, and Math) as well as a score ranging from 160 to 760 for Evidence-Based Reading and Writing and for Math. Your overall PSAT score will range from 320 to 1520 and is calculated by adding your two area scores together.

In addition to your overall scores, you will receive subscores that provide a deeper analysis of your PSAT performance. The PSAT also gives you a percentile ranking, which allows you to compare your scores with those of other high school juniors who took the test. For example, a student with a percentile of 63 has earned a score better than 63 percent of that year's test takers.

WHERE AND WHEN TO TAKE THE PSAT

The PSAT is offered every year in mid-October. It is administered at your high school, not at a testing center. Homeschooled students can sign up at the nearest local high school. Most high schools administer the exam on a Saturday; some offer it on a Wednesday. Some high schools recommend that their sophomores take the test for additional practice, but sophomores who take the PSAT are not eligible to qualify for the National Merit Scholarship unless they are in an accelerated program and are preparing to graduate the following year. However, some schools will administer the test to their students only once (at the beginning of junior year). If this is the case, sophomores wanting to take the PSAT need to get permission from their guidance counselors.

WHY TAKE THE PSAT?

The PSAT/NMSQT stands for the Preliminary SAT/National Merit Scholarship Qualifying Test. It has three main functions:

1. The PSAT is excellent practice for the SAT. Although shorter than the SAT, it contains the same types of math, reading, and writing questions. It does not, however, contain an essay component. The PSAT also measures your score against those of your classmates and peers across the country, just as the SAT does.

2. Taking the PSAT also gives you a chance to qualify for several scholarship programs, most notably the National Merit Scholarship Program. Aside from the possibility of receiving tuition for college, the National Merit Scholarship program gives you recognition that is an impressive addition to your college applications.

3. The PSAT can help you stand out to colleges. Many schools purchase lists of high-scoring students and encourage these students to apply. A great score on the PSAT could get you noticed by colleges and earn you small perks such as meals during visits and waived application fees.

The top 50,000 scorers on the PSAT are recognized by the National Merit program and sent letters of commendation. More than 10,000 of these students share more than $47 million in National Merit Scholarship money. Only juniors who take the PSAT are eligible for National Merit Scholarships. The top 16,000 scorers become semifinalists, and approximately 15,000 semifinalists become finalists. Finally, almost 8,500 National Merit finalists receive National Merit Scholarships, with each award being up to $2,500 a year toward a college education. Many high scorers who don't receive National Merit Scholarships are awarded merit scholarships from the schools to which they apply based on their high scores. Whether you qualify as a commended student, a semifinalist, a finalist, or a full-fledged National Merit Scholar, it's definitely worth noting this achievement on your college applications.

For more information on the National Merit Scholarships and Special Scholarships, visit **www.nationalmerit.org**.

THE PSAT MATH TEST

The PSAT Math Test is broken down into a calculator section and a no-calculator section. Questions across the sections consist of multiple-choice, student-produced response (Grid-in), and more comprehensive multi-part math questions.

	Calculator Section	No-Calculator Section	Total
Duration (Minutes)	45	25	70
Multiple-Choice	27	13	40
Grid-In	4	4	8
Total	31	17	48

The PSAT Math Test is divided into four content areas: Heart of Algebra, Problem Solving and Data Analysis, Passport to Advanced Math, and Additional Topics in Math.

PSAT Math Test Content Area Distribution	
Heart of Algebra (16 questions)	Analyzing and fluently solving equations and systems of equations; creating expressions, equations, and inequalities to represent relationships between quantities and to solve problems; rearranging and interpreting formulas
Problem Solving and Data Analysis (16 questions)	Creating and analyzing relationships using ratios, proportions, percentages, and units; describing relationships shown graphically; summarizing qualitative and quantitative data
Passport to Advanced Math (14 questions)	Rewriting expressions using their structure; creating, analyzing, and fluently solving quadratic and higher-order equations; purposefully manipulating polynomials to solve problems
Additional Topics in Math (2 questions)	Making area and volume calculations in context; investigating lines, angles, triangles, and circles using theorems

A few math questions might look like something you'd expect to see on a science or history test. These "crossover" questions are designed to test your ability to use math in real-world scenarios. There are a total of 14 "crossover" questions that will contribute to subscores that span multiple tests. Seven of the questions will contribute to the Analysis in Science subscore, and seven will contribute to the Analysis in History/Social Studies subscore.

Finally, note that each multiple-choice and Grid-in math question is worth 1 point, regardless of difficulty level.

THE PSAT READING TEST

The PSAT Reading Test will focus on your comprehension and reasoning skills when presented with challenging extended prose passages taken from a variety of content areas.

PSAT Reading Test Overview	
Timing	60 minutes
Questions	47 passage-based multiple-choice questions
Passages	4 single passages and 1 set of paired passages
Passage Length	500–750 words per passage or passage set

Passages will draw from U.S. and World Literature, History/Social Studies, and Science. One set of History/Social Studies or Science passages will be paired. History/Social Studies and Science passages can also be accompanied by graphical representations of data such as charts, graphs, tables, and so on.

Reading Test Passage Types	
U.S. and World Literature	1 passage with 9 questions
History/Social Studies	2 passages or 1 passage and 1 paired-passage set with 9–10 questions each
Science	2 passages or 1 passage and 1 paired-passage set with 9–10 questions each

The multiple-choice questions for each passage will be arranged in order from the more general to the more specific so that you can actively engage with the entire passage before answering questions about details.

Skills Tested by Reading Test Questions	
Information and Ideas	Close reading, citing textual evidence, determining central ideas and themes

Skills Tested by Reading Test Questions	
Summarizing	Understanding relationships, interpreting words and phrases in context
Rhetoric	Analyzing word choice, assessing overall text structure, assessing part–whole relationships, analyzing point of view, determining purpose, analyzing arguments
Synthesis	Analyzing multiple texts, analyzing quantitative information

THE PSAT WRITING & LANGUAGE TEST

The PSAT Writing & Language Test will focus on your ability to revise and edit text from a range of content areas.

PSAT Writing & Language Test Overview	
Timing	35 minutes
Questions	44 passage-based multiple-choice questions
Passages	4 single passages with 11 questions each
Passage Length	400–450 words per passage

The PSAT Writing & Language Test will contain four single passages, one from each of the following subject areas: Careers, Humanities, History/Social Studies, and Science.

Writing & Language Passage Types	
Careers	Hot topics in "major fields of work" such as information technology and healthcare
Humanities	Arts and letters
History/Social Studies	Discussion of historical or social sciences topics such as anthropology, communication studies, economics, education, human geography, law, linguistics, political science, psychology, and sociology
Science	Exploration of concepts, findings, and discoveries in the natural sciences including Earth science, biology, chemistry, and physics

Passages will also vary in the type of text. A passage can be an argument, an informative or explanatory text, or a nonfiction narrative.

Writing & Language Passage Text Type Distribution	
Argument	1–2 passages
Informative/Explanatory Text	1–2 passages
Nonfiction Narrative	1 passage

Some passages and/or questions will refer to one or more informational graphics that represent data. Questions associated with these graphical representations will ask you to revise and edit the passage based on the data presented in the graphic.

The most prevalent question format on the PSAT Writing & Language Test will ask you to choose the best of three alternatives to an underlined portion of the passage or to decide that the current version is the best option. You will be asked to improve the development, organization, and diction in the passages to ensure they conform to conventional standards of English grammar, usage, and style.

Skills Tested by Writing & Language Test Questions	
Expression of Ideas (24 questions)	Development, organization, and effective language use
Standard English Conventions (20 questions)	Sentence structure, conventions of usage, and conventions of punctuation

TEST-TAKING STRATEGIES

You have already learned about the overall structure of the PSAT as well as the structure of the three tests it entails: Reading, Writing & Language, and Math. The strategies outlined in this section can be applied to any of these tests.

The PSAT is different from the tests you are used to taking in school. The good news is that you can use the PSAT's particular structure to your advantage.

For example, on a test given in school, you probably go through the questions in order. You spend more time on the harder questions than on the easier ones because harder questions are usually worth more points. You probably often show your work because your teacher tells you that how you approach a question is as important as getting the correct answer.

This approach is not optimal for the PSAT. On the PSAT, you benefit from moving around within a section if you come across tough questions, because the harder questions are worth the same number of points as the easier questions. It doesn't matter how you arrive at the correct answer—only that you bubble in the correct answer choice.

STRATEGY #1: TRIAGING THE TEST

You do not need to complete questions on the PSAT in order. Every student has different strengths and should attack the test with those strengths in mind. Your main objective on the PSAT should be to score as many points as you can. While approaching questions out of order may seem counter-intuitive, it is a surefire way to achieve your best score.

Just remember, you can skip around within each section, but you cannot work on a section other than the one you've been instructed to work on.

To triage the test effectively, do the following:

- First, work through all the easy questions that you can do quickly. Skip questions that are hard or time-consuming.

- For the Reading and Writing & Language Tests, start with the passage you find most manageable and work toward the one you find most challenging. You do not need to go in order.

- Second, work through the questions that are doable but time-consuming.

- Third, work through the hard questions.

- If you run out of time, pick a Letter of the Day for remaining questions.

A Letter of the Day is an answer choice letter (A, B, C, or D) that you choose before Test Day to select for questions you guess on.

STRATEGY #2: ELIMINATION

Even though there is no penalty for an incorrect answer on the PSAT, elimination is still a crucial strategy. If you can determine that one or more answer choices are definitely incorrect, you can increase your chances of getting the correct answer by paring the selection down.

To eliminate answer choices, do the following:

- Read each answer choice.

- Cross out the answer choices that are incorrect.

- Remember: there is no wrong-answer penalty, so take your best guess.

STRATEGY #3: GUESSING

Each question on the PSAT has four answer choices and no wrong-answer penalty. That means if you have no idea how to approach a question, you have a 25 percent chance of randomly choosing the correct answer. Even though there's a 75 percent chance of selecting the incorrect answer, you won't lose any points for doing so. The worst that can happen on the PSAT is that you'll earn zero points on a question, which means you should *always* at least take a guess, even when you have no idea what to do.

When guessing on a question, do the following:

- Always try to strategically eliminate answer choices before guessing.

- If you run out of time, or have no idea what a question is asking, pick a Letter of the Day.

COMMON TESTING MYTHS

Since its inception in 1971, the PSAT/NMSQT has gone through various revisions, but it has always been an integral part of helping high school students qualify for various scholarships. As a result of its significance and the changes it has undergone, a number of rumors and myths have circulated about the exam. In this section, we'll dispel some of the most common ones. As always, you can find the most up-to-date information about the redesigned PSAT at the College Board website (**www.collegeboard.org/delivering-opportunity/redesigned-psat-nmsqt**).

Myth: Colleges use PSAT scores to make admissions decisions.

Fact: Nothing could be further from the truth. When you take the PSAT, your scores are provided to a variety of organizations, including the National Merit Scholarship Corporation, that offer scholarships based on students' needs, merits, and backgrounds. Colleges can opt to receive lists of high-scoring PSAT students to target them with advertising. In short, a great score on the PSAT can help you get noticed by top colleges, but a terrible score won't have an adverse impact on your admissions decision.

Myth: There is a penalty for incorrect answers on the PSAT to discourage guessing.

Fact: While this statement was true a few years ago, it is no longer true. Older versions of the PSAT had a wrong-answer penalty so that students who guessed on questions would not have an advantage over students who left questions blank. This penalty has been removed; make sure you never leave a PSAT question blank!

Myth: Answer choice C is most likely to be the correct answer.

Fact: This rumor has roots in human psychology. Apparently, when people such as high school teachers, for example, design an exam, they have a slight bias toward answer choice C when assigning correct answers. While humans do write PSAT questions, a computer randomizes the distribution of correct choices; statistically, therefore, each answer choice is equally likely to be the correct answer.

Myth: **The PSAT is just like the SAT.**

Fact: The PSAT is a valuable tool to help you prepare for the SAT. However, there are important differences between the two exams. First, the PSAT is shorter than the SAT in terms of timing and the number of questions. Second, the PSAT does not include an essay section. Finally, you'll take the PSAT at your high school and not an established testing center. Most students find that their PSAT experience helps get them ready for the SAT, but remember that taking the PSAT should form only a small part of your SAT preparation.

Myth: **The PSAT is just like another test in school.**

Fact: While the PSAT covers some of the same content as your high school math, literature, and English classes, it also presents concepts in ways that are fundamentally different. While you might be able to answer a math question in a number of different ways on an algebra test, the PSAT places a heavy emphasis on working through questions as quickly and efficiently as possible.

Myth: **You have to get all the questions correct to get a perfect score.**

Fact: Many students have reported missing several questions on the PSAT and being pleasantly surprised to receive perfect scores. Their experience is not atypical; usually, you can miss a few questions and still get a coveted perfect score. The makers of the PSAT use a technique called scaling to ensure that a PSAT score conveys the same information from year to year, so you might be able to miss a couple more questions on a slightly harder PSAT exam and miss fewer questions on an easier PSAT exam and get the same scores. Keep a positive attitude throughout the PSAT, and in many cases, your scores will pleasantly surprise you.

Myth: **You can't prepare for the PSAT.**

Fact: You've already proven this myth false by buying this book. While the PSAT is designed to fairly test students, regardless of preparation, you can gain a huge advantage by familiarizing yourself with the structure and content of the exam. By working through the questions and practice tests available to you, you'll ensure that nothing on the PSAT catches you by surprise and that you do everything you can to maximize your score. Your Kaplan resources help you structure this practice in the most efficient way possible and provide you with helpful strategies and tips as well.

BOOK FEATURES

WELCOME TO KAPLAN!

Congratulations on taking this important step in your college admissions process! By studying with Kaplan, you'll maximize your score on the PSAT, a major factor in your overall college application.

Our experience shows that the greatest PSAT score increases result from active engagement in the preparation process. Kaplan will give you direction, focus your preparation, and teach you the specific skills and effective test-taking strategies you need to know for the PSAT. We will help you achieve your top performance on Test Day, but your effort is crucial. The more you invest in preparing for the PSAT, the greater your chances of achieving your target score and getting into your top-choice college.

Are you registered for the PSAT? Kaplan cannot register you for the official PSAT. If you have not already registered for the upcoming PSAT, talk to your high school guidance counselor or visit the College Board's website at **www.collegeboard.org** to register online and for information on registration deadlines, test sites, accommodations for students with disabilities, and fees.

The PSAT is administered on only two days in mid-October. Therefore, students should be registered well in advance of the test dates. Your high school guidance counselor may also have more information about registering for the PSAT. Homeschooled students can contact the guidance office of a local high school to make arrangements to take the exam at that school.

PRACTICE TESTS

Kaplan's practice tests are just like the actual PSAT. By taking a practice exam, you will prepare yourself for the actual Test Day experience. There are two practice tests included in this book. You can also download free practice tests from the College Board's website.

EXTRA PRACTICE

You need to reinforce what you learn in each chapter by consistently practicing the Kaplan Methods and Strategies. Each chapter contains a section called "On Your Own" that features additional practice questions to reinforce the concepts explained in that chapter. These questions are great practice for the real PSAT. Answers and Explanations are provided in the back of the book.

SMARTPOINTS

Each chapter contains a breakdown of SmartPoints. By studying the information released by the College Board, Kaplan has been able to determine how often certain topics are likely to show up on the PSAT, and therefore how many points these topics are worth on Test Day. If you master a given topic, you can expect to earn the corresponding number of SmartPoints on Test Day.

DIGITAL RESOURCES

To access your online resources:

1. Go to **kaptest.com/booksonline**.

2. Follow the on-screen instructions. Have this book available.

Join a Live Online Event

Kaplan's PSAT Live Online sessions are interactive, instructor-led prep lessons that you can participate in from anywhere you have Internet access.

PSAT Live Online sessions are held in our state-of-the-art visual classroom: actual lessons in real time, just like a physical classroom experience. Interact with your teacher using audio, chat, whiteboards, polling, and screen-sharing functionality. And just like courses at Kaplan centers, PSAT Live Online sessions are led by top Kaplan instructors.

To register for a PSAT Live Online event, visit **www.kaptest.com/PSAT/enroll**. From here you can view all of our PSAT course offerings—from prep courses to tutoring to free events.

PSAT Live Online events are scheduled to take place throughout the year. Please check the registration page with dates and times.

PSAT Practice Test

As part of your online resources, you have access to an additional full-length practice test. We recommend you complete this practice test after having gone through the contents of the book. After completing the practice test, you'll receive a detailed online score report. Use this to help you focus and review the sections in the book that pertain to your greatest opportunities for improvement.

PART ONE

Math

Heart of Algebra

BY THE END OF THIS UNIT, YOU WILL BE ABLE TO:

1. Apply the Kaplan Method for Math to Math questions on the PSAT
2. Solve linear equations and inequalities
3. Graph linear equations and inequalities
4. Solve systems of linear equations and inequalities
5. Translate word problems into math

CHAPTER 1

The Kaplan Method for Math & Linear Equations

 ## CHAPTER OBJECTIVES

By the end of this chapter, you will be able to:

1. Apply the Kaplan Method for Math to Heart of Algebra questions
2. Recognize, simplify, and solve linear equations efficiently
3. Translate complex word problems into equations
4. Interpret the most commonly tested types of linear graphs

SMARTPOINTS

Point Value	SmartPoint Category
Point Builder	Kaplan Method for Math
110 Points	Linear Equations

THE KAPLAN METHOD FOR MATH

Because the PSAT is a standardized test, students who approach each question in a consistent way will be rewarded on Test Day. Applying the same basic steps to every math question—whether it asks you about geometry, algebra, or even trigonometry—will help you avoid minor mistakes as well as tempting incorrect answer choices.

Use the Kaplan Method for Math for every math question on the PSAT. Its steps are applicable to every situation and reflect the best test-taking practices.

The Kaplan Method for Math has three steps:

Step 1: Read the question, identifying and organizing important information as you go

Step 2: Choose the best strategy to answer the question

Step 3: Check that you answered the *right* question

Let's examine each of these steps in more detail.

Step 1: Read the question, identifying and organizing important information as you go

This means asking yourself the following questions.

- **What information am I given?** Take a few seconds to jot down the information you are given and try to group similar items together.

- **What is the question asking?** Separate the question from the context. Word problems may include information that is unnecessary to solve the question. Feel free to discard any unnecessary information.

- **How are the answer choices different?** Reading answer choices carefully can help you spot the most efficient way to solve a multiple-choice math question. For example, if the answer choices in a question on the calculator section are decimals, then painstakingly rewriting your final answer as a simplified fraction is a waste of time; you can just use your calculator instead.

- **Should I label or draw a diagram?** If the question describes a shape or figure but doesn't provide one, sketch a diagram so you can see the shape or figure and add notes to it. If a figure is provided, take a few seconds to label it with information from the question.

✔ Expert Tip

Don't assume you understand a question as soon as you see it. Many students see an equation and immediately begin solving. Solving math questions without carefully reading can take you down the wrong path on Test Day.

Step 2: Choose the best strategy to answer the question

- **Look for patterns.** Every PSAT math question can be solved in a variety of ways, but not all strategies are created equally. To finish all of the questions, you'll need to solve questions as *efficiently* as possible. If you find yourself about to do time-consuming math, take a moment to look for time-saving shortcuts.

- **Pick numbers or use straightforward math.** While you can always solve a PSAT math question with what you've learned in school, doing so won't always be the fastest way. On questions that describe relationships between numbers (such as percentages) but don't actually use numbers, you can often save time on Test Day by using techniques such as Picking Numbers instead of straightforward math.

> ✔ **Expert Tip**
>
> The PSAT won't give you any extra points for solving a question the hard way.

Step 3: Check that you answered the *right* question

- When you get the final answer, **resist the urge to immediately bubble in the answer**. Take a moment to do the following:

  - Review the question stem

  - Check units of measurement

  - Double-check your work

- The PSAT will often ask you for quantities such as $x + 1$ or the product of x and y. **Be careful on these questions!** They often include tempting answer choices that correspond to the values of x or y individually. There's no partial credit on the PSAT, so take a moment at the end of every question to make sure you're answering the right question.

LINEAR EQUATIONS

Linear equations and linear graphs are some of the most common elements on the PSAT Math Test. They can be used to model relationships and changes such as those concerning time, temperature, or population.

The graphs of these equations are as important as the equations themselves. The graphs you will see most are either linear or lines of best fit. A sample graph is shown:

When working with a graph like this, you may not know anything about magnetization or cobalt ferrite, but you do see a graph with a straight line on it. That straight line is your clue that you're dealing with a linear equation.

Being able to work with, understand, and interpret linear equations will make up a substantial part of your Math score. In this chapter, we will explore all of those scenarios so you'll be ready to tackle linear equations in whatever form you encounter them on the test.

Many students inadvertently switch on "math autopilot" when solving linear equations, automatically running through the same set of steps on every equation without looking for the best way to solve the question. On the PSAT, however, every second counts. You will want to use the *most* efficient strategy for solving questions. To see this in action, take a look at the question that follows on the next page.

1. $\frac{1}{2}(3x + 17) = \frac{1}{6}(8x - 10)$

    Which value of *x* satisfies the equation above?

    A) −61

    B) −55

    C) −41

    D) −35

The following table shows Kaplan's strategic thinking on the left, along with suggested math scratchwork on the right. Keeping your notes organized is critical for success on the PSAT, so start practicing now setting up well-organized scratchwork.

Strategic Thinking	Math Scratchwork
Step 1: Read the question, identifying and organizing important information as you go This question is straightforward: you're being asked to solve the equation and find the correct value of *x*.	$\frac{1}{2}(3x + 17) = \frac{1}{6}(8x - 10)$
Step 2: Choose the best strategy to answer the question *Should you distribute those fractions first, or is there a faster way to solve?* By multiplying both sides of the equation by 6, you make the equation much simpler. Finish by using the distributive property, collecting like terms, and solving for *x*.	$6 \times \left[\frac{1}{2}(3x + 17) = \frac{1}{6}(8x - 10) \right]$ $3(3x + 17) = 8x - 10$ $9x + 51 = 8x - 10$ $x = -61$
Step 3: Check that you answered the *right* question You found the value of *x*, and it matches (A).	$x = -61$

You could have approached a question like this in many ways, but remember, the goal is to get the correct answer quickly. The faster you solve algebraic equations, the more time you'll be able to devote to challenging questions, setting you up to earn more points on Test Day.

> ✔ **Remember**
>
> As you practice, always ask yourself: "Is there a faster way to solve this question?" Use the Answers and Explanations at the back of this book to check!

When solving an equation, always keep in mind the fundamental principles of equality: because both sides of an equation are equal, you need to do the same thing to both sides so that equality is preserved. Try solving another linear equation for extra practice:

2. $-2(x - 3) = 17$

What value of x satisfies the equation shown?

A) $-\dfrac{23}{2}$

B) -10

C) -7

D) $-\dfrac{11}{2}$

Work through the Kaplan Method for Math step-by-step to solve this question. The following table shows Kaplan's strategic thinking on the left, along with suggested math scratchwork on the right.

Strategic Thinking	Math Scratchwork
Step 1: Read the question, identifying and organizing important information as you go This looks similar to the first question. It's asking you to solve the equation and find the correct value of x.	$-2(x - 3) = 17$
Step 2: Choose the best strategy to answer the question *What's the fastest way to solve this?* It doesn't look like there are many options. Use principles of equality and do the same thing to both sides until x is by itself. First, carefully distribute the -2. Next, subtract 6 from both sides and divide by -2.	$-2x + 6 = 17$ $-2x = 11$ $x = -\dfrac{11}{2}$
Step 3: Check that you answered the right question As requested, you've solved for x. Choice (D) is correct.	$x = -\dfrac{11}{2}$

Notice that some of the answer choices are not integers. The PSAT may challenge you by designing questions so that the answer is in a form you do not expect. If you arrive at an answer in an unusual form, don't be alarmed. Fractions and decimals are often correct on the PSAT.

Math

Looking carefully at how the PSAT uses fractions and decimals can guide your strategy in solving linear equations. The presence of fractions in the answer choices likely means you'll need to rely on techniques for combining and simplifying fractions to get to the correct answer. Seeing decimals in the answer choices, on the other hand, likely indicates that you can rely on your calculator and save time on Test Day.

Try to determine the best strategy for solving the next question.

3. $\dfrac{8}{7}\left(x - \dfrac{101}{220}\right) + 4\left(x + \dfrac{8}{9}\right) = 38$

Which approximate value of x satisfies the equation shown?

A) 4.29

B) 4.65

C) 6.6

D) 6.8

Work through the Kaplan Method for Math step-by-step to solve this question. The following table shows Kaplan's strategic thinking on the left, along with suggested math scratchwork on the right.

Strategic Thinking	Math Scratchwork
Step 1: Read the question, identifying and organizing important information as you go Notice a pattern? Again, the question is asking you to solve for x.	$\frac{8}{7}\left(x - \frac{101}{220}\right) + 4\left(x + \frac{8}{9}\right) = 38$
Step 2: Choose the best strategy to answer the question *How can you quickly solve this problem?* Clearing the fraction outside the parentheses is a smart move. Multiply both sides by 7. *What do you notice about the answer choices? How are they different from the answers in the last question?* The presence of decimals means your calculator will be a great asset here. Don't worry about common denominators. Divide the fractions. Because the answer choices are only written to two decimal places, write your intermediate steps to two places as well. Now distribute the numbers outside the parentheses, collect like terms, and solve for x.	$8\left(x - \frac{101}{220}\right) + 28\left(x + \frac{8}{9}\right) = 266$ $8(x - 0.46) + 28(x + 0.89) = 266$ $8x - 3.68 + 28x + 24.92 = 266$ $36x = 244.76$ $x = 6.8$
Step 3: Check that you answered the *right* question Double-check the question stem. Choice (D) is correct.	$x = 6.8$

Notice in the previous question that careful use of your calculator can eliminate the need to complete time-consuming tasks by hand. Be conscious of the format of the answer choices—decimal answers are a great clue that you can use your calculator.

✔ Note

Many graphing calculators have a built-in function that will let you input and solve algebraic equations like the previous one. Consider learning how to use it before Test Day by reading the instruction manual or searching online.

LINEAR WORD PROBLEMS (REAL-WORLD SCENARIOS)

Another way linear equations can be made to look complicated is for them to be disguised in real-world word problems, where it's up to you to extract and solve an equation. When you're answering these questions, you may run into trouble translating English into math. The following table shows some of the most common phrases and mathematical equivalents you're likely to see on the PSAT.

Word Problems Translation Table	
English	**Math**
equals, is, equivalent to, was, will be, has, costs, adds up to, the same as, as much as	$=$
times, of, multiplied by, product of, twice, double, by	$\times$
divided by, per, out of, each, ratio	$\div$
plus, added to, and, sum, combined, total, increased by	$+$
minus, subtracted from, smaller than, less than, fewer, decreased by, difference between	$-$
a number, how much, how many, what	x, n, etc.

Linear word problems are made more difficult by complex phrasing and extraneous information. Don't get frustrated—word problems can be broken down in predictable ways. To stay organized on Test Day, use the **Kaplan Strategy for Translating English into Math**:

- Define any variables, choosing letters that make sense

- Break sentences into short phrases

- Translate each phrase into a mathematical expression

- Put the expressions together to form an equation

Let's apply this to a straightforward example: Colin's age is three less than twice Jim's age.

- **Define any variables, choosing letters that make sense:** We'll choose C for Colin's age and J for Jim's age.

- **Break sentences into short phrases:** The information about Colin and the information about Jim seem like separate phrases.

- **Translate each phrase into a mathematical expression:** Colin's age $= C$; 3 less than twice Jim's age $= 2J - 3$.

- **Put the expressions together to form an equation:** Combine the results to get $C = 2J - 3$.

This strategy fits into the larger framework of the Kaplan Method for Math. When you get to **Step 2: Choose the best strategy to answer the question** and are trying to solve a word problem as efficiently as possible, switch over to this strategy to move forward quickly.

The Kaplan Strategy for Translating English into Math works every time. Apply it here to a test-like example:

4.   The number k can be determined in the following way: multiply m by 2, add $3n$ to the result, and subtract $(4m - 5n)$ from this sum. What is the value of k in terms of m and n ?

   A) $-2m - 3n$

   B) $-2m + 2n$

   C) $-2m + 8n$

   D) $6m - 2n$

Work through the Kaplan Method for Math step-by-step to solve this question. The following table shows Kaplan's strategic thinking on the left, along with suggested math scratchwork on the right.

Strategic Thinking	Math Scratchwork
Step 1: Read the question, identifying and organizing important information as you go The question is asking you to solve for k in terms of m and n. You're looking for what comes after $k =$.	
Step 2: Choose the best strategy to answer the question *Where should you start?* Go through each component of the Kaplan Strategy for Translating English into Math. *Do you need to choose variables?* No, the variables are already defined for you. *How can you logically break down this question?* Phrases about k and phrases about m and n are reasonable choices. Go ahead and translate:	
"k can be determined"	$k =$
"Multiply m by 2, add $3n$ to the result"	$2m + 3n$
"Subtract $(4m - 5n)$"	$-(4m - 5n)$
Combine the results.	$k = 2m + 3n - (4m - 5n)$
This doesn't look like an exact match for any of the answer choices. Can you simplify?	
Distribute the negative and combine like terms.	$k = 2m + 3n - 4m + 5n$
Step 3: Check that you answered the *right* question Perfect! Now you have an exact match for (C).	$k = -2m + 8n$

LINEAR GRAPHS

Working with equations algebraically is only half the battle. The PSAT will also expect you to work with graphs of linear equations, which means using lines in slope-intercept form and point-slope form.

One of the most important quantities you'll be working with when graphing a linear equation is the slope. Slope is given by the following equation: $m = \dfrac{y_2 - y_1}{x_2 - x_1}$, where (x_1, y_1) and (x_2, y_2) are coordinates of points on the line. To remember this, think: $\text{slope} = \dfrac{\text{rise}}{\text{run}}$.

One of the most common forms of a linear equation is *slope-intercept form*, which is used to describe the graph of a straight line. The formula is quickly recognizable: $y = mx + b$. The variables y and x represent the coordinates of a point on the graph through which the line passes, while m tells us what the slope of the line is and b represents the point at which the line intersects the y-axis.

Remember: a line with a positive slope runs up and to the right ("uphill"), and a line with a negative slope runs down and to the right ("downhill"). In the following figure, lines n and l have positive and negative slopes, respectively:

Occasionally, you will encounter a line with a slope of 0—meaning it does not rise or fall from left to right. These lines are easy to spot because they are horizontal and are parallel to the x-axis (line k in the figure shown). Lines that are parallel to the y-axis, such as line m in the figure, have slopes that are "undefined." The lines themselves exist, but their slopes cannot be calculated numerically.

The slope of a graph can also tell you valuable information about the rate of change of numbers and variables associated with the line. A positive slope signifies an increase in a variable, while a negative slope indicates a decrease. *Large* numerical values for slope indicate rapid changes, while *small* numerical values point to more gradual changes. Imagine that the balance in your checking account is B and that it changes with the number of days that go by, D. Think about how each of the following models would impact your life:

$$B = 100D + 75$$
$$B = 0.25D + 75$$
$$B = -100D + 75$$
$$B = -0.25D + 75$$

The first equation probably looks pretty good. The second equation isn't as great. An extra quarter a day isn't going to do much for you. The third equation would quickly drive you into bankruptcy, while the fourth equation might be cause for concern after a while.

The *y*-intercept, on the other hand, is often less significant, typically representing the initial condition in a model—that is, where the model begins. In the checking account example, the beginning balance was $75 in all four models. Notice, the *y*-intercept didn't change at all.

Look at the following question to see how the PSAT might test your ability to match a linear equation with its graph:

5. Which of the following shows the graph of the line $y = 4x + 7$?

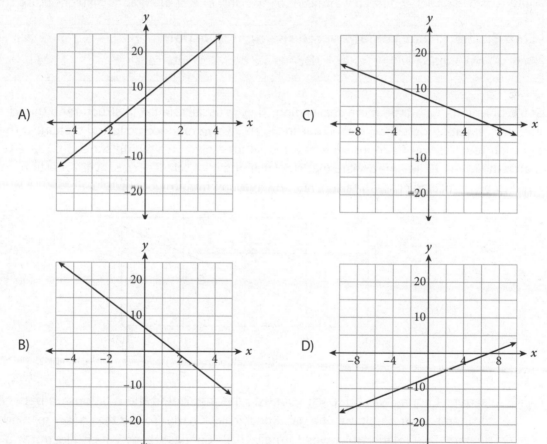

Approach this question by using the Kaplan Method for Math. Because there isn't any scratchwork required for a question like this, only the column containing Kaplan's strategic thinking is included in the following table. Try to ask yourself similar questions as you work through questions like this on Test Day.

Strategic Thinking
Step 1: Read the question, identifying and organizing important information as you go This question is asking you to match the linear equation to the appropriate graph.
Step 2: Choose the best strategy to answer the question *What is the fastest way to solve this? Should you use your graphing calculator, or can you eliminate some answer choices quickly?* Notice that the graphs are vastly different. You're looking for a graph that slopes up and to the right (positive slope) and has a *y*-intercept of +7. Only one of the graphs matches those criteria.
Step 3: Check that you answered the *right* question Only (A) has a graph with a positive slope and a positive *y*-intercept.

Some questions are a little more challenging. They're usually similar in structure to the "checking account" equation described earlier, but they can involve more complicated scenarios. This next question requires you to choose the best model for a given real-world situation. See if you can match the graph to an appropriate model. Watch out: it's a science "crossover" question, so you'll need to be particularly careful to separate the question from the context.

6. Jacques Charles was a French scientist who discovered the relationship between the temperature and volume of a gas. Specifically, Charles found that gases expand when heated. This relationship was formalized in Charles's Law, which illustrates a linear relationship between temperature and volume in gases. The graph here shows the volume of a sample of gas as it is cooled. If T is the temperature of the gas in °C and V is the volume in liters, which of the following equations, when plotted, could produce the graph shown?

   A) $V = 0.004T + 100$

   B) $V = 0.004T$

   C) $V = 0.004T + 1$

   D) $V = 0.004T - 0.25$

> ✔ **Note**
>
> Remember, the *x*-coordinate at the *y*-intercept will always be zero!

Although you may enjoy learning about history with your math, you don't need to waste time digesting extraneous information. The following table shows the strategic thinking that can help you solve this question. No scratchwork is necessary.

Strategic Thinking
Step 1: Read the question, identifying and organizing important information as you go
Only the last two sentences describe the graph. They are underlined here:
Jacques Charles was a French scientist who discovered the relationship between the temperature and volume of a gas. Specifically, Charles found that gases expand when heated. This relationship was formalized in Charles's Law, which illustrates a linear relationship between temperature and volume in gases. <u>The graph here shows the volume of a sample of gas as it is cooled. If T is the temperature of the gas in °C and V is the volume in liters, which of the following equations, when plotted, could produce the graph shown?</u>
Match the graph to the equation. Because V is on the y-axis and T is on the x-axis, the standard $y = mx + b$ equation should resemble $V = mT + b$. All you need to do now is figure out the slope and y-intercept.
Step 2: Choose the best strategy to answer the question
Should you graph each of the lines in the answer choices on your calculator? Is that the most efficient use of time?
Probably not. Notice that the answer choices describe very different lines.
What part is different in each answer choice?
Each option has a different y-intercept. To answer this complicated question, all you need to do is find the y-intercept of the graph and match it to an answer choice.
Where is the y-axis in the graph?
Notice the unusual orientation of the graph. The y-axis will always be at $x = 0$, but it does not have to be located at the far left of the graph. In this graph, the y-axis is offset and is located in the middle of the right side of the graph. In this case, the line intersects the y-axis at the point (0, 1). Therefore, you know you're looking for a line that has a y-intercept of 1.
Step 3: Check that you answered the *right* question
You can safely eliminate every answer choice except (C), the correct answer.

While scatterplots will be described in more detail in subsequent chapters, this next question shows that the principles covered here for graphing linear equations can be equally applied to the line of best fit on a scatterplot. See what you can conclude from the slope and *y*-intercept of the equation of the line of best fit. Note that this question is an example of a very complex word problem—don't be intimidated! If you can tackle this question, you'll be able to handle the most difficult PSAT word problems.

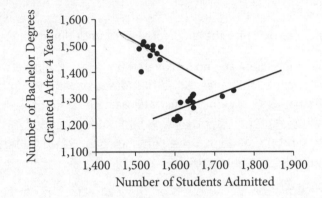

7. A university admissions department compiled data on students over a 25-year period. The department wanted to know how many students admitted in a given year graduated four years later with a degree. It noted that the number of students admitted showed a regular and consistent increase over the 25-year period. These data are plotted in the graph shown. Halfway through the data collection period, the general college enacted a policy that would allow students to take a year-long break during their studies. The college wants to model the relationship between the number of students admitted and the number of degrees attained in four years with a line of best fit before and after the policy change. Which of the following describes the best estimate for *m*, the slope of this line, before the change and after the change?

A) Before: $m = -1$; after: $m = 0$

B) Before: $m = 1$; after: $m = -\dfrac{1}{2}$

C) Before: $m = -1$; after: $m = \dfrac{3}{4}$

D) Before: $m = \dfrac{3}{4}$; after: $m = 0$

Use the Kaplan Method for Math to make short work of this question. The following table shows the strategic thinking that can help you solve complex questions like this one.

Strategic Thinking
Step 1: Read the question, identifying and organizing important information as you go In this case, the question is asking you to find the slope before and after the policy change. Because the number of students admitted increased over time, you know that data before the policy change are on the left side of the graph and data after the policy change are on the right side.
Step 2: Choose the best strategy to answer the question *How can you solve this efficiently? Do you notice any differences between the answer choices that would result in vastly different slopes? Do the signs tell you anything?* Because the line of best fit for the data collected before the policy change slopes down and to the right, you're looking for a negative slope. That eliminates choices B and D. Because the line of best fit for the data collected after the policy change slopes up and to the right, you know you need a positive slope. That eliminates A.
Step 3: Check that you answered the *right* question Because only one answer choice remains that describes the slopes of both lines correctly, you can confidently choose (C) without worrying about the numbers here.

Notice that even complicated-looking questions involving linear graphs often boil down to the same basic concepts of slope and *y*-intercept. Master those ideas and you'll be able to handle any linear graph you'll see on the PSAT.

Now you'll have a chance to try a few more test-like questions. Use the scaffolding as needed to guide you through the question and get the correct answer.

Some guidance is provided, but you'll need to fill in the missing parts of explanations or the step-by-step math to get to the correct answer. Don't worry—after going through the examples at the beginning of this chapter, these questions should be completely doable. If you find yourself struggling, however, review the worked examples again.

8. Ms. Walser's class had 18 students. She used three equally weighted tests to determine their final grades. The class average for the first test was 92, and the class average for the second test was 77. If the overall class average was 84, what was the average score for the third test?

    A) 74.3

    B) 77

    C) 83

    D) 84.3

The following table can help you structure your thinking as you work your way through this question. Kaplan's strategic thinking is provided, as are bits of structured scratchwork. If you're not sure how to approach a question like this, start at the top and work your way down.

Strategic Thinking	Math Scratchwork
Step 1: Read the question, identifying and organizing important information as you go You're solving for the average score on the third test. The number of students is extraneous information. Because the tests are equally weighted, just divide by 3 to calculate the final average.	
Step 2: Choose the best strategy to answer the question Use the Kaplan Strategy for Translating English into Math to get through this word problem quickly. *Can you give the variables names that make sense? Careful, T would give you trouble with Test Two and Test Three. Could you start at the beginning of the alphabet?* *How can you logically break this question apart into shorter sentences?* *Is it possible to translate each phrase into a math expression? Because you don't have a score for the third test, what should you do? Leave it as a variable?* *Almost there. Can you put all the pieces together? How can you use the average of the three scores to solve for the third test score?* Remember that the average is equal to the sum of the terms divided by the number of terms. Test Three should remain a variable because it is the quantity being solved for. *After you've plugged everything in, can you rearrange the equation to get the score on Test Three?*	Average on Test One = _____ Average on Test Two = _____ Average on Test Three = _____ Overall Average = _____ On Test One, the class scored an average of _____. On Test _____ the class scored an average of 77. The class's _____ average was 84. _____ = 92 _____ = 77 _____ = __ _____ = 84 (___ + ___ + ___)/3 = ___
Step 3: Check that you answered the *right* question Check your work. Does the variable you solved for correspond to the score on Test Three?	_____ = _____

Here's another test-like example to try:

9. A box of candies contains only chocolates, licorice sticks, peppermints, and gummy bears. If $\frac{1}{4}$ of the candies are chocolates, $\frac{1}{6}$ of the candies are gummy bears, $\frac{1}{3}$ are peppermints, and 9 are licorice sticks, what is the product of the number of peppermints and the number of chocolates?

    A) 12

    B) 36

    C) 72

    D) 108

The following table can help you structure your thinking as you work your way through this question. Kaplan's strategic thinking is provided, as are bits of structured scratchwork. If you're not sure how to approach a question like this, start at the top and work your way down.

Strategic Thinking	Math Scratchwork
Step 1: Read the question, identifying and organizing important information as you go You need to find the product of peppermints and chocolates.	
Step 2: Choose the best strategy to answer the question *How can you effectively translate this English into math?* Use the Kaplan Strategy for Translating English into Math. *Can you think of a variable to correspond to the total number of candies in the box? Be careful! Because chocolates, gummy bears, and peppermints are all defined in terms of the total number of candies, do they need their own variables?* How can each candy be written as a fraction of b? Break the question down into shorter phrases and translate into math. *Almost there. What should all of these candies add up to? Think about what variable they're all a fraction of.* At this point, solve for the number of candies in the box.	Total Candies = _____ $\frac{1}{4}b=$ _____ ____ $b=$ _____ ____ $b=$ _____ $9=$ _____ $\frac{1}{4}b+$ __ $b+$ __ $b+9=$ ____ $b=$ _____
Step 3: Check that you answered the *right* question Careful! Don't bubble in what you just solved for! You're looking for the product of chocolates and peppermints. Now multiply these candies together to get the final answer, (D).	chocolates $=\frac{1}{4}b=$ _____ peppermints $=$ __ $b=$ _____ product $=$ _____

Now that you've seen the variety of ways in which the PSAT can test you on linear equations, try the following three questions to check your understanding. Give yourself 3.5 minutes to answer the questions. Make sure you use the Kaplan Method for Math on every question. Remember, you'll need to emphasize speed and efficiency in addition to simply getting the correct answer.

10. Ibrahim has a contract for a cell phone plan that includes the following rates: the plan has a fixed cost of $50 a month, a data plan that provides 2 GB of data for free and $8 for each GB of data after that, and a text message plan that costs $0.10 per text message sent. Which of the following equations represents the amount of money in dollars that Ibrahim will spend per month as long as he uses at least 2 GB of data? (Assume $d =$ dollars, $g =$ number of GB of data used, and $t =$ number of text messages sent.)

A) $d = 50 + 8g + 0.1t$

B) $d = 50 + (8g - 2) + 0.1t$

C) $d = 50 + 8(g - 2) + 0.1t$

D) $d = 5,000 + 800g + 10t$

11. If $3(n - 2) = 6$, then what does $\dfrac{n - 2}{n + 2}$ equal?

12. A certain gym sells two membership packages. The first package, the Die-Hard Package, costs $250 for 6 months of unlimited use. The second package, the Personal Package, costs $130 initially plus $4 each day the member visits. How many visits would a person need to use for each package to cost the same amount over a 6-month period?

A)   2

B)   30

C)   96

D)   120

Answers and Explanations for this chapter begin on page 541.

ON YOUR OWN

The calculator icon means you are permitted to use a calculator to solve a question. It does not mean that you *should* use it, however.

1. A municipality charges two types of local taxes: a per capita tax, which is a flat fee that every person pays, and a local income tax, which is a percentage of the person's annual income, i. If a taxpayer's total tax bill is given by the function $T = 0.02i + 25$, then the value 0.02 best represents which of the following ?

   A) The per capita tax

   B) The taxpayer's annual income

   C) The total tax bill minus the per capita tax

   D) The amount of the income tax as a percentage

$$\frac{7(n-3)+11}{6} = \frac{18-(6+2n)}{8}$$

2. In the equation shown, what is the value of n ?

   A) $\dfrac{38}{17}$

   B) $\dfrac{38}{11}$

   C) $\dfrac{56}{11}$

   D) $\dfrac{94}{17}$

3. If $36 + 3(4x - 9) = c(2x + 1) + 25$ has no solution and c is a constant, what is the value of c ?

   A) -3

   B) 3

   C) 6

   D) 12

4. Jenna is renting a car while on a business trip. The cost is $54.95 per day, which is taxed at a rate of 6%. The car rental company charges an additional one-time, untaxed environmental impact fee of $10. Which of the following equations represents Jenna's total cost, in dollars, for renting the car for d days ?

   A) $c = (54.95 + 0.06d) + 10$

   B) $c = 1.06(54.95d) + 10$

   C) $c = 1.06(54.95d + 10)$

   D) $c = 1.06(54.95 + 10)d$

Price of One Can	Projected Number of Cans Sold
$0.75	10,000
$0.80	9,000
$0.85	8,000
$0.90	7,000
$0.95	6,000
$1.00	5,000

5. Which of the following equations best describes the relationship shown in the table, where n indicates the number of cans sold and p represents the price in dollars of one can?

A) $n = -20,000p + 25,000$

B) $n = -200p + 250$

C) $n = 200p + 250$

D) $n = 20,000p + 25,000$

Golf Balls

6. A driving range sells golf balls in different quantities. The figure shows the costs of the various quantities. According to the figure, what is the cost of a single golf ball?

A) $0.60

B) $1.67

C) $3.00

D) $5.00

7. Juan is on his school's archery team. In a match, he gets 12 arrows to shoot at a target. He gets 8 points if the arrow hits the inner circle of the target and 4 points if it hits the outer circle. Which of the following equations represents Juan's total score if a of his arrows hit the inner circle and the rest hit the outer circle?

A) $p = 8a$

B) $p = 8a + 4$

C) $p = 48 + 4a$

D) $p = 96 - 4a$

Shipping Cost

8. A freight company charges a flat insurance fee to deliver a package anywhere in the continental United States, plus an additional charge for each pound the package weighs. The graph shows the relationship between the weight of the package and the total cost to ship it. Based on the graph, how much would it cost to ship a 25-pound box?

A) $37.00

B) $48.00

C) $62.50

D) $74.50

Math

9. Which value of x makes the equation $\frac{2}{3}(x - 1) = 12$ true?

   A) 7

   B) 9

   C) 17

   D) 19

10. Sandy works at a tire store. She gets paid $70 for a day's work, plus a commission of $14 for each tire she sells. Which of the following equations represents the relationship between one day of Sandy's pay, y, and the number of tires she sells, x?

    A) $x = 14y + 70$

    B) $x = 70y + 14$

    C) $y = 14x + 70$

    D) $y = 70x + 14$

11. The value of a new car starts to depreciate as soon as it's purchased and driven for the first time. If the equation $y = -0.15x + 27,000$ represents the estimated value of a certain car, taking into account depreciation over time, what does 27,000 most likely represent?

    A) The depreciation rate

    B) The current value of the car

    C) The purchase price of the car

    D) The value of the car after 0.15 years of ownership

Carnival Spending

12. The figure shows the cost of going to a certain carnival. What does the y-intercept most likely represent?

    A) A flat entrance fee

    B) The cost of riding 8 rides

    C) The cost of attending the carnival 8 times

    D) The total cost of attending the carnival and riding 1 ride

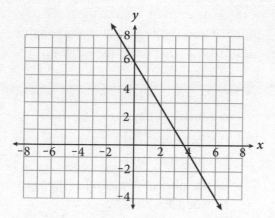

13. What is the slope of the line shown in the figure?

A) $-\dfrac{5}{3}$

B) $-\dfrac{3}{5}$

C) $\dfrac{3}{5}$

D) $\dfrac{5}{3}$

14. Which of the following does not represent a linear relationship?

A) $y = x$

B) $x - \dfrac{1}{4}y = 6$

C)

D)

x	y
−1	8
1	4
3	0
5	−4

15. If the equation of the line shown in the figure is written in the form $y = mx + b$, which of the following is true?

A) $m < 0$ and $b < 0$

B) $m < 0$ and $b > 0$

C) $m > 0$ and $b < 0$

D) $m > 0$ and $b > 0$

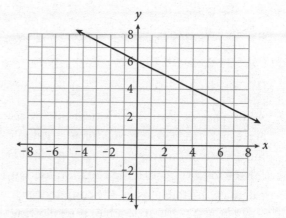

16. The figure shown represents which of the following equations?

A) $y = -2x + 6$

B) $y = -\dfrac{1}{2}x + 6$

C) $y = \dfrac{1}{2}x - 6$

D) $y = 2x - 6$

$$\frac{2}{3}(3h) - \frac{5}{2}(h - 1) = -\frac{1}{3}\left(\frac{3}{2}h\right) + 8$$

17. What is the value of h in the equation above?

   A) $h = -5.5$

   B) $h = 5.5$

   C) There is no value of h for which the equation is true.

   D) There are infinitely many values of h for which the equation is true.

18. A produce stand normally sells watermelons for $0.60 per pound. On Mondays, it sells watermelons at a 20% discount. The stand also sells sweet potatoes for $0.79 each. Which of the following represents the total cost, c, if a customer buys 4 sweet potatoes and a watermelon weighing p pounds on a Monday?

   A) $c = 0.2p + 0.79$

   B) $c = 0.48p + 3.16$

   C) $c = 0.6p + 0.79$

   D) $c = 0.6p + 3.16$

19. A company is hosting a business conference at a hotel. The hotel charges a flat rental rate for the use of the room plus a per person rate for the food service. If the equation used to calculate the total cost of the conference is $y = 15x + 325$, then which of the following most likely represents the number of people attending?

   A) x

   B) y

   C) 15

   D) 325

20. A machine running around the clock can produce 3,600 bolts per day. Based on this information, what could the equation $y = 150x$ represent?

   A) The number of bolts the machine can produce in x days

   B) The number of bolts the machine can produce in x hours

   C) The number of days it takes the machine to produce x bolts

   D) The number of hours it takes the machine to produce x bolts

21. The graph of which of the following linear equations has a slope of 0 ?

   A) $x = 0$

   B) $y = 2$

   C) $x = y$

   D) $x - y = 2$

22. Which of the following scenarios could be supported by the graph shown?

   A) As the temperature in a room decreases, the number of bacteria decreases.

   B) As the temperature in a room decreases, the number of bacteria increases.

   C) As the temperature in a room increases, the number of bacteria decreases.

   D) As the temperature in a room increases, the number of bacteria remains constant.

23. Which of the following figures could be the graph of the equation $ax + by = c$, given that $a > 0$, $b > 0$, and $c = b$?

A)

B)

C)

D)

24. Malik drew a linear graph that is increasing and has a negative x-intercept. Which of the following could be the equation Malik graphed?

A) $4x + 3y = 1$

B) $-x + 2y = -8$

C) $2x + 3y = -9$

D) $3x - 5y = -10$

25. When graphing a linear equation that is written in the form $y = mx + b$, the variable m represents the slope of the line, and b represents the y-intercept. Which of the following best describes how reversing the signs of m and b would affect the graph of this line?

A)   The graph will be a perfect reflection of the original line across the x-axis.

B)   The graph will be a perfect reflection of the original line across the y-axis.

C)   The new line will slant in the opposite direction, and the x-intercept will be reflected across the x-axis.

D)   The new line will slant in the opposite direction, and the y-intercept will be reflected across the y-axis.

26. For which of the following is it possible to have both a positive value of x and a negative value of x that satisfy the equation?

A) $36 - 5x = \dfrac{1}{4}x + 1$

B) $\dfrac{1}{3}x + 11 = 2x - 7$

C) $-\dfrac{1}{2}(x - 8) = \dfrac{2}{5}(10x + 15)$

D) $8\left(\dfrac{3}{4}x - 5\right) = -2(20 - 3x)$

27. A machine feeds a food pellet to a mouse once every 2.5 hours. If p is the number of pellets the mouse is fed over the course of d full days, which of the following equations defines p ?

A) $p = \dfrac{24d}{2.5}$

B) $p = 2.5d$

C) $p = \dfrac{2.5d}{24}$

D) $p = 2.5 \times 600d$

28. Karla is at the county fair and is playing a game in which she uses a magnet to catch toy fish. If the fish has a purple dot underneath, it is worth 2 points; if it has a green dot underneath, it is worth 5 points. Every fish has either a purple dot or a green dot. To play, it costs 50 cents for each attempt. If Karla catches f fish that have purple dots, the expression $2f + 5(8 - f)$ represents the total number of points she earns. Based on this expression, how much in dollars did Karla spend playing the fish game?

A) 2

B) 4

C) 5

D) 8

29. What was the initial amount of water in a barrel, in liters, if there are now x liters, y liters were spilled, and 6 liters were added?

A) $x - y + 6$

B) $y - x + 6$

C) $x + y + 6$

D) $y + x - 6$

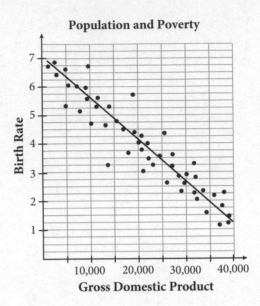

Population and Poverty

30. A historian conducted a study of 50 nations regarding the relationship between population and poverty. Specifically, she studied the birth rate, or number of children per woman, and the wealth of the nation measured as gross domestic product. The results are shown in the figure, along with a line of best fit for the data. What does the slope of the line of best fit illustrate about the relationship between birth rate and the wealth of a nation?

A) As the birth rate of a nation increases, the wealth increases.

B) As the birth rate of a nation decreases, the wealth decreases.

C) As the wealth of a nation increases, the birth rate decreases.

D) As the wealth of a nation decreases, the birth rate decreases.

$$\frac{9}{4}(y - 8) = \frac{27}{2}$$

31. What value of y satisfies the equation above?

32. For what value of y does the graph of $4x - \frac{1}{2}y = -12$ cross the y-axis?

CHAPTER 2

Systems of Equations

CHAPTER OBJECTIVES

By the end of this chapter, you will be able to:

1. Distinguish between independent and dependent equations

2. Solve two-variable systems of linear equations

3. Determine the most efficient way to solve systems of equations

4. Translate word problems into multiple equations

SMARTPOINTS

Point Value	SmartPoint Category
50 Points	Systems of Linear Equations

SYSTEMS OF EQUATIONS

The linear equations detailed in the previous chapter are well suited for modeling a variety of scenarios and for solving for a single variable in terms of another that is clearly defined (e.g., What is the cost of a data plan if you consume 4 GB of data in a month?). However, sometimes you will be given a set of multiple equations with multiple variables that are interdependent. For example, suppose a $50/month cell phone plan includes $0.05 text messages and $0.40 voice calls, with a cap of 1,000 combined text messages and voice calls.

This scenario can be represented by the following system of equations:

$$\$0.05t + \$0.40v = \$50$$
$$t + v = 1{,}000$$

Solving such a system would enable you to determine the maximum number of text messages and voice calls you could make under this plan, while optimizing total usage. To solve systems of equations, you'll need to rely on a different set of tools that builds on the algebra you're already familiar with. The following question shows an example of such a system in the context of a test-like question:

1. If $3r + 2s = 24$ and $r + s = 12$, what is the value of $r + 6$?

   A) 0

   B) 4

   C) 6

   D) 12

You might be tempted to switch on math autopilot at this point and employ substitution, solving the second equation for s in terms of r:

$$s = 12 - r$$

You could plug the resulting expression back into the other equation and eventually solve for r, but remember, the PSAT tests your ability to answer math questions in the most efficient way. The following table contains some strategic thinking designed to help you find the most efficient way to answer this question on Test Day, along with some suggested scratchwork.

Strategic Thinking	Math Scratchwork
Step 1: Read the question, identifying and organizing important information as you go In this case, you're looking for the value of *r*. There are two equations that involve *r* and *s*.	$3r + 2s = 24$ $r + s = 12$
Step 2: Choose the best strategy to answer the question *Is there any way you can make the first equation look like the second one? Does the quantity* r + s *exist in the first equation in some form?* *How can you effectively use both equations?* Once you've written the first equation in terms of *r* + *s*, substitute the value of *r* + *s* (which is 12) into the second equation and solve for *r*.	$3r + 2s = 24$ $r + 2r + 2s = 24$ $r + 2(r + s) = 24$ $r + 2(12) = 24$ $r = 0$
Step 3: Check that you answered the *right* question Be careful! The question isn't asking for the value of *r*. Add 6 to your result and you should see that (C) is the correct answer.	$r + 6 = 0 + 6$ $r + 6 = 6$

> ✔ **Note**
>
> Explanations for each simplifying step are not always included in this chapter. If you get stuck, review the information on simplifying and solving equations in chapter 1.

INDEPENDENT VERSUS DEPENDENT EQUATIONS

Generally, when you have a system involving *n* variables, you need *n independent* equations to solve for those variables. Thus, if you have a system of two variables, you need two independent equations. Three variables would require three independent equations, and so on.

Systems of equations are extremely useful in modeling and simulation. Complex mathematical problems, such as weather forecasting or crowd control predictions, often require 10 or more equations to be simultaneously solved for multiple variables. Fortunately, you won't encounter anything this daunting on Test Day.

Before we outline the process for solving two-variable systems of equations, let's clarify one of the key requirements. Earlier, it was stated that you need two independent equations to solve for two variables, but what exactly is an independent equation? Consider the equation $4x + 2y = 8$. You could use properties of equality to transform this equation in a number of different ways. For example, you could multiply both sides by 2, resulting in the equation $8x + 4y = 16$.

While it seems as though we've just created an additional equation, this is misleading, as the second equation has the same core variables and relationships as the first equation. This is termed a dependent equation, and two dependent equations cannot be used to solve for two variables. Look what happens when we try to use substitution. Start by isolating y in the original equation; the result is $y = 4 - 2x$.

Substituting that into the second equation, notice what happens:

$$8x + 4(4 - 2x) = 16$$
$$8x + 16 - 8x = 16$$
$$16 = 16$$

Although 16 does in fact equal 16, this doesn't bring us any closer to solving for either of the variables. In fact, if you arrive at a result like this when solving a system of equations, then the two equations are *dependent*. In this case, the system has infinitely many solutions because you could choose any number of possible values for x and y.

> ✔ **Note**
>
> When two equations are dependent, one equation can be obtained by algebraically manipulating the other equation. Graphically, dependent equations both describe the same line in the coordinate plane and therefore have the same slope and the same y-intercept.

At other times, you'll encounter equations that are fundamentally incompatible with each other. For example, if you have the two equations $4x + 2y = 8$ and $4x + 2y = 9$, it should be obvious that there are no values for x and y that will satisfy both equations at the same time. Doing so would violate fundamental laws of math. In this case, you would have a system of equations that has no solution. These two equations define parallel lines, which by definition never intersect.

Knowing how many solutions a system of equations has will tell you how graphing them in the same coordinate plane should look. Remember, the solution of a system of equations consists of the point or points where their graphs intersect.

If your system has...	then it will graph as...	Reasoning
no solution	two parallel lines	Parallel lines never intersect.
one solution	two lines intersecting at a single point	Two straight lines have only one intersection.
infinitely many solutions	a single line (one line directly on top of the other)	One equation is a manipulation of the other—their graphs are the same line.

Because you could encounter any of these three situations on Test Day, make sure you are familiar with all of them.

Math

Let's examine a sample question to investigate the requirements for solving a system of equations:

$$\begin{cases} \dfrac{1}{8}q + \dfrac{1}{5}s = 40 \\ zq + 8s = 1{,}600 \end{cases}$$

2. In the system of linear equations shown, z represents a constant. If the system of equations has infinitely many solutions, what is the value of z?

A) $\dfrac{1}{8}$

B) 5

C) 8

D) 40

Work through the Kaplan Method for Math step-by-step to solve this question. The following table shows Kaplan's strategic thinking on the left, along with suggested math scratchwork on the right.

Strategic Thinking	Math Scratchwork
Step 1: Read the question, identifying and organizing important information as you go You are looking for the value of z, given that the equation has infinitely many solutions. This means that the second equation should be the same as the first equation after some kind of algebraic manipulation.	
Step 2: Choose the best strategy to answer the question Look for ways to make the first equation resemble the second. The constant on the right gives you a strong clue: multiplying 40 by 40 gives 1,600. This also works well with the $\dfrac{1}{5}s$ term because multiplying by 40 yields $8s$.	$\dfrac{1}{8}q + \dfrac{1}{5}s = 40$ $zq + 8s = 1{,}600$ $40\left(\dfrac{1}{8}q + \dfrac{1}{5}s\right) = 40(40)$ $5q + 8s = 1{,}600$
Step 3: Check that you answered the *right* question Be careful! Choice D is a trap. The question isn't looking for the number you'd multiply the first equation by. Instead, it's looking for z, the coefficient of q. Because the number in front of q in your transformed equation is 5, you know that z must also be equal to 5, making (B) the correct answer.	$5q = zq$ $z = 5$

SOLVING SYSTEMS OF EQUATIONS: COMBINATION & SUBSTITUTION

Now that you understand the requirements that must be satisfied to solve a system of equations, let's look at some methods for solving these systems effectively. The two main methods for solving a system of linear equations are substitution and combination (sometimes referred to as *elimination by addition*).

Substitution is the most straightforward method for solving systems, and it can be applied in every situation. Unfortunately, it is often the longest and most time-consuming route for solving systems of equations as well. To use substitution, solve the simpler of the two equations for one variable, and then substitute the result into the other equation. You could use substitution to answer the following question, but you'll see that there's a quicker way: combination.

Combination involves adding the two equations together to eliminate a variable. Often, one or both of the equations must be multiplied by a constant before they are added together. Combination is often the best technique to use to solve a system of equations as it is usually faster than substitution.

Unfortunately, even though most students prefer substitution, systems of equations on the PSAT are often designed to be quickly solved with combination. To really boost your score on Test Day, practice combination as much as you can on Practice Tests and in homework questions so that it becomes second nature. As you work through the following question, be sure to think about which strategy will be more efficient:

3. If $6a + 6b = 30$ and $3a + 2b = 14$, then what are the values of a and b ?

   A) $a = 2; b = 2$

   B) $a = 4; b = 1$

   C) $a = 1; b = 4$

   D) $a = 3; b = 1$

Work through the Kaplan Method for Math step-by-step to solve this question. The following table shows Kaplan's strategic thinking on the left, along with suggested math scratchwork on the right.

Strategic Thinking	Math Scratchwork
Step 1: Read the question, identifying and organizing important information as you go You are given a system of two equations with two unknowns and asked to find the values of a and b.	$6a + 6b = 30$ $3a + 2b = 14$
Step 2: Choose the best strategy to answer the question Remember, while substitution could be used to answer this type of question, combination will often be faster. *What transformation will enable you to add the equations and eliminate a variable?* Combination often requires you to multiply one of your equations by a constant. In this case, notice what happens if you multiply the second equation by −3. *What's the next step in combination?* By arranging the equations vertically, you can simply add them, combining like terms along the way. Notice that $6b + (−6b) = 0b = 0$, and you've eliminated b from your equation. Your goal when using combination is to set the coefficient of the variable you are trying to eliminate to a number that is equal in magnitude and opposite in sign to the coefficient in the other equation. Now you can easily solve for a.	$(−3)(3a + 2b) = (14)(−3)$ $−9a − 6b = −42$ $6a + 6b = 30$ $+ \quad −9a − 6b = −42$ ───────────── $−3a + 0b = −12$ $−3a + 0b = −12$ $−3a = −12$ $a = 4$
Step 3: Check that you answered the *right* question Even though the question asks you for the values of a and b, each answer choice has a different value of a. There's no need to plug back in and find the correct value of b. Choice (B) is correct.	

Combination can also be used when the test makers ask you for the sum or difference of two variables as in the following question:

4. If $5c - 2b = 15$ and $3b - 4c = 12$, what is the value of $b + c$?

A) −27

B) −3

C) 8

D) 27

Work through the Kaplan Method for Math step-by-step to solve this question. The following table shows Kaplan's strategic thinking on the left, along with suggested math scratchwork on the right.

Strategic Thinking	Math Scratchwork
Step 1: Read the question, identifying and organizing important information as you go You are being asked to find the value of $b + c$. The question stem provides two equations involving b and c.	$5c - 2b = 15$ $3b - 4c = 12$
Step 2: Choose the best strategy to answer the question *How can you quickly and accurately answer the question? Why are the test makers asking for the quantity* b + c *and not the values of* b *and* c *independently?* The fact that you're solving for $b + c$ suggests that there's a time-saving shortcut to be found. Because you're not trying to get rid of a variable, see if you can add the equations to get a result that has $b + c$ equal to some numerical value. Before you add, don't forget to write the variable terms in the same order for each equation.	$\begin{array}{r} -2b + 5c = 15 \\ +\quad 3b - 4c = 12 \\ \hline b + c = 27 \end{array}$
Step 3: Check that you answered the *right* question Because you're asked to find the value of $b + c$, there's nothing more to do here. Choice (D) is correct.	$b + c = 27$

That was much easier and faster than substitution. With substitution, you could spend more than two minutes solving a question like this. However, a bit of analysis and combination gets the job done in much less time.

Math

TRANSLATING WORD PROBLEMS INTO MULTIPLE EQUATIONS

While solving systems of equations can be relatively straightforward once you get the hang of it, sometimes you'll encounter a complex word problem and will need to translate it into a system of equations and then solve. It sounds a lot scarier than it actually is. Remember to use the Kaplan Strategy for Translating English into Math to set up your equations, and then solve using either substitution or combination.

> ✔ **Note**
>
> The Kaplan Strategy for Translating English into Math can be found in chapter 12.

Let's take a look at an example:

5. At a snack stand, hot dogs cost $3.50 and hamburgers cost $5. If the snack stand sold 27 snacks and made $118.50 in revenue, how many hot dogs were sold? How many hamburgers?

    A) 16 hot dogs; 11 hamburgers

    B) 16 hot dogs; 16 hamburgers

    C) 11 hot dogs; 14 hamburgers

    D) 11 hot dogs; 16 hamburgers

Work through the Kaplan Method for Math step-by-step to solve this question. The following table shows Kaplan's strategic thinking on the left, along with suggested math scratchwork on the right.

Strategic Thinking	Math Scratchwork
Step 1: Read the question, identifying and organizing important information as you go You need to find the number of hot dogs and hamburgers sold.	
Step 2: Choose the best strategy to answer the question Use the Kaplan Strategy for Translating English into Math. *What variables should you use?* Because both snacks start with h, that's likely to be a confusing choice. Instead, use d for hot dogs and b for hamburgers. *How do you break apart the question into smaller phrases?* Break off each piece of relevant information into a separate phrase. *What should you do with the phrases?* Translating each phrase into a math expression will create the components of a system of equations. *What is the system of equations that will get you to the answer?* Assemble the math expressions you have to get the system of equations needed. *How can you best solve this system of equations?* In this case, you can use either substitution or combination to arrive at the numbers of hot dogs and hamburgers. To use combination, multiply the first equation by -5 to set it up. Continuing to solve, you see that $d = 11$. *What does this information enable you to do?* That immediately eliminates A and B. You now can plug 11 back into the first equation to get b.	$d =$ hot dogs sold $b =$ hamburgers sold hot dogs cost \$3.50 $\rightarrow 3.5d$ hamburgers cost \$5 $\rightarrow 5b$ snack stand sold 27 snacks $\rightarrow d + b = 27$ made \$118.50 in revenue $\rightarrow$ Total \$ $= 118.5$ $d + b = 27$ $3.5d + 5b = 118.5$ $\begin{array}{r} -5d - 5b = -135 \\ +\ \ 3.5d + 5b = 118.5 \\ \hline -1.5d + 0b = -16.5 \\ d = 11 \end{array}$ $d + b = 27$ $11 + b = 27$ $b = 16$
Step 3: Check that you answered the *right* question The only answer choice that meets these criteria is (D).	

Watch out for choice A, a trap answer designed to catch students who switched the variables, possibly due to choosing an ambiguous letter such as *h*. Choosing descriptive variable names might sound silly, but in the high-stakes environment of the PSAT, doing this can make the difference between a decent score and a National Merit Scholarship.

> ✔ **Note**
>
> Always choose variable names that make sense to you. Countless students struggle on multi-part questions due to disorganized notes. Don't let that happen to you. Move beyond *x* and *y* when selecting variable names.

Other questions of this type will simply ask you to choose from a series of answer choices that describes the system of equations—they won't actually ask you to calculate a solution! These questions can be great time-savers. Consider the following example:

6. A local airport has separate fees for commercial airliners and private planes to take into account the different rates of wear that each has on the facility. Commercial flights are charged a landing fee of $281 per flight, and private planes are charged a landing fee of $31 per flight. On a given day, a total of 312 planes landed at the airport, and $47,848 in landing fees was collected. Solving which of the following systems of equations yields the number of commercial airliners, *c*, and the number of private planes, *p*, that landed at the airport on the day in question?

    A) $c + p = 47,848$; $281c + 31p = 312$

    B) $c + p = 312$; $31c + 281p = 47,848$

    C) $c + p = 312$; $281c + 31p = 47,848$

    D) $c + p = 47,848$; $31c + 281p = 312$

Work through the Kaplan Method for Math step-by-step to solve this question. The following table shows Kaplan's strategic thinking on the left, along with suggested math scratchwork on the right.

Strategic Thinking	Math Scratchwork
Step 1: Read the question, identifying and organizing important information as you go You're asked for the system of equations that best represents the situation given.	
Step 2: Choose the best strategy to answer the question *What system of equations best models this scenario? What two equations should you construct?* You are given information about the total landing fees and the total number of planes. What quantities would add up to give you these totals? *What quantities combine to give you the total number of planes that landed at the airport?*	A total of 312 planes landed at the airport. $47,848 in landing fees were collected.
The number of private planes and airliners combined would yield the total number of planes. This immediately eliminates A and D.	$p + c = 312$
The cost for all of the commercial airliners could be represented by the cost of each airliner times the number of airliners.	$commercial = 281c$
Similarly, the cost for all the private planes could be represented by the cost of each plane times the number of planes.	$private = 31p$
The total amount of landing fees would then be both of these quantities added together. *Which answer choice has both of these equations in it?*	$47,848 = 281c + 31p$
Step 3: Check that you answered the *right* question If you chose (C), you're absolutely correct.	

Be careful! Choice B is close but switches the fee structure, drastically overcharging the private planes. Always pay close attention to the differences between answer choices to avoid traps on Test Day.

Now you'll have a chance to try a few more test-like questions. Use the scaffolding as needed to guide you through the question and get the correct answer.

Some guidance is provided, but you'll need to fill in the missing parts of explanations or the step-by-step math to get to the correct answer. Don't worry—after going through the examples at the beginning of this chapter, these questions should be completely doable. If you find yourself struggling, however, review the worked examples again.

7. A certain student cell phone plan charges $0.10 per text and $0.15 per picture, with no additional monthly fee. If a student sends a total of 75 texts and pictures in one month and is billed $8.90 for that month, how many more texts did he send than pictures?

    A) 19

    B) 28

    C) 36

    D) 47

The following table can help you structure your thinking as you go about answering this question. Kaplan's strategic thinking is provided, as are bits of structured scratchwork. If you're not sure how to approach a question like this, start at the top and work your way down.

Strategic Thinking	Math Scratchwork
Step 1: Read the question, identifying and organizing important information as you go You're asked how many more texts than pictures were sent.	
Step 2: Choose the best strategy to answer the question Use the Kaplan Strategy for Translating English into Math. Pick variables that match the context by using the letter that each word starts with. Next, break off each piece of relevant information into a separate phrase. *What should you do with the phrases?* Translating each phrase into a math expression will get you the components of a system of equations. *How can you best solve this system of equations?* You can use either substitution or combination to arrive at the text and picture counts. Remember to think critically about which approach would be faster in this situation. *How many texts were sent? How many pictures?* Solve for each variable. *Are you done?* You're not quite done. The question asks how many more texts were sent than pictures, so find the difference.	texts: ____ pictures: ____ _____ _____ _____ text cost: _____ picture cost: _____ total texts + pictures: _____ total bill: _____ . ____ + ____ = ____ ____ + ____ = texts: _____ pictures: _____ ____ − ____ = ____
Step 3: Check that you answered the *right* question If you answered (A), you're absolutely correct.	

8. Given $2x + 5y = 49$ and $5x + 3y = 94$, what is the product of x and y?

Larger numbers don't make this question any different; just be careful with the arithmetic. Again, the following table can help you structure your thinking as you go about answering this question. Kaplan's strategic thinking is provided, as are bits of structured scratchwork. If you're not sure how to approach a question like this, start at the top and work your way down.

Strategic Thinking	Math Scratchwork
Step 1: Read the question, identifying and organizing important information as you go You're asked to find the product of *x* and *y*.	
Step 2: Choose the best strategy to answer the question *What's the quickest route to the answer?* You have coefficients on all four variable terms and large constants on the right sides of the equations, so combination will likely be faster than substitution. *How do you cancel out one of the variables?* Although you can often get away with manipulating only one equation, you'll need to adjust both here. The *x* coefficients are 2 and 5. No integer will multiply by 2 to get 5 and vice versa, but what about multiplying both equations by numbers that will get you a common multiple on both *x* terms? Don't forget to make one of them negative. *What is the next step?* Carry out combination as usual, being especially careful with the larger numbers. *What's the value of* y*?* Straightforward algebra from your combined equations should reveal the value of *y*. *How about* x*?* Plug your *y* value back into one of the original equations and solve for *x*. Lastly, multiply *x* and *y* together.	$2x + 5y = 49$ $5x + 3y = 94$ ___ (___ + ___ = ___) ___ (___ + ___ = ___) $y = $ ___ $x = $ ___ $xy = $ ___ × ___ = ___
Step 3: Check that you answered the *right* question If your answer is 51, you're correct!	$xy = $ ___

Now that you've seen the variety of ways in which the PSAT can test you on systems of linear equations, try the following questions to check your understanding. Give yourself 4.5 minutes to tackle the following three questions:

$$\begin{cases} 8x + 4y = 17 \\ \dfrac{1}{5}x + zy = \dfrac{1}{2} \end{cases}$$

9. In the system of linear equations shown, z is a constant. If the system has no solution, what is the value of z?

   A) $\dfrac{1}{10}$

   B) $\dfrac{1}{4}$

   C) 8

   D) 10

10. If x and y are both integers such that $x + 6 = 17$ and $y + 9 = 12$, what is the value of $x + y$?

11. Sixty people attended a concert. Children's tickets sold for $8 each, and adults' tickets sold for $12 each. If $624 was collected in ticket money, what is the product of the number of children and the number of adults who attended the concert?

   A) 275

   B) 779

   C) 864

   D) 900

Answers and Explanations for this chapter begin on page 548.

ON YOUR OWN

1. Guests at a wedding had two meal choices, chicken or vegetarian. The catering company charges $12.75 for each chicken dish and $9.50 for each vegetarian dish. If 62 people attended the wedding and the catering bill was $725.25, which of the following systems of equations could be used to find the number of people who ordered chicken, c, and the number of people who ordered vegetarian, v, assuming everyone ordered a meal?

    A) $\begin{cases} c + v = 725.25 \\ 12.75c + 9.5v = 62 \end{cases}$

    B) $\begin{cases} c + v = 62 \\ 12.75c + 9.5v = \dfrac{725.25}{2} \end{cases}$

    C) $\begin{cases} c + v = 62 \\ 12.75c + 9.5v = 725.25 \end{cases}$

    D) $\begin{cases} c + v = 62 \\ 12.75c + 9.5v = 725.25 \times 2 \end{cases}$

    $$\begin{cases} 2x - 4y = 14 \\ 5x + 4y = 21 \end{cases}$$

2. What is the y-coordinate of the solution to the system of equations shown?

    A) -1
    B) 0
    C) $\dfrac{7}{3}$
    D) 5

$$\begin{cases} 2x + 3y = 8 - y \\ x - 6y = 10 \end{cases}$$

3. If (x, y) is a solution to the system of equations shown above, then what is the value of $x - y$?

    A) $-\dfrac{3}{4}$
    B) $\dfrac{19}{4}$
    C) $\dfrac{11}{2}$
    D) $\dfrac{25}{4}$

4. A television set costs $25 less than twice the cost of a radio. If the television and radio together cost $200, how much more does the television cost than the radio?

    A) $50
    B) $75
    C) $100
    D) $125

5. Two turkey burgers and a bottle of water cost $3.25. If three turkey burgers and a bottle of water cost $4.50, what is the cost of two bottles of water?

    A) $0.75
    B) $1.25
    C) $1.50
    D) $3.00

$$\begin{cases} 3x - 4y = 10 \\ 6x + wy = 16 \end{cases}$$

6. For which of the following values of w will the system of equations above have no solution?

A) -8

B) -4

C) 4

D) 8

$$\begin{cases} \dfrac{1}{2}x - \dfrac{2}{3}y = c \\ 6x - 8y = -1 \end{cases}$$

7. If the system of linear equations shown has infinitely many solutions, and c is a constant, what is the value of c ?

A) $-\dfrac{1}{2}$

B) $-\dfrac{1}{12}$

C) 2

D) 12

8. At a certain restaurant, there are 25 tables, and each table has either 2 or 4 chairs. If a total of 86 chairs accompany the 25 tables, how many tables have exactly 4 chairs?

A) 12

B) 15

C) 18

D) 21

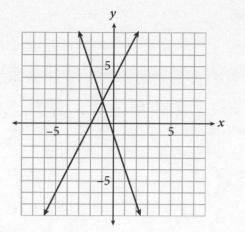

9. If (x, y) is the solution to the system of equations graphed in the figure, what is the value of $x + y$?

A) -2

B) -1

C) 1

D) 4

Problem Solving & Data Analysis

BY THE END OF THIS UNIT, YOU WILL BE ABLE TO:

1. Apply the Kaplan Method for Multi-Part Math Questions

2. Use rates, ratios, proportions, and percentages

3. Interpret and extract information from scatterplots and two-way tables

4. Analyze simple and complex data sets using descriptive statistics

CHAPTER 3

Rates, Ratios, Proportions, and Percentages

 ## CHAPTER OBJECTIVES

By the end of this chapter, you will be able to:

1. Use the Kaplan Method for Multi-Part Math Questions to answer Problem Solving and Data Analysis questions effectively

2. Solve multi-part question sets involving rates, ratios, and proportions

3. Use appropriate formulas to find percentages and single or multiple percent changes

SMARTPOINTS

Point Value	SmartPoint Category
Point Builder	Kaplan Method for Multi-Part Math Questions
80 Points	Rates, Ratios, Proportions, and Percentages

The PSAT contains multiple-choice and grid-in questions, as well as multi-part math question sets. These question sets have multiple parts that are based on the same scenario and may require more analysis and planning than a typical multiple-choice question. To help you answer these questions effectively, use the Kaplan Method for Multi-Part Math Questions.

KAPLAN METHOD FOR MULTI-PART MATH QUESTIONS

Step 1: Read the first question in the set, looking for clues

Step 2: Identify and organize the information you need

Step 3: Based on what you know, plan your steps to navigate the first question

Step 4: Solve, step-by-step, checking units as you go

Step 5: Did I answer the *right* question?

Step 6: Repeat for remaining questions, incorporating results from the previous question if possible

The next few pages will walk you through each step in more detail.

Step 1: Read the first question in the set, looking for clues

- **Focus all your energy here** instead of diluting it over the whole set of questions; solving a multi-part question in pieces is far simpler than trying to solve all the questions in the set at once. Further, you may be able to use the results from earlier parts to solve subsequent ones. Don't even consider the later parts of the question set until you've solved the first part.

- **Watch for hints** about what information you'll actually need to use to answer the questions. Underlining key quantities is often helpful to separate what's important from extraneous information.

Step 2: Identify and organize the information you need

If you think this sounds like the Kaplan Method for Math, you're absolutely correct. You'll use some of those same skills. The difference: a multi-part math question is just more involved with multiple pieces.

- **What information am I given?** Jot down key notes, and group related quantities to develop your strategy.

- **What am I solving for?** This is your target. As you work your way through subsequent steps, keep your target at the front of your mind. This will help you avoid unnecessary work (and subsequent time loss). You'll sometimes need to tackle these questions from both ends, so always keep your goal in mind.

> ✔ **Expert Tip**
>
> Many students freeze when they encounter a question with multiple steps and seemingly massive amounts of information. Don't worry! Take each piece one at a time, and you won't be intimidated.

Step 3: Based on what you know, plan your steps to navigate the first question

- **What pieces am I missing?** Many students become frustrated when faced with a roadblock such as missing information, but it's an easy fix. Sometimes you'll need to do an intermediate calculation to reveal the missing piece or pieces of the puzzle.

Step 4: Solve, step-by-step, checking units as you go

- **Work quickly but carefully**, just as you've done on other PSAT math questions.

Step 5: Did I answer the *right* question?

- As is the case with the Kaplan Method for Math, **make sure your final answer is the requested answer**.

- Review the first question in the set.

- Double-check your units and your work.

Step 6: Repeat for remaining questions, incorporating results from the previous question if possible

- Now take your results from the first question and think critically about whether they fit into the subsequent questions in the set. Previous results won't always be applicable, but when they are, they often lead to huge time savings. But be careful—don't round results from the first question in your calculations for the second question—only the final answer should be rounded.

When you've finished, congratulate yourself for persevering through such a challenging task. A multi-part math question is likely to be one of the toughest on the PSAT. If you can ace these questions, you'll be poised for a great score on Test Day. Don't worry if the Kaplan Method seems complicated; we'll walk through an example shortly.

> ✔ **Expert Tip**
>
> Because these question sets take substantially more time, consider saving multi-part math questions for last.

RATES, MEASUREMENT, AND UNIT CONVERSIONS

By now, you've become adept at using algebra to answer many PSAT math questions, which is great, because you'll need those algebra skills to answer questions involving rates. You're likely already familiar with many different rates—kilometers per hour, meters per second, and even miles per gallon are all considered rates.

A fundamental equation related to rates is "Distance = rate × time" (a.k.a. the DIRT equation— **D**istance **I**s **R**ate × **T**ime). If you have two of the three components of the equation, you can easily find the third. An upcoming multi-part math example demonstrates this nicely.

You'll notice units of measurement are important for rate questions (and others that require a unit conversion) and, therefore, also an opportunity to fall for trap answers if you're not careful. How can you avoid this? Use the factor-label method (also known as dimensional analysis). The factor-label method is a simple yet powerful way to ensure you're doing your calculations correctly and getting an answer with the requested units.

For example, suppose you're asked to find the number of cups there are in two gallons. First, identify your starting quantity's units (gallons), and then identify the end quantity's units (cups). The next step is to piece together a path of relationships that will convert gallons into cups, canceling out units as you go. Keep in mind that you will often have multiple stepping stones between your starting and ending quantities, so don't panic if you can't get directly from gallons to cups.

The test makers won't expect you to know English measurements by heart. Instead, they'll provide conversion factors when needed. For example, a gallon is the same as 4 quarts, every quart contains 2 pints, and a pint equals 2 cups. And there you have it! Your map from gallons to cups is complete. The last step is to put it together as a giant multiplication question. Each relationship, called a conversion factor, is written as a fraction. The basic rules of fraction multiplication apply, so you can cancel a unit that appears in both the numerator and denominator.

> ✔ **Note**
>
> The PSAT will not require you to memorize conversions for conventional units. If the test asks you to convert miles into inches, for example, you will be provided with enough conversion factors to answer the question.

Follow along as we convert from gallons to quarts to pints to cups using the factor-label method:

$$2 \text{ gallons} \times \frac{4 \text{ quarts}}{1 \text{ gallon}} \times \frac{2 \text{ pints}}{1 \text{ quart}} \times \frac{2 \text{ cups}}{1 \text{ pint}} = (2 \times 4 \times 2 \times 2) \text{ cups} = 32 \text{ cups}$$

The DIRT equation is actually a variation of this process. Suppose you travel at 60 mph for 5 hours. You would calculate the distance traveled using the equation $d = rt = \dfrac{60 \text{ mi}}{1 \text{ h}} \times 5 \text{ h} = 300$ miles.

The units for hours cancel out, leaving only miles, which is precisely what you're looking for, a distance. This built-in check is a great way to ensure your path to the answer is correct. If your units are off, check your steps for mistakes along the way. The PSAT will never ask you for a quantity such as miles^4 or gallons^3, so if you end up with funky units like that, you've made an error somewhere in your work.

> ✔ **Note**
>
> When using the factor-label method, don't be afraid to flip fractions and rates to make the units cancel out as needed.

The following question demonstrates the factor-label method in a test-like question:

1. A homeowner wants to buy 81 square feet of grass for his yard, but the vendor he uses only sells grass by the square yard. How many square yards of grass does the homeowner need? (1 yard = 3 feet)

    A)   9

    B)   27

    C)   243

    D)   729

Work through the Kaplan Method for Math step-by-step to solve this question. The following table shows Kaplan's strategic thinking on the left, along with suggested math scratchwork on the right.

Strategic Thinking	Math Scratchwork
Step 1: Read the question, identifying and organizing important information as you go You're asked how many square yards of grass the homeowner needs. You know he needs 81 square feet of grass.	81 ft^2 grass needed
Step 2: Choose the best strategy to answer the question *How do you convert from square feet to square yards?*	Use factor-label method
What are the starting and ending quantity units? Which conversion factors are needed? You're starting with square feet and need to convert to square yards. You know that 1 yd = 3 ft, but be careful: 1 yd^2 is not the same as 3 ft^2. Consider each feet-to-yards conversion separately. You'll need to multiply by your conversion factor twice. Remember your rules for exponents: to cancel out ft^2, you'll need to divide by ft^2.	starting qty: 81 ft^2 end qty: $? \text{ yd}^2$ $\dfrac{81 \text{ ft}^2}{1} \times \dfrac{1 \text{ yd}}{3 \text{ ft}} \times \dfrac{1 \text{ yd}}{3 \text{ ft}} = \dfrac{81}{9} \text{ yd}^2$ $= 9 \text{ yd}^2$
Step 3: Check that you answered the *right* question You've correctly converted from square feet to square yards to get the correct answer, (A).	9 yd^2

> ✔ **Note**
>
> The conversion from feet to yards is not the same as the conversion from square feet to square yards (or cubic feet to cubic yards). Trap answers will often use incorrect conversion factors. Be particularly careful when dealing with area or volume conversions that have multiple dimensions.

Next, you'll walk through a test-like multi-part question that involves rates. Follow along with the Kaplan Method and think about how knowledge of rates and conversion factors is used to get to the answer.

Remember, even though these questions have multiple parts, you'll rely on the same math skills you'd use in a simple multiple-choice question to solve each part. If you find that there are missing pieces or missing quantities, use techniques such as the factor-label method to bridge the gap. Also keep in mind that you may be able to use the answer from one part as a shortcut to answering the next part. If you do, don't round until the final answer, especially on grid-in questions.

Questions 2 and 3 refer to the following information.

Three business professionals are traveling to New York City for a conference. Mr. Black is taking a train from Philadelphia that leaves at 7:00 a.m. Eastern Time (ET), Ms. Weiss will begin driving in from Newark at 6:15 a.m. ET, and Dr. Grey plans to catch a plane from Chicago that departs at 8:30 a.m. Central Time (one hour behind ET).

2. With traffic, Ms. Weiss averages a speed of 25 mph for the length of her 20-mile commute. Mr. Black's train will get to NYC, a 100-mile journey, at 8:15 a.m. ET. How much longer, in minutes, will Mr. Black travel than Ms. Weiss?

3. Dr. Grey's flight is delayed 45 minutes. If the plane flies at 332 mph for the 830-mile flight, how many hours after Ms. Weiss arrives will Dr. Grey arrive? Round your answer to the nearest tenth of an hour.

Work through the Kaplan Method for Multi-Part Math Questions step-by-step to solve this set of questions. The following table shows Kaplan's strategic thinking on the left, along with suggested math scratchwork on the right.

Strategic Thinking	Math Scratchwork
Step 1: Read the first question in the set, looking for clues You know the travel start times of the three colleagues, as well as Ms. Weiss's speed and commute length and Mr. Black's commute length and arrival time.	Departure times: B: 7:00 a.m. ET W: 6:15 a.m. ET G: 8:30 a.m. CT W: 25 mph, 20 mi traveled B: 100 mi traveled, arrives at 8:15 ET
Step 2: Identify and organize the information you need *What do you need to find for this question? Of the information given, what will help answer the question? What can you dismiss?* You're asked to find the time between Ms. Weiss and Mr. Black's arrivals. Because the first question asks only about Mr. Black and Ms. Weiss, you can disregard any information about Dr. Grey for now. To answer this question, you need Mr. Black's and Ms. Weiss's travel times. *What about Mr. Black's speed?* This question asks for the difference in arrival times. Because you're given Mr. Black's travel time, finding his speed is not necessary.	B travel time: ? W travel time: ? disregard G for now
Step 3: Based on what you know, plan your steps to navigate the first question *How do you find Mr. Black's travel time? What about Ms. Weiss's?* Finding Mr. Black's travel time is straightforward; just take the difference between his departure and arrival times. You can use the DIRT equation to find Ms. Weiss's travel time.	B: start @ 7:00 a.m., arrive @ 8:15 a.m. W: $d = rt$

Strategic Thinking	Math Scratchwork
Step 4: Solve, step-by-step, checking units as you go *What is Mr. Black's travel time? What's Ms. Weiss's?* You know it took Mr. Black 75 minutes. For Ms. Weiss, plug her given speed (rate) and distance traveled into the DIRT equation, then solve for *t*. *How much longer will Mr. Black spend traveling?* Find the difference in travel times, making sure your answer is in the units requested (minutes).	B: 7:00 a.m. – 8:15 a.m. = 1 h 15 min = 75 min W: 20 mi = 25 mi/h × *t* $t = \dfrac{20}{25}$ h = 0.8 h = 48 min 75 min – 48 min = 27 min
Step 5: Did I answer the *right* question? Mr. Black will travel 27 minutes longer than Ms. Weiss.	27 min

✔ **Note**

You might be given extra information on questions like these. If you don't need it to get to the answer, then don't worry about it.

Now on to Step 6: Repeat for remaining questions in the set. Kaplan's strategic thinking is on the left, along with suggested math scratchwork on the right.

Strategic Thinking	Math Scratchwork
Step 1: Read the second question in the set, looking for clues From the introduction, you know Dr. Grey's flight was supposed to depart at 8:30 a.m. CT. This question tells you there is a 45-minute delay, as well as Dr. Grey's speed and distance traveled. You found Ms. Weiss's travel time in the previous question.	8:30 a.m. CT planned start, delayed 45 min plane speed: 332 mi/h distance covered: 830 mi W travel: 48 min

Math

Strategic Thinking	Math Scratchwork
Step 2: Identify and organize the information you need You need to determine how many hours separate the arrival times of Ms. Weiss and Dr. Grey.	W arrival: ? G arrival: ?
Step 3: Based on what you know, plan your steps to navigate the second question *What calculations will yield Dr. Grey's travel time?* You're given Dr. Grey's speed and distance, so you can use the DIRT equation to find his time in transit. Then add this time to his start time, taking the delay and time zone change into account.	G travel time: ? $d = rt$ + 45 min (delay), + 1 h (time zone)
Step 4: Solve, step-by-step, checking units as you go *How long is Dr. Grey's flight?* Plug the rate and distance into the DIRT equation and solve for time. *What effect do the delay and time zone change have on his arrival time?* Add 45 minutes to the initial start time to account for the delay, and then add the 2 hours and 30 minutes flight time. Add another hour for the time zone change. *At what time did Ms. Weiss arrive in New York? How many hours before Dr. Grey's arrival is this?* Add 48 minutes to Ms. Weiss's start time to yield her arrival time. Lastly, find the difference between the two colleagues' arrival times.	$d = rt$ 830 mi = 332 mi/h × t t = 2.5 h (2 h 30 min) G: 8:30 a.m. → 9:15 a.m. (delay) + 2 h 30 min flt = 11:45 a.m. CT → 12:45 p.m. ET W: 6:15 a.m. ET + 48 min = 7:03 a.m. ET 7:03 a.m. ET vs. 12:45 p.m. ET: diff = 5 h 42 min
Step 5: Did I answer the *right* question? Adjust your answer so it's in the requested format.	5 h 42 min = $5\frac{42}{60}$ h = 5.7 h

As you just saw, using the Kaplan Method for Multi-Part Math Questions makes an intimidating question far more straightforward. You'll have a chance to try it yourself later in this chapter.

RATIOS AND PROPORTIONS

Ratios and proportions are quite common in everyday life. Whether it's making a double batch of meatballs or calculating the odds of winning the lottery, you'll find that ratios and proportions are invaluable in myriad situations.

A **ratio** is a comparison of one quantity to another. When writing ratios, you can compare part of a group to another part of that group, or you can compare a part of the group to the whole group. Suppose you have a bowl of apples and oranges. You can write ratios that compare apples to oranges (part to part), apples to total fruit (part to whole), and oranges to total fruit (part to whole).

You can also combine ratios. If you have two ratios, $a:b$ and $b:c$, you can derive $a:c$ by finding a common multiple of the b terms. Take a look at the following table to see this in action:

a	:	b	:	c
3	:	4		
		3	:	5
9	:	12		
		12	:	20
9	:			20

What's a common multiple of the b terms? The number 12 is a good choice because it's the least common multiple of 3 and 4, thus reducing the need to simplify later. Where do you go from there? Multiply each ratio by the factor (use 3 for $a:b$ and 4 for $b:c$) that will get you to $b = 12$.

The ratio $a:c$ equals 9:20. Notice we didn't merely say $a:c$ is 3:5; this would be incorrect on Test Day (and likely a wrong-answer trap!).

A **proportion** is simply two ratios set equal to each other. Proportions are an efficient way to solve certain questions, but you must exercise caution when setting them up. Watching the units of each piece of the proportion will help you with this. Sometimes the PSAT will ask you to determine whether certain proportions are equivalent—check this by cross-multiplying. You'll get results that are much easier to compare.

If $\dfrac{a}{b} = \dfrac{c}{d}$, then: $ad = bc$, $\dfrac{a}{c} = \dfrac{b}{d}$, $\dfrac{d}{b} = \dfrac{c}{a}$, $\dfrac{b}{a} = \dfrac{d}{c}$, BUT $\dfrac{a}{d} \neq \dfrac{c}{b}$

Each derived ratio shown except the last one is simply a manipulation of the first, so all except the last are correct. You can verify this via cross-multiplication ($ad = bc$).

Alternatively, pick numerical values for a, b, c, and d; then simplify and confirm the two sides of the equation are equal. For example, take the two equivalent fractions $\dfrac{2}{3}$ and $\dfrac{6}{9}$ ($a = 2$, $b = 3$, $c = 6$, $d = 9$).

Cross-multiplication gives $2 \times 9 = 3 \times 6$, which is a true statement. Dividing a and b by c and d gives $\dfrac{2}{6} = \dfrac{3}{9}$, also true, and so on. However, attempting to equate $\dfrac{a}{d}\left(\dfrac{2}{9}\right)$ and $\dfrac{b}{c}\left(\dfrac{3}{6}\right)$ will not work.

Let's take a look at a test-like question that involves ratios:

4. A researcher is optimizing solvent conditions for a chemical reaction. The conventional protocols use either 7 parts dioxane (an organic solvent) and 3 parts water or 5 parts water and 2 parts methanol. The researcher wants to see what happens when she uses dioxane and methanol without deviating from the given protocols. What ratio of methanol to dioxane should she use?

    A) 35:6

    B) 7:2

    C) 2:7

    D) 6:35

Work through the Kaplan Method for Math step-by-step to solve this question. The following table shows Kaplan's strategic thinking on the left, along with suggested math scratchwork on the right.

Strategic Thinking	Math Scratchwork
Step 1: Read the question, identifying and organizing important information as you go You need the ratio of methanol to dioxane. You're given two ratios: dioxane to water and water to methanol.	D:W = 7:3 W:M = 5:2
Step 2: Choose the best strategy to answer the question *How can you directly compare methanol to dioxane? What's a common multiple of the two water components?* The two given ratios both contain water, but the water components are not identical. However, they share a common multiple: 15. Multiply each ratio by the factor that will make the water part equal 15. *What does the combined ratio look like?* Merging the two ratios lets you compare dioxane to methanol directly.	D:W = 7:3 W:M = 5:2 common multiple: 5 × 3 = 15 (7:3) × 5 = 35:15 (5:2) × 3 = 15:6 D:W:M = 35:15:6 D:M = 35:6
Step 3: Check that you answered the *right* question The question asks for methanol to dioxane, so flip your ratio, and you're done. Choice (D) is correct. Watch out for trap answer A. You aren't looking for dioxane to methanol.	M:D = 6:35

✔ **Note**

Beware of trap answers that contain incorrect ratios. Always confirm that you've found the ratio requested.

PERCENTAGES

Percentages aren't just for test grades; you'll find them frequently throughout life—discount pricing in stores, income tax brackets, and stock price trackers all use percents in some form. It's critical that you know how to use them correctly, especially on Test Day.

Suppose you have a bag containing 10 blue marbles and 15 pink marbles, and you're asked what percent of the marbles are pink. You can determine this easily by using the formula Percent $= \dfrac{\text{part}}{\text{whole}} \times 100\%$. Plug 15 in for the part and 10 + 15 (= 25) for the whole to get $\dfrac{15}{25} \times 100\% = 60\%$ pink marbles.

Another easy way to solve many percent questions is to use the following statement: (blank) percent of (blank) is (blank). Translating from English into math, you obtain (blank)% × (blank) = (blank). As you saw with the DIRT equation in the rates section, knowledge of any two quantities will unlock the third.

> ✔ **Note**
>
> The percent formula requires the percent component to be in decimal form. Remember to move the decimal point appropriately before using this formula.

You might also be asked to determine the **percent change** in a given situation. Fortunately, you can find this easily using a variant of the percent formula:

$$\text{Percent increase or decrease} = \frac{\text{amount of increase or decrease}}{\text{original amount}} \times 100\%$$

Sometimes more than one change will occur. Be especially careful here, as it can be tempting to take a shortcut by just adding two percent changes together (which will almost always lead to an incorrect answer). Instead, you'll need to find the total amount of the increase or decrease and calculate accordingly. We'll demonstrate this in an upcoming question.

The following is a test-like question involving percentages:

5. Ethanol is almost always mixed with gasoline to reduce automobile emissions. Most tanks of gasoline are 15% ethanol by volume. An oil company tries decreasing the ethanol content to 6% to lower the cost of gas. If a car with a 14-gallon tank is filled with the 15% blend, and a second car with a 10-gallon tank is filled with the 6% blend, how many times more ethanol is in the first car than in the second car?

    A) 1.5

    B) 2.5

    C) 3.5

    D) 4.0

Work through the Kaplan Method for Math step-by-step to solve this question. The following table shows Kaplan's strategic thinking on the left, along with suggested math scratchwork on the right.

Strategic Thinking	Math Scratchwork
Step 1: Read the question, identifying and organizing important information as you go You need to find how many times more ethanol is in the 15% tank. The question supplies information about a 14-gallon tank and a 10-gallon tank, each containing a different ethanol/gasoline blend.	14 gal tank: 15% ethanol 10 gal tank: 6% ethanol
Step 2: Choose the best strategy to answer the question *What formula can you use to get to the answer?* *How much ethanol is in the 14-gallon tank? How much ethanol is in the 10-gallon tank?* Plug the appropriate values into the percent formula. Remember to move the decimal points of your percents to get their decimal forms. *How many times more ethanol is in the larger tank?* Set up an equation to show 0.6 times a number equals 2.1. Solving for Z gives 3.5; that is, the larger tank contains 3.5 times more ethanol than the smaller one.	_____ % of _____ is _____ 0.15×14 gal $= 2.1$ gal 0.06×10 gal $= 0.6$ gal 0.6 gal $\times Z = 2.1$ gal $Z = \dfrac{2.1 \text{ gal}}{0.6 \text{ gal}} = 3.5$
Step 3: Check that you answered the *right* question The question asks for how many times more ethanol is in the 14-gallon tank, which is what you found: 3.5 matches (C).	

✔ **Note**

Resist the urge to merely take the difference between the two ethanol quantities. Make sure you're answering the question posed.

Here's an example of a multi-part question that tests your percentage expertise.

Questions 6 and 7 refer to the following information.

A bank normally offers a compound annual interest rate of 0.25% on any savings account with a minimum balance of $5,000. The bank is currently offering college students a higher rate, 0.42%, with a $1,000 minimum balance. Assume the average balances are kept constant at the required minima (e.g., all interest is withdrawn) for the following.

6. How much more interest does the regular account earn after three years than the student account?

7. What is the minimum balance a student would need to maintain to earn the same amount of interest in one year as would be earned by saving the minimum required balance in the regular account? Round your answer to the nearest dollar.

Work through the Kaplan Method for Multi-Part Math Questions step-by-step to solve this question. The following table shows Kaplan's strategic thinking on the left, along with suggested math scratchwork on the right.

Strategic Thinking	Math Scratchwork
Step 1: Read the first question in the set, looking for clues The intro provides information on two account types.	regular acct: 0.25%, $5,000 min student acct: 0.42%, $1,000 min
Step 2: Identify and organize the information you need You need to find how much more interest the $5,000 account will have after three years.	difference in interest: ?
Step 3: Based on what you know, plan your steps to navigate the first question *What pieces needed to find the answer are missing? How do you find the difference in interest?* You'll need the amount of interest that each account accrues after three years. Use the three-part percent formula to find annual interest, then find the interest after three years, then take the difference.	reg. int. = ? stu. int. = ? reg. int. × 3 = ? stu. int. × 3 = ? reg. − stu. = ? (blank)% of (blank) is (blank)

Strategic Thinking	Math Scratchwork
Step 4: Solve, step-by-step, checking units as you go	
How much interest does each account earn after one year? After three years?	$0.0025 \times \$5,000 = \$12.50$ $0.0042 \times \$1,000 = \$4.20$
Plug in appropriate values. Remember to adjust the decimal point on the percents appropriately. Triple the interest amounts to get the total accrued interest after three years.	$\$12.50 \times 3 = \$37.50$ $\$4.20 \times 3 = \$12.60$
What's the difference in interest earned?	
Subtract.	$\$37.50 - \$12.60 = \$24.90$
Step 5: Did I answer the *right* question?	
You've found how much more interest the regular account makes after three years, so you're done with the first question.	24.9

✔ **Note**

Disregard the 0 in the hundredths place when gridding in your answer.

The first part of the question set is finished! Now on to Step 6: Repeat for the other question in the set. Kaplan's strategic thinking is on the left, along with suggested math scratchwork on the right.

Strategic Thinking	Math Scratchwork
Step 1: Read the second question in the set, looking for clues No new information here, but some pieces from the first part of the question set might be useful.	
Step 2: Identify and organize the information you need *What does the second question ask you to find? Is there any information from the first question that will help?* The second question asks for the student account balance that will yield the same interest as a regular account at the minimum balance. You know the interest rates for a regular account and a student account at their respective minimum balances. You also know the interest earned annually (from the first question).	reg. acct: 0.25%, $12.50/yr stu. acct: 0.42%, $4.20/yr
Step 3: Based on what you know, plan your steps to navigate the second question *How can you determine when the two accounts will earn the same interest? Will algebra work here?* To answer the second question, you'll need to find when annual student interest equals annual regular interest. Set up equations with interest earned as a function of the account balance, one for each account. You already know what the regular account makes in interest annually, so it's just a matter of finding when the student equation equals that value.	Int. = rate × balance
Step 4: Solve, step-by-step, checking units as you go *When does the student account earn $12.50 in interest per year?* Plug 12.5 in for your dependent variable, then solve for *x*.	reg.: $y = 0.0025x$ $12.5 = 0.0025 \times 5,000$ stu.: $y = 0.0042x$ $12.5 = 0.0042x$ $x = 2,976.19$
Step 5: Did I answer the *right* question? The second question asks for the balance a student account needs to make the same interest as a regular account. Round to the nearest dollar, and you're done!	2,976

Now you'll have a chance to try a few test-like questions in a scaffolded way. We've provided some guidance, but you'll need to fill in the missing parts of explanations or the step-by-step math to get to the correct answer. Don't worry—after going through the worked examples at the beginning of this section, these questions should be completely doable.

8. Fuel efficiency is a measure of how many miles a car can go using a specified amount of fuel. It can change depending on the speed driven and how often the driver brakes and then accelerates, as well as other factors. Jack is taking a road trip. If he travels 180 miles at 40 miles per gallon and then another 105 miles at 35 miles per gallon, how many gallons of fuel has his car consumed?

    A) 1.5

    B) 3.0

    C) 4.5

    D) 7.5

The following table can help you structure your thinking as you go about solving this question. Kaplan's strategic thinking is provided, as are bits of structured scratchwork.

Strategic Thinking	Math Scratchwork
Step 1: Read the question, identifying and organizing important information as you go	
You need to find the amount of fuel Jack's car consumed. The question provides information about two legs of Jack's trip.	___ mi @ ___ mpg ___ mi @ ___ mpg
Step 2: Choose the best strategy to answer the question	
What hint does the unit "miles per gallon" give you? Is there a standard equation you can use?	___ = ___ × ___
The unit mpg is a rate, so straightforward math using the DIRT equation is appropriate.	Leg 1: ___ = ___ × t $t =$ ___
180 miles is clearly a distance, and 40 miles per gallon is your rate. Therefore, you need to find the time. Don't forget your units. Repeat for the second leg.	Leg 2: ___ = ___ × t $t =$ ___
The ultimate goal is to find the total fuel consumption. Add the two gallon figures together.	___ + ___ = ___
Step 3: Check that you answered the *right* question	
If your answer is (D), you're correct!	fuel consumed: ___ gal

Here's another test-like example to try:

9. Financial advisers are often hired to manage people's retirement accounts by shifting
    how money is invested in stocks and bonds. During a particularly volatile stock market
    period, a financial adviser makes a number of changes to a client's stock allocation.
    She first decreases this allocation by 25%, then increases it by 10%, then increases
    it by an additional 50%. What is the approximate net percent increase in this client's
    stock allocation?

    A) 20%

    B) 24%

    C) 30%

    D) 35%

The following table can help you structure your thinking as you go about answering this question. Kaplan's strategic thinking is provided, as are bits of structured scratchwork. If you're not sure how to approach a question like this, start at the top and work your way down.

Strategic Thinking	Math Scratchwork
Step 1: Read the question, identifying and organizing important information as you go You need to find the net percent change in this client's stock allocation. The question provides a series of percent changes that this allocation undergoes.	start → _____ → _____ → _____ → end
Step 2: Choose the best strategy to answer the question *What kind of question is this? What's a good starting point for calculations?* This is a percent change question. You aren't given a concrete starting point, so pick a starting number that's easy to use with percents, and get ready for a series of three-part percent formula calculations. *How many shares are left after each change?* Plug in the starting share count and the new percent, then solve for the new share count. Using the percent left in your calculation instead of the percent change will save you a step. When you compute the second and third changes, remember to use the final share count from the previous calculation, not the original number of shares. *Am I finished?* You found the final stock share count, now you need to find the percent change.	assume _____ shares @ start after − 25%: _____% × _____ = _____ shares left: _____ after + 10%: _____% × _____ = _____ shares left: _____ after + 50%: _____% × _____ = _____ shares left: _____ _____ × 100% = _____
Step 3: Check that you answered the *right* question If you chose (B), you're correct.	net change: _____%

Now try your hand at a multi-part question.

Math

Questions 10 and 11 refer to the following information.

An artist is creating a rectangular tile mosaic. Her desired pattern uses 5 green tiles and 3 blue tiles per square foot of mosaic.

10. If the artist's entire mosaic is 12 feet by 18 feet, how many more green tiles than blue will she need?

11. The artist discovers her tile vendor has a very limited supply of green tiles, so she alters her design so that it requires 2 green tiles and 3 blue tiles per square foot of mosaic. She also decides to add red tiles to her mosaic. How many red tiles will the artist need to make the ratio of red tiles to green tiles 3:4 ?

The following table can help you structure your thinking as you go about answering this question. Kaplan's strategic thinking is provided, as are bits of structured scratchwork. If you're not sure how to approach a question like this, start at the top and work your way down.

Strategic Thinking	Math Scratchwork
Step 1: Read the first question in the set, looking for clues Included are the size of the mosaic and the ratio of green to blue tiles.	mosaic dimensions: ___ × ___ green:blue → ___:___
Step 2: Identify and organize the information you need You must find how many more green tiles than blue tiles the artist will use.	diff. between green & blue: ?
Step 3: Based on what you know, plan your steps to navigate the first question *What's missing? What calculations will get you the tile counts? How are the mosaic dimensions important?* You're missing the number of green tiles and blue tiles, as well as the number of times the pattern appears in the mosaic. You know the pattern appears once per square foot of mosaic, so finding the mosaic area will tell you how many times the pattern repeats. Multiply this number by the tile ratio to find how many of each color the artist needs, then take the difference.	# green tiles: ? # blue tiles: ? # pattern appearances: ? A = ? A × green:blue = # green: # blue

Strategic Thinking	Math Scratchwork
Step 4: Solve, step-by-step, checking units as you go *What's the area of the mosaic?* Use the rectangle area formula to find the area of the mosaic (and the number of times the pattern repeats). *How many green tiles and blue tiles will the artist require? How many more green will she need?* Multiply the area by each number in the tile ratio, and then take the difference.	$A = \underline{\quad} \times \underline{\quad} = \underline{\quad}$ green: $\underline{\quad} \times \underline{\quad} = \underline{\quad}$ blue: $\underline{\quad} \times \underline{\quad} = \underline{\quad}$ $\underline{\quad}$ green $- \underline{\quad}$ blue $= \underline{\quad}$
Step 5: Did I answer the *right* question? If you came up with 432 more green tiles, great job! You're correct.	difference: $\underline{\quad}$

Fantastic! Now repeat for the other question in the set. Once again, Kaplan's strategic thinking is provided in the table that follows, as are bits of structured scratchwork. If you're not sure how to approach the second part, start at the top and work your way down.

Math

Strategic Thinking	Math Scratchwork
Step 1: Read the second question in the set, looking for clues You know the new ratio of green to blue tiles and what the ratio of red to green tiles should be, as well as the area of the mosaic (from the previous question).	green:blue → ____ : ____ red:green → ____ : ____ area: ____
Step 2: Identify and organize the information you need To answer this question, you need to find how many red tiles are required to make the ratio of red to green 3:4.	# red tiles: ?
Step 3: Based on what you know, plan your steps to navigate the second question *Anything missing? How does the new green:blue ratio affect the green tile count?* The ratios here are different, so you'll need new tile counts for green and red (blue stays constant). First, find the adjusted number of green tiles needed. Then determine the number of red tiles needed to satisfy the given ratio using a proportion that compares red to green.	# green tiles: ? # red tiles: ?
Step 4: Solve, step-by-step, checking units as you go *Given the new green:blue ratio, how many green tiles are now needed?* Multiply the number of pattern appearances from the first question by the green tile component of the adjusted ratio. *What red tile count will satisfy the desired red:green ratio? Could a proportion be useful?* Set up a proportion using the red:green ratio and the new green tile count to find the number of red tiles required. Be careful when setting it up.	# green: ____ × ____ = ____ $\dfrac{red}{green} : \dfrac{?}{?} = \dfrac{?}{?} \rightarrow$ ____ = ____ ____ = ____
Step 5: Did I answer the *right* question? Did you get 324 red tiles? If so, congrats! You're correct.	____ red tiles

Now that you've seen the variety of ways in which the PSAT can test you on ratios, rates, proportions, and percentages, try the following questions to check your understanding. Give yourself 5 minutes to answer the following four questions. Make sure you use the Kaplan Method for Math as often as you can (as well as the Kaplan Method for Multi-Part Math Questions when necessary). Remember, you want to emphasize speed and efficiency in addition to simply getting the correct answer.

12. An engineer is monitoring construction of a 75-foot escalator. The difference in height between the two floors being connected was originally supposed to be 40 feet, but due to a calculation error, this figure must be reduced by 25%. The angle between the escalator and the floor must not change in order to comply with the building code. What is the change in length in feet between the original escalator measurement and its corrected value?

A) 18.75

B) 25

C) 56.25

D) 100

13. Grocery stores often sell larger quantities of certain foods at reduced prices so that customers ultimately get more food for less money. Suppose an 8-ounce can of pineapple sells for $0.72 and a 20-ounce can costs $1.10. How many more cents does the 8-ounce can cost per ounce than the 20-ounce can?

Questions 14 and 15 refer to the following information.

An electronics store is having a Black Friday Blowout sale. All items are 40% off, and the first 50 customers will receive an additional 25% off the reduced prices.

14. Two people purchase a home theater system that normally costs $2,200. The first person is one of the first 50 customers. The second person arrives much later in the day. How much more, in dollars, does the first customer save than the second customer?

15. In addition to price reductions, the store is offering to pay part of the sales tax on customers' purchases: instead of paying the regular 6.35% sales tax, customers pay only half this rate. Assuming the same conditions from the previous question and that you are among the first 50 in the store, what is the total difference in price between the reduced price (with reduced tax) and the full price with standard tax? Round your answer to the nearest dollar.

Answers and Explanations for this chapter begin on page 552.

ON YOUR OWN

You may use your calculator for all questions in this section.

1. During fairly heavy traffic, the number of cars that can safely pass through a stoplight during a left turn signal is directly proportional to the length of time in seconds that the signal is green. If 9 cars can safely pass through a light that lasts 36 seconds, how many cars can safely pass through a light that lasts 24 seconds?

    A) 4

    B) 6

    C) 7

    D) 8

2. For every 4,000 snowblowers produced by a snowblower factory, exactly 8 are defective. At this rate, how many snowblowers were produced during a period in which exactly 18 snowblowers were defective?

    A)   6,000

    B)   9,000

    C)   12,000

    D)   18,000

3. The average college student reads prose text written in English at a rate of about 5 words per second. If the pages of Jorge's world history textbook contain an average of 500 words per page, how long will it take him to read a 45-page chapter?

    A)   50 minutes

    B)   1 hour, 15 minutes

    C)   1 hour, 25 minutes

    D)   1 hour, 40 minutes

4. According to data provided by the College Board, the cost of tuition and fees for a private nonprofit four-year college in 1988 was approximately $15,800 (in 2013 dollars). In 2013, the cost of tuition and fees at the same type of college was approximately $30,100. If the cost of education experiences the same total percent increase over the next 25 years, approximately how much will tuition and fees at a private nonprofit four-year college cost (in 2013 dollars)?

    A) $44,400

    B) $45,800

    C) $57,300

    D) $66,200

5. A radiology center administers magnetic resonance images (MRIs) to check for abnormalities in a patient's body. One MRI scan typically produces about 3.6 gigabits of data. Every night, for 8 hours, the hospital backs up the files of the scans on a secure remote server. The hospital computers can upload the images at a rate of 2 megabits per second. What is the maximum number of MRI scans that the hospital can upload to the remote server each night? (1 gigabit = 1,024 megabits)

A)   15

B)   16

C)   56

D)   202

6. A chef is preparing ingredients to make a large quiche. The recipe calls for 5 cups of milk and 2 eggs. There is also a lower-fat option that calls for 4 cups of water and 3 eggs. The caterer wants to see what happens when he uses both milk and water. To keep the same ratio of liquid to eggs, what ratio of milk to water should he use?

A)   1:1

B)   5:4

C)   8:15

D)   15:8

Questions 7 and 8 refer to the following information.

Verona owns a landscaping company, and she is mulching all of the flowerbeds at the houses in a planned retirement community. The figure shows the layout of the community and the times that Verona started mulching the flowerbeds at two of the houses. According to the architect's plans for the community, the flowerbed for each house is approximately 0.006 acres in size.

7. How many minutes will it take Verona to mulch all of the flowerbeds in the community?

8. Verona uses a landscaper's wagon that holds about 15 bags of mulch. Each bag of mulch covers 24 square feet of flowerbed. How many times, including the first time, will Verona need to fill the wagon, assuming she loads 15 bags of mulch each time? (1 acre = 43,560 square feet)

9. A cybercafé is a place that provides Internet access to the public, usually for a fee, along with snacks and drinks. Suppose a cybercafé charges a base rate of $25 to join for a year, an additional $0.30 per visit for the first 50 visits, and $0.10 for every visit after that. How much does the cybercafé charge for a year in which 72 visits are made?

A) $32.20

B) $36.60

C) $42.20

D) $46.60

10. A high school's Environment Club receives a certain amount of money from the school to host an all-day Going Green Teach-In. The club budgets 40% for a guest speaker, 25% for educational materials, 20% to rent a hotel conference room, and the remainder for lunch. If the club plans to spend $225 on lunch for the participants, how much does it plan to spend on the guest speaker?

A) $375

B) $450

C) $525

D) $600

Bead Content of Necklace

11. A certain necklace is made up of beads of the following colors: red, blue, orange, indigo, silver, and clear. The necklace contains 120 beads. According to the pie chart shown, how many beads of the necklace are not blue?

A) 20

B) 24

C) 80

D) 96

12. Most of the world uses the metric system of measurements. The United States uses the standard system, also called the English system. Luca is from a country that uses the metric system and is visiting his cousin Drew in the United States. He gives Drew a family recipe for bread. The recipe is for 1 loaf and calls for 180 milliliters of milk. Drew wants to make 5 loaves. If 1 U.S. cup equals 236.588 milliliters, how many cups of milk will Drew need?

A) $\frac{3}{4}$

B) $1\frac{1}{3}$

C) $3\frac{4}{5}$

D) $6\frac{1}{2}$

13. The Occupational Safety and Health Act (OSHA) was passed in 1970 to "assure safe and healthful working conditions." Its provisions cover all non-farm employers. Some small businesses, however, are exempt from certain reporting and inspection requirements if they have fewer than 10 employees. A certain city has 2,625 businesses in its jurisdiction and has a ratio of 5:2 of businesses that are exempt from inspections to those that are not exempt. Of the businesses that were required to have inspections, 12% had safety violations and were required to address the deficiencies. How many covered businesses did not have to address any OSHA safety issues?

A)   90

B)   315

C)   660

D)   2,310

14. Carmen is a traffic engineer. The city she works for recently added a number of new intersections with stoplights and wants to redesign the traffic system. The distance between the new intersections increases as one moves down Main Street. Carmen has been given the task of determining the length of the green lights at the intersections along Main Street, according to the following guidelines:

- The length of each green light should be greater than or equal to 8 seconds but less than or equal to 30 seconds.

- Each green light should be at least 25% longer than the one at the intersection before it.

- The length of each green light must be a whole second.

Which list of light lengths meets the city guidelines and includes as many intersections as possible?

A)   8, 12, 16, 20, 25, 30

B)   8, 10, 13, 17, 22, 28

C)   8, 10, 12.5, 16, 20, 25

D)   8, 10, 12, 15, 18, 22, 27

15. An average consumer car can travel 120 miles per hour under controlled conditions. An average race car can travel 210 miles per hour. How many more miles can the race car travel in 30 seconds than the consumer car?

A) $\dfrac{3}{4}$

B) 1

C) $\dfrac{3}{2}$

D) 45

16. An Internet provider charges k dollars for the first hour of use in a month and m dollars per hour for every additional hour used that month. If Jared paid $65.50 for his Internet use in one month, which of the following expressions represents the number of hours he used the Internet that month?

A) $\dfrac{65.50}{k + m}$

B) $\dfrac{65.50 - k}{m}$

C) $\dfrac{65.50 - k - m}{m}$

D) $\dfrac{65.50 - k + m}{m}$

17. Engine oil often contains additives that are designed to prevent certain common engine problems. One such additive is zinc, which reduces engine wear. Company A's oil contains 4% zinc, and Company B's oil contains 9%. Suppose a car uses 8 pints of Company B's oil and a truck uses 6 quarts of Company A's oil. How many times more zinc is in the car's oil pan than in the truck's? (1 quart = 2 pints)

A) 0.34

B) 0.67

C) 1.5

D) 3

18. When a consignment store gets a used piece of furniture to sell, it researches the original price and then marks the used piece down 40%. Every 30 days after that, the price is marked down an additional 20% until it is sold. The store gets a piece of used furniture on July 15. If the original price of the furniture was $1,050, and it is sold on October 5, what is the final selling price, not including tax?

A) $258.05

B) $322.56

C) $403.20

D) $630.00

19. In the United States, the maintenance and construction of airports, transit systems, and major roadways is largely funded through a federal tax on gasoline. Based on the 2011 statistics given below, what was the federal gasoline tax rate in cents per gallon?

- The average motor vehicle was driven approximately 11,340 miles per year.

- The national average fuel economy for noncommercial vehicles was 21.4 miles per gallon.

- The average American household owned 1.75 vehicles.

- The average household paid $170.63 annually in federal gasoline taxes.

A)   1.2

B)   5.43

C)   7.97

D)   18.4

20. An amusement park is building a scale model of an airplane for a 3-D ride. The real airplane measures 220 feet, 6 inches from nose to tail. The amusement park plans to make the ride 36 feet, 9 inches long. If the wingspan of the real plane is 176.5 feet, how long in inches should the wingspan on the ride be?

(1 foot = 12 inches)

A)   7 feet, 3 inches

B)   29 feet, 5 inches

C)   35 feet, 2 inches

D)   45 feet, 11 inches

Questions 21 and 22 refer to the following information.

Three planes depart from three different airports at 8:00 a.m., all traveling to Fort Lauderdale International Airport (FLL). The first plane is a small passenger plane that must travel 110 miles to reach FLL. The second plane is a large passenger plane that must travel 825 miles. The third plane is a cargo plane that must travel 640 miles.

21. The small passenger plane traveled at an average speed of 200 miles per hour. The cargo plane arrived at FLL at 9:15 a.m. How many minutes before the cargo plane arrived did the small passenger plane arrive?

22. For the first $\frac{1}{3}$ of the distance of the trip, the large passenger plane flew through fairly heavy cloud cover at an average speed of 300 miles per hour. For the remaining portion of the trip, the sky was clear and the plane flew at an average speed of 500 miles per hour. Due to a backlog of planes at the Fort Lauderdale airport, it was forced to circle overhead in a holding pattern for 35 minutes after arriving at the airport. At what time did the large passenger plane land at FLL? Use only digits for your answer (for example, enter 11:15 as 1115).

Math

Questions 23 and 24 refer to the following information.

A hedge fund usually consists of a small group of investors that employs aggressive, high-risk methods of investing in hopes of earning large capital gains. They always require a large minimum investment. Hedge fund portfolio managers usually charge a percentage of the value of the portfolio as a management fee. A certain company charges an annual fee of 3.5% with a minimum initial investment of $100,000 for lower-risk portfolios and an annual fee of 1.25% with a minimum investment of $250,000 for higher-risk portfolios.

23. If Christi manages one of each type of portfolio that is opened with only the minimum initial investment, and neither portfolio gains or loses money over 4 years, what is the difference in total fees that Christi will collect between the two portfolios?

24. What percent gain would the higher-risk portfolio need to make in 1 year for the annual fee to be as much as that of the lower-risk portfolio? Enter your answer as a decimal number (for example, enter 25% as .25).

Questions 25 and 26 refer to the following information.

An infomercial is advertising a new product that has just been made available in stores. The retail price of the item is $160. If you purchase the product through the infomercial, you receive 10% off the in-store retail price, and you do not have to pay sales tax. The company is also offering an additional 20% off the discounted infomercial price to the first 250 callers.

25. If the sales tax in your state is 5.5%, how much would you save by purchasing the item through the infomercial as one of the first 250 callers?

26. Malik is one of the first 250 callers and buys 5 of the item. He calls back later and is the 410th caller and buys 3 more. What is the average price that Malik paid per item?

Questions 27 and 28 refer to the following information.

A chemical solvent is a substance that dissolves another. For example, acetone is a solvent and is the primary ingredient in fingernail polish remover. It is also one of the few solvents that will safely remove adhesives from skin. The following table shows the chemical makeup of 1 mole (a unit of measure commonly used in chemistry) of acetone:

Chemical Makeup of 1 Mole of Acetone		
Element	Number of Moles	Mass per Mole (grams)
Oxygen	1	15.9994
Carbon	3	12.0107
Hydrogen	6	1.00794

27. Oxygen makes up what percent of the mass of 1 mole of acetone? Round your answer to the nearest whole percent.

28. If a chemist starts with 1,800 grams of acetone and uses 871.1871 grams, how many moles of carbon are left? Round your answer to the nearest whole mole.

Questions 29 and 30 refer to the following information.

Great Britain has not adopted the euro as its form of currency and instead utilizes the British pound. Rosslyn is from Great Britain but is vacationing throughout Europe. When she arrives in France, she realizes she forgot to exchange her British pounds for euros. Her bank does not exist in France, so she must use a local bank, which charges a 5% fee to exchange money for noncustomers.

29. Rosslyn wants to get 1,800 euros. The bank representative tells her that the total amount she will need, including the exchange fee, is 1,512 pounds. What is the current exchange rate from euros to British pounds?

30. When she returns to Great Britain, Rosslyn converts the 65 euros she has left back to British pounds at her own bank, where there is no fee to exchange the money. She is informed that the euros-to-pounds exchange rate has increased slightly over the course of her vacation. If Rosslyn lost a total of 74 pounds, including the fee she paid to the bank in France, what was the new euros-to-pounds exchange rate?

Passport to Advanced Math

BY THE END OF THIS UNIT, YOU WILL BE ABLE TO:

1. Simplify, solve, and rewrite expressions and equations involving polynomials, radicals, and exponents

2. Solve a formula for a given variable

3. Solve function questions graphically and algebraically

4. Combine multiple functions

5. Solve quadratic equations with and without a calculator

6. Connect quadratic equations to features of a parabola

CHAPTER 4

Exponents, Radicals, Polynomials, and Rational Expressions and Equations

CHAPTER OBJECTIVES

By the end of this chapter, you will be able to:

1. Simplify and solve expressions and equations involving exponents and/or radicals

2. Perform arithmetic operations on polynomials

3. Simplify expressions using polynomial long division and find polynomial remainders

4. Simplify and solve rational expressions and equations

5. Solve a formula for a given variable

SMARTPOINTS

Point Value	SmartPoint Category
80 Points	Exponents

INTRODUCTION TO EXPONENTS AND RADICALS

We often turn to our calculators to solve difficult radical and exponent questions, especially in math-intensive classes. However, being too calculator dependent can cost you time and points on the PSAT. Further, on the PSAT, many radical and exponent questions are structured in such a way that your calculator can't help you, even if it is allowed.

This chapter will review algebra and arithmetic rules that you may have learned at some point but likely haven't used in a while. This chapter will reacquaint you with the formulas and procedures you'll need to simplify even the toughest expressions and equations on the PSAT. We'll start with exponents.

Questions involving exponents often look intimidating, but when you know the rules governing them, you'll see that there are plenty of shortcuts. First, it's important to understand the anatomy of a term that has an exponent. This term is comprised of two pieces: a base and an exponent (also called a power). The base is the number in larger type and is the value being multiplied by itself. The exponent, written as a superscript, shows you how many times the base is being multiplied by itself.

$$\text{Base} \Rightarrow 3^4 \Leftarrow \text{Exponent} \text{ is the same as } 3 \times 3 \times 3 \times 3$$

The following table lists the rules you'll need to handle any exponent question you'll see on the PSAT.

Rule	Example
When multiplying two terms with the same base, add the exponents.	$a^b \times a^c = a^{(b+c)} \rightarrow 4^2 \times 4^3 = 4^{2+3} = 4^5$
When dividing two terms with the same base, subtract the exponents.	$\dfrac{a^b}{a^c} = a^{(b-c)} \rightarrow \dfrac{4^3}{4^2} = 4^{3-2} = 4^1$
When raising a power to another power, multiply the exponents.	$(a^b)^c = a^{(bc)} \rightarrow (4^3)^2 = 4^{3 \times 2} = 4^6;$ $(2x^2)^3 = 2^{1 \times 3} x^{2 \times 3} = 8x^6$
When raising a product to a power, apply the power to all factors in the product.	$(ab)^c = a^c \times b^c \rightarrow (2m)^3 = 2^3 \times m^3 = 8m^3$
Any term raised to the zero power equals 1.	$a^0 = 1 \rightarrow 4^0 = 1$
A base raised to a negative exponent can be rewritten as the reciprocal raised to the positive of the original exponent.	$a^{-b} = \dfrac{1}{a^b}; \dfrac{1}{a^{-b}} = a^b \rightarrow 4^{-2} = \dfrac{1}{4^2}; \dfrac{1}{4^{-2}} = 4^2$

✔ **Note**

Raising an expression involving addition or subtraction to a power, such as $(a + b)^2$, requires a special process called FOIL, which you'll learn about in chapter 6. You *cannot* merely distribute the exponent; this will certainly lead you to a trap answer.

Different things happen to different kinds of numbers when they are raised to powers. Compare the locations and values of the variables and numbers on the following number line to the results in the table for a summary.

$$\xleftarrow{\hspace{1cm}} \underset{w}{\;} \;\; \underset{-1}{\;} \;\; \underset{x}{\;} \;\; \underset{0}{\;} \;\; \underset{y}{\;} \;\; \underset{1}{\;} \;\; \underset{z}{\;} \xrightarrow{\hspace{1cm}}$$

Quantity	Even Exponent Result	Odd Exponent Result	Example
w	positive, absolute value increases	negative, absolute value increases	$(-5)^2 = 25; (-5)^3 = -125$
-1	always 1	always -1	n/a
x	positive, absolute value decreases	negative, absolute value decreases	$\left(-\dfrac{1}{2}\right)^2 = \dfrac{1}{4}; \left(-\dfrac{1}{2}\right)^3 = -\dfrac{1}{8}$
0	always 0	always 0	n/a
y	positive, absolute value decreases	positive, absolute value decreases	$\left(\dfrac{1}{4}\right)^2 = \dfrac{1}{16}; \left(\dfrac{1}{4}\right)^3 = \dfrac{1}{64}$
1	always 1	always 1	n/a
z	positive, absolute value increases	positive, absolute value increases	$3^2 = 9; 3^3 = 27$

1. Which expression is equivalent to $(-3a^5b^4)^3$?

    A) $-27a^{15}b^{12}$

    B) $-9a^8b^7$

    C) $-3a^8b^7$

    D) $-3a^{15}b^{12}$

Use the Kaplan Method for Math to solve this question, working through it step-by-step. The following table shows Kaplan's strategic thinking on the left, along with suggested math scratchwork on the right.

Strategic Thinking	Math Scratchwork
Step 1: Read the question, identifying and organizing important information as you go You need to find the expression that is equivalent to the one given.	
Step 2: Choose the best strategy to answer the question *What's the first step in simplifying this expression?* Follow the order of operations. Cube each term within the parentheses, then simplify.	$(-3a^5b^4)^3$ $= (-3)^3 \times (a^5)^3 \times (b^4)^3$ $= -27a^{15}b^{12}$
Step 3: Check that you answered the *right* question Choice (A) is a match.	

> ✔ **Note**
>
> Once you get to $-27a^{15}b^{12}$, there are no like bases or exponents, so your work is done.

2. Which of the following has the same value as $\dfrac{6^4 \times 36^3}{4^5}$?

   A) $\dfrac{3^9}{2}$

   B) 3^{10}

   C) $2^2 \times 3^9$

   D) $\dfrac{3^{12}}{2^2}$

Work through the Kaplan Method for Math step-by-step to solve this question. The following table shows Kaplan's strategic thinking on the left, along with suggested math scratchwork on the right.

Strategic Thinking	Math Scratchwork
Step 1: Read the question, identifying and organizing important information as you go You're asked to identify the expression that has the same value as the one presented; this means you need to simplify it.	
Step 2: Choose the best strategy to answer the question As written, you can't combine the bases or the exponents. However, $36 = 6^2$, so rewrite the numerator to reflect this relationship. Then combine the bases in the numerator by adding the exponents. The bases are now being raised to the same power, 5, so rewrite the expression using a single exponent. Then simplify by dividing.	$\dfrac{6^4 \times 36^3}{4^5} = \dfrac{\left(6^2\right)^2 \times 36^3}{4^5}$ $= \dfrac{36^2 \times 36^3}{4^5}$ $\dfrac{36^5}{4^5} = \left(\dfrac{36}{4}\right)^5$ $= 9^5$
Step 3: Check that you answered the *right* question Although 9^5 is correct, it's not one of the answer choices, so you'll need to simplify even further. Rewrite 9 as 3^2 and then use exponent rules to simplify. The result is 3^{10}, which is (B).	$9^5 = \left(3^2\right)^5 = 3^{10}$

✔ **Note**

A calculator could probably handle numbers the size of those in the previous question, but what if the question is in the no-calculator section? Knowing exponent rules for Test Day is critical.

RADICALS

A radical can be written using a fractional exponent. You can think of addition and subtraction (and multiplication and division) as opposites; similarly, raising a number to a power and taking the root of the number are another opposite pair. Specifically, when you raise a term to the nth power, taking the nth root will return the original term. Consider, for example, $3^4 = 3 \times 3 \times 3 \times 3 = 81$. If you take the fourth root of 81 (that is, determine the number that can be multiplied by itself four times to get 81), you will arrive at the original term: $\sqrt[4]{81} = \sqrt[4]{3 \times 3 \times 3 \times 3} = 3$.

Radicals can be intimidating at first, but remembering the basic rules for radicals can make them much easier to tackle. The following table contains all the formulas you'll need to know to achieve "radical" success on the PSAT.

Rule	Example
When a fraction is under a radical, you can rewrite it using two radicals: one containing the numerator and the other containing the denominator.	$\sqrt{\dfrac{a}{b}} = \dfrac{\sqrt{a}}{\sqrt{b}} \rightarrow \sqrt{\dfrac{4}{9}} = \dfrac{\sqrt{4}}{\sqrt{9}} = \dfrac{2}{3}$
Two factors under a single radical can be rewritten as separate radicals multiplied together.	$\sqrt{ab} = \sqrt{a} \times \sqrt{b} \rightarrow \sqrt{75} = \sqrt{25} \times \sqrt{3} = 5\sqrt{3}$
A radical can be written using a fractional exponent.	$\sqrt{a} = a^{\frac{1}{2}}, \sqrt[3]{a} = a^{\frac{1}{3}} \rightarrow \sqrt{289} = 289^{\frac{1}{2}}$
When you have a fractional exponent, the numerator is the power to which the base is raised, and the denominator is the root to be taken.	$a^{\frac{b}{c}} = \sqrt[c]{a^b} \rightarrow 5^{\frac{2}{3}} = \sqrt[3]{5^2}$
When a number is squared, the original number can be positive or negative, but the square root of a number can only be positive.	If $a^2 = 81$, then $a = \pm 9$, BUT $\sqrt{81} = 9$ only.

✔ **Note**

Note this difference: by definition, the square root of a number is positive. However, when you take the square root to solve for a variable, you get two solutions: one that is positive and one that is negative. For instance, by definition $\sqrt{4} = 2$. However, if you are solving $x^2 = 4$, x will have two solutions: $x = \pm 2$.

Math

It is not considered proper notation to leave a radical in the denominator of a fraction. However, it's sometimes better to keep them through intermediate steps to make the math easier (and sometimes the radical is eliminated along the way). Once all manipulations are complete, the denominator can be rationalized to remove a remaining radical by multiplying both the numerator and denominator by that same radical.

1. Original Fraction	2. Rationalization	3. Intermediate Math	4. Resulting Fraction
$\dfrac{x}{\sqrt{5}}$	$\dfrac{x}{\sqrt{5}} \times \dfrac{\sqrt{5}}{\sqrt{5}}$	$\dfrac{x\sqrt{5}}{\sqrt{5 \times 5}} = \dfrac{x\sqrt{5}}{\sqrt{25}} = \dfrac{x\sqrt{5}}{5}$	$\dfrac{x\sqrt{5}}{5}$
$\dfrac{14}{\sqrt{x^2+2}}$	$\dfrac{14}{\sqrt{x^2+2}} \times \dfrac{\sqrt{x^2+2}}{\sqrt{x^2+2}}$	$\dfrac{14\sqrt{x^2+2}}{\sqrt{(x^2+2)(x^2+2)}} = \dfrac{14\sqrt{x^2+2}}{\sqrt{(x^2+2)^2}}$	$\dfrac{14\sqrt{x^2+2}}{x^2+2}$

Sometimes, you'll have an expression such as $2 + \sqrt{5}$ in the denominator. To rationalize this, multiply by its conjugate, which is found by negating the second term; in this case, the conjugate is $2 - \sqrt{5}$.

As a general rule of thumb, you are not likely to see a radical in the denominator of the answer choices on the PSAT, so you'll need to be comfortable with rationalizing expressions that contain radicals.

> ✔ **Note**
>
> When you rationalize a denominator, you are not changing the value of the expression; you're only changing the expression's appearance. This is because the numerator and the denominator of the fraction that you multiply by are the same, which means you're simply multiplying by 1.

Ready to take on a test-like question that involves radicals? Take a look at the following:

3. If $\sqrt[4]{x} - 8 = -2$, what is the value of $x + 4$?

    A)   629

    B)   1,300

    C)   1,628

    D)   2,405

Work through the Kaplan Method for Math step-by-step to solve this question. The following table shows Kaplan's strategic thinking on the left, along with suggested math scratchwork on the right.

Strategic Thinking	Math Scratchwork
Step 1: Read the question, identifying and organizing important information as you go All you need to do is solve for *x*.	
Step 2: Choose the best strategy to answer the question *What should you do first?* Solving a radical equation is similar to solving a linear equation, so start by isolating the variable term on one side. *What operation will remove the root from the left side of the equation?* To undo the radical, apply the exponent that corresponds to the root (4 in this case) to each side.	$\sqrt[4]{x} - 8 = -2$ $\sqrt[4]{x} = 6$ $\left(\sqrt[4]{x}\right)^4 = 6^4$ $x = 6^1$ $x = 1,296$
Step 3: Check that you answered the *right* question You've found *x*, so add 4 and you'll be done. The correct answer is (B).	$x + 4 = 1,300$

POLYNOMIALS

By now you're used to seeing equations, exponents, and variables; another important topic you are sure to see on the PSAT is polynomials. A **polynomial** is an expression comprised of variables, exponents, and coefficients, and the only operations involved are addition, subtraction, multiplication, division (by constants *only*), and non-negative integer exponents. A polynomial can have one or multiple terms. The following table contains examples of polynomial expressions and non-polynomial expressions.

Polynomial	$23x^2$	$\dfrac{x}{5} - 6$	$y^{11} - 2y^6 + \dfrac{2}{3}xy^3 - 4x^2$	47
Not a Polynomial	$\dfrac{10}{z} + 13$	x^3y^{-6}	$\dfrac{1}{x^2}$	$\dfrac{4}{y - 3}$

> ✔ **Note**
>
> Remember that a constant, such as 47, is considered a polynomial; this is the same as $47x^0$. Also, keep in mind that for an expression to be a polynomial, division by a constant is allowed, but division by a variable is not.

Identifying **like terms** is an important skill that will serve you well on Test Day. To simplify polynomial expressions, you combine like terms just as you did with linear expressions and equations (*x* terms with *x* terms, constants with constants). To have like terms, the types of variables present and their exponents must match. For example, $2xy$ and $-4xy$ are like terms; *x* and *y* are present in both and their corresponding exponents are identical. However, $2x^2y$ and $3xy$ are not like terms because the exponents on *x* do not match. A few more examples follow:

Like terms	$7x, 3x, 5x$	3, 15, 900	$xy^2, 7xy^2, -2xy^2$
Not like terms	$3, x, x^2$	$4x, 4y, 4z$	$xy^2, x^{2y}, 2xy$

You can also **evaluate** a polynomial expression (just like any other expression) for given values in its domain. For example, suppose you're given the polynomial expression $x^3 + 5x^2 + 1$. At $x = -1$, the value of the expression is $(-1)^3 + 5(-1)^2 + 1$, which simplifies to $-1 + 5 + 1 = 5$.

A polynomial can be named based on its **degree**. For a single-variable polynomial, the degree is the highest power on the variable. For example, the degree of $3x^4 - 2x^3 + x^2 - 5x + 2$ is 4 because the highest power of *x* is 4. For a multivariable polynomial, the degree is the highest sum of the exponents on any one term. For example, the degree of $3x^2y^2 - 5x^2y + x^3$ is 4 because the sum of the exponents in the term $3x^2y^2$ equals 4.

On Test Day, you might be asked about the nature of the **zeros** or **roots** of a polynomial. Simply put, zeros are the *x*-intercepts of a polynomial's graph, which can be found by setting each factor of the polynomial equal to 0. For example, in the polynomial equation $y = (x + 6)(x - 2)^2$, you would have three equations: $x + 6 = 0$, $x - 2 = 0$, and $x - 2 = 0$ (because $x - 2$ is squared, that binomial appears twice in the equation). Solving for *x* in each yields -6, 2, and 2; we say that the equation has two zeros: -6 and 2. Zeros can have varying levels of **multiplicity**, which is the number of times that a factor appears in the polynomial equation. In the preceding example, $x + 6$ appears once in the equation, so its corresponding zero (-6) is called a **simple zero**. Because $x - 2$ appears twice in the equation, its corresponding zero (2) is called a **double zero**.

You can recognize the multiplicity of a zero from the polynomial's graph as well. Following is the graph of $y = (x + 6)(x - 2)^2$:

When a polynomial has a simple zero (multiplicity 1) or any zero with an odd multiplicity, its graph will cross the *x*-axis (as it does at $x = -6$ in the graph above). When a polynomial has a double zero (multiplicity 2) or any zero with an even multiplicity, it just touches the *x*-axis (as it does at $x = 2$ in the graph above).

Use your knowledge of polynomials to answer the following test-like question:

4. If *A* and *B* are polynomial expressions such that $A = 24xy + 13$ and $B = 8xy + 1$, how much greater is *A* than *B* ?

    A) $32xy + 14$

    B) $16xy + 14$

    C) $16xy + 12$

    D) $32xy + 13$

Use the Kaplan Method for Math to solve this question, working through it step-by-step. The following table shows Kaplan's strategic thinking on the left, along with suggested math scratchwork on the right.

Strategic Thinking	Math Scratchwork
Step 1: Read the question, identifying and organizing important information as you go Don't let the unusual wording fool you. To find how much greater A is, just do what you would do for two numbers: subtract the smaller from the larger.	$A - B$
Step 2: Choose the best strategy to answer the question *What's your first step?* Substitute the correct expressions for A and B. Distribute the -1 outside the second set of parentheses. Be careful here; this is an easy place to make a mistake. *And afterward?* Combine like terms. Rearranging so that like terms are next to each other helps here.	$(24xy + 13) - (8xy + 1)$ $= 24xy + 13 - 8xy - 1$ $= 24xy - 8xy + 13 - 1$ $= 16xy + 12$
Step 3: Check that you answered the *right* question No further simplification is possible; the correct answer is (C), so you're done.	

Adding and subtracting polynomials are straightforward operations, but what about multiplying and dividing them? These operations are a little tougher but (fortunately) far from impossible.

Multiplying polynomials is just like multiplying ordinary numbers except you want to pay special attention to distributing and combining like terms. Take the expression $(3x^3 + 5x)(2x^2 + x - 17)$ as an example. All you need to do is distribute each term in the first set of parentheses to each term in the second set. Distribute the $3x^3$ first, then repeat with $5x$:

The following table shows the product for each step:

1	2	3
$3x^3 \cdot 2x^2 = 6x^5$	$3x^3 \cdot x = 3x^4$	$3x^3 \cdot (-17) = -51x^3$
4	**5**	**6**
$5x \cdot 2x^2 = 10x^3$	$5x \cdot x = 5x^2$	$5x \cdot (-17) = -85x$

All that's left to do now is write out the expression and combine any like terms:

$$6x^5 + 3x^4 - 51x^3 + 10x^3 + 5x^2 - 85x$$

$$= 6x^5 + 3x^4 - 41x^3 + 5x^2 - 85x$$

Although it is relatively straightforward to add, subtract, and multiply polynomials, dividing polynomial expressions requires a different, more involved process called **polynomial long division**. Polynomial long division is just like regular long division except, as the name suggests, you use polynomials in place of numbers.

Suppose you want to divide $x^3 + 3x + 7$ by $x + 4$. You can set this up as a long division problem:

$$x + 4 \overline{) x^3 + 0x^2 + 3x + 7}$$

Notice that even though the dividend does not have an x^2 term, a placeholder is used to keep the terms organized. Because $0x^2$ is equal to 0, adding this placeholder term doesn't change the value of the polynomial. Start by dividing the first term of the dividend by the first term of the divisor to get x^2. Multiply the entire divisor by x^2 and subtract this product from the dividend:

$$
\begin{array}{r}
x^2 \\
x + 4 \overline{) x^3 + 0x^2 + 3x + 7} \\
-(x^3 + 4x^2) \\
\hline
-4x^2 + 3x + 7
\end{array}
$$

Continue by dividing the next term, $-4x^2$, by the first term of the divisor. Bring down leftover terms as needed. Multiply the quotient, $-4x$, by the entire divisor and then subtract:

$$
\begin{array}{r}
x^2 - 4x \\
x + 4 \overline{)\, x^3 + 0x^2 + 3x + 7} \\
-(x^3 + 4x^2) \\
\hline
-4x^2 + 3x + 7 \\
-(-4x^2 - 16x) \\
\hline
19x + 7
\end{array}
$$

Finally, repeat this process with the $19x + 7$:

$$
\begin{array}{r}
x^2 - 4x + 19 \\
x + 4 \overline{)\, x^3 + 0x^2 + 3x + 7} \\
-(x^3 + 4x^2) \\
\hline
-4x^2 + 3x + 7 \\
-(-4x^2 - 16x) \\
\hline
19x + 7 \\
-(19x + 76) \\
\hline
-69
\end{array}
$$

When all is said and done, the quotient is $x^2 - 4x + 19$ with a remainder of -69; the remainder is written over the divisor in a separate term. Thus, the final answer is $x^2 - 4x + 19 - \dfrac{69}{x + 4}$.

This is a topic many students tend to forget soon after it's tested in math class, so make sure you spend sufficient time brushing up on it.

✔ **Note**

You can use polynomial long division to determine whether a binomial is a factor of a polynomial. If the remainder in the previous example had been 0, then $x + 4$ would have been a factor of the polynomial $x^3 + 3x + 7$.

Let's try a polynomial long division question:

5.   What is the remainder when $8a^2 + 3$ is divided by $2a + 1$?

   A) -5

   B) -1

   C) 1

   D) 5

Work through the Kaplan Method for Math step-by-step to solve this question. The following table shows Kaplan's strategic thinking on the left, along with suggested math scratchwork on the right.

Strategic Thinking	Math Scratchwork
1: Read the question, identifying and organizing important information as you go You must find the remainder when $8a^2 + 3$ is divided by $2a + 1$.	
Step 2: Choose the best strategy to answer the question Write as a polynomial long division problem. Once it's set up, work carefully through each step until you get to the end.	$$\begin{array}{r} 4a - 2 \\ 2a+1\overline{\smash{\big)}\,8a^2 + 0a + 3} \\ \underline{-(8a^2 + 4a)} \\ -4a + 3 \\ \underline{-(-4a - 2)} \\ 5 \end{array}$$
Step 3: Check that you answered the *right* question You get 5 for the remainder, which is (D).	

Math

RATIONAL EXPRESSIONS

A **rational expression** is simply a ratio (or fraction) of polynomials. In other words, it is a fraction with a polynomial as the numerator and another polynomial as the denominator. The rules that govern fractions and polynomials also govern rational expressions, so if you know these well, you'll be in good shape when you encounter one on Test Day.

There are a few important tidbits to remember about rational expressions; these are summarized here. They are also true for rational equations.

- For an expression to be rational, the numerator and denominator must both be polynomials.

- Like polynomials, rational expressions are also designated certain degrees based on the term with the highest variable exponent sum. For instance, the expression $\frac{1-2x}{3x^2+3}$ has a first-degree numerator and a second-degree denominator.

- Because rational expressions by definition can have polynomial denominators, they will often be undefined for certain values. For example, the expression $\frac{x-4}{x+2}$ is defined for all values of x except -2. This is because when $x = -2$, the denominator of the expression is 0, which would make the expression undefined.

- Factors in a rational expression can be canceled when simplifying, but under no circumstances can you do the same with individual terms. Consider, for instance, the expression $\frac{x^2-x-6}{x^2+5x+6}$.

  Many students will attempt to cancel the x^2, x, and 6 terms to give $\frac{1-1-1}{1+5+1} = \frac{-1}{7}$, which is *never* correct. Don't even think about trying this on Test Day.

- Like fractions, rational expressions can be proper or improper. A proper rational expression has a lower-degree numerator than denominator $\left(\text{e.g., } \frac{1-x}{x^2+3}\right)$, and an improper one has a higher-degree numerator than denominator $\left(\text{e.g., } \frac{x^2+3}{1-x}\right)$. The latter can be simplified using polynomial long division.

✔ Note

For those who are curious, the correct way to simplify $\frac{x^2-x-6}{x^2+5x+6}$ is to factor, which you'll learn about in chapter 10. For now, know that this equals $\frac{(x+2)(x-3)}{(x+2)(x+3)}$. Cancel the $x+2$ factors to get $\frac{x-3}{x+3}$.

SOLVING RATIONAL EQUATIONS

Rational equations are just like rational expressions except for one difference: they have an equal sign. They follow the same rules as rational expressions. The steps you take to solve the more friendly-looking linear equations apply to rational equations as well.

When solving rational equations, beware of **extraneous solutions**—solutions derived that don't satisfy the original equation. This happens when the derived solution causes 0 in the denominator of *any* of the terms in the equation (because division by 0 is not possible). Take the equation $\dfrac{1}{x + 4} + \dfrac{1}{x - 4} = \dfrac{8}{(x + 4)(x - 4)}$, for instance. After multiplying both sides by the common denominator $(x + 4)(x - 4)$, you have $(x - 4) + (x + 4) = 8$. Solving for x yields $2x = 8$, which simplifies to $x = 4$. However, when 4 is substituted for x, you get 0 in the denominator of both the second and third terms of the equation, so 4 is an extraneous solution. Therefore, this equation is said to have no solution.

> ✔ **Note**
>
> Whenever you encounter an equation with variables in a denominator or under a radical, make sure you check the solutions by plugging the values back into the original equation.

6. Which value of x satisfies the equation $\dfrac{4}{x} + \dfrac{2}{x - 8} = \dfrac{-2}{x^2 - 8x}$?

   A)   −1

   B)   1

   C)   4

   D)   5

Work through the Kaplan Method for Math step-by-step to solve this question. The following table shows Kaplan's strategic thinking on the left, along with suggested math scratchwork on the right.

Strategic Thinking	Math Scratchwork
Step 1: Read the question, identifying and organizing important information as you go You're asked to determine which value of x satisfies the equation.	
Step 2: Choose the best strategy to answer the question Start by identifying a common denominator. By factoring x out of the denominator of the term on the right side of the equation, you'll see that the common denominator across all three terms is $x(x - 8)$. Multiply the entire equation by this expression, then distribute properly and solve for x.	$x^2 - 8x \rightarrow x(x - 8)$ $x(x - 8)\left(\dfrac{4}{x} + \dfrac{2}{x - 8} = \dfrac{-2}{x(x - 8)}\right)$ $\begin{aligned} 4(x - 8) + 2x &= -2 \\ 4x - 32 + 2x &= -2 \\ 6x &= 30 \\ x &= 5 \end{aligned}$
Step 3: Check that you answered the *right* question Because "no solution" is not a choice, you can be confident that 5 is not an extraneous solution. Choice (D) is therefore correct.	

✔ **NOTE**

Extraneous solutions are solutions that cause the entire expression to become undefined. Look out for zeros in denominators and negatives under square roots.

MODELING REAL-WORLD APPLICATIONS USING POLYNOMIAL, RADICAL, AND RATIONAL EQUATIONS

A typical rational equation that models a real-world scenario (and that you're likely to see on Test Day) involves rates. Recall from chapter 3 that distance is the product of rate and time ($d = rt$); this equation will serve you well when solving rational equations involving rates. In some cases, you may want to change d to W (for work), as some questions ask how long it will take to complete some kind of work or a specific task. The good news is that the math doesn't change. For example, you can calculate a combined rate by rewriting $W = rt$ as $r = \dfrac{W}{t}$ for each person (or machine) working on a job and then adding the rates together.

Here's an example: Suppose machine A can complete a job in 2 hours and machine B can do the same job in 4 hours. You want to know how long it will take to do this job if both machines work together. Their rates would be $r_A = \dfrac{W_A}{t_A} = \dfrac{1}{2}$ job per hour and $r_B = \dfrac{W_B}{t_B} = \dfrac{1}{4}$ job per hour, respectively. The combined rate would be $\dfrac{3}{4}$ job per hour, which means $t_{total} = \dfrac{W_{total}}{r_{total}} = \dfrac{1}{\frac{3}{4}} = \dfrac{4}{3}$. Thus, it will take $\dfrac{4}{3}$ hours to complete the job if A and B work together.

Ready for a real-world example? Check out the following question:

7. Ankeet needs to back up a large quantity of financial data for his firm. He has access to two systems that can assist with the task. One system is three times as fast as the other. If Ankeet uses both systems together, the backup will be complete in 12 hours. If the equation $\dfrac{1}{h} + \dfrac{3}{h} = \dfrac{1}{12}$ represents the situation, what does $\dfrac{3}{h}$ represent?

A) The time, in hours, that it takes the faster system to complete the full data backup when working alone

B) The portion of the data backup that the faster system will complete in 1 hour

C) The time, in hours, that it takes the slower system to complete the full data backup when working alone

D) The portion of the data backup that the faster system will complete in 3 hours

There's no scratchwork for this question, but Kaplan's strategic thinking is provided in the table. Follow along as we reason through the question to get the correct answer.

Strategic Thinking
Step 1: Read the question, identifying and organizing important information as you go You must determine the significance of $\dfrac{3}{h}$ in the given situation.
Step 2: Choose the best strategy to answer the question The left side of the equation shows the sum of the two systems' task completion rates. A rate cannot also be a quantity of time, so eliminate A and C. To determine which remaining choice is correct, think carefully. When the machines work together, they complete the job in 12 hours; put another way, they complete $\dfrac{1}{12}$ of the job in 1 hour. Because the right side of the equation represents the portion of the job that will be done in 1 hour, the terms on the left represent the portion of the job that is done by each system in 1 hour. The faster system is three times as fast as the other, so it will complete three times as much work. Therefore, $\dfrac{3}{h}$ is the portion of the job completed by the faster system in 1 hour.
Step 3: Check that you answered the *right* question The portion of the job that the faster system will complete in 1 hour is $\dfrac{3}{h}$. Choice (B) is correct.

SOLVING A FORMULA OR EQUATION FOR A GIVEN VARIABLE

If you've ever taken a chemistry or physics course, you probably noticed that many real-world situations can't be represented by simple linear equations. There are frequently radicals, exponents, and fractions galore. For example, the root-mean-square velocity for particles in a gas can be described by the following equation:

$$v = \sqrt{\frac{3kT}{m}}$$

In this equation, v represents the root-mean-square velocity, k is the Boltzmann constant, T is the temperature in degrees Kelvin, and m is the mass of 1 molecule of the gas. It's a great equation if you have k, T, and m and are looking for v. However, if you're looking for a different quantity, having that unknown buried among others (and under a radical to boot) can be unnerving, but unearthing it is easier than it appears. Let's say we're given v, k, and m but need to find T. First, square both sides to eliminate the radical to yield $v^2 = \frac{3kT}{m}$. Next, isolate T by multiplying both sides by m and dividing by $3k$; the result is $\frac{mv^2}{3k} = T$.

At this point, you can plug in the values of m, v, and k to solve for T. Sometimes the PSAT will have you do just that: solve for the numerical value of a variable of interest. In other situations, you'll need to rearrange an equation so that a different variable is isolated. The same rules of algebra you've used all along apply. The difference: you're manipulating solely variables.

Now you'll have a chance to try a few more test-like questions. Some guidance is provided, but you'll need to fill in the missing parts of explanations or the step-by-step math to get to the correct answer. Don't worry—after going through the examples at the beginning of this chapter, these questions should be completely doable. If you're still struggling, review the worked examples in this chapter.

8. A plasma is a gas composed of positively charged atom nuclei and negatively charged electrons. When a plasma is at equilibrium, the density of charge oscillates (shifts back and forth) at what is called the plasma frequency, which can be found using the following formula:

$$\omega_p = \sqrt{\frac{ne^2}{m_e \varepsilon_0}}$$

In the formula, n is the number of electrons present, e is electric charge, m_e is the mass of a single electron, and ε_0 is permittivity of free space. Which of the following equations correctly shows the electric charge in terms of the other variables?

A) $e = \sqrt{\dfrac{\omega_p^2 m_e \varepsilon_0}{n}}$

B) $e = \sqrt{\dfrac{\omega_p^2}{n m_e \varepsilon_0}}$

C) $e = \dfrac{\omega_p^2 m_e \varepsilon_0}{n}$

D) $e = \dfrac{ne^2}{\omega_p^2 m_e}$

Use the scaffolding below as your map through the question. Kaplan's strategic thinking is on the left, and bits of scratchwork are on the right. If you aren't sure where to start, fill in the blanks in the table as you work from top to bottom.

Strategic Thinking	Math Scratchwork
Step 1: Read the question, identifying and organizing important information as you go You need to identify the equation that represents electric charge. Translation: solve the given equation for e.	
Step 2: Choose the best strategy to answer the question *There are several variables and unusual symbols. How should this be solved?* Don't let the strange Greek letters intimidate you; just treat them as you would "normal" variables. Start by undoing the radical so you can get to what's underneath, then isolate the correct variable. Related note: don't panic if you've never heard of "permittivity of free space." If you don't need it to answer the question, don't sweat it.	$\omega_p = \sqrt{\dfrac{ne^2}{m_e \varepsilon_O}}$ _____ = _____ _____ = _____ _____ = _____ _____ = _____
Step 3: Check that you answered the *right* question Did you get (A)? If so, you're absolutely correct.	____

✔ **Note**

Beware of look-alike variables; it's easy to mistake ε_0 for e in this question. Make sure you keep them straight in your scratchwork.

9. What is the value of the remainder when $6x^3 - 4x^2 + 3$ is divided by $x - 1$?

Use the scaffolding that follows as your map through the question. Kaplan's strategic thinking is on the left, and bits of scratchwork are on the right. If you aren't sure where to start, fill in the blanks in the table as you work from top to bottom.

Strategic Thinking	Math Scratchwork
Step 1: Read the question, identifying and organizing important information as you go You need to divide the first polynomial by the second.	
Step 2: Choose the best strategy to answer the question *Can anything be factored out of the first polynomial?* Possibly, but it would likely take time you don't have. Polynomial long division will prevent wasted time. Fill in the blanks on the right to get to the answer.	$-\overline{\big)\rule{0pt}{1em}\qquad}$ $-(\ \ -\ \ )$ ____ $-(\ \ -\ \ )$ ____ $-(\ \ -\ \ )$ Remainder: _____
Step 3: Check that you answered the *right* question If your answer is 5, congrats! You're correct.	____

10. Which of the following is the correct simplification of $\dfrac{\sqrt{3x^2 y^3}}{4\sqrt{5xy^3}}$?

A) $\dfrac{\sqrt{15}}{20}$

B) $\dfrac{\sqrt{15x}}{20}$

C) $\dfrac{y\sqrt{15x}}{20}$

D) $\dfrac{xy^2\sqrt{15x}}{40}$

Use the scaffolding that follows as your map through the question. Kaplan's strategic thinking is on the left, and bits of scratchwork are on the right.

Strategic Thinking	Math Scratchwork
Step 1: Read the question, identifying and organizing important information as you go You need to correctly simplify the given expression.	$\dfrac{\sqrt{3x^2 y^3}}{4\sqrt{5xy^3}}$
Step 2: Choose the best strategy to answer the question *There's no real equation. What route should you take?* Use your exponent and radical rules to get to the answer. You can remove squares from under the radical now, but there's a faster route: split the numerator's radical terms so each is under a separate radical; repeat with the denominator. Doing this makes canceling easier and lessens the chance of making a careless error. Don't forget to rationalize the denominator, if necessary.	$\dfrac{\sqrt{} \times \sqrt{} \times \sqrt{}}{\underline{} \times \sqrt{} \times \sqrt{} \times \sqrt{}}$ $= \dfrac{\sqrt{} \times \sqrt{}}{\underline{} \times \sqrt{}}$ $\dfrac{\sqrt{} \times \sqrt{}}{\underline{} \times \sqrt{}} \times \dfrac{\sqrt{}}{\sqrt{}}$ $= \dfrac{\sqrt{} \times \sqrt{} \times \sqrt{}}{\underline{} \times \sqrt{} \times \sqrt{}}$ $= \dfrac{\sqrt{}}{\underline{} \times \sqrt{}}$
Step 3: Check that you answered the *right* question Did you get (B)? If so, you're absolutely correct.	$\underline{}$

Now that you've seen the variety of ways in which the PSAT can test you on the topics in this chapter, try the following questions to check your understanding. Give yourself 3.5 minutes to tackle the following three questions. Make sure you use the Kaplan Method for Math as often as you can. Remember, you want to emphasize speed and efficiency in addition to simply getting the correct answer.

11. The electromagnetic spectrum encompasses all types of light, both visible and invisible. A light's wavelength is inversely proportional to its damage capability and can be found using the equation $c = \lambda v$, where c is the speed of light in a vacuum in meters per second (3×10^8 m/s), λ (lambda) is wavelength in meters, and v (nu) is frequency in reciprocal seconds (s^{-1}). Suppose environmental scientists are scanning for ozone layer depletion and discover an unusually high concentration of ultraviolet light near Los Angeles. If this light has a wavelength of 150 nanometers (1 m = 1×10^9 nm), what is its frequency in s^{-1}?

   A) 2×10^7

   B) 3×10^7

   C) 2×10^{15}

   D) 3×10^{15}

12. Which of the following expressions is equivalent to $\dfrac{2 - \sqrt{3}}{2 + \sqrt{3}}$?

   A) $7 - 4\sqrt{3}$

   B) 1

   C) 7

   D) $7 + 4\sqrt{3}$

13. If $n^3 = -8$, what is the value of $\dfrac{(n^2)^3}{\dfrac{1}{n^2}}$?

Answers and Explanations for this chapter begin on page 561.

ON YOUR OWN

1. Which of the following is equivalent to the expression $\dfrac{9^4 \times 3^2}{9^5}$?

   A) 0

   B) 1

   C) 3

   D) 9

2. What is the resulting coefficient of x after multiplying $-x + 4$ by $x - 5$?

   A) -9

   B) -1

   C) 1

   D) 9

3. Which of the following is equivalent to the expression $\dfrac{3}{k^{-\frac{2}{5}}}$ above?

   A) $\sqrt[5]{\dfrac{k^2}{3}}$

   B) $3\sqrt{k^5}$

   C) $3\sqrt[5]{k^2}$

   D) $\sqrt{3k^5}$

4. The expression $\dfrac{x^{\frac{3}{2}}}{\sqrt{x}}$ is equivalent to which of the following?

   A) $\sqrt{x}$

   B) 1

   C) x

   D) x^3

5. What is the quotient of $\dfrac{8x^2 + 14x + 3}{4x + 1}$?

   A) $2x + 1$

   B) $2x + 3$

   C) $4x + 3$

   D) $4x + 7$

$$v = \sqrt[3]{\dfrac{P}{0.02}}$$

6. The power generated by a windmill is related to the velocity of the wind by the equation shown above, where P is the power in watts and v is the wind velocity in miles per hour. What is the wind velocity when the windmill is generating 160 watts of power?

   A) 20 mph

   B) 32 mph

   C) 64 mph

   D) 89 mph

$$t = 2\pi\sqrt{\frac{L}{32}}$$

7. The period of a pendulum is the amount of time that it takes for the pendulum to swing back and forth to complete one full cycle. The period t in seconds depends on the length L of the pendulum in feet and is defined by the equation above. Which equation defines the length of the pendulum in terms of its period?

   A) $L = \dfrac{8t^2}{\pi^2}$

   B) $L = \dfrac{\pi^2 t^2}{8}$

   C) $L = \dfrac{8t^2}{\pi}$

   D) $L = \dfrac{16t^2}{\pi}$

Box 1

$x - 1$

$x + 1$

x

Box 2

$y - 1$

$y + 1$

y

8. The length of Box 2 (y) shown above is twice the length of Box 1 (x). Which expression shows the difference in the volumes of the two boxes?

   A) $2x^3 - 2x$

   B) $7x^3 - x$

   C) $7x^3 - 2x$

   D) $8x^3 - 2x$

9. If $M = 12x^2 + 4x - 7$ and $N = 5x^2 - x + 8$, then which of the following equals $M - N$?

   A) $7x^2 + 3x + 1$

   B) $7x^2 + 5x + 1$

   C) $7x^2 + 3x - 15$

   D) $7x^2 + 5x - 15$

10. The value of $6x + 5$ is how much more than the value of $6x - 1$?

    A) 4

    B) 6

    C) $6x - 4$

    D) $6x + 6$

11. Which of the following is the reduced form of $\dfrac{2x + 6y}{10x - 16}$?

    A) $\dfrac{x + 3y}{5x - 8}$

    B) $\dfrac{x + 6y}{5x - 16}$

    C) $\dfrac{1}{5} - \dfrac{3y}{8}$

    D) $\dfrac{1 + 3y}{-3}$

12. What is the difference when $\dfrac{3x + 1}{x + 3}$ is subtracted from $\dfrac{4x - 9}{x + 3}$?

    A) $\dfrac{-x + 10}{x + 3}$

    B) $\dfrac{x - 10}{x + 3}$

    C) $\dfrac{x - 8}{x + 3}$

    D) $\dfrac{x - 8}{2x + 6}$

13. Which of the following represents $9^{\frac{3}{2}}$ as an integer?

   A)   3

   B)   9

   C)   27

   D)   81

14. When a liquid leaks onto a level surface, it generally spreads out equally in all directions, so the puddle is usually in the shape of a circle. When a hazardous chemical leaks like this, it is important to know how long it has been leaking to determine the possible risk to nearby water sources, vegetation, animals, and people. For a certain chemical, the equation $d = 1.25\sqrt{m - 1}$, where d represents the diameter of the puddle in inches, can be used to find the number of minutes, $m \geq 1$, that have passed since the leak began. If the diameter of a puddle created by a leak is 3 feet, about how many minutes has the liquid been leaking? (1 foot = 12 inches)

   A)   8

   B)   15

   C)   830

   D)   2,026

15. For all a and b, what is the product of $(a - b)^2$ and $(a + b)$?

   A) $a^2 - b^2$

   B) $a^3 - b^3$

   C) $a^3 - ab^2 + a^2b - b^3$

   D) $a^3 - a^2b - ab^2 + b^3$

16. If A and B are given by $A = 25x^2 + 10x - 45$ and $B = -12x^2 - 32x + 24$, what is $\frac{3}{5}A + \frac{1}{2}B$?

   A) $2x^2 - 6x - 3$

   B) $2x^2 - 6x + 20$

   C) $9x^2 - 10x - 15$

   D) $21x^2 + 22x - 39$

17. If $x > 1$, which of the following must be true?

   A) $\dfrac{\sqrt{x}}{x} - 1 < 0$

   B) $\dfrac{x}{\sqrt{x}} < 1$

   C) $2\sqrt{x} < x$

   D) $\sqrt{x} + x > x^2$

18. If $x > 4$ and $\dfrac{18}{\sqrt{x - 4}} = 6$, what is the value of x?

CHAPTER 5

Functions

CHAPTER OBJECTIVES

By the end of this chapter, you will be able to:

1. Use function notation to answer questions containing equations, tables, and/or graphs

2. Interpret functions and functional statements that represent real-world scenarios

3. Combine functions using basic operations and compute compositions of functions

4. Determine when a function is increasing, decreasing, or constant and apply transformations to a given function or functions

SMARTPOINTS

Point Value	SmartPoint Category
50 points	Functions

FUNCTIONS

Functions act as rules that transform inputs into outputs, and they differ from equations in that each input must have only one corresponding output. For example, imagine a robot: every time you give it an apple, it promptly cuts that apple into three slices. The following table summarizes the first few inputs and their corresponding outputs.

Domain, x: # apples given to robot	Range, f(x): # slices returned by robot
0	0
1	3
2	6
3	9

From the table, you see that the output will always be triple the input, and you can express that relationship as the function $f(x) = 3x$ (read "f of x equals three x").

PSAT questions, especially those involving real-world situations, might ask you to derive the equation of a function, so you'll need to be familiar with the standard forms. Following is the standard form of a linear function:

$$f(x) = kx + f(0)$$

The input, or **domain**, is the value represented by x. Sometimes the domain will be constrained by the question (e.g., x must be an integer). Other times, the domain could be defined by real-world conditions. For example, if x represents the time elapsed since the start of a race, the domain would need to exclude negative numbers. The output, or **range**, is what results from substituting a domain value into the function and is represented by f(x). The initial amount, or **y-intercept**, is represented by f(0)—the value of the function at the very beginning. If you think this looks familiar, you're absolutely right. It's just a dressed-up version of the standard $y = mx + b$ equation you've already seen. Take a look at the following table for a translation:

Function Notation	What It Represents	Slope-Intercept Counterpart
f(x)	dependent variable or output	y
k	rate of change, slope	m
f(0)	y-intercept or initial quantity in a word problem	b

As you might have guessed, an exponential equation has a standard function notation as well. Here we've used g in place of f for visual clarity. Know that the letter used to represent a function (f, g, h, etc.) is sometimes arbitrarily chosen.

$$g(x) = g(0)(1 + r)^x$$

Just as before, $g(0)$ represents the initial amount and r represents the growth (or decay) rate. Recognizing that function notation is a variation of something you already know will go a long way toward reducing nerves on Test Day. You should also note that graphing functions is a straightforward process. In the examples above, just replace $f(x)$ or $g(x)$ with y and enter it into your graphing calculator.

> ✔ **Note**
>
> A quick way to determine whether an equation is a function is to conduct the vertical line test: if a vertical line passes through the graph of the equation more than once for any given value of x, the equation is not a function.

Below is an example of a test-like question about functions:

1. If $f(x) = x^2 - x$ for all $x \leq -1$ and $f(x) = 0$ for all $x > -1$, which of the following could not be a value of $f(x)$?

   A) -4

   B) 0

   C) 2

   D) 4

Use the Kaplan Method for Math to solve this question, working through it step-by-step. The following table shows Kaplan's strategic thinking on the left, along with suggested math scratchwork on the right.

Strategic Thinking	Math Scratchwork
Step 1: Read the question, identifying and organizing important information as you go The question is asking for the answer choice that could *not* be in the range of this function.	
Step 2: Choose the best strategy to answer the question *How can you determine which of the four choices is not part of the range?* You'll need to examine each piece of the domain individually to learn more. First, summarize each piece of the domain description. *Can you use the domain information to eliminate any answer choices? What happens when x > −1?* Because the range is 0 when $x > −1$, you can eliminate B. *Would your knowledge of number properties be helpful for the second domain component?* Absolutely. Because the range $x^2 − x$ only applies when $x \leq −1$, you only need to consider what happens when a negative number less than −1 is substituted for x. No matter what number you use, your output will always be positive. Eliminate C and D.	domain $x \leq −1$: range $= x^2 − x$ domain $x > −1$: range $= 0$ $(\text{negative})^2 − \text{negative} \rightarrow$ $\text{positive} + \text{positive} \rightarrow \text{positive}$
Step 3: Check that you answered the *right* question The range of $f(x)$ consists of only positive numbers, so (A) is correct.	−4 is not positive

Once broken into simpler pieces, this function question became much easier. Read on for more information about other ways the PSAT can test your knowledge of functions.

> ✔ **Note**
>
> You might be tempted to plug the answer choices in and solve for x, but this will cost you valuable time. Use this strategy only if you can't approach the question in any other way. The PSAT will reward you for knowing the quickest way to answer the question, which in this case involves knowing number properties.

FUNCTIONS DEFINED BY TABLES AND GRAPHS

The ability to interpret the graph of a function will serve you well on Test Day. To interpret graphs of functions, you'll need to utilize the same skills you use to interpret "regular" equations on the coordinate plane, so this material shouldn't be completely foreign.

You know from the first part of this chapter that a function is merely a dressed-up equation, so translating from function to "regular" notation or vice versa is a straightforward process. Consider the following brief example:

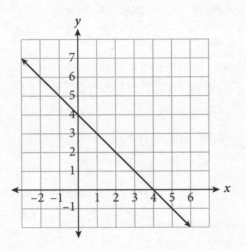

Suppose you're asked to find the value of x for which $f(x) = 6$. Because $f(x)$ represents the output value, or range, translate this as "When does the y-value equal 6?" To answer the question, find 6 on the y-axis, then trace over to the function (the line). Read the corresponding x-value: it's -2, so when $f(x) = 6$, x must be -2.

The PSAT might also present functions in the form of tables. These may or may not have an equation associated with them, but regardless, you'll need to be adept at extracting the information necessary to answer questions. Most of the time the table will have just two columns, one for the domain and another for the range.

> **✔ Note**
>
> Remember: A value of $f(x)$ corresponds to a location along the y-axis. A value of x corresponds to a location on the x-axis.

Now let's try a test-like example:

2. In the figure shown, what is the value of $f(0) + g\left(\dfrac{1}{2}\right)$?

    A) -4

    B)   6

    C)   10

    D)   14

Work through the Kaplan Method for Math step-by-step to solve this question. The following table shows Kaplan's strategic thinking on the left, along with suggested math scratchwork on the right.

Math

Strategic Thinking	Math Scratchwork
Step 1: Read the question, identifying and organizing important information as you go You're asked to determine the value of $f(0) + g\left(\frac{1}{2}\right)$. In other words, you need to find the y-value of function f when $x = 0$ and the y-value of function g when $x = \frac{1}{2}$, then add those values together.	
Step 2: Choose the best strategy to answer the question *How can you find f(0)?* Start with $f(x)$. Locate the spot on the graph of $f(x)$ where $x = 0$. At that point, the y-value is 4. Therefore, $f(0) = 4$. *What about* $g\left(\frac{1}{2}\right)$? Repeat the previous process for $g(x)$ when $x = \frac{1}{2}$; at this x-value, $y = 10$. In function notation, $g\left(\frac{1}{2}\right) = 10$. The hard part is over; now just add the values together.	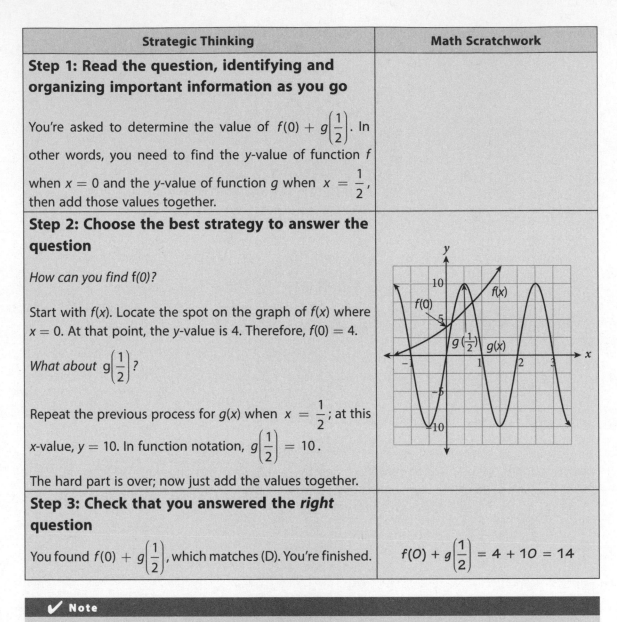
Step 3: Check that you answered the *right* question You found $f(0) + g\left(\frac{1}{2}\right)$, which matches (D). You're finished.	$f(0) + g\left(\frac{1}{2}\right) = 4 + 10 = 14$

✔ **Note**

Watch your axis scales; just like scatterplot questions, questions involving graphs of functions often contain trap answers for students who misread the axes.

Although this question would have been much simpler if the graph had labeled the points or given you an equation to plug values into, it wouldn't have tested your knowledge of functions. Your ability to figure out what questions about functions are actually asking is key to solving them correctly on Test Day.

Try out a question in which a function is presented in the form of a table:

Game	Number of students
1	5
2	11
3	21
4	35
5	53
6	75
7	101
8	131

3. West Valley High School is keeping track of how many students show up to the home football games wearing face paint in the school colors. To encourage participation, there is a prize giveaway at each game. As the prizes get more exciting, participation begins to increase. If j represents the game number and $f(j)$ represents the number of students in face paint at game j, which of the following functions best describes the information in the table?

A) $f(j) = j + 4$

B) $f(j) = 2j + 5$

C) $f(j) = \dfrac{1}{2}j^2 + 7$

D) $f(j) = 2j^2 + 3$

Work through the Kaplan Method for Math step-by-step to solve this question. The following table shows Kaplan's strategic thinking on the left, along with suggested math scratchwork on the right.

Strategic Thinking	Math Scratchwork
Step 1: Read the question, identifying and organizing important information as you go The question is asking which function accurately depicts the relationship between the game number and how many students show up in face paint.	
Step 2: Choose the best strategy to answer the question The question stem tells you what *f* and *j* represent and provides a table relating the two variables. *Can you eliminate any obviously incorrect answers right away?* Choices A and B are linear functions. Because the number of students does not increase by a constant amount, we can safely eliminate these choices. *How can you best evaluate the remaining answer choices?* Try plugging a pair of data points from the table into the remaining choices. The point (8, 131) invalidates C, so eliminate it. *There's only one answer choice left. Am I done?* You know (D) must be correct, but plug in (8, 131) to confirm.	f = number of students j = the game number A and B disagree w/table use (8, 131) C: $131 = \dfrac{1}{2} \times 8^2 + 7$ $131 = \dfrac{1}{2} \times 64 + 7$ $131 = 32 + 7$ $131 \neq 39$ D: $131 = 2 \times 8^2 + 3$ $131 = 2 \times 64 + 3$ $131 = 128 + 3$ $131 = 131$
Step 3: Check that you answered the *right* question The only function that fits all the entries in the table is (D).	

✔ **Note**

When you have only one answer choice remaining, it isn't necessary to evaluate it. If you've done your math correctly up until that point, you know the remaining answer choice *has* to be correct. However, if you're at all worried that you made a mistake earlier, check the remaining answer choice to validate your math.

REAL-WORLD APPLICATION OF FUNCTIONS

Because functions are equations, you have a great deal of flexibility in working with them. For example, order of operations (PEMDAS) and the basic rules of algebra apply to functions just as they do to equations. You learned in Unit 1 that equations can represent real-world situations in convenient ways, and the same is true for functions.

For example, suppose a homeowner wants to determine the cost of installing a certain amount of carpet in her living room. In prose, this would quickly become awkward to handle, as a description would need to account for the cost per square foot, fixed installation fee, and sales tax to get the final cost. However, you can easily express this as a function.

Suppose that, in the homeowner example, carpet costs \$0.86 per square foot, the installer charges a \$29 installation fee, and sales tax on the total cost is 7%. Using your algebra and function knowledge, you can describe this situation in which the cost, c, is a function of square footage, f. The equation would be $c = 1.07(0.86f + 29)$. In function notation, this becomes $c(f) = 1.07(0.86f + 29)$, where $c(f)$ is shorthand for "cost as a function of square footage." The following table summarizes what each piece of the function represents in the scenario:

English	Overall cost	Square footage	Material cost	Installation fee	Sales tax
Math	c	f	$0.86f$	29	1.07

> ✔ **Note**
>
> Why does a 7% tax translate to 1.07? Using 0.07 would only provide the sales tax due. Because the function is meant to express the total cost, 1.07 is used to retain the carpet cost and installation fee while introducing the sales tax. Think of it as 100% (the original price) + the 7% sales tax on top. In decimal form, $1 + 0.07 = 1.07$.

This test-like question will test your ability to write a function and use it to solve a problem:

4. A country club allows its members to host private parties. The price is a function of a number of variables. First, members are charged a fixed fee of $1,000 during the peak season (spring, summer, fall) and $500 during the winter months. Members must also pay a certain additional amount for each attendee (not including the member himself): $150 per guest in the peak season and $120 per guest in the winter. An administrative fee of 20% of the guest cost is added to account for logistics, and a 6% sales tax is added to the final bill. How much would a member save by holding a party for 85 guests in winter instead of spring? Round your answer to the nearest dollar.

A word problem like this is a great time to reach for the Kaplan Strategy for Translating English into Math. The following table shows Kaplan's strategic thinking on the left, along with suggested math scratchwork on the right.

Strategic Thinking	Math Scratchwork
Step 1: Read the question, identifying and organizing important information as you go You're asked to find the difference in cost between a winter and spring party for 85 people.	
Step 2: Choose the best strategy to answer the question *How do you sort through all the words?* Use the Kaplan Strategy for Translating English into Math to extract what you need. *What variables need to be defined?* You have a cost, c, which is a function of guests, g, in attendance outside the winter months. In winter the cost is w, which is also a function of guests. *What other information is provided?* The question provides several numbers; break it apart to get each numerical piece by itself. *What math pieces can I get from the small phrases?*	$c =$ *cost of party (peak)* $w =$ *cost of party (winter)* $g =$ *guests* $\$150$ *per guest (peak)* $\$120$ *per guest (winter)* $\$1,000$ *rental fee (peak)* $\$500$ *rental fee (winter)* 20% *admin. fee on guest cost* 6% *sales tax on entire cost*

Strategic Thinking	Math Scratchwork
Examine the question carefully to ensure the right figures are being combined. This is an easy place to inadvertently switch a peak season figure with one from winter. *What function represents the total cost during the peak season?*	fixed fees: 1,000 (peak), 500 (winter) guest cost: 150g (peak), 120g (winter) fee: $(1 + 0.2) \times$ guest cost tax: $(1 + 0.06) \times$ total price
Put the pieces together to get your function. Remember to add 1 onto your percents so you're calculating the total cost and not the administrative charge or tax alone. Repeat the same process for the winter season, but make sure not to confuse any quantities. *How much will the party for 85 people cost in spring?*	$\begin{aligned} c(g) &= 1.06(1.2(150g) + 1,000) \\ &= 1.06(180g + 1,000) \\ &= 190.8g + 1,060 \end{aligned}$ $\begin{aligned} w(g) &= 1.06(1.2(120g) + 500) \\ &= 1.06(144g + 500) \\ &= 152.64g + 530 \end{aligned}$
Plug 85 into the appropriate function. *How much would the same party cost in the winter?*	$\begin{aligned} c(85) &= 190.8 \times 85 + 1060 \\ &= 16,218 + 1060 \\ &= 17,278 \end{aligned}$
Plug 85 into the appropriate function. *How can you find the amount of savings?*	$\begin{aligned} w(85) &= 152.64 \times 85 + 530 \\ &= 12,974.4 + 530 \\ &= 13,504.4 \end{aligned}$
Subtract the winter costs from peak costs.	$c(85) - w(85) = 3,773.6$
Step 3: Check that you answered the *right* question	
Round your answer to the nearest dollar.	3,774

✔ **Note**

On Test Day, it would take considerable time to write out everything in this scratchwork column verbatim; use good judgment when doing scratchwork, and abbreviate when you can. For clarity, we've included more than the average student would write.

Notice that even with a more difficult word problem, the Kaplan Strategy for Translating English into Math gets the job done. You also should have noticed how function notation can help keep your scratchwork clear and organized.

MULTIPLE FUNCTIONS

There are several ways in which the PSAT might ask you to juggle multiple functions simultaneously. Fortunately, the rules governing what to do are easy to understand. To start, we'll look at how to combine functions. This technique simply involves adding, subtracting, multiplying, and/or dividing the functions in play. Check out the following table for a synopsis of how to combine functions with the four basic operations (and how to make them look less intimidating):

When you see . . .	convert it to . . .
$(f + g)(x)$	$f(x) + g(x)$
$(f - g)(x)$	$f(x) - g(x)$
$(fg)(x)$	$f(x) \times g(x)$
$\left(\dfrac{f}{g}\right)(x)$	$\dfrac{f(x)}{g(x)}$

You'll have a chance to solve a problem involving combined functions shortly.

A more challenging type of function question that you're likely to see is a **composition of functions** or **nested functions**. Questions involving a composition of functions require that you find an output value for one function and use the result as the input for another function to get the final solution. A composition of functions can be written as $f(g(x))$ or $(f \circ g)(x)$. The first is read as f of g of x, and the second, f composed with g of x. To answer these questions, start with the innermost parentheses and work your way out.

> ✔ **Note**
>
> You might see a composition of functions written as $(f \circ g)(x)$. Just remember that it's the same as $f(g(x))$, and solve as you would normally, working from the inside outward.

Suppose $f(x) = 8x$ and $g(x) = x + 3$. To find the value of $f(g(1))$, your steps would be as follows:

1. Determine $g(1)$, the innermost function when $x = 1$.

2. By substituting 1 for x in $g(x)$, you find that $g(1) = 1 + 3 = 4$. Now rewrite $f(g(1))$ as $f(4)$.

3. Find $f(4)$, the outer function when $x = 4$. Substituting 4 for x in function f, the final answer is $8(4) = 32$.

> ✔ **Note**
>
> Note that $f(g(x))$ does *not* equal $g(f(x))$. Not only is interchanging these incorrect, but this practice might also lead you to a trap answer on Test Day.

On Test Day, you might see **piecewise functions**. A piecewise function is a function that is defined, literally, by multiple pieces. What breaks a function into pieces are different rules that govern different parts of the function's domain. Here's an example:

$$f(x) = \begin{cases} 1, & \text{if } x \leq -2 \\ x^2, & \text{if } -2 < x < 3 \\ 3, & \text{if } x = 3 \\ -3x + 11, & \text{if } x > 3 \end{cases}$$

In the function shown, the behavior of the graph depends on the domain. Linear, quadratic, and even a single-point interval make up this function. Each "rule" is written inside the open bracket in "pieces." To the right is the domain interval for which each "rule" applies. On the graph, an open dot indicates that a point is not included in the interval; a closed dot indicates one that is. Note that the different inequality signs used in the domain constraints dictate whether a dot is open or closed on the graph. For a single-point interval, an equal sign is used.

To evaluate a piecewise function, first determine to which piece of the domain the input value belongs, and then substitute the value into the corresponding rule. For example, in the function above, $f(2) = (2)^2 = 4$, because the input value 2 is between -2 and 3 (the second piece of the domain). Similarly, $f(5) = -3(5) + 11 = -4$ because the input value 5 is greater than 3 (the last piece of the domain). You can confirm these values by looking at the graph. At $x = 2$, the point on the graph is $(2, 4)$, and at $x = 5$, the point on the graph is $(5, -4)$.

Math

Give this function question a try:

5. Given that $f(x) = 2x + 1$ and $g(x) = \dfrac{x + 2}{3}$, what is the value of $(fg)(-5)$?

A) -6

B) -2

C) 3

D) 9

Appearances can be deceiving. At first glance, this question looks tough, but the following table will clarify anything confusing. Kaplan's strategic thinking is on the left, along with suggested math scratchwork on the right.

Strategic Thinking	Math Scratchwork
Step 1: Read the question, identifying and organizing important information as you go Read carefully to see what the question is asking. You need to find the product (fg) of the results when each function is evaluated at $x = -5$.	
Step 2: Choose the best strategy to answer the question You could multiply the two functions together and then evaluate the result, but it's quicker to evaluate each function separately and then multiply.	$f(-5) = 2(-5) + 1$ $\qquad = -10 + 1$ $\qquad = -9$ $g(-5) = \dfrac{(-5) + 2}{3}$ $\qquad = \dfrac{-3}{3}$ $\qquad = -1$
Step 3: Check that you answered the *right* question The question is asking for the product (fg), which is 9, (D).	$(fg)(-5) = -9 \times (-1) = 9$

Let's look at a sample test-like question involving a composition of functions:

6. If $f(x) = x^2 + 17$ and $g(x) = \dfrac{3x}{x+1}$, where $x \neq -1$, what is the value of $g(f(3))$?

   A) $\dfrac{26}{9}$

   B) $\dfrac{299}{16}$

   C) 26

   D) $\dfrac{113}{4}$

Use the Kaplan Method for Math to solve this question, working through it step-by-step. The following table shows Kaplan's strategic thinking on the left, along with suggested math scratchwork on the right.

Strategic Thinking	Math Scratchwork
Step 1: Read the question, identifying and organizing important information as you go The question is asking for the value of $g(f(3))$.	
Step 2: Choose the best strategy to answer the question You have a composition of functions, so start with the innermost set of parentheses. Substitute 3 for x in $f(x)$. Next, simplify using order of operations until you get a single value for $f(3)$. *How do you use f(3) to solve for g(f(3))?* You know $f(3) = 26$, so substitute 26 wherever you see $f(3)$ to yield $g(26)$. In other words, plug in the first "output" as the new "input" of the second function. *The answer choices do not include $\dfrac{78}{27}$, however. How can you simplify this expression?* Both 78 and 27 are multiples of 3, so you can reduce to $\dfrac{26}{9}$.	$f(x) = x^2 + 17$ $f(3) = (3)^2 + 17$ $ = 9 + 17$ $ = 26$ $g(26) = \dfrac{3(26)}{26 + 1}$ $ = \dfrac{78}{27}$ $\dfrac{78}{27} = \dfrac{26}{9}$
Step 3: Check that you answered the *right* question The fraction $\dfrac{26}{9}$ matches (A).	

Math

DESCRIBING FUNCTION BEHAVIOR AND PERFORMING TRANSFORMATIONS

When describing the graph of a function or an interval (a specific segment) of a function, the trend of the relationship between the *x*- and *y*-values while reading the graph from left to right is often important. Three terms you are sure to see in more difficult function questions are **increasing**, **decreasing**, and **constant**. Let's look at what these terms mean and how they apply to PSAT questions:

- **Increasing** functions have *y*-values that *increase* as the corresponding *x*-values increase.

- **Decreasing** functions have *y*-values that *decrease* as the corresponding *x*-values increase.

- **Constant** functions have *y*-values that *stay the same* as the *x*-values increase.

The PSAT can ask about function trends in a variety of ways. The most basic would be to examine a function's behavior and determine whether (and where) the function is increasing, decreasing, or constant. Tougher questions might ask you to identify the trend and then explain what it means in the context of a real-life situation presented in the question, or to identify the effect a transformation would have on the trend of a function.

A function **transformation** occurs when a change is made to the function's equation or graph. Transformations include translations (moving a graph up/down, left/right), reflections (flips about an axis or other line), and expansions/compressions (stretching or squashing horizontally or vertically). How do you know which is occurring? The following table provides some rules for guidance when altering a hypothetical function $f(x)$.

Algebraic Change	Corresponding Graphical Change	Graph	Algebraic Change	Corresponding Graphical Change	Graph
$f(x)$	N/A—original function		$f(x + a)$	$f(x)$ moves left a units	
$f(x) + a$	$f(x)$ moves up a units		$f(x - a)$	$f(x)$ moves right a units	

Algebraic Change	Corresponding Graphical Change	Graph	Algebraic Change	Corresponding Graphical Change	Graph
$f(x) - a$	$f(x)$ moves down a units		$-f(x)$	$f(x)$ reflected over the x-axis (top-to-bottom)	
$f(-x)$	$f(x)$ reflected over the y-axis (left-to-right)		$af(x)$ $(0 < a < 1)$	$f(x)$ undergoes vertical compression	
$f(ax)$ $(0 < a < 1)$	$f(x)$ undergoes horizontal expansion		$af(x)$ $(a > 1)$	$f(x)$ undergoes vertical expansion	
$f(ax)$ $(a > 1)$	$f(x)$ undergoes horizontal compression				

If you forget what a particular transformation looks like, you can always plug in a few values for x and plot the points to determine the effect on the function's graph.

✔ Expert Tip

Adding or subtracting inside the parentheses of a function will always effect a horizontal change (e.g., shift left/right, horizontal reflection); if the alteration is outside, you're looking at a vertical change.

Try out this function transformation question:

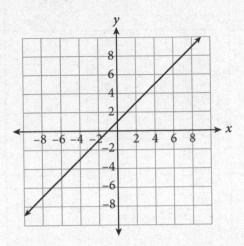

7. The graph above represents the function $f(x)$. Which of the following choices corresponds to $f(x - 2) - 5$?

> ✔ **Note**
>
> Note that the slope of the function post-translation is identical to that of the original function. Translations only shift a function and do not impact slope.

Use the Kaplan Method for Math to solve this question, working through it step-by-step. The following table shows Kaplan's strategic thinking on the left, along with suggested math scratchwork on the right.

Strategic Thinking	Math Scratchwork
Step 1: Read the question, identifying and organizing important information as you go You must determine which graph shows the transformation specified in the question stem.	
Step 2: Choose the best strategy to answer the question *How do you begin solving?* First, determine what the transformation is. Next, identify a couple of easy points on the initial function and apply the transformation "instructions" to them. The *y*-intercept is a good choice here. *On which graph do the transformed points lie?* Determine which answer's graph contains the new coordinates.	graph moves 2 units right and 5 units down (0, 1) becomes (2, −4) (1, 2) becomes (3, −3) new points fall on the graph of (B)
Step 3: Check that you answered the *right* question The only matching graph is (B).	

> ✔ **Expert Tip**
>
> If you're better with algebra, plug the transformation changes into the original function instead of picking points. Substituting $x − 2$ for x and subtracting another 5 gives $y = [(x − 2) + 1] − 5 = x − 6$. The graph of $y = x − 6$ clearly corresponds to (B).

Now you'll have a chance to try a couple test-like questions in a scaffolded way. We've provided some guidance, but you'll need to fill in the missing parts of explanations or the step-by-step math in order to get to the correct answer. Don't worry—after going through the worked examples at the beginning of this section, these questions should be completely doable.

8. Scientists are modeling population trends and have noticed that when a certain bacterial population changes, the change is based on a linear function of the amount of time elapsed in seconds. When $t = 21$ seconds, the population is 8 colonies, and when $t = 35$ seconds, the population is 10 colonies. Which of the following best describes $f(t)$?

A) $f(t) = \dfrac{1}{3}t + 1$

B) $f(t) = \dfrac{1}{5}t + 3$

C) $f(t) = \dfrac{1}{7}t + 5$

D) $f(t) = 7(t - 5)$

The following table can help you structure your thinking as you go about solving this question. Kaplan's strategic thinking is provided, as are bits of structured scratchwork. If you're not sure how to approach a question like this, start at the top and work your way down.

Strategic Thinking	Math Scratchwork
Step 1: Read the question, identifying and organizing important information as you go You need to find the function that describes the population increase observed.	$f(t) = ?$
Step 2: Choose the best strategy to answer the question *What form do all the functions take? What is different about each one?* All the answer choices are linear functions, and the slope is different for each one. *To use the slope formula, what do you need?* You need two ordered pairs to plug into the formula. Use the information provided to write two ordered pairs in the form (time, number of colonies). Then calculate the slope.	$(21, \underline{\quad})$ and $(\underline{\quad}, \underline{\quad})$ slope: $m = \dfrac{y_2 - y_1}{x_2 - x_1} = \underline{\quad\quad} = \underline{\quad}$
Step 3: Check that you answered the *right* question If you picked (C), you were right! You can check by plugging one or both of your points into this equation.	

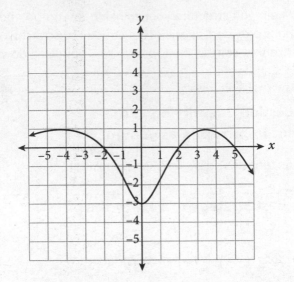

9. The figure shows the graph of $r(x)$. What is one value of x for which $r(x) = 0$?

The following table can help you structure your thinking as you go about answering this question. Kaplan's strategic thinking is provided, as are bits of structured scratchwork. If you're not sure how to approach a question like this, start at the top and work your way down.

Strategic Thinking	Math Scratchwork
Step 1: Read the question, identifying and organizing important information as you go	
You need to find a value of x for which $r(x) = 0$.	$r(x) = 0$ at $x = ?$
Step 2: Choose the best strategy to answer the question	
What information does the question provide? What does "r(x) = 0" mean graphically?	when $r(x) = 0$, $y = $ _____
You have a graph of the function $r(x)$; you must determine where $y = 0$ for the function $r(x)$.	when $y = 0$, $x = $ _____, _____, _____
Step 3: Check that you answered the *right* question	
Did you get −2, 2, and 5? If so, you're right! Because Grid-in answers can only be positive, choose either 2 or 5. Either answer is correct.	

Now that you've seen the variety of ways in which the PSAT can test you on functions, try the following questions to check your understanding. Give yourself 3.5 minutes to tackle the following three questions. Make sure you use the Kaplan Method for Math as often as you can. Remember, you want to emphasize speed and efficiency in addition to simply getting the correct answer.

10. For the two functions $f(x)$ and $g(x)$, tables of values follow. What is the value of $f(g(1))$?

x	f(x)
−2	8
−1	6
0	4
1	2

x	g(x)
−1	−4
1	0
2	2
4	6

A) 0

B) 2

C) 4

D) 6

11. A construction company plans to build a long row of houses, each with a certain number of brown shingles on its roof. The number of brown shingles on a house's roof, $f(h)$, is a function of its house number, h. The first few houses are shown here. If only brown shingles are used, how many shingles will the seventh house have?

A) 7

B) 27

C) 46

D) 60

Math

12. The function $f(x) = (x - 4)^2$ is shown here. Which of the following correctly depicts the transformation $g(x) = (-x + 2)^2 + 3$?

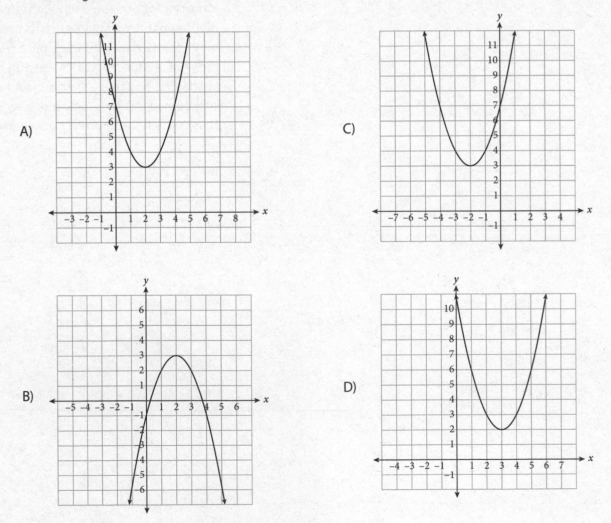

A)

B)

C)

D)

Answers and Explanations for this chapter begin on page 566.

ON YOUR OWN

1. An ecosystem is a network in which all living and nonliving things are connected. Components of an ecosystem are interdependent, meaning that a change in one component affects all other elements of the ecosystem. Biologists often study changes in ecosystems to predict other changes. A biologist studying the birth rate of a certain fish uses the function $b(n)$ to analyze the fish's effect on other parts of the ecosystem, where n is the number of eggs laid by the fish over a given period of time. Which of the following lists could represent a portion of the domain for the biologist's function?

    A) $\{\ldots -1{,}500, -1{,}000, -500, 0, 500, 1{,}000, 1{,}500 \ldots\}$

    B) $\{-1{,}500, -1{,}000, -500, 0, 500, 1{,}000, 1{,}500\}$

    C) $\{0, 0.25, 0.5, 0.75, 1, 1.25, 1.5 \ldots\}$

    D) $\{0, 500, 1{,}000, 1{,}500, 2{,}000 \ldots\}$

2. If $h(x) = 3x - 1$, what is the value of $h(5) - h(2)$?

    A) 3

    B) 8

    C) 9

    D) 14

3. The figure shown represents the function $q(x) = \sqrt{x}$. Which statement about the function is not true?

    A) $q(0) = 0$

    B) $q(2) = 4$

    C) The range of $q(x)$ is $y \geq 0$.

    D) The domain of $q(x)$ is $x \geq 0$.

4. A function is defined by the equation $f(x) = \dfrac{2}{5}x - 7$. For what value of x does $f(x) = 5$?

    A) -5

    B) 2

    C) 9

    D) 30

12 in.

8.5 in.

5. Tyree is dropping old pennies into a jar that contains a cleaning solution. As he adds more pennies, the height of the solution in the jar changes based on the number of pennies he adds. The figure shows this relationship after 50 pennies have been dropped in the jar. If the height of the solution in the jar was 5 inches before any pennies were added, which of the following linear functions represents the relationship between the number of pennies and the height of the solution in the jar?

A) $h(p) = 0.7p + 5$

B) $h(p) = 0.7p + 8.5$

C) $h(p) = 0.07p + 5$

D) $h(p) = 0.07p + 8.5$

x	$g(x)$
-2	1
0	2
1	3
4	2
6	1

x	$h(x)$
-2	4
-1	2
0	0
1	-2
2	-4

6. Several values for the functions $g(x)$ and $h(x)$ are shown in the tables. What is the value of $g(h(-2))$?

A) -2

B) 0

C) 2

D) 3

7. If the graph of $R(x)$ passes through the point $(-2, 6)$, through which point does the graph of $-R(x + 5) + 1$ pass?

A) $(-7, -5)$

B) $(3, -5)$

C) $(3, 7)$

D) $(7, 7)$

$$c(t) = -0.05t^2 + 2t + 2$$

8. Doctors use the function shown to calculate the concentration, in parts per million, of a certain drug in a patient's bloodstream after t hours. How many more parts per million of the drug are in the bloodstream after 20 hours than after 10 hours?

9. Which set of ordered pairs could represent part of a function?

A) $\{(-4, -4), (-2, -2), (0, 0), (-2, 2), (-4, 4)\}$

B) $\{(-4, -2), (-2, 0), (0, 2), (2, 0), (4, -2)\}$

C) $\{(-2, 0), (0, -2), (2, 0), (0, 2), (4, 2)\}$

D) $\{(-2, -4), (-2, -2), (-2, 0), (-2, 2), (-2, 4)\}$

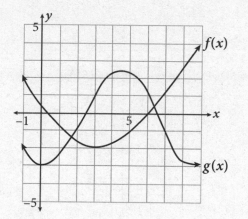

10. The graph of $f(x)$ is shown here. Which of the following represents the domain and range of the function?

    A) Domain: $f(x) \geq 5$; range: all real numbers

    B) Domain: $f(x) \leq 5$; range: all real numbers

    C) Domain: all real numbers; range: $f(x) \geq 5$

    D) Domain: all real numbers; range: $f(x) \leq 5$

11. If $g(x) = \dfrac{2}{5}x + 3$, which of the following statements is always true?

    A) $g(x) < 0$

    B) $g(x) > 0$

    C) $g(x) < 0$ when $x < 0$

    D) $g(x) > 0$ when $x > 0$

12. In the figure shown, what is the value of $f(3) - g(3)$?

    A) -3

    B) 0

    C) 3

    D) 6

13. If $f(x) = -4x + 1$ and $g(x) = \sqrt{x} + 2.5$, what is the value of $(f \circ g)\left(\dfrac{1}{4}\right)$?

    A) -11

    B) 0

    C) 2.5

    D) 3

14. The graph of $g(x)$ is shown in the figure. If $k(x) = -g(x) - 1$, which of the following statements is true?

    A) The range of $k(x)$ is $-5 \leq y \leq 1$.

    B) The minimum value of $k(x)$ is -4.

    C) The coordinates of point A on the function $k(x)$ are $(2, 0)$.

    D) The graph of $k(x)$ is increasing between $x = 0$ and $x = 1$.

15. If $f(x) = -x + 5$ and $g(x) = x^2$, which of the following is not in the range of $f(g(x))$?

    A) -11

    B) 0

    C) 1

    D) 9

CHAPTER 6

Quadratic Equations

CHAPTER OBJECTIVES

By the end of this chapter, you will be able to:

1. Solve quadratic equations via algebra, graphing, or the quadratic formula

2. Sketch the graph of a given quadratic equation

3. Identify how various components of a quadratic equation are significant to its graph or a real-world scenario

SMARTPOINTS

Point Value	SmartPoint Category
40 Points	Quadratics

INTRODUCTION TO QUADRATIC EQUATIONS

A quadratic equation or expression is simply one that contains a squared variable (x^2) as the highest-order term (also called highest-powered term). In standard form, a quadratic equation is written as $ax^2 + bx + c = 0$, where a, b, and c are constants. However, quadratics can be written in a variety of other forms as well, such as the following:

$$x^2 - 9 = 0 \qquad 2r^2 - 8r + 10 = 4 \qquad 2(x - 3)^2 = 8 \qquad (x - 2)(x + 3) = 6$$

> ✔ **Note**
>
> At first glance, the last equation might not look quadratic, but it is; it's merely masquerading as a product of binomials. You'll learn a strategy for unveiling its x^2 term shortly.

All quadratic equations have 0, 1, or 2 real solutions. When you are asked to find the solutions of a quadratic equation, all you need to do is equate the variable to a constant. Solutions might also be called roots, x-intercepts, or zeros.

Before you can solve, however, there is a step you must always complete: **set the equation equal to 0**. In other words, move everything to one side of the equation so that 0 is the only thing left on the other side. Once the quadratic equation is equal to 0, you can take one of three routes to determine how many solutions it has: **algebra**, **graphing**, or the **quadratic formula**. Read on for more information about these three techniques.

SOLVING QUADRATICS ALGEBRAICALLY

Using algebra is often necessary when working with quadratic equations, so getting comfortable with it is critical. We'll start with a technique that is highly useful for manipulating quadratics: FOIL. **FOIL is essential for putting a quadratic into standard form.**

> ✔ **Expert Tip**
>
> If you get stuck on the algebra in a question about a quadratic equation, Picking Numbers can often help. Just remember that it might take more time than the algebraic route, so use good judgment if you're in a bind—and remember that you can always skip the question and revisit it later.

FOIL

Whenever you see a pair of binomials on the PSAT, your default algebra strategy should be FOIL, which stands for **F**irst, **O**uter, **I**nner, **L**ast. This acronym helps ensure that you don't forget any terms when distributing. Multiply the first terms in each binomial together, then repeat with the outer, inner, and last terms. Then add the four products together, combining like terms as needed. Here is a generic scheme for the FOIL procedure:

$$(a + b)(c + d) = ac + ad + bc + bd$$
$$(\text{Binomial 1})(\text{Binomial 2}) = \textbf{F}\text{irst} + \textbf{O}\text{uter} + \textbf{I}\text{nner} + \textbf{L}\text{ast}$$

It is often tempting to FOIL in your head, but this is risky: it is very easy to lose a negative sign or switch a pair of coefficients (and arrive at a trap answer). Show *all* of your work when using FOIL.

Factoring

Factoring, also known as reverse-FOILing, allows you to go from a quadratic to a product of two binomials. This is a very powerful tool; once you have a binomial pair, you're a few short algebraic steps away from finding the solution(s). The factoring process for a quadratic equation that is written in standard form ($ax^2 + bx + c$) is demonstrated in the following table:

Step	Scratchwork
Starting point: notice a, the coefficient in front of x^2, is equal to 1, a great condition for factoring.	$x^2 + 5x + 6 = 0 \rightarrow (x \pm \text{?})(x \pm \text{?}) = 0$
1. What are the factors of c? Remember to include negatives.	factors of 6: 1 & 6, −1 & −6, 2 & 3, −2 & −3
2. Which factor pair, when added, equals b, the coefficient in front of x?	$2 + 3 = 5$
3. Write as a product of binomials.	$(x + 2)(x + 3) = 0$
4. Split the product of binomials into two equations set equal to 0.	$x + 2 = 0, x + 3 = 0$
5. Solve each equation.	$x = -2, x = -3$

Factoring is easiest when a is 1, so whenever possible, try to simplify the expression so that is the case. In addition, if you see nice-looking numbers (integers, simple fractions) in the answer choices, this is a clue that factoring is possible. If you're ever not sure that you've done your factoring correctly, go ahead and FOIL to check your work. You should get the expression you started with.

✔ **Note**

Sometimes, the two binomials factors will be identical. In this case, the quadratic equation will have only one real solution (because the two solutions are identical).

Completing the Square

For more difficult quadratics, you'll need to turn to a more advanced strategy: **completing the square**. In this process, you'll create a perfect square trinomial, which has the form $(x + h)^2 = k$, where h and k are constants. This route takes some practice to master but will pay dividends when you sail through the most challenging quadratic equation questions on Test Day. The following table illustrates the procedure along with a corresponding example (even though the equation could have been factored).

Step	Scratchwork
Starting point	$x^2 + 6x - 7 = 0$
1. Move the constant to the opposite side.	$x^2 + 6x = 7$
2. Divide b by 2, then square the quotient.	$b = 6;\ \left(\dfrac{b}{2}\right)^2 = \left(\dfrac{6}{2}\right)^2 = (3)^2 = 9$
3. Add the number from the previous step to both sides of the equation, then factor.	$x^2 + 6x + 9 = 7 + 9 \rightarrow (x + 3)(x + 3) = 16 \rightarrow$ $(x + 3)^2 = 16$
4. Take the square root of both sides.	$\sqrt{(x + 3)^2} = \pm\sqrt{16} \rightarrow x + 3 = \pm 4$
5. Split the product into two equations and solve each one.	$x + 3 = 4,\ x + 3 = -4 \rightarrow x = 1,\ x = -7$

A note about completing the square: a needs to be 1 to use this process. You can divide the first term by a to convert the coefficient to 1, but if you start getting strange-looking fractions, it may be easier to use the quadratic formula instead.

Grouping

Although less commonly seen than other strategies, **grouping** is useful with more challenging quadratics, especially when the leading coefficient (the value of a) is not 1. You'll need two x terms to use this route. The goal of grouping is to identify the greatest common factor (GCF) of the first two terms, repeat for the second two terms, then finally combine the two GCFs into a separate binomial. Check out the following example:

Step	Scratchwork
Starting point	$2x^2 - 7x - 15 = 0$
1. You need to split the x term in two; the sum of the new terms' coefficients must equal b, and their product must equal ac.	$a \times c = 2 \times (-15) = -30,\ b = -7$ new x term coefficients: 3 and -10 $2x^2 - 10x + 3x - 15 = 0$
2. What's the GCF of the first pair of terms? How about the second pair of terms?	GCF of $2x^2$ and $-10x$ is $2x$ GCF of $3x$ and -15 is 3
3. Factor out the GCFs for each pair of terms.	$2x^2 - 10x + 3x - 15 = 0$ $2x(x - 5) + 3(x - 5) = 0$

Step	Scratchwork
4. Factor out the newly formed binomial and combine the GCFs into another factor.	$2x(x - 5) + 3(x - 5) = 0$ $(2x + 3)(x - 5) = 0$
5. Split into two equations and solve as usual.	$2x + 3 = 0,\ x - 5 + 0 \rightarrow x = -\dfrac{3}{2},\ x = 5$

Straightforward Math

Sometimes you can get away with not having to FOIL or factor extensively, but you need to be able to spot patterns or trends. Don't resort to complex techniques when some easy simplification will get the job done. Equations similar to the following examples are highly likely to appear on the PSAT.

No Middle Term	No Last Term	Squared Binomial
$x^2 - 9 = 0$	$x^2 - 9x = 0$	$(x - 3)^2 = 9$
$x^2 = 9$	$x(x - 9) = 0$	$(x - 3) = \pm\sqrt{9}$
$x = \pm\sqrt{9}$	$x = 0,\ x - 9 = 0$	$(x - 3) = \pm 3$
$x = \pm 3$	$x = 0,\ x = 9$	$x - 3 = 3 \rightarrow x = 6$ $x - 3 = -3 \rightarrow x = 0$

✔ **Expert Tip**

You can also factor $x^2 - 9$ to get $(x + 3)(x - 3)$; this is called a difference of squares. Note that this only works when the terms are being subtracted.

Quadratic Formula

The quadratic formula can be used to solve any quadratic equation. However, because the math can often get complicated, use this as a last resort or when you need to find exact (i.e., not rounded, fractions, and/or radicals) solutions. If you see square roots in the answer choices, this is a clue to use the quadratic formula.

The quadratic formula that follows yields solutions to a quadratic equation that is written in standard form, $ax^2 + bx + c = 0$:

$$x = \frac{-b \pm \sqrt{b^2 - 4ac}}{2a}$$

The $\pm$ sign that follows $-b$ indicates that you will have two solutions, so remember to find both.

The expression under the radical ($b^2 - 4ac$) is called the discriminant, and its value determines the number of real solutions. If this quantity is positive, the equation has two distinct real solutions; if it is equal to 0, there is only one distinct real solution; and if it is negative, there are no real solutions.

> ✔ **Note**
>
> Being flexible and familiar with your strengths on Test Day is essential. By doing so, you can identify the path to the answer to a quadratics question that is the most efficient for you.

On the next few pages, you'll get to try applying some of these strategies to test-like PSAT questions. Let's start with a FOIL question:

1. Which of the following is an equivalent form of the expression $(x - 4)(x + 2)$?

   A) $x^2 - 8x - 2$

   B) $x^2 - 2x - 8$

   C) $x^2 + 2x - 8$

   D) $x^2 - 2x + 8$

Work through the Kaplan Method for Math step-by-step to solve this question. The following table shows Kaplan's strategic thinking on the left, along with suggested math scratchwork on the right.

Strategic Thinking	Math Scratchwork
Step 1: Read the question, identifying and organizing important information as you go You're asked to identify the quadratic expression equivalent to $(x - 4)(x + 2)$.	
Step 2: Choose the best strategy to answer the question *Are you presented with anything familiar in the question stem? How about in the answer choices? What's the best route to the answer?* You have a product of two binomials in the stem and quadratic expressions written in standard form in the answer choices, so FOIL is the quickest route. Follow the standard FOIL procedure, then simplify.	$(x-4)(x+2)$ First + Outer + Inner + Last $= (x)(x)+(2)(x)+(-4)(x)+(-4)(2)$ $= x^2+(-2x)+(-8)$ $= x^2 - 2x - 8$
Step 3: Check that you answered the *right* question You correctly expanded the quadratic using FOIL and got an exact match for (B), the correct answer.	$x^2 - 2x - 8$

Use the strategies you've learned in this section to simplify the rational expression that follows:

2. Which of the following is equivalent to $\dfrac{x^2 - 4x + 4}{2x^2 + 4x - 16}$?

A) $\dfrac{1}{2}$

B) $\dfrac{x}{x + 4}$

C) $-\dfrac{2 - x}{2(x + 4)}$

D) $\dfrac{x^2 - 4x + 4}{x^2 + 2x - 8}$

Work through the Kaplan Method for Math step-by-step to solve this question. The following table shows Kaplan's strategic thinking on the left, along with suggested math scratchwork on the right.

Strategic Thinking	Math Scratchwork
Step 1: Read the question, identifying and organizing important information as you go You need to find the simplified expression that is equivalent to the one given.	
Step 2: Choose the best strategy to answer the question *What familiar pieces do you see?* There are a few x^2 terms, so you should be thinking about quadratics and factoring. Also, whenever you're given a fraction, think about ways to cancel terms. *What should be done first?* Examine the numerator first. It's an example of a perfect square trinomial, so it's easy to factor. The denominator is a bit more involved. Factor out the 2 to get 1 for the x^2 coefficient, then factor the quadratic as usual. If the numerator and denominator have any factors in common, cancel those factors. *The answer doesn't match any of the choices. Did I make a mistake?* Not necessarily. In this case, you'll notice your choice is very close to (C); all you need to do is factor a -1 out of your answer's numerator to get the whole expression to match.	$\dfrac{x^2 - 4x + 4}{2x^2 + 4x - 16}$ $\dfrac{(x-2)(x-2)}{2(x^2 + 2x - 8)}$ $\dfrac{(x-2)(x-2)}{2(x+4)(x-2)}$ $\dfrac{(x-2)}{2(x+4)}$ $\dfrac{(-1)(-x+2)}{2(x+4)}$ $\dfrac{(-1)(2-x)}{2(x+4)}$
Step 3: Check that you answered the *right* question After factoring out a negative, the expression matches (C).	$-\dfrac{2-x}{2(x+4)}$

✔ **Expert Tip**

Something seemingly trivial like a negative sign can separate your answer from the correct answer. If you've checked your math for errors but found none, look for ways to alter your answer's appearance so that it matches an answer choice. When in doubt, pick numbers and plug a few test cases into your expression and the answer choices to find a match.

3. What value of x satisfies the equation $4x^2 + 24x = -8$?

A) $-3 - \sqrt{7}$

B) $3 - \sqrt{7}$

C) 3

D) $3 + \sqrt{7}$

This question is full of radicals, but don't panic. You can use the Kaplan Method for Math to efficiently tackle this kind of question on Test Day. The following table shows Kaplan's strategic thinking on the left, along with suggested math scratchwork on the right.

Strategic Thinking	Math Scratchwork
Step 1: Read the question, identifying and organizing important information as you go The question asks for a solution to the given equation.	
Step 2: Choose the best strategy to answer the question The equation is a quadratic, so think about factoring. Remember to first put the equation in standard form. *How can you make factoring easier here?* Divide both sides of the equation by 4 to get an x^2 coefficient of 1. *The number 2 does not have factors that add up to 6. What can you do besides factoring?* You only have three terms with no perfect squares, so grouping and square rooting are out. Try completing the square instead. *Now that you have two possible values of x, what should you do next?* Identify the solution that is among the answer choices.	$4x^2 + 24x + 8 = 0$ $4(x^2 + 6x + 2) = 0$ $x^2 + 6x + 2 = 0$ $x^2 + 6x = -2$ $\left(\dfrac{b}{2}\right)^2 = \left(\dfrac{6}{2}\right)^2 = 3^2 = 9$ $x^2 + 6x + 9 = -2 + 9$ $(x + 3)^2 = 7$ $x + 3 = \pm\sqrt{7}$ $x = -3 \pm \sqrt{7}$ $x = -3 + \sqrt{7}$ or $x = -3 - \sqrt{7}$
Step 3: Check that you answered the *right* question One of your solutions is an exact match for (A), the correct answer.	

CONNECTIONS BETWEEN QUADRATICS AND PARABOLAS

A quadratic function is simply a quadratic equation set equal to y or $f(x)$ instead of 0. To solve one of these, you would follow the same procedure as before: substitute 0 for y, or $f(x)$, then solve using one of the three methods demonstrated (algebra, graphing, quadratic formula). Consider the graphical connection: when you set y equal to 0, you're really finding the x-intercepts.

The graph of every quadratic equation (or function) is a parabola, which is a symmetric U-shaped graph that opens either up or down. To determine whether a parabola will open up or down, examine the value of a in the equation. If a is positive, the parabola will open up; if a is negative, it will open down. Take a look at the examples below to see this graphically.

Like quadratic equations, quadratic functions will have zero, one, or two real solutions, corresponding to the number of times the parabola crosses the x-axis. As you saw with previous examples, graphing is a powerful way to determine the number of solutions a quadratic function has.

Two Real Solutions	One Real Solution	No Real Solutions

There are three algebraic forms that a quadratic equation can take: standard, factored, and vertex. Each is provided in the following table along with some features that are revealed by writing the equation in that particular form.

Standard	Factored	Vertex
$y = ax^2 + bx + c$	$y = a(x - m)(x - n)$	$y = a(x - h)^2 + k$
y-intercept is c.	Solutions are m and n.	Vertex is (h, k).
In real-world contexts, starting quantity is c.	x-intercepts are m and n.	Minimum/maximum of function is k.
Format used to solve via quadratic formula.	Vertex is halfway between m and n.	Axis of symmetry is given by $x = h$.

You've already seen standard and factored forms earlier in this chapter, but vertex form might be new to you. In vertex form, a is the same as the a from standard form, and h and k are the coordinates of the **vertex** (h, k). If a quadratic function is not in vertex form, you can still find the x-coordinate of the vertex by plugging the appropriate values into the equation $h = \dfrac{-b}{2a}$, which is also the equation for the axis of symmetry (see graph that follows). Once you determine h, plug this value into the quadratic function and solve for y to determine k, the y-coordinate of the vertex.

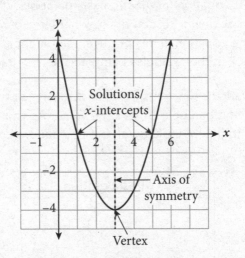

In addition to familiarity with the various forms a quadratic equation/function can take, you should have a foundational knowledge of the structure of a parabola. Some of the basic pieces you could be asked about on Test Day are shown above. You already know how to determine the solutions and the vertex, and finding the axis of symmetry is straightforward. The **equation of the axis of symmetry** of a parabola is $x = h$, where h is the x-coordinate of the vertex.

✔ **Note**

The formula for a parabola's axis of symmetry is easy to remember: it's the quadratic formula without the radical component. If the x-intercepts are rational numbers, you can also determine the axis of symmetry by finding the midpoint, the point exactly halfway between.

Take some time to explore the questions on the next several pages to test your new wealth of quadratic knowledge.

A question like this next one could arise in either the calculator or the no-calculator section. Think critically about how you'd solve it in either case.

4.   Will the graph of $f(x) = \dfrac{5}{2}x - 2$ intersect the graph of $f(x) = \dfrac{1}{2}x^2 + 2x - 3$?

   A)   Yes, only at the vertex of the parabola

   B)   Yes, once on each side of the vertex

   C)   Yes, twice to the right of the vertex

   D)   No, the graphs will not intersect

Work through the Kaplan Method for Math step-by-step to solve this question. The following table shows Kaplan's strategic thinking on the left, along with suggested math scratchwork on the right. Because this question could occur in either the calculator or the no-calculator section, graphical and algebraic solutions are included.

Strategic Thinking	Math Scratchwork
Step 1: Read the question, identifying and organizing important information as you go You are given a linear function and a quadratic function and asked whether their graphs intersect.	$f(x) = \dfrac{5}{2}x - 2$ $f(x) = \dfrac{1}{2}x^2 + 2x - 3$
Step 2: Choose the best strategy to answer the question *What should you find first, the vertex or the intersection points?* Because the equations may not even intersect, ignore the vertex for now. You can always find it later, if need be. *How can you discover whether these intersect without graphing?* Set the equations equal to each other and combine all of your terms on one side to get a quadratic in standard form. Factor to find the solutions. *Your quadratic has two solutions; what does this mean?* The two graphs intersect at two points so you can eliminate A and D.	$\dfrac{5}{2}x - 2 = \dfrac{1}{2}x^2 + 2x - 3$ $0 = \dfrac{1}{2}x^2 - \dfrac{1}{2}x - 1$ $0 = \dfrac{1}{2}(x^2 - x - 2)$ $0 = x^2 - x - 2$ $0 = (x + 1)(x - 2)$ $x = -1$ and $x = 2$

Strategic Thinking	Math Scratchwork
How can you determine where the vertex of the parabola is? Use the formulas for h and k. Putting a parabola in standard form into vertex form is too time-consuming. *Where are the points of intersection with respect to the vertex?* Compare the two solutions you found earlier to the x-coordinate of the vertex. They are both to the right of the vertex. The correct answer is (C). *How can your calculator make this question much easier?* You can simply graph the equations on the same graph and visually estimate the vertex and intersection points. Make sure you set an appropriate viewing window. You need to be able to see the vertex of the parabola and the points where the graphs intersect (if they do). Upon further investigation, it is clear that there are two intersection points to the right of the vertex, which matches (C).	$h = \dfrac{-b}{2a} = \dfrac{-2}{2(1/2)} = \dfrac{-2}{1} = -2$ $k = f(-2) = \dfrac{1}{2}(-2)^2 + 2(-2) - 3$ $= \dfrac{1}{2}(4) - 4 - 3$ $= 2 - 4 - 3 = -5$ Vertex: $(-2, -5)$
Step 3: Check that you answered the *right* question Using either method, you found that the line intersects the parabola at two locations to the right of the vertex, which is what the question asked for.	

✔ **Expert Tip**

Sometimes questions involving complex algebra or simplification will appear in the calculator section. Avoid autopilot. Use your calculator to cut out as much algebra as you can. Remember, you don't get extra points for solving questions the hard way on the PSAT!

In one final type of quadratic-related question, you may be asked to match a function to a graph, or vice versa. An example of this follows; unfortunately, it is not likely to appear in the calculator section of the test:

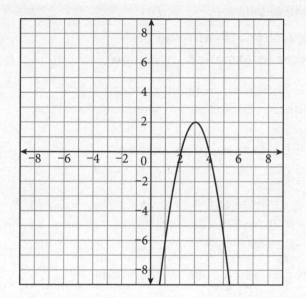

5. Which of the following represents the function shown in the graph?

A) $f(x) = -(x - 3)^2 + 2$

B) $f(x) = -2(x - 3)^2 + 2$

C) $f(x) = -2(x + 3)^2 + 2$

D) $f(x) = -(x + 3)^2 + 2$

Use the Kaplan Method for Math to work through this question step-by-step. The following table shows Kaplan's strategic thinking on the left, along with suggested math scratchwork on the right.

Strategic Thinking	Math Scratchwork
Step 1: Read the question, identifying and organizing important information as you go Notice that the answer choices all represent quadratic functions written in vertex form. Your task is to determine which matches the graph.	
Step 2: Choose the best strategy to answer the question *Use what you know about vertex form to systematically eliminate choices. What is the vertex of the function in the graph? Which choices can you eliminate?* *How might you determine which remaining function matches without using a calculator?* Check a few key points. The graph crosses the *x*-axis at $x = 2$ and $x = 4$. Check those points first.	vertex $= (3, 2)$ Eliminate C and D. key points: $(2, 0)$ and $(4, 0)$ Choice A: $f(2) = -(2 - 3)^2 + 2 = -1 + 2 = 1$ $1 \neq 0$ Eliminate A. Choice B: $f(2) = -(2 - 3)^2 + 2 = -2 + 2 = 0$ $0 = 0$
Step 3: Check that you answered the *right* question Choice (B) must be the correct answer.	

✔ **Note**

Remember to check for differences in the *a* values of the answer choices. In the previous example, all the choices have a negative *a*, so *a* isn't much help here. However, it might help you eliminate incorrect answers on Test Day, so always check it.

GRAPHING QUADRATICS ON A CALCULATOR

At this point, you've become quite an expert at working with quadratics on paper. In this part, we'll explore how you can use your calculator to efficiently graph quadratics. Calculators can be great time-savers *when you're allowed to use them*.

Graphing

All quadratic equations can be solved by graphing, unless they happen to have imaginary solutions. That said, you might ask why you need to learn all the algebra techniques. There are a few reasons why graphing shouldn't be the first option you turn to:

- Remember, there's a no-calculator section on the PSAT; graphing isn't an option here.

- Graphing is often slower because entering complex equations and then zooming in to find points of interest can be tedious.

- It is easy to accidentally mistype when you're being timed—a misplaced parenthesis or negative sign will likely lead to a trap answer choice.

However, if you have complicated algebra ahead (e.g., fractional coefficients), decimals in the answer choices, or time-consuming obstacles to overcome, graphing can be a viable alternative to solving quadratic equations algebraically. Here is a set of straightforward steps for graphing on a calculator:

1. Manipulate the equation so that it equals 0.

2. Substitute $y =$ for the 0.

3. Enter the equation into your calculator.

4. Trace the graph to approximate the *x*-intercepts (usually the answer choices will be sufficiently different to warrant an approximation over an exact value) or use your calculator's built-in capability to find the *x*-intercepts exactly.

Graphing on the TI-83/84

While on the home screen, press [Y=]. Then enter the function to be graphed. Press [GRAPH] and allow the function to plot. If you can't see everything or want to make sure there isn't something hiding, consider pressing [WINDOW] to set your own manual parameters or hitting [ZOOM] to quickly zoom in and out. If you want to simply investigate your graph, press [TRACE] and use the right and left arrow keys to move around on the graph. If you type in any *x*-value and press [ENTER], the *y*-value will be returned on screen.

Determining Solutions on the TI-83/84

Once you have your graph on screen, you're ready to find solutions. Press [2ND] [TRACE] to pull up the CALC menu, which has options for finding points of interest. Select option 2:ZERO by highlighting and pressing [ENTER]. You will be taken back to the graph. Use the arrow keys to move to the left of the x-intercept (zero) that you want to calculate. Once you are just to the left of only the zero you are interested in, press [ENTER]—this is called the Left Bound. Next, move to the right of that zero only, careful not to go past any others, and press [ENTER]—this is called the Right Bound. Finally, the calculator will ask you to "Guess," so move left or right to approximate this zero, and press [ENTER].

Because you've already set the quadratic equation equal to zero, you know the zeros that your calculator returns will be the solutions to the overall equation.

> ✔ **Note**
>
> Take the time to get comfortable with your calculator functions regardless of what calculator you have. You can find great instructions and even video demonstrations on the Internet.

Next, you'll get to try a sample test-like question that could be solved via graphing or the quadratic formula. Choose wisely. In almost every case, graphing will be faster, but familiarize yourself with the quadratic formula approach in case you encounter a question like this in the no-calculator section:

6. Which of the following are the real values of x that satisfy $3x^2 + 2x + 4 = 5x$?

   A) 3 and -2

   B) $\dfrac{3}{5}$ and $-\dfrac{2}{5}$

   C) 0

   D) No real solutions

Work through the Kaplan Method for Math step-by-step to solve this question. The following table shows Kaplan's strategic thinking on the left, along with suggested math scratchwork on the right.

Strategic Thinking	Math Scratchwork
Step 1: Read the question, identifying and organizing important information as you go You need to identify the values of x that satisfy the given equation.	
Step 2: Choose the best strategy to answer the question With quadratics, you have a few options: solve algebraically, graphically, or via the quadratic formula. *What is the first step?* Set the quadratic equal to 0 by subtracting $5x$ from each side of the equation. Once there, you'll see that solving algebraically is not wise, as the equation doesn't look easy to factor. Graphing and the quadratic formula will be quicker.	$3x^2 + 2x + 4 = 5x$ $3x^2 - 3x + 4 = 0$
Graphical Approach After plugging $y = 3x^2 - 3x + 4$ into your calculator, you get the graph on the right. The graph does not cross the x-axis, so there are no real solutions.	 $f(x) = 3x^2 - 3x + 4$

Math

Strategic Thinking	Math Scratchwork
Quadratic Formula (No-Calculator) Approach Plug in the coefficients and the constant carefully. It helps to jot down the numbers you'll be using: $a = 3$, $b = -3$, and $c = 4$. You'll notice that the discriminant will be negative, meaning there are no real solutions. Don't worry about simplifying—that's beyond the scope of this question.	$x = \dfrac{-b \pm \sqrt{b^2 - 4ac}}{2a}$ $x = \dfrac{3 \pm \sqrt{(-3)^2 - 4(3)(4)}}{2(3)}$ $x = \dfrac{3 \pm \sqrt{9 - 48}}{6}$ $x = \dfrac{3 \pm \sqrt{-39}}{6}$
Step 3: Check that you answered the *right* question This equation has no real solutions, which is (D).	

✔ **Note**

Don't worry if graphing is still somewhat foreign to you; the next section has more examples to get you comfortable with this route.

Nicely done! Take a look at another example:

7. The equation $\dfrac{1}{3}(3x^2 + kx - 9) = 9$ is satisfied when $x = 4$ and when $x = -3$. What is the value of $2k$?

A) -6

B) -3

C) $-\dfrac{1}{3}$

D) 3

Although this question seems more complicated than others you've seen in this chapter, if you use the Kaplan Method for Math, you'll arrive at the correct answer. The following table shows Kaplan's strategic thinking on the left, along with suggested math scratchwork on the right.

Strategic Thinking	Math Scratchwork
Step 1: Read the question, identifying and organizing important information as you go You're asked to find the value of $2k$.	
Step 2: Choose the best strategy to answer the question Notice that the equation in the question stem is not in standard form. Distributing the $\frac{1}{3}$ won't result in unmanageable fractions, so doing so won't cost you a lot of time. After distributing, set the equation equal to 0.	$\frac{1}{3}(3x^2 + kx - 9) = 9$ $x^2 + \frac{1}{3}kx - 3 = 9$ $x^2 + \frac{1}{3}kx - 12 = 0$
The "normal" routes to the solutions (factoring, etc.) would be difficult to take here because of the presence of k. Instead, use the solutions to construct and FOIL two binomials.	$(x - 4)(x + 3) = 0$ $x^2 - x - 12 = 0$
The quadratic expressions must be equal because they share the same solutions. Set them equal to each other, and then use algebra to solve for k.	$x^2 + \frac{1}{3}kx - 12 = x^2 - x - 12$ $\frac{1}{3}kx = -x$ $\frac{1}{3}k = -1$ $k = -3$
Step 3: Check that you answered the _right_ question Be careful! Many students will bubble in choice B. You're asked for $2k$. Multiply your previous result by 2, and select (A), the correct response.	$k = -3$ $2k = -6$

As demonstrated, even the most daunting quadratic equation questions are made more straightforward by using the Kaplan Method for Math.

Now you'll have a chance to try a few test-like questions in a scaffolded way. We've provided some guidance, but you'll need to fill in the missing parts of explanations or the step-by-step math in order to get to the correct answer. Don't worry—after going through the worked examples at the beginning of this section, these questions should be completely doable.

8. A projectile is launched from a cannon on top of a building. Its height in feet can be described as a function of elapsed time according to the following quadratic equation: $f(t) = -16t^2 + 128t + 320$. What is the product of the maximum height of the projectile and the time it takes the projectile to hit the ground?

    A)   2,048

    B)   3,842

    C)   4,096

    D)   5,760

Use the following scaffolding as your map through the question. If you aren't sure where to start, answer the questions in italics and fill in the blanks in the table as you work from top to bottom.

Strategic Thinking	Math Scratchwork
Step 1: Read the question, identifying and organizing important information as you go You're asked to find the product of the maximum height and the time the object takes to hit the ground.	
Step 2: Choose the best strategy to answer the question *How can you approach this systematically? What component of the parabola would correspond to the maximum height?* Hint: this parabola opens down. You know the maximum height would be at the vertex. *Which coordinate would give height, h or k?* *Are you finished? Make sure you calculate the time it takes to hit the ground. What height will the projectile be at when it hits the ground?* The projectile will be at a height of zero. Set up an equation and solve for the time. Hint: you can easily factor this quadratic. *What are the possible solutions for t? Which of these solutions doesn't make sense in the context of the question? Is there anything left to do here?*	$h = \dfrac{-b}{2a} = $ _____ $k = f(h)$ $k = -16(\_\_)^2 + 128(\_\_) + 320$ $k = $ _____ $0 = $ _____ $0 = (_____)(_____)$ $t = $ _____ $t = $ _____
Step 3: Check that you answered the *right* question *Did you calculate the product of the maximum height and the time the projectile spent in the air?* If you answered (D), you're absolutely right.	product = _____ × _____ = _____

9. Which of the following functions has *x*-intercepts at $x = -2$ and $x = 5$?

A) $f(x) = (x + 2)(x - 5) + 2$

B) $f(x) = \left(x - \dfrac{3}{2}\right)^2 - \dfrac{49}{4}$

C) $f(x) = (x - 5) + (x - 2)$

D) $f(x) = \left(x + \dfrac{3}{2}\right)^2 - \dfrac{49}{4}$

Use the scaffolding that follows as your map through the question. If you aren't sure where to start, answer the questions in italics and fill in the blanks in the table as you work from top to bottom.

Strategic Thinking	Math Scratchwork
Step 1: Read the question, identifying and organizing important information as you go You're asked to find the function that crosses the *x*-axis at the *x*-values of −2 and 5.	
Step 2: Choose the best strategy to answer the question *What will the y-coordinate of your function be at the x-intercept?* The *y*-coordinate will be 0 when the function crosses the *x*-axis. *Can you eliminate any answer choices quickly by plugging in x values? Can you immediately tell that some choices will not have zeroes at these x values?* Yes! Start with the ones that are easy to calculate. As soon as you get a nonzero result, go ahead and eliminate the answer choice.	$f(-2) = $ _____ $f(5) = $ _____ A: $f(-2) = $ _____ C: $f(5) = $ _____

Strategic Thinking	Math Scratchwork
Now that you've got it down to two choices, look critically at them. What is the same in both choices? Notice that in each case, you'll be subtracting $\frac{49}{4}$. *What is a decimal approximation for $\frac{49}{4}$? Don't worry about accuracy . . . what two integers is it between?* *Now use number properties to narrow it down. If you're look-ing for f(x) = 0, you'll need to subtract $\frac{49}{4}$ from something pretty close to that decimal value. Are you looking for a number greater or less than 5^2? Should you add or subtract $\frac{3}{2}$ when you plug in x = 5?* *Do you need to go any further?* No. There are no other possible matching answer choices.	_____ $< \frac{49}{4} <$ _____ $5^2 =$ _____ which is much _____ than $\frac{49}{4}$. Therefore, you should (add / subtract) $\frac{3}{2}$.
Step 3: Check that you answered the *right* question If your answer is (B), you're correct! Choice D would result in a squared quantity that is much greater than 25, such that subtracting $\frac{49}{4}$ would never give you a zero.	

✔ **Expert Tip**

Notice that we didn't do a lot of calculating in the previous question. Remember, the PSAT tests math and critical thinking, not computation. Don't calculate a quantity unless you absolutely have to. Calculations take time and are often unnecessary to eliminate answer choices. Instead, think about the relationships between numbers.

Now that you've seen the variety of ways in which the PSAT can test you on quadratics, try the following questions to check your understanding. Give yourself 4 minutes to tackle the following four questions. Make sure you use the Kaplan Method for Math as often as you can. Remember, you want to emphasize speed and efficiency in addition to simply getting the correct answer.

10. What positive value(s) of z satisfy the equation $4z^2 + 32z - 81 = -1$?

    A) 2

    B) 2 and -10

    C) 4 and 2

    D) None of the above

11. If a quadratic function $f(x)$ has solutions a and b such that $a < 0$, $b > 0$, and $|b| > |a|$, which of the following could be $f(x)$?

    A) $4x^2 + 4x - 24$

    B) $-x^2 + x + 6$

    C) $-x^2 - x + 6$

    D) $3x^2 - 6x$

12. The non-negative difference between the zeros of $g(x) = -2x^2 + 16x - 32$ is equal to what value ?

13. Which equation represents the axis of symmetry of the graph of the quadratic function $h(x) = 2x^2 + 4x - 5$?

    A) $x = 2$

    B) $x = 1$

    C) $x = -1$

    D) $x = 0$

Answers and Explanations for this chapter begin on page 570.

ON YOUR OWN

1. Which of the following are solutions to the quadratic equation $(x + 1)^2 = \dfrac{1}{25}$?

   A) $x = -6, x = 4$

   B) $x = -\dfrac{24}{25}$

   C) $x = -\dfrac{6}{5}, x = -\dfrac{4}{5}$

   D) $x = \dfrac{4}{5}, x = \dfrac{6}{5}$

2. The factored form of a quadratic equation is $y = (x + 2)(x - 7)$, and the standard form is $y = x^2 - 5x - 14$. Which of the following statements accurately describes the graph of y ?

   A) The x-intercepts are -7 and 2, and the y-intercept is -14.

   B) The x-intercepts are -2 and 7, and the y-intercept is -14.

   C) The x-intercepts are -7 and 2, and the y-intercept is 14.

   D) The x-intercepts are -2 and 7, and the y-intercept is 14.

3. The following quadratic equations are all representations of the graph shown. Which equation best reveals the values of the x-intercepts of the graph?

   A) $y = \dfrac{3}{4}x^2 - \dfrac{1}{2}x - 2$

   B) $y + \dfrac{25}{12} = \dfrac{1}{12}(3x - 1)^2$

   C) $y = \dfrac{1}{12}(3x - 1)^2 - \dfrac{25}{12}$

   D) $y = \dfrac{1}{4}(3x + 4)(x - 2)$

4. If $x^2 + 8x = 48$ and $x > 0$, what is the value of $x - 5$?

   A) -9

   B) -1

   C) 4

   D) 7

5. Which of the following equations has the same solutions as $x^2 + 6x + 17 = 0$?

   A) $y = (x - 3)^2 - 26$

   B) $y = (x - 3)^2 + 8$

   C) $y = (x + 3)^2 + 8$

   D) $y = (x + 3)^2 + 17$

$$\begin{cases} y = 3x \\ x^2 - y^2 = -288 \end{cases}$$

6. If (x, y) is a solution to the system of equations shown here, what is the value of x^2?

   A)   6

   B)   36

   C)   144

   D)   1,296

7. Which of the following are the roots of the equation $x^2 + 8x - 3 = 0$?

   A) $-4 \pm \sqrt{19}$

   B) $-4 \pm \sqrt{3}$

   C) $4 \pm \sqrt{3}$

   D) $4 \pm \sqrt{19}$

8. If a catapult is used to throw a lead ball, the path of the ball can be modeled by a quadratic equation, $y = ax^2 + bx + c$, where x is the horizontal distance that the ball travels and y is the height of the ball. If one of these catapult-launched lead balls travels 150 feet before hitting the ground and reaches a maximum height of 45 feet, which of the following equations represents its path?

   A) $y = -0.008x^2 + 1.2x$

   B) $y = -0.008x^2 - 150x$

   C) $y = 45x^2 + 150x$

   D) $y = 125x^2 + 25x$

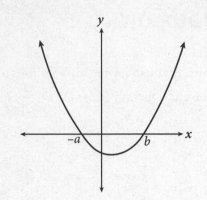

9. If the distance from $-a$ to b in the figure shown is 10, which of the following could be the factored form of the graph's equation?

   A) $y = (x - 7)(x - 3)$

   B) $y = (x - 7)(x + 3)$

   C) $y = (x - 8)(x - 2)$

   D) $y = (x - 1)(x + 10)$

10. If $y = ax^2 + bx + c$ represents the equation of the graph shown in the figure, which of the following statements is not true?

    A)   The value of a is a negative number.

    B)   The value of c is a negative number.

    C)   The graph is increasing for $x < 3$ and decreasing for $x > 3$.

    D)   The zeros of the equation are $x = -2$ and $x = 8$.

11. Which of the following equations could represent a parabola that has a minimum value of -3 and whose axis of symmetry is the line $x = 2$?

    A) $y = (x - 3)^2 + 2$

    B) $y = (x + 3)^2 + 2$

    C) $y = (x - 2)^2 - 3$

    D) $y = (x + 2)^2 - 3$

12. If the axis of symmetry of the parabola given by the equation $y = -(x + 5)^2 + 1$ is $x = p$, then what is the value of p ?

    A) -5

    B) -1

    C) 1

    D) 5

Shawna's Throw

13. Shawna throws a baseball into the air. The equation $h = -12t^2 + 36t + 4$ represents the height of the ball in feet, t seconds after it was thrown. The graph of part of the equation is shown in the previous figure. Which of the following equations could represent the height of a second ball that was thrown by Meagan, if Meagan's ball did not go as high as Shawna's ball?

    A) $h = -12t^2 + 35t + 7$

    B) $h = -12t^2 + 37t + 3$

    C) $h = -3(2t - 1)^2 + 35$

    D) $h = -3(2t - 2)^2 + 28$

14. Given the equation $y = -2(x - 6)^2 + 5$, which of the following statements is not true?

    A) The y-intercept is $(0, 5)$.

    B) The axis of symmetry is $x = 6$.

    C) The vertex is $(6, 5)$.

    D) The parabola opens downward.

15. The x-coordinates of the solutions to a system of equations are -8 and -3. Which of the following could be the system?

    A) $\begin{cases} y = -x - 1 \\ y = (x - 8)^2 - 3 \end{cases}$

    B) $\begin{cases} y = x + 8 \\ y = (x + 3)^2 - 8 \end{cases}$

    C) $\begin{cases} y = x + 8 \\ y = (x + 3)^2 - 2 \end{cases}$

    D) $\begin{cases} y = -x - 1 \\ y = (x + 5)^2 - 2 \end{cases}$

    $$\begin{cases} y = x + 1 \\ y = \dfrac{1}{2}x^2 - x - \dfrac{3}{2} \end{cases}$$

16. If (a, b) is a solution to the system of equations shown, what is the value of a, given that $u > 0$?

Additional Topics in Math

BY THE END OF THIS UNIT, YOU WILL BE ABLE TO:

1. Solve geometry questions involving lines, angles, triangles, and other complex shapes

2. Use special right triangles and Pythagorean triplets to save time on Test Day

3. Solve for unknown parts of circles

4. Interpret 3-D figures and solve problems using formulas for volume

CHAPTER 7

Geometry

CHAPTER OBJECTIVES

By the end of this chapter, you will be able to:

1. Apply the properties of lines and angles to solve geometry questions

2. Use the Pythagorean theorem, Pythagorean triplets, and special right triangles to answer questions involving triangles

3. Use concepts and theorems about congruence and similarity to solve problems about lines, angles, and triangles

4. Identify simple shapes within complex figures and use them to solve questions

5. Apply theorems about circles to find arc lengths, angle measures, chord lengths, and areas of sectors

6. Create or use an equation with two variables to solve a problem about a circle in the coordinate plane

7. Solve problems using volume formulas

SMARTPOINTS

Point Value	SmartPoint Category
40 Points	Geometry

LINES AND ANGLES

Lines and angles are the foundation of PSAT geometry. Therefore, mastering their basic rules will make solving these questions, as well as related geometry questions, easier. With the knowledge you'll gain from this chapter, you will be able to quickly identify geometric relationships, build upon the information given in the question, and often bypass complex algebra.

Familiarity with angle types will often unlock information that is not explicitly given in a question. This makes getting to the answer much easier for even the toughest geometry questions. First, let's take a look at the types of angles you should be able to recognize:

Angle Type	Angle Measurement	Example
Acute	Less than 90°	
Right	90°	
Obtuse	Between 90° and 180°	
Straight	180°	

More often than not, you'll work with multiple angles in a single question. Therefore, it's worth noting two likely familiar terms that involve working with two or more angles: complementary and supplementary angles. Two angles are **complementary** if their measures add up to 90°; if their measures add up to 180°, the angles are **supplementary**.

> ✔ **Note**
>
> Two angles need *not* be adjacent to be complementary or supplementary.

Intersecting lines create angles with special relationships you'll need to know as well. When two lines intersect, adjacent angles are supplementary, and **vertical** angles (two angles opposite a vertex) are equal, or **congruent**. Take a look at the following figure for an example.

The angles marked $a°$ and $b°$ are supplementary; therefore, $a + b = 180$. The angle marked $a°$ is vertical (and thus equal) to the one marked 60°, so $a = 60$. With this new information, you can find b: $a + b = 60 + b = 180$, so $b = 120$.

> ✔ **Note**
>
> Unless otherwise noted, figures on the PSAT are drawn to scale. Be especially careful when you see "<u>Note:</u> Figure not drawn to scale."

When two parallel lines are intersected by another line (called a **transversal**), all acute angles are equal, and all obtuse angles are equal. Additionally, **corresponding angles** are angles that are in the same position but on different parallel lines/transversal intersections; they are also equal. Furthermore, **alternate interior angles** and **alternate exterior angles** are equal. Alternate interior angles are angles that are positioned between the two parallel lines on opposite sides of the transversal, whereas alternate exterior angles are positioned on the outside of the parallel lines on opposite sides of the transversal. Consider the following figure:

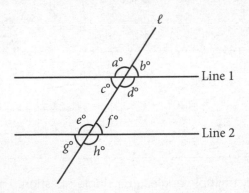

- Line 1 and Line 2 are parallel and cut by transversal ℓ.
- Angles a, d, e, and h are obtuse and equal.
- Angles b, c, f, and g are acute and equal.
- Angle pairs (b and f), (c and g), (a and e), and (d and h) are corresponding angles.
- Angle pairs (a and h) and (b and g) are alternate exterior angles.
- Angle pairs (d and e) and (c and f) are alternate interior angles.

Below is a summary of the essential theorems related to parallel lines that you'll need to know. Notice that the converse of most of these theorems is also true.

Angle Theorem	Definition
Alternate Interior Angles	• If two parallel lines are cut by a transversal, the alternate interior angles are congruent. • If two lines are cut by a transversal and the alternate interior angles are congruent, the lines are parallel.
Alternate Exterior Angles	• If two parallel lines are cut by a transversal, the alternate exterior angles are congruent. • If two lines are cut by a transversal and the alternate exterior angles are congruent, the lines are parallel.
Corresponding Angles	• If two parallel lines are cut by a transversal, the corresponding angles are congruent. • If two lines are cut by a transversal and the corresponding angles are congruent, the lines are parallel.
Vertical Angles	• If two parallel lines are cut by a transversal, the vertical angles are congruent.

✔ **Note**

Parallel lines cut by a transversal are powerful: even if you know only one angle measure, you can get the other seven in mere seconds by knowing these rules.

TRIANGLES

Lines and angles form the basis of triangles—some of the most commonly occurring shapes on the PSAT. Luckily, triangle questions usually don't involve a lot of complex algebra and are a great way to earn a few quick points on Test Day. Having a good command of triangle properties will help you recognize and solve these questions quickly. Many seemingly difficult questions will become easier once you can confidently speak the language of triangles.

All triangles follow the rules listed here, regardless of the type of triangle, so take the time now to get comfortable with these rules.

Triangle Theorem	Definition
Triangle Sum and Exterior Angle Theorems	• Interior angles add up to 180°. • An exterior angle equals the sum of the two opposite interior angles.
Isosceles Triangle Theorem	• If two sides of a triangle are congruent, the angles opposite them are congruent. • If two angles of a triangle are congruent, the sides opposite them are congruent.
Triangle Inequality Theorem	• The sum of the lengths of any two sides of a triangle must be greater than the length of the third side. • The difference of the lengths of any two sides of a triangle must be less than the length of the third side.
Side-Angle Relationship	• In a triangle, the longest side is across from the largest angle. • In a triangle, the largest angle is across from the longest side.
Mid-Segment Theorem	• A triangle mid-segment (or midline) is parallel to one side of the triangle and joins the midpoints of the other two sides. • The mid-segment's length is half the length of the side to which it is parallel.

The corresponding angles and side lengths of **congruent triangles** are equal. **Similar triangles** have the same angle measurements and proportional sides. In the figure below, $\triangle ABC$ and $\triangle DEF$ have the same angle measurements, so the side lengths can be set up as the following proportion: $\frac{A}{D} = \frac{B}{E} = \frac{C}{F}$.

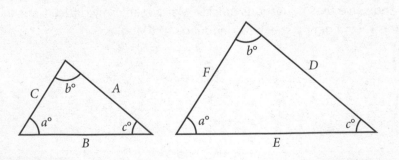

Math

Drawing multiple heights in one triangle creates similar triangles, as shown in the diagram below. When you encounter a question like this, redrawing the similar triangles with their angles and sides in the same positions will help keep information in order.

COMPLEX FIGURES

Complex figures are also a recurring PSAT geometry topic, particularly ones that involve triangles. A complex figure is not a shape such as a dodecahedron. Instead, a complex figure is usually a larger shape that is composed of multiple (familiar) shapes; these can be obvious or cleverly hidden. These figures can always be broken down into squares, rectangles, triangles, and/or circles. No matter how convoluted the figure, following the below guidelines will lead you to the correct answer on Test Day:

- Transfer information from the question stem to the figure. If a figure isn't provided, draw one!

- Break the figure into familiar shapes.

- Determine how one line segment can play multiple roles in a figure. For example, if a circle and triangle overlap correctly, the circle's radius might be the triangle's hypotenuse.

- Work from the shape with the most information to the shape with the least information.

Now use your knowledge of lines, angles, and triangles to answer a test-like question:

1. In the figure above, lines *l* and *m* are parallel and x = 40. What is the value of y + z ?

A) 220

B) 140

C) 120

D) 70

Work through the Kaplan Method for Math step-by-step to solve this question. The following table shows Kaplan's strategic thinking on the left, along with suggested math scratchwork on the right.

Strategic Thinking	Math Scratchwork
Step 1: Read the question, identifying and organizing important information as you go You need to determine the value of $y + z$.	
Step 2: Choose the best strategy to answer the question *Which line relationships will help you solve this question?* Parallel lines are being cut by a transversal. Therefore, you know the angle where A and l intersect corresponds to the one marked $z°$, so they are equal. The former is labeled $w°$ here. A, B, and l make a triangle, which has an interior angle sum of 180°, but you're only given one angle, $x = 40$. The sum of the two unknown angles of the triangle must be 140°, and because you're looking for the sum of y and z (not y and z separately), you can just pick numbers for the triangle's unknown angles. Suppose both are 70°. This means that the angles supplementary to these (y and w) must both be 110°. Remembering that $w = z$, you can substitute 110 for z as well as y. Add y and z to get $110 + 110 = 220$.	 $z = w$ $y = w = 110$ $y + w = y + z = 110 + 110 = 220$
Step 3: Check that you answered the *right* question You found $y + z$, so you're done. Choice (A) is correct.	

✔ **Expert Tip**

The PSAT rewards students who can think flexibly about variables. If you need $y + z$, don't waste time trying to find y and z individually (it's sometimes impossible, as in this question!). Stay focused on what the question asks.

Let's try another test-like question. Refer back to the properties and theorems as needed.

2. Which of the following is not true of the figure above?

A) $\overline{AB} \neq \overline{BC} \neq \overline{CA}$

B) $\overline{BC} < \overline{CA} < \overline{AB}$

C) $\overline{AB} = \sqrt{\overline{BC}^2 + \overline{CA}^2}$

D) $\overline{BC} + \overline{AB} > \overline{CA}$

There's no scratchwork for this question, but Kaplan's strategic thinking is provided in the table. Follow along as we reason through the question to get the correct answer.

Strategic Thinking
Step 1: Read the question, identifying and organizing important information as you go You need to identify the false statement.
Step 2: Choose the best strategy to answer the question *What does the question give you?* The question stem doesn't have information in it, but the figure gives the interior angles of a triangle. *How are the side lengths and interior angles related to one another?* None of the interior angles are equal, so none of the sides of the triangle are equal. Eliminate A. *What theorem can you apply to choice B?* The longest side of a triangle is opposite the largest angle, so arrange the angles in ascending order: 47°, 65°, 68°. The corresponding opposite sides are $\overline{BC}$, $\overline{CA}$, $\overline{AB}$, so B is true; eliminate it. *How can you evaluate choice (C)? Is there another way to view the relationship?* The equation in (C) should look familiar; it's a derivative of the Pythagorean theorem (square both sides to eliminate the radical). The Pythagorean theorem may be used only with right triangles, so this relationship is false.
Step 3: Check that you answered the *right* question Choice (C) is a false statement. There is no need to check D; move on to the next question.

THE PYTHAGOREAN THEOREM, PYTHAGOREAN TRIPLETS, AND SPECIAL RIGHT TRIANGLES

The Pythagorean theorem is one of the most fundamental equations in geometry, and it will be of great use to you on the PSAT. Common Pythagorean triplets and special right triangle ratios that originate from this formula will also serve you well on Test Day.

The **Pythagorean theorem** is an important triangle topic that you are probably familiar with already. If you know the lengths of any two sides of a right triangle, you can use the Pythagorean theorem equation to find the missing side. The equation is expressed as $a^2 + b^2 = c^2$, where a and b are the shorter sides of the triangle (called legs) and c is the hypotenuse, which is always across from the right angle of the triangle.

> ✔ **Note**
>
> The Pythagorean theorem can only be applied to right triangles.

Consider an example: A right triangle has a leg of length 9 and a hypotenuse of length 14. To find the missing leg, plug the known values into the Pythagorean theorem: $9^2 + b^2 = 14^2$. This simplifies to $81 + b^2 = 196$, which becomes $b^2 = 115$. Take the square root of both sides to get $b = \sqrt{115}$. Because no factors of 115 are perfect squares, $b = \sqrt{115}$ is the answer.

> ✔ **Note**
>
> Wait to simplify radicals until you have your final answer. Leave answers in radical form unless a question says otherwise or the answer choices are written as decimals.

Because time is such a premium on the PSAT, time-saving strategies are invaluable, and there are two that will come in handy on triangle questions. The first is knowing common **Pythagorean triplets**, which are right triangles that happen to have integer sides. These triangles show up *very* frequently on the PSAT. The two most common are 3-4-5 and 5-12-13. Multiples of these (e.g., 6-8-10 and 10-24-26) can also pop up, so watch out for them as well. The beauty of these triplets is that if you see any two sides, you can automatically fill in the third without having to resort to the time-consuming Pythagorean theorem.

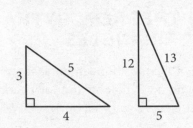

The second time-saving strategy involves recognizing **special right triangles**. Like Pythagorean triplets, special right triangles involve a ratio comparing the lengths of a right triangle's legs and hypotenuse, but with these triangles, you only need to know one side in order to calculate the other two. These triangles are defined by their angles.

The ratio of the sides of a **45-45-90** triangle is $x:x:x\sqrt{2}$, where x is the length of each leg and $x\sqrt{2}$ is the length of the hypotenuse.

The ratio of the sides of a **30-60-90** triangle is $x:x\sqrt{3}:2x$, where x is the shorter leg, $x\sqrt{3}$ is the longer leg, and $2x$ is the hypotenuse.

While the Pythagorean theorem can always be used to solve right triangle questions, it is not always the most efficient way to proceed. Further, many students make errors when simplifying radicals and exponents. The Pythagorean triplets and special right triangles allow you to save time and avoid those mistakes. Use them whenever possible!

✔ **Note**

Although you will be given the special right triangle ratios on Test Day, you can save yourself some time by memorizing them. That way, you won't have to keep flipping back to the formula page! You should also commit Pythagorean triplets to memory to bypass the Pythagorean theorem on Test Day.

AREA OF A TRIANGLE

On Test Day, you might also be asked to find the area of a triangle or to use the area of a triangle to find something else. The area of a triangle can be determined using $A = \frac{1}{2}bh$, where b is the triangle base and h is the triangle height.

When you have a right triangle, you can use the legs as the base and the height. If the triangle isn't a right triangle, you'll need to draw the height in, as demonstrated in the figure shown. Remember that the height *must* be perpendicular to the base.

A final note about triangles: You are likely to see triangle questions involving real-world situations. But don't fret: All you need to do is follow the Kaplan Strategy for Translating English into Math. Extract the geometry information you need, then solve!

Take a look at another test-like triangle question:

3. Owen has a rectangular field that he would like to split into two triangular fields—one for planting grain and one for planting vegetables—by building a fence from one corner of the field to the opposite corner. If the area of the field is 540 square meters and the length of the field is 36 meters, how many meters of fence will Owen need?

Work through the Kaplan Method for Math step-by-step to solve this question. The following table shows Kaplan's strategic thinking on the left, along with suggested math scratchwork on the right.

Strategic Thinking	Math Scratchwork
Step 1: Read the question, identifying and organizing important information as you go You need to find the length of the fence (the diagonal of the rectangular field).	
Step 2: Choose the best strategy to answer the question Draw a figure to visualize the situation. Sketch the rectangle and label what you know. The area of a rectangle is the product of its length and width. Because you know the length and the area, you can find the width.	 36 $A = 540 = 36 \times w$ $w = 540 \div 36 = 15$
The diagonal of the rectangle is also the hypotenuse of a right triangle with legs of lengths 15 and 36. This is a multiple of the 5-12-13 Pythagorean triplet. Multiply 3 by 13 to find the length of the hypotenuse (and that of the diagonal of the rectangle). Note that if you didn't recognize the multiple of the Pythagorean triplet, you could have used the Pythagorean theorem to find the length of the diagonal.	15 36 $15 = 5 \times 3$ $36 = 12 \times 3$ $\text{diagonal} = 13 \times 3 = 39$
Step 3: Check that you answered the *right* question The question asks for the length of the fence, which is represented by the diagonal, so you're done. Grid in 39 and move on.	39

TRIANGLE CONGRUENCE THEOREMS

Many students ask why they need to learn how to do proofs when they take geometry. Although you will likely not need them in college (unless you're a math or computer science major), there is a fundamental skill that comes with constructing proofs: the ability to construct an argument effectively for a statement or position. This skill is critical in numerous situations and fields—for criminal cases in law, research proposals in science, treatment plans in medicine, and others—so it's a powerful tool to have in your skill set.

That being said, there's no question that proofs can be unnerving. The good news: You will *not* need to construct a complete proof on the PSAT. The language of certain questions might still be slightly intimidating, but it will be far more manageable than a full-blown proof.

There are several theorems that can be used to prove two triangles are congruent; these are summarized in the following table. Make sure you are comfortable with all of them—you may need to determine that two triangles are congruent in order to find a side length or an angle measure in one or both of the triangles.

Triangle Congruence Theorem	Notation	Diagram
If three sides of one triangle are congruent to the corresponding sides of another triangle, then the two triangles are congruent.	SSS (side-side-side)	
If two sides and the included angle of one triangle are congruent to the corresponding parts of another triangle, then the two triangles are congruent.	SAS (side-angle-side)	
If two angles and the non-included side of one triangle are congruent to the corresponding parts of another triangle, then the two triangles are congruent.	AAS (angle-angle-side)	
If two angles and the included side of one triangle are congruent to the corresponding parts of another triangle, then the two triangles are congruent.	ASA (angle-side-angle)	
If the hypotenuse and leg of one right triangle are congruent to the corresponding parts of another right triangle, then the two triangles are congruent.	HL (hypotenuse-leg)	
An angle or line segment is congruent to itself.	Reflexive Property	
Corresponding parts of congruent triangles are congruent.	CPCTC	

✔ **Note**

There are two bogus congruence "theorems" to watch out for: AAA and SSA. Two triangles with identical angles are always similar, but they aren't necessarily congruent. If you have two triangles with two adjacent congruent sides and a congruent angle outside them, the third side can be two different lengths. SSA is valid only with right triangles, in which case you call it HL. Never use AAA.

QUADRILATERAL THEOREMS

Quadrilaterals are four-sided figures, with interior angles that add up to 360°. You will likely not see a question solely about quadrilaterals; if a quadrilateral appears at all, it will likely contain hidden triangles. However, the properties of the quadrilateral will allow you to deduce information about the triangles present, so make sure you know the basic properties of the most common quadrilaterals.

Given the high likelihood of a Test Day geometry question containing hidden triangles, you should familiarize yourself with the types of quadrilaterals that are most likely to have useful triangles within.

Parallelogram Theorems	Properties
Parallelogram	<ul><li>Both pairs of sides are parallel.</li><li>Both pairs of sides are congruent.</li><li>Both pairs of opposite angles are congruent.</li><li>An angle is supplementary to both angles adjacent to it.</li><li>The diagonals bisect each other.</li></ul>
Rhombus	<ul><li>It has all the properties of a parallelogram.</li><li>All four sides are congruent.</li><li>Diagonals bisect angles and are perpendicular.</li></ul>
Rectangle	<ul><li>It has all the properties of a parallelogram.</li><li>All angles are right angles.</li><li>Diagonals are congruent.</li></ul>
Square	<ul><li>It has all the properties of a parallelogram, rhombus, and rectangle.</li><li>All sides are congruent.</li></ul>

A word of caution: Do not make any assumptions about a test figure that go beyond the information provided in the question. It's tempting to assume a quadrilateral is a rectangle or other more "friendly" shape, but unless this is proven or stated in the question (or indicated in the figure), don't do it!

INTRODUCTION TO CIRCLES

You already know the PSAT can ask a variety of questions about lines, angles, and triangles; it can also test you on your knowledge of circles. Keep reading for a refresher on these ubiquitous shapes.

Circle Anatomy and Basic Formulas

There are a number of circle traits you should know for Test Day:

- **Radius (r):** The distance from the center of a circle to its edge

- **Chord:** A line segment that connects two points on a circle

- **Diameter (d):** A chord that passes through the center of a circle. The diameter is always the longest chord a circle can have and is twice the length of the radius.

- **Circumference (C):** The distance around a circle; the equivalent of a polygon's perimeter. Find this using the formula $C = 2\pi r = \pi d$.

- **Area:** The space a circle takes up, just like a polygon. A circle's area is found by computing $A = \pi r^2$.

- Every circle contains 360°. You'll find out more on this fact's utility shortly.

As the formulas demonstrate, the radius is often key to unlocking several other components of a circle. Therefore, your first step for many circle questions will be to find the radius.

Circles on the Coordinate Plane and Their Equations

When you have a circle on the coordinate plane, you can describe it with an equation. The equation of a circle in **standard form** is as follows:

$$(x - h)^2 + (y - k)^2 = r^2$$

In this equation, r is the radius of the circle, and h and k are the x- and y-coordinates of the circle's center, respectively: (h, k).

> **✔ Note**
>
> A circle is one of the four conic sections, which are made by slicing a double cone with a plane. The parabola is another conic section that you read about in chapter 6. The ellipse and hyperbola (with standard forms $\frac{(x-h)^2}{a^2} + \frac{(y-k)^2}{b^2} = 1$ and $\frac{(x-h)^2}{a^2} - \frac{(y-k)^2}{b^2} = 1$, respectively) will not be tested on the PSAT. Watch out for them in trap answer choices, however!

You might also see what is referred to as **general form**:

$$x^2 + y^2 + Cx + Dy + E = 0$$

At first glance, the general form probably doesn't resemble the equation of a circle, but the fact that you have an x^2 term and a y^2 term with coefficients of 1 is your indicator that the equation does indeed graph as a circle. To convert to standard form, complete the square for the x terms, then repeat for the y terms. Refer to chapter 6 for a review of completing the square.

> ✔ **Note**
>
> The x^2 and y^2 terms in the equation of a circle occasionally have coefficients other than 1 (but the coefficients must be equal). If this is the case, simply divide all terms in the equation by the coefficient to eliminate them.

Ready to try a circle question?

4. A circle in the standard coordinate plane is given by the equation $(x - 5)^2 + y^2 = 38$. What are the radius of the circle and the coordinates of the circle's center?

   A) radius: $\sqrt{38}$; center: $(-5, 0)$

   B) radius: 19; center: $(5, 0)$

   C) radius: 38; center: $(5, 0)$

   D) radius: $\sqrt{38}$; center: $(5, 0)$

There's no scratchwork for this question, but Kaplan's strategic thinking is provided in the table. Follow along as we reason through the question to get the correct answer.

Strategic Thinking
Step 1: Read the question, identifying and organizing important information as you go
You're asked for the radius and coordinates of the center of the circle.
Step 2: Choose the best strategy to answer the question
What is the radius of the circle?
The equation of a circle written in standard form is $(x - h)^2 + (y - k)^2 = r^2$, so the radius must be $\sqrt{38}$. Eliminate B and C.
Where is the center of the circle?
The sign in the parentheses indicates subtraction. Therefore, the x-coordinate is 5. The presence of y^2 by itself tells you that the y-coordinate is 0, because y^2 can be written as $(y - 0)^2$, making the coordinates of the center $(5, 0)$. Eliminate A.
Step 3: Check that you answered the *right* question
Choice (D) is the only answer that matches both pieces.

Circle Ratios: Arcs, Central Angles, and Sectors

The PSAT can ask you about parts of circles as well. There are three partial components that can be made in a circle: arcs, central angles, and sectors. These circle pieces are frequently used in proportions with their whole counterparts, so the ability to set up ratios and proportions correctly is of utmost importance for these questions.

- An **arc** is part of a circle's circumference. Both chords and radii can cut a circle into arcs. The number of arcs present depends on how many chords and/or radii are present. If only two arcs are present, the smaller arc is called the **minor arc** and the larger one is the **major arc**. If a diameter cuts the circle in half, the two formed arcs are called **semicircles**. An arc length can never be greater than the circle's circumference.

- When radii cut a circle into multiple (but not necessarily equal) pieces, the angle at the center of the circle contained by the radii is the **central angle**. Because a full circle contains 360°, a central angle measure cannot be greater than this.

- Radii splitting a circle into pieces can also create **sectors**, which are parts of the circle's area. The area of a sector cannot be greater than its circle's total area.

Here's a summary of the ratios formed by these three parts and their whole counterparts:

$$\frac{\text{arc length}}{\text{circumference}} = \frac{\text{central angle}}{360°} = \frac{\text{sector area}}{\text{circle area}}$$

Notice that all of these ratios are equal. Intuitively, this should make sense: When you slice a pizza into four equal slices, each piece should have $\frac{1}{4}$ of the cheese, sauce, crust, and toppings. If you slice a circle into four equal pieces, the same principle applies: Each piece should have $\frac{1}{4}$ of the degrees, circumference, and area.

Inscribed Angle Theorem

An angle whose vertex is on the edge of the circle is called an **inscribed angle**. As this vertex moves along the edge, the measure of the inscribed angle remains constant as long as the minor arc created (in other words, isolated or **subtended** by the chords) does not change. When the chords that create an inscribed angle subtend the same minor arc that a pair of radii do, a special relationship appears: The central angle measure is twice that of the inscribed angle.

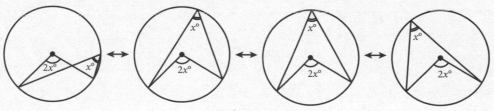

x remains constant

Arcs Formed Between Parallel Chords

Another theorem states that two parallel chords will intercept two congruent arcs; see the following diagram for an example. The congruent arcs will be between the chords.

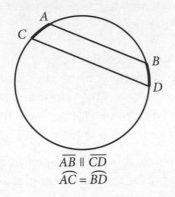

$$\overline{AB} \parallel \overline{CD}$$
$$\overset{\frown}{AC} = \overset{\frown}{BD}$$

Tangent Lines

A **tangent line** touches a circle at exactly one point and is perpendicular to a circle's radius at the point of contact. The following diagram demonstrates what this looks like:

The presence of a right angle opens up the opportunity to draw otherwise hidden shapes, so pay special attention to tangents when they're mentioned. They often come up in complex figure questions.

The next question will give you a chance to see how these properties of circles can be tested on the PSAT.

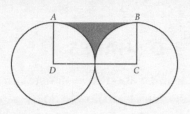

5. In the figure above, *ABCD* is a rectangle, and $\overline{DA}$ and $\overline{CB}$ are radii of the circles shown. If $\overline{AB} = 4$, what is the perimeter of the shaded region?

   A) $2\pi + 4$

   B) $4\pi + 4$

   C) $4\pi + 8$

   D) $8\pi + 8$

Work through the Kaplan Method for Math step-by-step to solve this question. The following table shows Kaplan's strategic thinking on the left, along with suggested math scratchwork on the right.

Strategic Thinking	Math Scratchwork
Step 1: Read the question, identifying and organizing important information as you go You must calculate the perimeter of the shaded area.	
Step 2: Choose the best strategy to answer the question Use your complex figure expertise to break this down. You'll notice the top of the shaded piece is also the top of the rectangle. In addition, each curved side is an arc of one of the circles. *How do you find the length of each piece?* The rectangle component is easy. $\overline{AB}$ is the top of both the rectangle and the shaded region, so that part of the shaded region's perimeter is 4. All four of the rectangle's angles are 90°, two of which are central angles in the circles. This means the arcs are $\frac{90°}{360°}$, or $\frac{1}{4}$ of the circumference of one of the circles. You'll notice $\overline{CD}$ is two radii combined (and equal to $\overline{AB}$); because the circles are congruent, the two radii make up a diameter of one circle. This means the circles' circumferences are both 4π, and each curved piece of the shaded region is π. Double to account for both, then add to 4 to get $2\pi + 4$.	perimeter comprised of a rectangle length and two circle arcs shaded area's top = $\overline{AB}$ = 4 $C = \pi d = 4\pi$ $\frac{1}{4}C = \pi$; therefore, one curved side = π $P = \pi + \pi + 4$ = $2\pi + 4$
Step 3: Check that you answered the *right* question The correct answer is (A).	

INTRODUCTION TO 3-D SHAPES

Over the last several pages, you learned about two-dimensional (2-D) shapes and how to tackle PSAT questions involving them. Now you'll learn how to do the same for questions containing three-dimensional (3-D) shapes, also called solids. There are several different types of solids that might appear on Test Day—rectangular solids, cubes, cylinders, prisms, spheres, cones, pyramids—so it is critical that you be familiar with them.

The following is a diagram showing the basic anatomy of a 3-D shape:

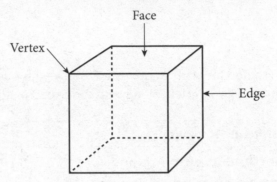

A **face** (or **surface**) is a 2-D shape that acts as one of the sides of the solid. Two faces meet at a line segment called an **edge**, and three faces meet at a single point called a **vertex**.

Keep reading for more on types of 3-D shapes and questions you could be asked about them.

Volume

Volume is the amount of 3-D space occupied by a solid. This is analogous to the area of a 2-D shape like a triangle or circle. You can find the volume of many 3-D shapes by finding the area of the base and multiplying it by the height. We've highlighted the base area components of the formulas in the following table using parentheses:

Rectangular Solid	Cube	Right Cylinder
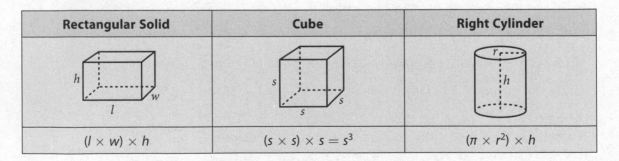		
$(l \times w) \times h$	$(s \times s) \times s = s^3$	$(\pi \times r^2) \times h$

These three 3-D shapes are prisms. Almost all prisms on the PSAT are right prisms; that is, all faces are perpendicular to those with which they share edges.

Following are some examples of less commonly seen prisms:

Triangular Prism	Hexagonal Prism	Decagonal Prism

Like the rectangular solids, cubes, and cylinders you saw earlier, these right prisms use the same general volume formula ($V = A_{base} \times h$).

> ✔ **Note**
>
> You might not be told explicitly the area of the base of a prism, in which case you'll need to rely on your two-dimensional geometry expertise to find it before calculating the volume.

More complicated 3-D shapes include the right pyramid, right cone, and sphere. The vertex of a right pyramid or right cone will always be centered above the middle of the base. Their volume formulas are similar to those of prisms, albeit with different coefficients.

> ✔ **Note**
>
> Some of these formulas might look daunting, but don't fret—you won't have to memorize them for Test Day. They'll be provided on the reference page at the beginning of each math section.

Right (Square) Pyramid	Right Cone	Sphere
$\dfrac{1}{3} \times (l \times w) \times h$	$\dfrac{1}{3} \times (\pi \times r^2) \times h$	$\dfrac{4}{3} \times \pi \times r^3$

> ✔ **Note**
>
> A right pyramid can have any regular polygon as its base; the square variety is the one you're most likely to see. Also note that the vertex above the base of a right pyramid or cone is not necessarily formed by an intersection of exactly three faces, as in prisms, but it is still a single point and is still called a vertex.

Surface Area

Surface area is the sum of the areas of all faces of a solid. You might liken this to determining the amount of wrapping paper needed to cover all faces of a solid.

To calculate the surface area of a solid, simply find the area of each face using your 2-D geometry skills, then add them all together.

> ✔ **Note**
>
> You won't be expected to know the surface area formulas for right pyramids, right cones, and spheres; they'll be provided if you need them. However, you could be asked to find the surface area of a prism, in which case you'll be given enough information to find the area of each surface of the solid.

You might think that finding the surface area of a solid with many sides, such as a 10-sided right octagonal prism, is a tall order. However, you can save time by noticing a vital trait: This prism has two identical octagonal faces and eight identical rectangular faces. Don't waste time finding the area of each of the 10 sides; find the area of one octagonal face and one rectangular face instead. Once complete, multiply the area of the octagonal face by 2 and the area of the rectangular face by 8, add the products together, and you're done! The same is true for other 3-D shapes such as rectangular solids (including cubes), other right prisms, and certain pyramids.

If you're ready to test your knowledge of 3-D shapes, check out the next question:

6. Sabine bought 10 right cylindrical candles as party favors and plans to wrap them such that the gift paper wraps around the candle height exactly once with no overlap. She wants to leave an extra 3 inches of wrapping paper past each end of the candles so she can tie both ends with a bit of ribbon. If each candle has a diameter of 4 inches and is 8 inches tall, how many square inches of wrapping paper will Sabine need to wrap one candle?

A) 32π

B) 40π

C) 56π

D) 64π

Work through the Kaplan Method for Math step-by-step to solve this question. The following table shows Kaplan's strategic thinking on the left, along with suggested math scratchwork on the right.

Strategic Thinking	Math Scratchwork
Step 1: Read the question, identifying and organizing important information as you go You need to find the amount of wrapping paper Sabine needs to wrap one of her candles.	
Step 2: Choose the best strategy to answer the question Covering a 3-D shape (with gift wrap here) implies surface area, but be careful: one piece of gift wrap is not identical to the surface area of one of the candles because the circular top and bottom will not be covered exactly. The gift wrap will be in the shape of a rectangle. The question states that Sabine will leave extra gift wrap at both ends, so remember to take this into account. The rectangle length shares an edge with the circular top of the candle; therefore, the length is equal to the top's circumference.	*(diagram: rectangle labeled 4π in across the top, 3 in, 8 in, and 3 in on the right side)* C is rect. length, h is rect. width $d = 4$ in → $C = 4\pi$ in, $h = 8$ in gift wrap for one candle: 4π in × (3 in + 8 in + 3 in) = 56π in^2
Step 3: Check that you answered the *right* question Nicely done! You've found the amount of gift wrap Sabine needs for one candle, which is (C).	56π in^2

Now you'll have a chance to try a few more test-like geometry questions in a scaffolded way. We've provided some guidance, but you'll need to fill in the missing parts of explanations or the step-by-step math in order to get to the correct answer:

7. In △ACB above, what is the measure of an angle that is supplementary to ∠ACB?

    A)   65°

    B)   85°

    C)   95°

    D)   115°

Use the following scaffolding as your map through the question. Fill in the blanks in the table as you work from top to bottom.

Strategic Thinking	Math Scratchwork
Step 1: Read the question, identifying and organizing important information as you go You need to find the measure of an angle that is supplementary to ∠ACB.	
Step 2: Choose the best strategy to answer the question Remember the rule of interior angles of a triangle: The three angles must add to 180°. Create an equation that sets the angles equal to 180. Then solve for *x*. *Am I done?* Be careful here; you are looking for the measure of an angle that is supplementary to ∠ACB, not the value of *x*. Determine m∠ACB, then subtract from 180.	___ + ___ + ___ = ___ ___ + ___ = ___ ___ = ___ ___ = ___ m∠ACB = ___ supp. ∠ = 180 − ___ = ___
Step 3: Check that you answered the *right* question If you got (C), you are correct.	

8. The size of a TV is dictated by the length of its diagonal. Whitney would like to purchase a new TV, but must first determine the maximum size TV she can mount on her living room wall. She would like a 3-inch space on each side of the TV, effectively creating a frame of empty space around the TV that is 3 inches wide on each side. If the rectangular wall space Whitney plans to use for her TV is 28.25 inches by 53 inches, what is the largest size TV (in inches) that she can fit on the wall? Round your answer to the nearest inch.

The following table can help you structure your thinking as you go about solving this problem. The Kaplan strategic thinking is provided, as are bits of structured scratchwork. If you're not sure how to approach a question like this, start at the top and work your way down.

Strategic Thinking	Math Scratchwork
Step 1: Read the question, identifying and organizing important information as you go You're asked for the largest size TV Whitney can mount on her wall; in other words, you need to calculate the length of its diagonal.	
Step 2: Choose the best strategy to answer the question First, draw a rectangle to represent the wall space. Next, draw another rectangle inside the first to represent the TV. Label the diagram with the information the question provides. Subtract the width of the empty wall space from the given dimensions. Once there, use the Pythagorean theorem to find the diagonal of the TV area, and then subtract the area of the picture from it.	 wall space: _____ × _____ TV space: _____ × _____ _____^{2} × _____^{2} = _____^{2} _____ + _____ = _____
Step 3: Check that you answered the *right* question If you got 52, you're correct!	_____

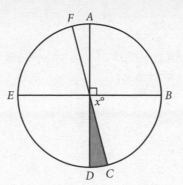

9. In the circle above, $\overline{AD}$, $\overline{BE}$, and $\overline{CF}$ are diameters. If the shaded area is equal to $\frac{1}{18}$ of the area of the circle, what is the value of x?

Use the scaffolding that follows as your map through the question. Fill in the blanks in the table as you work from top to bottom.

Strategic Thinking	Math Scratchwork
Step 1: Read the question, identifying and organizing important information as you go You need to find the value of x.	
Step 2: Choose the best strategy to answer the question The shaded area is a sector for which the question has provided information. This is your cue that you should be thinking about circle proportions. Use degrees and sector/circle area. You know the number of degrees in a full circle, as well as the ratio of the shaded area to the entire circle area. Use a variable other than x to represent the shaded part's central angle to avoid confusion later. The sector marked by A and B is 90°. Because $\overline{AD}$ is a diameter, you know this sector combined with the shaded sector and the one marked by x must add to 180°. From here you can find x.	 $\dfrac{y}{\underline{}} = \dfrac{\underline{}}{\underline{}}$ $\underline{}\, y = \underline{}$ $y = \underline{}$ $x + \underline{} + \underline{} = 180$ $x = \underline{}$
Step 3: Check that you answered the *right* question Did you get 70? If so, you're absolutely correct.	

10. The ratio of the lengths of the radii of two spheres is 1:2. Which of the following ratios correctly compares their volumes?

A) $1:\dfrac{4}{3}$

B) 1:2

C) 1:4

D) 1:8

Work through the Kaplan Method for Math step-by-step to solve this question. The following table shows Kaplan's strategic thinking on the left, along with suggested math scratchwork on the right.

Strategic Thinking	Math Scratchwork
Step 1: Read the question, identifying and organizing important information as you go You need to determine the ratio of the volume of the two spheres. A ratio comparing their radii is given.	
Step 2: Choose the best strategy to answer the question Pick your own radii to make this question less abstract; just be sure they obey the given ratio. Compute the volumes of the corresponding spheres and then use the volumes to write a second ratio, reducing as necessary.	$r_1 = \_\_\,, r_2 = \_\_\,, V_{cylinder} = \_\_\_\_$ $V_1 = \_\_\_\_ \times (\ \ )^3 = \_\_\_\_$ $V_2 = \_\_\_\_ \times (\ \ )^3 = \_\_\_\_$ ratio: $\_\_\_\_$ to $\_\_\_\_ = \_\_\_:\_\_\_$
Step 3: Check that you answered the *right* question Did you get (D)? If so, you're absolutely correct.	

Now that you've seen the variety of ways in which the PSAT can test your geometry skills, try the following questions to check your understanding. Give yourself 5 minutes to answer the following four questions. Make sure you use the Kaplan Method for Math as often as you can. Remember, you want to emphasize speed and efficiency in addition to simply getting the correct answer.

11. △*SNO* is a triangle with vertices (0, 0), (4, 0), and (0, −3). When △*SNO* is reflected over the *y*-axis and then shifted up five units, △*ICE* is formed. What is the equation of the line that forms the hypotenuse of △*ICE*?

A) $y = -\dfrac{3}{4}x + 2$

B) $y = -\dfrac{3}{4}x - 3$

C) $y = \dfrac{3}{4}x + 2$

D) $y = \dfrac{3}{4}x - 3$

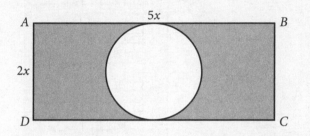

13. In the figure above, both $\overline{AB}$ and $\overline{DC}$ are tangent to the circle, and *ABCD* is a rectangle with side lengths 2*x* and 5*x*. What is the area of the shaded region?

A) $10x^2 - \pi x^2$

B) $10\pi x^2$

C) $10x^2 - 2\pi x$

D) $9\pi x^2$

14. The base of a certain right square pyramid paperweight has a diagonal of length $2\sqrt{2}$ centimeters, and the paperweight's height is 50% larger than the base edges. If the paperweight is placed inside a rectangular box full of water with dimensions of 2 cm × 4 cm × 6 cm, how many cubic centimeters of water will remain once the paperweight is completely submerged?

Note: Figure not drawn to scale.

12. If the area of △*ABC* is $8\sqrt{3}$, what is the length of *AB*?

A)   4

B)   6

C)   7

D)   8

Answers and Explanations for this chapter begin on page 576.

Math

ON YOUR OWN

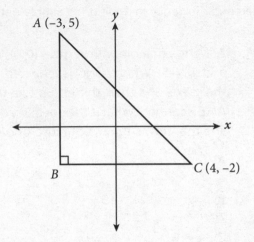

1. The figure above shows a ladder propped against the side of a building. If the base of the ladder is 17 feet from the building, how long in feet is the ladder?

   A) 17

   B) $17\sqrt{2}$

   C) $17\sqrt{3}$

   D) 34

2. What is the measure in degrees of angle ACB in the figure above?

   A) 35

   B) 40

   C) 45

   D) 50

3. The figure above shows the route of Gina's trip from her apartment to her gym. Gina travels 7 miles from W to X, 24 miles from X to Y, and 3 miles from Y to Z. If she were able to travel from W to Z directly, how much shorter, in miles, would the trip be?

A) 8
B) 10
C) 14
D) 26

4. In the figure above, the length of $\overline{JK}$ is 2, and M is the midpoint of $\overline{JL}$. What is the length of $\overline{KL}$?

A) $2\sqrt{3}$
B) 4
C) $4\sqrt{3}$
D) $2\sqrt{13}$

5. The area of a right triangle is 48 square inches. If the longer leg is 4 inches more than the shorter leg, what is the length in square inches of the hypotenuse?

A) 12
B) $4\sqrt{13}$
C) 20
D) 208

6. $\triangle CAT$ is similar to triangle $\triangle DOG$. $\triangle CAT$ has side lengths of 7, 12, and 15. If the perimeter of $\triangle DOG$ is 51, then what is the length of its longest side?

A) 10.5
B) 15
C) 18
D) 22.5

7. $\triangle POR$ and $\triangle STU$ are similar triangles plotted on a coordinate plane. The vertices of $\triangle PQR$ are $P(-4, 2)$, $Q(1, 2)$, and $R(-4, 7)$. If $\triangle STU$ has vertices $S(-6, -2)$ and $T(3, -2)$, then what is the area in square units of $\triangle STU$?

Note: Figure not drawn to scale.

8. Similar triangles can be used to find the height of tall objects using shadow lengths because the sun shines on objects at the same angle. Based on the diagram above, what is the height of the telephone pole, assuming that it meets the ground at a 90° angle?

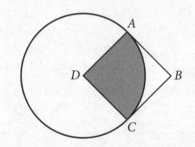

9. If the measure of ∠AOC is 100° and $\overline{OC} = 9$, what is the length of $\widehat{ABC}$?

   A) 4π

   B) 5π

   C) 9π

   D) 18π

10. In the figure above, D is the center of the circle, and the perimeter of square ABCD is 24. What is the area of the shaded sector?

   A) 9π

   B) 18π

   C) 24π

   D) 36π

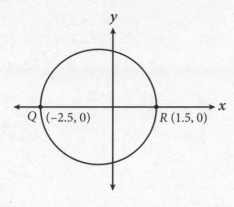

11. The circle shown above has diameter $\overline{QR}$. Which of the following represents the equation of the circle?

    A) $(x - 0.5)^2 + y^2 = 4$

    B) $(x + 0.5)^2 + y^2 = 4$

    C) $(x - 2.5)^2 + (y + 1.5)^2 = 0$

    D) $(x + 2.5)^2 + (y - 1.5)^2 = 0$

$$x^2 + y^2 + 4x - 12y = 41$$

12. What is the diameter of the circle with the equation given above?

    A) 9

    B) 18

    C) 41

    D) 81

13. Milk is poured from a full rectangular container with dimensions 4 inches by 9 inches by 10 inches into a cylindrical container with a diameter of 6 inches. Assuming the milk does not overflow the container, how many inches high will the milk reach?

    A) 3π

    B) 10

    C) $\dfrac{40}{\pi}$

    D) 24

14. The Pyramid of Cestius in Rome serves as a tomb for Gaius Cestius, a wealthy Roman magistrate. The marble structure is a right square pyramid with a square base that stands approximately 37 meters high. If the volume of the pyramid is 11,100 cubic meters, then what is the length in meters of one side of the base?

    A) 17

    B) 30

    C) 36

    D) 45

15. A company wants to install new air conditioners in their building. The building has the dimensions shown in the figure above. To buy the most efficient air-conditioning unit, the company needs to know the total volume of space inside the building in cubic feet. What is the volume?

    A) 220,000 ft^3

    B) 280,000 ft^3

    C) 5,940,000 ft^3

    D) 7,560,000 ft^3

16. How many units longer is the diameter of a sphere that has a volume of 36π cubic units than one with a volume of $\dfrac{4}{3}\pi$ cubic units?

    A) 2

    B) 4

    C) 5

    D) 8

PART TWO

Reading

Reading

BY THE END OF THIS UNIT, YOU WILL BE ABLE TO:

1. Apply the Kaplan Method for Reading Comprehension

2. Identify Reading Test question types and apply the appropriate strategies to correctly answer them

The Kaplan Method for Reading Comprehension and Reading Test Passage Types

CHAPTER OBJECTIVES

By the end of this chapter, you will be able to:

1. Identify the three types of passages on the PSAT Reading Test

2. Passage Map passages using the Kaplan Method for Reading Comprehension, identifying key words and central ideas across passage types

3. Predict an answer and find its match among the answer choices using a Passage Map

SMARTPOINTS

Point Value	SmartPoint Category
Point Builder	The Kaplan Method for Reading Comprehension
Point Builder	Passage Mapping
Point Builder	U.S. and World Literature Passages
Point Builder	History/Social Studies Passages
Point Builder	Science Passages

OVERVIEW OF THE PSAT READING TEST PASSAGE TYPES

PSAT Reading Test Passage Distribution	
U.S. and World Literature	1 passage; 9 questions
History/Social Studies	2 passages OR 1 passage and 1 paired-passage set; 9–10 questions each
Science	2 passages OR 1 passage and 1 paired-passage set; 9–10 questions each

It is imperative that you use the Kaplan Method for Reading Comprehension for every passage on the PSAT Reading Test. Doing so ensures that you spend your time efficiently and maximize your opportunity to earn points.

THE KAPLAN METHOD FOR READING COMPREHENSION

The Kaplan Method for Reading Comprehension consists of three steps:

Step 1: Read actively

Step 2: Examine the question stem

Step 3: Predict and answer

Let's take a closer look at each step.

Step 1: Read actively

Active reading means:

- Ask questions and take notes *as* you read the passage. Asking questions about the passage and taking notes are integral parts of your approach to acing the PSAT Reading Test.

You should ask questions such as:

- Why did the author write this word/detail/sentence/paragraph?

- Is the author taking a side? If so, what side is he or she taking?

- What are the tone and purpose of the passage?

Reading & Writing

Make sure you remember to:

- Identify the passage type

- Take notes, circle key words, and underline key phrases

> ✔ **Expert Tip**
>
> Questions will range from general to specific. By using clues in the question stem to identify what the question is looking for, you will be better able to complete Step 3 of the Kaplan Method for Reading Comprehension.

Step 2: Examine the question stem

This means you should:

- Identify key words and line references in the question stem

- Apply question type strategies as necessary

Step 3: Predict and answer

This means you should:

- Predict an answer before looking at the answer choices, also known as "predict before you peek"

- Select the best match

Predicting before you peek helps you:

- Eliminate the possibility of falling into wrong-answer traps

PASSAGE MAPPING

Step 1 of the Kaplan Method for Reading Comprehension dictates that you must take notes as you read the passage. We call these notes a Passage Map because they guide you through the passage and will lead you to the correct answers.

> ✔ **On Test Day**
>
> A Passage Map should not replace the occasional underline or circle—it is important that you underline, circle, *and* take notes to create the most effective Passage Map.

Make sure you pay attention and take note of the following when you map the passage:

- The "why" or the central idea of the passage—in other words, the thesis statement

- The transitions or changes in direction in a passage's logic

- The author's opinions and other opinions the author cites

- The author's tone and purpose

While Passage Mapping may seem time-consuming at first, with practice it will become second nature by Test Day, and your overall PSAT Reading Test timing will greatly improve because you'll spend less time searching the passage for answers to the questions.

> ✔ **Remember**
>
> The PSAT Reading Test is an open-book test! The answer is always in the passage.

Just as the passages span different genres, your approach to them will also vary from subject to subject. The approach for each type of PSAT Reading Test passage will be addressed in this chapter.

Now, let's look at the specific passage types individually.

U.S. AND WORLD LITERATURE PASSAGES

There will be a single U.S. and World Literature passage on the PSAT. It is different from the other passages because:

- There will be multiple characters and, therefore, multiple opinions
- The tone will be nuanced and emotion-based, rather than informative or explanatory

As you read a U.S. and World Literature passage, you should:

1. Identify the characters and evaluate how the author describes them

    - What do the characters want?

    - What are the characters doing?

    - What adjectives describe each character?

2. Assess the characters' opinions of each other and themselves

    - Do they like each other? Dislike each other?

    - Why does each character make a particular decision or take a particular course of action?

    - What do these decisions or actions tell you about a character?

3. Identify the themes of the story

    - What are the "turning points" in the passage?

    - Is there a moral to the story?

> ✔ **Remember**
>
> Because U.S. and World Literature passages have multiple characters with multiple opinions, remember to keep straight who said what.

Let's look at the following example of an abbreviated U.S. and World Literature passage and question set. After the mapped passage, the left column contains questions similar to those you'll see on the PSAT Reading Test on Test Day. The column on the right features the strategic thinking a test expert employs when approaching the passage and questions presented. Note how a test expert can quickly condense the entire passage into a few words and use his or her Passage Map to ask questions that build a prediction for the correct answer.

> ✔ **EXPERT TIP**
>
> **Some paragraphs are longer than others. If you are mapping a very long paragraph, you can write two or three short notes rather than try to fit everything into just one long note.**

Strategic Thinking
Step 1: Read actively
Read the passage and the notes provided. Remember, a well-crafted Passage Map should summarize the central idea of each paragraph as well as important topics or themes. Your notes for U.S. and World Literature passages should focus on characters. Use your Passage Map to help you answer each question.

Questions 1–2 are based on the following passage.

In this excerpt from a short story, the narrator describes an afternoon visit to the farm of Mrs. Hight and her daughter, Esther.

¶1: Mrs. H - stroke, widow, owned farm

Mrs. Hight, like myself, was tired and thirsty. I brought a drink of water, and remembered some fruit that was left from my lunch. She revived
Line vigorously, and told me the history of her later
(5) years since she had been struck in the prime of her life by a paralyzing stroke, and her husband had died and left her with Esther and a mortgage on their farm. There was only one field of good land, but they owned a large area of pasture and
(10) some woodland. Esther had always been laughed at for her belief in sheep-raising when one by one their neighbors were giving up their flocks. When everything had come to the point of despair she had raised some money and bought all the sheep

¶1, cont.: E - raised sheep, succeeded

(15) she could, insisting that Maine lambs were as good as any, and that there was a straight path by sea to the Boston market. By tending her flock herself she had managed to succeed; she had paid off the mortgage five years ago, and now what they did
(20) not spend was in the bank. "It has been stubborn work, day and night, summer and winter, and now she's beginning to get along in years," said the old mother. "She's tended me along with the sheep, and she's been good right along, but she should have
(25) been a teacher."

¶1, cont.: mom, Mrs. H. describes determination of daughter, E (theme)

Questions	Strategic Thinking
1. The main purpose of the passage is to A) suggest some of the essential attributes of a character. B) show that people's lives are determined by events beyond their control. C) identify the major causes of Mrs. Hight's unhappiness. D) recount an incident that changed the narrator's life.	**Step 2: Examine the question stem** *What are the key words or clues in the question stem?* "Main purpose" **Step 3: Predict and answer** *What is the main purpose of the passage?* To relay Mrs. Hight's positive opinion of her daughter, Esther *Which answer choice matches this?* Choice (A)
2. Mrs. Hight's description of Esther's sheep-raising efforts in lines 20–25 reveals her daughter's A) desire to succeed no matter what the cost. B) humility and grace in accepting defeat. C) considerable regard for her neighbors' opinions. D) calm determination in meeting difficulties.	**Step 2: Examine the question stem** *What are the key words in the question stem?* "Sheep-raising efforts" and the line numbers **Step 3: Predict and answer** *Raising the sheep is described as what kind of work?* "Stubborn work" (lines 20–21) *How does Mrs. Hight describe Esther's attitude toward the work?* She says that "she's been good right along" (line 24). *What can you predict?* Esther did not give up, despite having been "laughed at" (lines 10–11). *Which answer choice does this match?* Choice (D)

HISTORY/SOCIAL STUDIES PASSAGES

The History/Social Studies portion of the PSAT Reading Test will consist of either two single History/Social Studies passages or one single History/Social Studies passage and one History/Social Studies paired-passage set. History/Social Studies passages are different from other passage types because:

- The passage will have a clearly stated topic, a well-defined scope, and a specific purpose.

- There will be at least one primary source passage that uses antiquated language.

Because History/Social Studies passages can be densely written, you should:

1. Identify the topic and scope of the passage
   - You can usually find the topic and scope in the first paragraph.

2. Identify the topic sentence of each succeeding paragraph
   - What does this paragraph accomplish? Does it provide evidence to support a previous statement? Or does it introduce questions about an earlier claim?

3. Summarize the purpose of the passage
   - Some common purposes include: to inform, to refute, to promote, to explore.

> ✔ **Note**
>
> **Resist the temptation to reread large portions of the passage. Your Passage Map can help you predict and answer questions correctly without having to dive completely back into the text. Doing so will save you time on Test Day!**

Let's look at the following example of an abbreviated History/Social Studies passage and question set. After the mapped passage, the left column contains questions similar to those you'll see on the PSAT Reading Test on Test Day. The column on the right features the strategic thinking a test expert employs when approaching the passage and questions presented. Note how a test expert can quickly condense the entire passage into a few words and use his or her Passage Map to ask questions that build a prediction for the correct answer.

Strategic Thinking
Step 1: Read actively
Read the passage and the notes provided. Remember, a well-crafted Passage Map should summarize the central idea of each paragraph as well as important topics or themes. Use your Passage Map to help you answer each question.

Questions 3–4 are based on the following passage.

The following passage is an adaptation of an excerpt from *Up From Slavery: An Autobiography* by Booker T. Washington.

¶1: author believes rights will come (purpose)

Line

My own belief is, although I have never before said so in so many words, that the time will come when African Americans in the South will (5) be accorded the political rights which his ability, character and material possessions entitle him to. I think, though, that the opportunity to freely exercise such political rights will not come in any large degree through outside or artificial forcing, (10) but will be accorded to African Americans by white people themselves, and that they will protect him in the exercise of those rights. Just as soon as the South gets over the old feeling that it is being forced by "foreigners," or "aliens" to do something which it does not want to do, I believe that the change in the (15) direction that I have indicated is going to begin. In fact, there are indications that it is already beginning to a slight degree.

¶1 cont.: change will begin soon, when S doesn't feel forced

Questions	Strategic Thinking
3. This passage can best be described as A) a description of a state of affairs intolerable to the author. B) a statement of belief about society and how it will change. C) a declaration of basic rights and a roadmap to achieve them. D) a call to action to correct an injustice.	**Step 2: Examine the question stem** *What are the key words in the question stem?* There are none; it's about the passage as a whole. **Step 3: Predict and answer** *Look at the Passage Map notes. What is the author's purpose for writing this passage?* Change will happen *Which choice matches this prediction?* Choice (B)
4. According to the passage, "the political rights" mentioned in line 4 will come about through A) increased political pressure on those denying the rights. B) additional laws mandating those rights. C) peer pressure designed to embarrass anyone denying those rights. D) a natural evolution of society.	**Step 2: Examine the question stem** *What clues are in the question stem?* The quoted phrase and line number **Step 3: Predict and answer** *According to the passage and your notes, how does the South feel?* Forced *So when will "the political rights" come about?* When the South stops feeling forced *Which answer choice does this match?* Choice (D)

SCIENCE PASSAGES

The PSAT Reading Test will contain either two single Science passages or one single Science passage and one set of paired Science passages. Science passages differ from other passage types because:

- They often contain a lot of jargon and technical terms.

- They can utilize unfamiliar terms and concepts.

While Science passages can be tricky due to unfamiliar language, you will never need to employ knowledge outside of the passage when answering questions. Use the following strategy when approaching Science passages on the PSAT:

1. Locate the central idea in the first paragraph.

2. Note how each paragraph relates to the central idea. Does the paragraph…

   - Explain?

   - Support?

   - Refute?

   - Summarize?

3. Don't be distracted by jargon or technical terms.

   - Unfamiliar terms will generally be defined within the passage or in a footnote.

Let's look at the following example of an abbreviated Science passage and question set. After the mapped passage, the left column contains questions similar to those you'll see on the PSAT Reading Test on Test Day. The column on the right features the strategic thinking a test expert employs when approaching the passage and questions presented. Note how a test expert can quickly condense the entire passage into a few words and use his or her Passage Map to ask questions that build a prediction for the correct answer.

> ✔ **Remember**
>
> **When you encounter more than one theory or idea, paraphrase each in as few words as possible in your Passage Map.**

Strategic Thinking
Step 1: Read actively
Read the passage and the notes provided. Remember, a well-crafted Passage Map should summarize the central idea of each paragraph as well as important topics or themes. Your notes for Science passages should focus on the passage's central idea and how each paragraph relates to that idea. Use your Passage Map to help you answer each question.

Questions 5–6 are based on the following passage.

This passage is adapted from an essay about the characteristics of lunar eclipses.

Many people are aware of the beauty of a solar eclipse, but are surprised to learn that lunar eclipses are often just as spectacular and are both more
Line common and easier to observe. The filtering and
(5) refraction of light from the Earth's atmosphere during a lunar eclipse creates stunning color effects that range from dark brown to red, orange, and yellow. Each of these light shows is unique since they are the result of the amount of dust and cloud
(10) cover in the Earth's atmosphere at the time of the eclipse. While total solar eclipses last only for a few minutes and can be seen only in a small area of a few kilometers, total lunar eclipses can last for several hours and can be seen over much of the
(15) planet. In fact, the beauty and stability of lunar eclipses make them a favorite of both amateur and professional photographers.

Lunar eclipses generally occur two to three times a year and are possible only when the Moon is in its
(20) full phase. When we see the Moon, we are actually seeing sunlight reflected off the surface of the Moon. When the Earth is positioned in between the Moon and the Sun, however, the Earth's shadow falls on the Moon and a lunar eclipse occurs.
(25) To better understand this process, it's helpful to imagine the Earth's shadow on the Moon as a pair of nested cones, with the Earth at the apex of the cones, and the Moon at their bases. The outer, more diffuse cone of shadow is called the penumbral
(30) shadow, while the inner, darker cone is the umbral shadow.

¶1: lun ecl more common than solar ecl (central idea), created by light filt & refract

¶2: info about how lunar ecl occurs

Questions	Strategic Thinking
5. According to the passage, the colors of a lunar eclipse are the result of A) the penumbral shadow. B) the stability of lunar eclipses. C) filtering and refraction of light. D) the sunlight reflected off the moon.	**Step 2: Examine the question stem** *What key words are in the question stem?* "The colors of a lunar eclipse" **Step 3: Predict and answer** *Look at the Passage Map notes. Where does the author discuss how lunar eclipses are created?* The first paragraph *What are the colors the result of?* "The filtering and refraction of light" (lines 4–5) *Which answer choice matches this prediction?* Choice (C)
6. In lines 26–27, the phrase "pair of nested cones" serves to A) offer support for a previous statement. B) describe the diffraction of light through the atmosphere. C) explain why lunar eclipses are favorites of photographers. D) provide a concrete example to help readers visualize a phenomenon.	**Step 2: Examine the question stem** *What clue is in this question stem?* A phrase from the passage and a line reference **Step 3: Predict and answer** *Read around the cited line reference. What does the author state before introducing this phrase?* "To better understand this process, it's helpful to imagine . . ." (lines 25–26) *Which answer choice matches this?* Choice (D)

You have seen the ways in which the PSAT presents Reading passages and the way a PSAT expert approaches these types of questions.

You will use the Kaplan Method for Reading Comprehension to complete this section. Part of the test-like passage has been mapped already. Your first step is to complete the Passage Map. Then you will continue to use the Kaplan Method for Reading Comprehension and the strategies discussed in this chapter to answer the questions. Strategic thinking questions have been included to guide you—some of the answers have been filled in, but you will have to fill in the answers to others.

Use your answers to the strategic thinking questions to select the correct answer, just as you will on Test Day.

Strategic Thinking
Step 1: Read actively
The passage below is partially mapped. Read the passage and the first part of the Passage Map. Then complete the Passage Map on your own. Remember to focus on the central ideas of each paragraph as well as the central idea of the overall passage. Use your Passage Map as a reference when you're answering questions.

Questions 7–8 are based on the following passage.

The following passage discusses the scientific classification of the giant panda.

¶1: panda classification controversy

Line

Ever since European scientists came upon the giant panda in the middle of the nineteenth century, a controversy has raged among Western biologists over its relation to other species. While (5) the general public tends to view the giant panda as a kind of living teddy bear, taxonomists have not been sure how to classify this enigmatic animal. At different times, the panda has been placed with bears in the *Ursidae* family, with raccoons in the (10) *Procyonidae* family, and in its own *Ailuropodidae* family.

¶2: homologous trait categorization

Biologists who classify animal species have tried to categorize the panda according to whether its traits are "homologous" or "analogous" to similar (15) traits in other species. Homologous traits are those that species have in common because they have descended from a common ancestor. For instance, every species of cat has the homologous trait of

possessing only four toes on its hind foot because (20) every member of the cat family descended from a common feline ancestor with the same four toes. The greater the number of shared homologous traits between two species, the more closely they are related. A cat and a lion have more homologous (25) traits than a cat and a human, for example, so cats and lions have a closer biological relationship.

What appears to be a homologous trait may only be an analogous trait, however. An analogous trait is a trait that two species have in common (30) not because they are descended from a common ancestor, but because they have different ancestors that developed in similar ways in response to their environment. The eagle and the butterfly, for example, both possess the trait of wings but are not (35) closely related.

Questions	Strategic Thinking
7. How do the second and third paragraphs differ? A) The second paragraph focuses on the similarities between cats and lions, while the third paragraph focuses on the similarities between eagles and butterflies. B) The second paragraph focuses on homologous traits in common between pandas and bears, while the third paragraph focuses on analogous traits in common between pandas and raccoons. C) The second paragraph explains and gives examples of homologous traits, while the third paragraph explains and gives examples of analogous traits. D) The second paragraph explains and gives examples of analogous traits, while the third paragraph explains and gives examples of homologous traits.	**Step 2: Examine the question stem** *What are the clues in this question stem?* "Second and third paragraphs differ" **Step 3: Predict and answer** *Look at your Passage Map. What does the second paragraph discuss?* _____ _____ _____ *Look at your Passage Map. What does the third paragraph discuss?* _____ _____ _____ *Which answer choice matches?* _____
8. The people described in line 12 ("Biologists who classify animal species") are most likely called A) classicists. B) taxonomists. C) botanists. D) geneticists.	**Step 2: Examine the question stem** *What are the clues in the question stem?* _____ _____ _____ **Step 3: Predict and answer** *Where does the author first discuss classification of pandas?* _____ _____ *What word does the author use to describe those who classify?* _____ _____ *Which answer choice matches this prediction?* ___ _____

Now, try a test-like PSAT Reading passage and question set on your own. Give yourself 6 minutes to read the passage and answer the questions.

Questions 9–11 are based on the following passage.

The following passage, adapted from an article in an encyclopedia of American culture, addresses some of the influences of the automobile on American life.

Few developments have so greatly affected American life as the automobile. Indeed, it would be hard to overestimate its impact. Since mass
Line production of the automobile became feasible in the
(5) early twentieth century, the car has had a significant effect on nearly every facet of American life, including how we work, where we live, and what we believe.

Interestingly, it was the process of building cars
(10) rather than the cars themselves that first brought a sea change to the American workplace. In 1914, a Ford plant in Highland Park, Michigan, used the first electric conveyor belt, greatly increasing the efficiency of automobile manufacturing. Assem-
(15) bly lines for the production of automobiles were quickly adopted and became highly mechanized, providing a new model for industrial business. In contrast to European manufacturers, which employed a higher percentage of skilled labor-
(20) ers to produce fewer and costlier cars, American companies focused on turning out a large quantity of affordable cars utilizing less-skilled laborers. Assembly-line production was a mixed blessing, as it enabled higher productivity and more afford-
(25) able cars but resulted in less-satisfied workers with less-interesting jobs. The value of efficiency was emphasized over personal pride and investment in the work.

As cars became more popular, their effect on
(30) population distribution was likewise profound. Unlike railroads, which helped concentrate the population in cities, the automobile contributed to urban sprawl and, eventually, to the rise of sub-urbs. People no longer needed to live near public
(35) transportation lines or within walking distance of

their jobs, and so were drawn to outlying areas with less congestion and lower property taxes. Business districts became less centralized for similar reasons. Sadly, this movement toward suburbs exacerbated
(40) social stratification. Since cars were initially af-fordable only to wealthier people, the upper and middle classes moved out of cities. Many businesses followed, attracted by the educated, well-trained workforce. As good jobs also moved out of cit-
(45) ies, the people who remained were further disad-vantaged and even less able to leave. Though few anticipated it in the heady early days of suburban growth, by the century's end cars had helped to further entrench social divisions in America by
(50) making possible great physical distances between rich and poor.

Automobile ownership has also transformed our individual lives and values. Historian James Flink has observed that automobiles particularly altered
(55) the work patterns and recreational opportunities of farmers and other rural inhabitants by reducing the isolation that had been characteristic of life in the country. Of course, there were also profound changes in the recreational activities of suburban
(60) and urban dwellers. For example, the 1950s saw a huge increase in drive-in movie theaters, fast-food establishments, supermarkets, and shopping centers—most facets of how we ate, shopped, and played changed to accommodate the car. Family
(65) life was also affected: Cars changed dating behavior by allowing teenagers more independence from parental supervision and control, and they provided women with more freedom to leave the home. This personal mobility and autonomy afforded by the car
(70) has become an integral part of American culture.

9. The author refers to European and American manufacturing practices in lines 18–22 primarily to

A) demonstrate the quality difference between European and American cars.

B) argue for a return to a less mechanized but less efficient factory system.

C) highlight the positive and negative effects of the automobile on the American workplace.

D) suggest that greater efficiency and more skilled laborers can improve the American workplace.

10. In lines 31–34 ("Unlike . . . suburbs"), what distinction does the author draw between the two types of transportation?

A) Railroads are a more efficient mode of transportation than automobiles.

B) Automobiles allow greater flexibility, while railroads operate on a fixed schedule.

C) Railroads promote clustered populations, while automobiles promote dispersed populations.

D) Automobiles replaced railroads as the preferred American mode of transportation.

11. As used in line 30, "profound" most nearly means

A) absolute.

B) unintelligible.

C) far-reaching.

D) thoughtful.

Answers and Explanations for this chapter begin on page 583.

ON YOUR OWN

Questions 1–9 are based on the following passage.

The following is adapted from a short story first published in 1921. The author was a Native American woman.

It was summer on the western plains, and fields of golden sunflowers, facing eastward, greeted the rising sun. Blue-Star Woman, with windshorn braids of white
Line hair over each ear, sat in the shade of her log hut before
(5) an open fire. Lonely but unmolested, she dwelt here like the ground squirrel that took its abode nearby—both through the easy tolerance of the landowner. As the Indian woman held a skillet over the burning embers, a large round cake, with long slashes in its center, baked
(10) and crowded the capacity of the frying pan.

In deep abstraction, Blue-Star Woman prepared her morning meal. "Who am I?" had become the obsessing riddle of her life. She was no longer a young woman, being in her fifty-third year; yet now it was required of her,
(15) in the eyes of the white man's law, to give proof of her membership in the Sioux tribe in order to get her share of tribal land. The unwritten law of heart prompted her naturally to say, "I am a being. I am Blue-Star Woman. A piece of earth is my birthright."

(20) It was taught for reasons now forgotten that an Indian should never pronounce his or her name in answer to any inquiry. It was probably a means of protection in the days of black magic; be that as it may, Blue-Star Woman lived in times when this teaching was disregarded. It
(25) gained her nothing, however, to pronounce her name to the government official to whom she applied for her share of tribal land. His persistent question was always, "Who are your parents?" Blue-Star Woman was left an orphan at a tender age, so she did not remember them.

(30) They were long-gone to the spirit-land—and she could not understand why they should be recalled to earth on her account. It was another one of the old, old teachings of her race that the names of the dead should not be idly spoken—in fact, it was considered a sac-
(35) rilege to mention carelessly the name of any departed one, especially in disputes over worldly possessions. The unfortunate circumstances of her early childhood, together with the lack of written records of a roving people, placed a formidable barrier between her and
(40) her heritage. The fact was, events of far greater importance to the tribe than her reincarnation had passed unrecorded in books. The verbal reports of the old-time men and women of the tribe were varied—some were contradictory.

(45) Blue-Star Woman was unable to find even a twig of her family tree . . . Blue-Star Woman was her individual name. For untold ages the Indian race had not used family names—a newborn child was given a brand-new name. Blue-Star Woman was proud to write her name
(50) for which she would not be required to substitute another's upon her marriage, as is the custom of civilized peoples. "The times are changed now," she muttered under her breath. "My individual name seems to mean nothing." Looking out into space, she saw the nodding
(55) sunflowers, and they acquiesced with her . . . With fried bread and black coffee she regaled herself, and once again her mind reverted to her riddle. "This also puzzles me," thought she to herself. "Once a wise leader of our people, addressing a president of this country, said:
(60) 'I am a man. You are another. The Great Spirit is our witness!' This is simple and easy to understand, but the times are changed—the white man's laws are strange."

1. The primary purpose of the passage is to

   A) highlight the differences between the laws of two cultures.

   B) describe the impact of a changing world on a woman.

   C) illustrate the danger of living apart from society.

   D) show the futility of preserving ancient myths in modern times.

2. The author most likely mentions the "ground squirrel" in line 6 in order to

   A) suggest Blue-Star Woman's profound relationship with nature.

   B) demonstrate Blue-Star Woman's keen observation of her surroundings.

   C) show Blue-Star Woman's adaptability to squalid living conditions.

   D) indicate Blue-Star Woman's overwhelming loneliness.

3. As used in line 7, "tolerance" most nearly means

   A) neglect.

   B) fortitude.

   C) permission.

   D) open-mindedness.

4. As used in line 11, "abstraction" most nearly means

   A) reverie.

   B) happiness.

   C) uncertainty.

   D) self-reflection.

5. The phrase in lines 53–54 ("My individual name seems to mean nothing") most nearly reflects Blue-Star Woman's

   A) devastating loss of privilege and good reputation among her people.

   B) sad comprehension that cherished old customs are losing their relevance.

   C) great dismay that she has no children to carry on the family name.

   D) unsettling realization that no member of the tribe remembers her.

6. Which choice provides the best support for the answer to the previous question?

   A) Lines 13–17 ("She . . . land")

   B) Lines 23–25 ("Blue-Star Woman . . . name")

   C) Lines 42–44 ("The . . . contradictory")

   D) Lines 58–62 ("'Once . . . strange'")

7. The second paragraph suggests that "the white man's law" in line 15 differs from the "unwritten law of heart" in line 17 in that the latter

   A) suggests that every person deserves land of his or her own.

   B) has practical consequences for Blue-Star Woman.

   C) considers each human being to be different.

   D) places restrictions on who can and cannot own land.

8. Which choice best describes the government official's treatment of Blue-Star Woman's situation?

   A) The official tries his best to accommodate Blue-Star Woman's circumstances.

   B) The official lacks cultural empathy and is unable to understand Blue-Star Woman's difficulties.

   C) The official solves Blue-Star Woman's dilemma by the end of the passage.

   D) The official is suspicious of Blue-Star Woman's motives.

9. Which choice provides the best support for the answer to the previous question?

   A) Lines 11–13 ("In . . . life")

   B) Lines 24–27 ("It . . . land")

   C) Lines 32–36 ("It . . . possessions")

   D) Lines 40–42 ("The . . . books")

CHAPTER 9

Synthesis Questions and the Kaplan Method for Infographics

 ## CHAPTER OBJECTIVES

By the end of this chapter, you will be able to:

1. Apply the Kaplan Strategy for Paired Passages to History/Social Studies and Science paired passages and question sets

2. Synthesize, compare, and contrast information from two different but related passages

3. Use the Kaplan Method for Infographics to analyze quantitative information and infographics

4. Combine information from infographics and text to answer questions about charts and graphs

SMARTPOINTS

Point Value	SmartPoint Category
Point Builder	The Kaplan Method for Infographics
25 Points	Quantitative Synthesis
20 Points	Paired Passage Synthesis

SYNTHESIS QUESTIONS

There are two types of Synthesis questions on the PSAT:

1. Questions that ask you to synthesize information from both passages of a Paired Passage set

2. Questions that are associated with an infographic

Synthesis questions require you to analyze information from separate sources and then understand how those sources relate to each other.

Let's take a closer look at the two types of Synthesis questions.

PAIRED PASSAGES

There will be exactly one set of Paired Passages on the PSAT Reading Test. These passages will be either History/Social Studies passages or Science passages.

The Kaplan Strategy for Paired Passages helps you attack each pair you face by dividing and conquering, rather than processing two different passages and 9–10 questions all at once:

- Read Passage 1, then answer its questions.

- Read Passage 2, then answer its questions.

- Answer questions about both passages.

By reading Passage 1 and answering its questions before moving on to Passage 2, you avoid falling into wrong-answer traps that reference the text of Passage 2. Furthermore, by addressing each passage individually, you will have a better sense of the central idea and purpose of each passage. This will help you answer questions that ask you to synthesize information about both passages.

> ✔ **Remember**
>
> **Even though the individual passages are shorter in a Paired Passage set, you should still map both of them. Overall, there is still too much information to remember effectively in your head. Your Passage Maps will save you time by helping you locate key details.**

Fortunately, questions in a Paired Passage set that ask about only one of the passages will be no different from questions you've seen and answered about single passages. Use the same methods and strategies you've been using to answer these questions.

Other questions in a Paired Passage set are Synthesis questions. These questions will ask you about both passages. You may be asked to identify similarities or differences between the passages or how the author of one passage may respond to a point made by the author of the other passage.

Reading & Writing

THE KAPLAN METHOD FOR INFOGRAPHICS

The PSAT Reading Test will contain two passages that include infographics. One History/Social Studies passage (or Paired Passage set) and one Science passage (or Paired Passage set) will include infographics. Infographics will convey or expand on information related to the passages. Questions about infographics may ask you to read data, to draw conclusions from the data, or to combine information from the infographic and the passage text.

The Kaplan Method for Infographics consists of three steps:

Step 1: Read the question

Step 2: Examine the infographic

Step 3: Predict and answer

Let's take a closer look at each step.

> **✔ Expert Tip**
>
> Expert test takers consider infographics as part of the corresponding passages, so they make sure to take notes on the infographic as part of their Passage Map.

Step 1: Read the question

Assess the question stem for information that will help you zero in on the specific parts of the infographic that apply to the question.

Step 2: Examine the infographic

Make sure to:

- Identify units of measurement, labels, and titles
- Circle parts of the infographic that relate directly to the question

> **✔ Expert Tip**
>
> For more data-heavy infographics, you should also make note of any trends in the data or relationships between variables.

Step 3: Predict and answer

Just as in Step 3 of the Kaplan Method for Reading Comprehension, do not look at the answer choices until you've used the infographic to make a prediction.

Let's look at the following example of a test-like passage and question set. After the mapped passage, the left column contains questions similar to those you'll see on the PSAT Reading Test on Test Day. The column on the right features the strategic thinking a test expert employs when approaching the passage and questions presented. Pay attention to how test experts vary the approach to answer different question types.

Strategic Thinking

Step 1: Read actively

Read the paired passages and the notes provided. Remember, a well-crafted Passage Map should summarize the central idea of each paragraph as well as important topics or themes. Use your Passage Map to help you answer each question.

> ✔ **Remember**
>
> When answering Paired Passage questions, first read and answer questions about Passage 1. Then read and answer questions about Passage 2. Finally, answer the questions about both passages.

Questions 1–3 are based on the following passages and supplementary material.

Passage 1 recommends more action to address the problem of obesity in the United States. Passage 2 questions how the issue of obesity has been portrayed.

Passage 1

¶1: obesity -> disease; ↑ rate = ↑ costs

Researchers have consistently proven obesity to be a leading risk factor for several diseases, includ-
Line ing diabetes, hypertension, coronary heart disease, and many types of cancer. Disturbingly, obesity is
(5) on the rise. From 1960 to 2000, the obesity rate rose from 13.3 to 30.9 percent of the population and jumped nearly 75 percent from 1991 to 2001 alone. As the prevalence of obesity increases, so too do the economic consequences of the condition. Missed
(10) work and the escalating expense of health care are part of the hundred-billion-dollar-plus total cost of obesity that affects the nation's economy. Intensi-

¶1, cont.: gov't should do more

fied government efforts to address obesity and its consequences would benefit not only the nation's
(15) economy, but also the well-being of its citizens.

Passage 2

¶1: US obesity ↑: stats ignore gov't actions = incomplete pic

The United States of America is getting fatter. Statistics show that obesity rates more than doubled from 1960 to 2000. However, advocates who cite such statistics and demand government action
(20) ignore existing initiatives. The U.S. government has responded to the obesity epidemic by creating many programs aimed at obesity awareness, prevention, and control. In addition, its healthcare system continues to improve and respond to the

(25) needs of the obese population. Statistics describing rising obesity rates are alarmist and neglect existing antiobesity efforts, as well as the nonquantitative factors that affect health. Fighting obesity is a noble objective, but the overzealous use of statistics
(30) contributes to an incomplete and ultimately inaccurate portrayal of the situation.

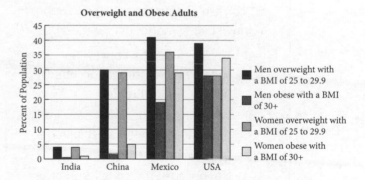

Overweight and Obese Adults

Reading & Writing

Questions	Strategic Thinking
1. One difference between the responses described in the passages is that, unlike the author of Passage 1, the author of Passage 2 A) suggests that new government efforts to combat obesity would be largely ineffective. B) recommends conducting additional research before intensifying government efforts. C) cites existing programs and improved healthcare efforts that already address the problem. D) claims fighting obesity should not be a national concern.	**Step 2: Examine the question stem** *What is this question asking you to do?* Describe one of the differences between the opinions of the authors of the two passages. **Step 3: Predict and answer** *Review your Passage Map to find each author's central idea. How do the authors' opinions differ?* Author 1 claims the government should do more to combat obesity. Author 2 states the government already has programs to this effect and argues that statistics about obesity can be misleading. *Which answer choice matches your prediction?* Choice (C)
2. Are the benefits of addressing the consequences of obesity described in Passage 1 consistent with the main conclusion drawn by the author of Passage 2? A) Yes, because the conclusion suggests that addressing obesity has societal value. B) Yes, because the conclusion implies that government is best suited to pursue such goals. C) No, because the conclusion offers alternative benefits associated with a different approach. D) No, because the conclusion focuses only on the use of statistics to evaluate the problem.	**Step 2: Examine the question stem** *What is this question asking you to do?* Compare part of one passage with the conclusion of another passage **Step 3: Predict and answer** *What is the conclusion in Passage 2?* Fighting obesity is good, but statistics can be misleading. *Does this conclusion match the benefits mentioned in Passage 1?* Yes. Lines 14–15 state that fighting obesity would help the "nation's economy" and "the well-being of its citizens." *Which answer choice best matches your prediction?* Choice (A)

Questions	Strategic Thinking
3. Based on the information in Passage 2 and the chart, it can be reasonably inferred that A) obesity rates for U.S. women are increasing more rapidly than are the rates for U.S. men. B) in the United States, the proportion of overweight men to overweight women suggests that existing initiatives are more effective for women. C) the statistics displayed in the graph suggest a serious problem, but don't present a complete picture. D) governments in other countries have spent too much time fighting obesity.	**Step 1: Read the question** *Assess the question for clues to determine what parts of the infographic are needed for this question.* **Step 2: Examine the infographic** *What are the units of measurement, labels, or titles?* The units on the *y*-axis are population percentages. The labels on the *x*-axis are four countries: India, China, Mexico, and USA. The key also provides labels for the four different categories: men and women who are overweight and obese. The title of the chart is "Overweight and Obese Adults." **Step 3: Predict and answer** *What part(s) of the infographic should you circle?* This question does not specify what information is needed from the infographic, so just note any overall trends. For instance, the overweight and obese percentages are relatively high in the USA (and Mexico) compared to the other countries depicted. *This question requires you to evaluate each answer choice. Keep in mind the conclusion of Passage 2.* Choice A is incorrect because the chart does not display change over time, so it's impossible to know whether the rates are increasing more rapidly. Choice B is incorrect because no information is given concerning the relative effectiveness of initiatives according to gender. There could be many other causes for the difference in percentages. Choice D is incorrect because neither the infographic nor the text addresses government actions in other countries. *Which is the correct answer?* Choice (C)

You have seen the ways in which the PSAT tests you on Synthesis questions in Reading passages and the way a PSAT expert approaches these types of questions.

You will use the Kaplan Method for Reading Comprehension to complete this section. Part of the test-like passage has been mapped already. Your first step is to complete the Passage Map. Then you will continue to use the Kaplan Method for Reading Comprehension and the strategies discussed in this chapter to answer the questions. Strategic thinking questions have been included to guide you—some of the answers have been filled in, but you will have to fill in the answers to others.

Use your answers to the strategic thinking questions to select the correct answer, just as you will on Test Day.

When answering Paired Passage questions, remember to first read and answer questions about Passage 1. Then read and answer questions about Passage 2. Finally, answer the questions about both passages.

Strategic Thinking

Step 1: Read actively

The paired passage set below is partially mapped. Read the first passage and its Passage Map. Then complete the Passage Map for the second passage on your own. Remember to focus on the central ideas of each paragraph as well as the central idea of the overall passage. Use your Passage Map as a reference when you're answering questions.

Questions 4–6 are based on the following passages and supplementary material.

The following passages both argue for changes related to the American election system, but differ in their recommendations about how to achieve reform.

Passage 1

In the United States, we should make it an urgent priority to reform the process of campaigning for elective office. The vast sums necessary to
Line mount credible presidential and congressional
(5) campaigns are especially detrimental. They threaten to limit the pool of candidates to the very wealthy and also give disproportionate influence to lobbyists and other special interests. We should also change the length of such campaigns. In the United
(10) Kingdom, campaigns for parliamentary elections last for weeks; in the United States, the process lasts for well over a year. Finally, the two major parties should establish norms for campaign advertising, with the goal of sharply curtailing "attack ads."

¶1: argue U.S. reform campaigns; why: costly, too long, ads mean

Passage 2

(15) American elections would be more democratic if candidates were required to debate and if everyone eligible to vote were required to do so. Under the present system, a candidate with the advantages of incumbency or widespread name recognition is
(20) free to sidestep an opponent's challenge to debate. This puts the opponent at a disadvantage and compromises the goals of our two-party system. Debates needn't play the determining role in elections, but they should be an important factor as the public
(25) evaluates candidates' positions on issues. Of course, a well-informed public is irrelevant if people don't vote. Many foreign countries have a far higher election turnout than we do in the United States. We should consider legislation requiring people to vote
(30) in national elections. Citizenship has its privileges, but it also involves responsibilities.

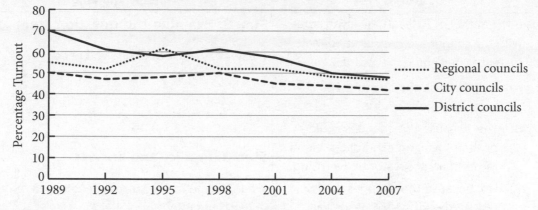

Voter Turnout at Selected Local Elections

.... Regional councils
- - - - - City councils
———— District councils

Don't get distracted by less important details. If you're stuck, review the Sample Passage Map Notes in the Answers and Explanations for this chapter on page 586.

Questions	Strategic Thinking
4. The arguments presented in Passage 1 and Passage 2 share what element? A) Recommendation of changes to campaign finance rules B) Citation of supporting evidence from foreign countries C) Recommendation of a mix of voluntary and required actions D) Support of an expanded debate schedule	**Step 2: Examine the question stem** *What is this question asking you to do?* Find an argumentative element shared by both passages. *Keep in mind the argument made in each passage.* Author 1 argues that U.S. campaigns should be reformed. Likewise, author 2 argues for two changes that would make U.S. elections more democratic. However, note that the question asks for an element both arguments have in common. **Step 3: Predict and answer** *What element do both authors employ when making their arguments?* Passage 1 cites United Kingdom affairs while Passage 2 describes the election turnout in foreign countries. *Which answer matches this?*_____

Reading & Writing

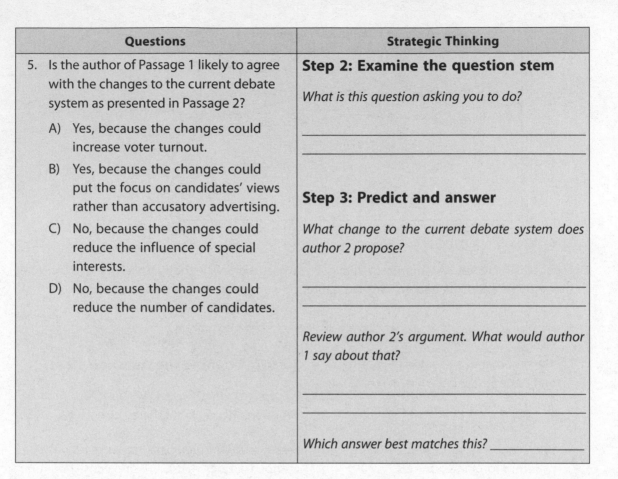

Questions	Strategic Thinking
5. Is the author of Passage 1 likely to agree with the changes to the current debate system as presented in Passage 2? A) Yes, because the changes could increase voter turnout. B) Yes, because the changes could put the focus on candidates' views rather than accusatory advertising. C) No, because the changes could reduce the influence of special interests. D) No, because the changes could reduce the number of candidates.	**Step 2: Examine the question stem** *What is this question asking you to do?* _____ _____ **Step 3: Predict and answer** *What change to the current debate system does author 2 propose?* _____ _____ *Review author 2's argument. What would author 1 say about that?* _____ _____ *Which answer best matches this?* _____

Questions	Strategic Thinking
6. Based on the information in Passage 2 and the graphic, which answer choice, if true, would weaken the argument made by the author of Passage 2? A) The graph shows voter turnout in the United States before and after campaigns began and lasting over a year. B) The graph shows voter turnout after campaign reforms have been enacted. C) The graph shows voter turnout in the European Union before and after mandatory voting laws were enacted in 1998. D) The graph shows voter turnout in the European Union after laws requiring citizens to vote were repealed in 1989.	**Step 1: Read the question** *Assess the question for clues to determine what parts of the infographic are needed for this question.* **Step 2: Examine the infographic** *What are the units of measurement, labels, or titles? Is there any important information you are not given in this infographic?* _____ _____ *What part(s) of the infographic should you circle? This question does not specify what information is needed from the infographic, so just note any overall trends.* **Step 3: Predict and answer** *What trend do you notice in the graph?* _____ *What recommendation did author 2 make about voting in national elections?* _____ *What situation could make the data in the graph weaken the argument that required voting in national elections would make the U.S. more democratic?* _____ *Which answer choice matches this?_____*

Now, try a test-like PSAT Reading passage on your own. Give yourself 6 minutes to read the passage and answer the questions.

Remember to first read and answer questions about Passage 1. Then read and answer questions about Passage 2. Finally, answer the questions about both passages.

Questions 7–9 are based on the following passages and supplementary material.

The infringement of one species on the habitat of another can cause serious biological and environmental damage, especially when this infringement is caused by human intervention. To what extent should we work to prevent this? The following passages address differing aspects of this issue.

Passage 1

A plant or animal species is considered invasive when it spreads to an area where it does not natu-rally occur, causing economic or environmental

Line harm. Biologists have long recognized that invasive
(5) species can present problems for native ecosystems, but recent developments have intensified their con-cern. In May 2002, hundreds of invasive northern snakehead fish were found in a Maryland pond, having been spawned by a pair of fish released by
(10) a man who had bought them at a live fish market. Unlike native fish, which have natural predators to keep their populations in check, snakeheads, which evolved in Asia, can destroy ecosystems where they have no natural predators by eating huge amounts
(15) of smaller fish and plant life. Their ability to survive for up to four days out of water and to "walk" with their fins on land for short distances has made their potential spread especially worrisome.

Measures that have been taken to contain the
(20) spread of invasive fish include banning the impor-tation or possession of snakeheads, draining ponds or lakes where they have been found, poisoning ponds with herbicides and pesticides, and inspect-ing pet stores to make sure they are not illegally
(25) selling the fish. The United States, however, does not appear to be acting swiftly enough either to prevent the further spread of invasive fish or, more generally, to minimize other plant or animal inva-sions in the future. Although laws are now in place
(30) to prevent the introduction and spread of invasive species, they were slow to be enacted, despite ample evidence from Australia and elsewhere that non-native animals can cause severe and irreversible environmental harm.

(35) The number of scientists and environmentalists who recognize invasive species as a serious environ-mental problem, however, is increasing. If scien-tists, government officials, and the general popula-tion work together and make it a priority to identify
(40) and prevent the spread of invasive species in the early stages where containment or eradication is still feasible, we may at least be able to minimize the unwelcome impact of exotic species on native ecosystems.

Passage 2

(45) Lately, much attention has been focused on the snakehead fish and other invasive species. Environmentalists issue dire warnings about the disappearing habitats of native species and sug-gest that ecological disaster will follow if we do not
(50) take immediate action to contain exotic plant and animal invasions whenever and wherever they are perceived as a threat. While they are surely right that the uncontrolled spread of nonnative plants and animals may have undesirable consequences
(55) for the ecosystem, they seem to forget that the environmental concerns raised by invasive species must be weighed against many other environmental issues competing for adequate funding. The discov-ery of snakehead fish in Maryland, for instance, was
(60) highly publicized and prompted a great expenditure of time and resources to eradicate them, and the spread of carp in the Great Lakes has likewise been addressed at great cost. While these fish do pose

very real problems, pollution, deforestation, and a
(65) host of other environmental problems are at least
as worthy of funding. The fact that invasive species
are currently a "hot topic" in the media does not
mean they should overshadow larger environmental issues, even if discussion of the larger issues
(70) has become more mundane. Containing invasive
species is a worthwhile goal, but it is not the only
worthwhile environmental goal.

Scientific evidence is lacking about what containment measures work and about how serious the
(75) threat posed by various invasive species actually
is. Recently, the discovery of a single snakehead
fish in one lake prompted officials to drain and

refill the lake at a cost of more than $10,000, yet
no additional snakeheads were even found there.
(80) Instead of taking drastic and expensive measures
every time a potential problem is reported, we
should strive for a balance between environmental
protection and economic responsibility. Scientific
data can be valuable because they alert us to an is-
(85) sue we should watch closely, but simply identifying
an environmental threat does not mean we should
automatically give it priority over other important
issues. Instead, scientific data should be treated as
just that—data that allow us to make informed and
(90) balanced policy decisions after reflecting on the
consequences of various courses of action.

Year	Annual Spending in $1,000s of Dollars		
	2010	2011	2012
Environmental Protection Agency	$6,663,000	$6,848,000	$6,071,000
National Invasive Species Council	$2,207,000	$2,238,000	$2,221,000
Total	$8,870,000	$9,086,000	$8,292,000

7. One difference between the assessment of environmental issues described in the two passages is that unlike the author of Passage 1, the author of Passage 2

   A) minimizes the risk associated with invasive species.

   B) considers invasive species as only one of a number of environmental concerns.

   C) questions whether scientific data have a role when larger economic or environmental issues are concerned.

   D) argues that the legislative response to the threat posed by invasive species has been rapid and effective.

8. The authors of Passage 1 and Passage 2 would most likely agree on which of the following statements?

   A) Greater expenditures to reduce the impact of invasive species are justified.

   B) The economic benefits of environmental protection must be weighed against the severity of the environmental threat.

   C) Effective use of the media can increase public awareness of mundane environmental issues.

   D) Efforts by scientists and environmentalists to contain environmental damage are worth continuing.

9. Based on the information in Passage 1 and the graphic, it can be reasonably inferred that the author considers spending by the National Invasive Species Council to be

   A) continually overshadowed by spending on other environmental issues.

   B) an important part of a coalition working to prevent the spread of invasive species.

   C) less effective than the EPA in combatting invasive species.

   D) most effective when the council works in partnership with the EPA.

Answers and Explanations for this chapter begin on page 586.

ON YOUR OWN

The following questions provide an opportunity to practice the concepts and strategic thinking covered in this chapter. While many of the questions pertain to Synthesis, some touch on other concepts tested on the Reading Test to ensure that your practice is test-like, with a variety of question types per passage.

Questions 1–10 are based on the following passages and supplementary materials.

In the 1980s to early 1990s, Biosphere 2 was a highly anticipated scientific endeavor in which people were going to live for years in an isolated, completely self-contained environment composed of five biomes. Passage 1 explains problems with the project, while Passage 2 describes the experiment in light of its media coverage.

Passage 1

In 1984, great fanfare and optimism accompanied the funding of an ecosystem research project called "Biosphere 2." The project's mission was to
Line create an airlock-sealed habitat that could support a
(5) human crew for several years without contact with or resources from the outside world. Less than a decade later, however, enthusiasm for the project had almost entirely eroded after serious questions were raised about adherence to that mission.
(10) The problems that hampered expectations for the project from the start involved the construction of the Biosphere itself. Shaping bodies of water to have waves and tidal changes posed troublesome issues. During the mission, unforeseen difficulties
(15) included overstocked fish dying and clogging filtration systems. Unanticipated condensation made the "desert" too wet. Populations of greenhouse ants and cockroaches exploded. Morning glories overran the "rainforest," blocking out other plants.
(20) These issues did not draw media fire, however, until it was revealed that the project team had allowed an injured member to leave and return, carrying new material inside. Although the administrators claimed the only new supplies brought in were plas-
(25) tic bags, other sources accused mission members of bringing food and other items. More criticism was raised when it was learned that the project had been pumping oxygen inside, to make up for a fail-

ure in the balance of the system that resulted in the
(30) amount of oxygen steadily declining. This scrutiny only intensified when these same administrators denied having tampered with the project. As an unfortunate result, doubts regarding the integrity of all the scientific data generated by the project ham-
(35) pered the perceived value of the overall project.

Passage 2

An amazing undertaking, despite its ultimate failure, Biosphere 2 was a colossal Arizona-desert space-age ark devoted to exploration and experimentation. As promised by its promoters,
(40) Biosphere 2 inhabitants would produce all their own food and oxygen and recycle their own waste. However, despite currying the initial favor of media sources, the project became riddled with controversy. The story of its start is an awkward page of
(45) scientific history but also incidentally a chronicle of the metamorphosis of media relations from auspicious beginnings to recriminating endings.

Promoters of Biosphere 2 were not shy about putting the project into the public eye and on the
(50) radar of the scientific community. In July 1987, SBV and The Institute of Ecotechnics held the First International Workshop on Closed Ecological Systems in conjunction with the Royal Society in London. This workshop brought together for the
(55) first time pioneers in the field from Russia, NASA, and Europe's biological life support programs. The architectural-engineering team of Allen, Augustine, Hawes, and Dempster authored the preliminary Biosphere 2 designs. In addition, Biosphere 2 was
(60) from the beginning consistently propped up by the press. Biosphere 2 came to be regarded as an

indicator of the possibility of human habitation in space. Even as many scientists worked to temper such lofty goals, the media dubbed Biosphere 2 the
(65) most exciting scientific project undertaken since the moon landing. But, in the aftermath, the project's first crew emerged from a supposed two-year isolation only to be greeted by a swirl of negative attention and controversy. The publications that had
(70) trumpeted the project quickly reversed direction. Frustrated with Biosphere 2's failures, the project's financiers fired their management team and, in a reversal of their own, lashed out at the same press they had once courted.

# of Publications from Biosphere 2 Center Research

1. As used in line 18, "exploded" most nearly means

   A) burst.

   B) increased.

   C) destroyed.

   D) opened.

2. The author of Passage 1 supports the claim about the Biosphere 2 project with

   A) hypothetical scenarios.

   B) analogous situations.

   C) supporting details.

   D) comparative analyses.

3. The main structure used in the second paragraph of Passage 1 can best be described as

   A) cause-and-effect.

   B) sequential.

   C) compare and contrast.

   D) continuation.

4. The author of Passage 1 would most likely agree with which of the following statements?

   A) The Biosphere 2 project was doomed to fail despite the fanfare it generated.

   B) The problems with how the project was conducted call into question the usefulness of its results.

   C) The project should be reevaluated given the significant value of its scientific data.

   D) The problems associated with Biosphere 2 were directly caused by media bias.

5. As used in line 63, "temper" most nearly means

   A) anger.

   B) strengthen.

   C) calm.

   D) anneal.

6. The author of Passage 1 would most likely describe the statement in lines 39–41 ("As promised . . . waste") as a

   A) fair assessment of the project's results.

   B) clear example of the media hype surrounding the project.

   C) misleading statement regarding the project's outcome.

   D) compelling argument requiring a new review of the project.

7. Which choice provides the best evidence for the answer to the previous question?

   A) Lines 1–3 ("In 1984 . . . Biosphere 2'")

   B) Lines 14–16 ("During . . . systems")

   C) Lines 26–30 ("More criticism . . . declining")

   D) Lines 32–35 ("As an . . . project")

8. Passage 1 and Passage 2 differ mainly in that

   A) Passage 1 describes problems with Biosphere 2, while Passage 2 suggests possible solutions to those problems.

   B) Passage 1 relies on press reports for the basis of its argument, while Passage 2 provides internal documents to refute those claims.

   C) Passage 1 strikes a balance between initial optimism and subsequent pessimism, while Passage 2 remains neutral throughout.

   D) Passage 1 focuses on the internal causes of the problems with Biosphere 2, while Passage 2 focuses on how external perceptions of the project changed.

9. According to the chart, which of the following was the most consistently published research based on Biosphere 2?

   A) Human experiments

   B) Non-manipulative experiments

   C) Manipulative experiments

   D) None of the above

10. When read together, Passage 1 and Passage 2

   A) provide an overview of how the project was perceived and specific reasons for those perceptions.

   B) agree in their conclusions, but differ in their descriptions of how the project was initially viewed by outsiders.

   C) offer contrasting opinions on a controversial undertaking.

   D) demonstrate how both the media and administrators may hamper exciting scientific discoveries.

CHAPTER 10

Global and Command of Evidence Questions

CHAPTER OBJECTIVES

By the end of this chapter, you will be able to:

1. Locate appropriate textual evidence to support the answer to a previous question

2. Summarize the passage or key information and ideas within the passage

3. Identify central ideas and themes of a passage to answer questions about central ideas and themes

SMARTPOINTS

Point Value	SmartPoint Category
10 Points	Global
60 Points	Command of Evidence

GLOBAL QUESTIONS

Global questions require you to both identify explicit and determine implicit central ideas or themes in a text. If you pay attention to the big picture—the author's central idea and purpose—while reading PSAT Reading passages, you will be able to answer Global questions with little to no rereading of the passage. To fully understand the central ideas and themes of a passage, you must synthesize the different points the author makes with his or her thesis statement, which you should underline when Passage Mapping.

Global questions may also ask you to choose a correct summary of the passage as a whole or identify key information and ideas within the passage. When presented with this type of Global question, you can use your Passage Map, which is essentially a brief summary of what you have read.

> ✔ **On Test Day**
>
> The introductory text at the beginning of a PSAT Reading passage can be very helpful in determining the author's central ideas and themes. Make sure you take the time on Test Day to read this information—it orients you to the passage.

You can recognize Global questions because they typically do not reference line numbers or even individual paragraphs. To confidently answer Global questions, you need to not only identify the central idea or theme of the passage but also avoid choosing answers that summarize secondary or supplementary points.

Note that there is a slight difference between nonfiction and fiction passages. Science and History/Social Studies passages are nonfiction and will have a definite central idea and thesis statement; U.S. and World Literature passages are fiction and will have a central theme but no thesis statement.

> ✔ **Remember**
>
> History/Social Studies and Science passages on the PSAT Reading Test are just well-written essays or article excerpts. You can normally find the thesis statement of a well-written piece at the end of the introductory paragraph.

COMMAND OF EVIDENCE QUESTIONS

A Command of Evidence question relies on your answer to the question that precedes it. These questions require you to identify the portion of the text that provides the best evidence for the conclusion you reached when selecting your answer to the previous question.

Kaplan's Strategy for Command of Evidence questions involves retracing your steps; that is, you must return to the previous question to ensure you answer the Command of Evidence question correctly.

To answer Command of Evidence questions efficiently and correctly, employ the following Kaplan Strategy:

- When you see a question asking you to choose the best evidence to support your answer to the previous question, review how you selected that answer.

- Avoid answers that provide evidence for incorrect answers to the previous question.

- The correct answer will support why the previous question's answer is correct.

> ✔ **Expert Tip**
>
> You can recognize Command of Evidence questions easily. The question stem usually reads, "Which choice provides the best evidence for the answer to the previous question?" Furthermore, the answer choices are always line numbers with parentheses containing the first and last word of the intended selection. Answer choices are listed in the order they appear in the passage.

Command of Evidence questions ask that you cite the textual evidence that best supports, disputes, strengthens, or weakens a given claim or point. Whether the argument is supported or not, the use of textual evidence is the same. The evidence can be personal stories, scientific facts, tone, writing style, or infographics. It is important to identify the appropriate aspect of the text used for Command of Evidence questions and not to make assumptions beyond what is written.

The first step to approaching a Command of Evidence question is to make sure you answered the previous question—no matter its type—correctly. If you answer the question preceding a Command of Evidence question incorrectly, you have a smaller chance of selecting the correct answer.

> ✔ **Remember**
>
> There is no incorrect answer penalty on the PSAT, so even if you have no idea of how to approach a question, take your best guess and move on.

Let's look at the following example of a test-like passage and question set. After the mapped passage, the left column contains questions similar to those you'll see on the PSAT Reading Test on Test Day. The column on the right features the strategic thinking test experts employ when approaching the passage and questions presented. Pay attention to how test experts vary the approach to answer different question types.

Strategic Thinking

Step 1: Read actively

Read the passage and the notes provided. Remember, a well-crafted Passage Map should summarize the central idea of each paragraph as well as important topics or themes. Use your Passage Map to help you answer each question.

Questions 1–3 are based on the following passage.

The following, adapted from an English novel published in 1907, describes the family environment and early childhood of Rickie Elliot, a boy with a mild physical disability.

¶1: Rickie doesn't like suburbs

Some people spend their lives in a suburb, and not for any urgent reason. This had been the fate of Rickie. He had opened his eyes to filmy heavens,
Line and taken his first walk on asphalt. He had seen
(5) civilization as a row of semi-detached villas, and society as a state in which men do not know the men who live next door. He had himself become part of the gray monotony that surrounds all cities. There was no necessity for this—it was only rather
(10) convenient to his father.

¶2: description of Rickie's father

Mr. Elliot was a barrister. In appearance he resembled his son, being weakly and lame, with hollow little cheeks, a broad white band of forehead, and stiff impoverished hair. His voice, which he did
(15) not transmit, was very suave, with a fine command of cynical intonation. By altering it ever so little he could make people wince, especially if they were simple or poor. Nor did he transmit his eyes. Their peculiar flatness, as if the soul looked through
(20) dirty windowpanes, the unkindness of them, the cowardice, the fear in them, were to trouble the world no longer.

¶3: description of Rickie's mother

He married a girl whose voice was beautiful. There was no caress in it yet all who heard it were
(25) soothed, as though the world held some unexpected blessing. She called to her dogs one night over invisible waters, and he, a tourist up on the bridge, thought "that is extraordinarily adequate." In time he discovered that her figure, face, and thoughts

(30) were adequate also, and as she was not impossible socially, he married her. "I have taken a plunge," he told his family. The family, hostile at first, had not a word to say when the woman was introduced to them; and his sister declared that the plunge had
(35) been taken from the opposite bank.

¶3, cont.: Mr. E not excited about marriage

Things only went right for a little time. Though beautiful without and within, Mrs. Elliot had not the gift of making her home beautiful; and one day, when she bought a carpet for the dining room that
(40) clashed, he laughed gently, said he "really couldn't," and departed. Departure is perhaps too strong a word. In Mrs. Elliot's mouth it became, "My husband has to sleep more in town." He often came down to see them, nearly always unexpectedly, and
(45) occasionally they went to see him. "Father's house," as Rickie called it, only had three rooms, but these were full of books and pictures and flowers; and the flowers, instead of being squashed down into the vases as they were in mummy's house, rose
(50) gracefully from frames of lead which lay coiled at the bottom, as doubtless the sea serpent has to lie, coiled at the bottom of the sea. Once he was let to lift a frame out—only once, for he dropped some water on a creton.* "I think he's going to have
(55) taste," said Mr. Elliot languidly. "It is quite possible," his wife replied. She had not taken off her hat and gloves, nor even pulled up her veil. Mr. Elliot laughed, and soon afterwards another lady came in, and they went away.

¶4: mom- bad taste, dad- left

¶4, cont.: parents lived apart

¶4, cont.: father has new lady

*here, a piece of furniture covered with a cotton fabric

Questions	Strategic Thinking
1. Mr. Elliot is described as being A) monotonous and opportunistic. B) superficial and condescending. C) tasteful and classy. D) weak and generous.	**Step 2: Examine the question stem** *What kind of question is this?* A Global question *How do you know?* It asks about the description of a character mentioned throughout the passage. **Step 3: Predict and answer** *What is the general characterization of Mr. Elliot?* Negative *Which answer choice contains two negative adjectives that reflect Mr. Elliot's personality?* Choice (B)
2. According to the passage, the family's life in the suburbs is described as A) an impersonal and unfortunate situation chosen to accommodate Mr. Elliot. B) a dull environment from which Mr. Elliot wanted to escape. C) an impoverished but friendly upbringing for Rickie. D) oppressive to Mrs. Elliot, but something she endured in order to please her husband.	**Step 2: Examine the question stem** *What kind of question is this?* A Detail question *How do you know?* "According to the passage" **Step 3: Predict and answer** *In what part of the passage does the author mention the suburbs?* The first paragraph *What is Rickie's attitude toward the suburbs?* Negative *Why does the family live in the suburbs?* Because it's "convenient" (line 10) for Mr. Elliot *Which answer choice matches this?* Choice (A)

Questions	Strategic Thinking
3. Which choice provides the best evidence for the answer to the previous question? A) Lines 1–2 ("Some . . . reason") B) Lines 3–7 ("He had opened . . . next door") C) Lines 7–8 ("He had himself . . . cities") D) Lines 9–10 ("There was . . . father")	**Step 2: Examine the question stem** *What kind of question is this?* A Command of Evidence question *How do you know?* The question stem's wording *What key words are in the question stem's wording?* "Best evidence for the answer to the previous question" and the answer choices use line citations **Step 3: Predict and answer** *Where did you find the answer to the previous question?* The first paragraph *Who insists that the family live in the suburbs?* Mr. Elliot *Which answer choice matches this?* Choice (D)

✔ **Note**

Remember the Kaplan Strategy for Command of Evidence questions: review how you selected the answer to the previous question, and avoid answer choices that provide evidence for incorrect answer choices to it. The correct answer will support why the previous question's answer is correct.

You have seen the ways in which the PSAT tests you on Citing Textual Evidence and Global Questions in Reading passages and the way a PSAT expert approaches these types of questions.

You will use the Kaplan Method for Reading Comprehension to complete this section. Part of the test-like passage has been mapped already. Your first step is to complete the Passage Map. Then you will continue to use the Kaplan Method for Reading Comprehension and the strategies discussed in this chapter to answer the questions. Strategic thinking questions have been included to guide you—some of the answers have been filled in, but you will have to fill in the answers to others.

Use your answers to the strategic thinking questions to select the correct answer, just as you will on Test Day.

Strategic Thinking
Step 1: Read actively
The passage below is partially mapped. Read the passage and the first part of the Passage Map. Then complete the Passage Map on your own. Remember to focus on the central ideas of each paragraph as well as the central idea of the overall passage. Use your Passage Map as a reference when you're answering questions.

Questions 4–6 are based on the following passage.

Paleontology is the study of life from prehistoric or geological times through the use of fossils. The following is adapted from a magazine article written by a paleontologist for a general interest magazine.

¶1: description of sedimentary = water made

Of the thousands of different kinds of rocks on Earth's surface, the sedimentary, or "water-made,"
rocks hold the most information for paleontologists
Line and other fossil collectors because water plays such
(5) an important role in the making of fossils. Because water-made rocks are common and fossils are easy to find and extract in many locations, many people overlook these fascinating objects. This is quite a shame because fossils can act as windows into the
(10) past for the informed observer.

¶2: types of sedimentary rocks

Sandstone, limestone, and shale are three of the most common water-made rocks, and they all can play a role in fossil creation. Shale is composed of mud—often distinct layers that have dried
(15) together—and is usually formed by erosion from landmasses. By contrast, sandstone and limestone often come from the ocean bottom. Sandstone is made up of grains of sand that, with the help of water, have adhered to one another over time, often

(20) trapping and fossilizing simple sea creatures and plants in the process. Limestone is a more complex category. Sometimes, the lime that occurs naturally in water settles to the bottom of a body of water and hardens into rock. Of more interest to fossil
(25) hunters is the limestone that forms when the shells of water animals, like crab or shrimp, pile up on the bottom of a body of water and eventually become a layer of stone. Limestone formed through such accretion is actually a composite of
(30) myriad fossilized shells.

Unlike the slow but inevitable creation of fossilized limestone on the ocean floor, the creation of fossils in shale requires a rather incredible sequence of circumstances. Consider the fossilized
(35) footprint of a dinosaur. It starts when a dinosaur steps in semisoft mud. In mud that is too soft, the footprint will simply disappear as the mud levels out, while mud that is too dry will not take a print at all. Under the right circumstances, however,
(40) the print will be captured in the drying dirt when the sun comes out. In the meantime, the print can easily be ruined or obscured by the tracks of other

animals or even the delicate touch of a fallen leaf or branch. If the print somehow survives these dan-
(45) gers, a reasonably dry environment will eventually harden the mud to form rock. Incredibly, many such fragile offerings have been produced through this process and found by paleontologists.

Fossils in any form of sedimentary rock act
(50) as a vital source of information about animals, insects, and plants from long ago. Many parts of Earth's surface are dominated by metamorphic or volcanic rocks rather than sedimentary rocks, and so have a dearth of fossils. Such places, blank slates
(55) to the paleontologist, serve to remind us of the gift of the water-made rock and our good fortune in having so much of it on our planet.

Don't get distracted by less important details. While there is a lot going on in this passage, your additions to the Passage Map should note the rocks' roles in fossil creation as well as the definitions of unfamiliar terms such as "sedimentary rocks." If you're stuck, review the Suggested Passage Map Notes in the Answers and Explanations for this chapter on page 589.

Questions	Strategic Thinking
4. Throughout the passage, the author advocates that A) fossil collecting is an ideal hobby suitable for many people. B) fossils found in limestone and shale are more useful to paleontologists than those found in sandstone. C) few people are qualified to understand the story told by Earth's record. D) knowledge about Earth's geological history is important.	**Step 2: Examine the question stem** *What kind of question is this?* A Global question *How do you know?* "Throughout the passage" and no line numbers **Step 3: Predict and answer** *What is the central idea of the passage?* Fossils are very helpful in understanding Earth. *Which answer choice matches this?* _____

Questions	Strategic Thinking
5. The author notes in lines 21–22 that limestone "is a more complex category" because A) it is formed in both landmasses and on the ocean floor. B) fossils formed in limestone require a very particular process. C) many of its forms are of little interest to paleontologists. D) it can be formed through a variety of processes.	**Step 2: Examine the question stem** *What kind of question is this?* A Rhetoric question *How do you know?* The line reference and quotation **Step 3: Predict and answer** *Read around the cited lines. Why does the author note that "limestone is a more complex category"?* _____ _____ *Which answer choice matches this?* _____
6. Which choice provides the best evidence for the answer to the previous question? A) Lines 16–17 ("By contrast . . . bottom") B) Lines 24–28 ("Of . . . stone") C) Lines 28–30 ("Limestone . . . shells") D) Lines 49–51 ("Fossils . . . ago")	**Step 2: Examine the question stem** *What kind of question is this?* _____ _____ *How do you know?* _____ _____ **Step 3: Predict and answer** *Where did you find the answer to the previous question?* _____ *Which answer choice matches this?* _____

Now, try a test-like PSAT Reading passage on your own. Give yourself 6 minutes to read the passage and answer the questions.

Questions 7–9 are based on the following passage.

This passage, about the decline of the Norse colonies that once existed in Greenland, is from a comprehensive research report examining this anthropological mystery.

In 1721, the Norwegian missionary Hans Egede discovered that the two known Norse settlements on Greenland were completely deserted. Ever since,
Line the reasons behind the decline and eventual disap-
(5) pearance of these people have been greatly debated. Greenland, established by the charismatic outlaw Eric the Red in about 986 c.e., was a colony of Norway by 1000 c.e. complete with a church hierarchy and trading community. After several relatively
(10) prosperous centuries, the colony had fallen on hard times and was not heard from in Europe, but it wasn't until Egede's discovery that the complete downfall of the settlement was confirmed.

Throughout the nineteenth century, research-
(15) ers attributed the demise of the Norse colonies to war between the colonies and Inuit groups. This is based largely on evidence from the work *Description of Greenland*, written by Norse settler Ivar Bardarson around 1364, which describes strained
(20) relationships between the Norse settlers and the Inuits who had recently come to Greenland. However, because there is no archeological evidence of a war or a massacre, and the extensive body of Inuit oral history tells of no such event, modern
(25) scholars give little credence to these theories.

New theories about the reason for the decline of the Norse colonies are being proposed partially because the amount of information available is rapidly increasing. Advances in paleoclimatology, for ex-
(30) ample, have increased the breadth and clarity of our picture of the region. Most notably, recent analyses of the central Greenland ice core, coupled with data obtained from plant material and sea sediments, have indicated severe climate changes in the region
(35) that some are now calling a "mini ice age." Such studies point toward a particularly warm period for

Greenland that occurred between the years 800 c.e. and 1300 c.e., which was then followed—unfortunately for those inhabiting even the most temperate
(40) portions of the island—by a steady decline in overall temperatures that lasted for nearly 600 years. The rise and fall of the Norse colonies in Greenland, not surprisingly, roughly mirrors this climate-based chronology. Researchers have also found useful
(45) data in a most surprising place—fly remains. The insect, not native to the island, was brought over inadvertently on Norse ships. Flies survived in the warm and unsanitary conditions of the Norse dwellings and barns and died out when these were no
(50) longer inhabited. By carbon dating the fly remains, researchers have tracked the occupation of the settlements and confirmed that the human population began to decline around 1350 c.e.

Changing economic conditions likely also
(55) conspired against the settlers. The colonies had founded a moderately successful trading economy based on exporting whale ivory, especially important given their need for the imported wood and iron that were in short supply on the island.
(60) Unfortunately, inexpensive and plentiful Asian and African elephant ivory flooded the European market during the fourteenth century, destroying Greenland's standing in the European economy. At the same time, the trading fleet of the Ger-
(65) man Hanseatic League supplanted the previously dominant Norwegian shipping fleets. Because the German merchants had little interest in the Norse colonists, Greenland soon found itself visited by fewer and fewer ships each year until its inhabitants
(70) were completely isolated by 1480 c.e.

Cultural and sociological factors may have also contributed to the demise of the Norse settlements. The Inuit tribes, while recent immigrants to Greenland, had come from nearby areas to the west and
(75) had time-tested strategies to cope with the severe

environment. The Norse settlers, however, seem to have viewed themselves as fundamentally European and did not adopt Inuit techniques. Inuit apparel, for example, was far more appropriate for the cold, (80) damp environment; the remains from even the last surviving Norse settlements indicate a costume that was undeniably European in design. Likewise, the Norse settlers failed to adopt Inuit hunting techniques and tools, such as the toggle harpoon, which (85) made it possible to capture calorie-rich seal meat. Instead, the Norse relied on the farming styles that had been so successful for their European ancestors, albeit in a radically different climate. It seems likely that this stubborn cultural inflexibility (90) prevented the Norse civilization in Greenland from adapting to increasingly severe environmental and economic conditions.

7. The main purpose of the passage is to

   A) explain possible theories explaining a historical event.

   B) refute a commonly held belief about a group of people.

   C) chronicle the conflict between immigrant settlers and a country's indigenous people.

   D) analyze the motivations behind a number of conflicting explanations.

8. The author implies that, during the period in which the Norse settlements were initially founded, the climate in the region was

   A) uncharacteristically mild.

   B) typically inhospitable.

   C) unusually harsh.

   D) increasingly cold.

9. Which choice provides the best evidence for the answer to the previous question?

   A) Lines 31–34 ("Most notably . . . region")

   B) Lines 35–38 ("Such studies . . . 1300 c.e.")

   C) Lines 38–41 ("which was . . . 600 years")

   D) Lines 41–44 ("The rise . . . chronology")

Answers and Explanations for this chapter begin on page 589.

ON YOUR OWN

The following questions provide an opportunity to practice the concepts and strategic thinking covered in this chapter. While many of the questions pertain to Citing Textual Evidence and Global questions, some touch on other concepts tested on the Reading Test to ensure that your practice is test-like, with a variety of question types per passage.

Questions 1–9 are based on the following passage.

In the following excerpt from a novella, Rosemary, an elderly woman, reminisces about her childhood as she waits for her grandson to wake up.

Rosemary sat at her kitchen table, working a crossword puzzle. Crosswords were nice; they filled the time, and kept the mind active. She needed just
Line one word to complete this morning's puzzle; the
(5) clue was "a Swiss river," and the first of its three letters was "A." Unfortunately, Rosemary had no idea what the name of the river was, and could not look it up. Her atlas was on her desk, and the desk was in the guest room, currently being occupied by her
(10) grandson Victor. Looking up over the tops of her bifocals, Rosemary glanced at the kitchen clock: It was almost 10 a.m. *Land sakes!* Did the boy intend to sleep all day? She noticed that the arthritis in her wrist was throbbing, and put down her pen. At 87
(15) years of age, she was glad she could still write at all. She had decided long ago that growing old was like slowly turning to stone; you couldn't take anything for granted. She stood up slowly, painfully, and started walking to the guest room.
(20) The trip, though only a distance of about 25 feet, seemed to take a long while. Late in her ninth decade now, Rosemary often experienced an expanded sense of time, with present and past tense intermingling in her mind. One minute she
(25) was padding in her slippers across the living room carpet, the next she was back on the farm where she'd grown up, a sturdy little girl treading the path behind the barn just before dawn. In her mind's eye, she could still pick her way among the stones in the
(30) darkness, more than 70 years later. . . . Rosemary arrived at the door to the guest room. It stood slightly ajar, and she peered through the opening. Victor lay sleeping on his side, his arms bent, his

expression slightly pained. *Get up, lazy bones,*
(35) she wanted to say. Even in childhood, Rosemary had never slept past 4 a.m.; there were too many chores to do. How different things were for Victor's generation! Her youngest grandson behaved as if he had never done a chore in his life. Twenty-one
(40) years old, he had driven down to Florida to visit Rosemary in his shiny new car, a gift from his doting parents. Victor would finish college soon, and his future appeared bright—if he ever got out of bed, that is.
(45) Something Victor had said last night over dinner had disturbed her. Now what was it? Oh yes; he had been talking about one of his college courses—a "gut," he had called it. When she had asked him to explain the term, Victor had said it was a course
(50) that you took simply because it was easy to pass. Rosemary, who had not even had a high school education, found the term repellent. If she had been allowed to continue her studies, she would never have taken a "gut." . . . The memory flooded back
(55) then, still painful as an open wound all these years later. It was the first day of high school. She had graduated from grammar school the previous year, but her father had forbidden her to go on to high school that fall, saying she was needed on the farm.
(60) After much tearful pleading, she had gotten him to promise that next year, she could start high school. She had endured a whole year of chores instead of books, with animals and rough farmhands for company instead of people her own age. Now, at
(65) last, the glorious day was at hand. She had put on her best dress (she owned two), her heart racing in anticipation.

But her father was waiting for her as she came downstairs.

(70)   "Where do you think you're going?" he asked.

"To high school, Papa."

"No you're not. Take that thing off and get back to work."

"But Papa, you promised!"

(75)   "*Do as I say!*" he thundered.

There was no arguing with Papa when he spoke that way. Tearfully, she had trudged upstairs to change clothes. Rosemary still wondered what her life would have been like if her father had not

(80) been waiting at the bottom of the stairs that day, or if somehow she had found the strength to defy him. . . .

Suddenly, Victor stirred, without waking, and mumbled something unintelligible. Jarred from her

(85) reverie, Rosemary stared at Victor. She wondered if he were having a nightmare.

1. Rosemary's attitude toward the physical afflictions of old age can best be described as one of

   A) acceptance.

   B) sadness.

   C) resentment.

   D) anxiety.

2. Rosemary's walk to the guest room in lines 20–28 reveals that she

   A) feels nostalgia for her family.

   B) is anxious about Victor.

   C) is determined to conquer her ailments.

   D) has an elastic perception of time.

3. Rosemary's memory of the day she finally prepared to start high school indicates that she had

   A) anticipated her father's command to stay home.

   B) hesitated over her choice of clothes.

   C) done especially well in grammar school.

   D) strongly desired to continue her education.

4. Which choice provides the best evidence for the answer to the previous question?

   A) Lines 10–13 ("Looking up . . . day")

   B) Lines 48–52 ("When she . . . repellent")

   C) Lines 60–61 ("After much . . . high school")

   D) Lines 83–86 ("Suddenly . . . nightmare")

5. The author includes Rosemary's thoughts regarding her grandson in lines 38–44 ("Her youngest . . . that is") in order to

   A) emphasize Rosemary's dislike of her grandson.

   B) demonstrate that Rosemary's grandson does not appreciate how fortunate he is.

   C) set up a juxtaposition between Rosemary's grandson's opportunities and Rosemary's own struggles.

   D) explain why Rosemary is waiting for him to get out of bed.

6. Which choice provides the best evidence for the answer to the previous question?

   A) Lines 1–3 ("Rosemary sat . . . active")

   B) Lines 34–38 ("*Get up* . . . generation")

   C) Lines 52–54 ("If . . . 'gut'")

   D) Lines 65–67 ("She had . . . anticipation")

7. As used in line 27, "sturdy" most nearly means

   A) stoic.

   B) physically strong.

   C) capable.

   D) flighty.

8. "If he ever got out of bed" in lines 43–44 suggests that Rosemary thinks Victor

   A) lacks a sense of humor.

   B) is ashamed of what he said last night.

   C) is promising but undisciplined.

   D) works himself to exhaustion.

9. The passage as a whole is most concerned with

   A) Rosemary's affectionate concern for Victor.

   B) Rosemary's struggle to suppress painful memories.

   C) the abusive treatment Rosemary suffered at the hands of her father.

   D) the interplay in Rosemary's mind between past and present.

CHAPTER 11

Connections and Vocab-in-Context Questions

CHAPTER OBJECTIVES

By the end of this chapter, you will be able to:

1. Identify and answer Connections questions that ask about explicit cause-and-effect, compare-and-contrast, and sequenced relationships in a passage

2. Identify and answer Connections questions that ask about implicit cause-and-effect, compare-and-contrast, and sequenced relationships in a passage

3. Interpret words and phrases in context to answer test-like questions

SMARTPOINTS

Point Value	SmartPoint Category
10 Points	Connections
60 Points	Vocab-in-Context

CONNECTIONS QUESTIONS

Before we jump into the specifics about inferring connections—explicit and implicit—let's look at different kinds of connections that can exist in a PSAT Reading passage.

Connections questions ask about how two events, characters, or ideas are related. The three most common connection types are:

1. **Cause-and-Effect** connections require you to identify an action or condition that brings about a predictable result. You can identify cause-and-effect relationships by the key words *caused by*, *results in*, *because*, and *therefore*.

2. **Compare-and-Contrast** connections highlight the similarities or differences between two items. Common compare-and-contrast key words are *similar*, *different*, *despite*, and *like*.

3. **Sequential** connections describe the chronology, or order, in which the items are arranged or occur. Key words include *first*, *second*, *following*, and *after*.

EXPLICIT CONNECTIONS QUESTIONS

Some Connections questions will ask about explicit information; the question stem will provide one part of the relationship and ask you to find the other part. In an Explicit Connections question, the wording of the correct answer will be very similar to the wording of the passage.

> ✔ **Remember**
>
> Don't forget Step 2 of the Kaplan Method for Reading Comprehension: Examine the question stem.

IMPLICIT CONNECTIONS QUESTIONS

Questions about implicit connections, like those about explicit connections, ask you to identify how items are related. However, unlike Explicit Connections questions, Implicit Connections questions require you to find a relationship that may not be directly stated in the passage.

When answering Implicit Connections questions, describe the relationship being tested in your own words by using key words such as *because*, *although*, and *in order to*.

> ✔ **Expert Tip**
>
> Eliminating answer choices that are clearly incorrect will help you answer even the toughest Implicit Connections questions correctly.

Prepare

Reading & Writing

VOCAB-IN-CONTEXT QUESTIONS

Vocab-in-Context questions require you to deduce the meaning of a word or phrase by using the context in which the word or phrase appears. You can recognize Vocab-in-Context questions because the wording of the question stem is often like this: "As used in line 7, 'clairvoyant' most nearly means . . . "

> ✔ **Expert Tip**
>
> Some Vocab-in-Context questions ask about infrequently used words that you don't know or that may not have a common meaning. Approach these questions exactly the same way you would any other Vocab-in-Context question—by using the Kaplan Strategy.

Kaplan's Strategy for Vocab-in-Context questions relies heavily on Step 3 of the Kaplan Method for Reading Comprehension: Predict and answer.

To answer Vocab-in-Context questions efficiently and correctly, employ the following Kaplan Strategy:

- Pretend the word is a blank in the sentence
- Predict what word could be substituted for the blank
- Select the answer choice that best matches your prediction

> ✔ **Real-World Application**
>
> You can use the Kaplan Strategy for Vocab-in-Context questions outside of the test preparation context. It works for texts you read for school and in your free time.

Let's look at the following example of a test-like passage and question set. After the mapped passage, the left column contains questions similar to those you'll see on the PSAT Reading Test on Test Day. The column on the right features the strategic thinking test experts employ when approaching the passage and questions presented. Pay attention to how test experts vary the approach to answer different question types.

Strategic Thinking

Step 1: Read actively

Read the passage and the notes provided. Remember, a well-crafted Passage Map should summarize the central idea of each paragraph, as well as important topics or themes. Use your Passage Map to help you answer each question.

Questions 1–3 are based on the following passage.

The following excerpt is from a speech delivered in 1873 by Susan B. Anthony, a leader in the women's rights movement of the nineteenth century.

Friends and fellow-citizens: I stand before you tonight under indictment for the alleged crime of having voted at the last Presidential election, with-
Line out having a lawful right to vote. It shall be my work
(5) this evening to prove to you that in thus voting, I not only committed no crime, but, instead, simply exercised my citizen's rights, guaranteed to me and all United States citizens by the National Constitution, beyond the power of any State to deny.
(10) The preamble of the Federal Constitution says: "We, the people of the United States, in order to form a more perfect union, establish justice, insure domestic tranquillity, provide for the common defense, promote the general welfare, and secure
(15) the blessings of liberty to ourselves and our posterity, do ordain and establish this Constitution for the United States of America."

It was we, the people; not we, the white male citizens; nor yet we, the male citizens; but we, the
(20) whole people, who formed the Union. And we formed it, not to give the blessings of liberty, but to secure them; not to the half of ourselves and the half of our posterity, but to the whole people—women as well as men. And it is a downright
(25) mockery to talk to women of their enjoyment of the blessings of liberty while they are denied the use of the only means of securing them provided by this democratic-republican government—the ballot.

For any State to make sex a qualification that
(30) must ever result in the disfranchisement* of one entire half of the people is a violation of the supreme law of the land. By it the blessings of liberty

are forever withheld from women and their female posterity. To them this government had no just
(35) powers derived from the consent of the governed. To them this government is not a democracy. It is not a republic. It is an odious aristocracy; a hateful oligarchy of sex; this oligarchy of sex, which makes father, brothers, husband, sons, the oligarchs over
(40) the mother and sisters, the wife and daughters of every household—which ordains all men sovereigns, all women subjects, carries dissension, discord and rebellion into every home of the nation. Webster, Worcester and Bouvier all define a citizen
(45) to be a person in the United States, entitled to vote and hold office.

The one question left to be settled now is: Are women persons? And I hardly believe any of our opponents will have the hardihood to say they are
(50) not. Being persons, then, women are citizens; and no State has a right to make any law, or to enforce any old law, that shall abridge their privileges or immunities. Hence, every discrimination against women in the constitutions and laws of the several
(55) States is today null and void, precisely as is every one against African Americans.

disfranchisement: to deprive of the right to vote

Margin notes:

¶1: voting isn't a crime

¶2: Const. guarantees right

¶3: "we the people" includes women

¶4: should be unlawful to prevent women from voting

¶5: women are citizens

Questions	Strategic Thinking
1. In line 7, "exercised" most nearly means A) used. B) practiced. C) angered. D) trained.	**Step 2: Examine the question stem** *What kind of question is this?* A Vocab-in-Context question *How do you know?* The question uses the phrase "most nearly means." **Step 3: Predict and answer** *Pretend "exercised" is blank in the sentence from the passage. What word or phrase can you substitute for the blank?* Acted within *Which answer choice matches your prediction?* Choice (A)
2. The author suggests that without the lawful right to vote, women A) can still hold elected office. B) cannot be considered citizens. C) can still receive the blessings of liberty. D) cannot consent to be governed.	**Step 2: Examine the question stem** *What kind of question is this?* An Implicit Connections question *How do you know?* By using the word "suggests," the question stem describes a "cause," so the correct answer must describe an implied effect. **Step 3: Predict and answer** *Which paragraph discusses the results of disfranchisement?* Paragraph 4 *What is the cause of women not being able to vote, according to the passage?* Government has no "just powers derived from the consent . . ." (lines 34–35) *Which choice best matches this?* Choice (D)

Questions	Strategic Thinking
3. Based on the passage, which of the following is necessary to secure the blessings of liberty? A) A republic B) The ballot C) A constitution D) The people	**Step 2: Examine the question stem** *What kind of question is this?* An Explicit Connections question *How do you know?* Because the question stem is asking for a cause "based on the passage," the correct answer must describe a stated cause. **Step 3: Predict and answer** *Where in the passage does the author discuss this relationship?* The last sentence of the third paragraph *What question describes this relationship?* What has to happen to secure liberty? *Which choice best matches this?* Choice (B)

Reading & Writing

You have seen the ways in which the PSAT tests you on Connections and Vocab-in-Context questions in Reading passages and the way a PSAT expert approaches these types of questions.

You will use the Kaplan Method for Reading Comprehension to complete this section. Part of the test-like passage has been mapped already. Your first step is to complete the Passage Map. Then you will continue to use the Kaplan Method for Reading Comprehension and the strategies discussed in this chapter to answer the questions. Strategic thinking questions have been included to guide you—some of the answers have been filled in, but you will have to fill in the answers to others.

Use your answers to the strategic thinking questions to select the correct answer, just as you will on Test Day.

Strategic Thinking
Step 1: Read actively
The passage below is partially mapped. Read the passage and the first part of the Passage Map. Then complete the Passage Map on your own. Remember to focus on the central ideas of each paragraph as well as the central idea of the overall passage. Use your Passage Map as a reference when you're answering questions.

Questions 4–6 are based on the following passage.

James Weldon Johnson was a poet, diplomat, composer, and historian of African American culture who wrote around the turn of the twentieth century. In this narrative passage, Johnson recalls his first experience of hearing rag-time jazz.

When I had somewhat collected my senses, I realized that in a large back room into which the main room opened, there was a young fellow sing-
Line ing a song, accompanied on the piano by a short,
(5) thickset young man. After each verse, he did some dance steps, which brought forth great applause and a shower of small coins at his feet. After the singer had responded to a rousing encore, the stout man at the piano began to run his fingers up and down the
(10) keyboard. This he did in a manner which indicated that he was a master of a good deal of technique. Then he began to play; and such playing! I stopped talking to listen. It was music of a kind I had never heard before. It was music that demanded physi-
(15) cal response, patting of the feet, drumming of the fingers, or nodding of the head in time with the beat. The dissonant harmonies, the audacious

¶1: new kind of music

resolutions, often consisting of an abrupt jump from one key to another, the intricate rhythms
(20) in which the accents fell in the most unexpected places, but in which the beat was never lost, produced a most curious effect. . . .

This was rag-time music, then a novelty in New York, and just growing to be a rage, which has not
(25) yet subsided. It was originated in the questionable resorts about Memphis and St. Louis by black piano players who knew no more of the theory of music than they did of the theory of the universe, but were guided by natural musical instinct and
(30) talent. It made its way to Chicago, where it was popular some time before it reached New York. These players often improvised simple and, at times, vulgar words to fit the melodies. This was the beginning of the rag-time song. . . .

(35) American musicians, instead of investigating rag-time, attempt to ignore it, or dismiss it with a contemptuous word. But that has always been the course of scholasticism in every branch of art. Whatever new thing the *people* like is

¶2: ragtime history

¶3: American critics dislike ragtime, but the public and Europeans like it

(40) pooh-poohed; whatever is *popular* is spoken of
as not worth the while. The fact is, nothing great
or enduring, especially in music, has ever sprung
full-fledged and unprecedented from the brain of
any master; the best that he gives to the world he
(45) gathers from the hearts of the people, and runs
it through the alembic* of his genius. In spite of
the bans which musicians and music teachers
have placed upon it, the people still demand and
enjoy rag-time. One thing cannot be denied; it is
(50) music which possesses at least one strong element
of greatness: it appeals universally; not only the
American, but the English, the French, and even
the German people find delight in it. In fact, there
is not a corner of the civilized world in which it is
(55) not known, and this proves its originality; for if it
were an imitation, the people of Europe, anyhow,
would not have found it a novelty. . . .

I became so interested in both the music and
the player that I left the table where I was sitting,
(60) and made my way through the hall into the back
room, where I could see as well as hear. I talked to

93, cont.: ragtime popular all over

the piano player between the musical numbers
and found out that he was just a natural musician,
never having taken a lesson in his life. Not only
(65) could he play almost anything he heard, but he
could accompany singers in songs he had never
heard. He had, by ear alone, composed some
pieces, several of which he played over for me;
each of them was properly proportioned and
(70) balanced. I began to wonder what this man with
such a lavish natural endowment would have done
had he been trained. Perhaps he wouldn't have
done anything at all; he might have become, at
best, a mediocre imitator of the great masters in
(75) what they have already done to a finish, or one of
the modern innovators who strive after originality
by seeing how cleverly they can dodge about
through the rules of harmony and at the same
time avoid melody. It is certain that he would not
(80) have been so delightful as he was in rag-time.

alembic: scientific apparatus used in the process
of distillation

Don't get distracted by less important details. While there is a lot going on in this passage, your
additions to the Passage Map should show that the author considers ragtime musicians without
training to be more delightful. If you're stuck, review the Suggested Passage Map Notes in the
Answers and Explanations for this chapter on page 592.

Questions	Strategic Thinking
4. In line 19, "intricate" most nearly means A) innate. B) elaborate. C) complex. D) ornate.	**Step 2: Examine the question stem** *What kind of question is this?* A Vocab-in-Context question *How do you know?* The question uses the phrase "most nearly means." **Step 3: Predict and answer** *Pretend "intricate" is blank in the sentence from the passage. What word or phrase can you substitute for the blank?* Complicated *Which answer choice matches your prediction?* _____
5. According to the author, the "most curious effect" (lines 21–22) was most likely the result of A) tension between surprising and familiar elements. B) conflicts between scholastic and popular music. C) differences between natural and trained techniques. D) contrast between simple and lavish melodies.	**Step 2: Examine the question stem** *What kind of question is this?* A Connections question about an implicit relationship *How do you know?* The words "most likely" in the question stem indicate that this is a Connections question. The question stem describes an effect and asks for the cause. **Step 3: Predict and answer** *What was the cause of the "curious effect"?* _____ *Which answer choice best matches this?* _____

Questions	Strategic Thinking

6. Based on the passage, which choice best describes the reason for the author's opinion that the piano player was "a natural musician" (line 63)?
 	
  A) He might have become a mediocre imitator.
 	
  B) He could play and compose by ear.
 	
  C) He cleverly dodged the rules of harmony.
 	
  D) He was a master of technique.
	Step 2: Examine the question stem
	
	What kind of question is this? An Inference question asking about an explicit relationship
	
	How do you know? _____
	
	_____
	
	_____
	
	Step 3: Predict and answer
	
	Why does the author think the piano player was a "natural musician"?
	
	_____
	
	Which answer choice best matches this?
	_____

Now, try a test-like PSAT Reading passage on your own. Give yourself 6 minutes to read the passage and answer the questions.

Questions 7–10 are based on the following passage.

This passage, about infant language acquisition, was adapted from a research paper that explores early childhood development.

For an infant just beginning to interact with the surrounding world, it is imperative that he quickly become proficient in his native language.
Line While developing a vocabulary and the ability to
(5) communicate using it are obviously important steps in this process, an infant must first be able to learn from the various streams of audible communication around him. To that end, during the course of even the first few months of development, an
(10) infant will begin to absorb the rhythmic patterns and sequences of sounds that characterize his language, and will begin to differentiate between the meanings of various pitch and stress changes.

However, it is important to recognize that such
(15) learning does not take place in a vacuum. Infants must confront these language acquisition challenges in an environment where, quite frequently, several streams of communication or noise are occurring simultaneously. In other words, infants must not
(20) only learn how to segment individual speech streams into their component words, but they must also be able to distinguish between concurrent streams of sound.

Consider, for example, an infant being spoken
(25) to by his mother. Before he can learn from the nuances of his mother's speech, he must first separate that speech from the sounds of the dishwasher, the family dog, the bus stopping on the street outside, and, quite possibly, background
(30) noise in the form of speech: a newscaster on the television down the hall or siblings playing in an adjacent room.

How exactly do infants wade through such a murky conglomeration of audible stimuli? While
(35) most infants are capable of separating out two different voices despite the presence of additional, competing streams of sound, this capability is predicated upon several specific conditions.

First, infants are better able to learn from a
(40) particular speech stream when that voice is louder than any of the competing streams of background speech; when two voices are of equal amplitude, infants typically demonstrate little preference for one stream over the other. Most likely, equally loud
(45) competing voice streams, for the infant, become combined into a single stream that necessarily contains unfamiliar patterns and sounds that can quite easily induce confusion. Secondly, an infant is more likely to attend to a particular voice stream
(50) if it is perceived as more familiar than another stream. When an infant, for example, is presented with a voice stream spoken by his mother and a background stream delivered by an unfamiliar voice, usually he can easily separate out her voice
(55) from the distraction of the background stream. By using these simple yet important cues, an infant can become quite adept at concentrating on a single stream of communication and, therefore, is capable of quickly learning the invaluable characteristics
(60) and rules of his native language.

7. According to the information in paragraph 5, whether an infant is able to distinguish a certain voice depends partially on whether that voice is

   A) noncompetitive.

   B) in a vacuum.

   C) nuanced.

   D) familiar.

8. As used in line 38, "predicated upon" most nearly means

   A) predicted by.

   B) expressed by.

   C) replaced by.

   D) influenced by.

9. Based on the passage, which choice best describes the relationship between language acquisition and distinct speech streams?

   A) Acquiring language helps an infant to distinguish speech streams.

   B) Acquiring language requires an infant to disregard speech streams.

   C) Distinguishing speech streams improves an infant's capacity for language acquisition.

   D) Distinguishing speech streams reduces an infant's capacity for language acquisition.

10. As used in line 49, "attend to" most nearly means

   A) care for.

   B) participate in.

   C) listen to.

   D) cope with.

Answers and Explanations for this chapter begin on page 592.

ON YOUR OWN

The following questions provide an opportunity to practice the concepts and strategic thinking covered in this chapter. While many of the questions pertain to Connections and Vocab-in-Context questions, some touch on other concepts tested on the Reading Test to ensure that your practice is test-like, with a variety of question types per passage.

Questions 1–9 are based on the following passage.

This passage is an excerpt adapted from the novel *You Can't Go Home Again* by Thomas Wolfe. (©1934, 1937, 1938, 1939, 1940 by Maxwell Perkins as Executor of the Estate of Thomas Wolfe. Reprinted by permission of HarperCollins Publishers.)

It was late afternoon and the shadows were slanting swiftly eastward when George Webber came to his senses somewhere in the wilds of the
Line upper Bronx. . . . All he could remember was that
(5) suddenly he felt hungry and stopped and looked about him and realized where he was. His dazed look gave way to one of amazement and incredulity, and his mouth began to stretch into a broad grin. In his hand he still held the rectangular slip of crisp
(10) yellow paper. . . .

It was a check for five hundred dollars. His book had been accepted, and this was an advance against his royalties.

So he was happier than he had ever been in all
(15) his life. Fame, at last, was knocking at his door and wooing him with her sweet blandishments. . . . The next weeks and months were filled with the excitement of the impending event. The book would not be published till the fall, but meanwhile there was
(20) much work to do. Foxhall Edwards had made some suggestions for cutting and revising the manuscript, and, although George at first objected, he surprised himself in the end by agreeing with Edwards. . . .

George had called his novel *Home to Our*
(25) *Mountains*, and in it he had packed everything he knew about his home town in Old Catawba. . . . He had distilled every line of it out of his own experience of life. And, now that the issue was decided, he sometimes trembled when he thought that it would
(30) only be a matter of months before the whole world knew what he had written. He loathed the thought of giving pain to anyone, and that he might do so

had never occurred to him until now. . . . Of course it was fiction, but it was made as all honest fiction
(35) must be, from the stuff of human life. Some people might recognize themselves and be offended, and then what would he do? Would he have to go around in smoked glasses and false whiskers? He comforted himself with the hope that his charac-
(40) terizations were not so true as, in another mood, he liked to think they were, and he thought that perhaps no one would notice anything.

Rodney's Magazine, too, had become interested in the young author and was going to publish a
(45) story, a chapter from the book. . . . This news added immensely to his excitement. He was eager to see his name in print, and in the happy interval of expectancy he felt like a kind of universal Don Juan, for he literally loved everybody—his fellow instruc-
(50) tors at the school, his drab students, the little shop-keepers in all the stores, even the nameless hordes that thronged the streets. *Rodney's,* of course, was the greatest and finest publishing house in all the world, and Foxhall Edwards was the greatest editor
(55) and the finest man that ever was. George had liked him instinctively from the first, and now, like an old and intimate friend, he was calling him Fox. George knew that Fox believed in him, and the editor's faith and confidence . . . restored his self-respect and
(60) charged him with energy for new work.

Already his next novel was begun and was beginning to take shape within him. . . . He dreaded the prospect of buckling down in earnest to write it, for he knew the agony of it. . . . While the fury of
(65) creation was upon him, it meant sixty cigarettes a day, twenty cups of coffee, meals snatched anyhow and anywhere and at whatever time of day or night he happened to remember he was hungry. It meant

sleeplessness, and miles of walking to bring on the
(70) physical fatigue without which he could not sleep, then
nightmares, nerves, and exhaustion in the morning. As
he said to Fox:

"There are better ways to write a book, but this, God
help me, is mine, and you'll have to learn to put up with
(75) it."

When *Rodney's Magazine* came out with the story,
George fully expected convulsions of the earth, falling
meteors, suspension of traffic in the streets, and a general strike. But nothing happened. A few of his friends
(80) mentioned it, but that was all. For several days he felt
let down, but then his common sense reassured him
that people couldn't really tell much about a new author
from a short piece in a magazine. The book would show
them who he was and what he could do. . . . He could
(85) afford to wait a little longer for the fame which he was
certain would soon be his.

1. Through describing George Webber's
   experiences, what central idea does the author
   establish about life as a writer?

   A) Like most professions, work as a writer
      eventually settles into predictable
      routine that usually requires hardly any
      exhaustive effort to maintain.

   B) A young author's big break—such as
      getting one's first book published—is a
      complex experience that can have the
      writer at the mercy of the full range of
      human emotions.

   C) A young author's big break is usually
      the final hurdle one must overcome to
      bask in the fame and money that being a
      successful author brings.

   D) A traditional marker of success such as
      getting one's first book published does
      not always lead to a long career as an au-
      thor; in fact, many young authors never
      again publish.

2. Throughout the passage, George Webber is
   described as

   A) a young author who is hungry for the
      fame, recognition, and wealth that a
      career as a fiction writer could potentially
      provide.

   B) a young author who is wary of the
      corrupting influences of fame, recognition,
      and wealth.

   C) a seasoned writer who has grown tired of
      the literary and publishing worlds.

   D) a nonfiction author who chronicles life in
      small-town America.

3. George's new book, *Home to Our Mountains*,
   is described as

   A) a memoir about George's time growing
      up in his hometown, Old Catawba.

   B) a novel that was inspired by George's
      time growing up in his hometown, Old
      Catawba.

   C) a novel based on life in a small town
      George once visited.

   D) set in a small town, most of the details of
      which were invented by George to suit
      the purposes of his story.

4. Which choice provides the best evidence for
   the answer to the previous question?

   A) Lines 11–13 ("His . . . royalties")

   B) Lines 18–23 ("The . . . Edwards")

   C) Lines 24–28 ("George . . . life")

   D) Lines 76–80 ("When . . . all")

5. As used in line 7, "incredulity" most nearly
   means

   A) disbelief.

   B) repudiation.

   C) conviction.

   D) fatigue.

6. Based on lines 28–42 ("And, now . . . notice anything"), what can the reader infer about the details of George's soon-to-be-released novel?

    A) George's experiences in Old Catawba informed his writing only sparingly, providing inspiration for bland details such as time and place.

    B) George based most of the novel's contents on experiences he had after he left his hometown, even though the novel is set in a town like Old Catawba.

    C) Most of the novel is based on real events, and the characters on real people, from the time of George's childhood in Old Catawba.

    D) George looked beyond Old Catawba when he sought inspiration for the novel.

7. When writing a new work, George

    A) has a different creative process for every work he creates.

    B) has a creative process that is arduous and difficult, but he relishes the opportunity to produce something new.

    C) has learned how to control his creative periods, resulting in pleasantly predictable experiences when he writes new work.

    D) has a creative process that takes a heavy toll on his mind and body and is not necessarily something he looks forward to.

8. Which choice provides the best evidence for the answer to the previous question?

    A) Lines 1–6 ("It . . . was")

    B) Lines 61–71 ("Already . . . morning")

    C) Lines 76–79 ("When . . . strike")

    D) Lines 83–86 ("The . . . his")

9. As used in line 64, "fury" most nearly means

    A) indignation.

    B) agitation.

    C) serenity.

    D) animosity.

CHAPTER 12

Rhetoric

CHAPTER OBJECTIVES

By the end of this chapter, you will be able to:

1. Determine the author's purpose and point of view in a given passage

2. Determine why the author uses a certain word or phrase in a given passage

3. Evaluate both the overall and part-to-whole text structure of a given test-like passage

4. Distinguish between claims and counterclaims and evaluate the use of evidence to support the author's reasoning

SMARTPOINTS

Point Value	SmartPoint Category
60 Points	Rhetoric

RHETORIC QUESTIONS: ANALYZING PURPOSE

Overall, rhetoric refers to the language the author uses, especially in order to persuade or influence the reader.

Some Analyzing Purpose questions ask about the purpose of the passage as a whole. Every author has a reason for writing. To identify that reason—or purpose—ask these two questions:

- Why did the author write this passage?

- What does the author want the reader to think about this topic?

Other Analyzing Purpose questions will ask you to identify the purpose of part of a passage, usually one or more paragraphs. To answer this type of question, read around the cited portion, review your Passage Map, and ask these two questions:

- What is the function of this section?

- How does this section help achieve the author's purpose?

RHETORIC QUESTIONS: ANALYZING POINT OF VIEW

The author's point of view is closely tied to the purpose of the passage. Though some authors are neutral, most authors have an opinion, or point of view. Questions that ask you to analyze point of view require you to establish the author's perspective and how that perspective affects the content and the style of the passage. That is, you need to figure out not only what the author says, but also how the author says it. Mapping the passage will help you determine the author's point of view.

As you map a passage, ask:

- Is the author's tone positive, negative, or neutral?

- Does the author want things to change or stay the same?

- Is the author addressing supporters or opponents?

RHETORIC QUESTIONS: ANALYZING WORD CHOICE

Rhetoric questions about word choice ask about how a particular word or phrase affects your understanding of the author's purpose and point of view.

Don't confuse Analyzing Word Choice questions with Vocab-in-Context questions, which ask about the meaning of a word or phrase. Analyzing Word Choice questions ask about the function of a word or phrase within the passage; that is, why did the author use this word or phrase?

To answer Analyzing Word Choice questions, ask what the function of the cited word or phrase is. Common functions of words or phrases include the following:

- Setting a mood
- Conveying an emotion
- Building to a conclusion
- Calling to action
- Stating an opinion

> ✔ **Remember**
>
> Correct answers to Analyzing Word Choice questions will always be in line with the author's overall purpose.

RHETORIC QUESTIONS: ANALYZING TEXT STRUCTURE

Some Rhetoric questions will require you to analyze the structure of the passage. The PSAT Reading Test will ask about two kinds of text structures:

1. **Overall text structure** refers to how the information within a passage is organized. Some common text structures are cause-and-effect, compare-and-contrast, sequence, problem-and-solution, and description.

2. **Part-whole relationships** describe how a particular part of the passage (e.g., a sentence, quotation, or paragraph) relates to the overall text. When asked about a part-whole relationship, make sure you determine what function the part plays in the passage.

> ✔ **Expert Tip**
>
> Include the structure of the passage in your Passage Map. Identifying the structure of the text will make it easier to understand and analyze its content.

RHETORIC QUESTIONS: ANALYZING ARGUMENTS

Other Rhetoric questions will ask you to analyze arguments within the text for both their form and content.

Questions that ask you to analyze a text's arguments vary in scope. There are three types of Analyzing Arguments questions. You may be asked to:

1. **Analyze claims and counterclaims.** A claim is not an opinion but rather the main point or thesis of a passage the author promotes. A counterclaim is the opposite of a claim—it will negate or disagree with the thesis or central idea of the passage.

2. **Assess reasoning.** The reasoning of a passage is composed of the statements offering support for claims and counterclaims. On the PSAT Reading test, you may be asked whether an author's or a character's reasoning is *sound*—that is, whether the argument is valid and the reasoning for the argument is true.

3. **Analyze evidence.** Evidence can be facts, reasons, statistics, and other information the author employs to *support* a claim or counterclaim. You will have to assess how and why this evidence is used.

Let's look at the following example of a test-like passage and question set. After the mapped passage, the left column contains questions similar to those you'll see on the Reading Test on Test Day. The column on the right features the strategic thinking test experts employ when approaching the passage and questions presented. Pay attention to how test experts vary the approach to answer different question types.

Strategic Thinking

Step 1: Read actively

Read the passage and the notes provided. Remember, a well-crafted Passage Map should summarize the central idea of each paragraph as well as important topics or themes. Use your Passage Map to help you answer each question.

Questions 1–3 are based on the following passage.

The following passage about evolutionary science was excerpted from the writings of a well-known biologist.

There is something intrinsically fascinating about the idea of evolution. What principles govern the evolution of species? And what does evolution
Line tell us about the place of *Homo sapiens* in the grand
(5) order of things? The writer George Bernard Shaw held that a mystical guiding force impels life to evolve toward eventual perfection. Modern scientists may not believe in this guiding force or in the possibility of perfection, but many would agree that
(10) life has been improving itself through evolution for billions of years. (Note that this conveniently makes *Homo sapiens*, a very recent product of evolution, one of the newest and most improved versions of life.) In the view of these scientists, constant
(15) competition among species is the engine that drives the process of evolution and propels life upward. In order to win one day's struggle and live to fight another day, a species always has to adapt, be a little faster, a little stronger, and a little smarter than its
(20) competitors and its predecessors.

¶1: original theory: species' competition = evolution

No less an eminence than Charles Darwin put forth the idea that species were in constant competition with each other. To Darwin, nature was a surface covered with thousands of sharp wedges,
(25) all packed together and jostling for the same space. Those wedges that fared best moved toward the center of the surface, improving their position by knocking other wedges away with violent blows. The standard example that textbooks give of such
(30) competitive wedging is the interaction between the brachiopods and the clams. Clams were long held to be ancient undersea competitors with brachiopods due to the fact that the two species inhabited the same ecological niche. Clams are abundant
(35) today, whereas brachiopods (dominant in ancient times) are not. Modern clams are also physiologically more complex than brachiopods are. The standard interpretation of these facts is that the clams' physiology was an evolutionary improve-
(40) ment that gave them the ability to "knock away" the brachiopods.

¶2: evolutionary improvements, ex: clams

Reading & Writing

In recent years, however, the prominent natural-ists Stephen Jay Gould and C. Brad Calloway have challenged the validity of this example as well as the
(45) model it was meant to support. Gould and Callo-way found that over most of geological time, clams and brachiopods went their separate ways. Never did the population of brachiopods dip as that of the clams rose, or vice versa. In fact, the two popula-
(50) tions often grew simultaneously, which belies the notion that they were fighting fiercely over the same narrow turf and resources. That there are so many more clams than brachiopods today seems rather to be a consequence of mass dyings that occurred
(55) in the Permian period. Whatever caused the mass dyings—some scientists theorize that either there were massive ecological or geological changes, or a comet crashed down from the heavens—clams were simply able to weather the storm much better than
(60) the brachiopods.

Out of these observations, Gould and Calloway drew a number of far-reaching conclusions. For instance, they suggested that direct competition between species was far less frequent than Darwin

¶3: G & C → clams & brach. didn't compete

(65) thought. Perhaps nature was really a very large surface on which there were very few wedges, and the wedges consequently did not bang incessantly against each other. Perhaps the problem facing these wedges was rather that the surface
(70) continually altered its shape, and they had to struggle independently to stay in a good position on the surface as it changed. In this alternate model, competition between species is not the impetus for evolutionary adaptation—changes
(75) in the environment (geological and climatic variations) are.

So where does that leave *Homo sapiens* if evolu-tion is a response to sudden, unpredictable, and sweeping changes in the environment rather than
(80) the result of a perpetual struggle? No longer are we the kings of the mountain who clawed our way to the top by advancing beyond other species. We are instead those who took to the mountains when floods began to rage below and then discovered
(85) that living high up has its definite advantages . . . so long as our mountain doesn't decide to turn into a volcano.

¶4: new theory: changes in environ. = evolution

¶5: humans must also adapt to environ.

Questions	Strategic Thinking
1. The main purpose of the second and third paragraphs is to A) question a standard theory in light of new scientific research. B) provide an example of how evolutionary science has changed its focus. C) highlight the difference between theoretical thinking and empirical data. D) argue for caution before accepting a new scientific theory.	**Step 2: Examine the question stem** *What kind of question is this?* A Rhetoric question in which you are asked to analyze the purpose of part of the passage, specifically paragraphs 2–3 *How do you know?* The question uses the phrase "main purpose of." **Step 3: Predict and answer** *Review the Passage Map for the cited paragraphs. What is the author trying to accomplish with these paragraphs?* Predict: Question Darwin's theory after Gould and Calloway's discoveries *Which is the correct answer?* Choice (A)

Questions	Strategic Thinking
2. The stance the author takes in the passage toward *Homo sapiens* is best described as A) a skeptic questioning a cherished belief. B) an advocate seeking recognition for a new idea. C) a philosopher outlining an ethical position. D) a scientist presenting evidence for a hypothesis.	**Step 2: Examine the question stem** *What kind of question is this?* A Rhetoric question in which you are asked to analyze point of view *How do you know?* The question stem asks about the author's "stance." **Step 3: Predict and answer** *Which paragraph(s) mention(s) "Homo sapiens"?* The first and last paragraphs *What does the author conclude about* Homo sapiens? Predict: Not "the kings of the mountain" anymore (line 81) *Is this positive, negative, or neutral in tone?* Negative *Which is the correct answer?* Choice (A)
3. The author's use of the phrase "No less an eminence than Charles Darwin" in line 21 is primarily meant to convey A) Darwin's age when he developed his ideas about evolution. B) the author's skepticism toward Darwin's ideas about evolution. C) Darwin's importance to the field of evolutionary science. D) the author's respect for Darwin's historical significance.	**Step 2: Examine the question stem** *What kind of question is this?* A Rhetoric question in which you are asked to analyze word choice *How do you know?* The question stem asks about the purpose of a phrase. **Step 3: Predict and answer** *Read around the cited lines. What is the author letting you know about Darwin?* Predict: He is very important in the history of evolutionary science. *Which is the correct answer?* Choice (C)

You have seen the ways in which the PSAT tests you on Rhetoric in Reading passages and the way a PSAT expert approaches these types of questions.

You will use the Kaplan Method for Reading Comprehension to complete this section. Part of the test-like passage has been mapped already. Your first step is to complete the Passage Map. Then you will continue to use the Kaplan Method for Reading Comprehension and the strategies discussed in this chapter to answer the questions. Strategic thinking questions have been included to guide you—some of the answers have been filled in, but you will have to fill in the answers to others.

Use your answers to the strategic thinking questions to select the correct answer, just as you will on Test Day.

Strategic Thinking
Step 1: Read actively The passage below is partially mapped. Read the passage and the first part of the Passage Map. Then complete the Passage Map on your own. Remember to focus on the central ideas of each paragraph as well as the central idea of the overall passage. Use your Passage Map as a reference when you're answering questions.

Questions 4–6 are based on the following passage.

This passage, about the formative years of the American media, was adapted from an essay on the relationship between newspapers and popular culture by Walter Fox.

Throughout American history, newspapers have played a crucial role in shaping our cultural life. The colonial press of the early 18th century in America,
Line although on the whole limited in circulation and
(5) dependent upon rather primitive technology, first established just how powerful newspapers could be as instruments of social change by moving the colonists to revolt against the British throne. Later, in the mid-1800s during a period known as the
(10) "penny press" era, the first newspapers designed for the "common man" came into print, constituting a journalistic revolution of sorts roughly comparable to President Andrew Jackson's political triumph for the American middle class over the 40 years of gov-
(15) ernment dominated by a more aristocratic, upper-class elite. Yet, the formative significance of these periods in the constitution of the American press aside, it was the last few decades of the nineteenth century that produced the most profound change in
(20) the relationship between the American press and its readership.

¶1: changed rel. between U.S. press & readers

Whereas before, especially during slower news times, newspapers occupied a relatively ancillary position in American life, by 1900, such publica-
(25) tions had become one of the primary determinants of public opinion. Although this transformation was undoubtedly fueled by the substantive social changes taking place throughout the nation, name-ly those of industrialization and the mass migra-
(30) tions that altered the American urban landscape, there were smaller technological breakthroughs in printing that also helped newspapers become more pervasive voices in society. In particular, by the turn of the 19th century, electronic printing
(35) presses were being used to churn out papers at pre-viously unheard of costs. Additionally, newsprint prices fell dramatically and full-color printing techniques became cheap, allowing for striking visual images to adorn even the most mundane
(40) stories. But to look at these two areas of change, one social and the other technological, as separate catalysts is to miss the point; it was their union that created a massive newspaper readership that has only grown over the past century.

¶2: some causes = indust. & urban landscape

(45) Of particular significance during this period is the fact that this readership was not only enormous, but also largely composed of immigrants and former migrant farmers and laborers who had flocked to the growing cities by the hundreds of thousands only to *(50)* hold a rather uncertain rung on the American economic ladder. This social positioning created a mass newspaper audience fervently reliant upon the relative immediacy of media reports to inform their constantly changing, unstable lives. The daily papers began *(55)* to augment impressively comprehensive worldwide news coverage with more sensational human-interest stories, a combination that proved to be particularly appealing for the new American urban culture. Thus, by the first decades of the twentieth *(60)* century, the American press was already the outspoken generator of American popular culture that it is today: a social position that would only be expanded with the advent of radio and television.

Don't get distracted by less important details. While there is a lot going on in this passage, your additions to the Passage Map should continue to note the relationship between the press and pop culture. If you're stuck, review the suggested Passage Map notes in the Answers and Explanations for this chapter on page 595.

Questions	Strategic Thinking
4. The author mentions all of the following to support his thesis EXCEPT A) increased readership. B) industrialization. C) the changing urban landscape. D) technological innovation.	**Step 2: Examine the question stem** *What kind of question is this?* A Rhetoric question in which you are asked to analyze arguments; specifically, various pieces of evidence *How do you know?* The question stem refers to the author's thesis and what he uses to support it. **Step 3: Predict and answer** *Look at your Passage Map notes, including any information you may have underlined or circled. Which answer choice(s) can you eliminate because they are mentioned to support the thesis?* Choice B is mentioned in line 29, C is referenced in line 30, and D is mentioned in line 31. *Which is the correct answer?*_____

Reading & Writing

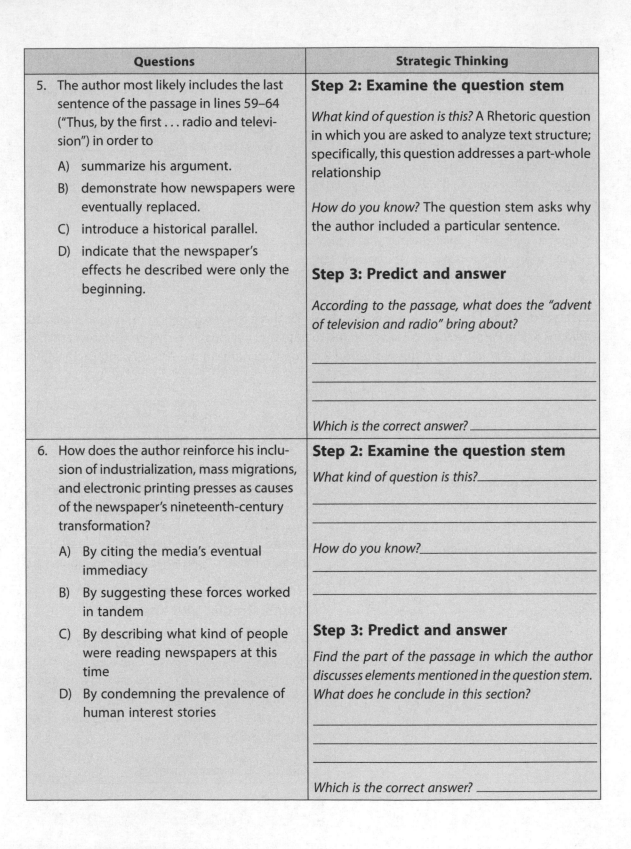

Questions	Strategic Thinking
5. The author most likely includes the last sentence of the passage in lines 59–64 ("Thus, by the first . . . radio and television") in order to A) summarize his argument. B) demonstrate how newspapers were eventually replaced. C) introduce a historical parallel. D) indicate that the newspaper's effects he described were only the beginning.	**Step 2: Examine the question stem** *What kind of question is this?* A Rhetoric question in which you are asked to analyze text structure; specifically, this question addresses a part-whole relationship *How do you know?* The question stem asks why the author included a particular sentence. **Step 3: Predict and answer** *According to the passage, what does the "advent of television and radio" bring about?* _____ _____ _____ *Which is the correct answer?* _____
6. How does the author reinforce his inclusion of industrialization, mass migrations, and electronic printing presses as causes of the newspaper's nineteenth-century transformation? A) By citing the media's eventual immediacy B) By suggesting these forces worked in tandem C) By describing what kind of people were reading newspapers at this time D) By condemning the prevalence of human interest stories	**Step 2: Examine the question stem** *What kind of question is this?* _____ _____ _____ *How do you know?* _____ _____ _____ **Step 3: Predict and answer** *Find the part of the passage in which the author discusses elements mentioned in the question stem. What does he conclude in this section?* _____ _____ _____ *Which is the correct answer?* _____

Reading & Writing

Now, try a test-like Reading passage on your own. Give yourself 6 minutes to read the passage and answer the questions.

Questions 7–9 are based on the following passage.

The following passage was written in 1992 by France Bequette, a writer who specializes in environmental issues.

The ozone layer, the fragile layer of gas surrounding our planet between 7 and 30 miles above the Earth's surface, is being rapidly depleted.
Line Seasonally occurring holes in the ozone layer have
(5) appeared over the Poles and, recently, over densely populated temperate regions of the northern hemisphere. The threat is serious because the ozone layer protects the Earth from the sun's ultraviolet radiation, which is harmful to all living organisms.

(10) Even though the layer is many miles thick, the atmosphere in it is tenuous and the total amount of ozone, compared with other atmospheric gases, is small. Ozone is highly reactive to chlorine, hydrogen, and nitrogen. Of these, chlorine is the most
(15) dangerous since it is very stable and long-lived. When chlorine compounds reach the stratosphere, they bond with and destroy ozone molecules, with subsequent repercussions for life on Earth.

In 1958, researchers began noticing seasonal
(20) variations in the ozone layer above the South Pole. Between June and October the ozone content steadily fell, followed by a sudden increase in November. These fluctuations appeared to result from the natural effects of wind and temperature.
(25) However, while the low October levels remained constant until 1979, the total ozone content over the Pole was steadily diminishing. In 1985, public awareness was finally roused by reports of a "hole" in the layer.

(30) The culprits responsible for the hole were identified as compounds known as chlorofluorocarbons, or CFCs. CFCs are compounds of chlorine and fluorine. Nonflammable, nontoxic, and noncorrosive, they have been widely used in industry since
(35) the 1950s, mostly as refrigerants and propellants and components in making plastic foam and insulation.

In 1989 CFCs represented a sizable market valued at over $1.5 billion and a labor force of 1.6 million. But with CFCs implicated in ozone depletion,
(40) the question arose as to whether we were willing to risk increases in cases of skin cancer and eye ailments, even a lowering of the human immune defense system—all effects of further loss of the ozone layer. And not only humans would suffer; so would
(45) plant life. Phytoplankton, the first link in the ocean food chain and vital to the survival of most marine species, would not be able to survive near the ocean surface, which is where these organisms grow.

In 1990, 70 countries agreed to stop produc-
(50) ing CFCs by the year 2000. In late 1991, however, scientists noticed a depletion of the ozone layer over the Arctic. In 1992, it was announced that the layer was depleting faster than expected and that it was also declining over the northern hemisphere.
(55) Scientists believe that natural events are making the problem worse. The Pinatubo volcano in the Philippines, which erupted in June 1991, released 12 million tons of damaging volcanic gases into the atmosphere.

(60) Even if the whole world agreed today to stop all production and use of CFCs, this would not solve the problem. A single chlorine molecule can destroy 10,000–100,000 molecules of ozone. Furthermore, CFCs have a lifespan of 75–400 years
(65) and they take ten years to reach the ozone layer. In other words, what we are experiencing today results from CFCs emitted ten years ago.

Researchers are working hard to find substitute products. Some are too dangerous because they are
(70) highly flammable; others may prove to be toxic and to contribute to the greenhouse effect (and to the process of global warming). Nevertheless, even if there is no denying that the atmosphere is in a state of disturbance, nobody can say that the situation
(75) will not improve, either in the short or the long term, especially if we ourselves lend a hand.

7. The author's reference to the long life of chlorine molecules in lines 14–15 is meant to show that

   A) there is more than adequate time to develop a long-term strategy against ozone loss.

   B) the long-term effects of ozone loss on human health may never be known.

   C) it is doubtful that normal levels of ozone can ever be reestablished.

   D) the positive effects of actions taken against ozone loss will be gradual.

8. In paragraph 6 (lines 49–59), the author cites the evidence of changes in the ozone layer over the Northern Hemisphere to indicate that

   A) the dangers of ozone depletion appear to be intensifying.

   B) ozone depletion is posing an immediate threat to many marine species.

   C) scientists are unsure about the ultimate effects of ozone loss on plants.

   D) CFCs are not the primary cause of ozone depletion in such areas.

9. In the final paragraph, the author tries to emphasize that

   A) researchers are unlikely to find effective substitutes for CFCs.

   B) human action can alleviate the decline of the ozone layer.

   C) people must learn to live with the damaging effects of industrial pollutants.

   D) people have more control over ozone depletion than over the greenhouse effect.

Answers and Explanations for this chapter begin on page 595.

ON YOUR OWN

The following questions provide an opportunity to practice the concepts and strategic thinking covered in this chapter. While many of the questions pertain to Rhetoric questions, some touch on other concepts tested on the Reading Test to ensure that your practice is test-like, with a variety of question types per passage.

Reading & Writing

Questions 1–10 are based on the following passage.

The following passage is adapted from a psychologist's discussion of the development of the human brain.

Although the brain comprises only 2 percent of the human body's average weight, the billions of neurons and trillions of synaptic connections that

Line are the human brain constitute a truly impressive
(5) organ. In terms of what it can do, the human brain is in some ways unable to match the brain functioning of "lower" animals; in other ways, its capabilities are quite unrivaled. Salmon, caribou, and migrating birds, for example, have navigational abilities
(10) unparalleled in our own species, and even dogs and cats have senses of hearing and smell known only, in human form, to comic book superheroes. Yet, no other animal on the planet can communicate, solve problems, or think abstractly about itself and
(15) the future as we do. While these relative strengths and weaknesses can be attributed to the unique and sophisticated structure of the human brain, neuroscientists also have traced these characteristics to the human brain's remarkable flexibility, or what
(20) researchers call plasticity.

Encased in a hard, protective skull that by the age of two is already 80 percent of its eventual adult size, the human brain has little room for size expansion even while the rest of the body, especially dur-
(25) ing adolescence, is experiencing significant changes in physical appearance. The first few years of a child's life are a time of rapid brain growth. At birth, each neuron in the cerebral cortex has an estimated 2,500 synapses; by age three, this number blossoms
(30) to 15,000 synapses per neuron. The average adult, however, has about half that number of synapses. Nevertheless, the human brain's plasticity allows for marked capacity changes because of usage, practice,

and experience throughout one's life. This idea that
(35) the human brain continues to develop and, some might say, improve over the course of one's life is a relatively new concept. Neuroscientists, even after brain size was no longer considered a direct determiner of brain capacity, once believed that the
(40) basic structure and abilities of the adult brain are developed early in life and not subject to change. Although psychologist William James suggested as early as 1890 that "organic matter, especially nervous tissue, seems endowed with a very extraor-
(45) dinary degree of plasticity," this idea went largely ignored for many years. Then, several provocative experiments dramatically complicated conventional thinking about the human brain.

In the 1920s, researcher Karl Lashley provided
(50) evidence of changes in the neural pathways of rhesus monkeys. By the 1960s, researchers began to explore cases in which older adults who had suffered massive strokes were able to regain functioning, demonstrating that the brain was
(55) much more malleable than previously believed. Modern researchers have also found evidence that the brain is able to rewire itself following damage. One of these experiments, for example, examined the various effects an enriched environment, in this
(60) case an "amusement park" for rats, could have on brain development. Researchers kept one group of rats in an empty cage, devoid of any stimulus, while another group lived in a cage filled with ladders, platforms, boxes, and other toys. Over
(65) the course of the experiment, researchers used magnetic resonance imaging technology to observe the brain development of the two groups. Those rats that lived in the enriched environment full of stimuli developed heavier, thicker brains with more
(70) neurons and synaptic connections—the cellular activity by which the brain functions—than those

that were deprived. Such results were then found to be even more noticeable in humans. Whereas it was once believed that the brain's physical (75) structure was permanent, this experiment and other contemporary findings show that the brain continues to create new neural pathways and alter existing ones in order to adapt to new experiences, learn new information, and create new memories. (80) As we gain new experiences, some connections are strengthened while others are eliminated in a process called "synaptic pruning." Frequently used neurons develop stronger connections; those rarely (or never) used eventually die. By developing new (85) connections and pruning away weak ones, the brain is able to adapt to the changing environment, thus confirming an essential point: one's life experiences and environment not only mold the brain's particular architecture but can also continue to (90) expand its capacity to function.

1. What is the author's central idea in this passage?

   A) The brain's capability to grow and develop is greatly limited after childhood.

   B) The science of studying the brain has come a long way in the past century.

   C) The human brain is remarkably flexible and is able to develop new synapses and pathways well into adulthood.

   D) Despite many decades of studying brain development and dynamics, scientists are no closer to unlocking the brain's secrets than they were a hundred years ago.

2. According to the passage, which choice best describes the number of synapses per neuron of a three-year-old compared to that of an average adult?

   A) Three-year-olds have twice as many synapses per neuron as the average adult.

   B) Three-year-olds have half as many synapses per neuron as the average adult.

   C) Three-year-olds and adults tend to have about the same number of synapses per neuron.

   D) Scientists are unable to tell how many synapses per neuron people have.

3. Which choice provides the best evidence for the answer to the previous question?

   A) Lines 21–26 ("Encased in . . . physical appearance")

   B) Lines 27–31 ("At birth . . . number of synapses")

   C) Lines 51–55 ("By the 1960s . . . previously believed")

   D) Lines 80–84 ("As we gain . . . eventually die")

4. As used in line 17, "sophisticated" most nearly means

   A) messy.

   B) intricate.

   C) unknowable.

   D) challenging.

5. As used in line 33, "marked" most nearly means

   A) pronounced.

   B) modest.

   C) infinitesimal.

   D) eye-catching.

6. Based on lines 58–73 ("One of these experiments . . . noticeable in humans"), the reader can conclude that

   A) experiments with rats tell us little about the human brain.

   B) scientists were mistaken in their hypothesis that an enriched environment would affect brain growth.

   C) surprisingly, environments devoid of enrichment actually boost brain growth.

   D) an enriched environment abundant in stimuli positively impacts the development of brains in rats as well as humans.

7. Which choice best describes the scientific consensus on brain flexibility and development beyond childhood?

   A) No one suspected the brain's ability to develop and grow throughout a person's life until the past fifty years.

   B) Scientists have been convinced of the brain's flexibility for a very long time, but the experiments to prove this flexibility were only recently developed.

   C) The brain's flexibility was hypothesized more than a century ago, but the concept did not gain proof until later in the twentieth century.

   D) Few scientists are convinced that the human brain retains any elasticity beyond childhood.

8. Which choice provides the best evidence for the answer to the previous question?

   A) Lines 15–20 ("While these . . . plasticity")

   B) Lines 37–48 ("Neuroscientists . . . human brain")

   C) Lines 61–67 ("Researchers . . . two groups")

   D) Lines 84–90 ("By developing . . . function")

9. As used in line 59, "enriched" most nearly means

   A) wealthy.

   B) enhanced.

   C) streamlined.

   D) clean.

10. As used in line 89, "architecture" most nearly means

    A) silhouette.

    B) façade.

    C) edifice.

    D) configuration.

PART THREE

Writing

Writing & Language: Expression of Ideas

BY THE END OF THIS UNIT, YOU WILL BE ABLE TO:

1. Apply the Kaplan Method for Writing & Language

2. Evaluate the effectiveness and clarity of a given passage

3. Identify proper and effective language use

4. Utilize the standard conventions of usage in written English

CHAPTER 13

The Kaplan Methods for Writing & Language and Infographics

CHAPTER OBJECTIVES

By the end of this chapter, you will be able to:

1. Distinguish among the three different Writing & Language text types

2. Identify issues in a passage and select the correct answer by applying the Kaplan Method for Writing & Language

3. Identify and analyze quantitative information and infographics

4. Synthesize information from infographics and text

SMARTPOINTS

Point Value	SmartPoint Category
Point Builder	The Kaplan Method for Writing & Language
Point Builder	The Kaplan Method for Infographics
10 Points	Quantitative

OVERVIEW OF THE WRITING & LANGUAGE PASSAGE TYPES

You will see four Writing & Language passages on Test Day, each of which will have 11 questions. Recognizing the text type of a Writing & Language passage helps you focus on the questions as they relate to the passage's general purpose. Knowing the overarching aim of the passage will help you answer questions more efficiently and accurately.

Writing & Language Passage Types	
1–2 Argumentative texts	Author will advocate a point, idea, or proposal.
1–2 Informative/Explanatory texts	Author will explain, describe, or analyze a topic in order to impart information without necessarily advocating.
1 Nonfiction Narrative text	Author will use a story-like approach to convey information or ideas.

✔ **Remember**

The PSAT rewards critical thinking in context. Pay attention to the text type to answer Writing & Language questions more efficiently.

Let's look at three short Writing & Language passage excerpts (without errors) and see how a PSAT expert identifies the text type of each. The left column features the passage excerpt, while the right column demonstrates the strategic thinking a test expert employs when identifying Writing & Language text types.

Reading & Writing

Passages	Strategic Thinking
It has long been believed that the best system of government is one in which everyone in a given society would vote on each and every law. Such a system of referendum would prevent corrupt politicians from serving their own self-interests when voting on a law. In the past, such a system could only be considered for small communities, as it would be impossible to execute efficiently on a large scale. However, the existence of modern technology renders this objection moot. If our society so desires it, all of us may one day cast votes on individual laws from the comfort of our homes.	*What does the opening phrase "It has long been believed" suggest?* The author might be challenging a belief or advocating something against that belief. *What does the word "however" indicate?* A change in direction in the passage *What is the author advocating?* Voting from home *Which text type is this?* Argumentative
Some psychologists believe that humans have developed special nervous systems capable of recognizing subtle expressions out of necessity, due to the weight of such recognition in human communication. To test this theory, researchers showed photographs of people displaying emotions of joy, anger, and surprise to a group of trained pigeons. The birds were not only able to distinguish between expressions but were also able to match each correctly to the same expression displayed by photographs with different faces. While the experiment's results do not conclusively prove that the pigeons can comprehend the meaning of the tested expressions, it does cast doubt upon the theory proposed by the psychologists.	*What does the introductory phrase "Some psychologists believe" indicate?* That the author is reporting on a behavior or phenomenon *What other phrases indicate this "reporting" approach?* "To test this theory, researchers . . ." and "While the experiment's results . . ." *What is the author describing in this passage?* A theory of expression recognition *Which text type is this?* Informative/Explanatory

Passages	Strategic Thinking
When studying ancient history in this university many years ago, I had as a special subject "Greece in the Period of the Persian Wars." I collected 15 or 20 volumes on my shelves and took it for granted that there, recorded in these volumes, I had all the facts relating to my subject. Let us assume—it was very nearly true—that those volumes contained all the facts about it that were then known or could be known. It never occurred to me to inquire by what accident or process of attrition that minute selection of facts, out of all the myriad facts that must have once been known to somebody, had survived to become the facts of history. I suspect that even today one of the fascinations of ancient and medieval history is that it gives us the illusion of having all the facts at our disposal within a manageable compass: the nagging distinction between the facts of history and other facts about the past vanishes because the few known facts are all facts of history.	*How is this passage different from the previous two passages?* It is written in the first person. *How do you know?* The author uses personal pronouns such as "I" and "me." *Which text type is this?* Nonfiction narrative

THE KAPLAN METHOD FOR WRITING & LANGUAGE

The Kaplan Method for Writing & Language is the method you will use to boost your score on the Writing & Language Test. By understanding what the question is looking for, how it relates to the passage, and the questions you should ask yourself on Test Day, you will maximize the number of points you earn. Use the Kaplan Method for Writing & Language for every PSAT Writing & Language Test passage and question you encounter, whether practicing, completing your homework, working on a Practice Test, or taking the actual exam on Test Day.

The Kaplan Method for Writing & Language has three steps:

Step 1: Read the passage and identify the issue

- If there's an infographic, apply the Kaplan Method for Infographics.

Step 2: Eliminate answer choices that do not address the issue

Step 3: Plug in the remaining answer choices and select the most correct, concise, and relevant one

✔ **On Test Day**

The PSAT will expect you to be able to recognize errors in organization, pronouns, agreement, comparisons, development, sentence structure, modifiers, verbs, wordiness, style, tone, and syntax.

Reading & Writing

Let's take a closer look at each step.

Step 1: Read the passage and identify the issue

This means:

- Rather than reading the whole passage and then answering all of the questions, you can answer questions as you read because they are mostly embedded in the text itself.

- When you see a number, stop reading and look at the question. If you can answer it with what you've read so far, do so. If you need more information, keep reading until you have enough context to answer the question.

Step 2: Eliminate answer choices that do not address the issue

Eliminating answer choices that do not address the issue:

- Increases your odds of getting the correct answer by removing obviously incorrect answer choices

Step 3: Plug in the remaining answer choices and select the most correct, concise, and relevant one

Correct, concise, and relevant means that the answer choice you select:

- Makes sense when read with the correction
- Is as short as possible while retaining the information in the text
- Relates well to the passage overall

> **✔ Remember**
>
> There is no incorrect answer penalty on the PSAT. When in doubt, eliminate what you can and then guess. You won't lose points for guessing.

The correct answer will NOT:

- Change the intended meaning of the original sentence, paragraph, or passage
- Introduce new grammatical errors

> **✔ On Test Day**
>
> If you have to guess, eliminate answer choices that are clearly incorrect and then choose the shortest one—the PSAT rewards students who know how to be concise.

You will see four Writing & Language passages on Test Day, each of which will have 11 questions. When you encounter a Writing & Language question, use the Kaplan Method, asking yourself a series of strategic thinking questions.

By asking these strategic thinking questions, you will be able to select the correct answer choice more easily and efficiently. Pausing to ask yourself questions before answering each question may seem like it takes a lot of time, but it actually saves you time by preventing you from weighing the four answer choices against each other; it's better to ask questions that lead you directly to the correct answer than to debate which of four answers seems the least incorrect.

Let's look at the following Writing & Language passage and questions. After the passage, there are two columns. The left column contains test-like questions. The column on the right features the strategic thinking a test expert employs when approaching the passage and questions presented.

Question	Strategic Thinking
Interest in developing wind power as an alternative renewable energy source has increased in recent years. In the eastern United States, exposed summits or ridge crests in the Appalachian Mountains have high wind power potential, and **1** numerous wind power projects are being proposed by power companies. While generally supportive of energy development from renewable sources, the U.S. Fish & Wildlife Service, state wildlife agencies, nongovernmental organizations, and the public are concerned about potential impacts of wind power development on wildlife.	**Step 1: Read the passage and identify the issue** *Can you identify a grammatical issue?* No, the underlined phrase is grammatically correct. *When there is no apparent grammatical issue, check style, tone, and syntax. Are there any style, tone, or syntax errors?* The sentence is written in the passive voice: the subject—"power companies"—comes after the object: "wind power projects."

1. A) NO CHANGE
   B) numerous wind power projects have been proposed.
   C) numerous wind power projects will be proposed.
   D) power companies have proposed numerous wind power projects.
	Step 2: Eliminate answer choices that do not address the issue
	
	Which answer choice(s) can you eliminate? Eliminate B and C because they just change the verb tense rather than addressing the error.
	
	Step 3: Plug in the remaining answer choices and select the most correct, concise, and relevant one
	
	Which is the correct answer? Choice (D)

THE KAPLAN METHOD FOR INFOGRAPHICS

The PSAT Writing & Language Test will contain one or more passages and/or questions that include one or more infographics. Each infographic will convey or expand on information from the passage.

The Kaplan Method for Infographics has three steps:

Step 1: Read the question

Step 2: Examine the infographic

Step 3: Predict and answer

Let's examine these steps a bit more closely.

Step 1: Read the question

Analyze the question stem for information that will help you zero in on the specific parts of the infographic that apply to the question.

Step 2: Examine the infographic

Make sure to:

- Circle parts of the infographic that relate directly to the question

- Identify units of measurement, labels, and titles

> ✔ **Expert Tip**
>
> For more data-heavy infographics, you should also make note of any present variables or categories, trends in the data, or relationships between variables.

Step 3: Predict and answer

Just as in Step 3 of the Kaplan Method for Reading Comprehension, do not look at the answer choices until you've used the infographic to make a prediction. Asking questions and taking time to assess the given information before answering the test question will increase your chances of selecting the correct answer. Infographics vary in format—there can be tables, graphs, charts, and so on—so be flexible when you ask yourself these critical-thinking questions.

When you apply the Kaplan Method for Infographics, keep in mind that infographics will either represent data described in the passage or present new data that expand on what the passage is about.

Let's look at the following Writing & Language infographic and questions. After the passage, there are two columns. The left column contains test-like questions. The column on the right features the strategic thinking a test expert employs when approaching the infographic and questions presented.

Question	Strategic Thinking

Reduction of Flying Animals in the Appalachians

Species	2007	2008	2009	2010
Kestrel	415	383	320	268
Bat	543	421	267	233
Eagle	58	45	34	33
Hawk	196	138	85	85

Step 1: Read the question

Assess the question to determine what part of the infographic to focus on.

What information in the question stem corresponds to the infographic? The years 2007 to 2010

2. Assume that from 2007 to 2010, the number of wind power projects in the Appalachians increased. According to the table, during that same time period

A) bat and bird populations decreased.

B) bat and bird populations increased.

C) bat and bird populations decreased and then increased.

D) bat and bird populations did not change.

Step 2: Examine the infographic

What are the units of measurement, labels, or titles? The units in the table are numbers. They aren't labeled, so you'll need to look for context; don't blindly make assumptions. Because the numbers go down, and the title of the graph is "Reduction of Flying Animals in the Appalachians," you can conclude that these must be populations.

Step 3: Predict and answer

Now that you understand the table, reread the question. Based on the question, what parts of the table do you need to look at? The number of each species as the years progress

Which is the correct answer? Choice (A)

Reading & Writing

You have seen the ways in which the PSAT tests you on Writing & Language and Infographics in Writing & Language passages and the way a PSAT expert approaches these types of questions.

Use the Kaplan Method for Writing & Language to answer the three questions that accompany the following Writing & Language passage excerpt. Remember to look at the strategic thinking questions that have been laid out for you—some of the answers have been filled in, but you will have to complete the answers to others.

Use your answers to the strategic thinking questions to select the correct answer, just as you will on Test Day.

Questions 3–5 are based on the following passage.

Migrant Birds and Wind Power

During their seasonal migration, there are **3** large numbers migrating through the mountainous landforms used for wind power. Wind power development could potentially impact populations of several species. Baseline information on nocturnally migrating birds and bats has been collected at some wind power development sites in the Appalachians, generally within a single season. However, a stronger scientific basis is critically needed to assess and mitigate risks at a regional scale.

The United States Geological Survey (USGS) is studying the distribution and flight patterns of birds and bats that migrate at night. Researchers analyze weather surveillance radar data (NEXRAD) to allow for a broad view of spring and fall migration through the Appalachians and **4** assessing the response of migrant birds to mountain ridges and other prominent landforms. Although NEXRAD data **5** provide information on the broad-scale spatial and temporal patterns of nocturnal migration through the region, the devices generally do not detect bird or bat targets within the altitudinal zone potentially occupied by wind turbines. Therefore, researchers are using two complementary ground-based techniques—acoustic detection and portable radar sampling—to obtain site-specific information on the abundance and flight characteristics of nocturnal migrants in lower airspace.

Questions	Strategic Thinking
3. A) NO CHANGE B) large amounts C) innumerable birds and bats D) birds and bats	**Step 1: Read the passage and identify the issue** *Can you identify an issue?* There's a modifier issue—as written, the sentence states that large numbers are migrating, not the actual birds and bats. **Step 2: Eliminate answer choices that do not address the issue** *Which answer choice(s) can you eliminate?* _____ **Step 3: Plug in the remaining answer choices and select the most correct, concise, and relevant one** *Do any of the remaining answer choices change the original meaning? Which one(s)?* _____ *Which is the correct answer?* _____

Reading & Writing

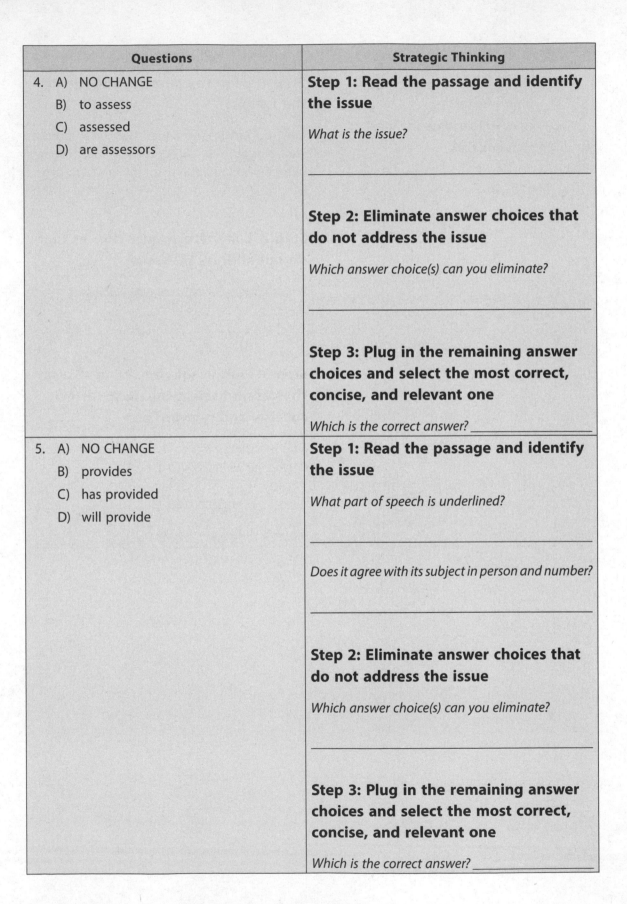

Questions	Strategic Thinking
4. A) NO CHANGE B) to assess C) assessed D) are assessors	**Step 1: Read the passage and identify the issue** *What is the issue?* _____ **Step 2: Eliminate answer choices that do not address the issue** *Which answer choice(s) can you eliminate?* _____ **Step 3: Plug in the remaining answer choices and select the most correct, concise, and relevant one** *Which is the correct answer?* _____
5. A) NO CHANGE B) provides C) has provided D) will provide	**Step 1: Read the passage and identify the issue** *What part of speech is underlined?* _____ *Does it agree with its subject in person and number?* _____ **Step 2: Eliminate answer choices that do not address the issue** *Which answer choice(s) can you eliminate?* _____ **Step 3: Plug in the remaining answer choices and select the most correct, concise, and relevant one** *Which is the correct answer?* _____

Now, try a test-like Writing & Language passage and infographic on your own. Give yourself 5 minutes to read the passage and answer the questions.

Questions 6–14 are based on the following passage and supplementary materials.

Business Entities

In the business sector of New York City, giant corporations conduct their business in colossal towers. But what about the individual who wants to operate a business without being subject to the whims of corporate shareholders? How can such an individual realize her dreams to own a business, perhaps not equal in size to large corporations, but at least their rival in ambition? **6** Life goes on, for the eager entrepreneur has two options.

For the confident entrepreneur looking to succeed on her own, there is *sole proprietorship*. In a sole proprietorship, there is one owner who is "solely" responsible for the business and any decisions regarding **7** it's operation. Of course, as with all choices in life, **8** it does not come without its share of disadvantages. Sole proprietorships aren't seen as separate **9** from their owners, so credit may be a problem, especially if you don't have a lot of financial assets on hand. You're fine if the business is lucrative, but if not, sole proprietorships can be a scary proposition because being the only boss also means taking on any and all debt that your business incurs.

6. A) NO CHANGE
   B) Never fear,
   C) Don't worry,
   D) In fact,

7. A) NO CHANGE
   B) their
   C) its
   D) its'

8. A) NO CHANGE
   B) sole proprietorship
   C) business
   D) an operation

9. A) NO CHANGE
   B) with
   C) between
   D) by

If our entrepreneur is lucky enough to have a group of like-minded acquaintances with **10** <u>who</u> to start her company, she and her associates might instead opt to form a partnership. A partnership sacrifices some of the operational freedom that comes with a sole proprietorship, as you now have a bunch of "friends" to convince before you can have things your way on any business decisions that need to be **11** <u>made however</u> these same individuals will also be chipping in on expenses and sharing responsibility for any debt that the business may incur.

12 <u>Profits are shared with your partners</u> on payday, but the extra support they can provide if the business struggles helps to make up for that. **13** <u>Partnerships, however, are less lucrative for the individual than sole proprietorships.</u>

10. A) NO CHANGE
    B) who's
    C) whose
    D) whom

11. A) NO CHANGE
    B) made, however
    C) made; however,
    D) made, however,

12. A) NO CHANGE
    B) You will share profits with your partners
    C) Profits will be shared with your partners
    D) Partners will share your profits

13. Which choice best reflects the data in the graph?
    A) NO CHANGE
    B) Sole proprietorships, however, are more lucrative for the individual than partnerships.
    C) Partnerships, however, have a lower net income per person than sole proprietorships.
    D) Partnerships are also more lucrative for the individual than are sole proprietorships.

While the partnership seems to alleviate many of the problems that plague the sole proprietorship, it does have its share of disadvantages. In a sole proprietorship, the business could be sold if you, the owner, desire it, but a partnership requires consent from your partners before **14** it can take place. Moreover, unlike corporations, which come with limited liability for their shareholders, if the business runs deeply into debt, you are still responsible for your complete share of the debt, even if you do have others to share that debt with. When viewed in this light, the "evil corporations" surrounding us may be a necessary evil indeed.

14. A) NO CHANGE
    B) a partnership
    C) this consent
    D) this sale

Answers and Explanations for this chapter begin on page 598.

Partnership Versus Sole Proprietorship Net Income, 2002–2005

ON YOUR OWN

Questions 1–11 are based on the following passage and supplementary materials.

The North American Suburb

The North American suburb is an architectural and civic phenomenon distinct from suburban areas in any other part of the world. It was **1** <u>a counterreaction to</u> the need, especially keen after World War II, to "get away" from the city and all the noise, pollution, and general nastiness that went along with it. Cities were where the factories were, and the factories before modern pollution and safety standards were horrific things to behold. Of those who could **2** <u>get out, many did.</u>

Suburban communities, however, were not **3** <u>sufficient by themselves to support life.</u> The people who lived in them needed to work, shop, and socialize, and most of the active part of their lives remained fixed in urban centers. **4** <u>Paradoxically, suburbs were clustered around their parent cities, with the suburban inhabitants avoiding the city center.</u>

1. A) NO CHANGE
   B) an avoidance of
   C) a response to
   D) an intensifier of

2. A) NO CHANGE
   B) get out many did.
   C) get out . . . many did.
   D) get out; many did.

3. A) NO CHANGE
   B) self-sufficient.
   C) entirely sufficient by themselves to support life.
   D) sufficiently able to adequately support life by themselves.

4. A) NO CHANGE
   B) Therefore, suburbs were unnecessarily far from their parent cities, hampering suburban inhabitants' intent to commute to the city for work and play.
   C) Therefore, suburbs were clustered around their parent cities, with suburban inhabitants commuting daily to the city center for work and play.
   D) Suburbs therefore developed the amenities needed for suburbanites who were unwilling to ever go back into the city.

All this seems perfectly logical and inevitable. The suburb should be the ambiguous halfway point between city and country—away from the noise, congestion, and pollution but not so far away that there's no access to culture, to income, to all the exciting **5** pitfalls of urban life. In reality, though, few suburbs have actually approached this ideal. Moreover, the structure of the **6** modern suburb, while offering a respite from city pollution, has created health and environmental risks of its own.

Suburban zoning laws **7** have forced the separation of living and commercial spaces. As such, the city dweller's fond experience of walking down the block to the neighborhood café may be rare or entirely alien to a suburbanite. Should suburban dwellers, on a Saturday morning, desire a change of scenery and a cup of coffee, they must get in their cars and drive some distance. **8** Come to think of it, nearly everything aside from the nearby houses and the occasional neighborhood park requires an automobile trip. All of this driving comes at the cost of pollution and a lack of daily exercise. Surely, we must begin to balance the appeal and freedom of the car with ecological and civic responsibility.

5. A) NO CHANGE
    B) drawbacks
    C) perils
    D) benefits

6. A) NO CHANGE
    B) modern suburb while offering a respite from city pollution has created
    C) modern suburb, (while offering a respite from city pollution) has created
    D) modern suburb; while offering a respite from city pollution; has created

7. A) NO CHANGE
    B) has
    C) having
    D) had

8. A) NO CHANGE
    B) As fate would have it, nearly everything
    C) Contrary to popular belief, nearly everything
    D) In fact, nearly everything

Reading & Writing

[1] Some have charged that America doesn't need any more of these bland developments, that these projects line construction companies' pockets without contributing much to the value and diversity of American culture. [2] **9** <u>I, however, think that the problem of suburbs can be described as one of degree rather than kind.</u> [3] We don't need to abandon suburbs altogether; instead, we need to more knowingly pursue that ideal of the best of city and country. [4] Suburbs could be fascinating and beautiful places; we need only exercise our power to determine the nature of the places in which we live. **10** **11**

City and Suburb Rates of Growth

Population Growth (%)

■ Primary cities　▨ Suburbs

9. A)　NO CHANGE

B)　I, however, believe that the problem of the suburbs should be described as one of degree rather than kind.

C)　I, however, see the problem of suburbs as one of degree rather than kind.

D)　I, however, think that one can see the problem of suburbs as one of degree rather than kind.

10. Which answer choice best describes the data in the graph as it relates to the passage?

A)　Despite the growing awareness of the shortcomings of suburban living, America's suburban population continues to grow faster than that of the country's primary cities.

B)　It also seems that Americans' opinions of the suburbs are objectively changing—from 2010 to 2011, population growth in cities outstripped growth in the suburbs.

C)　Suburbs may have their naysayers, but the fact remains that it is hard to detect any change in where Americans are settling.

D)　Contrary to continued positive perceptions of the suburbs, population growth swung back in favor of primary cities in the early twenty-first century.

11. What is the best placement for the sentence featured in the answer to the previous question?

A)　After sentence 1

B)　After sentence 2

C)　After sentence 3

D)　After sentence 4

Writing & Language: Standard English Conventions

BY THE END OF THIS UNIT, YOU WILL BE ABLE TO:

1. Recognize correct and incorrect instances of conventions of usage and punctuation

2. Identify and correct errors in sentence structure

3. Identify and correct usage errors

CHAPTER 14

Conventions of Usage

CHAPTER OBJECTIVES

By the end of this chapter, you will be able to:

1. Recognize and correct errors in pronoun clarity, grammatical agreement, and logical comparison

2. Distinguish among commonly confused possessive determiners, contractions, and adverbs

3. Recognize and correct incorrectly constructed idioms and frequently misused words

SMARTPOINTS

Point Value	SmartPoint Category
40 Points	Usage

PRONOUNS

A pronoun is ambiguous if the noun to which it refers (its antecedent) is either missing or unclear. On the PSAT, you must be able to recognize either situation and make the appropriate correction. When you see an underlined pronoun, make sure you can find the specific noun to which it refers.

Missing Antecedent

- *When the flight arrived, **they** told the passengers to stay seated until the plane reached the gate.* (The pronoun *they* does not have an antecedent in this sentence.)

- *When the flight arrived, **the flight crew** told the passengers to stay seated until the plane reached the gate.* (Replacing the pronoun with a specific noun clarifies the meaning.)

Unclear Antecedent

- *Kayla asked Mia to drive Sree to the airport because **she** was running late.* (The pronoun *she* could refer to any of the three people mentioned in the sentence.)

- *Because Kayla was running late, **she** asked Mia to drive Sree to the airport.* (The pronoun *she* now unambiguously refers to Kayla.)

> ✔ **Definition**
>
> The **antecedent** is the noun that the pronoun replaces or stands in for elsewhere in the sentence. To identify the **antecedent** of a pronoun, check the nouns near the pronoun. Substitute those nouns for the pronoun to see which one makes sense.

AGREEMENT

Pronoun-Antecedent Agreement

Pronouns must agree with their antecedents not only in person and number, but also in gender. Only third-person pronouns make distinctions based on gender.

Gender	Example
Feminine	*Because Yvonne had a question, **she** raised her hand.*
Masculine	*Since **he** had lots of homework, Rico started working right away.*
Neutral	*The rain started slowly, but then **it** became a downpour.*
Unspecified	*If a traveler is lost, **he or she** should ask for directions.*

Reading & Writing

Pronoun-Case Agreement

There are three pronoun cases:

1. Subjective case: The pronoun is used as the subject.

2. Objective case: The pronoun is used as the object of a verb or a preposition.

3. Possessive case: The pronoun expresses ownership.

Subjective case	I, you, she, he, it, we, you, they, who
Objective case	me, you, her, him, it, us, you, them, whom
Possessive case	my, mine, your, yours, his, her, hers, its, our, ours, their, theirs, whose

> ✔ **Expert Tip**
>
> When there are two pronouns or a noun and a pronoun in a compound structure, drop the other noun to confirm which pronoun case to use. For example: *Leo and me walk into town.* Would you say, "Me walk into town"? No, you would say, "I walk into town." Therefore, the correct case is subjective and the original sentence should read *Leo and I walk into town.*

> ✔ **Remember**
>
> Use *who* when a sentence refers to *she, he,* or *I.* (*Quynh was the person **who** provided the best answer.*)
> Use *whom* when a sentence refers to *her, him,* or *me.* (*With **whom** did Aaron attend the event?*)

Subject-Verb Agreement

A verb must agree with its subject in person and number:

- Singular: *The **apple tastes** delicious.*

- Plural: ***Apples taste** delicious.*

The noun closest to a verb may not be its subject: *The **chair** with the cabriole legs **is** an antique.* The noun closest to the verb in this sentence (*is*, which is singular) is *legs*, which is plural. However, the verb's subject is *chair*, so the sentence is correct as written.

Only the conjunction *and* forms a compound subject requiring a plural verb form:

- *Saliyah **and** Taylor **are** in the running club.*

- ***Either** Saliyah **or** Taylor **is** in the running club.*

- ***Neither** Saliyah **nor** Taylor **is** in the running club.*

Noun-Number Agreement

Related nouns must be consistent in number:

- ***Students*** *applying for college must submit their **applications** on time.* (The sentence refers to multiple students, and they all must submit applications.)

FREQUENTLY CONFUSED WORDS

English contains many pairs of words that sound alike but are spelled differently and have different meanings.

ACCEPT/EXCEPT: To *accept* is to take or receive something that is offered: *My neighbor said he would accept my apology for trampling over his rose beds as long as I helped weed them in the spring.* To *except* is to leave out or exclude: *The soldier was excepted from combat duty because he had poor field vision. Except* is usually used as a preposition that means with the exception of, excluding: *When the receptionist found out that everyone except him had received a raise, he demanded a salary increase as well.*

AFFECT/EFFECT: To *affect* is to have an influence on something: *Eli refused to let the rain affect his plans for a picnic, so he sat under an umbrella and ate his sandwich.* An *affect* is an emotion or behavior: *The guidance counselor noticed that more outdoor time resulted in improved student affect.* To *effect* is to bring something about or cause something to happen: *The young activist received an award for effecting a change in her community.* An *effect* is an influence or a result: *The newspaper article about homeless animals had such an effect on Zarak that he brought home three kittens from the shelter. Affect* is most often used in its verb form, and *effect* is most often used in its noun form.

AFFLICT/INFLICT: To *afflict* is to torment or distress someone or something. It usually appears as a passive verb: *Jeff is afflicted with frequent migraine headaches.* To *inflict* is to impose punishment or suffering on someone or something: *No one dared displease the king, for he was known to inflict severe punishments on those who upset him.*

ALLUSION/ILLUSION: An *allusion* is an indirect reference to something, a hint: *The teacher's comment about the most enigmatic smile in art history was not lost on Sophie; this allusion could only be a reference to Leonardo da Vinci's* Mona Lisa. An *illusion* is a false, misleading, or deceptive appearance: *A magician creates the illusion that something has disappeared by hiding it faster than the eye can follow it.*

EMIGRATE/IMMIGRATE: To *emigrate* is to leave one country for another. It is usually used with the preposition *from: Many people emigrated from Europe in search of better living conditions.* To *immigrate* is to enter a country to take up permanent residence. It is usually used with the preposition *to: They immigrated to North America because land was plentiful.*

EMINENT/IMMINENT: Someone who is *eminent* is prominent or outstanding: *The eminent archeologist Dr. Wong has identified the artifact as prehistoric in origin.* Something that is *imminent* is likely to happen soon or is impending: *After being warned that the hurricane's arrival was imminent, beachfront residents left their homes immediately.*

LAY/LIE: To *lay* is to place or put something down and is usually followed by a "something"—a direct object: *Before she begins to paint, Emily lays all of her pencils, brushes, and paints on her worktable to avoid interruptions while she draws and paints.* One form, *laid*, serves as the simple past and the past participle of *lay*: *I laid my necklace on the counter, just where Rebecca had put hers.* To *lie* is to recline, to be in a lying position or at rest. This verb never takes a direct object: you do not lie anything down. The simple past form of *lie* is *lay*; the past participle is *lain*. Notice that the past form of *lie* is identical with the present form of *lay*. This coincidence complicates the task of distinguishing the related meanings of *lay* and *lie*: *Having laid the picnic cloth under the sycamore, they lay in the shady grass all last Sunday afternoon.*

RAISE/RISE: *Raise* means to lift up, or to cause to rise or grow, and it is paired with a direct object: you *raise* weights, roof beams, tomato plants, children. *Raise* is a regular verb. *The trade tariff on imported leather goods raised the prices of Italian shoes.* To *rise* is to get up, to go, to be built up. This verb is never paired with a direct object: you do not *rise* something. The past and past participle forms are irregular; *rose* is the simple past, and *risen* is the past participle. *Long-distance commuters must rise early and return home late.*

SET/SIT: The difference between *set* and *sit* is very similar to the difference between *lay* and *lie* and between *raise* and *rise*. To *set* is to put or place, settle or arrange something. However, *set* takes on other specific meanings when it is combined with several different prepositions, so always think carefully about the meaning of the word in the sentence. *Set* is an irregular verb because it has one form that serves as present tense, past tense, and past participle. *Set* usually has a direct object: you *set* a ladder against the fence, a value on family heirlooms, a date for the family reunion: *The professor set the students' chairs in a semicircle to promote open discussion.* To *sit* is to take a seat or to be in a seated position, to rest somewhere, or to occupy a place. This verb does not usually have a direct object: *The beach house sits on a hill at some distance from the shoreline.* When *sit* doesn't make sense, consider the word *sat*: *The usher sat us in the center seats of the third row from the stage.*

Other pairs of words do not sound alike but have similar meanings that are often confused:

AMONG/BETWEEN: The preposition *among* refers to collective arrangements; use it when referring to three or more people or items. *The soccer team shared dozens of oranges among themselves.* *Between* is also a preposition, but it refers to only two people or items: *Amy and Tonia split the tasks between them.*

AMOUNT/NUMBER: *Amount* is used in reference to mass nouns (also known as uncountable nouns): *The amount of bravery displayed was awe-inspiring.* *Number* is used in reference to countable nouns: *The recipe calls for a specific number of eggs.*

LESS/FEWER: *Less* should be used only with mass nouns, which are grammatically singular: *Diana's yard has less wildlife than mine.* One common misuse of *less* is a sign you probably encounter frequently at the supermarket: The *10 items or less* sign should actually be *10 items or fewer*, because the items are countable. *Fewer* should be used when referring to countable objects and concepts: *Diana's yard has fewer squirrels than mine.*

MUCH/MANY: *Much* modifies things that cannot be counted, often singular nouns: *Jim has much more money than I do. Many*, on the other hand, modifies things that can be counted, such as plural nouns: *Samantha has many awards in her collection.*

The PSAT will also test your ability to correctly use and identify possessive pronouns, contractions, and adverbs that sound the same:

ITS/IT'S: *Its* is a possessive pronoun like *his* and *hers*: *The rare book would be worth more if its cover weren't ripped. It's* is a contraction that can mean *it is, it has,* or *it was*: *It's been a long time since I last saw you.*

THEIR/THEY'RE/THERE: *Their* is a possessive form of the pronoun *they*: *The players respected their coach. They're* is a contraction of *they are*: *The students say they're planning to attend college. There* is used to introduce a sentence or indicate a location: *There was plenty of water in the well when we arrived there.*

THEIRS/THERE'S: *Theirs* is the possessive plural form of the pronoun *they*: *The team was ecstatic when it was announced that the prize was theirs. There's* is a contraction of *there is* or *there has*: *There's been a lot of rain this summer.*

WHOSE/WHO'S: *Whose* is a possessive pronoun used to refer to people or things: *Whose phone is ringing? Who's* is a contraction of *who is* or *who has*: *Who's planning to join us for dinner?*

COMPARISONS

The PSAT will test your ability to recognize and correct improper comparisons. There are three rules governing correct comparisons:

1. Compare logical things

The **price of tea** has risen sharply, while **coffee** has remained the same.

This sentence incorrectly compares *the price of tea* to *coffee*. The sentence should read: *The* **price of tea** *has risen sharply, while the* **price of coffee** *has remained the same.*

2. Use parallel structure

On a sunny day, I enjoy **hiking** *and* **to read** *outside.*

This sentence incorrectly uses the gerund verb form (*hiking*) and then switches to the infinitive verb form (*to read*). To correct the sentence, make sure the verb forms are consistent: *On a sunny day, I enjoy* **hiking** *and* **reading** *outside.*

Reading & Writing

3. Structure comparisons correctly

Some animals are **better** *at endurance running* **than** *they are at sprinting.*
Others are **as** *good at endurance running* **as** *they are at sprinting.*

Both of these sentences are correctly structured: the first with the use of *better . . . than,* and the second with the use of *as . . . as.*

When comparing like things, use adjectives that match the number of items being compared. When comparing two items or people, use the comparative form of the adjective. When comparing three or more items or people, use the superlative form.

Comparative	Superlative
Use when comparing two items	Use when comparing three or more items
better	best
more	most
newer	newest
older	oldest
shorter	shortest
taller	tallest
worse	worst
younger	youngest

IDIOMS

An **idiom** is a combination of words that must be used together to convey either a figurative or literal meaning. Idioms are tested in four ways on the PSAT:

1. Proper preposition usage in context

The three finalists will compete **for** *the grand prize: an all-inclusive cruise to Bali.*
Roger will compete **against** *Rafael in the final round of the tournament.*
I will compete **with** *Deborah in the synchronized swimming competition.*

2. Verb forms

The architect likes **to draft** *floor plans.*
The architect enjoys **drafting** *floor plans.*

3. Idiomatic expressions

Idiomatic expressions refer to words or phrases that must be used together to be correct.

*Simone will **either** continue sleeping **or** get up and get ready for school.*
***Neither** the principal **nor** the teachers will tolerate tardiness.*
*This fall, Shari is playing **not only** soccer **but also** field hockey.*

4. Implicit double negatives

Some words imply a negative and therefore cannot be paired with an explicit negative.

*Janie **cannot hardly** wait for summer vacation.*

This sentence is incorrect as written. It should read: *Janie **can hardly** wait for summer vacation.*

Frequently Tested Prepositions	Idiomatic Expressions	Words That Can't Be Paired with Negative Words
at	as . . . as	barely
by	between . . . and	hardly
for	both . . . and	scarcely
from	either . . . or	
of	neither . . . nor	
on	just as . . . so too	
to	not only . . . but also	
with	prefer . . . to	

Let's look at the following Writing & Language passage and questions. After the passage, there are two columns. The left column contains test-like questions. The column on the right features the strategic thinking a test expert employs when approaching the passage and questions presented.

Questions 1–4 are based on the following passage.

Woolly Mammoth

There is likely no animal that better captures the public's imagination of the prehistoric Ice Age than the woolly mammoth. Although remains of many mammoths have been discovered over the years, none have been found better preserved than the "Jarkov Mammoth" found on Siberia's Taimyr Peninsula in 1997. Soon after a 9-year-old boy out playing in the snowy hills first spotted the remains, scientists descended on the site. Then, after battling weeks of frigid weather and approximately 20,000 years' worth of dense frost coating the entire body of the mammoth, the assembled team finally completed a successful excavation. Important for numerous scientific reasons, the Jarkov Mammoth, in particular, **1** have helped scientists settle a debate that has been raging for many years concerning the possible reasons behind the sudden extinction of these ancient giants.

Woolly mammoths roamed the cold northern plains of the globe for much of the last 2 million years, including most of the Ice Age that began roughly 70,000 years ago. Then, quite suddenly, 10,000 years ago, a time that corresponds with the end of the Ice Age, the mammoths disappeared. Scientific theories explaining this rapid extinction ranged **2** from thoughts of meteor showers pelting Earth to massive volcanic eruptions. Today, however, partially through evidence taken from the Jarkov Mammoth, it is generally agreed that these creatures died out from a combination of changing climate, hunting pressures from humans, and probably even disease. In fact, scientists consider it likely that the rising temperatures accompanying the end of the Ice Age worked against the evolutionary adaptations made by the mammoths, including their signature woolly coats of dense fur. Indeed, the demise of the Jarkov Mammoth seems to have involved a deep patch of mud, perhaps a sign that these behemoths were unaccustomed to treading on increasingly softer ground.

Having adapted to the cold and snow that blanketed much of Earth during the Ice Age, the mammoth kept its enormous body at an optimal temperature with a covering of long, thick, dark hair and a layer of underfur. Typically, these herbivorous precursors to the modern-day elephant were about 12 feet long, 10 feet tall at the shoulders, and weighed nearly 6,000 pounds. The long, distinctively curved tusks of the mammoth were used for protection by all members of the species and specifically by the males to assert their dominance, much the same way **3** they utilize their own shorter, straighter toothy appendages. For a woolly mammoth living in the Ice Age, these tusks were particularly important **4** for digging through layers of ice in search of grass and other plant food. Although the eventual melting of these layers would seem to ease this search, the sudden change in climate apparently proved too much for the woolly mammoth to overcome.

Questions	Strategic Thinking
1. A) NO CHANGE B) had C) has D) having	**Step 1: Read the passage and identify the issue** *What is the issue?* The subject and verb do not agree. *What part of speech is underlined?* A third-person plural verb is underlined. *What is its subject?* The Jarkov Mammoth is the subject that matches the verb. *What is the subject's person and number?* The Jarkov Mammoth is a third-person singular noun. The underlined verb should be singular to match the singular noun. **Step 2: Eliminate answer choices that do not address the issue** *Which answer choice(s) can you eliminate?* Eliminate A because the subject and verb do not match. Eliminate B because the tense changes. Eliminate D because it creates a fragment. **Step 3: Plug in the remaining answer choices and select the most correct, concise, and relevant one** *Which is the correct answer?* Choice (C)

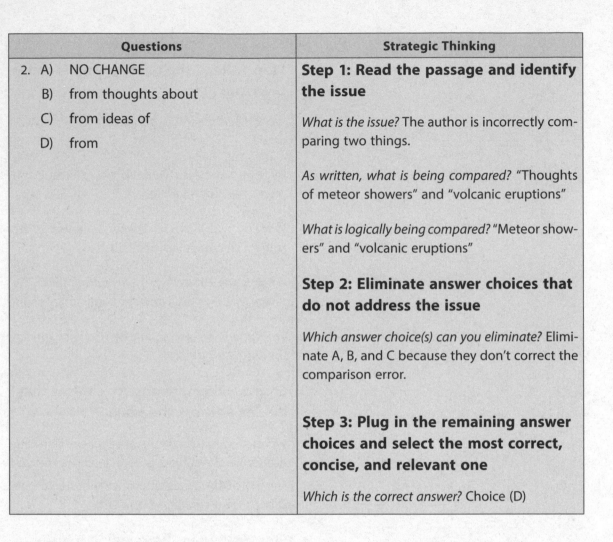

Questions	Strategic Thinking
2. A) NO CHANGE B) from thoughts about C) from ideas of D) from	**Step 1: Read the passage and identify the issue** *What is the issue?* The author is incorrectly comparing two things. *As written, what is being compared?* "Thoughts of meteor showers" and "volcanic eruptions" *What is logically being compared?* "Meteor showers" and "volcanic eruptions" **Step 2: Eliminate answer choices that do not address the issue** *Which answer choice(s) can you eliminate?* Eliminate A, B, and C because they don't correct the comparison error. **Step 3: Plug in the remaining answer choices and select the most correct, concise, and relevant one** *Which is the correct answer?* Choice (D)

Questions	Strategic Thinking
3. A) NO CHANGE B) today's elephants C) woolly mammoths D) scientists	**Step 1: Read the passage and identify the issue** *What is the issue?* The pronoun's antecedent is not clear. *How do you know?* The sentence talks about "all members of the species" and "males." **Step 2: Eliminate answer choices that do not address the issue** *Which answer choice(s) can you eliminate?* Eliminate A because it does not address the issue. Eliminate C because the writer is making a distinction between mammoths and something else. Eliminate D because scientists don't have "toothy appendages." **Step 3: Plug in the remaining answer choices and select the most correct, concise, and relevant one** *Which is the correct answer?* Choice (B)
4. A) NO CHANGE B) to dig C) at digging D) from digging	**Step 1: Read the passage and identify the issue** *What is the issue?* The underlined portion is an idiomatic phrase with a preposition. **Step 2: Eliminate answer choices that do not address the issue** *Which answer choice(s) can you eliminate?* Eliminate B, C, and D because none of them is grammatically correct in context. **Step 3: Plug in the remaining answer choices and select the most correct, concise, and relevant one** *Which is the correct answer?* Choice (A)

You have seen the ways in which the PSAT tests you on Conventions of Usage in Writing & Language passages and the way a PSAT expert approaches these types of questions.

Use the Kaplan Method for Writing & Language to answer the four questions that accompany the following Writing & Language passage excerpt. Remember to look at the strategic-thinking questions that have been laid out for you—some of the answers have been filled in, but you will have to complete the answers to others.

Use your answers to the strategic thinking questions to select the correct answer, just as you will on Test Day.

Questions 5–8 are based on the following passage.

Hudson River School

The first truly American art movement, called the Hudson River School, was formed by a group of landscape painters and emerged in the early nineteenth century. The first works in this style were created by Thomas Cole, Thomas Doughty, and Asher Durand, a trio of painters who worked during the 1820s in the Hudson River Valley and surrounding locations. Heavily influenced by European romanticism, these painters set out to convey the remoteness and splendor of the American wilderness. The strongly nationalistic tone of their paintings caught the spirit of the times, and within a generation, the movement had mushroomed to include landscape painters from all over the United States. Canvases celebrating such typically American scenes as Niagara Falls, Boston Harbor, and the expansion of the railroad into rural Pennsylvania **5** was greeted with enormous popular acclaim.

One factor contributing to the success of the Hudson River School was the rapid growth of American nationalism in the early nineteenth century. The War of 1812 had given the United States a new sense of pride in its identity, and as the nation continued to grow, there was a desire to compete with Europe on both economic and cultural grounds. The vast panoramas of the Hudson River School fit the bill perfectly **6** while providing a new movement in art that was unmistakably American in origin. The Hudson River School also arrived at a time when writers in the United States were turning their attention to the wilderness as a unique aspect of their nationality. The Hudson River School painters profited from this nostalgia because they effectively represented the continent the way it used to be. The view that the American character was formed by the frontier experience was widely held, and many **7** of them wrote about their concerns regarding an increasingly urbanized country.

In keeping with this nationalistic spirit, even the painting style of the Hudson River School exhibited a strong sense of American identity. Although many of the artists studied in Europe, their paintings show a desire to be free of European artistic rules. Regarding the natural landscape as a direct manifestation of God, the Hudson River School painters attempted to record what they saw as accurately as possible. Unlike European painters, who brought to their canvases the styles and techniques of centuries, the Hudson River School **8** painters sought neither to embellish nor to idealize their scenes, portraying nature with the objectivity and attention to detail of naturalists.

Questions	Strategic Thinking
5. A) NO CHANGE B) is C) are D) were	**Step 1: Read the passage and identify the issue** *What is the issue?* Subject-verb agreement *What is the subject of the underlined verb?* Canvases *Should the underlined verb be singular or plural?* Plural **Step 2: Eliminate answer choices that do not address the issue** *Which answer choice(s) can you eliminate?* Eliminate A and B because they feature singular verbs. Eliminate C because it is in present tense but the rest of the paragraph is written in past tense. **Step 3: Plug in the remaining answer choices and select the most correct, concise, and relevant one** *Which is the correct answer?* _____
6. A) NO CHANGE B) by providing C) in providing D) only providing	**Step 1: Read the passage and identify the issue** *What is the issue?* Preposition usage *How can you determine which preposition is correct?* By carefully reading the sentence to identify what meaning the preposition needs to convey **Step 2: Eliminate answer choices that do not address the issue** *Which answer choice(s) can you eliminate?* _____ **Step 3: Plug in the remaining answer choices and select the most correct, concise, and relevant one** *Which is the correct answer?* _____

Questions	Strategic Thinking
7. A) NO CHANGE B) painters C) writers D) Europeans	**Step 1: Read the passage and identify the issue** *What is the issue?* Pronoun ambiguity *How can you identify the correct antecedent?* By rereading enough of the passage to be able to determine who "were concerned" **Step 2: Eliminate answer choices that do not address the issue** *Which answer choice(s) can you eliminate?* _____ **Step 3: Plug in the remaining answer choices and select the most correct, concise, and relevant one** *Which is the correct answer?* _____
8. A) NO CHANGE B) canvases C) styles D) techniques	**Step 1: Read the passage and identify the issue** *What is the issue?* Comparing like things *What are the "painters" in the underlined portion being compared to?* _____ _____ **Step 2: Eliminate answer choices that do not address the issue** *Which answer choice(s) can you eliminate?* _____ **Step 3: Plug in the remaining answer choices and select the most correct, concise, and relevant one** *Which is the correct answer?* _____

Now try a test-like Writing & Language passage on your own. Give yourself 5 minutes to read the passage and answer the questions.

Questions 9–16 are based on the following passage.

1929 Stock Market Crash

On October 29, 1929, the stock market crashed in one of the [9] most worst financial panics in American history. The ensuing economic meltdown, known as the Great Depression, left Americans thinking about what went wrong and how to ensure that it would never happen again. To this day, economists study the speculative boom of the Roaring '20s, the crash, and the Great Depression, trying to find patterns that can be applied to today's economy.

After World War I, America, having proven itself a world power, began to reap the benefits of new technologies and investments opening everywhere. Mass production made all types of new gadgets, such as [10] vacuum cleaners and automobiles, available to more Americans because of cheaper prices. The same was true of stocks and bonds. Throughout the 1920s, many Americans, not just the rich, played the stock market. Laws of the day made this investment possible by requiring only 10 percent, or a "margin," of an investment to be paid immediately, with the rest payable over time. If something went wrong, however, investors would have to pay back the balance of [11] its loans.

Economists of the time worried about how much investing was being done by people who could not [12] hardly afford the losses if the market crashed, but government

9. A) NO CHANGE
    B) most worse
    C) worst
    D) more worse

10. A) NO CHANGE
    B) the vacuum cleaner and the automobiles
    C) the vacuum cleaner and automobiles
    D) vacuum cleaners or automobiles

11. A) NO CHANGE
    B) their
    C) one's
    D) the investor's

12. A) NO CHANGE
    B) barely afford
    C) scarcely afford
    D) afford

policy of the day called for nonintervention into business matters. Economists, nonetheless, sought a way to wean the people away from margin investing, but no laws were implemented for fear of causing a panic. As long as the stock prices continued to go up and investors continued to benefit, no one was willing to take action. History has taught us, however, that markets are cyclical in nature, and eventually even the strongest bull market* will begin to fail.

In this case, **13** it came in 1929. The year was filled with nervous tension as investors **14** which had bought a great quantity of stock on credit sought a way out of a market that was declining. Finally, on October 29, the pressure **15** in everyone trying to sell stock became too much, and the market began a downward spiral from which there would be no easy recovery.

The lessons of 1929 have taught investors that the stock market is no game. Laws have been passed that significantly reduce margin investing. In addition, many safeguards have been implemented to stem financial panic when the **16** market starts to decline. Although the economy will always have high and low points, the hope is that modifying people's behavior will prevent the raw panic that allowed the crash of '29 and the Great Depression to occur.

bull market: a successful market with confident investors

13. A) NO CHANGE
    B) the bull market
    C) the failure
    D) the cycle

14. A) NO CHANGE
    B) who
    C) whom
    D) those of whom who

15. A) NO CHANGE
    B) when
    C) on
    D) of

16. A) NO CHANGE
    B) markets starts
    C) market start
    D) market started

Answers and Explanations for this chapter begin on page 601.

ON YOUR OWN

The following questions provide an opportunity to practice the concepts and strategic thinking covered in this chapter. While many of the questions pertain to Conventions of Usage, some touch on other concepts tested on the Writing & Language Test to ensure that your practice is test-like, with a variety of question types per passage.

Questions 1–11 are based on the following passage.

Violence in Children's Entertainment

[1] In recent years, many parents have expressed concern that the atmosphere of violence **1** propagated by the American entertainment industry may be having a harmful effect on their children. [2] Certainly these parents are correct that **2** violent acts such as murder, have become the pervasive theme of everything from feature films to television cartoons. [3] But is this kind of depravity altogether new to the world of the **3** child. [4] Haven't parents for centuries been exposing their children to fairy tales that are at least as gory and violent? **4**

5 Consider, for example, the tale of "Little Red Riding Hood," a story of murder and mayhem that has been told to children—and repeated by them—for at least 300 years. In the earliest known version of the tale,

1. A) NO CHANGE
    B) secreted
    C) populated
    D) advocated

2. A) NO CHANGE
    B) violent acts; such as murder; have become
    C) violent acts, such as murder have become
    D) violent acts, such as murder, have become

3. A) NO CHANGE
    B) child?
    C) child!
    D) child;

4. For the sake of cohesion of this paragraph, sentence 2 should be placed
    A) where it is now.
    B) before sentence 1.
    C) after sentence 3.
    D) after sentence 4.

5. A) NO CHANGE
    B) Consider, for example, the tale of "Little Red Riding Hood," a story of murder and mayhem.
    C) Consider, for example, the tale of "Little Red Riding Hood."
    D) Consider, for example, the tale of "Little Red Riding Hood," a story told to children—and repeated by them—for at least 300 years.

both Granny and Little Red are devoured. **6** <u>Little Red is engaged in one of the most terrifying conversations in all literature when the wolf, having already eaten dear old Granny,</u> utters the chilling line: "All the better to eat you with!" Even Charles Dickens, an author whose own fictional world was hardly free of brutality against children, confessed that he deplored "the cruelty and treachery of that dissembling wolf who ate [Little Red's] grandmother without making any impression on his appetite, and then ate her [Little Red], after making a ferocious joke about his teeth." **7** <u>Believe it or not, but the version where both Grandmother and Little Red are eaten was not the worst version of the tale circulating in Charles Dickens's time.</u> In other parts of the world, children heard an even more horrifying story that concluded with the wolf collecting the grandmother's blood in bottles.

8 One theory suggests that fairy tales represent an attempt to deal with realistic threats in **9** <u>fantastic</u> terms. Living conditions for most families from Elizabethan times to the early nineteenth century made it impossible to shelter children from many of the harsher aspects of adult life. Families lived in cramped quarters

6. A) NO CHANGE

    B) Little Red is engaged in one of the most terrifying conversations in all literature when the wolf

    C) The wolf, having already eaten dear old Granny, engages Little Red in one of the most terrifying conversations in all literature when he

    D) The wolf, having already eaten dear old Granny,

7. A) NO CHANGE

    B) Yet, that was not the worst version of the tale circulating in Dickens's time.

    C) Yet, the version where both Grandmother and Little Red are eaten was not the worst version of the tale circulating in Dickens's time.

    D) Believe it or not, that was not the worst version of the tale circulating in Dickens's time.

8. Which choice, if inserted here, most effectively establishes the central idea of the paragraph?

    A) So why did the writers and tellers of fairy tales continually gloss over unsavory stories, avoiding themes of homicide, maiming, and lunacy?

    B) So why did Dickens continue to study—and mimic—the fairy tales he claimed to dislike?

    C) Theories for why fairy tales continually revisit these themes are hard to find.

    D) So why did the writers and tellers of fairy tales continually produce such unsavory stories, with their thinly veiled themes of homicide, maiming, and lunacy?

that precluded **10** any form of privacy. While prevailing notions of criminal justice required that punishment—whether flogging or imprisonment in stocks or even hanging or disembowelment—be conducted as a public spectacle. Fairy tales distanced this grisly reality by placing it in a context of unreal fantasies. But at the same time, the tales made children aware of dangers and wary of evil temptations. **11**

9. A) NO CHANGE
   B) caustic
   C) existent
   D) plausible

10. A) NO CHANGE
    B) any form of privacy, while prevailing notions
    C) any form of privacy while prevailing notions
    D) any form of privacy; while prevailing notions

11. Which choice most effectively concludes the paragraph and the passage?
    A) Indeed, fairy tales of old could do little to protect a child from the harshness of life and, at best, could only serve as a brief escape from the drudgery and danger that typified reality for most people.
    B) Thus, the fictionalized violence of fairy tales was simply the ancestor of the American entertainment industry.
    C) Thus, though parents today are concerned with violence in children's media, we can see that it is nothing new—and, in fact, that its origin was meant to help children rather than to harm them.
    D) Far from harming children, then, the fictionalized violence of fairy tales—as deplorable as it may seem in principle—is comparable to the film industry's violence today, in that it seems to have little effect on raising healthy children.

CHAPTER 15

Conventions of Punctuation

CHAPTER OBJECTIVES

By the end of this chapter, you will be able to:

1. Recognize and correct inappropriate uses of punctuation within and at the end of sentences

2. Identify and correct inappropriate uses of possessive nouns

3. Recognize and omit unnecessary punctuation

SMARTPOINTS

Point Value	SmartPoint Category
40 Points	Punctuation

END-OF-SENTENCE AND WITHIN-SENTENCE PUNCTUATION

The PSAT Writing & Language Test will require you to identify and correct inappropriate use of ending punctuation that deviates from the intent implied by the context. You will also have to identify and correct inappropriate colons, semicolons, and dashes when used to indicate breaks in thought within a sentence.

You can recognize Punctuation questions because the underlined portion of the text will include a punctuation mark. The answer choices will move that punctuation mark around or replace it with another punctuation mark.

Use **commas** to:

- Separate independent clauses connected by a FANBOYS conjunction (*for, and, nor, but, or, yet, so*)
  Jess finished her homework earlier than expected, so she started on a project that was due the following week.

- Separate an introductory or modifying phrase from the rest of the sentence
  Knowing that soccer practice would be especially strenuous, Tia filled up three water bottles and spent extra time stretching beforehand.

- Set off three or more items in a series or list
  Jeremiah packed a sleeping bag, a raincoat, and a lantern for his upcoming camping trip.

- Separate nonessential information from the rest of the sentence
  Professor Mann, who was the head of the English department, was known for including a wide variety of reading materials in the curriculum.

- Separate an independent and dependent clause
  Tyson arrived at school a few minutes early, which gave him time to clean his locker before class.

> **✔ Expert Tip**
>
> When you see an underlined comma, ask yourself, "Can the comma be replaced by a period or a semicolon?" If yes, the comma is grammatically incorrect and needs to be changed.

Use **semicolons** to:

- Join two independent clauses that are not connected by a FANBOYS conjunction
  Gaby knew that her term paper would take at least four more hours to write; she got started in study hall and then finished it at home.

- Separate items in a series or list if those items already include commas
  The team needed to bring uniforms, helmets, and gloves; oranges, almonds, and water; and hockey sticks, pucks, and skates.

> ✔ **Expert Tip**
>
> When you see an underlined semicolon, ask yourself, "Can the semicolon be replaced by a comma?" If yes, the semicolon is grammatically incorrect and needs to be changed. If the semicolon is separating two independent clauses and can be replaced with a period, it is grammatically correct.

Use **colons** to:

- Introduce and/or emphasize a short phrase, quotation, explanation, example, or list
  Sanjay had two important projects to complete: a science experiment and an expository essay.

Use **dashes** to:

- Indicate a hesitation or a break in thought
  Going to a history museum is a good way to begin researching prehistoric creatures—on second thought, heading to the library will likely be much more efficient.

> ✔ **Expert Tip**
>
> When you see an underlined colon or dash, ask yourself, "Has the author included a new idea by introducing or explaining something or by breaking his or her thought process?" If yes, the punctuation is often grammatically correct.

Let's look at the following Writing & Language passage and question. After the passage, there are two columns. The left column contains a test-like question. The column on the right features the strategic thinking a test expert employs when approaching the passage and question presented.

Question 1 is based on the following passage.

San Francisco Cable Cars

San Francisco's cable cars get their name from the long, heavy cable that runs beneath the streets along which the cars travel. This cable system resembles a giant laundry clothesline with a pulley at each end. Electricity turns the wheels of the **1** pulleys, they in turn make the cable move. Under its floor, each car has a powerful claw. The claw grips the cable when the car is ready to move, and it releases the cable when the car needs to stop. The cars themselves are not powered and don't generate any locomotion. Instead, they simply cling to the cable, which pulls them up and down San Francisco's steep hills.

Questions	Strategic Thinking
1. Which of the following is LEAST acceptable? A) NO CHANGE B) pulleys; they C) pulleys, and they D) pulleys. They	**Step 1: Read the passage and identify the issue** *What punctuation does the underlined segment include?* A comma *Can the comma be replaced by a period or semi-colon?* Yes, because the two clauses the comma connects are both independent. **Step 2: Eliminate answer choices that do not address the issue** *Which answer choice(s) can you eliminate?* The question asks for the LEAST acceptable answer. Choices B, C, and D all correct the error, so they can be eliminated. **Step 3: Plug in the remaining answer choices and select the most correct, concise, and relevant one** *Which is the correct answer?* Choice (A)

POSSESSIVE NOUNS AND PRONOUNS

Possessive nouns and pronouns indicate who or what possesses another noun or pronoun. Each follows different rules, and the PSAT will test both. These questions require you to identify both the singular and plural forms.

You can spot errors in possessive noun and pronoun construction by looking for the following:

- Two nouns in a row
- Context clues
- Pronouns with apostrophes
- Words that sound alike

Possessive Nouns		
Singular	sister's	*My oldest **sister's** soccer game is on Saturday.*
Plural	sisters'	*My two older **sisters'** soccer games are on Saturday.*

Questions about possessive pronouns often require you to watch out for contractions and sound-alike words.

Possessive Pronouns and Words to Watch Out For	
its = possessive	it's = it is/it has
their = possessive	there = location/place
whose = possessive	who's = who is/who has

Reading & Writing

Let's look at the following Writing & Language passage and question. After the passage, there are two columns. The left column contains a test-like question. The column on the right features the strategic thinking a test expert employs when approaching the passage and question presented.

Question 2 is based on the following passage.

The Discovery of Penicillin

In 1928, bacteriologist Dr. Alexander Fleming observed that a spot of mold had contaminated one of the glass plates on which he was growing a colony of bacteria. Instead of discarding the plate immediately, he noticed that bacteria were flourishing everywhere on the plate except in the **2** molds' vicinity. He decided to culture the mold and found that a broth filtered from it inhibited the growth of several species of bacteria. Nine years later, a team of scientists led by Howard Florey and Ernst Chain isolated the active antibacterial agent in Fleming's broth: penicillin. Florey and Chain went on to demonstrate that penicillin could cure bacterial infections in mice and in humans. Penicillin became a "miracle drug."

Question	Strategic Thinking
2. A) NO CHANGE B) mold C) molds D) mold's	**Step 1: Read the passage and identify the issue** *Are there any clues that suggest a grammatical issue?* Yes, an apostrophe is underlined. *What's the issue?* "Mold" should be singular, so the singular possessive is needed here. **Step 2: Eliminate answer choices that do not address the issue** *Which answer choice(s) can you eliminate?* Eliminate A because the sentence is incorrect as written. Eliminate B and C because they are both nouns and therefore cannot modify another noun. **Step 3: Plug in the remaining answer choices and select the most correct, concise, and relevant one** *Which is the correct answer?* Choice (D) because it properly forms a singular possessive and correctly modifies the noun "vicinity"

PARENTHETICAL/NONRESTRICTIVE ELEMENTS AND UNNECESSARY PUNCTUATION

Use **commas**, **dashes**, or **parentheses** to set off parenthetical or nonrestrictive information in a sentence.

> ### ✔ Definition
>
> Parenthetical or nonrestrictive information includes words or phrases that aren't essential to the sentence structure or content. Sometimes, however, this information is explanatory.

The PSAT will also ask you to recognize instances of unnecessary punctuation, particularly commas.

Do NOT use a comma to:

- Separate a subject from its predicate
- Separate a verb from its object or its subject, or a preposition from its object
- Set off restrictive elements
- Precede a dependent clause that comes after an independent clause
- Separate adjectives that work together to modify a noun

> ### ✔ Expert Tip
>
> To determine whether information is nonessential, read the sentence without the information. If the sentence still makes sense without the omitted words, then those words need to be set off with punctuation.

Let's look at the following Writing & Language passage and question. After the passage, there are two columns. The left column contains a test-like question. The column on the right features the strategic thinking a test expert employs when approaching the passage and question presented.

Question 3 is based on the following passage.

Raymond Carver

American **3** author, Raymond Carver, once said that everything we write is in some way autobiographical. This observation applies particularly to Carver's own work. In his seven books of short stories, Carver wrote almost exclusively about the working-class environment in which he grew up, portraying a neglected section of the American people with honesty and clarity. Born in the blue-collar town of Yakima, Washington, Carver was raised in a house where Zane Gray westerns and the local newspaper constituted the world of literature. After graduating from high school with Ds in English, he held a variety of jobs, ranging from scrubbing floors in a hospital to assembling bicycles at the local Sears. Few would have predicted that he would become a master of the short-story form, a literary figure mentioned in the same breath as Hemingway and Chekhov. And yet, it was in these humble surroundings that Carver found the inspiration for his unique narrative style: a plainspoken voice that enabled him to express the fears and aspirations of ordinary people.

Question	Strategic Thinking
3. A) NO CHANGE B) author, Raymond Carver once, C) author Raymond Carver once D) author Raymond Carver, once	**Step 1: Read the passage and identify the issue** *What clue is in the underlined section?* Commas setting off "Raymond Carter" *What do those commas tell you?* That if you delete the information within the commas, the sentence must still make sense logically *Does the sentence still make sense?* No, because "American author once said . . ." doesn't make sense. The sentence needs the information that is currently set off by commas. **Step 2: Eliminate answer choices that do not address the issue** *Which answer choice(s) can you eliminate?* Eliminate any answer with commas—B and D. **Step 3: Plug in the remaining answer choices and select the most correct, concise, and relevant one** *Which is the correct answer?* Choice (C) because it removes the commas around the necessary information

You have seen the ways in which the PSAT tests you on Punctuation in Writing & Language passages and the way a PSAT expert approaches these types of questions.

Use the Kaplan Method for Writing & Language to answer the four questions that accompany the following Writing & Language passage excerpt. Remember to look at the strategic thinking questions that have been laid out for you—some of the answers have been filled in, but you will have to complete the answers to others.

Use your answers to the strategic thinking questions to select the correct answer, just as you will on Test Day.

Questions 4–7 are based on the following passage.

The Sistine Chapel

One shudders to contemplate Michelangelo's reaction if he were to gaze up today at the famous frescoes* he painted on the ceiling of the Sistine Chapel over four centuries ago. A practical man, he would no doubt be unsurprised by the effects of time and environment on his masterpiece. He would be philosophical about the damage wrought by mineral salts left behind when rainwater leaked through the roof. The layers of dirt and soot from coal braziers that heated the chapel and from candles and incense burned during religious functions would—prior to their removal during restoration—likely have been taken in stride as **4** <u>well, however,</u> he would be appalled by the ravages recently inflicted on his work by restorers.

The Vatican restoration team reveled in inducing a jarringly colorful transformation in the frescoes with special cleaning solvents and computerized analysis equipment. However, this effect was **5** <u>not as they claimed achieved</u> merely by removing the dirt and animal glue (employed by earlier restorers to revive muted colors) from the frescoes; they removed Michelangelo's final touches as well. Gone from the ceiling is the quality of suppressed anger and thunderous pessimism so often commented on by admiring scholars. That quality was not an artifact of grime, not a misleading monochrome imposed on the ceiling by time, for Michelangelo himself applied a veil of glaze to the frescoes to darken them after he had deemed his work too bright. The master would have felt compelled to add a few more layers of glaze had the ceiling radiated forth as it does now. The solvents of the restorers, in addition to stripping away the shadows, reacted chemically with Michelangelo's pigments to produce hues the painter never beheld.

Of course, the restorers left open an avenue for the reversal of their progress toward color and brightness. Since the layers of animal glue were no longer there to serve as protection, the atmospheric pollutants from the city of Rome gained direct access to the frescoes. Significant darkening was already noticed in some of the restored work a mere four years after **6** <u>it's</u> completion. It remains to be seen whether the measure introduced to arrest this process—an extensive climate-control **7** <u>system—will</u> itself have any long-term effect on the chapel's ceiling.

fresco: a style of painting on plaster using water-based pigments

Question	Strategic Thinking
4. A) NO CHANGE B) well; however C) well. However D) well. However,	**Step 1: Read the passage and identify the issue** *What is the punctuation issue?* There is a comma joining two independent clauses. *How can you fix this?* Properly join the clauses or separate them into two sentences **Step 2: Eliminate answer choices that do not address the issue** *Which answer choice(s) can you eliminate?* Eliminate B and C because they fail to include the appropriate punctuation after the word "however." **Step 3: Plug in the remaining answer choices and select the most correct, concise, and relevant one** *Which is the correct answer?* _____
5. A) NO CHANGE B) not as they claimed, achieved C) not, as they claimed achieved D) not, as they claimed, achieved	**Step 1: Read the passage and identify the issue** *What is the grammatical issue?* There is missing punctuation—the sentence is confusing as written. *What part of the underlined segment is nonessential?* "As they claimed" **Step 2: Eliminate answer choices that do not address the issue** *Which answer choice(s) can you eliminate?* _____ **Step 3: Plug in the remaining answer choices and select the most correct, concise, and relevant one** *Which is the correct answer?*_____

Question	Strategic Thinking
6. A) NO CHANGE B) its C) their D) it is	**Step 1: Read the passage and identify the issue** *What is the grammatical issue? "It's" means "it is,"* which doesn't make sense in context. *What should "it's" be replaced with?* _____ **Step 2: Eliminate answer choices that do not address the issue** *Which answer choice(s) can you eliminate?* _____ **Step 3: Plug in the remaining answer choices and select the most correct, concise, and relevant one** *Which is the correct answer?* _____
7. A) NO CHANGE B) system will C) system, will D) system, and will	**Step 1: Read the passage and identify the issue** *What is the grammatical issue?* _____ **Step 2: Eliminate answer choices that do not address the issue** *Which answer choice(s) can you eliminate?* _____ **Step 3: Plug in the remaining answer choices and select the most correct, concise, and relevant one** *Which is the correct answer?* _____

Reading & Writing

Now try a test-like Writing & Language passage on your own. Give yourself 5 minutes to read the passage and answer the questions.

Questions 8–15 are based on the following passage.

Museums

City museums are places where people can learn about various cultures by studying objects of particular historical or artistic value. The increasingly popular "design museums" that are opening today perform quite a different function. Unlike most city **8** museums the design museum displays and assesses objects that are readily available to the general public. These museums place everyday household items under **9** spotlights. Breaking down the barriers between commerce and creative invention.

Critics have argued that design museums are often manipulated to serve as advertisements for new industrial technology. Their **10** role however is not simply a matter of merchandising—it is the honoring of **11** impressive, innovative products. The difference between the window of a department store and the showcase in a design museum is that the first tries to sell you something while the second informs you of the success of the attempt.

One advantage that the design museum has over other civic museums is that design museums are places where people feel familiar with the exhibits. Unlike the average art gallery patron, a design **12** museums visitor rarely feels intimidated or disoriented. This is partly

8. A) NO CHANGE
    B) museums; the
    C) museums: the
    D) museums, the

9. A) NO CHANGE
    B) spotlights; breaking
    C) spotlights, breaking
    D) spotlights breaking

10, A) NO CHANGE
    B) role; however, is
    C) role, however is
    D) role, however, is

11. A) NO CHANGE
    B) impressive innovative
    C) impressive, and innovative
    D) impressively innovative

12. A) NO CHANGE
    B) museums' visitor
    C) museum's visitor
    D) museum visitor's

because design museums clearly illustrate how and why mass-produced consumer objects work and look as they **13** do, and show how design contributes to the quality of our lives. For example, an exhibit involving a particular design of chair would not simply explain how it functions as a chair. It would also demonstrate how its various features combine to produce an artistic effect or redefine our manner of performing the basic act of being seated. Thus, the purpose of such an exhibit would be to present these concepts in novel **14** ways and to challenge, stimulate, and inform the viewer. An art gallery exhibit, on the other hand, would provide very little information about the chair and charge the visitor with understanding the exhibit on some abstract level.

Within the past decade, several new design museums have opened their doors. Each of these museums has responded in totally original ways to the public's growing interest in the field. London's Design Museum, for instance, displays a collection of mass-produced objects ranging from Zippo lighters to electric typewriters to a show of Norwegian sardine-tin labels. The options open to curators of design museums seem far less rigorous, conventionalized, and preprogrammed than those open to curators in charge of public galleries of paintings and sculpture. **15** Societies humorous aspects are better represented in the display of postmodern playthings or quirky Japanese vacuum cleaners in pastel colors than in an exhibition of Impressionist landscapes.

13. A) NO CHANGE
    B) do and show
    C) do: show
    D) do—show

14. A) NO CHANGE
    B) ways to challenge,
    C) ways; to challenge,
    D) ways—to challenge,

15. A) NO CHANGE
    B) Society's
    C) Societys'
    D) Societie's

Answers and Explanations for this chapter begin on page 604.

ON YOUR OWN

The following questions provide an opportunity to practice the concepts and strategic thinking covered in this chapter. While many of the questions pertain to Conventions of Punctuation, some touch on other concepts tested on the Writing & Language Test to ensure that your practice is test-like, with a variety of question types per passage.

Questions 1–11 are based on the following passage.

The Modern Professional

Despite the honor accorded them by society and the usually substantial monetary rewards they enjoy for their work, many modern professionals **1** complain and they feel demoralized. They don't command the respect of the public or enjoy special privileges as members of exclusive groups to the extent that professionals once did. This decline in the **2** profession's status is difficult for them to bear because, they vehemently **3** maintain, the knowledge and unique skills of professionals are as vital and indispensable to society as they have ever been.

Originally, being a professional meant practicing in one of the "learned professions," a category that included only law, theology, university scholarship, and (eventually) medicine **4** —long considered a practical art. Members of these groups distinguished themselves from the rest of society by their possession of certain special knowledge that brought with it power and abilities most others could not even fully fathom. **5** Aspirants, to a profession, were required not only to devote themselves to a demanding life of learning but also to adhere to a specifically tailored system of ethics to prevent the misuse of professional

1. A) NO CHANGE
    B) complain; they
    C) complain, and they
    D) complain that they

2. A) NO CHANGE
    B) professional
    C) professions'
    D) professions

3. A) NO CHANGE
    B) maintain the
    C) maintain. The
    D) maintain; the

4. A) NO CHANGE
    B) —considered a practical art.
    C) —for a long while considered to be a practical art.
    D) DELETE the underlined portion.

5. A) NO CHANGE
    B) Aspirants to a profession were
    C) Aspirants to a profession, were
    D) Aspirants, to a profession were

powers. The special deference and privileges these professionals received were their reward for using their knowledge in the service of others rather than of themselves.

[6] Because many of today's professionals would argue that this description still applies to them, the truth of the matter is that the professional scene has changed quite a bit since the days of the "learned professions." When the members of the professions began to organize themselves in the nineteenth century, establishing work standards and policing themselves to prevent the government from cleaning house for them, they proclaimed that they were doing this for the good of the public. The professional associations [7] that emerged from this structuring proved to be, however, far more advantageous to the professionals than to the general [8] populace. The associations began to function as [9] lobbies, and interest groups.

A further consequence of this organizing was that the elevated position of the professional gradually eroded as members of other occupations [10] jumped on the bandwagon. When just about any group could organize itself and call itself a profession, the concept of the professional as the possessor of special knowledge and abilities didn't seem to be as valid. Thus, many professions have had to struggle to [11] sustain and preserve the notion that their members provide a critical service to society that no one else can.

6. A) NO CHANGE
   B) As a result
   C) In addition
   D) Although

7. A) NO CHANGE
   B) who
   C) whom
   D) when

8. A) NO CHANGE
   B) populace because the
   C) populace, and the
   D) populace; the

9. A) NO CHANGE
   B) lobbies and, interest groups.
   C) lobbies and interest groups.
   D) lobbies, interest groups.

10. A) NO CHANGE
    B) claimed professional status
    C) joined in on the fun
    D) stated their wishes to be seen professionally

11. A) NO CHANGE
    B) sustain, and preserve
    C) preserve and sustain
    D) sustain

PART FOUR

Review

CHAPTER 16

Putting It All Together

KAPLAN METHOD FOR MATH

Step 1: Read the question, identifying and organizing important information as you go

Step 2: Choose the best strategy to answer the question

Step 3: Check that you answered the *right* question

Step 1: Read the question, identifying and organizing important information as you go

- **What information am I given?** Take a few seconds to jot down the information you are given and try to group similar items together.

- **Separate the question from the context.** Word problems may include information that is unnecessary to solve the question. Feel free to discard any unnecessary information.

- **How are the answer choices different?** Reading answer choices carefully can help you spot the most efficient way to solve a multiple-choice math question. For example, if the answer choices in a question on the calculator section are decimals, then painstakingly rewriting your final answer as a simplified fraction is a waste of time; you can just use your calculator instead.

- **Should I label or draw a diagram?** If the question describes a shape or figure but doesn't provide one, sketch a diagram so you can see the shape or figure and add notes to it. If a figure is provided, take a few seconds to label it with information from the question.

Step 2: Choose the best strategy to answer the question

- **Look for patterns.** Every PSAT math question can be solved in a variety of ways, but not all strategies are created equally. To finish all of the questions, you'll need to solve questions as *efficiently* as possible. If you find yourself about to do time-consuming math, take a moment to look for time-saving shortcuts.

- **Pick numbers or use straightforward math.** While you can always solve a PSAT math question with what you've learned in school, doing so won't always be the fastest way. On questions that describe relationships between numbers (such as percentages) but don't actually use numbers, you can often save time on Test Day by using a technique such as Picking Numbers instead of straightforward math.

Step 3: Check that you answered the *right* question

- When you get the final answer, **resist the urge to immediately bubble in the answer**. Take a moment to:
  - Review the question stem
  - Check units of measurement
  - Double-check your work

- The PSAT will often ask you for quantities such as $x + 1$ or the product of x and y. **Be careful on these questions!** They often include tempting answer choices that correspond to the values of x or y individually. There's no partial credit on the PSAT, so take a moment at the end of every question to make sure you're answering the right question.

KAPLAN METHOD FOR MULTI-PART MATH QUESTIONS

Step 1: Read the first question in the set, looking for clues

Step 2: Identify and organize the information you need

Step 3: Based on what you know, plan your steps to navigate the first question

Step 4: Solve, step-by-step, checking units as you go

Step 5: Did I answer the *right* question?

Step 6: Repeat for remaining questions, incorporating results from the previous question if possible

Step 1: Read the first question in the set, looking for clues

- **Focus all your energy here** instead of diluting it over the whole set of questions; solving a multi-part question in pieces is far simpler than trying to solve all the questions in the set at once. Furthermore, you may be able to use the results from earlier parts to solve subsequent ones. Don't even consider the later parts of the question set until you've solved the first part.

- **Watch for hints** about what information you'll actually need to use to answer the questions. Underlining key quantities is often helpful to separate what's important from extraneous information.

Step 2: Identify and organize the information you need

- **What information am I given?** Jot down key notes, and group related quantities to develop your strategy.

- **What am I solving for?** This is your target. As you work your way through subsequent steps, keep your target at the front of your mind. This will help you avoid unnecessary work (and subsequent time loss). You'll sometimes need to tackle these questions from both ends, so always keep your goal in mind.

Step 3: Based on what you know, plan your steps to navigate the first question

- **What pieces am I missing?** Many students become frustrated when faced with a roadblock such as missing information, but it's an easy fix. Sometimes you'll need to do an intermediate calculation to reveal the missing piece or pieces of the puzzle.

Step 4: Solve, step-by-step, checking units as you go

- **Work quickly but carefully**, just as you've done on other PSAT math questions.

Step 5: Did I answer the *right* question?

- As is the case with the Kaplan Method for Math, **make sure your final answer is the requested answer**.

- Review the first question in the set.

- Double-check your units and your work.

Step 6: Repeat for remaining questions, incorporating results from the previous question if possible

Now take your results from the first question and think critically about whether they fit into the subsequent questions in the set. Previous results won't always be applicable, but when they are, they often lead to huge time savings. But be careful—don't round results from the first question in your calculations for the second question—only the final answer should be rounded.

KAPLAN METHOD FOR READING COMPREHENSION

Step 1: Read actively

Step 2: Examine the question stem

Step 3: Predict and answer

Step 1: Read actively

Active reading means:

- Ask questions and take notes *as* you read the passage. Asking questions about the passage and taking notes are integral parts of your approach to acing the PSAT Reading Test.

Some of the questions you might want to ask include:

- Why did the author write this word/detail/sentence/paragraph?
- Is the author taking a side? If so, what side is he or she taking?
- What are the tone and purpose of the passage?

Make sure you remember to:

- Identify the passage type
- Take notes, circle key words, and underline key phrases

Step 2: Examine the question stem

This means you should:

- Identify key words and line references in the question stem
- Apply question-type strategies as necessary

Step 3: Predict and answer

This means you should:

- Predict an answer before looking at the answer choices, also known as "predict before you peek"
- Select the best match

Predicting before you peek helps you:

- Eliminate the possibility of falling into incorrect answer traps

KAPLAN METHOD FOR INFOGRAPHICS

Step 1: Read the question

Step 2: Examine the infographic

Step 3: Predict and answer

Step 1: Read the question

- Analyze the question stem for information that will help you zero in on the specific parts of the infographic that apply to the question.

Step 2: Examine the infographic

- Circle parts of the infographic that relate directly to the question.
- Identify units of measurement, labels, and titles.

Step 3: Predict and answer

- Do not look at the answer choices until you've used the infographic to make a prediction.

KAPLAN METHOD FOR WRITING & LANGUAGE

Step 1: Read the passage and identify the issue

- If there's an infographic, apply the Kaplan Method for Infographics.

Step 2: Eliminate answer choices that do not address the issue

Step 3: Plug in the remaining answer choices and select the most correct, concise, and relevant one

Step 1: Read the passage and identify the issue

This means:

- Rather than reading the whole passage and then answering all of the questions, you can answer questions as you read because they are mostly embedded in the text itself.
- When you see a number, stop reading and look at the question. If you can answer it with what you've read so far, do so. If you need more information, keep reading for context until you can answer the question.

Step 2: Eliminate answer choices that do not address the issue

Eliminating answer choices that do not address the issue:

- Increases your odds of getting the correct answer by removing obviously incorrect answer choices

Step 3: Plug in the remaining answer choices, and select the most correct, concise, and relevant one

Correct, concise, and relevant means that the answer choice you select:

- Makes sense when read with the correction
- Is as short as possible while retaining the information in the text
- Relates well to the passage overall

Answer choices should not:

- Change the intended meaning of the original sentence, paragraph, or passage

- Introduce new grammatical errors

KAPLAN STRATEGY FOR TRANSLATING ENGLISH INTO MATH

- Define any variables, choosing letters that make sense.

- Break sentences into short phrases.

- Translate each phrase into a mathematical expression.

- Put the expressions together to form an equation.

KAPLAN STRATEGY FOR COMMAND OF EVIDENCE QUESTIONS

- When you see a question asking you to choose the best evidence to support your answer to the previous question, review how you selected that answer.

- Avoid answers that provide evidence for incorrect answers to the previous question.

- The correct answer will support why the previous question's answer is correct.

KAPLAN STRATEGY FOR VOCAB-IN-CONTEXT QUESTIONS

- Pretend the word is a blank in the sentence.

- Predict what word could be substituted for the blank.

- Select the answer choice that best matches your prediction.

KAPLAN STRATEGY FOR PAIRED PASSAGES

- Read Passage 1, then answer its questions.

- Read Passage 2, then answer its questions.

- Answer questions about both passages.

COUNTDOWN TO TEST DAY

The Week Before the Test

- Finish up any required homework assignments, including online quizzes.

- Focus your additional practice on the question types and/or subject areas in which you usually score highest. Now is the time to sharpen your best skills, not cram new information.

- Make sure you are registered for the test. Remember, Kaplan cannot register you. If you missed the registration deadlines, you can request Waitlist Status on the test maker's website, collegeboard.org.

- Confirm the location of your test site. Never been there before? Make a practice run to make sure you know exactly how long it will take to get from your home to your test site. Build in extra time in case you hit traffic on the morning of the test.

- Get a great night's sleep the two days before the test.

The Day Before the Test

- Review the Kaplan Methods and Strategies, as well as the ReKap pages.

- Put new batteries in your calculator.

- Pack your backpack or bag for Test Day with the following items:

  - Photo ID

  - Registration slip or printout

  - Directions to your test site location

  - Five or more sharpened no. 2 pencils (no mechanical pencils)

  - Pencil sharpener

  - Eraser

  - Calculator

  - Extra batteries

  - Non prohibited timepiece

  - Tissues

  - Prepackaged snacks, like granola bars

  - Bottled water, juice, or sports drink

  - Sweatshirt, sweater, or jacket

The Night Before the Test

- No studying!

- Do something relaxing that will take your mind off the test, such as watching a movie or playing video games with friends.

- Set your alarm to wake up early enough so that you won't feel rushed.

- Go to bed early, but not too much earlier than you usually do. You want to fall asleep quickly, not spend hours tossing and turning.

The Morning of the Test

- Dress comfortably and in layers. You need to be prepared for any temperature.

- Eat a filling breakfast, but don't stray too far from your usual routine. If you normally aren't a breakfast eater, don't eat a huge meal, but make sure you have something substantial.

- Read something over breakfast. You need to warm up your brain so you don't go into the test cold. Read a few pages of a newspaper, magazine, or novel.

- Get to your test site early. There is likely to be some confusion about where to go and how to sign in, so allow yourself plenty of time, even if you are taking the test at your own school.

- Leave your cell phone at home or in your car's glove box. Many test sites do not allow them in the building.

- While you're waiting to sign in or be seated, read more of what you read over breakfast to stay in reading mode.

During the Test

- Be calm and confident. You're ready for this!

- Remember that while the PSAT is an almost three-hour marathon, it is also a series of shorter sections. Focus on the section you're working on at that moment; don't think about previous or upcoming sections.

- Use the Kaplan Methods and Strategies as often as you can.

- Don't linger too long on any one question. Mark it and come back to it later.

- Can't figure out an answer? Try to eliminate some choices and guess strategically. Remember, there is no penalty for an incorrect answer, so even if you can't eliminate any choices, you should take a guess.

- There will be plenty of questions you CAN answer, so spend your time on those first!

- Maintain good posture throughout the test. It will help you stay alert.

- If you find yourself losing concentration, getting frustrated, or stressing about the time, stop for 30 seconds. Close your eyes, put your pencil down, take a few deep breaths, and relax your shoulders. You'll be much more productive after taking a few moments to relax.

- Use your breaks effectively. During the five-minute breaks, go to the restroom, eat your snacks, and get your energy up for the next section.

After the Test

- Congratulate yourself! Also, reward yourself by doing something fun. You've earned it.

- Be aware that you can cancel your score if you got sick during the test or if something else happened that might have negatively affected your score. You have until the Wednesday following your test date. Request a score cancellation form from your test proctor or visit the test maker's website for more information. If you have questions about whether you should cancel your scores, call 1-800-KAP-TEST.

- Note that your scores will be available online approximately three to four weeks after your test and will be mailed to you with in approximately six weeks.

PART FIVE

Practice Tests

HOW TO SCORE YOUR PRACTICE TESTS

For each subject area in the practice test, convert your raw score, or the number of questions you answered correctly, to a scaled score using the table below. To get your raw score for Evidence-Based Reading & Writing, add the total number of Reading questions you answered correctly to the total number of Writing questions you answered correctly; for Math, add the number of questions you answered correctly for the Math—No-Calculator and Math—Calculator sections.

Evidence-Based Reading and Writing		Math		Evidence-Based Reading and Writing		Math	
TOTAL Raw Score	Scaled Score	Raw Score	Scaled Score	TOTAL Raw Score	Scaled Score	Raw Score	Scaled Score
0	160	0	160	46	490	46	750
1	160	1	190	47	490	47	760
2	180	2	210	48	500	48	760
3	190	3	240	49	510		
4	200	4	270	50	520		
5	210	5	290	51	520		
6	220	6	320	52	530		
7	230	7	340	53	540		
8	240	8	360	54	540		
9	250	9	370	55	540		
10	280	10	390	56	550		
11	280	11	400	57	550		
12	290	12	420	58	560		
13	300	13	430	59	560		
14	310	14	440	60	570		
15	320	15	460	61	580		
16	320	16	470	62	580		
17	340	17	480	63	580		
18	340	18	490	64	590		
19	350	19	500	65	590		
20	350	20	510	66	600		
21	360	21	520	67	610		
22	360	22	530	68	610		
23	360	23	540	69	620		
24	380	24	550	70	620		
25	380	25	560	71	630		
26	380	26	570	72	630		
27	390	27	580	73	640		
28	390	28	580	74	640		
29	400	29	590	75	640		
30	400	30	600	76	650		
31	420	31	610	77	660		
32	420	32	620	78	670		
33	420	33	630	79	680		
34	420	34	640	80	680		
35	430	35	650	81	690		
36	430	36	670	82	700		
37	440	37	680	83	710		
38	440	38	690	84	720		
39	450	39	710	85	720		
40	460	40	720	86	730		
41	460	41	730	87	740		
42	460	42	730	88	740		
43	470	43	740	89	750		
44	480	44	740	90	750		
45	480	45	750	91	760		

PSAT PRACTICE TEST 1 ANSWER SHEET

Remove (or photocopy) this answer sheet and use it to complete the test. See the answer key following the test when finished.

Start with number 1 for each section. If a section has fewer questions than answer spaces, leave the extra spaces blank.

SECTION

1

1. Ⓐ Ⓑ Ⓒ Ⓓ	13. Ⓐ Ⓑ Ⓒ Ⓓ	25. Ⓐ Ⓑ Ⓒ Ⓓ	37. Ⓐ Ⓑ Ⓒ Ⓓ
2. Ⓐ Ⓑ Ⓒ Ⓓ	14. Ⓐ Ⓑ Ⓒ Ⓓ	26. Ⓐ Ⓑ Ⓒ Ⓓ	38. Ⓐ Ⓑ Ⓒ Ⓓ
3. Ⓐ Ⓑ Ⓒ Ⓓ	15. Ⓐ Ⓑ Ⓒ Ⓓ	27. Ⓐ Ⓑ Ⓒ Ⓓ	39. Ⓐ Ⓑ Ⓒ Ⓓ
4. Ⓐ Ⓑ Ⓒ Ⓓ	16. Ⓐ Ⓑ Ⓒ Ⓓ	28. Ⓐ Ⓑ Ⓒ Ⓓ	40. Ⓐ Ⓑ Ⓒ Ⓓ
5. Ⓐ Ⓑ Ⓒ Ⓓ	17. Ⓐ Ⓑ Ⓒ Ⓓ	29. Ⓐ Ⓑ Ⓒ Ⓓ	41. Ⓐ Ⓑ Ⓒ Ⓓ
6. Ⓐ Ⓑ Ⓒ Ⓓ	18. Ⓐ Ⓑ Ⓒ Ⓓ	30. Ⓐ Ⓑ Ⓒ Ⓓ	42. Ⓐ Ⓑ Ⓒ Ⓓ
7. Ⓐ Ⓑ Ⓒ Ⓓ	19. Ⓐ Ⓑ Ⓒ Ⓓ	31. Ⓐ Ⓑ Ⓒ Ⓓ	43. Ⓐ Ⓑ Ⓒ Ⓓ
8. Ⓐ Ⓑ Ⓒ Ⓓ	20. Ⓐ Ⓑ Ⓒ Ⓓ	32. Ⓐ Ⓑ Ⓒ Ⓓ	44. Ⓐ Ⓑ Ⓒ Ⓓ
9. Ⓐ Ⓑ Ⓒ Ⓓ	21. Ⓐ Ⓑ Ⓒ Ⓓ	33. Ⓐ Ⓑ Ⓒ Ⓓ	45. Ⓐ Ⓑ Ⓒ Ⓓ
10. Ⓐ Ⓑ Ⓒ Ⓓ	22. Ⓐ Ⓑ Ⓒ Ⓓ	34. Ⓐ Ⓑ Ⓒ Ⓓ	46. Ⓐ Ⓑ Ⓒ Ⓓ
11. Ⓐ Ⓑ Ⓒ Ⓓ	23. Ⓐ Ⓑ Ⓒ Ⓓ	35. Ⓐ Ⓑ Ⓒ Ⓓ	47. Ⓐ Ⓑ Ⓒ Ⓓ
12. Ⓐ Ⓑ Ⓒ Ⓓ	24. Ⓐ Ⓑ Ⓒ Ⓓ	36. Ⓐ Ⓑ Ⓒ Ⓓ	

☐ # correct in Section 1

☐ # incorrect in Section 1

SECTION

2

1. Ⓐ Ⓑ Ⓒ Ⓓ	12. Ⓐ Ⓑ Ⓒ Ⓓ	23. Ⓐ Ⓑ Ⓒ Ⓓ	34. Ⓐ Ⓑ Ⓒ Ⓓ
2. Ⓐ Ⓑ Ⓒ Ⓓ	13. Ⓐ Ⓑ Ⓒ Ⓓ	24. Ⓐ Ⓑ Ⓒ Ⓓ	35. Ⓐ Ⓑ Ⓒ Ⓓ
3. Ⓐ Ⓑ Ⓒ Ⓓ	14. Ⓐ Ⓑ Ⓒ Ⓓ	25. Ⓐ Ⓑ Ⓒ Ⓓ	36. Ⓐ Ⓑ Ⓒ Ⓓ
4. Ⓐ Ⓓ Ⓓ Ⓓ	15. Ⓐ Ⓓ Ⓓ Ⓓ	26. Ⓐ Ⓓ Ⓓ Ⓓ	37. Ⓐ Ⓓ Ⓓ Ⓓ
5. Ⓐ Ⓑ Ⓒ Ⓓ	16. Ⓐ Ⓑ Ⓒ Ⓓ	27. Ⓐ Ⓑ Ⓒ Ⓓ	38. Ⓐ Ⓑ Ⓒ Ⓓ
6. Ⓐ Ⓑ Ⓒ Ⓓ	17. Ⓐ Ⓑ Ⓒ Ⓓ	28. Ⓐ Ⓑ Ⓒ Ⓓ	39. Ⓐ Ⓑ Ⓒ Ⓓ
7. Ⓐ Ⓑ Ⓒ Ⓓ	18. Ⓐ Ⓑ Ⓒ Ⓓ	29. Ⓐ Ⓑ Ⓒ Ⓓ	40. Ⓐ Ⓑ Ⓒ Ⓓ
8. Ⓐ Ⓑ Ⓒ Ⓓ	19. Ⓐ Ⓑ Ⓒ Ⓓ	30. Ⓐ Ⓑ Ⓒ Ⓓ	41. Ⓐ Ⓑ Ⓒ Ⓓ
9. Ⓐ Ⓑ Ⓒ Ⓓ	20. Ⓐ Ⓑ Ⓒ Ⓓ	31. Ⓐ Ⓑ Ⓒ Ⓓ	42. Ⓐ Ⓑ Ⓒ Ⓓ
10. Ⓐ Ⓑ Ⓒ Ⓓ	21. Ⓐ Ⓑ Ⓒ Ⓓ	32. Ⓐ Ⓑ Ⓒ Ⓓ	43. Ⓐ Ⓑ Ⓒ Ⓓ
11. Ⓐ Ⓑ Ⓒ Ⓓ	22. Ⓐ Ⓑ Ⓒ Ⓓ	33. Ⓐ Ⓑ Ⓒ Ⓓ	44. Ⓐ Ⓑ Ⓒ Ⓓ

☐ # correct in Section 2

☐ # incorrect in Section 2

Practice Tests

SECTION 3

1. Ⓐ Ⓑ Ⓒ Ⓓ
2. Ⓐ Ⓑ Ⓒ Ⓓ
3. Ⓐ Ⓑ Ⓒ Ⓓ
4. Ⓐ Ⓑ Ⓒ Ⓓ

5. Ⓐ Ⓑ Ⓒ Ⓓ
6. Ⓐ Ⓑ Ⓒ Ⓓ
7. Ⓐ Ⓑ Ⓒ Ⓓ
8. Ⓐ Ⓑ Ⓒ Ⓓ

9. Ⓐ Ⓑ Ⓒ Ⓓ
10. Ⓐ Ⓑ Ⓒ Ⓓ
11. Ⓐ Ⓑ Ⓒ Ⓓ
12. Ⓐ Ⓑ Ⓒ Ⓓ

13. Ⓐ Ⓑ Ⓒ Ⓓ

correct in Section 3

incorrect in Section 3

14. 15. 16. 17.

SECTION 4

1. Ⓐ Ⓑ Ⓒ Ⓓ
2. Ⓐ Ⓑ Ⓒ Ⓓ
3. Ⓐ Ⓑ Ⓒ Ⓓ
4. Ⓐ Ⓑ Ⓒ Ⓓ
5. Ⓐ Ⓑ Ⓒ Ⓓ
6. Ⓐ Ⓑ Ⓒ Ⓓ
7. Ⓐ Ⓑ Ⓒ Ⓓ

8. Ⓐ Ⓑ Ⓒ Ⓓ
9. Ⓐ Ⓑ Ⓒ Ⓓ
10. Ⓐ Ⓑ Ⓒ Ⓓ
11. Ⓐ Ⓑ Ⓒ Ⓓ
12. Ⓐ Ⓑ Ⓒ Ⓓ
13. Ⓐ Ⓑ Ⓒ Ⓓ
14. Ⓐ Ⓑ Ⓒ Ⓓ

15. Ⓐ Ⓑ Ⓒ Ⓓ
16. Ⓐ Ⓑ Ⓒ Ⓓ
17. Ⓐ Ⓑ Ⓒ Ⓓ
18. Ⓐ Ⓑ Ⓒ Ⓓ
19. Ⓐ Ⓑ Ⓒ Ⓓ
20. Ⓐ Ⓑ Ⓒ Ⓓ
21. Ⓐ Ⓑ Ⓒ Ⓓ

22. Ⓐ Ⓑ Ⓒ Ⓓ
23. Ⓐ Ⓑ Ⓒ Ⓓ
24. Ⓐ Ⓑ Ⓒ Ⓓ
25. Ⓐ Ⓑ Ⓒ Ⓓ
26. Ⓐ Ⓑ Ⓒ Ⓓ
27. Ⓐ Ⓑ Ⓒ Ⓓ

correct in Section 4

incorrect in Section 4

28. 29. 30. 31.

READING TEST

60 Minutes—47 Questions

This section corresponds to Section 1 of your answer sheet.

Directions: Read each passage or pair of passages, then answer the questions that follow. Choose your answers based on what the passage(s) and any accompanying graphics state or imply.

Questions 1–9 are based on the following passage.

The following passage is adapted from Charles Dickens's 1860 novel *Great Expectations*. In this scene, the narrator, a boy named Pip, eats breakfast with his older sister's acquaintance, Mr. Pumblechook. Pumblechook has agreed to take Pip to see Miss Havisham, a wealthy woman who has requested this visit, although Pip has never met her.

Mr. Pumblechook and I breakfasted at eight o'clock in the parlor behind the shop, while the shopman took his mug of tea and hunch of bread and butter
Line on a sack of peas in the front premises. I considered
(5) Mr. Pumblechook wretched company. Besides being possessed by my sister's idea that a mortifying and penitential character ought to be imparted to my diet,[1]—besides giving me as much crumb as possible in combination with as little butter, and putting
(10) such a quantity of warm water into my milk that it would have been more candid to have left the milk out altogether,—his conversation consisted of nothing but arithmetic. On my politely bidding him Good morning, he said, pompously, "Seven times nine,
(15) boy?" And how should I be able to answer, dodged in that way, in a strange place, on an empty stomach! I was hungry, but before I had swallowed a morsel, he began a running sum that lasted all through the breakfast. "Seven?" "And four?" "And eight?" . . . And
(20) so on. And after each figure was disposed of, it was as much as I could do to get a bite or a sup, before the next came; while he sat at his ease guessing nothing, and eating bacon and hot roll, in (if I may be allowed the expression) a gorging and gormandizing manner.

(25)   For such reasons, I was very glad when ten o'clock came and we started for Miss Havisham's; though I was not at all at my ease regarding the manner in which I should acquit myself under that lady's roof. Within a quarter of an hour we came to Miss
(30) Havisham's house, which was of old brick, and dismal, and had a great many iron bars to it. Some of the windows had been walled up; of those that remained, all the lower were rustily barred. There was a courtyard in front, and that was barred; so we
(35) had to wait, after ringing the bell, until some one should come to open it. While we waited at the gate, I peeped in (even then Mr. Pumblechook said, "And fourteen?" but I pretended not to hear him), and saw that at the side of the house there was a large
(40) brewery. No brewing was going on in it, and none seemed to have gone on for a long long time.

A window was raised, and a clear voice demanded "What name?" To which my conductor replied, "Pumblechook." The voice returned, "Quite right,"
(45) and the window was shut again, and a young lady came across the courtyard, with keys in her hand.

"This," said Mr. Pumblechook, "is Pip."

"This is Pip, is it?" returned the young lady, who was very pretty and seemed very proud; "come in, Pip."

(50)   Mr. Pumblechook was coming in also, when she stopped him with the gate.

"Oh!" she said. "Did you wish to see Miss Havisham?"

"If Miss Havisham wished to see me," returned
(55) Mr. Pumblechook, discomfited.

"Ah!" said the girl; "but you see she don't."

She said it so finally, and in such an

---

[1]Pip's sister indicated to Pumblechook that Pip should be grateful, even penitent (unreasonably so) for his help.

GO ON TO THE NEXT PAGE

undiscussible way, that Mr. Pumblechook, though in a condition of ruffled dignity, could not
(60) protest. But he eyed me severely,—as if I had done anything to him!—and departed with the words reproachfully delivered: "Boy! Let your behavior here be a credit unto them which brought you up by hand!"[2] I was not free from apprehension that
(65) he would come back to propound through the gate, "And sixteen?" But he didn't.

[2]Pumblechook is speaking of Pip's sister, who often boasts that she raised him "by hand."

1. According to the first paragraph, Pip's breakfast with Mr. Pumblechook is

   A) eaten on the run.

   B) small and of poor quality.

   C) better than Pip usually receives.

   D) carefully cooked and served.

2. As used in line 5, "wretched" most nearly means

   A) shameful.

   B) deprived.

   C) distressing.

   D) heartbroken.

3. Based on the passage, it can be inferred that Mr. Pumblechook

   A) has looked forward to his morning with Pip.

   B) is as uncomfortable as Pip is during breakfast.

   C) has known Pip and his sister for a very long time.

   D) is indifferent to Pip's discomfort during breakfast.

4. Which choice provides the best support for the answer to the previous question?

   A) Lines 1–4 ("Mr. Pumblechook . . . premises")

   B) Lines 5–13 ("Besides . . . arithmetic")

   C) Lines 43–44 ("To which my . . . Pumblechook")

   D) Lines 57–60 ("She said . . . protest")

5. What theme is communicated through the experiences of Pip, the narrator?

   A) The world can be a puzzling and sometimes cruel place.

   B) Young people are misunderstood by their elders.

   C) Mean-spirited people deserve to be treated harshly.

   D) The favors one receives in life should be reciprocated.

6. Which of the following is true when Mr. Pumblechook leaves Pip at Miss Havisham's house?

   A) Pip is excited to finally meet Miss Havisham.

   B) Pip is nervous about being away from his sister for so long.

   C) Pip is relieved to be away from Mr. Pumblechook.

   D) Pip is anxious about spending time with the young lady who greets them.

7. Which choice provides the best support for the answer to the previous question?

   A) Lines 1–4 ("Mr. Pumblechook . . . premises")

   B) Lines 42–43 ("A window . . . name")

   C) Lines 57–60 ("She said . . . protest")

   D) Lines 64–66 ("I was not . . . he didn't")

8. As used in line 59, "condition" most nearly means

   A) illness.

   B) prerequisite.

   C) state.

   D) limitation.

GO ON TO THE NEXT PAGE

Practice Tests

9. The function of the parenthetical comment in lines 23–24 is to reveal that

    A) Pip is usually more polite in his references to others.

    B) Mr. Pumblechook appreciates gourmet food.

    C) Pip is very angered that his own breakfast is so meager.

    D) Mr. Pumblechook has no qualms about overeating in public.

Questions 10–18 are based on the following passage.

This passage is adapted from Martin Luther King, Jr.'s "Letter from Birmingham Jail."

. . . I think I should give the reason for my being in Birmingham, since you have been influenced by the argument of "outsiders coming in." I have
Line the honor of serving as president of the Southern
(5) Christian Leadership Conference, an organization operating in every Southern state with headquarters in Atlanta, Georgia. We have some eighty-five affiliate organizations all across the South, one being the Alabama Christian Movement for
(10) Human Rights. Whenever necessary and possible we share staff, educational, and financial resources with our affiliates. Several months ago our local af-filiate here in Birmingham invited us to be on call to engage in a nonviolent direct action program if such
(15) were deemed necessary. We readily consented and when the hour came we lived up to our promises. So I am here, along with several members of my staff, because we were invited here. I am here because I have basic organizational ties here. Beyond this, I
(20) am in Birmingham because injustice is here. . . .

Moreover, I am cognizant of the interrelatedness of all communities and states. I cannot sit idly by in Atlanta and not be concerned about what happens in Birmingham. Injustice anywhere is a
(25) threat to justice everywhere. We are caught in an inescapable network of mutuality, tied in a single

garment of destiny. Whatever affects one directly affects all indirectly. Never again can we afford to live with the narrow, provincial "outside agitator"
(30) idea. Anyone who lives inside the United States can never be considered an outsider anywhere in this country. . . .

You may well ask, "Why direct action? Why sit-ins, marches, etc.? Isn't negotiation a better path?" You
(35) are exactly right in your call for negotiation. Indeed, this is the purpose of direct action. Nonviolent direct action seeks to create such a crisis and establish such creative tension that a community that has constantly refused to negotiate is forced to confront the issue. It
(40) seeks so to dramatize the issue that it can no longer be ignored. I just referred to the creation of tension as a part of the work of the nonviolent resister. This may sound rather shocking. But I must confess that I am not afraid of the word tension. I have earnestly
(45) worked and preached against violent tension, but there is a type of constructive nonviolent tension that is necessary for growth. Just as Socrates felt that it was necessary to create a tension in the mind so that individuals could rise from the bondage of myths and
(50) half-truths to the unfettered realm of creative analysis and objective appraisal, we must see the need of having nonviolent gadflies to create the kind of tension in society that will help men rise from the dark depths of prejudice and racism to the majestic
(55) heights of understanding and brotherhood. So the purpose of the direct action is to create a situation so crisis-packed that it will inevitably open the door to negotiation. We, therefore, concur with you in your call for negotiation. Too long has our beloved
(60) Southland been bogged down in the tragic attempt to live in monologue rather than dialogue. . . .

My friends, I must say to you that we have not made a single gain in civil rights without determined legal and nonviolent pressure.
(65) History is the long and tragic story of the fact that privileged groups seldom give up their privileges voluntarily. Individuals may see the moral light and voluntarily give up their unjust posture; but

GO ON TO THE NEXT PAGE

as Reinhold Niebuhr has reminded us, groups are
(70) more immoral than individuals.

We know through painful experience that freedom is never voluntarily given by the oppressor;
it must be demanded by the oppressed. . . . For
years now I have heard the word "Wait!" It rings in
(75) the ear of every African American with a piercing
familiarity. This "wait" has almost always meant
"never." It has been a tranquilizing thalidomide,
relieving the emotional stress for a moment, only
to give birth to an ill-formed infant of frustra-
(80) tion. We must come to see with the distinguished
jurist of yesterday that "justice too long delayed is
justice denied." We have waited for more than three
hundred and forty years for our constitutional and
God-given rights. The nations of Asia and Africa
(85) are moving with jet-like speed toward the goal of
political independence, and we still creep at horse
and buggy pace toward the gaining of a cup of coffee at a lunch counter. . . .

10. King's purpose for writing this letter is

A) to explain why he came to Birmingham to
   protest.

B) to launch a nonviolent protest movement in
   Birmingham.

C) to open an affiliate of the Southern
   Christian Leadership Conference in
   Birmingham.

D) to support fellow civil rights activists in
   Birmingham.

11. Which choice provides the best evidence for the
    answer to the previous question?

A) Lines 1–2 ("I think . . . in Birmingham")

B) Lines 3–7 ("I have . . . Atlanta, Georgia")

C) Lines 7–10 ("We have some . . . Rights")

D) Lines 24–25 ("Injustice anywhere . . .
   everywhere")

12. As used in lines 21–22, "interrelatedness of all
    communities and states" most nearly means that

A) King has personal connections to people in
   the town.

B) the Southern Christian Leadership
   Conference needs national support.

C) events in one part of the country affect
   everyone in the nation.

D) local civil rights groups operate independently of one another.

13. Based on paragraph 3, it can be reasonably inferred
    that King believed circumstances in Birmingham
    at the time

A) were unfair and wrong.

B) constituted an isolated event.

C) justified his arrest.

D) required federal intervention.

14. Which choice provides the best evidence for the
    answer to the previous question?

A) Lines 21–22 ("Moreover, . . . states")

B) Lines 24–25 ("Injustice anywhere . . .
   everywhere")

C) Lines 25–27 ("We are caught . . . destiny")

D) Lines 28–30 ("Never again . . . idea")

15. As used in line 40, "dramatize" most nearly means

A) to cast events in an appealing light.

B) to draw attention to significant events.

C) to exaggerate events to seem more
   important.

D) to turn events into a popular performance.

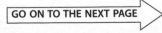 GO ON TO THE NEXT PAGE

16. Which choice most clearly paraphrases a claim made by King in paragraph 3?

  A) A failure to negotiate in the South has provoked secret action by civil rights activists.

  B) A focus on dialogue blinds reformers to the necessity for direct action to promote change.

  C) Direct action is necessary to motivate people to talk about prejudice and racism.

  D) Nonviolent protest encourages a sense of brotherhood and understanding among citizens.

17. Paragraph 4 best supports the claims made in paragraph 3 by

  A) arguing that nonviolent pressure is most likely to spur just action by individuals.

  B) clarifying that throughout history, privileged classes have been reluctant to let go of privilege.

  C) drawing a distinction between the morality of individuals and of groups.

  D) pointing out that few gains in civil rights have been made without nonviolent pressure.

18. King refers to "the gaining of a cup of coffee at a lunch counter" (lines 87–88) primarily to

  A) call attention to the sedative effect of delaying civil rights reform in the United States.

  B) emphasize that white Americans will not willingly end oppression against black Americans.

  C) describe the progress made toward the winning of equal rights in other countries.

  D) underscore the contrast between progress made in other countries and the United States.

Questions 19–28 are based on the following passages and supplementary material.

The idea of a World Bank became a reality in 1944, when delegates to the Bretton Woods Conference pledged to "outlaw practices which are agreed to be harmful to world prosperity." Passage 1 discusses the benefits of the World Bank, while Passage 2 focuses on the limited lifespan of the Bretton Woods system.

Passage 1

In 1944, 730 delegates from forty-four Allied nations met in Bretton Woods, New Hampshire, just as World War II was ending. They were attend-
Line ing an important conference. This mostly forgotten
(5) event shaped our modern world because delegates at the Bretton Woods Conference agreed on the establishment of an international banking system.

To ensure that all nations would prosper, the United States and other allied nations set rules
(10) for a postwar international economy. The Bretton Woods system created the International Monetary Fund (IMF). The IMF was founded as a kind of global central bank from which member countries could borrow money. The countries needed money
(15) to pay for their war costs. Today, the IMF facilitates international trade by ensuring the stability of the international monetary and financial system.

The Bretton Woods system also established the World Bank. Although the World Bank shares
(20) similarities with the IMF, the two institutions remain distinct. While the IMF maintains an orderly system of payments and receipts between nations, the World Bank is mainly a development institution. The World Bank initially gave loans to European countries dev-
(25) astated by World War II, and today it lends money and technical assistance specifically to economic projects in developing countries. For example, the World Bank might provide a low-interest loan to a country attempting to improve education or
(30) health. The goal of the World Bank is to "bridge the economic divide between poor and rich countries." In short, the organizations differ in their purposes. The Bank promotes economic and social progress so people can live better lives, while the IMF represents

GO ON TO THE NEXT PAGE ▷

(35) the entire world in its goal to foster global monetary cooperation and financial stability.

These two specific accomplishments of the Bretton Woods Conference were major. However, the Bretton Woods system particularly benefited (40) the United States. It effectively established the U.S. dollar as a global currency. A global currency is one that countries worldwide accept for all trade, or international transactions of buying and selling. Because only the U.S. could print dollars, the United (45) States became the primary power behind both the IMF and the World Bank. Today, global currencies include the U.S. dollar, the euro (European Union countries), and the yen (Japan).

The years after Bretton Woods have been (50) considered the golden age of the U.S. dollar. More importantly, the conference profoundly shaped foreign trade for decades to come.

Passage 2

The financial system established at the 1944 Bretton Woods Conference endured for many years. Even (55) after the United States abrogated agreements made at the conference, the nation continued to experience a powerful position in international trade by having other countries tie their currencies to the U.S. dollar. The world, however, is changing.

(60) In reality, the Bretton Woods system lasted only three decades. Then, in 1971, President Richard Nixon introduced a new economic policy by ending the convertibility of the dollar to gold. It marked the end of the Bretton Woods international monetary (65) framework, and the action resulted in worldwide financial crisis. Two cornerstones of Bretton Woods, however, endured: the International Monetary Fund (IMF) and the World Bank.

Since the collapse of the Bretton Woods system, (70) IMF members have been trading using a flexible exchange system. Namely, countries allow their exchange rates to fluctuate in response to changing conditions. The exchange rate between two currencies, such as the Japanese yen and the U.S. (75) dollar, for example, specifies how much one currency is worth in terms of the other. An exchange rate of 120 yen to dollars means that 120 yen are worth the same as one dollar.

Even so, the U.S. dollar has remained the most (80) widely used money for international trade, and having one currency for all trade may be better than using a flexible exchange system.

This seems to be the thinking of a powerful group of countries. The Group of Twenty (G20), which has (85) called for a new Bretton Woods, consists of governments and leaders from 20 of the world's largest economies including China, the United States, and the European Union. In 2009, for example, the G20 announced plans to create a new global currency (90) to replace the U.S. dollar's role as the anchor currency. Many believe that China's yuan, quickly climbing the financial ranks, is well on its way to becoming a major world reserve currency.

In fact, an earlier 1988 article in *The Economist* (95) stated, "30 years from now, Americans, Japanese, Europeans, and people in many other rich countries and some relatively poor ones will probably be paying for their shopping with the same currency."

The article predicted that the world supply of (100) currency would be set by a new central bank of the IMF. This prediction seems to be coming to fruition since the G20 indicated that a "world currency is in waiting." For an international construct such as the original Bretton Woods to last some 26 (105) years is nothing less than amazing. But move over Bretton Woods; a new world order in finance could be on the fast track.

GO ON TO THE NEXT PAGE ▷

Top 10 International Currencies						
(Percent Shares of Average Daily Currency Trading)						
	2007		2010		2013	
	Share	*Rank*	*Share*	*Rank*	*Share*	*Rank*
U.S. Dollar (USD)	85.6%	1	84.9%	1	87.0%	1
Euro (EUR)	37.0%	2	39.1%	2	33.4%	2
Japanese Yen (JPY)	17.2%	3	19.0%	3	23.0%	3
UK Pound (GBP)	14.9%	4	12.9%	4	11.8%	4
Australian Dollar (AUD)	6.6%	6	7.6%	5	8.6%	5
Swiss Franc (CHF)	6.8%	5	6.3%	6	5.2%	6
Canadian Dollar (CAD)	4.3%	7	5.3%	7	4.6%	7
Mexican Peso (MXN)	1.3%	12	1.3%	14	2.5%	8
Chinese Yuan (CNY)	0.5%	20	0.9%	17	2.2%	9
New Zealand Dollar	1.9%	11	1.6%	10	2.0%	10

Adapted from Mauldin Economics; Bank for International Settlements, September 2013 Triennial Central Bank Survey.

19. Based on Passage 1, it can reasonably be inferred that

A) world leaders recognized the need for markets to function independently.

B) Bretton Woods increased U.S. economic influence around the world.

C) the IMF and the World Bank work closely together to ensure prosperity.

D) the conclusion of World War II had little influence on events at Bretton Woods.

20. Which choice provides the best evidence for the answer to the previous question?

A) Lines 8–10 ("To ensure . . . economy")

B) Lines 10–12 ("The Bretton . . . Fund")

C) Lines 44–46 ("Because only . . . World Bank")

D) Lines 50–52 ("More importantly . . . to come")

21. As used in line 35, "foster" most nearly means

A) publicize.

B) rear.

C) stabilize.

D) encourage.

GO ON TO THE NEXT PAGE

22. Which statement best explains the difference between the purposes of the IMF and the World Bank?

   A) The IMF provides money to pay for war costs, while the World Bank offers assistance to rebuild countries recovering from war across the globe.

   B) The IMF encourages stability in the global financial system, while the World Bank promotes economic development in relatively poor nations.

   C) The IMF supports the U.S. dollar in international markets, while the World Bank provides low-interest loans to many nations around the world.

   D) The IMF offers governments advice about participation in global markets, while the World Bank encourages monetary cooperation between nations.

23. Based on the second paragraph in Passage 2, it can be reasonably inferred that

   A) the United States did not support the goals of the IMF and the World Bank.

   B) Bretton Woods was originally intended to last for three decades.

   C) President Nixon acted to reinforce the decisions made at Bretton Woods.

   D) some U.S. policy decisions differed from international consensus over Bretton Woods.

24. Which choice provides the best evidence for the answer to the previous question?

   A) Lines 60–61 ("In reality . . . three decades")

   B) Lines 61–63 ("Then, in 1971 . . . to gold")

   C) Lines 66–68 ("Two cornerstones . . . World Bank")

   D) Lines 69–71 ("Since the collapse . . . exchange system")

25. As used in line 90, "anchor" most nearly means

   A) key.

   B) fastening.

   C) rigid.

   D) supporting.

26. It can reasonably be inferred from both Passage 2 and the graphic that

   A) international markets are increasingly comfortable using the yuan as trade currency.

   B) the United States favors using the yuan as one of the world's reserve currencies.

   C) the G20 wants to replace the yuan and other currencies with a new global currency.

   D) the IMF continues to support the yuan and other currencies in a flexible exchange system.

27. Which statement most effectively compares the authors' purposes in both passages?

   A) Passage 1's purpose is to contrast the functions of the IMF and World Bank, while Passage 2's purpose is to outline the benefits of a flexible trade system to the United States.

   B) Passage 1's purpose is to describe the history of international trade in the 20th century, while Passage 2's purpose is to explain why the Bretton Woods system collapsed.

   C) Passage 1's purpose is to describe Bretton Woods' effect on the global economy, while Passage 2's purpose is to suggest that a new currency for global trade may soon be implemented.

   D) Passage 1's purpose is to promote the economic benefits of the IMF and World Bank, while Passage 2's purpose is to encourage the reestablishment of the Bretton Woods system.

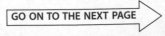 GO ON TO THE NEXT PAGE

28. Both passages support which generalization about the global economy?

A) U.S. influence on global trade has continued under a flexible exchange system.

B) The purposes of the International Monetary Fund and the World Bank are indirectly related.

C) The Group of Twenty represents the financial interests of the world's largest economies.

D) International institutions such as the IMF continue to influence economic trade and development.

Questions 29–38 are based on the following passage.

This passage is adapted from an article about treating paralysis.

According to a study conducted by the Christopher and Dana Reeve Foundation, more than six million people in the United States suffer from debilitating
Line paralysis. That's close to one person in every fifty
(5) who suffers from a loss of the ability to move or feel in areas of his or her body. Paralysis is often caused by illnesses, such as stroke or multiple sclerosis, or injuries to the spinal cord. Research scientists have made advances in the treatment of paralysis, which
(10) means retraining affected individuals to become as independent as possible. Patients learn how to use wheelchairs and prevent complications that are caused by restricted movement. This retraining is key in maintaining paralytics' quality of life; however, an actual
(15) cure for paralysis has remained elusive—until now.

In 2014, surgeons in Poland collaborated with the University College London's Institute of Neurology to treat a Polish man who was paralyzed from the chest down as a result of a spinal cord in-
(20) jury. The scientists chose this patient for their study because of the countless hours of physical therapy he had undergone with no signs of progress. Twenty-one months after their test subject's initial spinal cord injury, his condition was considered

(25) complete as defined by the American Spinal Injury Association (ASIA)'s Impairment Scale. This meant that he experienced no sensory or motor function in the segments of his spinal cord nearest to his injury.

(30) The doctors used a technique refined during forty years of spinal cord research on rats. They removed one of two of the patient's olfactory bulbs, which are structures found at the top of the human nose. From this structure, samples of olfactory ensheath-
(35) ing cells, responsible for a portion of the sense of smell, were harvested. These cells allow the olfactory system to renew its cells over the course of a human life. It is because of this constant regeneration that scientists chose these particular cells to implant into
(40) the patient's spinal cord. After being harvested, the cells were reproduced in a culture. Then, the cells were injected into the patient's spinal cord in 100 mini-injections above and below the location of his injury. Four strips of nerve tissue were then placed
(45) across a small gap in the spinal cord.

After surgery, the patient underwent a tailor-made neurorehabilitation program. In the nineteen months following the operation, not only did the patient experience no adverse effects, but his condi-
(50) tion improved from ASIA's class A to class C. Class C is considered an incomplete spinal cord injury, meaning that motor function is preserved to a certain extent and there is some muscle activity. The patient experienced increased stability in the trunk
(55) of his body, as well as partial recovery of voluntary movements in his lower extremities. As a result, he was able to increase the muscle mass in his thighs and regain sensation in those areas. In late 2014, he took his first steps with the support of only a walker.

(60) These exciting improvements suggest that the nerve grafts doctors placed in the patient's spinal cord bridged the injured area and prompted the regeneration of fibers. This was the first-ever clinical study that showed beneficial effects of cells transplanted into the
(65) spinal cord. The same team of scientists plans to treat ten more patients using this "smell cell" transplant technique. If they have continued success, patients around the world can have both their mobility and their hope restored.

Practice Tests

GO ON TO THE NEXT PAGE

29. The passage is primarily concerned with

    A) how various diseases and injuries can cause permanent paralysis.

    B) ways in which doctors and therapists work to improve patients' quality of life.

    C) one treatment being developed to return mobility to patients suffering paralysis.

    D) methods of physical therapy that can help patients with spinal cord injuries.

30. Based on the information in the passage, it can be inferred that the author

    A) believes more research should be done before patients with paralysis are subjected to the treatment described in the passage.

    B) feels that increased mobility will have a positive impact on patients suffering from all levels of paralysis.

    C) thinks that more scientists should study paralysis and ways to improve the quality of life for patients with limited mobility.

    D) was part of the research team that developed the new method of treating paralysis described in the passage.

31. Which choice provides the best support for the answer to the previous question?

    A) Lines 6–8 ("Paralysis is . . . spinal cord")

    B) Lines 16–20 ("In 2014 . . . injury")

    C) Lines 53–56 ("The patient . . . extremities")

    D) Lines 67–69 ("If they . . . restored")

32. As used in line 13, "restricted" most nearly means

    A) confidential.

    B) dependent.

    C) increased.

    D) limited.

33. In lines 46–47, the author's use of the word "tailor-made" helps reinforce the idea that

    A) the injected cells were from the patient and were therefore well-suited to work in his own body.

    B) spinal cord cells were replaced during the transplant portion of the individualized treatment.

    C) olfactory bulbs were removed from rats and placed in the patient's spinal cord during surgery.

    D) the method used by doctors to locate the damaged area required expertise and precision.

34. It can reasonably be inferred from the passage that

    A) the patient's treatment would have been more successful if scientists had used cells from another area of his body instead of from his olfactory bulbs.

    B) cells from olfactory bulbs will be used to cure diseases that affect areas of the body other than the spinal cord.

    C) the patient who received the experimental treatment using cells from olfactory bulbs would not have regained mobility without this treatment.

    D) soon doctors will be able to treat spinal injuries without time-consuming and demanding physical therapy.

35. Which choice provides the best evidence for the answer to the previous question?

    A) Lines 8–11 ("Research scientists . . . possible")

    B) Lines 20–22 ("The scientists . . . progress")

    C) Lines 31–33 ("They removed . . . nose")

    D) Lines 60–63 ("These exciting . . . fibers")

GO ON TO THE NEXT PAGE

36. As used in line 30, "refined" most nearly means

    A) advanced.

    B) improved.

    C) experienced.

    D) treated.

37. The success of the patient's treatment was due in large part to

    A) studies done on other patients.

    B) research conducted by other doctors in Poland.

    C) many experiments performed on rats.

    D) multiple attempts on various types of animals.

38. The procedure described in which cells from olfactory bulbs are injected into a damaged area of the spinal cord is most analogous to which of the following?

    A) Replacing a diseased organ in a patient with an organ from a donor who has the same tissue type

    B) Giving a patient with a high fever an injection of medication to bring the core body temperature down

    C) Placing a cast on a limb to hold the bone in place to encourage healing after suffering a break

    D) Grafting skin from a healthy area of the body and transplanting it to an area that has suffered severe burns

Questions 39–47 are based on the following passage and supplementary material.

The following passage is adapted from an essay about mercury in fish.

Mercury is an unusual element; it is a metal but is liquid at room temperature. It is also a neurotoxin and a teratogen, as it causes nerve damage

Line and birth defects. Mercury can be found just about
(5) everywhere; it is in soil, in air, in household items, and even in our food. Everyday objects, such as thermometers, light switches, and fluorescent light-bulbs, contain mercury in its elemental form. Batteries can also contain mercury, but they contain
(10) it in the form of the inorganic compound mercury chloride. Mercury can also exist as an organic compound, the most common of which is methyl-mercury. While we can take steps to avoid both elemental and inorganic mercury, it is much harder
(15) to avoid methylmercury.

Most of the mercury in the environment comes from the emissions of coal-burning power plants; coal contains small amounts of mercury, which are released into the air when coal burns. The concen-
(20) tration of mercury in the air from power plants is very low, so it is not immediately dangerous. However, the mercury is then washed out of the air by rain-storms and eventually ends up in lakes and oceans.

The mercury deposited in the water does not in-
(25) stantaneously get absorbed by fish, as elemental mer-cury does not easily diffuse through cell membranes. However, methylmercury diffuses into cells easily, and certain anaerobic bacteria in the water convert the elemental mercury to methylmercury as a by-
(30) product of their metabolic processes. Methylmer-cury released into the water by the bacteria diffuses into small single-celled organisms called plankton. Small shrimp and other small animals eat the plank-ton and absorb the methylmercury in the plankton
(35) during digestion. Small fish eat the shrimp and then larger fish eat the smaller fish; each time an animal preys on another animal, the predator absorbs the methylmercury. Because each animal excretes the methylmercury much more slowly than it absorbs
(40) it, methylmercury builds up in the animal over time and is passed on to whatever animal eats it, resulting in a process called bioaccumulation.

As people became aware of the bioaccumulation of mercury in fish, many reacted by eliminating
(45) seafood from their diet. However, seafood contains certain omega-3 fatty acids that are important for good health. People who do not eat enough of these fatty acids, especially eicosapentaenoic acid (EPA)

GO ON TO THE NEXT PAGE ▷

and docosahexaenoic acid (DHA), are more likely
(50) to have heart attacks than people who have enough
EPA and DHA in their diet. Because fish and shell-
fish, along with some algae, are the only sources of
these fatty acids, eliminating them from our diet
might have worse health effects than consuming
(55) small amounts of mercury.

Scientists have studied the effects of mercury by
conducting tests on animals and by studying various human populations and recording the amount
of mercury in their blood. By determining the lev-
(60) els of mercury consumption that cause any of the
known symptoms of mercury poisoning, they were
able to identify a safe level of mercury consumption. The current recommendation is for humans
to take in less than 0.1 microgram of mercury for
(65) every kilogram of weight per day. This means that
a 70-kilogram person (about 155 pounds) could
safely consume 7 micrograms of mercury per day.
Because haddock averages about 0.055 micrograms
of mercury per gram, that person could safely eat
(70) 127 grams (about 4.5 ounces) of haddock per day.
On the other hand, swordfish averages about 0.995
micrograms of mercury per gram of fish, so the
70-kilogram person could safely eat only about 7
grams (about one-quarter of an ounce) of swordfish
(75) per day.

Nutritionists recommend that, rather than
eliminate fish from our diet, we try to eat more of
the low-mercury fish and less of the high-mercury
fish. Low-mercury species tend to be smaller
(80) omnivorous fish while high-mercury species tend
to be the largest carnivorous fish. Awareness of
the particulars of this problem, accompanied by
mindful eating habits, will keep us on the best
course for healthy eating.

Species	Average Weight Range (grams)	Average Mercury Concentration (parts per billion)
Alaskan Pollock	227–1,000	31
Atlantic Haddock	900–1,800	55
Atlantic Herring	100–600	84
Chub Mackerel	100–750	88
Cod	800–4,000	111
Skipjack Tuna	2,000–10,000	144
Black-Striped Bass	6,820–15,900	152
Albacore Tuna	4,540–21,364	358
Marlin	180,000	485

39. The author of the passage would most likely agree
with which of the following statements?

A) Mercury poisoning is only one of many
concerns that should be considered when
choosing which fish to add to one's diet.

B) More should be done by scientists and
nutritionists to inform people about the
dangers of mercury poisoning.

C) Fish is an essential part of a healthy diet
and can be eaten safely if recommendations
for mercury consumption are kept in mind.

D) The mercury present in the air is more
dangerous to people than the mercury
consumed by eating fish with high mercury
levels.

40. Which choice provides the best evidence for the
answer to the previous question?

A) Lines 16–17 ("Most of . . . plants")

B) Lines 30–32 ("Methylmercury released . . .
plankton")

C) Lines 56–59 ("Scientists . . . their blood")

D) Lines 81–84 ("Awareness . . . eating")

GO ON TO THE NEXT PAGE

41. In addition to the levels of mercury in a specific species of fish, people should also consider which of the following when determining a safe level of consumption?

    A) Their own body weight

    B) Where the fish was caught

    C) The other meats they are eating

    D) What they ate the day before

42. As used in lines 19–20, "concentration" most nearly means

    A) focus.

    B) application.

    C) density.

    D) awareness.

43. The passage most strongly suggests which of the following statements is accurate?

    A) It is not possible to completely avoid environmental exposure to mercury.

    B) Inorganic mercury is more dangerous to humans than organic mercury.

    C) Most of the exposure to mercury experienced by humans comes from fish consumption.

    D) Mercury is one of the most abundant elements found in nature.

44. Which choice provides the best evidence for the answer to the previous question?

    A) Lines 1–2 ("Mercury is an unusual . . . temperature")

    B) Lines 4–6 ("Mercury . . . our food")

    C) Lines 19–21 ("The concentration . . . dangerous")

    D) Lines 27–30 ("However, methylmercury . . . processes")

45. Which of the following pieces of evidence would most strengthen the author's line of reasoning?

    A) More examples in paragraph 1 of places mercury is found

    B) Details in paragraph 2 about the levels of mercury found in the air

    C) An explanation in paragraph 4 of how to treat mercury poisoning

    D) More examples in paragraph 5 of how many micrograms of mercury people of different weights could eat

46. As used in line 82, "particulars" most nearly means

    A) data.

    B) specifics.

    C) points.

    D) evidence.

47. Based on the information in the passage and the graphic, which of the following statements is true?

    A) The fish with the lowest average weight is the safest to eat.

    B) A person can safely eat more marlin than albacore tuna in one day.

    C) Eating large fish carries a lower risk of mercury poisoning than eating small fish.

    D) A person can safely eat more Alaskan pollock than black striped bass in one day.

Practice Tests

WRITING AND LANGUAGE TEST

35 Minutes—44 Questions

This section corresponds to Section 2 of your answer sheet.

Directions: Each passage in this section is followed by several questions. Some questions will reference an underlined portion in the passage; others will ask you to consider a part of a passage or the passage as a whole. For each question, choose the answer that reflects the best use of grammar, punctuation, and style. If a passage or question is accompanied by a graphic, take the graphic into account in choosing your response(s). Some questions will have "NO CHANGE" as a possible response. Choose that answer if you think the best choice is to leave the sentence as written.

Questions 1–11 are based on the following passage and supplementary material.

The UN: Promoting World Peace

The United Nations (UN) is perhaps the most important political contribution of the 20th century. Some may argue that the work of the UN **1** ; an international peacekeeping organization—has proven futile, given persisting global conflict. But the UN's worldwide influence demands a closer look. This organization's

1. A) NO CHANGE
    B) —an international peacekeeping organization;
    C) —an international peacekeeping organization—
    D) ; an international peacekeeping organization,

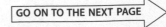

global impact is undeniable. The UN is a strong political organization determined to create opportunities for its member nations to enjoy a peaceful and productive world. **2**

3 Decades ago, provoked by the events of World Wars I and II, world leaders began imagining a politically neutral force for international peace. The UN was born in 1945 with 51 participating nations. It was to be a collective political authority for global peace and security. Today, 193 nations are UN members. **4** In keeping with the original hope, the UN still strives toward peaceful international relations.

Understandably, no single organization can perfectly solve the world's countless, complex problems. But the UN has offered consistent relief for many of the past half-century's most difficult disasters and conflicts. It also provides a safe space for international conversation.

2. Which choice would most clearly end the paragraph with a restatement of the author's claim?

A) The UN is an organization dedicated to advancing social and political justice around the world.

B) Those who argue otherwise are not well educated about geopolitical issues in the 20th century or today.

C) The UN has had its share of corruption over the years, but it has a well-earned reputation of effectively settling international disputes.

D) A better understanding of the UN suggests that the UN enables far greater peace in today's world than could have been possible otherwise.

3. A) NO CHANGE
   B) Recently,
   C) Consequently,
   D) In other words,

4. A) NO CHANGE
   B) In having kept with the original hope, the UN still strives toward peaceful international relations.
   C) In keeping with the original hope, the UN still strived toward peaceful international relations.
   D) In keeping with the original hope, the UN still strove toward peaceful international relations.

GO ON TO THE NEXT PAGE

Practice Tests

Moreover, it advocates for issues such as justice, trade, hunger relief, human rights, health, and gender **5** equality, the UN also coordinates care for those displaced by disaster and conflict, **6** dictates environmental protection, and works toward conflict reconciliation.

7 The UN's budget, goals, and personnel count have significantly expanded to meet more needs. **8** The year 2014 witnessed the UN peacekeeping force grow to over 100,000 strong. These uniformed, volunteer, civilian personnel represent 128 nations. The UN's budget has also grown over the years to support an international court system, as well as countless agencies, committees, and centers addressing sociopolitical

5. A) NO CHANGE
   B) equality. The UN
   C) equality: the UN
   D) equality, The UN

6. A) NO CHANGE
   B) prefers
   C) promotes
   D) celebrates

7. Which choice provides the most logical introduction to the paragraph?
   A) NO CHANGE
   B) The UN has developed over the years, but critics charge it has met with limited success.
   C) The responsibilities of the UN have expanded in recent years in response to challenging events.
   D) The UN has maintained a quiet but effective voice on the world stage in spite of criticism.

8. Which choice best completes the sentence with accurate data based on the graphic?
   A) NO CHANGE
   B) The year 2010 led to an increase of approximately 100,000 in the UN peacekeeping force.
   C) The year 2010 saw the UN peacekeeping force grow to approximately 100,000 strong.
   D) The year 2010 saw the UN peacekeeping force decrease to just over 100,000 strong.

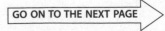 GO ON TO THE NEXT PAGE

Practice Tests

topics. Today's UN does big things, and it functions with remarkable organization and efficiency. Critics highlight shortcomings to discount the UN's effectiveness. But considering the countless disasters to which the UN has responded over its six decades of existence, today's world might enjoy **9** far less peace, freedom, and safety without the UN.

[1] From promoting overarching sociopolitical change to offering food and care for displaced groups, the UN serves to protect human rights. [2] Equally **10** quotable are its initiatives to foster international collaboration, justice, and peace. [3] The UN provided aid to the Philippines after the disastrous 2013 typhoon. [4]Certainly, this work is not finished. [5] But no other organization compares with the work and influence of the UN. [6] This brave endeavor to insist on and strive for peace, whatever the obstacles, has indeed united hundreds of once-divided nations. [7] Today, with eleven Nobel Peace Prizes to its name, the UN is undoubtedly an irreplaceable and profoundly successful force for peace. **11**

9. A) NO CHANGE
   B) considerably less peace, less freedom, and less safety
   C) much less peace, less freedom, and less safety
   D) significantly less peace and freedom, and less safety

10. A) NO CHANGE
    B) luminous
    C) noteworthy
    D) repeatable

11. Which sentence should be removed to improve the focus of the concluding paragraph?
    A) Sentence 1
    B) Sentence 3
    C) Sentence 5
    D) Sentence 6

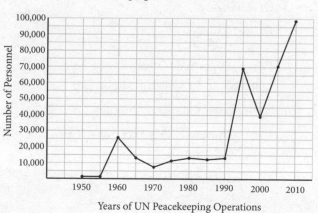

UN Peacekeeping Personnel Numbers Since 1950

Number of Personnel (y-axis: 10,000 to 100,000)

Years of UN Peacekeeping Operations (x-axis: 1950 to 2010)

Questions 12–22 are based on the following passage.

DNA Analysis in a Day

Jane Saunders, a forensic DNA specialist, arrives at work and finds a request waiting for her: She needs to determine if the DNA of a fingernail with a few skin cells on it [12] match any records in the criminal database.

"Human DNA is a long, double-stranded [13] molecule; each strand consists of a complementary set of nucleotides," she explains. "DNA has four nucleotides: [14] adenine (A), thymine (T), guanine (G), and, cytosine (C). On each strand is a sequence of nucleotides that 'match,' or pair up with the nucleotides on the other, or complementary, strand. [15] On the other hand, when there is an adenine on one strand, there is a thymine on the complementary strand, and where there is guanine on one strand, there is cytosine on the complementary strand."

She begins by [16] moving the DNA from the rest of the sample, transferring it to a [17] reaction tube. She adds a solution of primers, DNA polymerase, and nucleotides. Her goal is to separate the two strands of the DNA molecules and then make complementary copies of each strand.

12. A) NO CHANGE
    B) matches
    C) has matched
    D) will be matching

13. A) NO CHANGE
    B) molecule, each strand consists
    C) molecule each strand consists
    D) molecule but each strand consists

14. A) NO CHANGE
    B) adenine (A), thymine (T), guanine (G), and cytosine (C).
    C) adenine (A), thymine (T) guanine (G) and cytosine (C).
    D) adenine (A) thymine (T), guanine (G) and cytosine (C).

15. A) NO CHANGE
    B) Specifically,
    C) However,
    D) Similarly,

16. A) NO CHANGE
    B) reviewing
    C) changing
    D) detaching

17. Which choice most effectively combines the sentences at the underlined portion?
    A) reaction tube since she adds
    B) reaction tube, however, she adds
    C) reaction tube, and adding
    D) reaction tube, she adds

GO ON TO THE NEXT PAGE
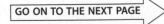

18 The process of testing the DNA includes several steps and many changes in temperature. After mixing the primers, DNA polymerase, and nucleotides with the evidence DNA, Saunders closes the reaction tube and puts it in a thermocycler. It is programmed to raise the temperature to 94°C to separate the double strands into single strands, and then lower the temperature to 59°C to attach the primers to the single strands. Finally, it raises the temperature to 72°C for the DNA polymerase to build the complementary strands. The thermocycler holds each temperature for one minute and repeats the cycle of three temperatures for at least 30 cycles. At the end of each cycle, the number of DNA segments containing the sequence marked by the primers doubles. If the original sample contains only 100 DNA strands, **19** the absolute final sample will have billions of segments.

18. Which sentence most effectively establishes the central idea?

    A) NO CHANGE

    B) The object of testing the DNA is to re-create many strands of the DNA in question.

    C) Saunders uses a variety of machines in order to analyze the DNA.

    D) Saunders would be unable to identify the DNA without the thermocycler.

19. A) NO CHANGE

    B) absolutely the final sample

    C) the final sample

    D) the most final sample

GO ON TO THE NEXT PAGE

[1] After a short lunch break, Saunders needs to separate and identify the copied DNA segments. [2] She had used primers that bind to 13 specific sites in human DNA called short tandem repeats, or STRs. [3] The 13 STRs are segments of four nucleotides that repeat, such as GATAGATAGATA. [4] "Now here's where the real magic happens!" Saunders says excitedly. [5] "Most DNA is identical for all humans. [6] But STRs vary greatly. [7] The chances of any two humans—other than identical twins—having the same set of 13 STRs is less than one in one trillion." **20**

Saunders knows that the detectives will be **21** prepared to hear her findings, so she sits down at her desk to compare her results with the criminal database in the hopes of finding a match. **22** Is it possible that too much time is spent identifying DNA in cases that are relatively easy to solve?

20. Where should sentence 1 be placed to make the paragraph feel cohesive?

    A) Where it is now

    B) After sentence 2

    C) After sentence 3

    D) After sentence 4

21. A) NO CHANGE

    B) eager

    C) impatient

    D) conditioned

22. At this point, the writer wants to add a conclusion that best reflects Jane's feelings conveyed in the passage. Which choice accomplishes that?

    A) NO CHANGE

    B) It takes a good deal of work and expense to identify DNA in the world of modern forensics.

    C) She takes pride in the fact that her scientific expertise plays such a key role in bringing criminals to justice.

    D) She marvels at how far science has come in DNA analysis.

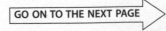

Questions 23–33 are based on the following passage.

Will Your Start-Up Succeed?

According to research from Harvard Business School, the majority of small businesses [23] <u>fail in fact</u> the success rate for a first-time company owner is a meager 18 percent. With odds so dismal, why would anyone become a business entrepreneur?

[24] <u>Many people desire the freedom of being their own boss, but to be successful, an entrepreneur must also be productive, persistent, and creative.</u> Veteran entrepreneurs achieve a higher 30 percent success rate, so the most predictive factor for success appears to be the number of innovations that a person has "pushed out." More specifically, the people who succeed at building a robust start-up are the ones who have previously tried. Finally, many entrepreneurs [25] <u>grab</u> the idea for their business by solving practical problems, and it's more than luck; 320 new entrepreneurs out of 100,000 *do* succeed by starting a company at the right time in the right industry.

23. A) NO CHANGE
    B) fail, in fact,
    C) fail; in fact,
    D) fail: in fact

24. Which sentence most effectively establishes the central idea?

    A) NO CHANGE
    B) The Small Business Administration defines a small business as one with fewer than 500 employees and less than $7 million in sales annually.
    C) Many small businesses fail because company founders are not realistic about the amount of time it takes for a company to become profitable.
    D) Running a small business can take up a lot more time than punching a clock for someone else and might not be enjoyable for everyone.

25. A) NO CHANGE
    B) derive
    C) achieve
    D) grasp

GO ON TO THE NEXT PAGE ▷

Practice Tests

Mitch Gomez is evidence of this data. He 26 <u>did graduate</u> from college with a degree in accounting. "I quickly realized that I have too big of a personality to be content practicing accounting," he laughs. He first built a successful insurance claims 27 <u>service, and next</u> founded his own independent insurance agency. "I continually employ my accounting skills, but I've ascertained that I'm an even more effective salesperson."

Similarly, Barbara Vital, the woman behind Vital Studio, explains, "I love spending as much time with my family as possible." Vital saw an opportunity to 28 <u>launch</u> a monogramming business when her two young sons started school, so she founded a company that offers monogrammed backpacks and water bottles for kids, as well as 29 <u>totes, rain boots; and</u> baseball caps for college students. What is the secret to Vital's success? "I'm always learning how to incorporate social media and add functionality to my product website to keep customers happy," she says.

Finally, Chris Roth is an entrepreneur who can step out of his comfort zone. Always seeking a new 30 <u>challenge his company</u> designed and manufactured technology to keep the nozzles of water misting systems clean. Roth has also established a corporate travel agency and

26. A) NO CHANGE
    B) has graduated
    C) graduated
    D) would have graduated

27. A) NO CHANGE
    B) service. And next
    C) service and next
    D) service; and next

28. A) NO CHANGE
    B) present
    C) propel
    D) impact

29. A) NO CHANGE
    B) totes; rain boots; and
    C) totes, rain boots, and,
    D) totes, rain boots, and

30. A) NO CHANGE
    B) challenge: his company
    C) challenge; his company
    D) challenge, his company

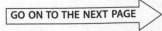

a truck customization company, most recently claiming he has become an innovator who beat the odds by "striving to serve customers better than my competition." **31** Large companies often employ corporate travel agencies to arrange travel for their employees and clients.

Gomez, Vital, and Roth **32** agrees that although being an entrepreneur can be a formidable challenge, exceptionally skillful entrepreneurs have important strategies for success, including stretching **33** his personal boundaries and recovering from failures. "And nothing beats being your own boss," adds Gomez.

31. Which sentence would best support the central idea?

A) NO CHANGE

B) Savvy entrepreneurs know which risks are worth taking and which risks can tank their business before their doors open.

C) Now Roth's small business installs water misters on restaurant patios and even sets up misting stations at outdoor music festivals.

D) Many new small businesses fail because company founders fail to do market research and identify the needs of their community.

32. A) NO CHANGE

B) agree

C) should agree

D) had agreed

33. A) NO CHANGE

B) their

C) our

D) her

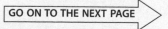GO ON TO THE NEXT PAGE

Questions 34–44 are based on the following passage and supplementary material.

Edgard Varèse's Influence

Today's music, from rock to jazz, has many [34] influences. And perhaps none is as unique as the ideas from French composer Edgard Varèse. Called "the father of electronic music," he approached compositions from a different theoretical perspective than classical composers such as Bartók and Debussy. He called his [35] works "organized sound"; they did not [36] endear melodies but waged assaults of percussion, piano, and human voices. He thought of sounds as having intelligence and treated music spatially, as "sound objects floating in space."

His unique vision can be credited to his education in science. Born in 1883 in France, Varèse was raised by a great-uncle and grandfather in the Burgundy region. He was interested in classical music and composed his first opera as a teenager. While the family lived [37] in Italy he studied engineering in Turin, where he learned math and science and was inspired by the work of the artist Leonardo da Vinci.

In 1903, he returned to France to study music at the Paris Conservatory. There, he composed the radical percussion performance piece *Ionisation*, which featured cymbals, snares, bass drum, xylophone, and sirens wailing. Later compositions were scored for the theremin, a new electronic instrument controlled by [38] the player's hands waving over its antennae, which sense their position.

34. A) NO CHANGE
    B) influences, and perhaps none is as
    C) influences, but perhaps none is as
    D) influences. Or perhaps none is as

35. A) NO CHANGE
    B) works "organized sound": They
    C) works "organized sound", they
    D) works—"organized sound"—they

36. A) NO CHANGE
    B) amplify
    C) deprive
    D) employ

37. A) NO CHANGE
    B) in Italy, he studied engineering in Turin, where he
    C) in Italy he studied engineering in Turin where he
    D) in Italy, he studied engineering in Turin; where he

38. A) NO CHANGE
    B) the players' hands
    C) the players hands
    D) the player's hands'

Practice Tests

No composer had ever scored any music for the theremin before.

In his thirties, Varèse moved to New York City, where he played piano in a café and conducted other composers' works until his own compositions gained success. His piece *Amériques* was performed in Philadelphia in 1926. Varèse went on to travel to the western United States, where he recorded, lectured, and collaborated with other musicians. By the 1950s, he was using tape recordings in **39** contention with symphonic performance. His piece *Déserts* was aired on a radio program amid selections by Mozart and Tchaikovsky but was received by listeners with hostility. **40**

Varèse's ideas were more forward-thinking than could be realized. One of his most ambitious scores, called *Espace*, was a choral symphony with multilingual lyrics, which was to be sung simultaneously by choirs in Paris, Moscow, Peking, and New York. He wanted the timing to be orchestrated by radio, but radio technology did not support worldwide transmission. If only Varèse **41** had had the Internet!

39. A) NO CHANGE
    B) conjunction
    C) appropriation
    D) supplication

40. If added to the paragraph, which fact would best support the author's claims?
    A) The critical response to his 1926 performance in Philadelphia
    B) The selections by Mozart and Tchaikovsky that were played on the radio
    C) Which specific states he traveled to in the western United States
    D) The cities in which the radio program was aired

41. A) NO CHANGE
    B) would have had
    C) would have
    D) have had

Practice Tests

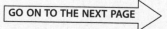

Although many of [42] their written compositions were lost in a fire in 1918, many modern musicians and composers have been influenced by Varèse, including Frank Zappa, John Luther Adams, and John Cage, who wrote that Varèse is "more relevant to present musical necessity than even the Viennese masters." [43] Despite being less famous than Stravinsky or Shostakovich, his impact is undeniable. [44] Varèse's love of science and mathematics is shown in his later compositions, but less so in his early works.

Composer	Number of Surviving Works
Edgard Varèse	14
Benjamin Britten	84
Charles Ives	106
Igor Stravinsky	129
Arnold Schoenberg	290
Dmitri Shostakovich	320

42. A) NO CHANGE
    B) its
    C) our
    D) his

43. Which choice most accurately and effectively represents the information in the graph?
    A) NO CHANGE
    B) Despite having fewer surviving works than his contemporaries, his impact is undeniable.
    C) Even though he wrote pieces using a wider range of instruments than other composers, his impact is undeniable.
    D) Even though far fewer of his works are now performed compared with those of his contemporaries, his impact is undeniable.

44. Which sentence best summarizes the central idea?
    A) NO CHANGE
    B) In contrast with his newfound popularity, Varèse's early works have long been ignored due to increasing critical hostility.
    C) Varèse and his innovative compositions became an inspiration for artists seeking to challenge traditional musical beliefs.
    D) Though Varèse's contemporary critics failed to call him a "Viennese master," this distinction is changing.

IF YOU FINISH BEFORE TIME IS CALLED, YOU MAY CHECK YOUR WORK ON THIS SECTION ONLY. DO NOT TURN TO ANY OTHER SECTION IN THE TEST. **STOP**

MATH TEST

25 Minutes—17 Questions

NO-CALCULATOR SECTION

This section corresponds to Section 3 of your answer sheet.

Directions: For this section, solve each question and select the best answer choice. The available space on each page may be used for scratch work.

Notes:

1. Calculator use is NOT permitted.
2. All numbers used are real numbers, and all variables used represent real numbers, unless otherwise indicated.
3. Figures are drawn to scale and lie in a plane unless otherwise indicated.
4. Unless stated otherwise, the domain of any function f is assumed to be the set of all real numbers x, for which $f(x)$ is a real number.

Information:

$A = \pi r^2$
$C = 2\pi r$

$A = lw$

$A = \frac{1}{2}bh$

$c^2 = a^2 + b^2$

Special Right Triangles

$V = lwh$

$V = \pi r^2 h$

$V = \frac{4}{3}\pi r^3$

$V = \frac{1}{3}\pi r^2 h$

$V = \frac{1}{3}lwh$

The sum of the degree measures of the angles in a triangle is 180.

The number of degrees of arc in a circle is 360.

The number of radians of arc in a circle is 2π.

GO ON TO THE NEXT PAGE

$$\frac{4(n-2)+5}{2} = \frac{13-(9+4n)}{4}$$

1. In the equation above, what is the value of n ?

    A) $\dfrac{5}{6}$

    B) $\dfrac{5}{2}$

    C) There is no value of n that satisfies the equation.

    D) There are infinitely many values of n that satisfy the equation.

$$\frac{18x^3 + 9x^2 - 36x}{9x^2}$$

2. Which of the following is equivalent to the expression above?

    A) $2x - \dfrac{4}{x}$

    B) $18x^3 - 36x$

    C) $2x + 1 - \dfrac{4}{x}$

    D) $18x^3 - 36x + 1$

3. The figure above shows the graph of $f(x)$. For which value(s) of x does $f(x)$ equal 0?

    A) -3 and 3

    B) -1 and 1

    C) -1, 1, and 2

    D) 2 only

4. Which of the following systems of inequalities has no solution?

    A) $\begin{cases} y \geq x \\ y \leq 2x \end{cases}$

    B) $\begin{cases} y \geq x \\ y \leq -x \end{cases}$

    C) $\begin{cases} y \geq x+1 \\ y \leq x-1 \end{cases}$

    D) $\begin{cases} y \geq -x+1 \\ y \leq x-1 \end{cases}$

GO ON TO THE NEXT PAGE

5. At what value(s) of x do the graphs of $y = -2x + 1$ and $y = 2x^2 + 5x + 4$ intersect?

    A) -8 and $\dfrac{1}{2}$

    B) -3 and $-\dfrac{1}{2}$

    C) -3 and 3

    D) $-\dfrac{1}{2}$ and 3

6. If line P shown in the graph is reflected over the x-axis and shifted up 3 units, what is the new y-intercept?

    A) $(0, -4)$

    B) $(0, -2)$

    C) $(0, 2)$

    D) $(0, 4)$

7. Which of the following are roots of the equation $3x^2 - 6x - 5 = 0$?

    A) $1 \pm 2\sqrt{6}$

    B) $\dfrac{1 \pm 2\sqrt{2}}{3}$

    C) $\dfrac{3 \pm 2\sqrt{2}}{3}$

    D) $\dfrac{3 \pm 2\sqrt{6}}{3}$

8. If $m = \dfrac{1}{n^{-\frac{1}{4}}}$, where both $m > 0$ and $n > 0$, which of the following gives n in terms of m?

    A) $n = m^4$

    B) $n = \dfrac{1}{m^4}$

    C) $n = \dfrac{1}{\sqrt[4]{m}}$

    D) $n = m^{\frac{1}{4}}$

$$\begin{cases} y = 3x - 1 \\ y = \dfrac{5x + 8}{2} \end{cases}$$

9. If (x, y) represents the solution to the system of equations shown above, what is the value of y?

    A) 10

    B) 19

    C) 29

    D) 31

10. If $0 < \dfrac{d}{2} + 1 \le \dfrac{8}{5}$, which of the following is not a possible value of d?

    A) -2

    B) $-\dfrac{6}{5}$

    C) 0

    D) $\dfrac{6}{5}$

 GO ON TO THE NEXT PAGE

Practice Tests

11. Mae-Ling made 15 shots during a basketball game. Some were 3-pointers and others were worth 2 points each. If *s* shots were 3-pointers, which expression represents her total score?

   A) $3s$

   B) $s + 30$

   C) $3s + 2$

   D) $5s + 30$

12. If $\frac{1}{2}y - \frac{3}{5}x = -16$, what is the value of $6x - 5y$?

   A) 32

   B) 80

   C) 96

   D) 160

13. If $f(g(2)) = -1$ and $f(x) = x + 1$, then which of the following could define $g(x)$?

   A) $g(x) = x - 6$

   B) $g(x) = x - 4$

   C) $g(x) = x - 2$

   D) $g(x) = x - 1$

GO ON TO THE NEXT PAGE

Directions: For questions 14–17, enter your responses into the appropriate grid on your answer sheet, in accordance with the following:

1. You will receive credit only if the circles are filled in correctly, but you may write your answers in the boxes above each grid to help you fill in the circles accurately.

2. Don't mark more than one circle per column.

3. None of the questions with grid-in responses will have a negative solution.

4. Only grid in a single answer, even if there is more than one correct answer to a given question.

5. A **mixed number** must be gridded as a decimal or an improper fraction. For example, you would grid $7\frac{1}{2}$ as 7.5 or $\frac{15}{2}$.

    (Were you to grid it as ⟨7 1 / 2⟩, this response would be read as $\frac{71}{2}$.)

6. A **decimal** that has more digits than there are places on the grid may be either rounded or truncated, but every column in the grid must be filled in order to receive credit.

GO ON TO THE NEXT PAGE ⟩

$$k(10x - 5) = 2(3 + x) - 7$$

14. If the equation above has infinitely many solutions and k is a constant, what is the value of k?

15. A right triangle has leg lengths of 18 and 24 and a hypotenuse of $15n$. What is the value of n?

$$\frac{\sqrt{x} \cdot x^{\frac{5}{4}} \cdot x^2}{\sqrt[4]{x^3}}$$

16. If the expression above is combined into a single power of x with a positive exponent, what is that exponent?

17. If the equation of the parabola shown in the graph is written in standard quadratic form, $y = ax^2 + bx + c$, and $a = -1$, then what is the value of b?

MATH TEST

45 Minutes—31 Questions

CALCULATOR SECTION

This section corresponds to Section 4 of your answer sheet.

Directions: For this section, solve each question and select the best answer choice. The available space on each page may be used for scratch work.

Notes:

1. Calculator use is permitted.
2. All numbers used are real numbers, and all variables used represent real numbers, unless otherwise indicated.
3. Figures are drawn to scale and lie in a plane unless otherwise indicated.
4. Unless stated otherwise, the domain of any function f is assumed to be the set of all real numbers x, for which $f(x)$ is a real number.

Information:

The sum of the degree measures of the angles in a triangle is 180.

The number of degrees of arc in a circle is 360.

The number of radians of arc in a circle is 2π.

GO ON TO THE NEXT PAGE

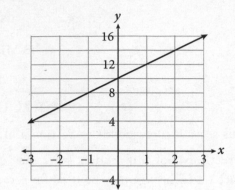

1. The scatterplot above shows data collected from 10 major league baseball players comparing the average weekly time each one spent in batting practice and the number of home runs he hit in a single season. The line of best fit for the data is also shown. What does the slope of the line represent in this context?

   A) The estimated time spent in batting practice by a player who hits 0 home runs

   B) The estimated number of single-season home runs hit by a player who spends 0 hours in batting practice

   C) The estimated increase in time that a player spends in batting practice for each home run that he hits in a single season

   D) The estimated increase in the number of single-season home runs hit by a player for each hour he spends in batting practice

2. Where will the line shown in the graph above intersect the *x*-axis?

   A) −5.5

   B) −5

   C) −4.5

   D) −4

3. The function $f(x)$ is defined as $f(x) = -3g(x)$, where $g(x) = x + 2$. What is the value of $f(5)$?

   A) −21

   B) −1

   C) 4

   D) 7

GO ON TO THE NEXT PAGE

Number of Nights

Average Position

4. The graph above shows the average cost of back surgery followed by a hospital stay in the United States. The hospital charges for the surgery itself plus all the costs associated with recovery care for each night the patient remains in the hospital. Based on the graph, what is the average cost per night spent in the hospital?

   A) $2,600

   B) $4,000

   C) $6,600

   D) $8,000

5. The figure above represents a click-through rate curve, which shows the relationship between a search result position in a list of Internet search results and the number of people who clicked on advertisements on that result's page. Which of the following regression types would be the best model for this data?

   A) A linear function

   B) A quadratic function

   C) A polynomial function

   D) An exponential function

GO ON TO THE NEXT PAGE

Practice Tests

6. Kudzu is a vine-like plant that grows indigenously in Asia. It was brought over to the United States in the early 20th century to help combat soil erosion. As can often happen when foreign species are introduced into a non-native habitat, kudzu growth exploded and it became invasive. In one area of Virginia, kudzu covered approximately 3,200 acres of a farmer's cropland, so he tried a new herbicide. After two weeks of use, 2,800 acres of the farmer's cropland were free of the kudzu. Based on these results, and assuming the same general conditions, how many of the 30,000 acres of kudzu-infested cropland in that region would still be covered if all the farmers in the entire region had used the herbicide?

   A)   3,750

   B)   4,000

   C)   26,000

   D)   26,250

x	−2	−1	0	1	2	3
$g(x)$	5	3	1	−1	−3	−5
$h(x)$	−3	−2	−1	0	1	2

7. Several values for the functions $g(x)$ and $h(x)$ are shown in the table. What is the value of $g(h(3))$?

   A)   −5

   B)   −3

   C)   −1

   D)   2

8. A business's "break-even point" is the point at which revenue (sales) equals expenses. When a company breaks even, no profit is being made, but the company is not losing any money either. Suppose a manufacturer buys materials for producing a particular item at a cost of $4.85 per unit and has fixed monthly expenses of $11,625 related to this item. The manufacturer sells this particular item to several retailers for $9.50 per unit. How many units must the manufacturer sell per month to reach the break-even point for this item?

   A)   810

   B)   1,225

   C)   2,100

   D)   2,500

9. Crude oil is sold by the barrel, which refers to both the physical container and a unit of measure, abbreviated as bbl. One barrel holds 42 gallons and, consequently, 1 bbl = 42 gallons. An oil company is filling an order for 2,500 barrels. The machine the company uses to fill the barrels pumps at a rate of 37.5 gallons per minute. If the oil company has 8 machines working simultaneously, how long will it take to fill all the barrels in the order?

   A)   5 hours and 50 minutes

   B)   12 hours and 45 minutes

   C)   28 hours and 30 minutes

   D)   46 hours and 40 minutes

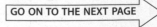
GO ON TO THE NEXT PAGE

	Jan	Feb	Mar	Apr
Company A	54	146	238	330
Company B	15	30	60	120

10. Company A and Company B are selling two similar toys. The sales figures for each toy are recorded in the table above. The marketing department at Company A predicts that its monthly sales for this particular toy will continue to be higher than Company B's through the end of the year. Based on the data in the table, and assuming that each company sustains the pattern of growth the data suggests, which company will sell more of this toy in December of that year and how much more?

A) Company A; 182

B) Company A; 978

C) Company B; 29,654

D) Company B; 60,282

$$5(x - 2) - 3x \ \boxed{} \ 4x - 6$$

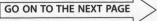

11. Which symbol correctly completes the inequality whose solution is shown above?

A) <

B) >

C) ≤

D) ≥

Questions 12 and 13 refer to the following information.

A student is drawing the human skeleton to scale for a school assignment. The assignment permits the student to omit all bones under a certain size because they would be too small to draw. The longest bone in the human body is the femur, or thighbone, with an average length of 19.9 inches. The tenth longest bone is the sternum, or breastbone, with an average length of 6.7 inches.

12. If the scale factor of the drawing is one-eighth, about how long in inches should the student draw the femur?

A) 2

B) 2.5

C) 2.8

D) 3

13. The student draws the femur, but then realizes she drew it too long, at 3.5 inches. She doesn't want to erase and start over, so she decides she will adjust the scale factor to match her current drawing instead. Based on the new scale factor, about how long in inches should she draw the sternum?

A) 0.8

B) 1

C) 1.2

D) 1.5

Practice Tests

GO ON TO THE NEXT PAGE

14. If a line that passes through the ordered pairs $(4 - c, 2c)$ and $(-c, -8)$ has a slope of $\frac{1}{2}$, what is the value of c?

A) −5

B) −3

C) −2

D) 2

From	Distance to LHR
DCA	3,718
MIA	4,470

15. Two airplanes departed from different airports at 5:30 AM, both traveling nonstop to London Heathrow Airport (LHR). The distances the planes traveled are recorded in the table. The Washington, D.C. (DCA) flight flew through moderate cloud cover and as a result only averaged 338 mph. The flight from Miami (MIA) had good weather conditions for the first two-thirds of the trip and averaged 596 mph, but then encountered some turbulence and only averaged 447 mph for the last part of the trip. Which plane arrived first and how long was it at the London airport before the other plane arrived?

A) MIA; 2 hours, 40 minutes

B) MIA; 3 hours, 30 minutes

C) DCA; 1 hour, 20 minutes

D) DCA; 3 hours, 40 minutes

16. Which of the following quadratic equations has no solution?

A) $0 = -3(x + 1)(x - 8)$

B) $0 = 3(x + 1)(x - 8)$

C) $0 = -3(x + 1)^2 + 8$

D) $0 = 3(x + 1)^2 + 8$

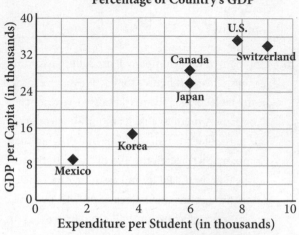

Annual Expenditures per Student as a Percentage of Country's GDP

Adapted from the Organization for Economic Cooperation and Development (OECD), 2003.

17. A student looked at the graph above and determined based on the data that spending more money per student causes the gross domestic product (GDP) to increase. Which of the following statements is true?

A) The student is correct; the data shows that increased spending on students causes an increase in the GDP.

B) The student is incorrect; the data shows that having a higher GDP causes an increase in the amount of money a country spends on students.

C) The student is incorrect; there is no correlation and, therefore, no causation between GDP and expenditures on students.

D) The student is incorrect; the two variables are correlated, but changes in one do not necessarily cause changes in the other.

GO ON TO THE NEXT PAGE

18. In chemistry, the combined gas law formula

$\dfrac{p_1 V_1}{T_1} = \dfrac{p_2 V_2}{T_2}$ gives the relationship between the

volumes, temperatures, and pressures for two fixed amounts of gas. Which of the following gives p_2 in terms of the other variables?

A) $p_1 = p_2$

B) $\dfrac{p_1 T}{V} = p_2$

C) $\dfrac{p_1 V_1 T_2}{T_1 V_2} = p_2$

D) $\dfrac{p_1 V_1 V_2}{T_1 T_2} = p_2$

19. An object's weight is dependent upon the gravitational force being exerted upon the object. If 1 pound on Earth is equal to 0.377 pounds on Mars and 2.364 pounds on Jupiter, and 1 ton is equal to 2,000 pounds, how many more pounds does an object weighing 1.5 tons on Earth weigh on Jupiter than on Mars?

A) 1,131

B) 4,092

C) 5,961

D) 7,092

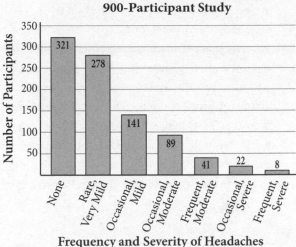

Clinical Trial: Headache Side Effect 900-Participant Study

Frequency and Severity of Headaches

20. When a drug company wants to introduce a new drug, it must subject the drug to rigorous testing. The final stage of this testing is human clinical trials, in which progressively larger groups of volunteers are given the drug and carefully monitored. One aspect of this monitoring is keeping track of the frequency and severity of side effects. The figure above shows the results for the side effect of headaches for a certain drug. According to the trial guidelines, all moderate and severe headaches are considered to be adverse reactions. Which of the following best describes the data?

A) The data is symmetric with over 50% of participants having adverse reactions.

B) The data is skewed to the right with over 50% of participants having adverse reactions.

C) The data is skewed to the right with over 75% of participants failing to have adverse reactions.

D) The data is skewed to the right with approximately 50% of participants having no reaction at all.

GO ON TO THE NEXT PAGE ▷

21. In the legal field, "reciprocity" means that an attorney can take and pass a bar exam in one state and be allowed to practice law in a different state that permits such reciprocity. Each state bar association decides with which other states it will allow reciprocity. For example, Pennsylvania allows reciprocity with the District of Columbia. It costs $25 less than 3 times as much to take the bar in Pennsylvania than in D.C. If both bar exams together cost $775, how much less expensive is it to take the bar exam in D.C. than in Pennsylvania?

A) $200

B) $275

C) $375

D) $575

Driver's Education Test Results

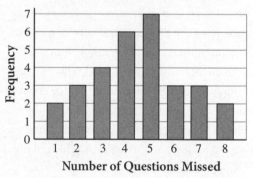

Number of Questions Missed

22. Mr. Juno took his driver's education class to the Department of Motor Vehicles to take their driver's license test. The number of questions missed by each student in the class is recorded in the bar graph above. Which of the following statements is true?

A) More than half of the students missed 5 or more questions.

B) The mean number of questions missed was between 4 and 5.

C) More students missed 3 questions than any other number of questions.

D) Thirty-six students from Mr. Juno's class took the driver's license test that day.

23. If the graph of the equation $y = ax^2 + bx + c$ passes through the points $(0, 2)$, $(-6, -7)$, and $(8, -14)$, what is the value of $a + b + c$?

A) -19

B) -2

C) 1.75

D) 2.25

24. A bakery sells three sizes of muffins—mini, regular, and jumbo. The baker plans daily muffin counts based on the size of his pans and how they fit in the oven, which results in the following ratios: mini to regular equals 5 to 2, and regular to jumbo equals 5 to 4. When the bakery caters events, it usually offers only the regular size, but it recently decided to offer a mix of mini and jumbo instead of regular. If the baker wants to keep the sizes in the same ratio as his daily counts, what ratio of mini to jumbo should he use?

A) 1:1

B) 4:2

C) 5:2

D) 25:8

$$\begin{cases} \dfrac{1}{3}x + \dfrac{1}{2}y = 5 \\ kx - 4y = 16 \end{cases}$$

25. If the system of linear equations shown above has no solution, and k is a constant, what is the value of k ?

A) $-\dfrac{8}{3}$

B) -2

C) $\dfrac{1}{3}$

D) 3

GO ON TO THE NEXT PAGE
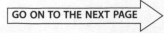

26. What is the value of $3^{90} \times 27^{90} \div \left(\dfrac{1}{9}\right)^{30}$?

    A) 9^{60}

    B) 9^{120}

    C) 9^{150}

    D) 9^{210}

27. If a right cone is three times as wide at its base as it is tall, and the volume of the cone is 384π cubic inches, what is the diameter in inches of the base of the cone?

    A) 8

    B) 12

    C) 16

    D) 24

GO ON TO THE NEXT PAGE

Directions: For questions 28–31, enter your responses into the appropriate grid on your answer sheet, in accordance with the following:

1. You will receive credit only if the circles are filled in correctly, but you may write your answers in the boxes above each grid to help you fill in the circles accurately.

2. Don't mark more than one circle per column.

3. None of the questions with grid-in responses will have a negative solution.

4. Only grid in a single answer, even if there is more than one correct answer to a given question.

5. A **mixed number** must be gridded as a decimal or an improper fraction. For example, you would grid $7\frac{1}{2}$ as 7.5 or $\frac{15}{2}$.

   (Were you to grid it as $\boxed{7\ 1\ /\ 2}$, this response would be read as $\frac{71}{2}$.)

6. A **decimal** that has more digits than there are places on the grid may be either rounded or truncated, but every column in the grid must be filled in order to receive credit.

28. Nine data points were used to generate the scatterplot shown above. Assuming all whole number values for the data points, what is the maximum value in the range of the data?

29. If $Ax + By = C$ is the standard form of the line that passes through the points $(-4, 1)$ and $(3, -2)$, where A is an integer greater than 1, what is the value of B?

Questions 30 and 31 refer to the following information.

The Great Depression began in 1929 and lasted until 1939. It was a period of extreme poverty, marked by low prices and high unemployment. The main catalytic event to the Great Depression was the Wall Street Crash (stock market crash). The Dow, which measures the health of the stock market, started Black Thursday (October 24, 1929) at approximately 306 points.

30. The stock market had been in steady decline since its record high the month before. If the market had declined by 19.5% between its record high and opening on Black Thursday, what was the approximate value of the Dow at its record high? Round your answer to the nearest whole point.

31. By the end of business on Black Thursday, the Dow had dropped by 2%. Over the course of Friday and the half-day Saturday session, there was no significant change. Unfortunately, the market lost 13% on Black Monday, followed by another 12% on Black Tuesday. What was the total percent decrease from opening on Black Thursday to closing on Black Tuesday? Round your answer to the nearest whole percent and ignore the percent sign when entering your answer.

Practice Tests

ANSWER KEY
READING TEST

1. B	14. B	27. C	40. D
2. C	15. B	28. D	41. A
3. D	16. C	29. C	42. C
4. B	17. D	30. B	43. A
5. A	18. D	31. D	44. B
6. C	19. B	32. D	45. D
7. D	20. C	33. A	46. B
8. C	21. D	34. C	47. D
9. A	22. B	35. B	
10. A	23. D	36. B	
11. A	24. B	37. C	
12. C	25. A	38. D	
13. A	26. A	39. C	

WRITING AND LANGUAGE TEST

1. C	12. B	23. C	34. C
2. D	13. A	24. A	35. A
3. A	14. B	25. B	36. D
4. A	15. B	26. C	37. B
5. B	16. D	27. C	38. A
6. C	17. C	28. A	39. B
7. A	18. A	29. D	40. A
8. C	19. C	30. D	41. A
9. A	20. A	31. C	42. D
10. C	21. B	32. B	43. B
11. B	22. C	33. B	44. C

MATH—NO-CALCULATOR TEST

1. A	6. D	11. B	16. 3
2. C	7. D	12. D	17. 6
3. B	8. A	13. B	
4. C	9. C	14. 1/5 or .2	
5. B	10. A	15. 2	

MATH—CALCULATOR TEST

1. D	11. A	21. C	31. 25
2. B	12. B	22. B	
3. A	13. C	23. C	
4. B	14. B	24. D	
5. D	15. A	25. A	
6. A	16. D	26. D	
7. B	17. D	27. D	
8. D	18. C	28. 85	
9. A	19. C	29. 7	
10. C	20. C	30. 380	

ANSWERS AND EXPLANATIONS

READING TEST

Great Expectations

Suggested Passage Map notes:

¶1: Pip eating paltry breakfast, Mr. P making him do math while he eats, Pip does not like Mr. P

¶2: Pip visiting Miss H, Miss H's house in disrepair

¶3-9: lady let's in Pip, makes Mr. P go away

¶10: Pip happy to be rid of Mr. P for now

1. B   Difficulty: Easy

Category: Detail

Getting to the Answer: Examine the description of breakfast in the first paragraph before choosing the correct answer. In lines 8-9, Pip uses "crumb" and "little butter" to describe what he ate, and he also says in line 10 that "a quantity of warm water" had been added to his milk. Therefore, it's clear that Pip's breakfast with Mr. Pumblechook is (B), "small and of poor quality."

2. C   Difficulty: Medium

Category: Vocab-in-Context

Getting to the Answer: Eliminate answer choices that might be synonyms of "wretched" but don't make sense in the context of the passage. When Pip describes Mr. Pumblechook's company to be "wretched," he means "distressing," or causing misery. Choice (C) is the correct answer.

3. D   Difficulty: Medium

Category: Inference

Getting to the Answer: Review the passage for details that reveal Mr. Pumblechook's attitude. By his actions, you can infer that Mr. Pumblechook is indifferent to Pip's discomfort. Choice (D) is the correct answer.

4. B   Difficulty: Medium

Category: Command of Evidence

Getting to the Answer: Find each answer choice in the passage. Think about your answer for the previous question, and determine which lines provide the strongest support for that answer. In the first paragraph, Pip describes how Mr. Pumblechook offers him a meager breakfast and quizzes him on arithmetic during their meal rather than making conversation. Choice (B) is the correct answer.

5. A   Difficulty: Hard

Category: Global

Getting to the Answer: Study the answer choices. Eliminate any that go too far in their interpretation of characters and events in the passage. Though B seems to reflect what might be true of Pip and Mr. Pumblechook's relationship, and one might believe that C and D are true, the correct answer is (A). This theme most clearly reflects the message conveyed through Pip's experiences in this passage.

6. C   Difficulty: Medium

Category: Inference

Getting to the Answer: Think about details in the passage that relate to the characters' relationships. What do they reveal about how Pip probably feels at the end of the passage? It is reasonable to infer that Pip is relieved when he is no longer in Mr. Pumblechook's company. Therefore, (C) is the correct answer.

7. D   Difficulty: Hard

Category: Command of Evidence

Getting to the Answer: Locate each answer in the passage, and decide which one provides the best support for the answer to the previous question. At the end of the passage, Pip "was not free from apprehension" (line 64) that Mr. Pumblechook would return but then tells the reader that no return took place. Choice (D) best supports the idea that Pip is relieved to be away from Mr. Pumblechook.

8. C   Difficulty: Easy

Category: Vocab-in-Context

Getting to the Answer: Substitute each answer choice for "condition." The correct answer will not change the meaning of the sentence. Choice (C) is the correct answer. The narrator says that Mr. Pumblechook is "in a condition of ruffled dignity" (line 59). In this context, "state" means the same as "condition."

9. A   Difficulty: Medium

Category: Rhetoric

Getting to the Answer: Think of what the parenthetical comment by Pip tells you about his personality. In a sense, Pip is apologizing for what he is about to say of Mr. Pumblechook. The parenthetical comment reveals that Pip is usually more polite in his references to others. Choice (A) is the correct answer.

"Letter from Birmingham Jail"

Suggested Passage Map notes:

¶1: MLK states why he is in Birmingham, history of SCLC, in Birmingham due to injustice

¶2: MLK cannot let injustice continue, we are one people

¶3: MLK explains why peaceful protests are needed, benefits of tension to open negotiations

¶4: nonviolent pressure only way to enact change

¶5: justice must be demanded by the oppressed

10. A   Difficulty: Medium

Category: Rhetoric

Getting to the Answer: Avoid answer choices that deal with related issues but do not address the main purpose of the letter. The passage as a whole addresses why King came to Birmingham, and then builds on his explanation for being in Birmingham to explore his cause. Choice (A) is correct.

11. A   Difficulty: Easy

Category: Command of Evidence

Getting to the Answer: Choose the answer that relates directly to the purpose you identified in the previous question. King begins the letter by stating, "I think I should give the reason for my being in Birmingham," which clearly explains his purpose for writing the letter from the jail. Choice (A) is correct.

12. C   Difficulty: Easy

Category: Vocab-in-Context

Getting to the Answer: Read the complete sentence and the surrounding paragraph to best understand the meaning of the phrase within its greater context. In the paragraph, King goes on to explain that events in Birmingham must necessarily concern him. He states that an injustice in one place threatens justice everywhere, and even writes, "Whatever affects one directly affects all indirectly" (lines 27-28). This suggests that events in Birmingham affect people throughout the nation. Choice (C) is correct, as it explains that the "interrelatedness of all communities and states" refers to the idea that events in one part of the country affect the entire nation.

13. A   Difficulty: Easy

Category: Inference

Getting to the Answer: Predict King's opinions before reviewing the answer choices. The correct answer can be inferred directly from King's views as expressed in the paragraph. In this paragraph, King refers specifically to injustice and how it affects people everywhere. From this, you can most clearly infer that King considered circumstances in Birmingham to be unfair and wrong. Choice (A) is correct.

14. B　　Difficulty: Easy

Category: Command of Evidence

Getting to the Answer: Review the answer to the previous question. Read the answer choices to identify the one whose rhetoric provides clear support for the inference. Although the entire paragraph provides general support and context for the inference, only (B) suggests that circumstances in Birmingham were unjust, that is, unfair and wrong.

15. B　　Difficulty: Medium

Category: Vocab-in-Context

Getting to the Answer: Before viewing the answer choices, think about the purpose of the word in the sentence, and form an alternate explanation of the word. Then identify the answer choice that best reflects that meaning and intent. King says that direct action in Birmingham aims to "dramatize the issue that it can no longer be ignored." This suggests that the issue, or events, in Birmingham are of great significance and demand attention that they have not received. Therefore, (B) is correct.

16. C　　Difficulty: Hard

Category: Rhetoric

Getting to the Answer: Consider the overall thrust of King's argument in this paragraph. Choose the answer that encapsulates this idea. In paragraph 3, King responds to charges that activists should focus on negotiation, not direct action. He argues that direct action is needed to spur negotiations. King reasons that nonviolent protests create the tension between forces in society needed to bring people to the table to discuss the relevant issues of prejudice and racism. His claim in the paragraph is that direct action is needed to spur negotiation, making choice (C) correct.

17. D　　Difficulty: Hard

Category: Rhetoric

Getting to the Answer: Identify an idea in paragraph 4 that provides clear support to the claim

made in the previous paragraph. In paragraph 3, King claims that nonviolent direct action is needed to prompt negotiations on civil rights. In paragraph 4, he supports that argument by explaining that no gains have been made in civil rights without such nonviolent action, as choice (D) states.

18. D　　Difficulty: Medium

Category: Rhetoric

Getting to the Answer: Read the complete paragraph to best understand the context and purpose of the cited line. The correct answer will identify what the phrase helps achieve in the paragraph. At the start of the paragraph, King argues that oppressors do not willingly give more freedom to the people whom they oppress. He goes on to explain the delay tactics that have kept African Americans from winning equal rights, and concludes that oppressed peoples in other nations are winning independence while African Americans still cannot get a cup of coffee at a lunch counter. The phrase helps King underscore the contrast between these two scenarios, so (D) is the correct answer.

Paired Passages—Bretton Woods

Suggested Passage Map notes:

Passage 1

¶1: background of Bretton Woods

¶2: created IMF to facilitate international trade

¶3: created World Bank to give loans to war affected countries, bridge rich and poor countries

¶4: BW made U.S. dollar global currency

¶5: shaped foreign trade

¶6: BW made U.S. powerful

Passage 2

¶1: BW only lasted 3 decades, Nixon changed economic policy

¶2: BW collapsed, IMF began flexible exchange system for currency

Practice Tests

¶3: U.S. dollar still widely used

¶4: G20 wants to create global currency

¶5-6: predicts worldwide currency, new world order in finance coming

19. B   Difficulty: Medium

Category: Inference

Getting to the Answer: Remember that you are being asked to choose an inference suggested by Passage 1, not a statement of fact. The passage notes that the U.S. dollar became a global currency that nations around the world accept for trade, leaving the United States in a stronger position to influence international markets. Choice (B) is the correct answer.

20. C   Difficulty: Medium

Category: Command of Evidence

Getting to the Answer: The correct choice should support your answer to the previous question. Consider which choice best shows a clear relationship with your answer to the item above. Choice (C) explicitly states the United States became the "primary power" behind the institutions established at Bretton Woods.

21. D   Difficulty: Medium

Category: Vocab-in-Context

Getting to the Answer: Predict an answer based on the context of the passage. The correct answer should not alter the meaning of the sentence in the passage. Then choose the option that best fits your prediction. The passage states that the IMF gives loans to member countries to ensure their continued stability. Choice (D) is correct because it most closely reflects the IMF's goals of proactively promoting global economic growth and stability.

22. B   Difficulty: Medium

Category: Connections

Getting to the Answer: Locate information in the passage that accurately summarizes the purposes of both institutions. Then ask yourself how these purposes differ. Both institutions encourage economic growth. However, Passage 1 notes that the IMF maintains payments and receipts between nations. The World Bank, on the other hand, focuses on "economic and social progress" (line 33) in individual countries. Choice (B) is the correct answer.

23. D   Difficulty: Hard

Category: Inference

Getting to the Answer: Eliminate any answer choices that are not suggested in the passage. Choice (D) is correct. The paragraph states that President Nixon's decision broke with the Bretton Woods framework. It can be reasonably inferred that the decision differed from the consensus of other nations, given the fact that many nations had agreed to Bretton Woods.

24. B   Difficulty: Medium

Category: Command of Evidence

Getting to the Answer: The answer choice should support your answer to the previous question. The paragraph states that President Nixon's decision "marked the end" of the Bretton Woods framework, which best supports the inference that the United States did not have the support of other nations. The correct answer is (B).

25. A   Difficulty: Medium

Category: Vocab-in-Context

Getting to the Answer: Reread the sentence in which the word appears and decide which meaning makes the most sense in context. The sentence is referring to a new global currency that might take the place of the U.S. dollar as the major, or key, currency. Therefore, (A) is the correct definition of "anchor" in this context.

26. A   Difficulty: Hard

Category: Synthesis

Getting to the Answer: Study the yuan's percent share of use in daily trading relative to other currencies in the graphic over time. What does this suggest about global views of the yuan? Passage 2 explicitly states that the yuan is "becoming a major world reserve currency" (lines 92-93). This is supported by the data in the chart, which shows the yuan's percent share of use in daily trading climbing from 0.5% in 2007 to 2.2% in 2013. Choice (A) is correct.

27. C   Difficulty: Medium

Category: Synthesis

Getting to the Answer: Identify the overall purpose of each passage. Then consider which answer choice accurately describes these purposes. Choice (C) is the correct answer. Passage 1 focuses on the effects of Bretton Woods, while Passage 2 focuses on the reasons why the international economy may transition to a new global currency.

28. D   Difficulty: Medium

Category: Synthesis

Getting to the Answer: Keep in mind that the correct answer will be a statement that is evident in both passages. The role of the IMF is mentioned prominently in both passages. Therefore, (D) is the correct answer.

Treatment for Paralysis Passage

Suggested Passage Map notes:

¶1: six million U.S. people paralyzed; causes of paralysis
¶2: patient in Poland became subject of study
¶3: spinal cord research on rats, now used to develop treatment
¶4: patient responded well to treatment
¶5: future benefits of treatment

29. C   Difficulty: Easy

Category: Global

Getting to the Answer: Keep in mind that the correct answer will be supported by all of the informa-

tion in the text rather than just a few details. The passage is concerned with one experimental treatment that doctors are exploring to help paralyzed patients regain mobility. Choice (C) is the correct answer.

30. B   Difficulty: Medium

Category: Inference

Getting to the Answer: Consider the main points the author makes throughout the passage. The correct answer will be directly related to these points, even if it is not directly stated in the passage. Choice (B) is the correct answer. It can be inferred that the author feels that increased mobility will have a positive impact on patients suffering from all levels of paralysis.

31. D   Difficulty: Easy

Category: Command of Evidence

Getting to the Answer: Locate each answer choice in the passage. Decide which one provides the best support for the answer to the previous question. In the last line of the passage, the author says that paralyzed patients "can have both their mobility and their hope restored" (lines 68-69). This answer, (D), offers the strongest support for the answer to the previous question.

32. D   Difficulty: Easy

Category: Vocab-in-Context

Getting to the Answer: The correct answer will not only be a synonym for "restricted" but will also make sense in the context of the sentence in the passage. Eliminate answers, such as A, that are synonyms for "restricted" but do not make sense in context. Here, the author is explaining that patients in wheelchairs must learn to prevent complications from restricted movement. In this context, "restricted" most nearly means "limited," answer choice (D).

33. A   Difficulty: Hard

Category: Rhetoric

Getting to the Answer: Locate lines 46-47 in the passage, and then read the paragraph that comes before it. This will help you identify why the author chose "tailor-made" to describe the patient's treatment. The patient received his own cells during the treatment, meaning that the treatment was tailored to his own body. Choice (A) fits this situation and is therefore the correct answer.

34. C   Difficulty: Hard

Category: Inference

Getting to the Answer: Remember that when a question is asking you to infer something, the answer is not stated explicitly in the passage. In paragraph 2, the author explains that the patient who received the experimental treatment had not seen an increase in mobility despite "countless hours" (line 21) of physical therapy. Therefore, it is logical to infer that the patient would not have regained mobility without this experimental treatment. Choice (C) is the correct answer.

35. B   Difficulty: Medium

Category: Command of Evidence

Getting to the Answer: Think about how you selected the correct answer for the previous question. Use that information to help you choose the correct answer to this question. In paragraph 2, the author explains that the patient selected for the experimental treatment had not regained mobility despite intensive physical therapy. This provides the strongest support for the answer to the previous question, so (B) is correct.

36. B   Difficulty: Easy

Category: Vocab-in-Context

Getting to the Answer: Substitute each of the answer choices for "refined." Select the one that makes the most sense in context and does not change the meaning of the sentence. In this context, "refined" most nearly means "improved." Choice (B) is the correct answer.

37. C   Difficulty: Easy

Category: Inference

Getting to the Answer: Skim the passage and look for details about how doctors came to use the treatment described. In paragraph 3, the author explains that the doctors used a technique that was developed during years of research on rats. Therefore, (C) is the correct answer.

38. D   Difficulty: Medium

Category: Connections

Getting to the Answer: Compare and contrast each answer choice with the procedure described in the passage. As in the procedure described in the passage, skin transplants for burn victims involve taking tissue containing healthy cells from one area of the body and using it to repair damage done to another area. Choice (D) is the correct answer.

Mercury in Fish Passage

Suggested Passage Map notes:

¶1: what mercury is, uses for mercury
¶2: causes of mercury pollution
¶3: water affected by mercury, issue for many organisms
¶4: consumption of mercury-laden seafood, risks and benefits
¶5: explanation of safe levels of mercury based on bodyweight and fish type
¶6: nutritionists' recommendations

39. C   Difficulty: Medium

Category: Inference

Getting to the Answer: The correct answer will be directly supported by the evidence in the passage. Avoid answers like A and B that go beyond what can logically be inferred about the author. The author explains how mercury gets into the fish that humans eat and goes on to say that it is possible to eat fish that contain mercury without getting mercury poisoning. Choice (C) is the correct answer because it is directly supported by the evidence in the passage.

40. D   Difficulty: Medium

Category: Command of Evidence

Getting to the Answer: The correct answer will provide direct support for the answer to the previous question. Avoid answers like B that include relevant details but do not provide direct support. In the last paragraph, the author says that nutritionists recommend eating low-mercury fish instead of eliminating fish altogether, adding that an awareness of the issues with mercury can help us make healthy eating choices. This statement supports the answer to the previous question, so (D) is the correct answer.

41. A   Difficulty: Easy

Category: Detail

Getting to the Answer: Review the details provided in the passage about how to determine a safe level of mercury consumption. In paragraph 5, the author explains that humans should consume less than 0.1 microgram of mercury for every kilogram of their own weight. Therefore, (A) is the correct answer.

42. C   Difficulty: Easy

Category: Vocab-In-Context

Getting to the Answer: Eliminate answer choices that are synonyms for "concentration" but do not make sense in context. In this sentence, the author is describing the amount of mercury in the air from power plants. "Concentration" most nearly means "density" in this context, so (C) is the correct answer.

43. A   Difficulty: Medium

Category: Inference

Getting to the Answer: Eliminate any answer choices that are not directly supported by information in the passage. The passage strongly suggests that it is

impossible to avoid exposure to mercury completely. Therefore, (A) is the correct answer.

44. B   Difficulty: Easy

Category: Command of Evidence

Getting to the Answer: Locate each of the answer choices in the passage. The correct answer should provide support for the answer to the previous question. In paragraph 1, the author explains that mercury can be found in many places. This supports the conclusion that it is impossible to avoid mercury completely. Choice (B) is the correct answer.

45. D   Difficulty: Hard

Category: Rhetoric

Getting to the Answer: Consider one of the central ideas of the passage. The correct answer would help provide additional support for this idea. One central idea in the passage is that people can eat fish if they know what mercury levels are safe for human consumption. The author states that scientists have determined safe mercury levels by studying at what point symptoms of mercury poisoning occur. However, the author only provides one example weight of how many micrograms of mercury a person could eat. Therefore, (D) is the correct answer.

46. B   Difficulty: Easy

Category: Vocab-In-Context

Getting to the Answer: Reread the sentence and replace "particulars" with each answer choice. Though the answer choices are similar in meaning to a certain degree, one of them makes the most sense when substituted for "particulars." In this context, "particulars" most nearly means "specifics"; therefore, (B) is the correct answer.

47. D   Difficulty: Hard

Category: Synthesis

Getting to the Answer: Remember that the correct answer will be supported by information in both the passage and the graphic. Refer to the passage to draw conclusions about the information in the graphic. The passage states that it is safe to eat fish that contain mercury as long as certain guidelines are followed regarding daily consumption. The graphic shows that Alaskan pollock has the lowest concentration of mercury of the fish listed. Therefore, (D) is the correct answer; a person can safely eat more Alaskan pollock than black-striped bass in one day.

WRITING AND LANGUAGE TEST

The UN: Promoting World Peace

1. C   **Difficulty:** Medium

Category: Punctuation

Getting to the Answer: Examine the passage to determine whether the current punctuation is incorrect. Then consider which set of punctuation marks correctly emphasizes the selected part of the sentence. The dashes provide emphasis for the idea that the UN is a peacekeeping organization; the dashes help set off this part of the sentence from the remaining content. The correct answer is (C).

2. D   **Difficulty:** Hard

Category: Development

Getting to the Answer: Review the main points made so far. The correct answer should touch on or summarize previous ideas in the paragraph. Choice (D) is correct. This concluding sentence effectively summarizes the ideas that compose the paragraph's main claim.

3. A   **Difficulty:** Medium

Category: Organization

Getting to the Answer: Read the previous paragraph and identify the word or phrase that is the best transition between the two paragraphs. The previous paragraph describes the UN today, and the paragraph beginning with the phrase in question explains the origins of the UN in the 1940s. Choice (A) indicates the correct shift in time period and provides the most effective transition between paragraphs.

4. A   **Difficulty:** Medium

Category: Usage

Getting to the Answer: Pay close attention to the context of the previous sentence to help you establish the correct verb tense for this particular sentence. The correct answer is (A). It uses the present tense to logically follow the previous sentence that refers to the UN in the present tense, as well.

5. B   **Difficulty:** Easy

Category: Punctuation

Getting to the Answer: Watch out for choices that may create a run-on sentence. The correct choice is (B), which provides a clear separation between one complete sentence and the next.

6. C   **Difficulty:** Easy

Category: Effective Language Use

Getting to the Answer: Substitute each choice in the complete paragraph. The correct answer will most appropriately fit within the context of the sentence and the paragraph. The correct answer is (C). The UN encourages, or promotes, environmental protection.

7. A   **Difficulty:** Medium

Category: Development

Getting to the Answer: The correct choice should introduce a central idea that is supported by subsequent sentences in the paragraph. The correct answer is (A). The expansion of the UN's budget, goals, and personnel number connects to specific evidence in the rest of the paragraph.

8. C   Difficulty: Medium

Category: Quantitative

Getting to the Answer: Notice that the graphic gives specific information about the increases and decreases in the UN peacekeeping force over a period of time. Study the answer choices to find the one that best relates to the paragraph while using accurate information from the graphic. The graphic shows data through the year 2010 and does not indicate that personnel levels rose above 100,000. Choice (C) is the correct answer.

9. A   Difficulty: Medium

Category: Effective Language Use

Getting to the Answer: Watch out for unnecessarily wordy choices like B. The correct answer is (A) because it effectively communicates an idea without additional words that distract from the content.

10. C   Difficulty: Easy

Category: Effective Language Use

Getting to the Answer: Look at the context of the sentence in which the word appears as well as the paragraph itself to choose the answer that works best. Choice (C), "noteworthy," is synonymous with "worth mentioning," which clearly fits within the context of the paragraph and the author's intent to highlight the accomplishments of the UN.

11. B   Difficulty: Medium

Category: Development

Getting to the Answer: Read the entire paragraph. Identify the sentence that is least relevant to the paragraph's topic and purpose. The purpose of this paragraph is to sum up the central ideas of the passage. Choice (B) introduces a detail that, while important, does not summarize the central ideas of the passage and therefore detracts from the paragraph's focus.

DNA Analysis in a Day

12. B   Difficulty: Easy

Category: Usage

Getting to the Answer: Read the sentence and notice that the verb in question is in a clause with intervening prepositional phrases that come between the subject and the verb. Check to see what the subject is and whether the verb agrees with the subject. The verb "match" is in a plural form, but the subject is "DNA," not one of the other nouns in the prepositional phrases. "DNA" is singular. Choice (B) is the correct answer because it is the singular form of the verb "to match."

13. A   Difficulty: Medium

Category: Punctuation

Getting to the Answer: Read the sentence to determine whether the two clauses separated by the semicolon are independent or not. If they are both independent, a semicolon is the appropriate punctuation. Be careful of answer choices with inappropriate transition words. A semicolon is the correct way to separate two independent but related clauses, so (A) is the correct answer.

14. B   Difficulty: Easy

Category: Punctuation

Getting to the Answer: Study the words in a series and see where a comma might need to be inserted or eliminated. Choice (B) is correct.

15. B   Difficulty: Hard

Category: Organization

Getting to the Answer: When you see an underlined transition, identify how the sentence relates to the previous one to determine what kind of transition is appropriate. Choice (B) is correct because the sentence to which the transition belongs provides more detail about a general statement that preceded it.

16. D   Difficulty: Easy

Category: Effective Language Use

Getting to the Answer: Imagine that the sentence has a blank where the word in question is. Read the entire paragraph for context and predict what word could complete the blank. Review the answer choices to find the word closest in meaning to your prediction. The paragraph later states that Jane Saunders's goal is to separate the two strands of DNA. Only answer choice (D) has the correct connotation and fits within the context of the sentence.

17. C   Difficulty: Medium

Category: Effective Language Use

Getting to the Answer: It is important to combine sentences in order to vary sentence structures. But the correct choice should not only be the most effective way to combine the two sentences; it must also be in parallel construction with the first sentence. Watch out for choices that may have incorrect transition words as well. Choice (C) is the correct answer. It joins the sentences concisely and correctly because the verb "adding" is in parallel construction with the earlier verbs "detaching" and "transferring." The subject in both sentences is the same, "she," so it can be dropped when combining the two sentences.

18. A   Difficulty: Medium

Category: Development

Getting to the Answer: Read the entire paragraph and then put each answer choice at the beginning. Choose the one that makes the most sense and is further explained by subsequent details in the paragraph. The paragraph discusses the process of identifying DNA, which is lengthy and involves changing the temperature of the DNA several times. Choice (A) is closest to this summation of what is to follow and is the correct answer.

19. C   Difficulty: Easy

Category: Effective Language Use

Getting to the Answer: Watch out for choices that are wordy or redundant. Choice (C) is the most concise and effective way of stating the information in the passage.

20. A   Difficulty: Medium

Category: Organization

Getting to the Answer: Consider the function of this sentence. At what point in the paragraph should this function be employed? The sentence is setting the scene, so it should be placed where it is now, at the beginning of the paragraph. To place it later would make the meaning of the paragraph unclear. Choice (A) is the correct answer.

21. B   Difficulty: Easy

Category: Effective Language Use

Getting to the Answer: Think about the connotations of each answer choice, and be sure to pick the one that fits with the context of the sentence. Substitute each answer choice for the word to see which word works best. "Eager" best reflects how the detectives would be feeling while waiting for important test results. They would be eagerly anticipating this important information and would want it as quickly as possible. Choice (B) is the correct answer.

22. C   Difficulty: Hard

Category: Development

Getting to the Answer: Decide which sentence sounds like the most appropriate way to conclude the passage. The rhetorical question currently in the passage (choice A) introduces an opinion that the passage never reveals; there is no sign that Jane Saunders would feel this way. Likewise, there is no indication in the passage of how expensive modern DNA analysis is (choice B), nor that Saunders marvels about how far science has come in DNA analysis (choice D). Choice (C) is the correct answer; it presents a fairly natural way for Saunders to feel given her accomplishments for the day.

Will Your Start-Up Succeed?

23. C   Difficulty: Medium

Category: Sentence Formation

Getting to the Answer: Check to see whether there are two independent clauses within this sentence. Two independent clauses without punctuation indicate a run-on sentence. As written, this is a run-on sentence. Choice (C) is the correct answer because it separates the two complete but related thoughts with a semicolon.

24. A   Difficulty: Medium

Category: Development

Getting to the Answer: Eliminate answers that might contain details related to the central idea but do not properly express the central idea. This paragraph is mostly about the characteristics of people who are successful entrepreneurs. Choice (A) is the correct answer because it introduces the main idea by summarizing the traits people must have to achieve success as a business owner.

25. B   Difficulty: Hard

Category: Effective Language Use

Getting to the Answer: Eliminate answers such as D that mean nearly the same thing as "grab" but do not clarify the meaning of the sentence. In this context, "derive" best clarifies the meaning of the sentence, which explains how entrepreneurs get ideas for their businesses. Choice (B) is the correct answer.

26. C   Difficulty: Easy

Category: Usage

Getting to the Answer: Read the rest of the paragraph and pay attention to the verb tense used. The verbs in the rest of this paragraph are in past tense. "Graduated" is the past tense of the verb "to graduate"; therefore, (C) is the correct answer.

27. C   Difficulty: Medium

Category: Punctuation

Getting to the Answer: Examine the structure of the whole sentence. Consider whether the punctuation is correct or even necessary. The subject of this sentence is "he," and it is followed by a compound predicate containing the verbs "built" and "founded." When a compound predicate contains only two items, a comma should not separate either verb from the subject. No punctuation is necessary, so (C) is the correct answer.

28. A   Difficulty: Medium

Category: Effective Language Use

Getting to the Answer: Replace the underlined word with each answer choice. Consider which word makes the most sense in context and conveys the clearest meaning. The sentence discusses how Vital began her own business. In this context, "launch" conveys the most precise meaning because it connotes the start of a major endeavor. Choice (A) is the correct answer because no change is needed.

29. D   Difficulty: Easy

Category: Punctuation

Getting to the Answer: This sentence contains a list of items in a series. Think about the rules of punctuation for items in a series. Items in a series should be separated by commas, with a comma following each word except the last item in the series. The word "and" is not an item in the series and, therefore, should not be followed by a comma. Therefore, (D) is the correct answer.

30. D   Difficulty: Easy

Category: Punctuation

Getting to the Answer: Identify the main elements of this sentence, such as the subject, predicate, and any restrictive or nonrestrictive clauses. Remember that a nonrestrictive clause should be set off with a comma. The clause "always seeking a new challenge" is nonrestrictive and should be set off from the rest of the sentence with a comma. Choice (D) is the correct answer.

31. C   Difficulty: Hard

Category: Development

Getting to the Answer: Identify the central idea of the paragraph. Read each answer choice and consider which sentence could be added to the paragraph to provide support for the central idea you identified. This paragraph is mostly about Chris Roth, an entrepreneur who now has several companies. (C) is the correct answer because it provides specific details about one of the companies Roth owns.

32. B   Difficulty: Easy

Category: Usage

Getting to the Answer: Read the entire sentence. Identify the subject and determine whether it is plural or singular. Determine the correct verb tense for the sentence. The subject of this sentence is plural (Gomez, Vital, and Roth), so the verb must be plural, as well. (B) is the correct answer because "agree" is the plural present tense of the verb "to agree."

33. B   Difficulty: Easy

Category: Usage

Getting to the Answer: Read the entire sentence and identify the antecedent for the underlined pronoun. The correct answer will be the pronoun that is in agreement with the antecedent. In this sentence, the antecedent is "entrepreneurs," which requires a third-person plural pronoun. Therefore, (B) is the correct answer.

Edgard Varèse's Influence

34. C   Difficulty: Medium

Category: Sentence Formation

Getting to the Answer: Read the two sentences connected by the underlined portion and decide

which answer choice creates a grammatically correct and logical sentence. Choice (C) is correct. Using the coordinating conjunction "but" with a comma to combine the sentences shows that the second portion, which mentions Varèse as being unique, stands in contrast to the first portion, which mentions many influential artists. The other options, featuring "and" and "or," do not show this necessary contrast.

35. A   Difficulty: Hard

Category: Punctuation

Getting to the Answer: Reread the entire sentence to assess how the punctuation in the answer choices affects how each portion of the sentence relates to one another. The correct answer is (A). The semicolon correctly links the two independent clauses that have a direct relationship with one another.

36. D   Difficulty: Medium

Category: Effective Language Use

Getting to the Answer: Read the sentence for context clues, and think about the author's intention. Then determine which answer provides the most appropriate word choice. "Employ" is the only word that matches the meaning of the sentence, which states that Varèse did not use traditional melodies. Thus, choice (D) is correct.

37. B   Difficulty: Medium

Category: Punctuation

Getting to the Answer: Reread the sentence to determine how each portion relates to the others. Then examine how the punctuation in the answer choices affects these relationships. The portion of the sentence discussing the family's move to Italy is an introductory element and needs a comma to offset it from the rest of the sentence. The portion discussing what Varèse learned in Turin is a parenthetical element and also requires a comma. Therefore, choice (B) is correct.

38. A   Difficulty: Medium

Category: Punctuation

Getting to the Answer: Review the sentence for context clues and to assess the subject's ownership of the objects in the sentence. Then determine which form of the possessive noun correctly reflects this ownership. The hands in the sentence belong to a single player using a single theremin; therefore, the correct answer will use the singular possessive noun "player's." Choice (A) is correct.

39. B   Difficulty: Medium

Category: Effective Language Use

Getting to the Answer: Read the sentence for context clues. Decide on the answer choice that makes the sentence's meaning precise and clear. "Conjunction" is the only word that relates to two things occurring at the same time to create a single outcome, which is the intended meaning of the sentence. Choice (B) is correct.

40. A   Difficulty: Hard

Category: Development

Getting to the Answer: Assess the central idea of the introductory sentence in the paragraph, and determine which additional fact noted in the answer choices would have the greatest benefit to the reader. The introductory sentence states that Varèse worked in New York until he secured his first success. Describing the critical reaction to the next event mentioned would help strengthen the idea that the Philadelphia performance was a successful event in Varèse's career. Choice (A) is the correct answer.

41. A   Difficulty: Hard

Category: Usage

Getting to the Answer: Consider what kind of situation the author is presenting here, and decide which tense of the verb "has" creates a grammatically correct sentence that reflects this meaning. Keep in mind the time of the events in the sentence. The

sentence imagines a situation in which Varèse had been able to use the Internet, an unrealistic action. The double "had had" is correct; it describes past-tense actions that might have occurred in the past but didn't. Choice (A) is correct.

42. D   Difficulty: Easy

Category: Usage

Getting to the Answer: Read the entire sentence to figure out who is the owner of the burned compositions. Then select the proper personal pronoun for this antecedent. Choice (D) is the correct singular possessive pronoun because the burned compositions belonged to Varèse, one person, and not a group of artists.

43. B   Difficulty: Medium

Category: Quantitative

Getting to the Answer: Study the information in the graphic to determine which answer choice most accurately finishes the sentence. Choice (B) is correct because it accurately reflects information included in the graphic.

44. C   Difficulty: Medium

Category: Development

Getting to the Answer: After reading the final paragraph, examine each answer choice to determine which best summarizes the paragraph's overall message. Choice (C) is correct. It is the one sentence that sets up the idea that Varèse's challenging work has been an inspiration to many later artists, an idea supported by the rest of the paragraph.

MATH—NO-CALCULATOR TEST

1. A   Difficulty: Easy

Category: Heart of Algebra / Linear Equations

Getting to the Answer: You could start by cross-multiplying to get rid of the denominators, but simplifying the numerators first will make the calculations easier. Don't forget to distribute the negative to both terms in the parentheses on the right-hand side of the equation.

$$\frac{4(n - 2) + 5}{2} = \frac{13 - (9 + 4n)}{4}$$

$$\frac{4n - 8 + 5}{2} = \frac{13 - 9 - 4n}{4}$$

$$\frac{4n - 3}{2} = \frac{4 - 4n}{4}$$

$$4(4n - 3) = 2(4 - 4n)$$

$$16n - 12 = 8 - 8n$$

$$16n = 20 - 8n$$

$$24n = 20$$

$$n = \frac{20}{24} = \frac{5}{6}$$

Choice (A) is correct.

2. C   Difficulty: Easy

Category: Passport to Advanced Math / Exponents

Getting to the Answer: Don't be tempted—you can't simply cancel one term when a polynomial is divided by a monomial. You can, however, split the expression into three terms, each with a denominator of $9x^2$, and simplify. You could also use polynomial long division to answer the question. Use whichever method gets you to the answer more quickly on Test Day.

$$\frac{18x^3 + 9x^2 - 36x}{9x^2} = \frac{18x^3}{9x^2} + \frac{9x^2}{9x^2} - \frac{36x}{9x^2}$$

$$= 2x + 1 - \frac{4}{x}$$

Choice (C) is correct.

3. B   Difficulty: Easy

Category: Passport to Advanced Math / Functions

Getting to the Answer: When using function notation, $f(x)$ is simply another way of saying y, so this question is asking you to find the value(s) of x for which $y = 0$, or in other words, where the graph crosses

the x-axis. Don't be tempted by the flat parts of the graph—they have a slope of 0, but the function itself does not equal 0 here (it equals -4). The graph crosses the x-axis at the points $(-1, 0)$ and $(1, 0)$, so the values of x for which $f(x) = 0$ are -1 and 1, (B).

4. C   Difficulty: Medium

Category: Heart of Algebra / Inequalities

Getting to the Answer: You don't need to use algebra to answer this question, and you also don't need to graph each system. Instead, think about how the graphs would look. The only time a system of linear inequalities has no solution is when it consists of two parallel lines shaded in opposite directions. All the inequalities are written in slope-intercept form, so look for parallel lines (two lines that have the same slope but different y-intercepts). The slopes in A are different ($m = 1$ and $m = 2$), so eliminate this choice. The same is true for B ($m = 1$ and $m = -1$) and D ($m = -1$ and $m = 1$). This means (C) must be correct ($m = 1$ and $m = 1$, $b = 1$ and $b = -1$). The graph of the system is shown here:

Because the shading never overlaps, the system has no solution.

5. B   Difficulty: Medium

Category: Passport to Advanced Math / Quadratics

Getting to the Answer: Although this question asks where the graphs intersect, it is not necessary to actually graph them. The point(s) at which the two graphs intersect are the points where the two equations are equal to each other. So, set the equations equal and use algebra to solve for x. Because the question only asks for the x-values, you don't need to substitute the results back into the equations to solve for y:

$$-2x + 1 = 2x^2 + 5x + 4$$
$$-2x = 2x^2 + 5x + 3$$
$$0 = 2x^2 + 7x + 3$$
$$0 = (2x + 1)(x + 3)$$

Now that the equation is factored, use the Zero-Product Property to solve for x:

$$2x + 1 = 0 \quad \text{and} \quad x + 3 = 0$$
$$2x = -1 \qquad\qquad x = -3$$
$$x = -\frac{1}{2}$$

Choice (B) is correct.

6. D   Difficulty: Medium

Category: Heart of Algebra / Linear Equations

Getting to the Answer: You can approach this question conceptually or concretely. When dealing with simple transformations, drawing a quick sketch is most likely the safest approach. You are only concerned about the y-intercept, so keep your focus there. When the graph is reflected over the x-axis, the y-intercept will go from $(0, -1)$ to $(0, 1)$. Next, the line is shifted up 3 units, which adds 3 to the y-coordinates of all the points on the line, making the new y-intercept $(0, 4)$. Choice (D) is correct. A sketch follows:

7. D   Difficulty: Medium

Category: Passport to Advanced Math / Quadratics

Getting to the Answer: The roots of an equation are the same as its solutions. Take a peek at the answer

choices—they contain radicals, which tells you that the equation can't be factored. Instead, either complete the square or solve the equation using the quadratic formula, whichever you are most comfortable with. The equation is already written in the form $y = ax^2 + bx + c$ and the coefficients are fairly small, so using the quadratic formula is probably the quickest method. Jot down the values that you'll need: $a = 3$, $b = -6$, and $c = -5$. Then, substitute these values into the quadratic formula and simplify:

$$x = \frac{-b \pm \sqrt{b^2 - 4ac}}{2a}$$
$$= \frac{-(-6) \pm \sqrt{(-6)^2 - 4(3)(-5)}}{2(3)}$$
$$= \frac{6 \pm \sqrt{36 + 60}}{6}$$
$$= \frac{6 \pm \sqrt{96}}{6}$$

This is not one of the answer choices, so simplify the radical. To do this, look for a perfect square that divides into 96 and take its square root. Then, if possible, cancel any factors that are common to the numerator and the denominator:

$$x = \frac{6 \pm \sqrt{16 \times 6}}{6}$$
$$= \frac{6 \pm 4\sqrt{6}}{6}$$
$$= \frac{\cancel{2}(3 \pm 2\sqrt{6})}{\cancel{2}(3)}$$
$$= \frac{3 \pm 2\sqrt{6}}{3}$$

Choice (D) is correct. Be careful—you can't simplify the answer any further because you cannot divide the square root of 6 by 3.

8. A   Difficulty: Medium

Category: Passport to Advanced Math / Exponents

Getting to the Answer: When you write an equation in terms of a specific variable, you are simply solving the equation for that variable. To do this, you'll need to use the property that raising a quantity to the one-fourth power is the same as taking its fourth root and that applying a negative exponent to a quantity is the same as writing its reciprocal. Rewrite the equation using these properties, and then solve for n using inverse operations. Note that the inverse of taking a fourth root of a quantity is raising the quantity to the fourth power:

$$m = \frac{1}{n^{-\frac{1}{4}}}$$

$$m = \frac{\sqrt[4]{n}}{1}$$

$$(m)^4 = \left(\sqrt[4]{n}\right)^4$$

$$m^4 = n$$

Choice (A) is correct.

9.   C   Difficulty: Medium

Category: Heart of Algebra / Systems of Linear Equations

Getting to the Answer: When a system consists of two equations already written in terms of y, the quickest way to solve the system is to set the equations equal to each other and then use inverse operations. Don't let the fraction intimidate you—you can write the first equation as a fraction over 1 and use cross-multiplication:

$$\frac{3x - 1}{1} = \frac{5x + 8}{2}$$
$$2(3x - 1) = 5x + 8$$
$$6x - 2 = 5x + 8$$
$$6x = 5x + 10$$
$$x = 10$$

Don't let A fool you—the question is asking for the value of y, not the value of x. To find y, substitute 10 for x in either equation and simplify:

$$y = 3(10) - 1$$
$$= 30 - 1$$
$$= 29$$

Choice (C) is correct.

10.   A   Difficulty: Medium

Category: Heart of Algebra / Inequalities

Getting to the Answer: You don't need to separate this compound inequality into pieces. Just remember, whatever you do to one piece, you must do to all three pieces. The fractions in this question make it look more complicated than it really is, so start by clearing them. To do this, multiply everything by the least common denominator, 10:

$$0 < \frac{d}{2} + 1 \leq \frac{8}{5}$$
$$10(0) < 10\left(\frac{d}{2} + 1\right) \leq \left(\frac{8}{5}\right)10$$
$$0 < 5d + 10 \leq 16$$
$$-10 < 5d \leq 6$$
$$-2 < d \leq \frac{6}{5}$$

Now, read the inequality symbols carefully. The value of d is between -2 and $\frac{6}{5}$, not including -2 because of the $<$ symbol, so (A) is the correct answer. Don't let C fool you—you can't have a 0 *denominator* in a rational expression, but in this expression, the variable is in the numerator, so it *can* equal 0.

11.   B   Difficulty: Medium

Category: Heart of Algebra / Linear Equations

Getting to the Answer: The key to answering this type of question is determining how many results fit in each category. Here, you need to know how many shots were 3-pointers and how many were 2-pointers. Mae-Ling successfully made 15 shots total and s were 3-pointers, so the rest, or $15 - s$, must have been 2-pointers. Write the expression in words first: points per 3-pointers (3) times number of shots that were 3-pointers (s), plus points per regular goal (2) times number of regular goals ($15 - s$). Now, translate from English into math: $3s + 2(15 - s)$. This is not one of the answer choices, so simplify the expression by distributing the 2 and then combining like terms: $3s + 2(15 - s) = 3s + 30 - 2s = s + 30$. This matches (B).

12. D   Difficulty: Medium

Category: Heart of Algebra / Linear Equations

Getting to the Answer: There is only one equation given and it has two variables. This means that you don't have enough information to solve for either variable. Instead, look for the relationship between the left side of the equation and the other expression that you are trying to find. The expression you are trying to find $(6x - 5y)$ has the x-term first and then the y-term, so start by reversing the order of the terms on the left side of the given equation. Also, notice that the x term in $6x - 5y$ is not negative, so multiply the equation by -1:

$$\frac{1}{2}y - \frac{3}{5}x = -16 \rightarrow -\frac{3}{5}x + \frac{1}{2}y = -16$$

$$-1\left(-\frac{3}{5}x + \frac{1}{2}y = -16\right) \rightarrow \frac{3}{5}x - \frac{1}{2}y = 16$$

Finally, there are no fractions in the desired expression, so clear the fractions by multiplying both sides of the equation by 10. This yields the expression that you are looking for, so no further work is required—just read the value on the right-hand side of the equation, which is 160:

$$10\left(\frac{3}{5}x - \frac{1}{2}y\right) = 16(10)$$

$$6x - 5y = 160$$

Choice (D) is correct.

13. B   Difficulty: Medium

Category: Passport to Advanced Math / Functions

Getting to the Answer: Understanding the language of functions will make questions that seem complicated much more doable. When you know the output of a function (or in this question, a composition of two functions), you can work backward to find the input. Because $g(x)$ is the inside function

for this composition, its output becomes the input for $f(x)$. Unfortunately, you don't have any information about g yet. You do know, however, that f of some number, $g(2)$, is -1, so set $f(x)$ equal to -1 and solve for x:

$$-1 = x + 1$$

$$-2 = x$$

You now know that $f(-2) = -1$. In the equation for the composition, $g(2)$ represents x, so you also know that $g(2)$ must be -2. Your only option now is to use brute force to determine which equation for g, when evaluated at 2, results in -2.

Choice A: $g(2) = 2 - 6 = -4$ (not -2), so eliminate.

Choice B: $g(2) = 2 - 4 = -2$

You don't need to go any further; (B) is correct.

You could check your answer by working forward, starting with $g(2)$:

$$g(2) = 2 - 4 = -2$$

$$f(g(2)) = f(-2) = -2 + 1 = -1$$

14. 1/5 or .2   Difficulty: Medium

Category: Heart of Algebra / Linear Equations

Getting to the Answer: There are two variables but only one equation, so you can't actually solve the equation for k. Instead, recall that an equation has infinitely many solutions when the left side is identical to the right side. When this happens, everything cancels out and you get $0 = 0$, which is always true. Start by simplifying the right-hand side of the equation. Don't simplify the left side because k is already in a good position:

$$k(10x - 5) = 2(3 + x) - 7$$

$$k(10x - 5) = 6 + 2x - 7$$

$$k(10x - 5) = 2x - 1$$

Next, compare the left side of the equation to the right side. Rather than distributing the k, notice that $2x$ is a fifth of $10x$ and -1 is a fifth of -5, so if k were

$\frac{1}{5}$ (or 0.2), then both sides of the equation would equal $2x - 1$, and it would therefore have infinitely many solutions. Thus, k is $\frac{1}{5}$ or .2.

15. 2   Difficulty: Medium

Category: Additional Topics in Math / Geometry

Getting to the Answer: You could use the Pythagorean theorem to solve this, but it will save valuable time on Test Day if you recognize that this question is testing your knowledge of Pythagorean triples. The triangle is a right triangle with leg lengths of 18 and 24, which, when divided by 6, are in the proportion 3:4. This means that the triangle is a scaled up 3:4:5 right triangle with a scale factor of 6. To keep the same proportion, the hypotenuse must be $5 \times 6 = 30$. For $15n$ to equal 30, n must be 2.

16. 3   Difficulty: Hard

Category: Passport to Advanced Math / Exponents

Getting to the Answer: You need to use rules of exponents to simplify the expression. Before you can do that, you must rewrite the radicals as fraction exponents. Use the phrase "power over root" to help you convert the radicals: $\sqrt{x} = \sqrt[\text{root} \to 2]{x^{1 \leftarrow \text{power}}} = x^{\frac{1}{2}}$ and $\sqrt[\text{root} \to 4]{x^{3 \leftarrow \text{power}}} = x^{\frac{3}{4}}$. Then use rules of exponents to simplify the expression. Add the exponents of the factors that are being multiplied and subtract the exponent of the factor that is being divided:

$$\frac{\sqrt{x} \cdot x^{\frac{5}{4}} \cdot x^2}{\sqrt[4]{x^3}} = \frac{x^{\frac{1}{2}} \cdot x^{\frac{5}{4}} \cdot x^{\frac{2}{1}}}{x^{\frac{3}{4}}}$$

$$= x^{\frac{1}{2} + \frac{5}{4} + \frac{2}{1} - \frac{3}{4}}$$

$$= x^{\frac{2}{4} + \frac{5}{4} + \frac{8}{4} - \frac{3}{4}}$$

$$= x^{\frac{12}{4}} = x^3$$

The exponent of the simplified expression is 3.

17. 6   Difficulty: Hard

Category: Passport to Advanced Math / Quadratics

Getting to the Answer: When you are given the graph of a parabola, try to use what you know about intercepts, the vertex, and the axis of symmetry to answer the question. Here, you could try to use points from the graph to find its equation, but this is not necessary because the question only asks for the value of b. As a shortcut, recall that you can find the vertex of a parabola using the formula $x = -\frac{b}{2a}$ (the quadratic formula without the radical part). You are given that $a = -1$. Now look at the graph—the vertex of the parabola is (3, 8), so substitute 3 for x, -1 for a, and solve for b:

$$3 = -\frac{b}{2(-1)}$$

$$3 = -\left(\frac{b}{-2}\right)$$

$$3 = \frac{b}{2}$$

$$3(2) = b$$

$$6 = b$$

As an alternate method, you could plug the value of a and the vertex (from the graph) into vertex form of a quadratic equation and simplify:

$$y = a(x - h)^2 + k$$

$$= -1(x - 3)^2 + 8$$

$$= -1(x^2 - 6x + 9) + 8$$

$$= -x^2 + 6x - 9 + 8$$

$$= -x^2 + 6x - 1$$

The coefficient of x is b, so $b = 6$.

MATH—CALCULATOR TEST

1. D   Difficulty: Easy

Category: Problem Solving and Data Analysis / Scatterplots

Strategic Advice: You don't need to know the slope of the line of best fit to answer the question, so don't waste valuable time trying to find it. Instead, use the labels on the axes to determine the meaning of the slope.

Getting to the Answer: Graphically, slope is the ratio of the change in the *y*-values (rise) to the change in the *x*-values (run). In a real-world scenario, this is the same as the unit rate. In this context, the rise describes the change in the number of home runs hit in a single season, and the run describes the change in the number of hours a player spends in batting practice. Thus, the unit rate, or slope, represents the estimated increase (since the data trends upward) in the number of single-season home runs hit by a player for each hour he spends in batting practice.

2. B   Difficulty: Easy

Category: Heart of Algebra / Linear Equations

Getting to the Answer: Finding an *x*-intercept is easy when you know the equation of the line—it's the value of *x* when *y* is 0. Notice that the answer choices are very close together. This means you shouldn't just estimate visually. Take the time to do the math. Everything you need to write the equation is shown on the graph—just pay careful attention to how the grid lines are labeled. The *y*-intercept is 10 and the line rises 2 units and runs 1 unit from one point to the next, so the slope is $\frac{2}{1} - 2$. This means the equation of the line, in slope-intercept form, is $y = 2x + 10$. Now, set the equation equal to zero and solve for *x*:

$$0 = 2x + 10$$
$$-10 = 2x$$
$$-5 = x$$

The line will intersect the *x*-axis at −5, which is (B).

3. A   Difficulty: Easy

Category: Passport to Advanced Math / Functions

Getting to the Answer: When you see an expression like *f*(*x*), it means to substitute the given value for *x* in the function's equation. When there is more

than one function involved, pay careful attention to which function should be evaluated first. You are looking for the value of *f*(*x*) at *x* = 5. Because *f*(*x*) is defined in terms of *g*(*x*), evaluate *g*(5) first by substituting 5 for *x* in the expression *x* + 2:

$$g(5) = 5 + 2 = 7$$
$$f(5) = -3g(5) = -3(7) = -21$$

This means (A) is correct.

4. B   Difficulty: Medium

Category: Heart of Algebra / Linear Equations

Getting to the Answer: The cost per night in the hospital is the same as the unit rate, which is represented by the slope of the line. Use the grid lines and the axis labels to count the rise and the run from the *y*-intercept of the line (0, 26,000) to the next point that hits an intersection of two grid lines, (2, 34,000). Pay careful attention to how the grid lines are marked (by 2s on the *x*-axis and by 2,000s on the *y*-axis). The line rises 8,000 units and runs 2 units, so the slope is $\frac{8,000}{2}$, which means it costs an average of $4,000 per night to stay in the hospital.

Note that you could also use the slope formula and the two points to find the slope:

$$\frac{34,000 - 26,000}{2 - 0} = \frac{8,000}{2} = 4,000$$

Choice (B) is correct.

5. D   Difficulty: Medium

Category: Problem Solving and Data Analysis / Scatterplots

Getting to the Answer: You aren't given much information to go on except the shape of the graph, so you'll need to think about what the shape means. Remember, linear functions increase at a constant rate, exponential functions increase at either an increasing or decreasing rate, gradually at first and then more quickly or vice versa, and quadratics and polynomials reverse direction one or more times. The graph begins by decreasing extremely quickly, but then it almost (but not quite) levels off. Therefore, it can't be linear and because it doesn't change direction, an exponential function, (D), would be the best model for the data.

6. A   **Difficulty:** Medium

Category: Problem Solving and Data Analysis / Statistics and Probability

Getting to the Answer: This is a science crossover question. Read the first three sentences quickly—they are simply describing the context. The second half of the paragraph poses the question, so read that more carefully. In the sample, 2,800 out of 3,200 acres were free of kudzu after applying the herbicide. This is $\frac{2,800}{3,200} = 0.875 = 87.5\%$ of the area. For the whole region, assuming the same general conditions, 0.875(30,000) = 26,250 acres should be free of the kudzu. Be careful—this is not the answer. The question asks how much of the cropland would *still be covered* by kudzu, so subtract to get 30,000 − 26,250 = 3,750 acres, (A).

7. B   **Difficulty:** Medium

Category: Passport to Advanced Math / Functions

Getting to the Answer: The notation $g(h(x))$ indicates a composition of two functions, which can be read "g of h of x." It means that the output when x is substituted in $h(x)$ becomes the input for $g(x)$. First, use the top and bottom rows of the table to find that $h(3)$ is 2. This is your new input. Now, use the top and middle rows of the table to find $g(2)$, which is −3, (B).

8. D   **Difficulty:** Medium

Category: Heart of Algebra / Linear Equations

Getting to the Answer: Assign a variable to the unknown, and then create an equation that represents the scenario. Let n be the number of units the manufacturer sells in a month. Sales must equal expenses for the manufacturer to break even (sales = expenses). The sales are equal to the selling price ($9.50) times the number of units sold

(n), so write 9.5n on one side of the equal sign. The monthly expenses are the fixed expenses ($11,625) plus the amount paid for the materials needed to produce one unit ($4.85) times the number of units (n), so write 11,625 + 4.85n on the other side of the equal sign. Then, solve for n:

$$9.5n = 11,625 + 4.85n$$
$$4.65n = 11,625$$
$$n = 2,500$$

Choice (D) is correct.

9. A   **Difficulty:** Medium

Category: Problem Solving and Data Analysis / Rates, Ratios, Proportions, and Percentages

Getting to the Answer: Let the units in this question guide you to the answer. You can do one conversion at a time or all of them at once. Just be sure to line up the units so they'll cancel correctly. The company uses 8 machines, each of which pumps at a rate of 37.5 gallons per minute, so the rate is actually 8 × 37.5 = 300 gallons per minute. Find the total number of gallons needed, and then use the rate to find the time:

$$2,500 \text{ bbl} \times \frac{42 \text{ gal}}{1 \text{ bbl}} \times \frac{1 \text{ min}}{300 \text{ gal}} = 350 \text{ min}$$

The answers are given in hours and minutes, so change 350 minutes to 350 ÷ 60 = 5.833 hours, which is 5 hours and 50 minutes, (A).

10. C   **Difficulty:** Medium

Category: Problem Solving and Data Analysis / Functions

Getting to the Answer: Look for a pattern for the sales of each company. Then apply that pattern to see which one will sell more in the last month of the year. Writing a function that represents each pattern will also help, but you have to be careful that you evaluate the function at the correct input value. Company A's sales can be represented by a linear function because each month the company sells 92 more of the toy than the month before, which is a constant difference. The sales can be represented by the function $f(t) = 92t + 54$, where t is the number of months *after January*. December is 11 months (not 12) after January, so during the last month of the year Company A should sell $f(11) = 92(11) + 54 = 1,066$ of the toy. Company B's sales can be represented by an exponential function because the sales are doubling each month, which is a constant ratio (2 for doubling). The function is $g(t) = 15(2)^t$, where t is again the number of months *after January*. In December, Company B should sell $g(11) = 15(2)^{11} = 30,720$. This means that in December, Company B should sell $30,720 - 1,066 = 29,654$ more of the toy than Company A. Choice (C) is correct.

11. A   Difficulty: Medium

Category: Heart of Algebra / Inequalities

Getting to the Answer: Apply logic to this question first, and then algebra. The dot at the beginning of the shaded portion is an open dot, so -2 is not included in the solution set of the inequality. This means you can eliminate C and D because those symbols *would* include the endpoint. Don't immediately choose B just because the arrow is pointing to the right, which typically indicates *greater than*. When dealing with an inequality, if you multiply or divide by a negative number, you must flip the symbol, so the answer is not necessarily what you might think. Because you were able to eliminate two of the choices, the quickest approach is to pick one of the remaining symbols, plug it in, and see if it works. If it does, choose that answer. If it doesn't, then it must be the other symbol. Try (A):

$$5(x - 2) - 3x < 4x - 6$$
$$5x - 10 - 3x < 4x - 6$$
$$2x - 10 < 4x - 6$$
$$-2x < 4$$
$$x > -2$$

The resulting inequality, $x > -2$, means all the values on the number line greater than (or to the right of) -2, so the initial inequality symbol must have been $<$. Choice (A) is correct.

12. B   Difficulty: Easy

Category: Problem Solving and Data Analysis / Rates, Ratios, Proportions, and Percents

Getting to the Answer: When a question involves scale factors, set up a proportion and solve for the missing value:

$$\frac{1}{8} = \frac{x}{19.9}$$
$$8x = 19.9$$
$$x = 2.4875 \approx 2.5$$

Choice (B) is correct.

13. C   Difficulty: Easy

Category: Problem Solving and Data Analysis / Rates, Ratios, Proportions, and Percents

Getting to the Answer: Don't make this question harder than it actually is. You don't need to find the new scale factor. Instead, use the length that the student drew the femur and the actual length to set up and solve a new proportion:

$$\frac{\text{drawing of sternum}}{\text{actual sternum}} = \frac{\text{drawing of femur}}{\text{actual femur}}$$
$$\frac{x}{6.7} = \frac{3.5}{19.9}$$
$$23.45 = 19.9x$$
$$1.1783 = x$$
$$x \approx 1.2$$

Choice (C) is correct.

14. B   Difficulty: Medium

Category: Heart of Algebra / Linear Equations

Getting to the Answer: Given two points (even when the coordinates are variables), the slope of the line between the points can be found using the formula $m = \dfrac{y_2 - y_1}{x_2 - x_1}$. You are given a numerical value for the slope and a pair of ordered pairs that have variables in them. To find the value of c, plug the points into the slope formula, and then solve for c. Be careful of all the negative signs:

$$m = \frac{y_2 - y_1}{x_2 - x_1}$$

$$\frac{1}{2} = \frac{-8 - 2c}{-c - (4 - c)}$$

$$\frac{1}{2} = \frac{-8 - 2c}{-c - 4 + c}$$

$$\frac{1}{2} = \frac{-8 - 2c}{-4}$$

$$1(-4) = 2(-8 - 2c)$$

$$-4 = -16 - 4c$$

$$12 = -4c$$

$$-3 = c$$

Choice (B) is correct.

15. A **Difficulty:** Medium

Category: Problem Solving and Data Analysis / Rates, Ratios, Proportions, and Percents

Getting to the Answer: Questions that involve distance, rate, and time can almost always be solved using the formula Distance = rate × time. Break the question into short steps (first part of trip, second part of trip). Start with the plane from DCA. Use the speed, or rate, of the plane, 338 mph, and its distance from London, 3,718 miles, to determine when it arrived. You don't know the time, so call it t:

$$\text{Distance} = \text{rate} \times \text{time}$$
$$3,718 = 338t$$
$$11 = t$$

It took the DCA flight 11 hours. Now determine how long it took the plane from MIA. You'll need to find the distance for each part of the trip—the question only tells you the total distance. Then, use the formula to find how long the plane flew at 596 mph and how long it flew at 447 mph:

First part of trip: *Second part of trip:*

$$\frac{2}{3} \times 4,470 = 2,980 \text{ mi} \quad \frac{1}{3} \times 4,470 = 1,490 \text{ mi}$$

$$2,980 = 596t \qquad\qquad 1,490 = 447t$$

$$5 = t \qquad\qquad\qquad 3.\overline{3} = t$$

This means it took the MIA flight 5 hours + 3 hours, 20 minutes = 8 hours, 20 minutes. So, the plane from MIA arrived first. It arrived 11 hours − 8 hours, 20 minutes = 2 hours, 40 minutes before the plane from DCA, making (A) correct.

16. D **Difficulty:** Medium

Category: Passport to Advanced Math / Quadratics

Getting to the Answer: The graph of every quadratic equation is a parabola, which may or may not cross the x-axis, depending on where its vertex is and which way it opens. When an equation has no solution, its graph does not cross the x-axis, so try to envision the graph of each of the answer choices (or you could graph each one in your graphing calculator, but this will probably take longer). Don't forget—if the equation is written in vertex form, $y = a(x - h)^2 + k$, then the vertex is (h, k) and the value of a tells you which way the parabola opens. When a quadratic equation is written in factored form, the factors tell you the x-intercepts, which means A and B (which are factored) must cross the x-axis, so eliminate them. Now, imagine the graph of the equation in C: The vertex is $(-1, 8)$ and a is negative, so the parabola opens downward and consequently must cross the x-axis. This means (D) must be correct. The vertex is also $(-1, 8)$, but a is positive, so the graph opens up and does not cross the x-axis.

17. D **Difficulty:** Medium

Category: Problem Solving and Data Analysis / Statistics and Probability

Getting to the Answer: The two variables are certainly correlated—as one goes up, the other goes up. A linear regression model would fit the data fairly well, so you can eliminate C. The spending is graphed on the x-axis, so it is the independent variable and therefore does not depend on the GDP, graphed on the y-axis, so you can eliminate B as well. The data does show that as spending on students increases, so does the GDP, but this is simply correlation, not causation. Without additional data, no statements can be made about whether spending more on students is the reason for the increased GDP, so (D) is correct.

18. C   Difficulty: Easy

Category: Passport to Advanced Math / Exponents

Getting to the Answer: Focus on the question at the very end—it's just asking you to solve the equation for p_2. Multiply both sides by T_2 to get rid of the denominator on the right-hand side of the equation. Then divide by V_2 to isolate p_2:

$$\frac{p_1 V_1}{T_1} = \frac{p_2 V_2}{T_2}$$

$$\frac{p_1 V_1 T_2}{T_1} = p_2 V_2$$

$$\frac{p_1 V_1 T_2}{T_1 V_2} = p_2$$

Stop here! You cannot cancel the V's and T's because the subscripts indicate that they are not the same variable. In math, subscripts do not behave the same way superscripts (exponents) do. Choice (C) is correct.

19. C   Difficulty: Medium

Category: Problem Solving and Data Analysis / Rates, Ratios, Proportions, and Percents

Getting to the Answer: The factor-label method (canceling units) is a great strategy for this question. You're starting with tons, so work from that unit, arranging conversions so that units cancel. To keep units straight, use an E for Earth, an M for Mars, and a J for Jupiter:

$$1.5 \; \cancel{T} \times \frac{2{,}000 \; \cancel{lb(E)}}{1 \cancel{T}} \times \frac{0.377 \; lb(M)}{1 \; \cancel{lb(E)}} = 1{,}131 \; lb \, (M)$$

$$1.5 \; \cancel{T} \times \frac{2{,}000 \; \cancel{lb(E)}}{1 \cancel{T}} \times \frac{2.364 \; lb(J)}{1 \; \cancel{lb(E)}} = 7{,}092 \; lb \, (J)$$

The object weighs 1,131 pounds on Mars and 7,092 pounds on Jupiter, so it weighs 7,092 − 1,131 = 5,961 more pounds on Jupiter, (C).

20. C   Difficulty: Medium

Category: Problem Solving and Data Analysis / Statistics and Probability

Getting to the Answer: Examine the shape of the data and familiarize yourself with the title and the axis labels on the graph. Data is *symmetric* if it is fairly evenly spread out, and it is *skewed* if it has a long tail on either side. Notice that the data is skewed to the right, so you can immediately eliminate A. Choices B, (C), and D all describe the data as skewed to the right, so you'll need to examine those statements more closely. For B, "adverse reactions" include the last four bars, which represent 89 + 41 + 22 + 8 = 160 participants total, which is not even close to 50% of 900, so eliminate B. Note that you don't need to add all the bar heights to find that there were 900 participants—the title of the graph tells you that. Now look at C—"failed to have adverse reactions" means "None" or "Mild" (the first three bars), which represent 900 − 160 = 740 of the 900 participants. 75% of 900 = 675, and 740 is more than 675, so (C) is correct. For D, the "None" column contains 320 participants, which does not equal approximately 50% of 900, so it too is incorrect.

21. C   Difficulty: Medium

Category: Heart of Algebra / Systems of Linear Equations

Getting to the Answer: Use the Kaplan Method for Translating English into Math. Write a system of equations with p = the cost in dollars of the Pennsylvania bar exam and d = the cost of the D.C. bar exam. The Pennsylvania bar exam (p) costs $25 less (−25) than 3 times as much ($3d$) as the D.C. bar exam, or $p = 3d - 25$. Together, both bar exams cost $775, so $d + p = 775$. The system is:

$$\begin{cases} p = 3d - 25 \\ d + p = 775 \end{cases}$$

The top equation is already solved for p, so substitute $3d − 25$ into the second equation for p, and solve for d:

$$d + (3d - 25) = 775$$
$$4d = 800$$
$$d = 200$$

Be careful—that's not the answer. The D.C. bar exam costs $200, which means the Pennsylvania bar exam costs $775 − $200 = $575. This means the D.C. bar exam is $575 − $200 = $375 less expensive than the Pennsylvania bar exam. Choice (C) is correct.

22. B   Difficulty: Medium

Category: Problem Solving and Data Analysis / Statistics and Probability

Getting to the Answer: Always read the axis labels carefully when a question involves a chart or graph. *Frequency*, which is plotted along the vertical axis, tells you how many students missed the number of questions indicated under each bar. Evaluate each statement as quickly as you can.

Choice A: Add the bar heights (frequencies) that represent students that missed 5 or more questions: 7 + 3 + 3 + 2 = 15. Then, find the total number of students represented, which is the number that missed less than 5 questions plus the 15 you just found: 2 + 3 + 4 + 6 = 15, plus the 15 you already found, for a total of 30 students. The statement is not true because 15 is exactly half (not more than half) of 30.

Choice (B): This calculation will take a bit of time so skip it for now.

Choice C: The tallest bar tells you which number of questions was missed most often, which was 5 questions, not 3 questions, so this statement is not true.

Choice D: The number of students from Mr. Juno's class who took the test that day is the sum of the heights of the bars, which you already know is 30, not 36.

This means (B) must be correct. Mark it and move on to the next question. (In case you're curious, find the mean by multiplying each number of questions missed by the corresponding frequency, adding all the products, and dividing by the total number of students, which you already know is 30:

$$\text{mean} = \frac{2 + 6 + 12 + 24 + 35 + 18 + 21 + 16}{30}$$
$$= \frac{134}{30} = 4.4\overline{6}$$

The mean is indeed between 4 and 5.)

23. C   Difficulty: Hard

Category: Passport to Advanced Math / Quadratics

Getting to the Answer: Writing quadratic equations can be tricky and time-consuming. If you know the roots, you can use factors to write the equation. If you don't know the roots, you need to create a system of equations to find the coefficients of the variable terms. You don't know the roots of this equation, so start with the point that has the nicest values (0, 2) and substitute them into the equation, $y = ax^2 + bx + c$, to get $2 = a(0)^2 + b(0) + c$, or $2 = c$. Now your equation looks like $y = ax^2 + bx + 2$. Next, use the other two points to create a system of two equations in two variables:

$$(-6, -7) \rightarrow -7 = a(-6)^2 + b(-6) + 2 \rightarrow -9 = 36a - 6b$$

$$(8, -14) \rightarrow -14 = a(8)^2 + b(8) + 2 \rightarrow -16 = 64a + 8b$$

You now have a system of equations to solve. If you multiply the top equation by 4 and the bottom equation by 3, and then add the equations, the b terms will eliminate each other:

$$4[-9 = 36a - 6b] \rightarrow -36 = 144a - 24b$$
$$3[-16 = 64a + 8b] \rightarrow \underline{-48 = 192a + 24b}$$
$$-84 = 336a$$
$$-0.25 = a$$

Now, find b by substituting $a = -0.25$ into either of the original equations. Using the top equation, you get:

$$-9 = 36(-0.25) - 6b$$
$$-9 = -9 - 6b$$
$$0 = 6b$$
$$0 = b$$

The value of $a + b + c$ is $(-0.25) + 0 + 2 = 1.75$, (C).

24. D   Difficulty: Hard

Category: Problem Solving and Data Analysis / Rates, Ratios, Proportions, and Percentages

Getting to the Answer: Read the question, organizing important information as you go. You need to find the ratio of mini muffins to jumbo muffins. You're given two ratios: mini to regular and regular to jumbo. Both of the given ratios contain regular muffin size units, but the regular amounts (2 and 5) are not identical. To directly compare them, find a common multiple (10). Multiply each ratio by the factor that will make the number of regular muffins equal to 10:

Mini to regular: (5:2) × (5:5) = 25:10

Regular to jumbo: (5:4) × (2:2) = 10:8

Now that the number of regular muffins is the same in both ratios (10), you can merge the two ratios to compare mini to jumbo directly: 25:10:8. So, the proper ratio of mini muffins to jumbo muffins is 25:8, which is (D).

25. A   Difficulty: Medium

Category: Heart of Algebra / Systems of Linear Equations

Getting to the Answer: Graphically, a system of linear equations that has no solution indicates two parallel lines, or in other words, two lines that have the same slope. So, write each of the equations in slope-intercept form ($y = mx + b$) and set their slopes (m) equal to each other to solve for k. Before finding the slopes, multiply the top equation by 6 to make it easier to manipulate:

$$6\left(\frac{1}{3}x + \frac{1}{2}y = 5\right) \rightarrow 2x + 3y = 30 \rightarrow y = -\frac{2}{3}x + 10$$

$$kx - 4y = 16 \rightarrow -4y = -kx + 16 \rightarrow y = \frac{k}{4}x - 4$$

The slope of the first line is $-\frac{2}{3}$, and the slope of the second line is $\frac{k}{4}$. Set them equal and solve for k:

$$-\frac{2}{3} = \frac{k}{4}$$
$$-8 = 3k$$
$$-\frac{8}{3} = k$$

Choice (A) is correct.

26. D   Difficulty: Hard

Category: Passport to Advanced Math / Exponents

Getting to the Answer: The numbers in some questions are simply too large to use a calculator (you get an "overflow" error message). Instead, you'll have to rely on rules of exponents. Notice that all of the base numbers have 3 as a factor, so rewrite everything in terms of 3. This will allow you to use the rules of exponents. Because 27 is the cube of 3, you can rewrite 27^{90} as a power of 3:

$$27^{90} = \left(3^3\right)^{90}$$
$$= 3^{3 \times 90}$$
$$= 3^{270}$$

Now the product should read: $3^{90} \times 3^{270}$, which is equal to $3^{90 + 270} = 3^{360}$. Repeat this process for the quantity that is being divided:

$$\left(\frac{1}{9}\right)^{30} = \left(\frac{1}{3^2}\right)^{30} = \left(3^{-2}\right)^{30} = 3^{-60}$$

Finally, use rules of exponents one more time to simplify the new expression:

$$\frac{3^{360}}{3^{-60}} = 3^{360 + 60} = 3^{420}$$

All the answer choices are given as powers of 9, so rewrite your answer as a power of 9:

$$3^{420} = 3^{2 \times 210} = \left(3^2\right)^{210} = 9^{210}$$

Choice (D) is correct.

27. D   **Difficulty:** Hard

Category: Additional Topics in Math / Geometry

Getting to the Answer: If needed, don't forget to check the formulas provided for you at the beginning of each math section. The volume of a right cone is given by $V = \frac{1}{3}\pi r^2 h$. Here, you only know the value of one of the variables, V, so you'll need to use the information in the question to somehow write r and h in terms of just one variable. If the cone is three times as wide at the base as it is tall, then call the diameter $3x$ and the height of the cone one-third of that, or x. The volume formula calls for the radius, which is half the diameter, or $\frac{3x}{2}$. Substitute these values into the formula and solve for x:

$$V = \frac{1}{3}\pi r^2 h$$

$$384\pi = \frac{1}{3}\pi\left(\frac{3}{2}x\right)^2 x$$

$$384 = \left(\frac{1}{3}\right)\left(\frac{9}{4}x^2\right)x$$

$$384 = \frac{3}{4}x^3$$

$$512 = x^3$$

$$\sqrt[3]{512} = x$$

$$8 = x$$

The question asks for the diameter of the base, which is $3x = 3(8) = 24$, choice (D).

28. 85   **Difficulty:** Easy

Category: Problem Solving and Data Analysis / Scatterplots

Getting to the Answer: The *range* of a set of data points is the set of outputs, which correspond to the y-values of the data points on the graph. To find the maximum value in the range of the data, look for the highest point on the graph, which is (250, 85). The y-value is 85, so 85 is the maximum value in the range.

29. 7   **Difficulty:** Hard

Category: Heart of Algebra / Linear Equations

Getting to the Answer: To write the equation of a line, you need two things: the slope and the y-intercept. Start by finding these, substituting them into slope-intercept form of a line ($y = mx + b$), and then manipulate the equation so that it is written in standard form. Use the given points, $(-4, 1)$ and $(3, -2)$, and the slope formula to find m:

$$m = \frac{y_2 - y_1}{x_2 - x_1} = \frac{-2 - 1}{3 - (-4)} = -\frac{3}{7}$$

Next, find the y-intercept, b, using the slope and one of the points:

$$y = -\frac{3}{7}x + b$$

$$1 = -\frac{3}{7}(-4) + b$$

$$1 = \frac{12}{7} + b$$

$$-\frac{5}{7} = b$$

Write the equation in slope-intercept form: $y = -\frac{3}{7}x - \frac{5}{7}$.

Now, rewrite the equation in the form $Ax + By = C$, making sure that A is a positive integer (a whole number greater than 0):

$$y = -\frac{3}{7}x - \frac{5}{7}$$

$$\frac{3}{7}x + y = -\frac{5}{7}$$

$$7\left(\frac{3}{7}x + y\right) = -\frac{5}{7}\bigg)7$$

$$3x + 7y = -5$$

The question asks for the value of B (the coefficient of y), so the correct answer is 7.

30. 380   **Difficulty:** Medium

Category: Problem Solving and Data Analysis / Rates, Ratios, Proportions, and Percents

Getting to the Answer: You can use the formula Percent × whole = part to solve this problem, but you will first need to think conceptually about what the question is asking. The question is asking for the Dow value *before* the 19.5% decrease to 306. This means that 306 represents 100 − 19.5 = 80.5% of what the stock market was at its record high. Fill these amounts into the equation and solve for the original whole, the record high Dow value:

$$0.805 \times w = 306$$
$$w = \frac{306}{0.805}$$
$$w = 380.124$$

Rounded to the nearest whole point, the record high was approximately 380 points.

31. 25   Difficulty: Hard

Category: Problem Solving and Data Analysis / Rates, Ratios, Proportions, and Percents

Getting to the Answer: Percent change is given by the ratio $\frac{\text{amount of change}}{\text{original amount}}$. To find the total percent change, you'll need to work your way through each of the days, and then use the ratio. Jot down the Dow value at the end of each day as you go. Do not round until you reach your final answer. First, calculate the value of the Dow at closing on Black Thursday: It opened at 306 and decreased by 2%, which means the value at the end of the day was 100 − 2 = 98% of the starting amount, or 306 × 0.98 = 299.88. Then, it decreased again on Monday by 13% to close at 100 − 13 = 87% of the opening amount, or 299.88 × 0.87 = 260.8956. Finally, it decreased on Tuesday by another 12% to end at 100 − 12 = 88% of the starting amount, or 260.8956 × 0.88 = 229.588. Now use the percent change formula to calculate the percent decrease from opening on Black Thursday (306) to closing on Black Tuesday (229.588):

$$\text{Percent decrease} = \frac{306 - 229.588}{306}$$
$$= \frac{76.412}{306} = 0.2497$$

The Dow had a total percent decrease of approximately 25% between opening on Black Thursday and closing on Black Tuesday.

PSAT PRACTICE TEST 2 ANSWER SHEET

Remove (or photocopy) this answer sheet and use it to complete the test. See the answer key following the test when finished.

Start with number 1 for each section. If a section has fewer questions than answer spaces, leave the extra spaces blank.

SECTION 1

1. Ⓐ Ⓑ Ⓒ Ⓓ
2. Ⓐ Ⓑ Ⓒ Ⓓ
3. Ⓐ Ⓑ Ⓒ Ⓓ
4. Ⓐ Ⓑ Ⓒ Ⓓ
5. Ⓐ Ⓑ Ⓒ Ⓓ
6. Ⓐ Ⓑ Ⓒ Ⓓ
7. Ⓐ Ⓑ Ⓒ Ⓓ
8. Ⓐ Ⓑ Ⓒ Ⓓ
9. Ⓐ Ⓑ Ⓒ Ⓓ
10. Ⓐ Ⓑ Ⓒ Ⓓ
11. Ⓐ Ⓑ Ⓒ Ⓓ
12. Ⓐ Ⓑ Ⓒ Ⓓ

13. Ⓐ Ⓑ Ⓒ Ⓓ
14. Ⓐ Ⓑ Ⓒ Ⓓ
15. Ⓐ Ⓑ Ⓒ Ⓓ
16. Ⓐ Ⓑ Ⓒ Ⓓ
17. Ⓐ Ⓑ Ⓒ Ⓓ
18. Ⓐ Ⓑ Ⓒ Ⓓ
19. Ⓐ Ⓑ Ⓒ Ⓓ
20. Ⓐ Ⓑ Ⓒ Ⓓ
21. Ⓐ Ⓑ Ⓒ Ⓓ
22. Ⓐ Ⓑ Ⓒ Ⓓ
23. Ⓐ Ⓑ Ⓒ Ⓓ
24. Ⓐ Ⓑ Ⓒ Ⓓ

25. Ⓐ Ⓑ Ⓒ Ⓓ
26. Ⓐ Ⓑ Ⓒ Ⓓ
27. Ⓐ Ⓑ Ⓒ Ⓓ
28. Ⓐ Ⓑ Ⓒ Ⓓ
29. Ⓐ Ⓑ Ⓒ Ⓓ
30. Ⓐ Ⓑ Ⓒ Ⓓ
31. Ⓐ Ⓑ Ⓒ Ⓓ
32. Ⓐ Ⓑ Ⓒ Ⓓ
33. Ⓐ Ⓑ Ⓒ Ⓓ
34. Ⓐ Ⓑ Ⓒ Ⓓ
35. Ⓐ Ⓑ Ⓒ Ⓓ
36. Ⓐ Ⓑ Ⓒ Ⓓ

37. Ⓐ Ⓑ Ⓒ Ⓓ
38. Ⓐ Ⓑ Ⓒ Ⓓ
39. Ⓐ Ⓑ Ⓒ Ⓓ
40. Ⓐ Ⓑ Ⓒ Ⓓ
41. Ⓐ Ⓑ Ⓒ Ⓓ
42. Ⓐ Ⓑ Ⓒ Ⓓ
43. Ⓐ Ⓑ Ⓒ Ⓓ
44. Ⓐ Ⓑ Ⓒ Ⓓ
45. Ⓐ Ⓑ Ⓒ Ⓓ
46. Ⓐ Ⓑ Ⓒ Ⓓ
47. Ⓐ Ⓑ Ⓒ Ⓓ

☐ # correct in Section 1

☐ # incorrect in Section 1

SECTION 2

1. Ⓐ Ⓑ Ⓒ Ⓓ
2. Ⓐ Ⓑ Ⓒ Ⓓ
3. Ⓐ Ⓑ Ⓒ Ⓓ
4. Ⓐ Ⓑ Ⓒ Ⓓ
5. Ⓐ Ⓑ Ⓒ Ⓓ
6. Ⓐ Ⓑ Ⓒ Ⓓ
7. Ⓐ Ⓑ Ⓒ Ⓓ
8. Ⓐ Ⓑ Ⓒ Ⓓ
9. Ⓐ Ⓑ Ⓒ Ⓓ
10. Ⓐ Ⓑ Ⓒ Ⓓ
11. Ⓐ Ⓑ Ⓒ Ⓓ

12. Ⓐ Ⓑ Ⓒ Ⓓ
13. Ⓐ Ⓑ Ⓒ Ⓓ
14. Ⓐ Ⓑ Ⓒ Ⓓ
15. Ⓐ Ⓑ Ⓒ Ⓓ
16. Ⓐ Ⓑ Ⓒ Ⓓ
17. Ⓐ Ⓑ Ⓒ Ⓓ
18. Ⓐ Ⓑ Ⓒ Ⓓ
19. Ⓐ Ⓑ Ⓒ Ⓓ
20. Ⓐ Ⓑ Ⓒ Ⓓ
21. Ⓐ Ⓑ Ⓒ Ⓓ
22. Ⓐ Ⓑ Ⓒ Ⓓ

23. Ⓐ Ⓑ Ⓒ Ⓓ
24. Ⓐ Ⓑ Ⓒ Ⓓ
25. Ⓐ Ⓑ Ⓒ Ⓓ
26. Ⓐ Ⓑ Ⓒ Ⓓ
27. Ⓐ Ⓑ Ⓒ Ⓓ
28. Ⓐ Ⓑ Ⓒ Ⓓ
29. Ⓐ Ⓑ Ⓒ Ⓓ
30. Ⓐ Ⓑ Ⓒ Ⓓ
31. Ⓐ Ⓑ Ⓒ Ⓓ
32. Ⓐ Ⓑ Ⓒ Ⓓ
33. Ⓐ Ⓑ Ⓒ Ⓓ

34. Ⓐ Ⓑ Ⓒ Ⓓ
35. Ⓐ Ⓑ Ⓒ Ⓓ
36. Ⓐ Ⓑ Ⓒ Ⓓ
37. Ⓐ Ⓑ Ⓒ Ⓓ
38. Ⓐ Ⓑ Ⓒ Ⓓ
39. Ⓐ Ⓑ Ⓒ Ⓓ
40. Ⓐ Ⓑ Ⓒ Ⓓ
41. Ⓐ Ⓑ Ⓒ Ⓓ
42. Ⓐ Ⓑ Ⓒ Ⓓ
43. Ⓐ Ⓑ Ⓒ Ⓓ
44. Ⓐ Ⓑ Ⓒ Ⓓ

☐ # correct in Section 2

☐ # incorrect in Section 2

Practice Tests

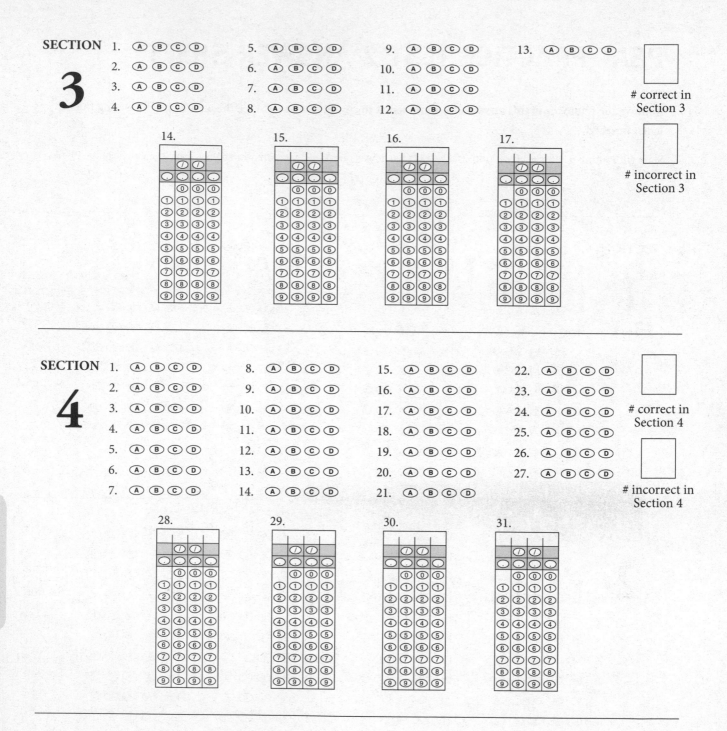

SECTION **3**

1. Ⓐ Ⓑ Ⓒ Ⓓ
2. Ⓐ Ⓑ Ⓒ Ⓓ
3. Ⓐ Ⓑ Ⓒ Ⓓ
4. Ⓐ Ⓑ Ⓒ Ⓓ
5. Ⓐ Ⓑ Ⓒ Ⓓ
6. Ⓐ Ⓑ Ⓒ Ⓓ
7. Ⓐ Ⓑ Ⓒ Ⓓ
8. Ⓐ Ⓑ Ⓒ Ⓓ
9. Ⓐ Ⓑ Ⓒ Ⓓ
10. Ⓐ Ⓑ Ⓒ Ⓓ
11. Ⓐ Ⓑ Ⓒ Ⓓ
12. Ⓐ Ⓑ Ⓒ Ⓓ
13. Ⓐ Ⓑ Ⓒ Ⓓ

correct in Section 3

incorrect in Section 3

14. 15. 16. 17.

SECTION **4**

1. Ⓐ Ⓑ Ⓒ Ⓓ
2. Ⓐ Ⓑ Ⓒ Ⓓ
3. Ⓐ Ⓑ Ⓒ Ⓓ
4. Ⓐ Ⓑ Ⓒ Ⓓ
5. Ⓐ Ⓑ Ⓒ Ⓓ
6. Ⓐ Ⓑ Ⓒ Ⓓ
7. Ⓐ Ⓑ Ⓒ Ⓓ
8. Ⓐ Ⓑ Ⓒ Ⓓ
9. Ⓐ Ⓑ Ⓒ Ⓓ
10. Ⓐ Ⓑ Ⓒ Ⓓ
11. Ⓐ Ⓑ Ⓒ Ⓓ
12. Ⓐ Ⓑ Ⓒ Ⓓ
13. Ⓐ Ⓑ Ⓒ Ⓓ
14. Ⓐ Ⓑ Ⓒ Ⓓ
15. Ⓐ Ⓑ Ⓒ Ⓓ
16. Ⓐ Ⓑ Ⓒ Ⓓ
17. Ⓐ Ⓑ Ⓒ Ⓓ
18. Ⓐ Ⓑ Ⓒ Ⓓ
19. Ⓐ Ⓑ Ⓒ Ⓓ
20. Ⓐ Ⓑ Ⓒ Ⓓ
21. Ⓐ Ⓑ Ⓒ Ⓓ
22. Ⓐ Ⓑ Ⓒ Ⓓ
23. Ⓐ Ⓑ Ⓒ Ⓓ
24. Ⓐ Ⓑ Ⓒ Ⓓ
25. Ⓐ Ⓑ Ⓒ Ⓓ
26. Ⓐ Ⓑ Ⓒ Ⓓ
27. Ⓐ Ⓑ Ⓒ Ⓓ

correct in Section 4

incorrect in Section 4

28. 29. 30. 31.

Practice Tests

READING TEST

60 Minutes—47 Questions

This section corresponds to Section 1 of your answer sheet.

Directions: Read each passage or pair of passages, then answer the questions that follow. Choose your answers based on what the passage(s) and any accompanying graphics state or imply.

Questions 1–9 are based on the following passage.

This passage is adapted from "Metamorphosis" by Franz Kafka, a famous story that combines elements of fantasy and reality. This excerpt begins with the protagonist realizing he has literally turned into a giant, beetle-like insect.

One morning, when Gregor Samsa woke from troubled dreams, he found himself transformed in his bed into a horrible vermin. He lay on his
Line armor-like back, and if he lifted his head a little
(5) he could see his brown belly, slightly domed and divided by arches into stiff sections. The bedding was hardly able to cover it and seemed ready to slide off any moment. His many legs, pitifully thin compared with the size of the rest of him, waved
(10) about helplessly as he looked.

"What's happened to me?" he thought. It wasn't a dream. His room, a proper human room although a little too small, lay peacefully between its four familiar walls. A collection of textile samples lay
(15) spread out on the table—Samsa was a travelling salesman—and above it there hung a picture that he had recently cut out of an illustrated magazine and housed in a nice, gilded frame. It showed a lady fitted out with a fur hat and fur boa who sat
(20) upright, raising a heavy fur muff that covered the whole of her lower arm towards the viewer.

Gregor then turned to look out the window at the dull weather. Drops of rain could be heard hitting the pane, which made him feel quite sad.
(25) "How about if I sleep a little bit longer and forget all this nonsense," he thought, but that was something he was unable to do because he was used to sleeping on his right, and in his present state couldn't get into that position. However hard he

(30) threw himself onto his right, he always rolled back to where he was. He must have tried it a hundred times, shut his eyes so that he wouldn't have to look at the floundering legs, and only stopped when he began to feel a mild, dull pain there that he had never felt before.

(35) He thought, "What a strenuous career it is that I've chosen! Travelling day in and day out. Doing business like this takes much more effort than doing your own business at home, and on top of that there's the curse of travelling, worries about
(40) making train connections, bad and irregular food, contact with different people all the time so that you can never get to know anyone or become friendly with them." He felt a slight itch up on his belly; pushed himself slowly up on his back
(45) towards the headboard so that he could lift his head better; found where the itch was, and saw that it was covered with lots of little white spots which he didn't know what to make of; and when he tried to feel the place with one of his legs he drew it quickly
(50) back because as soon as he touched it he was overcome by a cold shudder.

He slid back into his former position. "Getting up early all the time," he thought, "it makes you stupid. You've got to get enough sleep. Other
(55) travelling salesmen live a life of luxury. For instance, whenever I go back to the guest house during the morning to copy out the contract, these gentlemen are always still sitting there eating their breakfasts. I ought to just try that with my boss; I'd
(60) get kicked out on the spot. But who knows, maybe that would be the best thing for me. If I didn't have my parents to think about I'd have given in my notice a long time ago, I'd have gone up to the boss and told him just what I think, tell him everything I

GO ON TO THE NEXT PAGE ⟹

(65) would, let him know just what I feel. He'd fall right off his desk! And it's a funny sort of business to be sitting up there at your desk, talking down at your subordinates from up there, especially when you have to go right up close because the boss is hard

(70) of hearing. Well, there's still some hope; once I've got the money together to pay off my parents' debt to him—another five or six years I suppose—that's definitely what I'll do. That's when I'll make the big change. First of all though, I've got to get up, my

(75) train leaves at five."

1. According to the passage, Gregor initially believes his transformation is a

   A) curse.

   B) disease.

   C) nightmare.

   D) hoax.

2. As used in line 12, "proper" most nearly means

   A) called for by rules or conventions.

   B) showing politeness.

   C) naturally belonging or peculiar to.

   D) suitably appropriate.

3. The passage most strongly suggests which of the following about Gregor's attitude toward his profession?

   A) He is resentful.

   B) He is diligent.

   C) He is depressed.

   D) He is eager to please.

4. Which choice provides the best evidence for the answer to the previous question?

   A) Lines 14–18 ("A collection . . . gilded frame")

   B) Lines 22–24 ("Gregor then turned . . . quite sad")

   C) Lines 54–60 ("Other . . . the spot")

   D) Lines 66–70 ("And it's . . . hard of hearing")

5. What central idea does the passage communicate through Gregor's experiences?

   A) Imagination is a dangerous thing.

   B) People are fearful of change.

   C) Dreams become our reality.

   D) Humankind is a slave to work.

6. The passage most strongly suggests that which of the following is true of Gregor?

   A) He feels a strong sense of duty toward his family.

   B) He is unable to cope with change.

   C) He excels in his profession.

   D) He is fearful about his transformation.

7. Which choice provides the best evidence for the answer to the previous question?

   A) Lines 11–14 ("What's happened . . . familiar walls")

   B) Lines 22–24 ("Gregor then turned . . . quite sad")

   C) Lines 36–43 ("Doing business . . . with them")

   D) Lines 70–73 ("Well, there's still . . . what I'll do")

GO ON TO THE NEXT PAGE ⇒

8. As used in line 33, "floundering" most nearly means

   A) thrashing.

   B) painful.

   C) pitiful.

   D) trembling.

9. The function of the final sentence of the excerpt ("First of all though, I've got to get up, my train leaves at five") is to

   A) provide a resolution to the conflict Gregor faces.

   B) foreshadow the conflict between Gregor and his boss.

   C) illustrate Gregor's resilience and ability to move on.

   D) emphasize Gregor's extreme sense of duty.

Questions 10–18 are based on the following passage.

This passage is adapted from Hillary Rodham Clinton's speech titled "Women's Rights Are Human Rights," addressed to the United Nations Fourth World Conference on Women in 1995.

If there is one message that echoes forth from this conference, it is that human rights are women's rights. . . . And women's rights are human rights.
Line   Let us not forget that among those rights are the
(5) right to speak freely and the right to be heard.

Women must enjoy the right to participate fully in the social and political lives of their countries if we want freedom and democracy to thrive and endure.

It is indefensible that many women in
(10) nongovernmental organizations who wished to participate in this conference have not been able to attend— or have been prohibited from fully taking part.

Let me be clear. Freedom means the right of people to assemble, organize, and debate openly.
(15) It means respecting the views of those who may disagree with the views of their governments. It means not taking citizens away from their loved ones and jailing them, mistreating them, or denying them their freedom or dignity because of
(20) the peaceful expression of their ideas and opinions.

In my country, we recently celebrated the seventy-fifth anniversary of women's suffrage. It took one hundred and fifty years after the signing of our Declaration of Independence for women to
(25) win the right to vote. It took seventy-two years of organized struggle on the part of many courageous women and men.

It was one of America's most divisive philosophical wars. But it was also a bloodless war.
(30) Suffrage was achieved without a shot fired.

We have also been reminded, in V-J Day observances last weekend, of the good that comes when men and women join together to combat the forces of tyranny and build a better world.
(35)   We have seen peace prevail in most places for a half century. We have avoided another world war. But we have not solved older, deeply-rooted problems that continue to diminish the potential of half the world's population.
(40)   Now it is time to act on behalf of women everywhere.

If we take bold steps to better the lives of women, we will be taking bold steps to better the lives of children and families too. Families rely on mothers and
(45) wives for emotional support and care; families rely on women for labor in the home; and increasingly, families rely on women for income needed to raise healthy children and care for other relatives.

As long as discrimination and inequities remain
(50) so commonplace around the world—as long as girls and women are valued less, fed less, fed last, overworked, underpaid, not schooled and subjected to violence in and out of their homes— the potential of the human family to create a
(55) peaceful, prosperous world will not be realized.

Let this conference be our—and the world's— call to action.

And let us heed the call so that we can create a world in which every woman is treated with respect
(60) and dignity, every boy and girl is loved and cared for equally, and every family has the hope of a strong and stable future.

GO ON TO THE NEXT PAGE

Practice Tests

10. What is the primary purpose of the passage?

   A) To chastise those who have prevented women from attending the conference

   B) To argue that women continue to experience discrimination

   C) To explain that human rights are of more concern than women's rights

   D) To encourage people to think of women's rights as an issue important to all

11. Which choice provides the best evidence for the answer to the previous question?

   A) Lines 4–5 ("Let us . . . be heard")

   B) Lines 9–12 ("It is indefensible . . . taking part")

   C) Lines 37–39 ("But we have . . . population")

   D) Lines 44–48 ("Families . . . other relatives")

12. As used in line 28, "divisive" most nearly means

   A) conflict-producing.

   B) carefully watched.

   C) multi-purpose.

   D) time-consuming.

13. Based on the speech, with which statement would Clinton most likely agree?

   A) More men should be the primary caregivers of their children in order to provide career opportunities for women.

   B) Women do not need the support and cooperation of men as they work toward equality.

   C) Solutions for global problems would be found faster if women had more access to power.

   D) The American movement for women's suffrage should have been violent in order to achieve success more quickly.

14. Which choice provides the best evidence for the answer to the previous question?

   A) Lines 6–8 ("Women . . . endure")

   B) Line 30 ("Suffrage . . . shot fired")

   C) Lines 44–48 ("Families . . . relatives")

   D) Lines 49–55 ("As long . . . realized")

15. As used in line 26, "organized" most nearly means

   A) arranged.

   B) cooperative.

   C) hierarchical.

   D) patient.

16. Which claim does Clinton make in her speech?

   A) The conference itself is a model of nondiscrimination toward women.

   B) Democracy cannot prosper unless women can participate fully in it.

   C) Women's rights are restricted globally by the demands on them as parents.

   D) Women are being forced to provide income for their families as a result of sexism.

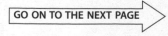

17. Clinton uses the example of V-J Day observations to support the argument that

A) campaigns succeed when they are nonviolent.

B) historical wrongs against women must be corrected.

C) many tragedies could have been avoided with more female participation.

D) cooperation between men and women leads to positive developments.

18. The fifth paragraph (lines 13–20) can be described as

A) a distillation of the author's main argument.

B) an acknowledgment of a counterargument.

C) a veiled criticism of a group.

D) a defense against an accusation.

Questions 19–28 are based on the following passages and supplementary material.

The following passages discuss the history and traditions associated with tea.

Passage 1

Europe was a coffee-drinking continent before it became a tea-drinking one. Tea was grown in China, thousands of miles away. The opening of trade
Line routes with the Far East in the fifteenth and sixteenth
(5) centuries gave Europeans their first taste of tea.

However, it was an unpromising start for the beverage, because shipments arrived stale, and European tea drinkers miscalculated the steeping time and measurements. This was a far cry from
(10) the Chinese preparation techniques, known as a "tea ceremony," which had strict steps and called for steeping in iron pots at precise temperatures and pouring into porcelain bowls.

China had a monopoly on the tea trade and
(15) kept their tea cultivation techniques secret. Yet as worldwide demand grew, tea caught on in

Europe. Some proprietors touted tea as a cure for maladies. Several European tea companies formed, including the English East India Company. In
(20) 1669, it imported 143.5 pounds of tea—very little compared to the 32 million pounds that were imported by 1834.

Europeans looked for ways to circumvent China's monopoly, but their attempts to grow the
(25) tea plant (Latin name *Camellia sinensis*) failed. Some plants perished in transit from the East. But most often the growing climate wasn't right, not even in the equatorial colonies that the British, Dutch, and French controlled. In 1763, the French
(30) Academy of Sciences gave up, declaring the tea plant unique to China and unable to be grown anywhere else. Swedish and English botanists grew tea in botanical gardens, but this was not enough to meet demand.

(35) After trial and error with a plant variety discovered in the Assam district of India, the British managed to establish a source to meet the growing demands of British tea drinkers. In May 1838, the first batch of India-grown tea shipped
(40) to London. The harvest was a mere 350 pounds and arrived in November. It sold for between 16 and 34 shillings per pound. Perfecting production methods took many years, but ultimately, India became the world's largest tea-producing country.
(45) By the early 1900s, annual production of India tea exceeded 350 million pounds. This voluminous source was a major factor in tea becoming the staple of European households that it is today.

Passage 2

In Europe, there's a long tradition of taking
(50) afternoon tea. Tea time, typically four o'clock, means not just enjoying a beverage, but taking time out to gather and socialize. The occasion is not identical across Europe, though; just about every culture has its own way of doing things.

(55) In France, for example, black tea is served with sugar, milk, or lemon and is almost always

Practice Tests

accompanied by a pastry. Rather than sweet pastries, the French prefer the savory kind, such as the *gougère*, or puff pastry, infused with cheese.

(60) Germans, by contrast, put a layer of slowly melting candy at the bottom of their teacup and top the tea with cream. German tea culture is strongest in the eastern part of the country, and during the week tea is served with cookies, while on the weekend

(65) or for special events, cakes are served. The Germans think of tea as a good cure for headaches and stress.

Russia also has a unique tea culture, rooted in the formalism of its aristocratic classes. Loose leaf black tea is served in a glass held by a *podstakannik*,

(70) an ornate holder with a handle typically made from silver or chrome—though sometimes it may be goldplated. Brewed separately, the tea is then diluted with boiled water and served strong. The strength of the tea is seen as a measure of the host's hospitality.

(75) Traditionally, tea is taken by the entire family and served after a large meal with jams and pastries.

Great Britain has a rich tradition of its own. Prior to the introduction of tea into Britain, the English had two main meals, breakfast and a sec-

(80) ond, dinner-like meal called "tea," which was held around noon. However, during the middle of the eighteenth century, dinner shifted to an evening meal at a late hour; it was then called "high tea." That meant the necessary introduction of an after-

(85) noon snack to tide one over, and "low tea" or "tea time" was introduced by British royalty. In present-day Britain, your afternoon tea might be served with scones and jam, small sandwiches, or cookies (called "biscuits"), depending on whether

(90) you're in Ireland, England, or Scotland.

Wherever they are and however they take it, Europeans know the value of savoring an afternoon cup of tea.

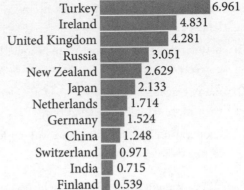

Average Annual Tea Consumption (Pounds per Person)

Country	Pounds
Turkey	6.961
Ireland	4.831
United Kingdom	4.281
Russia	3.051
New Zealand	2.629
Japan	2.133
Netherlands	1.714
Germany	1.524
China	1.248
Switzerland	0.971
India	0.715
Finland	0.539

Data from Euromonitor International and World Bank.

19. Based on the information provided in Passage 1, it can be inferred that

A) European nations tried to grow tea in their colonies.

B) European tea growers never learned Chinese cultivation techniques.

C) Europeans' purpose in opening trade routes with the Far East was to gain access to tea.

D) Europeans believed tea was ineffective as a treatment against illness.

20. Which choice provides the best evidence for the answer to the previous question?

A) Lines 6–9 ("However . . . measurements")

B) Lines 17–18 ("Some . . . maladies")

C) Lines 26–29 ("But . . . French controlled")

D) Lines 40–42 ("The harvest . . . per pound")

21. As used in line 23, "circumvent" most nearly means

A) destroy.

B) get around.

C) ignore.

D) compete with.

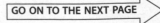

Practice Tests

22. It can be inferred from both Passage 1 and the graphic that

    A) English botanical gardens helped make the United Kingdom one of the highest tea-consuming countries in the world.

    B) if the French Academy of Sciences hadn't given up growing tea in 1763, France would be one of the highest tea-consuming countries in the world.

    C) Britain's success at growing tea in India in the 1800s helped make the United Kingdom one of the highest tea-consuming nations in the world.

    D) China's production of tea would be higher if Britain hadn't discovered a way to grow tea in India in the 1800s.

23. It is reasonable to infer, based on Passage 2, that

    A) serving tea is an important part of hosting guests in Russia.

    B) Germans generally avoid medicine for stress.

    C) drinking tea in modern Britain is confined to the upper classes.

    D) the usual hour for drinking tea varies across Europe.

24. Which choice provides the best evidence for the answer to the previous question?

    A) Lines 50–52 ("Tea time . . . socialize")

    B) Lines 65–66 ("The Germans . . . stress")

    C) Lines 73–74 ("The strength . . . hospitality")

    D) Lines 84–86 ("That meant . . . royalty")

25. As used in line 68, "aristocratic" most nearly means

    A) culinary.

    B) political.

    C) rigid.

    D) noble.

26. Compared with France's tradition of tea drinking, having tea in Germany

    A) is more formal.

    B) involves sweeter food.

    C) requires greater solitude.

    D) is more of a meal than a snack.

GO ON TO THE NEXT PAGE

27. Which statement is the most effective comparison of the two passages' purposes?

    A) Passage 1's purpose is to describe the early history of tea in Europe, while Passage 2's purpose is to compare European cultural practices relating to tea.

    B) Passage 1's purpose is to argue against the Chinese monopoly of tea, while Passage 2's purpose is to argue that Europeans perfected the art of tea drinking.

    C) Passage 1's purpose is to express admiration for the difficult task of tea cultivation, while Passage 2's purpose is to celebrate the rituals surrounding tea.

    D) Passage 1's purpose is to compare Chinese and European relationships with tea, while Passage 2's purpose is to describe the diffusion of tea culture in Europe.

28. Both passages support which generalization about tea?

    A) Tea drinking in Europe is less ritualized than in China.

    B) Coffee was once more popular in Europe than tea was.

    C) India grows a great deal of tea.

    D) Tea is a staple of European households.

Question 29–38 are based on the following passage.

The following passage is adapted from an article about the Spinosaurus, a theropod dinosaur that lived during the Cretaceous period.

At long last, paleontologists have solved a century-old mystery, piecing together information discovered by scientists from different times and places.

Line   The mystery began when, in 1911, German
(5) paleontologist Ernst Stromer discovered the first evidence of dinosaurs having lived in Egypt. Stromer, who expected to encounter fossils of early mammals, instead found bones that dated back to the Cretaceous period, some 97

(10) to 112 million years prior. His finding consisted of three large bones, which he preserved and transported back to Germany for examination. After careful consideration, he announced that he had discovered a new genus of sauropod, or a
(15) large, four-legged herbivore with a long neck. He called the genus Aegyptosaurus, which is Greek for Egyptian lizard. One of these Aegyptosaurs, he claimed, was the Spinosaurus. Tragically, the fossils that supported his claim were destroyed during
(20) a raid on Munich by the Royal Air Force during World War II. The scientific world was left with Stromer's notes and sketches, but no hard evidence that the Spinosaurus ever existed.

    It was not until 2008, when a cardboard box
(25) of bones was delivered to paleontologist Nizar Ibrahim by a nomad in Morocco's Sahara desert, that a clue to solving the mystery was revealed. Intrigued, Ibrahim took the bones to a university in Casablanca for further study. One specific bone
(30) struck him as interesting, as it contained a red line coursing through it. The following year, Ibrahim and his colleagues at Italy's Milan Natural History Museum were looking at bones that resembled the ones delivered the year before. An important
(35) clue was hidden in the cross-section they were examining, as it contained the same red line Ibrahim had seen in Morocco. Against all odds, the Italians were studying bones that belonged to the very same skeleton as the bones Ibrahim received
(40) in the desert. Together, these bones make up the partial skeleton of the very first Spinosaurus that humans have been able to discover since Stromer's fossils were destroyed.

    Ibrahim and his colleagues published a study
(45) describing the features of the dinosaur, which point to the Spinosaurus being the first known swimming dinosaur. At 36 feet long, this particular Spinosaurus had long front legs and short back legs, each with a paddle-shaped foot and claws that
(50) suggest a carnivorous diet. These features made the dinosaur a deft swimmer and excellent hunter, able to prey on large river fish.

    Scientists also discovered significant aquatic adaptations that made the Spinosaurus unique

GO ON TO THE NEXT PAGE ⟶

(55) compared to dinosaurs that lived on land but ate fish. Similar to a crocodile, the Spinosaurus had a long snout, with nostrils positioned so that the dinosaur could breathe while part of its head was submerged in water. Unlike predatory
(60) land dinosaurs, the Spinosaurus had powerful front legs. The weight of these legs would have made walking upright like a Tyrannosaurus Rex impossible, but in water, their strong legs gave the Spinosaurus the power it needed to swim quickly
(65) and hunt fiercely. Most notable, though, was the discovery of the Spinosaurus's massive sail. Made up of dorsal spines, the sail was mostly meant for display.

   Ibrahim and his fellow researchers used both
(70) modern digital modeling programs and Stromer's basic sketches to create and mount a life-size replica of the Spinosaurus skeleton. The sketches gave them a starting point, and by arranging and rearranging the excavated fossils they had in their
(75) possession, they were able to use technology to piece together hypothetical bone structures until the mystery of this semiaquatic dinosaur finally emerged from the murky depths of the past.

29. Which of the following best summarizes the central idea of this passage?

   A) Paleontologists were able to identify a new species of dinosaur after overcoming a series of obstacles.

   B) Most dinosaur fossils are found in pieces and must be reconstructed using the latest technology.

   C) The first evidence of the Spinosaurus was uncovered by German paleontologist Ernst Stromer.

   D) Fossils of an aquatic dinosaur called the Spinosaurus were first found in Egypt in the early twentieth century.

30. Based on the information in the passage, the author would most likely agree that

   A) aquatic dinosaurs were more vicious than dinosaurs that lived on land.

   B) too much emphasis is placed on creating realistic models of ancient dinosaurs.

   C) most mysteries presented by randomly found fossils are unlikely to be solved.

   D) the study of fossils and ancient life provides important scientific insights.

31. Which choice provides the best evidence for the answer to the previous question?

   A) Lines 13–15 ("After careful . . . long neck")

   B) Lines 53–56 ("Scientists also . . . ate fish")

   C) Lines 59–61 ("Unlike . . . front legs")

   D) Lines 72–78 ("The sketches . . . past")

32. As used in line 37, the phrase "against all odds" most nearly means

   A) by contrast.

   B) at the exact same time.

   C) to their dismay.

   D) despite low probability.

Practice Tests

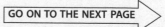
GO ON TO THE NEXT PAGE

33. The author uses the phrases "deft swimmer" and "excellent hunter" in line 51 to

   A) produce a clear visual image of the Spinosaurus.

   B) show how the Spinosaurus searched for prey.

   C) create an impression of a graceful but powerful animal.

   D) emphasize the differences between aquatic and land dinosaurs.

34. The information presented in the passage strongly suggests that Ibrahim

   A) chose to go into the field of paleontology after reading Stromer's work.

   B) was familiar with Stromer's work when he found the fossils with the red lines.

   C) did not have the proper training to solve the mystery of the Spinosaurus on his own.

   D) went on to study other aquatic dinosaurs after completing his research on the Spinosaurus.

35. Which choice provides the best evidence for the answer to the previous question?

   A) Lines 24–27 ("It was . . . revealed")

   B) Lines 44–47 ("Ibrahim . . . swimming dinosaur")

   C) Lines 53–56 ("Scientists . . . ate fish")

   D) Lines 69–72 ("Ibrahim and his fellow researchers . . . skeleton")

36. As used in line 76, "hypothetical" most nearly means

   A) imaginary.

   B) actual.

   C) possible.

   D) interesting.

37. Which statement best describes the relationship between Stromer's and Ibrahim's work with fossils?

   A) Stromer's work was dependent on Ibrahim's work.

   B) Stromer's work was contradicted by Ibrahim's work.

   C) Ibrahim's work built on Stromer's work.

   D) Ibrahim's work copied Stromer's work.

38. Which of the following is most similar to the methods used by Ibrahim to create a life-size replica of the Spinosaurus?

   A) An architect using computer software and drawings to create a scale model of a building

   B) A student building a model rocket from a kit in order to demonstrate propulsion

   C) A doctor using a microscope to study microorganisms unable to be seen with the naked eye

   D) A marine biologist creating an artificial reef in an aquarium to study fish

Questions 39–47 are based on the following passage and supplementary material.

The following passage is adapted from an essay about the intricacies and implications of laughter.

Today's technology and resources enable people to educate themselves on any topic imaginable, and human health is one of particular interest to all.
Line From diet fads to exercise trends, sleep studies
(5) to nutrition supplements, people strive to adopt healthier lifestyles. And while some people may associate diets and gym memberships with sheer enjoyment, most of the population tends to think of personal healthcare as a necessary but time-consuming,
(10) energy-draining, less-than-fun aspect of daily life.
    Yet for centuries, or perhaps for as long as conscious life has existed, sneaking suspicion has

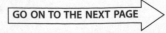 GO ON TO THE NEXT PAGE

suggested that fun, or more accurately, *funniness*, is essential to human health. Finally, in recent years
(15) this notion, often phrased in the adage, "Laughter is the best medicine," has materialized into scientific evidence.

When a person laughs, a chemical reaction in the brain produces hormones called endorphins.
(20) Other known endorphin-producing activities include exercise, physical pain, and certain food choices, but laughter's appearance on this list has drawn increasing empirical interest. Endorphins function as natural opiates for the human body,
(25) causing what are more commonly referred to as "good feelings." A boost of endorphins can thwart lethargy and promote the mental energy and positivity necessary to accomplish challenging tasks. Furthermore, recent data reveal that the
(30) laughter-induced endorphins are therapeutic and stress reducing.

This stress reduction alone indicates significant implications regarding the role of laughter in personal health. However, humor seems to address
(35) many other medical conditions as well. One study from Loma Linda University in California found that the act of laughing induced immediate and significant effects on senior adults' memory capacities. This result was in addition to declines
(40) in the patients' cortisol, or stress hormone, measurements. Another university study found that a mere quarter hour of laughter burns up to 40 calories. Pain tolerance, one group of Oxford researchers noticed, is also strengthened
(45) by laughter—probably due to the release of those same endorphins already described. And a group of Maryland scientists discovered that those who laugh more frequently seem to have stronger protection against heart disease, the illness that
(50) takes more lives annually than any other in America. Studies have shown that stress releases hormones that cause blood vessels to constrict, but

laughter, on the other hand, releases chemicals that cause blood vessels to dilate, or expand. This dilation
(55) can have the same positive effects on blood flow as aerobic exercise or drugs that help lower cholesterol.

Already from these reputable studies, empirical data indicates that laughter's health benefits include heart disease prevention, good physical exertion,
(60) memory retention, anxiety reduction, and pain resilience—not to mention laughter's more self-evident effects on social and psychological wellness. Many believe that these findings are only the beginning; these studies pave the way for more
(65) research with even stronger evidence regarding the powerful healing and preventative properties of laughter. As is true for most fields of science, far more can be learned.

As for how laughter is achieved, these studies
(70) used various methods to provoke or measure laughter or humor. Some used comedy films or television clips; others chose humor-gauging questionnaires and social—or group—laughter scenarios. Such variance suggests that the means
(75) by which people incorporate laughter into their daily routine matters less than the fact that they do incorporate it. However, it should be said that humor shared in an uplifting community probably offers greater benefits than that found on a screen.
(80) It is believed that young people begin to laugh less and less as they transition to adulthood. Time-pressed millennials might, in the interest of wellness, choose isolated exercise instead of social- or fun-oriented leisure activities. However,
(85) this growing pool of evidence exposes the reality that amusement, too, can powerfully nourish the health of both mind and body. Humor is no less relevant to well-being than a kale smoothie or track workout. But, then, some combination of
(90) the three might be most enjoyable (and, of course, beneficial) of all.

Practice Tests

GO ON TO THE NEXT PAGE ▷

Laughter and Its Effect on Pain

Adapted from I.M. Dunbar, et al., "Social Laughter Is Correlated with an Elevated Pain Threshold." © 2011 by The Royal Society of Biological Sciences.

39. The author would most likely characterize the study findings mentioned in the passage as

   A) irrelevant.

   B) very promising.

   C) inconclusive.

   D) mildly interesting.

40. Which choice provides the best evidence for the answer to the previous question?

   A) Lines 4–6 ("From diet . . . lifestyles")

   B) Lines 14–17 ("Finally, . . . evidence")

   C) Lines 18–19 ("When a person . . . endorphins")

   D) Lines 74–77 ("Such variance . . . incorporate it")

41. Which statement best explains the relationship between endorphin production and mental outlook?

   A) Increasing a person's amount of endorphins encourages a positive state of mind.

   B) The act of laughing produces endorphins, which can offer a person protection against heart disease.

   C) Research indicates that chemical reactions in the brain produce endorphins.

   D) If a person has more endorphins, he or she has a difficult time tolerating pain.

42. As used in line 57, "reputable" most nearly means

   A) honorable.

   B) distinguished.

   C) celebrated.

   D) credible.

43. Which of the following statements can be concluded from the passage?

   A) Laughing alone or in the company of others benefits people's health equally.

   B) There is reason for optimism about future research into laughter's health benefits.

   C) Public support for the idea that laughter is healthy is somewhat limited.

   D) Physical exercise is sufficient to maintain and improve mental health.

Practice Tests

GO ON TO THE NEXT PAGE

44. Which choice provides the best evidence for the answer to the previous question?

    A) Lines 11–14 ("Yet for centuries . . . health")

    B) Lines 32–35 ("This stress . . . well")

    C) Lines 63–67 ("Many believe . . . of laughter")

    D) Lines 87–91 ("Humor is . . . of all")

45. Which reason best explains why the author chose to discuss the function of endorphins in lines 23–26 ("Endorphins . . . 'good feelings'")?

    A) To reach a wider audience without a background in physiology

    B) To support the claim that laughter affects an individual's mental state

    C) To show that laughter is one of several endorphin-producing activities

    D) To demonstrate why scientists have an interest in studying laughter

46. As used in line 15, "adage" most nearly means

    A) remark.

    B) comment.

    C) cliché.

    D) proverb.

47. Which value shown on the graph most closely relates to the idea in line 78 that "humor shared in an uplifting community" increases resilience to pain?

    A) −25

    B)   0

    C) 20

    D) 75

Practice Tests

IF YOU FINISH BEFORE TIME IS CALLED, YOU MAY CHECK YOUR WORK ON THIS SECTION ONLY. DO NOT TURN TO ANY OTHER SECTION IN THE TEST.

WRITING AND LANGUAGE TEST

35 Minutes—44 Questions

This section corresponds to Section 2 of your answer sheet.

Directions: Each passage in this section is followed by several questions. Some questions will reference an underlined portion in the passage; others will ask you to consider a part of a passage or the passage as a whole. For each question, choose the answer that reflects the best use of grammar, punctuation, and style. If a passage or question is accompanied by a graphic, take the graphic into account in choosing your response(s). Some questions will have "NO CHANGE" as a possible response. Choose that answer if you think the best choice is to leave the sentence as written.

Questions 1–11 are based on the following passage.

From Here to the Stars

Gene Kranz hadn't slept in ages. **1** The flight director, pacing between rows of monitors in NASA's Mission Control Center, an impossible problem weighing heavy in his weary mind: Three astronauts were operating a crippled spacecraft nearly 200,000 miles from Earth. And time was running out.

Kranz was no stranger to **2** issues. After losing his father at an early age, Kranz turned to the stars for guidance—and found inspiration. His high school thesis was about the possibility of **3** space travel; an idea that prompted Kranz to set a path for the stars. Kranz pursued a degree in aeronautical engineering after high school graduation. After the Wright brothers

1. A) NO CHANGE
   B) The flight director paced
   C) The pacing flight director
   D) The flight director pacing

2. A) NO CHANGE
   B) adversity.
   C) deadlines.
   D) maladies.

3. A) NO CHANGE
   B) space travel: an idea
   C) space travel, an idea
   D) space travel. An idea

GO ON TO THE NEXT PAGE →

had pioneered powered, controlled flight only half a century earlier, aviation milestones like breaking the sound barrier changed the future of flight. Aeronautical engineering required a thorough understanding of 4 physics—like lift and drag on wings—as well as proficiency in mathematics to determine maximum weight on an aircraft. After graduating from Saint Louis University's Parks College of Engineering, Aviation, and Technology, Kranz piloted jets for the Air Force Reserve before performing research and development on missiles and rockets. Kranz later joined NASA and directed the successful *Apollo 11* mission to the moon in 1969.

    5 Without his unusual vest, no one would have noticed Kranz in the crowd. One year after the launch, the mood had drastically changed; there were no cheers, no celebratory pats on the back or teary-eyed congratulations. Coffee and adrenaline fueled the scientists and engineers communicating with the astronauts on *Apollo 13*. 6 Kranz was easy to spot among the avalanche of moving bodies and shifting papers. He was dressed, as ever, in his signature handmade

4. A) NO CHANGE
    B) physics; like lift and drag on wings, as well as proficiency
    C) physics like lift and drag on wings, as well as proficiency
    D) physics: like lift and drag on wings—as well as proficiency

5. Which sentence would serve as the most effective introduction to the paragraph?

    A) NO CHANGE
    B) During the mission, Kranz stood out as a pillar of strength in the chaos of the command center.
    C) Kranz earned the badges of honor that now adorned his vest.
    D) Kranz possessed more years of experience than anyone in the control center.

6. A) NO CHANGE
    B) Among the avalanche of moving bodies and shifting papers, it is easy to spot Kranz.
    C) Kranz easily spotted the avalanche of moving bodies and shifting papers.
    D) Kranz is easy to spot among the avalanche of moving bodies and shifting papers.

Practice Tests

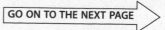
GO ON TO THE NEXT PAGE

vest. **7** The engineers looked to the calm man in the homemade vest.

Kranz's wife, Marta, had begun making vests at his request in the early '60s. **8** Their was power in a uniform, something Kranz understood from his years serving overseas. The vests served not as an authoritative mark or **9** sartorial flair, but a defining symbol for his team to rally behind. During the effort to save the *Apollo 13* crew, Kranz wore his white vest around the clock like perspiration-mottled battle armor.

10 Among meetings and calculations, Kranz and the NASA staff hatched a wild plan. By using the gravitational force of the moon, **11** it could slingshot the injured spacecraft back on an earthbound course. It was a long shot, of course, but also their best and only one. And, due to the tireless efforts of support staff on earth and the intrepid spirit of the *Apollo 13* crew, it worked. Six days after takeoff, all three astronauts splashed down safely in the Pacific Ocean.

Questions 12–22 are based on the following passage.

The UK and the Euro

[1] The United Kingdom is a longstanding member of the European Union (EU), a multinational political organization and economic world leader **12** elected over the course of the past half-century. [2] However, there is

7. Which sentence provides effective evidence to support the main focus of the paragraph?
   A) NO CHANGE
   B) Many of the men in the Mission Control Center had lengthy military careers.
   C) Kranz's thoughts returned to the many tribulations he had experienced.
   D) Several engineers joined together as a bastion of calm in a sea of uncertainty.

8. A) NO CHANGE
   B) They're was
   C) There was
   D) They were

9. A) NO CHANGE
   B) sanguine
   C) military
   D) martial

10. A) NO CHANGE
    B) In spite of
    C) Despite
    D) Between

11. A) NO CHANGE
    B) he
    C) they
    D) one

12. A) NO CHANGE
    B) determined
    C) advanced
    D) built

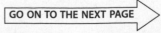
GO ON TO THE NEXT PAGE

one key feature of the EU in which the UK does not [13] participate; the monetary union known as the Eurozone, consisting of countries that share the euro as currency. [3] While the nation's public opinion has remained generally supportive of that decision, evidence suggests that the euro's benefits for the UK might, in fact, outweigh the risks. [4] When the EU first implemented the euro in 1999, intending to strengthen collective economy across the union, Britain was permitted exclusion and continued using the pound instead. [5] This, UK leaders hoped, would shield Britain from financial dangers that the euro might suffer. [14]

Proponents for avoiding the euro point [15] to faltering economies in the Eurozone region throughout the Eurozone. To join a massive, multinational economy would involve surrendering taxable wealth from one's own region to aid impoverished countries that may be some thousands of miles away. If a few economies in the Eurozone suffer, all of the participating nations suffer, too. Other proponents point to details of financial policy such as interest rates and territory responsibilities, fearing loss of agency and political traction. [16] The UK's taxable wealth would decrease if it assisted impoverished countries.

13. A) NO CHANGE
    B) participate: the monetary
    C) participate, the monetary
    D) participate. The monetary

14. To make this paragraph most logical, sentence 3 should be placed
    A) where it is now.
    B) after sentence 1.
    C) after sentence 4.
    D) after sentence 5.

15. Which choice best completes the sentence?
    A) NO CHANGE
    B) to financial dangers that the euro might suffer.
    C) to faltering economies in most if not all Eurozone countries.
    D) to financial dangers and faltering economies in Eurozone countries throughout Europe.

16. Which statement most clearly communicates the main claim of the paragraph?
    A) NO CHANGE
    B) Economic independence from impoverished countries would still be possible.
    C) The UK would take on significant economic risk if it adopted the euro as its currency.
    D) Euro adoption would require subsequent economic assistance on the UK's behalf.

Practice Tests

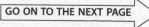
GO ON TO THE NEXT PAGE

But complications loom: the UK's current EU status may be untenable. In recent years, EU leaders seem to intend to transition all members **17** toward the Eurozone, for many reasons, this action appears necessary for protecting nations involved and ensuring the monetary union's long-term success. These conditions may potentially force the UK to choose either the security of its multidecade EU membership, or the pound and all it entails for Britain's economy. Enjoying both may not remain possible. **18** The UK wants to maintain the pound as its currency.

[1] Regarding Britain's intent to be protected from the Eurozone's economic dangers, this hope never quite materialized. [2] The UK saw economic downturns of its own during the euro's problematic years thus far. [3] Many families in the UK still struggle to pay their bills in the face of higher than normal unemployment rates. [4] It seems that regardless of shared currency, the economies of Britain and its Eurozone neighbors are too closely **19** intertwined for one to remain unscathed by another's crises. **20**

Perhaps this question of economic security has been the wrong one. Due to Britain's location and long-standing trade relationships with its neighbors, economies will persist to be somewhat reliant on each other, euro or not. **21** Furthermore, political security, power, and protection bear more significance for the future. If the UK hopes to maintain and expand its

17. A) NO CHANGE
    B) toward the Eurozone. For many reasons,
    C) toward the Eurozone, for many reasons.
    D) toward the Eurozone. For many reasons.

18. Which sentence most effectively concludes the paragraph?
    A) NO CHANGE
    B) All EU members may soon have to accept the euro.
    C) The UK faces a difficult decision regarding its EU membership.
    D) All member nations want to ensure the success of the EU.

19. A) NO CHANGE
    B) disparate
    C) identical
    D) relevant

20. Which sentence is least relevant to the central idea of this paragraph?
    A) Sentence 1
    B) Sentence 2
    C) Sentence 3
    D) Sentence 4

21. A) NO CHANGE
    B) Or,
    C) Also,
    D) However,

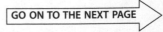

influential presence in world leadership, its association
and close involvement with greater Europe is invaluable.
Considering that the euro probably offers a lower risk
margin than many have supposed, the benefits of euro
22 adoption: to secure EU membership and strengthen
its cause, made Britain carefully reconsider.

Questions 23–33 are based on the following passage.

Coffee: The Buzz on Beans

Americans love coffee. **23** Some days you can find
a coffee shop in nearly every American city. But this
wasn't always true. How did coffee, which was first
grown in Africa over five hundred years ago, come to
America?

The coffee plant, from which makers get the
"cherries" that **24** is dried and roasted into what we
call beans, first appeared in the East African country
Ethiopia, in the province of Kaffa. From there, it spread
to the Arabian Peninsula, where the coffeehouse, or
qahveh khaneh in Arabic, was very popular. Like spices
and cloth, coffee was traded internationally as European
explorers reached far lands and **25** establishing shipping
routes. The first European coffeehouse opened in
Venice, Italy, in 1683, and not long after London
26 displayed over three hundred coffeehouses.

22. A) NO CHANGE
    B) adoption—to secure EU membership and
       strengthen its cause—
    C) adoption: to secure EU membership and
       strengthen its cause—
    D) adoption; to secure EU membership and
       strengthen its cause,

23. A) NO CHANGE
    B) Many
    C) The
    D) These

24. A) NO CHANGE
    B) are being dried and roasted
    C) are dried and roasted
    D) is being dried and roasted

25. A) NO CHANGE
    B) established
    C) having established
    D) was establishing

26. A) NO CHANGE
    B) bragged
    C) highlighted
    D) boasted

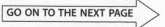
GO ON TO THE NEXT PAGE

There is no record of coffee being amongst the cargo of the *Mayflower*, which reached the New World in 1620. It was not until 1668 that the first written reference to coffee in America was made. The reference described a beverage made from roasted beans and flavored with sugar or honey, and cinnamon. Coffee was then chronicled in the New England colony's official records of 1670. In 1683, William Penn, who lived in a settlement on the Delaware River, wrote of buying supplies of coffee in a **27** New York market, he paid eighteen shillings and nine pence per pound. **28**

Coffeehouses like those in Europe were soon established in American colonies, and as America expanded westward, coffee consumption grew. In their settlement days, **29** Chicago St. Louis and New Orleans each had famous coffeehouses. By the mid-twentieth century, coffeehouses were abundant. In places like New York and San Francisco, they became **30** confused with counterculture, as a place where intellectuals and artists gathered to share ideas. In American homes, coffee was a social lubricant, bringing people together to socialize as afternoon tea had done in English society. With the

27. A) NO CHANGE
    B) New York market and William Penn
    C) New York market so he paid
    D) New York market, paying

28. Which choice best establishes a concluding sentence for the paragraph?
    A) Coffee's appearance in the historical record shows it was becoming more and more established in the New World.
    B) The colonies probably used more tea than coffee because there are records of it being imported from England.
    C) William Penn founded Pennsylvania Colony, which became the state of Pennsylvania after the Revolutionary War with England ended.
    D) The Mayflower did carry a number of items that the colonists needed for settlement, including animals and tools.

29. A) NO CHANGE
    B) Chicago, St. Louis, and New Orleans
    C) Chicago, St. Louis, and, New Orleans
    D) Chicago St. Louis and, New Orleans

30. A) NO CHANGE
    B) related
    C) associated
    D) coupled

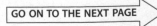

invention of the electric coffee pot, it became a common courtesy to ask a guest if she wanted "coffee or tea?"

31 There were many coffee shops in New York and in Chicago.

However, by the 1950s, U.S. manufacturing did to coffee what it had done to **32** other foods; produced it cheaply, mass-marketed it, and lowered its quality. Coffee was roasted and ground in manufacturing plants and freeze-dried for a long storage life, which compromised its flavor. An "evangelism" began to bring back the original bracing, dark-roasted taste of coffee, and spread quickly. **33** In every major city of the world, now travelers around the world, expect to be able to grab an uplifting, fresh, and delicious cup of coffee—and they can.

31. Which choice most effectively concludes the paragraph?

   A) NO CHANGE

   B) Electric coffee machines changed how people entertained at home.

   C) Over time, it was clear that coffee had become a part of everyday American life.

   D) People went to coffeehouses to discuss major issues.

32. A) NO CHANGE

   B) other foods produced

   C) other foods, produced

   D) other foods: produced

33. A) NO CHANGE

   B) Now travelers, in every major city of the world, around the world expect to be able to grab an uplifting, fresh, and delicious cup of coffee—and they can.

   C) Now in every major city of the world, travelers around the world expect to be able to grab an uplifting, fresh, and delicious cup of coffee—and they can.

   D) Now travelers around the world expect to be able to grab an uplifting, fresh, and delicious cup of coffee in every major city of the world—and they can.

Practice Tests

Questions 34–44 are based on the following passage and supplementary material.

Predicting Nature's Light Show

One of the most beautiful of nature's displays is the aurora borealis, commonly known as the Northern Lights. As **34** their informal name suggests, the best place to view this phenomenon **35** is the Northern Hemisphere. How far north one needs to be to witness auroras depends not on conditions here on Earth, but on the sun. **36**

As with hurricane season on Earth, the sun **37** observes a cycle of storm activity, called the solar cycle, which lasts approximately 11 years. Also referred to as the sunspot cycle, this period is caused by the amount of magnetic flux that rises to the surface of the sun, causing sunspots, or areas of intense magnetic activity. The magnetic energy is sometimes so great it causes a storm that explodes away from the sun's surface in a solar flare.

34. A) NO CHANGE
    B) an
    C) its
    D) that

35. A) NO CHANGE
    B) is through the Northern Hemisphere.
    C) is over the Northern Hemisphere.
    D) is in the Northern Hemisphere.

36. Which of the following would most strengthen the passage's introduction?
    A) A statement about the Kp-Index and other necessary tracking tools scientists use
    B) A mention that the National Oceanic and Atmospheric Administration monitors solar flares
    C) An explanation about why conditions on the sun rather than on Earth affect the Northern Lights
    D) A statement about what scientists think people should study before viewing auroras

37. A) NO CHANGE
    B) experiences
    C) perceives
    D) witnesses

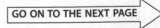

These powerful magnetic storms eject high-speed electrons and protons into space. Called a coronal mass ejection, this ejection is far more powerful than the hot gases the sun constantly emits. The speed at which the atoms are shot away from the sun is almost triple that of a normal solar wind. It takes this shot of energy one to three days to arrive at Earth's upper atmosphere. Once it arrives, it is captured by Earth's own magnetic field. It is this newly captured energy that causes the Northern Lights. **38** Interested scientists and interested amateurs in the Northern Hemisphere **39** use tools readily available to all in order to predict the likelihood of seeing auroras in their location at a specific time. One such tool is the Kp-Index, a number that determines the potential visibility of an aurora. The Kp-Index measures the energy added to Earth's magnetic field from the sun on a scale of 0–9, with 1 representing a solar calm and 5 or more indicating a magnetic storm, or solar flare. The magnetic fluctuations are measured in three-hour intervals (12 a.m. to 3 a.m., 3 a.m. to 6 a.m., and so on) so that deviations can be factored in and accurate data can be presented. **40**

38. A) NO CHANGE
    B) Interested scientists and amateurs
    C) Scientists and amateurs interested
    D) Scientists interested and amateurs

39. A) NO CHANGE
    B) use tools for prediction
    C) use specific tools to predict
    D) use all tools readily available to predict

40. Which of the following, if added to this paragraph, would best support the author's claims?
    A) The speeds of normal solar winds and coronal mass ejections
    B) The strength of Earth's magnetic field
    C) The temperature of normal solar wind
    D) The definition of coronal mass ejection

Practice Tests

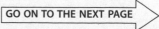
GO ON TO THE NEXT PAGE

Magnetometers, tools that measure the strength of Earth's magnetic field, are located around the world. When the energy from solar flares reaches Earth, the strength and direction of the energy **41** is recorded by these tools and analyzed by scientists at the National Oceanic and Atmospheric Administration, who calculate the difference between the average strength of the magnetic field and spikes due to solar flares. They plot this information on the Kp-Index and **42** update the public with information on viewing the auroras as well as other impacts solar flares may have on life on Earth. **43** While solar flares can sometimes have negative effects on our communications systems and weather patterns, the most common effect is also the most enchanting: a beautiful light show such as the solar flare that took place from **44** 9 p.m. to 6 p.m. on September 11.

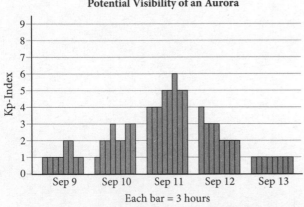

Potential Visibility of an Aurora

Each bar = 3 hours

Data from National Oceanic and Atmospheric Administration

41. A) NO CHANGE
    B) are
    C) will be
    D) has been

42. A) NO CHANGE
    B) update aurora viewing information
    C) update information on viewing the auroras
    D) update aurora viewing information for the public

43. A) NO CHANGE
    B) However,
    C) Since
    D) Whereas

44. Which choice completes the sentence with accurate data based on the graphic?

    A) NO CHANGE
    B) 12 a.m. on September 11 to 3 a.m. on September 12.
    C) 9 a.m. on September 10 to 12 p.m. on September 12.
    D) 9 a.m. on September 11 to 12 a.m. on September 12.

IF YOU FINISH BEFORE TIME IS CALLED, YOU MAY CHECK YOUR WORK ON THIS SECTION ONLY. DO NOT TURN TO ANY OTHER SECTION IN THE TEST. **STOP**

Practice Tests

MATH TEST

25 Minutes—17 Questions

NO-CALCULATOR SECTION

This section corresponds to Section 3 of your answer sheet.

Directions: For this section, solve each question and select the best answer choice. The available space on each page may be used for scratch work.

Notes:

1. Calculator use is NOT permitted.
2. All numbers used are real numbers, and all variables used represent real numbers, unless otherwise indicated.
3. Figures are drawn to scale and lie in a plane unless otherwise indicated.
4. Unless stated otherwise, the domain of any function f is assumed to be the set of all real numbers x, for which $f(x)$ is a real number.

Information:

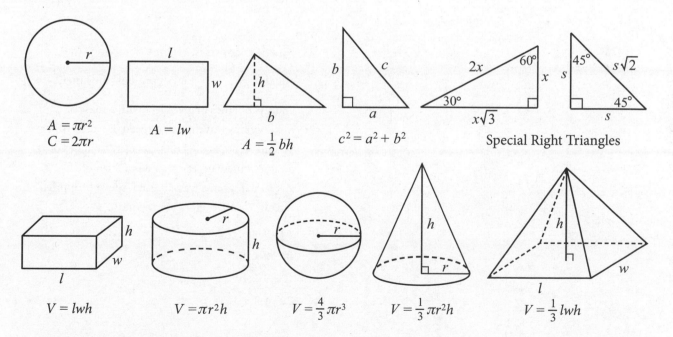

$A = \pi r^2$
$C = 2\pi r$

$A = lw$

$A = \frac{1}{2}bh$

$c^2 = a^2 + b^2$

Special Right Triangles

$V = lwh$

$V = \pi r^2 h$

$V = \frac{4}{3}\pi r^3$

$V = \frac{1}{3}\pi r^2 h$

$V = \frac{1}{3}lwh$

The sum of the degree measures of the angles in a triangle is 180.

The number of degrees of arc in a circle is 360.

The number of radians of arc in a circle is 2π.

GO ON TO THE NEXT PAGE ⟹

Practice Tests

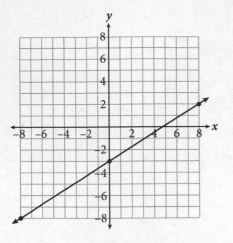

1. What is the average rate of change for the line graphed in the figure above?

    A) $\dfrac{3}{5}$

    B) $\dfrac{5}{8}$

    C) $\dfrac{8}{5}$

    D) $\dfrac{5}{3}$

2. Which of the following could be the factored form of the equation graphed in the figure above?

    A) $y = \dfrac{1}{5}(x - 2)(x + 6)$

    B) $y = \dfrac{1}{5}(x + 2)(x - 6)$

    C) $y = \dfrac{2}{3}(x - 1)(x + 5)$

    D) $y = \dfrac{2}{3}(x + 1)(x - 5)$

3. Kinetic energy is the energy of motion. The equation $E_K = \dfrac{1}{2}mv^2$ represents the kinetic energy in joules of an object with a mass of m kilograms traveling at a speed of v meters per second. What is the kinetic energy in joules of an unmanned aircraft that has a mass of 2×10^3 kilograms traveling at a speed of approximately 3×10^3 meters per second?

    A) 9×5^9

    B) 9×10^8

    C) 9×10^9

    D) 1.8×10^{10}

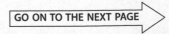
GO ON TO THE NEXT PAGE

$$\frac{3(k-1)+5}{2} = \frac{17-(8+k)}{4}$$

4. In the equation above, what is the value of k?

A) $\dfrac{9}{13}$

B) $\dfrac{5}{7}$

C) $\dfrac{8}{7}$

D) $\dfrac{8}{5}$

5. An environmental protection group had its members sign a pledge to try to reduce the amount of garbage they throw out by 3% each year. On the year that the pledge was signed, each person threw out an average of 1,800 pounds of garbage. Which exponential function could be used to model the average amount of garbage each person who signed the pledge should throw out each year after signing the pledge?

A) $y = 0.97 \times 1{,}800^t$

B) $y = 1{,}800 \times t^{0.97}$

C) $y = 1{,}800 \times 1.97^t$

D) $y = 1{,}800 \times 0.97^t$

6. If the equation of the line shown in the figure above is written in the form $\dfrac{y}{x} = m$, which of the following could be the value of m?

A) -3

B) $-\dfrac{1}{3}$

C) $\dfrac{1}{3}$

D) 3

7. If $4x^2 + 7x + 1$ is multiplied by $3x + 5$, what is the coefficient of x in the resulting polynomial?

A) 3

B) 12

C) 35

D) 38

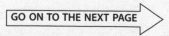 GO ON TO THE NEXT PAGE

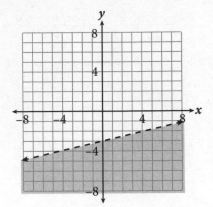

8. The figure above shows worldwide unemployment rates from 2004 to 2013. Which of the following statements is true?

    A) The graph is decreasing everywhere.

    B) The graph is increasing from 2007 to 2010.

    C) The graph is decreasing from 2004 to 2007 and from 2009 to 2011.

    D) The graph is increasing from 2007 to 2010 and decreasing from 2011 to 2013.

9. The solution to which inequality is represented in the graph above?

    A) $\frac{1}{4}x - y > 3$

    B) $\frac{1}{4}x - y < 3$

    C) $\frac{1}{4}x + y > -3$

    D) $\frac{1}{4}x + y < -3$

$$\frac{1}{2}(4a + 10b) = b$$

10. If (a, b) is a solution to the equation above, what is the ratio $\frac{b}{a}$, given that $a \neq 0$?

    A) -3

    B) -2

    C) $-\frac{1}{2}$

    D) $-\frac{1}{3}$

$$\begin{cases} \dfrac{1}{3}x + \dfrac{2}{3}y = -8 \\ ax + 6y = 15 \end{cases}$$

11. If the system of linear equations above has no solution, and a is a constant, what is the value of a?

A) $-\dfrac{1}{3}$

B) $\dfrac{1}{3}$

C) $\dfrac{3}{2}$

D) 3

12. A taxi in the city charges \$3.00 for the first $\dfrac{1}{4}$ mile, plus \$0.25 for each additional $\dfrac{1}{8}$ mile. Eric plans to spend no more than \$20 on a taxi ride around the city. Which inequality represents the number of miles, m, that Eric could travel without exceeding his limit?

A) $2.5 + 2m \le 20$

B) $3 + 0.25m \le 20$

C) $3 + 2m \le 20$

D) $12 + 2m \le 20$

13. A projectile is any moving object that is thrown near the Earth's surface. The path of the projectile is called the trajectory and can be modeled by a quadratic equation, assuming the only force acting on the motion is gravity (no friction). If a projectile is launched from a platform 8 feet above the ground with an initial velocity of 64 feet per second, then its trajectory can be modeled by the equation $h = -16t^2 + 64t + 8$, where h represents the height of the projectile t seconds after it was launched. Based on this model, what is the maximum height in feet that the projectile will reach?

A) 72

B) 80

C) 92

D) 108

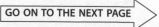
GO ON TO THE NEXT PAGE

Practice Tests

Directions: For questions 14–17, enter your responses into the appropriate grid on your answer sheet, in accordance with the following:

1. You will receive credit only if the circles are filled in correctly, but you may write your answers in the boxes above each grid to help you fill in the circles accurately.

2. Don't mark more than one circle per column.

3. None of the questions with grid-in responses will have a negative solution.

4. Only grid in a single answer, even if there is more than one correct answer to a given question.

5. A **mixed number** must be gridded as a decimal or an improper fraction. For example, you would grid $7\frac{1}{2}$ as 7.5 or $\frac{15}{2}$.

   (Were you to grid it as [7 1 / 2], this response would be read as $\frac{71}{2}$.)

6. A **decimal** that has more digits than there are places on the grid may be either rounded or truncated, but every column in the grid must be filled in order to receive credit.

GO ON TO THE NEXT PAGE ⟹

14. If $\frac{3}{4}x + \frac{5}{6}y = 12$, what is the value of $9x + 10y$?

15. How many degrees does the minute hand of an analogue clock rotate from 3:20 p.m. to 3:45 p.m.?

$$\frac{3x^{\frac{3}{2}} \cdot \left(16x^2\right)^3}{8x^{-\frac{1}{2}}}$$

16. What is the exponent on x when the expression above is written in simplest form?

17. An exponential function is given in the form $f(x) = a \cdot b^x$. If $f(0) = 3$ and $f(1) = 15$, what is the value of $f(-2)$?

IF YOU FINISH BEFORE TIME IS CALLED, YOU MAY CHECK YOUR WORK ON THIS SECTION ONLY. DO NOT TURN TO ANY OTHER SECTION IN THE TEST. STOP

Practice Tests

MATH TEST

45 Minutes—31 Questions

CALCULATOR SECTION

This section corresponds to Section 4 of your answer sheet.

Directions: For this section, solve each question and select the best answer choice. The available space on each page may be used for scratch work.

Notes:

1. Calculator use is permitted.
2. All numbers used are real numbers, and all variables used represent real numbers, unless otherwise indicated.
3. Figures are drawn to scale and lie in a plane unless otherwise indicated.
4. Unless stated otherwise, the domain of any function f is assumed to be the set of all real numbers x, for which $f(x)$ is a real number.

Information:

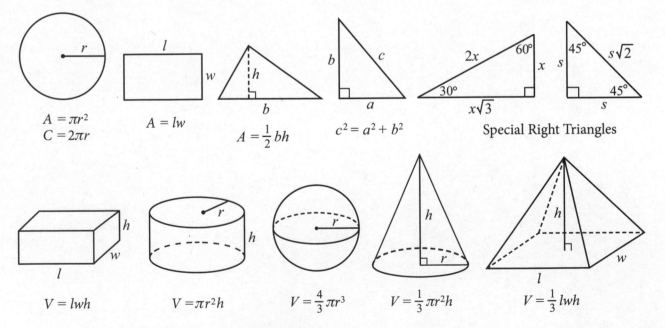

The sum of the degree measures of the angles in a triangle is 180.

The number of degrees of arc in a circle is 360.

The number of radians of arc in a circle is 2π.

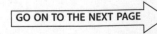

1. A home improvement store that sells carpeting charges a flat installation fee and a certain amount per square foot of carpet ordered. If the total cost for *f* square feet of carpet is given by the function $C(f) = 3.29f + 199$, then the value 3.29 best represents which of the following?

   A) The installation fee

   B) The cost of 1 square foot of carpet

   C) The number of square feet of carpet ordered

   D) The total cost not including the installation fee

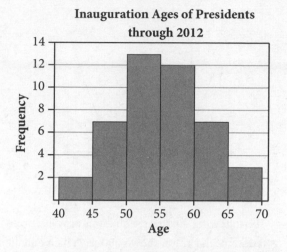

Inauguration Ages of Presidents through 2012

2. The United States Constitution requires that any candidate for the presidency be at least 35 years of age, although no president to date has been that young. The figure above shows the distribution of the ages of the presidents through 2012 at the time they were inaugurated. Based on the information shown, which of the following statements is true?

   A) The shape of the data is skewed to the left, so the mean age of the presidents is greater than the median.

   B) The shape of the data is fairly symmetric, so the mean age of the presidents is approximately equal to the median.

   C) The data has no clear shape, so it is impossible to make a reliable statement comparing the mean and the median.

   D) The same number of 55-or-older presidents have been inaugurated as ones who were younger than 55, so the mean age is exactly 55.

   $$\frac{1}{3}(5x - 8) = 3x + 4$$

3. Which value of *x* satisfies the equation above?

   A) −5

   B) −3

   C) −1

   D) 1

GO ON TO THE NEXT PAGE

Practice Tests

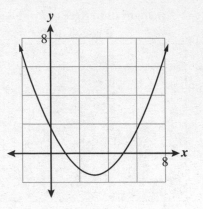

4. The following quadratic equations are all representations of the graph shown above. Which equation could you use to find the minimum value of the function, without doing any additional work?

A) $y = \dfrac{3}{8}(x - 3)^2 - \dfrac{3}{2}$

B) $y = \dfrac{3}{8}(x - 1)(x - 5)$

C) $y - \dfrac{15}{8} = \dfrac{3}{8}x^2 - \dfrac{9}{4}x$

D) $y = \dfrac{3}{8}x^2 - \dfrac{9}{4}x + \dfrac{15}{8}$

5. Marion is a city planner. The city she works for recently purchased new property on which it plans to build administrative offices. Marion has been given the task of sizing the lots for new buildings, using the following guidelines:

- The square footage of each lot should be greater than or equal to 3,000 square feet, but less than or equal to 15,000 square feet.

- Each lot size should be at least 30% greater in area than the size before it.

- To simplify tax assessment calculations, the square footage of each lot must be a multiple of 1,000 square feet.

Which list of lot sizes meets the city guidelines and includes as many lots as possible?

A)   3,000; 5,000; 10,000; 16,000

B)   3,000; 4,500; 6,000; 7,500; 10,000; 15,000

C)   3,000; 4,000; 6,000; 8,000; 11,000; 15,000

D)   3,000; 3,900; 5,100; 6,600; 8,600; 11,200; 14,600

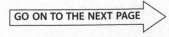

Practice Tests

6. After implementing several pollution reduction programs in a certain city, the EPA calculated that the air pollution should decrease by approximately 8% each year. What kind of function could be used to model the amount of air pollution in this city over the next several years, assuming no other significant changes?

A) A linear function

B) A quadratic function

C) A polynomial function

D) An exponential function

7. Escape velocity is the speed that a traveling object needs to break free of a planet's or moon's gravitational field without additional propulsion (for example, without using fuel). The formula used to calculate escape velocity is $v = \sqrt{\dfrac{2Gm}{r}}$, where G represents the universal gravitational constant, m is the mass of the body from which the object is escaping, and r is the distance between the object and the body's center of gravity. Which equation represents the value of r in terms of v, G, and m?

A) $r = \dfrac{2Gm}{v^2}$

B) $r = \dfrac{4G^2m^2}{v^2}$

C) $r = \sqrt{\dfrac{2Gm}{v}}$

D) $r = \sqrt{\dfrac{v}{2Gm}}$

8. A movie rental kiosk dispenses DVDs and Blu-rays. DVDs cost $2.00 per night and Blu-rays cost $3.50 per night. Between 5 p.m. and 9 p.m. on Saturday, the kiosk dispensed 209 movies and collected $562.00. Solving which system of equations would yield the number of DVDs, d, and the number of Blu-rays, b, that the kiosk dispensed during the 4-hour period?

A) $\begin{cases} d + b = 209 \\ 2d + 3.5b = \dfrac{562}{4} \end{cases}$

B) $\begin{cases} d + b = 562 \\ 2d + 3.5b = 209 \end{cases}$

C) $\begin{cases} d + b = 562 \\ 2d + 3.5b = 209 \times 4 \end{cases}$

D) $\begin{cases} d + b = 209 \\ 2d + 3.5b = 562 \end{cases}$

9. The United States Senate has two voting members for each of the 50 states. The 113th Congress had a 4:1 male-to-female ratio in the Senate. Forty-five of the male senators were Republican. Only 20% of the female senators were Republican. How many senators in the 113th Congress were Republican?

A) 20

B) 49

C) 55

D) 65

Practice Tests

GO ON TO THE NEXT PAGE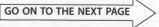

10. According to the *Project on Student Debt* prepared by The Institute for College Access and Success, 7 out of 10 students graduating in 2012 from a four-year college in the United States had student loan debt. The average amount borrowed per student was $29,400, which is up from $18,750 in 2004. If student debt experiences the same total percent increase over the next eight years, approximately how much will a college student graduating in 2020 owe, assuming she takes out student loans to pay for her education?

A) $40,100

B) $44,300

C) $46,100

D) $48,200

11. Annalisa has 10 beanbags to throw in a game. She gets 7 points if a beanbag lands in the smaller basket and 3 points if it lands in the larger basket. If she gets b beanbags into the larger basket and the rest into the smaller basket, which expression represents her total score?

A) $3b$

B) $3b + 7$

C) $30 + 4b$

D) $70 - 4b$

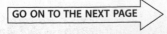

Questions 12 and 13 refer to the following information.

In a 2010 poll, surveyors asked registered voters in four different New York voting districts whether they would consider voting to ban fracking in the state. Hydraulic fracturing, or "fracking," is a mining process that involves splitting rocks underground to remove natural gas. According to ecologists, environmental damage can occur as a result of fracking, including contamination of water. The results of the 2010 survey are shown in the following table.

	In Favor of Ban	Against Ban	No Opinion	Total
District A	23,247	17,106	3,509	43,862
District B	13,024	12,760	2,117	27,901
District C	43,228	49,125	5,891	98,244
District D	30,563	29,771	3,205	63,539
Total	110,062	108,762	14,722	233,546

12. According to the data, which district had the smallest percentage of voters with no opinion on fracking?

A) District A

B) District B

C) District C

D) District D

13. A random follow-up survey was administered to 500 of the respondents in District C. They were asked if they planned to vote in the next election. The follow-up survey results were that 218 said they planned to vote, 174 said they did not plan to vote, and 108 said they were unsure. Based on the data from both the initial survey and the follow-up survey, which of the following is most likely an accurate statement?

A) Approximately 19,000 people in District C who support a ban on fracking can be expected to vote in the next election.

B) Approximately 21,000 people in District C who support a ban on fracking can be expected to vote in the next election.

C) Approximately 43,000 people in District C who support a ban on fracking can be expected to vote in the next election.

D) Approximately 48,000 people in District C who support a ban on fracking can be expected to vote in the next election.

GO ON TO THE NEXT PAGE >

Practice Tests

$$2x + 4y = 13$$
$$x - 3y = -11$$

14. Based on the system of equations above, what is the value of the sum of x and y?

    A) $-\dfrac{1}{2}$

    B) 3

    C) $3\dfrac{1}{2}$

    D) 4

	Bowling Scores		
	Ian	**Mae**	**Jin**
Game 1	160	110	120
Game 2	135	160	180
Game 3	185	140	105
Game 4	135	130	160
Game 5	185	110	135
Mean Score	160	130	140
Standard Deviation	22	19	27

15. Ian, Mae, and Jin bowled five games during a bowling tournament. The table above shows their scores. According to the data, which of the following conclusions is correct?

    A) Ian bowled the most consistently because the mean of his scores is the highest.

    B) Mae bowled the least consistently because the standard deviation of her scores is the lowest.

    C) Mae bowled the most consistently because the standard deviation of her scores is the lowest.

    D) Jin bowled the most consistently because the standard deviation of his scores is the highest.

16. Which of the following are solutions to the quadratic equation $(x + 3)^2 = 16$?

    A) $x = -19$ and $x = 13$

    B) $x = -7$ and $x = 1$

    C) $x = -1$ and $x = 1$

    D) $x = -1$ and $x = 7$

17. An architect is building a scale model of the Statue of Liberty. The real statue measures 305 feet, 6 inches from the bottom of the base to the tip of the torch. The architect plans to make her model 26 inches tall. If Lady Liberty's nose on the actual statue is 4 feet, 6 inches long, how long in inches should the nose on the model be?

    A) $\dfrac{1}{26}$

    B) $\dfrac{26}{141}$

    C) $\dfrac{18}{47}$

    D) $\dfrac{13}{27}$

18. If $f(x) = 3x + 5$, what is $f(6) - f(2)$?

    A) 11

    B) 12

    C) 17

    D) 23

GO ON TO THE NEXT PAGE

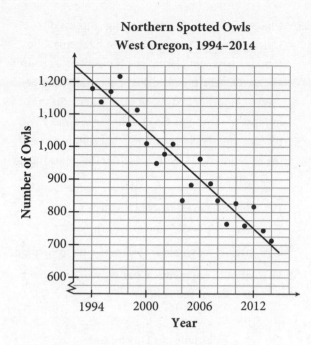

**Northern Spotted Owls
West Oregon, 1994–2014**

19. The United States Fish and Wildlife Service classifies animals whose populations are at low levels as either threatened or endangered. Endangered species are animals that are currently on the brink of extinction, whereas threatened species have a high probability of being on the brink in the near future. Since 1990, the Northern Spotted Owl has been listed as threatened. The figure above shows the populations of the Northern Spotted Owl in a certain region in Oregon from 1994 to 2014. Based on the line of best fit shown in the figure, which of the following values most accurately reflects the average change per year in the number of Northern Spotted Owls?

A) −25

B) −0.04

C)   0.04

D)   25

20. The x-coordinates of the solutions to a system of equations are −4 and 2. Which of the following could be the system?

A) $\begin{cases} y = 2x - 4 \\ y = (x + 4)^2 \end{cases}$

B) $\begin{cases} y = x - 2 \\ y = (x + 4)^2 + 2 \end{cases}$

C) $\begin{cases} y = x - 2 \\ y = (x - 4)^2 - 16 \end{cases}$

D) $\begin{cases} y = 2x - 4 \\ y = (x + 2)^2 - 16 \end{cases}$

Mice Litter Sample Data

21. The White-footed Mouse, named for its darker body fur and white feet, is primarily found on the east coast of the United States, living in warm, dry forests and brushland. A scientist in Virginia studied a sample of 200 white-footed mice to see how many offspring they had per birth. The results of the study are recorded in the figure above. Based on the data, given a population of 35,000 female white-footed mice living in Virginia, how many would you expect to have a litter of seven or more pups?

A)   3,325

B)   4,375

C)   7,700

D) 15,400

GO ON TO THE NEXT PAGE

Practice Tests

22. Human beings have a resting heart rate and an active heart rate. The resting heart rate is the rate at which the heart beats when a person is at rest, engaging in no activity. The active heart rate rises as activity rises. For a fairly active woman in her 20s, 8 minutes of moderate exercise results in a heart rate of about 90 beats per minute. After 20 minutes, the same woman's heart rate will be about 117 beats per minute. If the human heart rate increases at a constant rate as the time spent exercising increases, which of the following linear models represents this same woman's heart rate, r, after t minutes of moderate exercise?

A) $r = 0.15t - 5.3$

B) $r = 0.44t - 32$

C) $r = 2.25t + 72$

D) $r = 6.75t + 36$

23. Chantal buys new furniture using store credit, which offers five-year, no-interest financing. She sets up a payment plan to pay the debt off as soon as possible. The function $40x + y = 1,400$ can be used to model her payment plan, where x is the number of payments Chantal has made and y is the amount of debt remaining. If a solution to the equation is (21, 560), which of the following statements is true?

A) Chantal pays $21 per month.

B) Chantal pays $560 per month.

C) After 21 payments, $560 remains to be paid.

D) After 21 payments, Chantal will have paid off $560 of the debt.

Emails per Day by Age

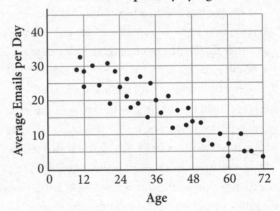

24. Which of the following equations best represents the trend of the data shown in the figure above?

A) $y = -2.4x + 30$

B) $y = -1.2x + 40$

C) $y = -0.8x + 40$

D) $y = -0.4x + 36$

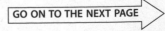
GO ON TO THE NEXT PAGE

25. The graph of $f(x)$ passes through the point (5, 1). Through which point does the graph of $-f(x + 3) - 2$ pass?

    A) $(-2, -1)$

    B) $(2, -3)$

    C) $(2, 1)$

    D) $(8, -3)$

26. When a certain kitchen appliance store decides to sell a floor model, it marks the retail price of the model down 25% and puts a "Floor Model Sale" sign on it. Every 30 days after that, the price is marked down an additional 10% until it is sold. The store decides to sell a floor model refrigerator on January 15th. If the retail price of the refrigerator was $1,500 and it is sold on April 2nd of the same year, what is the final selling price, not including tax?

    A) $820.13

    B) $825.00

    C) $911.25

    D) $1,012.50

27. When New York City built its 34th Street subway station, which has multiple underground levels, it built an elevator that runs along a diagonal track approximately 170 feet long to connect the upper and lower levels. The angle formed between the elevator track and the bottom level is just under 30 degrees. What is the approximate vertical distance in feet between the upper and lower levels of the subway station?

    A) 85

    B) 98

    C) 120

    D) 147

GO ON TO THE NEXT PAGE

Directions: For questions 28–31, enter your responses into the appropriate grid on your answer sheet, in accordance with the following:

1. You will receive credit only if the circles are filled in correctly, but you may write your answers in the boxes above each grid to help you fill in the circles accurately.

2. Don't mark more than one circle per column.

3. None of the questions with grid-in responses will have a negative solution.

4. Only grid in a single answer, even if there is more than one correct answer to a given question.

5. A **mixed number** must be gridded as a decimal or an improper fraction. For example, you would grid $7\frac{1}{2}$ as 7.5 or $\frac{15}{2}$.

(Were you to grid it as $\boxed{7\ 1\ /\ 2}$, this response would be read as $\frac{71}{2}$.)

6. A **decimal** that has more digits than there are places on the grid may be either rounded or truncated, but every column in the grid must be filled in order to receive credit.

Practice Tests

Boeing Jets	Coach	Business	First Class
747-400	310	52	12
767-300	151	26	6
777-200	194	37	16
777-300	227	52	8

28. The table above shows the seating configuration for several commercial airplanes. The day before a particular flight departs, a travel agent books the last seat available for a client. If the seat is on one of the two Boeing 777s, what is the probability that the seat is a Business Class seat, assuming that all seats have an equal chance of being the last one available?

29. Heating water accounts for a good portion of the average home's energy consumption. Tankless water heaters, which run on natural gas, are about 22% more energy efficient on average than electric hot water heaters. However, a tankless hot water heater typically costs significantly more. Suppose one tankless water heater costs $160 more than twice as much as a conventional hot water heater. If both water heaters cost $1,000 together, how many more dollars does the tankless water heater cost than the conventional one?

Questions 30 and 31 refer to the following information.

Daniel works for a pest control company and is spraying all the lawns in a neighborhood. The figure above shows the layout of the neighborhood and the times that Daniel started spraying the lawns at two of the houses. Each lawn in the neighborhood is approximately 0.2 acres in size and takes the same amount of time to spray.

30. How many minutes will it take Daniel to spray all of the lawns in the neighborhood?

31. Daniel uses a mobile spray rig that holds 20 gallons of liquid. It takes 1 gallon to spray 2,500 square feet of lawn. How many times, including the first time, will Daniel need to fill the spray rig, assuming he fills it to the very top each time? (1 acre = 43,560 square feet)

Practice Tests

ANSWER KEY
READING TEST

1. C	14. D	27. A	40. B
2. D	15. B	28. D	41. A
3. A	16. B	29. A	42. D
4. C	17. D	30. D	43. B
5. D	18. B	31. B	44. C
6. A	19. A	32. D	45. B
7. D	20. C	33. C	46. D
8. A	21. B	34. B	47. D
9. D	22. C	35. D	
10. D	23. A	36. C	
11. D	24. C	37. C	
12. A	25. D	38. A	
13. C	26. B	39. B	

WRITING AND LANGUAGE TEST

1. B	12. D	23. D	34. C
2. B	13. B	24. C	35. D
3. C	14. D	25. B	36. C
4. A	15. B	26. D	37. B
5. B	16. C	27. D	38. B
6. A	17. B	28. A	39. C
7. A	18. C	29. B	40. A
8. C	19. A	30. C	41. B
9. A	20. C	31. C	42. B
10. D	21. D	32. D	43. A
11. C	22. B	33. D	44. D

MATH—NO-CALCULATOR TEST

1. B	6. C	11. D	16. 8
2. D	7. D	12. A	17. 3/25 or .12
3. C	8. C	13. A	
4. B	9. A	14. 144	
5. D	10. C	15. 150	

MATH—CALCULATOR TEST

1. B	11. D	21. C	31. 4
2. B	12. D	22. C	
3. A	13. A	23. C	
4. A	14. B	24. D	
5. C	15. C	25. B	
6. D	16. B	26. C	
7. A	17. C	27. A	
8. D	18. B	28. 1/6 or .166 or .167	
9. B	19. A	29. 440	
10. C	20. D	30. 252	

ANSWERS & EXPLANATIONS

READING TEST

"Metamorphosis"

Suggested Passage Map notes:
¶1: Gregor woke up not himself
¶2: description of Gregor's room, job
¶3: thought sleep would make him normal, couldn't roll over
¶4: thought job stress was to blame for how he was
¶5: thinks he needs more sleep, wants more luxury but has to help parents

1. C Difficulty: Easy

Category: Detail

Getting to the Answer: Skim the passage to locate Gregor's first reaction to his transformation. The passage states in line 2 that Gregor woke "from troubled dreams." He only realizes "it wasn't a dream" after he has examined his new body and looked around his room to orient himself. Choice (C) is the correct answer. "Nightmare" describes a dream that is "troubled."

2. D Difficulty: Hard

Category: Vocab-in-Context

Getting to the Answer: Use context clues and tone to help determine the meaning of the word. Use the surrounding text to paint a mental picture of descriptive words. Finally, make sure the answer choice does not alter the meaning of the sentence when inserted. The paragraph in which the word appears describes an average room appropriate for a person. Therefore, (D) is the correct answer. "Proper" means "suitably appropriate" in this context.

3. A Difficulty: Medium

Category: Inference

Getting to the Answer: Look for Gregor's thoughts and statements about work. Use this as evidence of his attitude. Paragraphs 4 and 5 are essentially rants about Gregor's dissatisfaction with his job. He dislikes travelling, feels that he works much harder than others, and expresses anger toward his boss. Gregor feels that it is unfair that other salesmen have a life of "luxury" while he has to wake up early. Choice (A) is the correct answer. Gregor is resentful and bitter about his job.

4. C Difficulty: Medium

Category: Command of Evidence

Getting to the Answer: Review your answer to the previous question. Decide which lines of text give clues to how Gregor feels about his job. Choice (C) offers the best support. These lines describe Gregor's bitterness and the unfairness he perceives. He feels he works much harder than the other salesmen, but that he would be fired if he asked for better treatment or less work.

5. D Difficulty: Hard

Category: Global

Getting to the Answer: Ask yourself what purpose the author has in writing the passage. What main point does the majority of the excerpt support? The events in the passage show that despite a dramatic physical transformation, Gregor still plans to go to work. Gregor consistently expresses unhappiness and bitterness about his job but ignores his transformation into an insect because he feels he must still go to work or he will be fired. In this situation, (D) is the correct answer. Gregor's duty to his job overrides reason and sense when he plans to attend work despite the physical transformation that has left him inhuman and helpless.

6. A   **Difficulty:** Medium

Category: Inference

Getting to the Answer: Reread the text, looking for evidence to support each of the answer choices. Examine Gregor's thoughts and statements for clues about his personality. Based on Gregor's statements about his work, it is clear that he continues to work at a job he dislikes in order to support his parents. He largely ignores his physical transformation, and there is no evidence as to whether he excels at his work. Choice (A) is the correct answer.

7. D   **Difficulty:** Medium

Category: Command of Evidence

Getting to the Answer: Review your answer to the previous question. Read each choice and figure out which one provides specific support for that answer. Choice (D) provides the best support. These lines show that Gregor thinks it may be best to quit the job he hates, but he will continue to work until he can pay off his parents' debt.

8. A   **Difficulty:** Medium

Category: Vocab-in-Context

Getting to the Answer: Use context clues from the target sentence and surrounding sentence. Predict the meaning of the word and look for a match in the answer choices. Gregor is attempting to turn over in his bed, but finds his legs and body are useless and unable to turn him over into his preferred position. Choice (A) is the nearest match to the meaning of "floundering" in this context.

9. D   **Difficulty:** Medium

Category: Rhetoric

Getting to the Answer: Contrast Gregor's thoughts with the dark tone of the rest of the excerpt. Think about how this phrase adds to or supports the interpretations you made in previous questions. The author ends the excerpt with Gregor completely disregarding the fact that he is now an insect. Gregor plans to go to work as he always does, and the author draws attention to the absurdity of this decision. Choice (D) is the correct choice. The author uses the matter-of-fact tone in the sentence to emphasize that Gregor will ignore his physical condition and go to work because he has such a strong sense of duty to his family.

Hillary Rodham Clinton Speech

Suggested Passage Map notes:

¶1–4: women are equal and deserve to be treated as such

¶5: what freedom is

¶6–7: history of women fighting for equality

¶8–9: men and women do great things when they work together

¶10–14: must help women in other countries achieve equality and fight discrimination

10. D   **Difficulty:** Easy

Category: Rhetoric

Getting to the Answer: Consider the word choices Clinton uses throughout her speech. Notice any recurring themes. Choice (D) is the correct answer. Clinton says that working to improve the lives of women will improve others' lives as well.

11. D   **Difficulty:** Medium

Category: Command of Evidence

Getting to the Answer: Beware of answer choices that are only vaguely related to Clinton's point. The correct answer will follow her purpose closely. Clinton indicates that women's rights issues affect more than just women. Choice (D) is the best fit. These lines from the text provide concrete examples of how improving the lives of women improves their families' lives as well.

12. A   Difficulty: Medium

Category: Vocab-in-Context

Getting to the Answer: Sometimes you can recognize similarities between the word in question and a more familiar word. "Divisive" is similar to "divide" and "division," both of which have to do with things being split or made separate. Clinton is saying that though suffrage produced great conflict and divided people more than other philosophical wars, it was "bloodless." Choice (A) is correct; "divisive" means "conflict-producing."

13. C   Difficulty: Hard

Category: Inference

Getting to the Answer: You're being asked to decide which statement Clinton is most likely to agree with. Because the statement isn't explicitly mentioned in the speech, you must infer, or make a logical guess, based on information in the speech. Clinton states that the world would be improved if women were able to contribute more. She provides specific examples of her vision for an improved world. Choice (C) is correct, as it suggests that if women did not experience discrimination and had more power, the world would be better off.

14. D   Difficulty: Medium

Category: Command of Evidence

Getting to the Answer: Try paraphrasing the answer you chose for the previous test item. Then decide which quote from the speech supports this idea. Choice (D) provides the best evidence. This quote notes that women are discriminated against and that it is not just women who suffer from this discrimination; there are global problems that could benefit from women's ideas.

15. B   Difficulty: Hard

Category: Vocab-in-Context

Getting to the Answer: A word like "organized" can have several meanings, depending on the context.

Beware of choosing the most common meaning, as it may not fit this situation. Choice (B) successfully conveys the idea of the women's suffrage movement being one in which many different people worked together over a long period of time.

16. B   Difficulty: Hard

Category: Rhetoric

Getting to the Answer: Be careful to assess not only what topics are mentioned but also how Clinton discusses them. Choice (B) is supported by the passage, which claims "Women must enjoy the right to participate fully in the social and political lives of their countries if we want freedom and democracy to thrive and endure."

17. D   Difficulty: Medium

Category: Rhetoric

Getting to the Answer: Notice how the stem of the question doesn't ask you to find evidence for an argument; it instead gives you the evidence (the example of V-J Day) and then asks you to figure out what argument this evidence supports. Choice (D) is correct. Clinton mentions V-J Day as an example of something that resulted from cooperation between men and women.

18. B   Difficulty: Medium

Category: Detail

Getting to the Answer: Pay close attention to the words Clinton uses in the cited lines to describe problems that affect women. Clinton states that the problems that "diminish the potential" (line 38) of women are "older" (line 37) and "deeply-rooted" (line 37), making (B) the correct answer.

Paired Passages—Tea

Suggested Passage Map notes:

Passage 1

¶1: history of tea, Europe and China

¶2: tea not received well in Europe at first

¶3: China controlled tea production

¶4: Europe wanted to produce tea

¶5: finally had tea growing success in India

Passage 2

¶1: history of tea time in Europe

¶2: tea in France served with savory

¶3: tea in Germany served with sweet

¶4: tea in Russia sign of class

¶5: tea in GB

19. A   Difficulty: Medium

Category: Inference

Getting to the Answer: Be careful to choose an answer that is clearly supported by the information in the passage. The passage states that the climate was not right for growing tea "even in the equatorial colonies" (line 28). Choice (A) is the correct answer. Clearly, European tea-drinking nations tried to grow tea in their equatorial colonies; that's how they learned that the climate there wasn't right.

20. C   Difficulty: Medium

Category: Command of Evidence

Getting to the Answer: The correct answer will be the reason you were able to make the inference in the previous question. Choice (C) works logically. Europeans knew that tea would not grow well in their colonies; this leads to the conclusion that they tried.

21. B   Difficulty: Medium

Category: Vocab-in-Context

Getting to the Answer: You should be able to replace the original word with the correct answer in the sentence. The passage states that in order to "circumvent" the monopoly, European growers tried growing their own tea. It makes sense that Europeans' attempt at growing their own tea was a way to "get around" the Chinese monopoly. Therefore, (B) is the best choice.

22. C   Difficulty: Hard

Category: Synthesis

Getting to the Answer: Keep in mind that the graphic focuses on tea consumption, not tea production. The last paragraph of Passage 1 describes Britain's great success growing tea in India, which resulted in great increases in the amount of tea arriving in London. Therefore, (C) is a reasonable conclusion that may be drawn by synthesizing information in Passage 1 and the graphic.

23. A   Difficulty: Hard

Category: Inference

Getting to the Answer: Be careful to deduce only information that can reasonably be inferred from the passage. It can logically be inferred that hosting guests in Russia generally involves tea. Passage 2 emphasizes that Russian hosts are judged based on the strength of their tea and that Russians have elaborate tea-making equipment. Choice (A) is the correct answer.

24. C   Difficulty: Medium

Category: Command of Evidence

Getting to the Answer: Identify the country associated with the correct answer to the previous question and see what evidence fits. The passage states that Russian tea ceremonies are highly formal and that hosts are judged on their tea-making. Choice (C) is the correct answer. The referenced lines support the conclusions about Russia.

25. D **Difficulty:** Medium

Category: Vocab-in-Context

Getting to the Answer: Look for other words in this sentence that offer clues to the word's meaning. A "noble," or high-ranking, class is likely to have associations with formalism, so (D) is the correct answer.

26. B **Difficulty:** Easy

Category: Connections

Getting to the Answer: Make sure to compare only the two countries being asked about. Choice (B) is correct. The passage notes that cookies and cakes are served with tea in Germany, while foods served with tea in France are "savory" and include puff pastries with cheese.

27. A **Difficulty:** Easy

Category: Synthesis

Getting to the Answer: Look for true statements about Passage 1. Then do the same for Passage 2. Choice (A) is correct. Passage 1 focuses on an earlier period in European history, while Passage 2 compares different cultures within Europe.

28. D **Difficulty:** Medium

Category: Synthesis

Getting to the Answer: For this question, you're looking for a statement that is reflected in both passages. Choice (D) is the only choice supported by both passages.

Spinosaurus Passage

Suggested Passage Map notes:

¶1: Stromer discovered dinosaur fossils in Egypt, new genus, fossils destroyed in WWII, notes and sketches survived

¶2: Ibrahim rediscovered similar fossils, able to make partial skeleton

¶3: description of spinosaurus

¶4: spino unique—lived on land, hunted in water

¶5: Ibrahim used digital model and Stromer sketches to create replica

29. A **Difficulty:** Easy

Category: Global

Getting to the Answer: Look for the answer choice that describes an important idea that is supported throughout the text rather than a specific detail. The passage is mostly about how the mystery of the Spinosaurus fossils was decoded. Choice (A) is the best summary of the central idea of the passage.

30. D **Difficulty:** Medium

Category: Inference

Getting to the Answer: Think about the overall message of the passage and consider why the author would choose to write about this topic. The author's tone, or attitude, toward the topic of the passage demonstrates the point of view that the study of fossils and ancient life has value. Choice (D) is the correct answer. The evidence in the passage supports the idea that the author thinks the study of fossils and ancient life is important.

31. B **Difficulty:** Medium

Category: Command of Evidence

Getting to the Answer: Some answer choices may seem important. However, if they don't support your answer to the previous question, they aren't what you should choose. Choice (B) is correct. The author's use of the word "significant" in this quote shows that he or she thinks the study of fossils and ancient life is important.

32. D **Difficulty:** Medium

Category: Vocab-in-Context

Getting to the Answer: Though more than one answer choice might seem acceptable, one comes closest to meaning the same as the phrase in question. Earlier in the paragraph, the author explains that two different bones gathered at different times both had a red line coursing through them. This means that the bones were from the same animal. Choice (D) fits best. "Against all odds" most nearly means "despite low probability."

33. C   **Difficulty:** Medium

Category: Rhetoric

Getting to the Answer: Be careful to avoid answers that don't make sense in the context of the paragraph. These phrases help the author describe the animal in a generally positive way. Choice (C) is the correct answer.

34. B   **Difficulty:** Hard

Category: Inference

Getting to the Answer: Be careful of answers that make sense but are not implied by the information presented in the passage. Choice (B) is correct. The passage does not explicitly state how Ibrahim became familiar with Stromer's work, but it is implied that he was familiar with Stromer's work when he found the fossils with the red lines and used Stromer's sketches to aid with the modern digital models as mentioned in the last paragraph.

35. D   **Difficulty:** Hard

Category: Command of Evidence

Getting to the Answer: Eliminate any answer choices that have nothing to do with your answer to the previous question. Choice (D) is correct. It directly supports the inference that Ibrahim was familiar with Stromer's work, showing that he used Stromer's sketches to aid in creating his life-size replica of the Spinosaurus.

36. C   **Difficulty:** Easy

Category: Vocab-in-Context

Getting to the Answer: Ibrahim and his fellow researchers didn't know how the bones went together. They were making an educated guess with the help of technology and Stromer's sketches. Choice (C) is correct. "Hypothetical" in this sentence means "possible."

37. C   **Difficulty:** Easy

Category: Connections

Getting to the Answer: Think about the order in which Stromer and Ibrahim's work with the fossils oc-

curred. Choice (C) is correct. Ibrahim used Stromer's sketches to create his models of the Spinosaurus. He built on Stromer's work to complete his own.

38. A   **Difficulty:** Hard

Category: Connections

Getting to the Answer: Think about the process described in each answer choice and compare it to how Ibrahim went about building his replica of the Spinosaurus. Choice (A) is the right choice. An architect creating a model of a building would use tools and methods similar to those used by Ibrahim, such as drawings and digital technologies.

Laughter Passage

Suggested Passage Map notes:
¶1: people willing to try anything to be healthy
¶2: laughter important part of health
¶3: what happens to body when you laugh
¶4: humor helps many medical conditions, laugh more = better health
¶5: benefits of laughter
¶6: various methods to provoke laughter, best achieved in person, not through watching shows
¶7: laughter decreases with age

39. B   **Difficulty:** Easy

Category: Rhetoric

Getting to the Answer: When a question asks you about the point of view of an author, look for words and phrases in the passage that hint at the author's feelings or attitude toward the topic. Choice (B) is the correct answer because the author speaks quite positively of the studies throughout the passage.

40. B   **Difficulty:** Medium

Category: Command of Evidence

Getting to the Answer: Reread each quote in the context of the passage. Consider which one is the best evidence of the author's point of view toward laughter research. The word "Finally" in line 14 helps demonstrate that the author finds laughter research worthwhile. Choice (B) is the best answer.

41. A   Difficulty: Medium

Category: Connections

Getting to the Answer: Think about the connection the passage makes between laughter and the ability to accomplish challenging tasks. Choice (A) is correct. The passage notes that endorphin production is associated with "mental energy and positivity" (lines 27–28).

42. D   Difficulty: Medium

Category: Vocab-in-Context

Getting to the Answer: Notice that all of the answer choices are related to the word "reputable," but the correct answer will reflect the specific context in which the word is used. "Reputable" in this case indicates that the studies are official and are based on empirical data (data based on observation and experiment). This makes (D), "credible," the correct choice.

43. B   Difficulty: Hard

Category: Inference

Getting to the Answer: Eliminate any answer choices that are not suggested in the passage. Choice (B) is correct because early results of studies into laughter and health all seem to strengthen the relationship between the two.

44. C   Difficulty: Medium

Category: Command of Evidence

Getting to the Answer: Avoid answer choices like D that may not support a general conclusion you could take from the passage. Choice (C) is the correct answer. The author expects future research will yield stronger evidence in support of laughter's health benefits.

45. B   Difficulty: Hard

Category: Rhetoric

Getting to the Answer: Look at the verbs provided in each of the answer choices. Decide whether the author wanted to "reach," "support," "justify," or "show" by discussing the function of endorphins. After asserting that laughter produces endorphins, the author explains their function in order to help the reader understand why a positive mental state may result. Choice (B) is the correct answer.

46. D   Difficulty: Medium

Category: Vocab-in-Context

Getting to the Answer: Look carefully at the paragraph's context to help you decide on the correct answer choice. The phrase "'Laughter is the best medicine'" (lines 15–16) is an example of an adage, or proverb. Therefore, (D) is correct.

47. D   Difficulty: Hard

Category: Synthesis

Getting to the Answer: Decide whether the phrase "uplifting community" is a reference to a person alone or a group of people. Choice (D) is correct. The graph shows that shared humor with others most significantly increased pain tolerance in individuals.

WRITING & LANGUAGE TEST

From Here to the Stars

1. B   Difficulty: Medium

Category: Sentence Formation

Getting to the Answer: Read the sentence and determine whether it is grammatically complete. To form a grammatically complete sentence, you must have an independent clause prior to a colon. As written, the text that comes before the colon is not grammatically complete because it lacks an independent clause with a subject and predicate.

Choice (B) correctly adds a verb to the clause before the comma. It also correctly uses the past tense to match with the tense of "hadn't" in the first sentence of the passage.

2. B   Difficulty: Medium

Category: Effective Language Use

Getting to the Answer: Read the sentences surrounding the word to look for context clues. Watch out for near synonyms that are not quite correct. The word "issues" is not precise and does a poor job of conveying the meaning of the sentence. A better word, such as (B), "adversity," more precisely conveys hardship, difficulties, or painful situations.

3. C   Difficulty: Medium

Category: Punctuation

Getting to the Answer: Determine whether a clause is independent or dependent to decide between a comma and a semicolon. The clause is dependent, as it contains only a noun ("an idea") and a relative clause to modify it. A semicolon is used to separate two independent clauses, so it cannot be used here. A comma is the appropriate punctuation mark to separate the dependent clause from the independent clause in the sentence. Choice (C) is the correct answer.

4. A   Difficulty: Medium

Category: Punctuation

Getting to the Answer: Figure out the role of the underlined phrase in the sentence to find the correct punctuation. "Like lift and drag on wings" is a parenthetical element provided as an example. The sentence is correctly punctuated as written because it uses dashes to set off the parenthetical element. The answer is (A).

5. B   Difficulty: Hard

Category: Development

Getting to the Answer: Read the paragraph and summarize the main idea to predict an answer. Then look for an answer that matches your prediction. Choice (B) correctly establishes that Kranz stood out as a leader in a time of crisis.

6. A   Difficulty: Easy

Category: Usage

Getting to the Answer: Read the paragraph to establish the correct verb tense for the sentence. Other verbs in the paragraph, such as "were" and "fueled," are past tense and indicate that another past tense verb is needed for this sentence. Choice (A) is correct, because it uses the past tense "was" and logically transitions into the explanation about Kranz's vest making him easy to spot.

7. A   Difficulty: Hard

Category: Development

Getting to the Answer: Quickly summarize the main idea of the paragraph. Eliminate choices that may be accurate but do not support this primary focus. Choice (A) clearly supports the main focus of the paragraph by drawing attention to Kranz's role as a leader in Mission Control.

8. C   Difficulty: Easy

Category: Usage

Getting to the Answer: Be careful with homophones. Figure out the part of speech and what the target word refers to if it is a pronoun. "Their" is a possessive pronoun indicating ownership. "There" is a pronoun that replaces a place name. "They're" is a contraction that is short for "they are." Choice (C), "There," is the correct choice.

9. A   Difficulty: Hard

Category: Effective Language Use

Getting to the Answer: When faced with unfamiliar words, eliminate clearly incorrect answers first. The paragraph indicates that Kranz did not intend for the vest to be stylish. Kranz wore the vest as a military type of symbol, but the correct answer will need to be in contrast to that idea. Choice (A) is the correct answer. The word "sartorial" means "having to do with clothing."

10. D   Difficulty: Medium

Category: Usage

Getting to the Answer: Think about the commonly confused pair *between/among*. Consider which preposition is usually used to reference two distinct objects. Choice (D) appropriately selects the word "between" because the objects "meetings" and "calculations" are two distinct items. "Among" is used for more than two distinct items.

11. C   Difficulty: Medium

Category: Usage

Getting to the Answer: Read the target sentence and the sentence before it. Figure out whom or what the pronoun refers to and make sure it matches the antecedent in number. The plural antecedent is found in the previous sentence ("Kranz and the NASA staff") and is clearly plural. Choice (C) correctly uses a plural pronoun to refer to a plural antecedent.

The UK and the Euro

12. D   Difficulty: Medium

Category: Effective Language Use

Getting to the Answer: Read carefully to identify the context of the underlined word. Then choose the word that best fits the content of the sentence. You're looking for a word that suggests that the organization has developed over time, as is stated in the last part of the sentence. "Built," (D), best fits the context of the sentence.

13. B   Difficulty: Medium

Category: Punctuation

Getting to the Answer: Read the entire sentence to get a better sense for which punctuation would be correct. A colon will introduce an explanation of the "key feature," allowing the rest of the sentence to

elaborate on the preceding clause. Choice (B) is correct. In this case, the colon prompts the reader to see that the part of the sentence after the colon defines the phrase "key feature."

14. D   Difficulty: Medium

Category: Organization

Getting to the Answer: Watch out for any choices that would make the sentence seem out of place. Choice (D) is correct. Sentence 3 offers a transition to a specific discussion of those risks in the next paragraph.

15. B   Difficulty: Medium

Category: Effective Language Use

Getting to the Answer: Avoid choices that are redundant or that use more words than necessary to communicate an idea. All of the choices communicate the same idea, but one does so with greater economy of language. Choice (B) uses a minimal number of well-chosen words to revise the text.

16. C   Difficulty: Hard

Category: Development

Getting to the Answer: Watch out for answer choices that correctly identify supporting points but do not explain the main claim. The paragraph contains evidence, including decreased taxable wealth and decreased control over interest rates, to support the main claim. Choice (C) is correct. It expresses the main claim of the paragraph and is supported by the evidence.

17. B   Difficulty: Medium

Category: Sentence Formation

Getting to the Answer: Read the text carefully. Notice that the existing structure creates a run-on sentence. Then consider which answer choice will create two complete sentences. Choice (B) revises the run-on sentence to create two grammatically complete sentences.

18. C   Difficulty: Medium

Category: Development

Getting to the Answer: Find the main claim in the paragraph, and then come back to the question. The statement found in (C) best supports the paragraph statements that maintaining the current status may not be an option, and moving to the Eurozone may be in the best interest of the UK.

19. A   Difficulty: Easy

Category: Effective Language Use

Getting to the Answer: Watch out for choices that imply little relationship between the EU and the UK. "Intertwined" most accurately reflects the content of the text, because it implies a complex economic relationship between the UK and the Eurozone. Therefore, (A) is correct. No change is necessary.

20. C   Difficulty: Hard

Category: Development

Getting to the Answer: Find the central idea of the paragraph, and then come back to the question. The central idea in the paragraph is that economic downturns in the Eurozone also affect the UK. Choice (C) is correct.

21. D   Difficulty: Easy

Category: Organization

Getting to the Answer: Decide which transition word makes the most sense in the context of the sentence by reading each choice in the sentence. The correct choice should connect the two sentences as the text transitions from economic concerns to those of "security, power, and protection." The word "however" is the best transition because it provides a logical contrast between the ideas in the passage. Choice (D) is the correct answer.

22. B   Difficulty: Medium

Category: Punctuation

Getting to the Answer: Consider which punctuation will correctly set off the parenthetical information in this sentence. Dashes are often used to offset parenthetical sentence elements. Choice (B) is correct.

Coffee: The Buzz on Beans

23. D   Difficulty: Easy

Category: Usage

Getting to the Answer: Review each answer choice, and decide which makes the most sense in terms of what the first sentence says. Choice (D) is the correct answer. "These days" contrasts with the next sentence's use of "this wasn't always true."

24. C   Difficulty: Medium

Category: Usage

Getting to the Answer: Make sure that verbs agree with the subject. Check back and figure out what the subject is, and then see if it agrees. The word "cherries" requires a plural verb. Choice (C) is the correct answer.

25. B   Difficulty: Medium

Category: Sentence Formation

Getting to the Answer: Read the complete sentence carefully whenever you see a shift in tense or verb form. Decide whether this change is logically correct in the sentence. The verbs in a sentence need to be in parallel form. Choice (B) is in parallel form with the first verb "reached," so it is the correct answer.

26. D   Difficulty: Medium

Category: Effective Language Use

Getting to the Answer: Beware of some answer choices that may have similar meanings but do not fit into the context of this sentence. The word "boasted" is the best fit for the context of the sentence, so (D) is the correct answer.

27. D   **Difficulty:** Medium

Category: Sentence Formation

Getting to the Answer: Pay close attention to commas to ensure that they do not create run-on sentences. Notice that this sentence contains two complete thoughts. Choice (D) is the correct answer because it combines the two complete thoughts into one sentence in the best way.

28. A   **Difficulty:** Hard

Category: Development

Getting to the Answer: To find the best conclusion, look for the choice that summarizes the main points of the paragraph and best completes the paragraph. The paragraph begins by talking about the lack of record of coffee as cargo on the Mayflower and then introduces when it was first referenced. Choice (A) does the best job of retelling what the paragraph is about, therefore providing an effective conclusion.

29. B   **Difficulty:** Easy

Category: Punctuation

Getting to the Answer: Study the words in the series and see where commas might need to be placed or eliminated. Choice (B) is the correct answer.

30. C   **Difficulty:** Medium

Category: Effective Language Use

Getting to the Answer: Replace the word with the other answer choices. See which word works best in the context of the sentence. One answer choice indicates the correct relationship between coffeehouses and counterculture, and that is (C). "Associated" works best within the context of the sentence.

31. C   **Difficulty:** Medium

Category: Development

Getting to the Answer: To find the main topic of a paragraph, identify important details and summarize them in a sentence or two. Then find the answer

choice that is the closest to your summary. Choice (C) is the correct answer. The sentence best explains the increasing popularity of coffee in American life, the main topic of the paragraph.

32. D   **Difficulty:** Medium

Category: Punctuation

Getting to the Answer: Determine the relationship between the two parts of this sentence, and then consider the purpose of the various forms of punctuation. A colon indicates that the rest of the sentence will be a list or an explanation. Choice (D) is the correct answer, as it shows the correct relationship between both parts of the sentence.

33. D   **Difficulty:** Hard

Category: Sentence Formation

Getting to the Answer: Read the complete sentence carefully and look for sections that do not seem to follow logically. The modifiers need to be in the proper order so the sentence's meaning is clear; choice (D) is correct.

Predicting Nature's Light Show

34. C   **Difficulty:** Medium

Category: Usage

Getting to the Answer: Recall that a pronoun must agree with its antecedent, or the word to which it refers. Begin by identifying the antecedent of the pronoun. Then, check each choice against the antecedent to find the best match. The antecedent for the pronoun "their" is "this phenomenon," which appears in the main clause. The antecedent and its pronoun do not currently agree as "this phenomenon" is singular but "their" is plural. Although the *s* in "Lights" implies many lights, it is still considered a singular phenomenon and so requires a singular pronoun. Choice (C) is the correct answer.

35. D   Difficulty: Medium

Category: Effective Language Use

Getting to the Answer: Read each answer choice carefully to determine the correct preposition. Choice (D) is the correct answer because it correctly uses the preposition "in."

36. C   Difficulty: Medium

Category: Development

Getting to the Answer: Choice (C) is the correct answer because it provides additional information regarding how people are able to view auroras.

37. B   Difficulty: Hard

Category: Effective Language Use

Getting to the Answer: When choosing the correct verb, note how it alters the relationship between the subject, the "sun," and the stated action, in this case "storm activity." Choice (B) is correct. The verb "experiences" is the only one that states a direct action upon the subject, the sun, rather than the sun "observing" an action occurring externally, as suggested by the other verbs.

38. B   Difficulty: Easy

Category: Effective Language Use

Getting to the Answer: The adjective "interested" appears twice. The sentence would be more concise if it only appeared once before both nouns. That's choice (B). Note that C is incorrect because the scientists and amateurs are interested in the aurora borealis specifically, not in the entire Northern Hemisphere.

39. C   Difficulty: Hard

Category: Effective Language Use

Getting to the Answer: Generalized statements with inexact definitions that border on opinion have no place in a scientific essay. The tone and style must exhibit a reliance on verifiable statements. Because "readily available" cannot be quantified and implies

the author's opinion, using the word "specific" in (C) creates a more exact statement that precedes the information on the precise tools used.

40. A   Difficulty: Medium

Category: Development

Getting to the Answer: Reread the paragraph to understand the author's claims. Which answer choice provides a fact that would best support these claims? Make sure the answer choice does not digress from the progression of ideas. The speed of the solar flare is referenced as being three times the speed of normal solar winds, but neither exact speed is given. To make a stronger case for the author's statements, both speeds should be stated. Therefore, (A) is the correct answer.

41. B   Difficulty: Medium

Category: Usage

Getting to the Answer: Read closely to find the subject of the verb. Sometimes, the closest noun is not the subject. The subject of the sentence is "strength and direction," not "energy." Choice (B) is the correct answer because it matches the subject in number and maintains a consistent tense with the rest of the passage.

42. B   Difficulty: Hard

Category: Effective Language Use

Getting to the Answer: Eliminate extraneous and redundant information ("the public") and needless prepositions. Then reorder the verb and nouns to achieve the most efficient language possible. Making adjustments to the passage language as shown in (B) results in the most concise phrasing.

43. A   Difficulty: Hard

Category: Sentence Formation

Getting to the Answer: Consider the meanings of each introductory word carefully. Use the context clues in the rest of the sentence to choose the correct word. The context clues in the rest of the sentence reveal that the Northern Lights can create communication and weather problems and yet are still beautiful. Keeping the word "While" makes the most sense in this context, so (A) is the correct answer.

44. D   Difficulty: Hard

Category: Quantitative

Getting to the Answer: Reread paragraph 4 for information that will help you understand how to read the graphic. Use that information to calculate the precise start and end time for the solar flare as indicated in the graphic. The passage states that a solar flare is represented by any Kp-Index of 5 or higher. While there is one three-hour period where the Kp-Index reached 6, there is a consistent period where the chart shows readings of level 5 or higher. Choice (D) is the correct answer. This choice gives the complete time period showing a reading of level 5 or higher, according to the chart.

MATH—NO-CALCULATOR TEST

1. B   Difficulty: Easy

Category: Heart of Algebra / Linear Equations

Getting to the Answer: The average rate of change for a linear function is the same as the slope of the line. Find the slope of the line by either using the slope formula or by counting the rise and the run from one point to the next. If you start at $(0, -3)$, the line rises 5 units and runs 8 units to get to $(8, 2)$, so the slope, or average rate of change, is $\frac{5}{8}$.

2. D   Difficulty: Easy

Category: Passport to Advanced Math / Quadratics

Getting to the Answer: A root of an equation is an x-value that corresponds to a y-value of 0. The x-intercepts of the graph, and therefore the roots of the equation, are $x = -1$ and $x = 5$. When $x = -1$, the value of $x + 1$ is 0, so one of the factors is $x + 1$. When

$x = 5$, the value of $x - 5$ is 0, so the other factor is $x - 5$. The equation in (D) is the only one that contains these factors and is therefore correct.

3. C   Difficulty: Easy

Category: Passport to Advanced Math / Exponents

Getting to the Answer: Substitute the values given in the question into the formula. Then simplify using the rules of exponents. Remember, when raising a power to a power, you multiply the exponents:

$$
\begin{aligned}
KE &= \frac{1}{2}\left(2 \times 10^3\right)\left(3 \times 10^3\right)^2 \\
&= \frac{1}{2}\left(2 \times 10^3\right)\left(3^2 \times 10^{3 \times 2}\right) \\
&= \frac{1}{2} \times 2 \times 10^3 \times 9 \times 10^6 \\
&= 9 \times 10^{3+6} \\
&= 9 \times 10^9
\end{aligned}
$$

Choice (C) is correct.

4. B   Difficulty: Medium

Category: Heart of Algebra / Linear Equations

Getting to the Answer: Choose the best strategy to answer the question. You could start by cross-multiplying to get rid of the denominators, but simplifying the numerators first will make the calculations easier:

$$
\begin{aligned}
\frac{3(k-1) + 5}{2} &= \frac{17 - (8 + k)}{4} \\
\frac{3k - 3 + 5}{2} &= \frac{17 - 8 - k}{4} \\
\frac{3k + 2}{2} &= \frac{9 - k}{4} \\
4(3k + 2) &= 2(9 - k) \\
12k + 8 &= 18 - 2k \\
14k &= 10 \\
k &= \frac{10}{14} \\
&= \frac{5}{7}
\end{aligned}
$$

Choice (B) is correct.

5. D   **Difficulty:** Medium

Category: Passport to Advanced Math / Functions

Getting to the Answer: Whenever a quantity repeatedly increases or decreases by the same percentage (or fraction) over time, an exponential model can be used to represent the situation. Choice B is not an exponential equation, so you can eliminate it right away. The amount of garbage is decreasing, so the scenario represents exponential decay and you can use the form $y = a \times (1 - r)^t$, where a is the initial amount, r is the rate of decay, and t is time in years. The initial amount is 1,800, the rate is 3%, or 0.03, and t is an unknown quantity, so the correct equation is $y = 1,800 \times (1 - 0.03)^t$, which is equivalent to the equation $y = 1,800 \times 0.97^t$, (D).

6. C   **Difficulty:** Medium

Category: Heart of Algebra / Linear Equations

Getting to the Answer: The slope-intercept form of a line is $y = mx + b$. In this question, the graph passes through the origin, so b is 0. Because b is 0, the equation of this line in slope-intercept form is $y = mx$, which can be rewritten as $\frac{y}{x} = m$. Count the rise and the run from the origin, $(0, 0)$, to the next point, $(3, 1)$, to get a slope of $m = \frac{1}{3}$. This matches (C).

7. D   **Difficulty:** Medium

Category: Passport to Advanced Math / Exponents

Getting to the Answer: When multiplying polynomials, carefully multiply each term in the first factor by each term in the second factor. This question doesn't ask for the entire product, so check to make sure you answered the right question (the coefficient of x). After performing the initial multiplication, look for the x terms and add their coefficients. To save time, you do not need to simplify the other terms in the expression:

$$(4x^2 + 7x + 1)(3x + 5)$$
$$= 4x^2(3x + 5) + 7x(3x + 5) + 1(3x + 5)$$
$$= 12x^3 + 20x^2 + 21x^2 + \underline{35x + 3x} + 5$$

The coefficient of x is $35 + 3 = 38$, which is (D).

8. C   **Difficulty:** Medium

Category: Passport to Advanced Math / Functions

Getting to the Answer: A graph is *decreasing* when the slope is negative; it is *increasing* when the slope is positive. Eliminate A because there are some segments on the graph that have a positive slope. Eliminate B because the slope is negative, not positive, between 2009 and 2010. Choice (C) is correct because the slope is negative for each segment between 2004 and 2007 and also between 2009 and 2011.

9. A   **Difficulty:** Medium

Category: Heart of Algebra / Inequalities

Getting to the Answer: Don't answer this question too quickly. The shading is below the line, but that does not necessarily mean that the symbol in the equation will be the less than symbol (<). Start by writing the equation of the dashed line shown in the graph in slope-intercept form. Then use the shading to determine the correct inequality symbol. The slope of the line shown in the graph is $\frac{1}{4}$ and the y-intercept is -3, so the equation of the dashed line is $y = \frac{1}{4}x - 3$. The graph is shaded below the boundary line, so use the < symbol. When written in slope-intercept form, the inequality is $y < \frac{1}{4}x - 3$. The inequalities in the answer choices are given in standard form ($Ax + By = C$), so rewrite your answer in this form. Don't forget to reverse the inequality symbol if you multiply or divide by a negative number:

$$y < \frac{1}{4}x - 3$$

$$-\frac{1}{4}x + y < -3$$

$$\frac{1}{4}x - y > 3$$

Choice (A) is correct.

10. C   Difficulty: Medium

Category: Heart of Algebra / Linear Equations

Getting to the Answer: When you're given only one equation but two variables, chances are that you can't actually solve the equation (unless one variable happens to cancel out), but rather that you are going to need to manipulate it to look like the desired expression (which in this question is $\frac{b}{a}$). This type of question can't be planned out step-by-step—instead, start with basic algebraic manipulations and see where they take you. First, distribute the $\frac{1}{2}$ on the left side of the equation to get $2a + 5b = b$. There are two terms that have a b, so subtract $5b$ from both sides to get $2a = -4b$. You're hoping for plain b in the numerator, so divide both sides by -4 to get $\frac{2a}{-4} = b$. Finally, divide both sides by a to move the a into a denominator position under b. The result is $\frac{2}{-4} = \frac{b}{a}$, which means the ratio $\frac{b}{a}$ is $-\frac{2}{4}$, or $-\frac{1}{2}$, making (C) correct.

11. D   Difficulty: Hard

Category: Heart of Algebra / Systems of Linear Equations

Getting to the Answer: Graphically, a system of linear equations that has no solution indicates two parallel lines, or in other words, two lines that have the same slope. So, write each of the equations in slope-intercept form ($y = mx + b$) and set their slopes (m) equal to each other to solve for a. Before finding the slopes, multiply the top equation by 3 to make it easier to manipulate:

$$3\left(\frac{1}{3}x + \frac{2}{3}y = -8\right) \rightarrow x + 2y = -24 \rightarrow y = -\frac{1}{2}x - 12$$

$$ax + 6y = 15 \rightarrow 6y = -ax + 15 \rightarrow y = -\frac{a}{6}x + \frac{15}{6}$$

The slope of the first line is $-\frac{1}{2}$, and the slope of the second line is $-\frac{a}{6}$. Set them equal and solve:

$$-\frac{1}{2} = -\frac{a}{6}$$
$$-6(1) = -a(2)$$
$$-6 = -2a$$
$$3 = a$$

Choice (D) is correct.

12. A   Difficulty: Hard

Category: Heart of Algebra / Inequalities

Getting to the Answer: Pay careful attention to units, particularly when a question involves rates. The taxi charges $3.00 for the first $\frac{1}{4}$ mile, which is a flat fee, so write 3. The additional charge is $0.25 per $\frac{1}{8}$ mile, or 0.25 times 8 = $2.00 per mile. The number of miles after the first $\frac{1}{4}$ mile is $m - \frac{1}{4}$, so the cost of the trip, not including the first $\frac{1}{4}$ mile, is $2\left(m - \frac{1}{4}\right)$. This means the cost of the whole trip is $3 + 2\left(m - \frac{1}{4}\right)$. The clue "no more than $20" means that much or less, so use the symbol ≤. The inequality is $3 + 2\left(m - \frac{1}{4}\right) \le 20$, which simplifies to $2.5 + 2m \le 20$, (A).

13. A   Difficulty: Hard

Category: Passport to Advanced Math / Quadratics

Getting to the Answer: The quadratic equation is given in standard form, so use the method of completing the square to rewrite the equation in vertex form. Then, read the value of k to find the maximum height of the projectile:

$$h = -16t^2 + 64t + 8$$
$$= -16\left(t^2 - 4t + \underline{\quad}\right) + 8 - \underline{\quad}$$
$$= -16\left(t^2 - 4t + 4\right) + 8 - (-16 \times 4)$$
$$= -16(t - 2)^2 + 8 - (-64)$$
$$= -16(t - 2)^2 + 72$$

The vertex is (2, 72), so the maximum height is 72 feet, (A).

14. 144   Difficulty: Easy

Category: Heart of Algebra / Linear Equations

Getting to the Answer: There is only one equation given and it has two variables. This means that you don't have enough information to solve for either variable. Instead, look for the relationship between the left side of the equation and the other expression that you are trying to find. Start by clearing the fractions by multiplying both sides of the original equation by 12. This yields the expression that you are looking for, $9x + 10y$, so no further work is required—just read the value on the right-hand side of the equation:

$$\frac{3}{4}x + \frac{5}{6}y = 12$$
$$12\left(\frac{3}{4}x + \frac{5}{6}y\right) = 12(12)$$
$$9x + 10y = 144$$

15. 150   Difficulty: Medium

Category: Additional Topics in Math / Geometry

Getting to the Answer: There are 360 degrees in a circle. You need to figure out how many degrees each minute on the face of a clock represents. There are 60 minutes on the face of an analogue clock. This means that each minute represents $360 \div 60 = 6$ degrees. Between 3:20 and 3:45, 25 minutes go by, so the minute hand rotates $25 \times 6 = 150$ degrees.

16. 8   Difficulty: Hard

Category: Passport to Advanced Math / Exponents

Getting to the Answer: Read the question carefully to determine what part of the expression you need to simplify and what part you don't. Sometimes, you can work a simpler question and still arrive at the correct answer. The question only asks for the exponent on x, so you do not have to simplify the coefficients. Rewrite the expression without the coefficients and simplify using the rules of exponents:

$$\frac{3x^{\frac{3}{2}} \cdot \left(16x^2\right)^3}{8x^{-\frac{1}{2}}} \to \frac{x^{\frac{3}{2}} \cdot \left(x^2\right)^3}{x^{-\frac{1}{2}}}$$
$$= x^{\frac{3}{2}-\left(-\frac{1}{2}\right)} \cdot x^{2 \times 3}$$
$$= x^{\frac{3}{2}+\frac{1}{2}} \cdot x^6$$
$$= x^2 \cdot x^6$$
$$= x^8$$

The exponent on x is 8.

17. 3/25 or .12   Difficulty: Hard

Category: Passport to Advanced Math / Functions

Getting to the Answer: When a question involving a function provides one or more ordered pairs, substitute them into the function to see what information you can glean. Start with $x = 0$ because doing so often results in the elimination of a variable:

$$f(x) = a \cdot b^x$$
$$f(0) = a \cdot b^0$$
$$3 = a \cdot b^0$$
$$3 = a \cdot 1$$
$$3 = a$$

Now you know the value of a, so the equation looks like $f(x) = 3 \cdot b^x$. Substitute the second pair of values into the new equation:

$$f(x) = 3 \cdot b^x$$
$$f(1) = 3 \cdot b^1$$
$$15 = 3 \cdot b^1$$
$$15 = 3b$$
$$5 = b$$

The exponential function is $f(x) = 3 \cdot 5^x$. The final step is to find the value being asked for, $f(-2)$. Substitute -2 for x and simplify:

$$f(-2) = 3 \cdot 5^{-2} = \frac{3}{5^2} = \frac{3}{25}$$

Grid this in as 3/25 or 0.12.

MATH—CALCULATOR TEST

1. B   **Difficulty:** Easy

Category: Heart of Algebra / Linear Equations

Getting to the Answer: The total cost consists of a flat installation fee and a price per square foot. The installation fee is a one-time fee that does not depend on the number of feet ordered and therefore should not be multiplied by f. This means that 199 is the installation fee. The other expression in the equation, $3.29f$, represents the cost per square foot (the unit price) times the number of feet, f. Hence, 3.29 must represent the cost of 1 square foot of carpet, (B).

2. B   **Difficulty:** Easy

Category: Problem Solving and Data Analysis / Statistics and Probability

Getting to the Answer: Quickly read each answer choice. Cross out false statements as you go. Stop when you arrive at a true statement. There is no long "tail" of data on either side, so the shape is not skewed and you can eliminate A. The shape of the data *is* symmetric because the data is fairly evenly spread out, with about half of the ages above and half below the median. When the shape of a data set is symmetric, the mean is approximately equal to the median, so (B) is correct. Don't let D fool you—the *median* is 55, not the *mean*.

3. A   **Difficulty:** Easy

Category: Heart of Algebra / Linear Equations

Getting to the Answer: Think about the best strategy to answer the question. If you distribute the $\frac{1}{3}$, it creates messy numbers. Instead, clear the fraction

by multiplying both sides of the equation by 3. Then use inverse operations to solve for x:

$$\frac{1}{3}(5x - 8) = 3x + 4$$
$$5x - 8 = 3(3x + 4)$$
$$5x - 8 = 9x + 12$$
$$-4x = 20$$
$$x = -5$$

Choice (A) is correct.

4. A   **Difficulty:** Easy

Category: Passport to Advanced Math / Quadratics

Getting to the Answer: The minimum value of a quadratic function is equal to the y-value of the vertex of its graph, so vertex form, $y = a(x - h)^2 + k$, reveals the minimum without doing any additional work. Choice (A) is the only equation written in this form and therefore must be correct. The minimum value of this function is $-\frac{3}{2}$.

5. C   **Difficulty:** Medium

Category: Problem Solving and Data Analysis / Rates, Ratios, Proportions, and Percentages

Getting to the Answer: Start with the smallest possible lot size, 3,000 square feet. The next lot must be at least 30% larger, so multiply by 1.3 to get 3,900 square feet. Then, round up to the next thousand (which is not necessarily the nearest thousand) to meet the tax assessment requirement. You must always round up because rounding down would make the subsequent lot size less than 30% larger than the one before it. Continue this process until you reach the maximum square footage allowed, 15,000 square feet:

$$3{,}000 \times 1.3 = 3{,}900 \rightarrow 4{,}000$$
$$4{,}000 \times 1.3 = 5{,}200 \rightarrow 6{,}000$$
$$6{,}000 \times 1.3 = 7{,}800 \rightarrow 8{,}000$$
$$8{,}000 \times 1.3 = 10{,}400 \rightarrow 11{,}000$$
$$11{,}000 \times 1.3 = 14{,}300 \rightarrow 15{,}000$$

Choice (C) is correct.

6. D   **Difficulty:** Medium

Category: Problem Solving and Data Analysis / Functions

Getting to the Answer: Determine whether the change in the amount of pollution is a common difference (linear function) or a common ratio (exponential function), or if it changes direction (quadratic or polynomial function). Each year, the amount of pollution should be $100 - 8 = 92\%$ of the year before. You can write 92% as $\frac{92}{100}$, which represents a common ratio from one year to the next. This means that the best model is an exponential function, (D), of the form $y = a \cdot (0.92)^x$.

7. A   **Difficulty:** Medium

Category: Passport to Advanced Math / Exponents

Getting to the Answer: Don't spend too much time reading the scientific explanation of the equation. Solve for r using inverse operations. First, square both sides of the equation to remove the radical. Then, multiply both sides by r to get the r out of the denominator. Finally, divide both sides by v^2:

$$v = \sqrt{\frac{2Gm}{r}}$$

$$v^2 = \frac{2Gm}{r}$$

$$v^2 r = 2Gm$$

$$r = \frac{2Gm}{v^2}$$

This matches (A).

8. D   **Difficulty:** Medium

Category: Heart of Algebra / Systems of Linear Equations

Getting to the Answer: One equation should represent the total *number* of rentals, while the other equation represents the *cost* of the rentals. The number of DVDs plus the number of Blu-rays equals the total number of rentals, 209. Therefore, one equation is $d + b = 209$. This means you can eliminate choices B and C. Now write the cost equation: cost per DVD times number of DVDs ($2d$) plus cost per

Blu-ray times number of Blu-rays ($3.5b$) equals the total amount collected (562). The cost equation is $2d + 3.5b = 562$. Don't let A fool you. The question says nothing about the cost *per hour* so there is no reason to divide the cost by 4. Choice (D) is correct.

9. B   **Difficulty:** Medium

Category: Problem Solving and Data Analysis / Rates, Ratios, Proportions, and Percentages

Getting to the Answer: Break the question into short steps. *Step 1*: Find the number of female senators. *Step 2*: Use that number to find the number of female Republican senators. *Step 3*: Find the total number of Republican senators.

Each of the 50 states gets 2 voting members in the Senate, so there are $50 \times 2 = 100$ senators. The ratio of males to females in the 113th Congress was 4:1, so 4 parts male plus 1 part female equals a total of 100 senators. Write this as $4x + x = 100$, where x represents one part and therefore the number of females. Next, simplify and solve the equation to find that $x = 20$ female senators. To find the number of female senators that were Republican, multiply 20% (or 0.20) times 20 to get 4. Finally, add to get 45 male plus 4 female = 49 Republican senators in the 113th Congress, (B).

10. C   **Difficulty:** Medium

Category: Problem Solving and Data Analysis / Rates, Ratios, Proportions, and Percentages

Getting to the Answer: Find the percent increase by dividing the amount of change by the original amount. Then apply the same percent increase to the amount for 2012. The amount of increase is $29,400 - 18,750 = 10,650$, so the percent increase is $10,650 \div 18,750 = 0.568 = 56.8\%$ over 8 years. If the total percent increase over the next 8 years is the same, the average student who borrowed money will have loans totaling $29,400 \times 1.568 = 46,099.20$, or about \$46,100. Choice (C) is correct.

11. D   Difficulty: Medium

Category: Heart of Algebra / Linear Equations

Getting to the Answer: Write the expression in words first: points per large basket (3) times number of beanbags in large basket (*b*), plus points per small basket (7) times number of beanbags in small basket. If there are 10 beanbags total and *b* go into the larger basket, the rest, or $10 - b$, must go into the smaller basket. Now, translate the words to numbers, variables, and operations: $3b + 7(10 - b)$. This is not one of the answer choices, so simplify the expression by distributing the 7 and combining like terms: $3b + 7(10 - b) = 3b + 70 - 7b = 70 - 4b$. This matches (D).

12. D   Difficulty: Easy

Category: Problem Solving and Data Analysis / Statistics and Probability

Getting to the Answer: To calculate the percentage of the voters in each district who had no opinion on fracking, divide the number of voters in *that* district who had no opinion by the total number of voters in *that* district. Choice (D) is correct because $3,205 \div 63,539 \approx 0.05 = 5\%$, which is a lower percentage than in the other three districts that were polled (District A = 8%; District B = 7.6%; District C = 6%).

13. A   Difficulty: Medium

Category: Problem Solving and Data Analysis / Statistics and Probability

Getting to the Answer: Scan the answer choices quickly to narrow down the amount of information in the table that you need to analyze. Each choice makes a statement about people from District C who support a ban on fracking that can be expected to vote in the next election. To extrapolate from the follow-up survey sample, multiply the fraction of people from the follow-up survey who plan to vote in the upcoming election $\left(\dfrac{218}{500}\right)$ by the number of people in District C who support a ban on fracking (43,228) to get 18,847.408, or approximately 19,000 people. Choice (A) is correct.

14. B   Difficulty: Medium

Category: Heart of Algebra / Systems of Linear Equations

Getting to the Answer: Solve the system of equations using substitution. Then check that you answered the right question (find the sum of *x* and *y*). First, solve the second equation for *x* to get $x = 3y - 11$, then substitute this expression into the first equation to find *y*:

$$2x + 4y = 13$$
$$2(3y - 11) + 4y = 13$$
$$6y - 22 + 4y = 13$$
$$10y - 22 = 13$$
$$10y = 35$$
$$y = \frac{7}{2}$$

Now, substitute the result into $x = 3y - 11$ and simplify to find *x*:

$$x = 3\left(\frac{7}{2}\right) - 11$$
$$= \frac{21}{2} - 11$$
$$= -\frac{1}{2}$$

The question asks for the sum, so add *x* and *y* to get $-\dfrac{1}{2} + \dfrac{7}{2} = \dfrac{6}{2} = 3$, which is (B).

15. C   Difficulty: Medium

Category: Problem Solving and Data Analysis / Statistics and Probability

Getting to the Answer: The key word in the answer choices is "consistently," which relates to how spread out a player's scores are. Standard deviation, not mean, is a measure of spread, so you can eliminate choice A right away. A lower standard deviation indicates scores that are less spread out and therefore more consistent. Likewise, a higher standard deviation indicates scores that are more spread out and therefore less consistent. Notice the opposite nature of this relationship: lower standard deviation = more consistent; higher standard deviation = less consistent. Choice (C) is correct because the standard deviation of Mae's scores is the lowest, which means she bowled the most consistently.

16. B   Difficulty: Medium

Category: Passport to Advanced Math / Quadratics

Getting to the Answer: Notice the structure of the equation. The expression on the left side of the equation is the square of a quantity, so start by taking the square root of both sides. After taking the square roots, solve the resulting equations. Remember, $4^2 = 16$ and $(-4)^2 = 16$, so there will be *two* equations to solve:

$$(x + 3)^2 = 16$$
$$\sqrt{(x + 3)^2} = \sqrt{16}$$
$$x + 3 = \pm 4$$
$$x + 3 = 4 \rightarrow x = 1$$
$$x + 3 = -4 \rightarrow x = -7$$

Choice (B) is correct.

17. C   Difficulty: Medium

Category: Problem Solving and Data Analysis / Rates, Ratios, Proportions, and Percentages

Getting to the Answer: Pay careful attention to the units. You need to convert all of the dimensions to inches, and then set up and solve a proportion. The real statue's height is $305 \times 12 = 3,660 + 6 = 3,666$ inches; the length of the nose on the real statue is $4 \times 12 = 48 + 6 = 54$ inches; the height of the model statue is 26 inches; the length of the nose on the model is unknown:

$$\frac{3,666}{54} = \frac{26}{x}$$
$$3,666x = 26(54)$$
$$3,666x = 1,404$$
$$x = \frac{1,404}{3,666} = \frac{18}{47}$$

Choice (C) is correct.

18. B   Difficulty: Medium

Category: Passport to Advanced Math / Functions

Getting to the Answer: When evaluating a function, substitute the value inside the parentheses for x in the equation. Evaluate the function at $x = 6$ and at $x = 2$, and then subtract the second output from the first. Note that this is not the same as first subtracting $6 - 2$ and then evaluating the function at $x = 4$:

$$f(6) = 3(6) + 5 = 18 + 5 = 23$$
$$f(2) = 3(2) + 5 = 6 + 5 = 11$$
$$f(6) - f(2) = 23 - 11 = 12$$

Choice (B) is correct.

19. A   Difficulty: Medium

Category: Problem Solving and Data Analysis / Scatterplots

Getting to the Answer: Examine the graph, paying careful attention to units and labels. Here, the years increase by 2 for each grid line and the number of owls by 25. The average change per year is the same as the slope of the line of best fit. Find the slope of the line of best fit using the slope formula, $m = \dfrac{y_2 - y_1}{x_2 - x_1}$, and any two points that lie on (or very close to) the line. Using the two endpoints of the data, (1994, 1,200) and (2014, 700), the average change per year is $\dfrac{700 - 1,200}{2014 - 1994} = \dfrac{-500}{20} = -25$, which is (A). Pay careful attention to the sign of the answer—the number of owls is decreasing, so the rate of change is negative.

20. D   Difficulty: Medium

Category: Passport to Advanced Math / Quadratics

Getting to the Answer: The solution to a system of equations is the point(s) where their graphs intersect. You could solve this question algebraically, one system at a time, but this is not time efficient.

Instead, graph each pair of equations in your graphing calculator and look for the graphs that intersect at $x = -4$ and $x = 2$. The graphs of the equations in A and B don't intersect at all, so you can eliminate them right away. The graphs in C intersect, but both points of intersection have a positive x-coordinate. This means (D) must be correct. The graph looks like:

21. C   Difficulty: Medium

Category: Problem Solving and Data Analysis / Statistics and Probability

Getting to the Answer: Read the question, identifying parts of the graphic you need—the question asks about litters of 7 or more pups, so you'll only use the heights of the bars for 7, 8, and 9 pups. Start by finding the percent of the mice in the study that had a litter of 7 or more pups. Of the 200 mice in the sample, $25 + 14 + 5 = 44$ had a litter of 7 or more pups. This is $\frac{44}{200} = \frac{22}{100} = 22\%$ of the mice in the study. Given the same general conditions (such as living in the same geographic region), you would expect approximately the same results, so multiply the number of female mice in the whole population by the percent you found: $35,000 \times 0.22 = 7,700$, (C).

22. C   Difficulty: Medium

Category: Heart of Algebra / Linear Equations

Getting to the Answer: You'll need to interpret the information given in the question to write two ordered pairs. Then you can use the ordered pairs to find the slope and the y-intercept of the linear model. In an ordered pair, the independent variable is always written first. Here, the heart rate depends on the amount of exercise, so the ordered pairs should be written in the form (time, heart

rate). They are (8, 90) and (20, 117). Use these points in the slope formula, $m = \dfrac{y_2 - y_1}{x_2 - x_1}$, to find that $m = \dfrac{117 - 90}{20 - 8} = \dfrac{27}{12} = 2.25$. Then, substitute the slope (2.25) and either of the points into slope-intercept form and simply to find the y-intercept:

$$90 = 2.25(8) + b$$
$$90 = 18 + b$$
$$72 = b$$

Finally, write the equation using the slope and the y-intercept that you found to get $r = 2.25t + 72$. Note that the only choice with a slope of 2.25 is (C), so you could have eliminated the other three choices before finding the y-intercept and saved yourself a bit of time.

23. C   Difficulty: Medium

Category: Heart of Algebra / Linear Equations

Getting to the Answer: Pay careful attention to what the question tells you about the variables. The x-value is the number of payments already made, and the y-value is the amount of debt remaining (not how much has been paid). If a solution is (21, 560), the x-value is 21, which means Chantal has made 21 payments already. The y-value is 560, which means $560 is the amount of debt *left to be paid*, making (C) correct.

24. D   Difficulty: Hard

Category: Problem Solving and Data Analysis / Scatterplots

Getting to the Answer: A line that "represents the trend of the data" is another way of saying line of best fit. The trend of the data is clearly linear because the path of the dots does not turn around or curve, so draw a line of best fit on the graph. Remember, about half of the points should be above the line and half below.

Emails per Day by Age

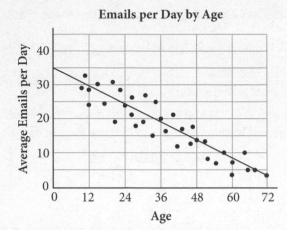

If you draw your line of best fit all the way to the y-axis, you'll save yourself a step by simply looking at the scatterplot to find the y-intercept. For this graph, it's about 35. This means you can eliminate choices B and C. Next, find the approximate slope using two points that lie on (or very close to) the line. You can use the y-intercept, (0, 35), as one of them to save time and estimate the second, such as (72, 4). Use the slope formula to find the slope:

$$m = \frac{y_2 - y_1}{x_2 - x_1} = \frac{4 - 35}{72 - 0} = \frac{-31}{72} \approx -0.43$$

The equation that has the closest slope and y-intercept is (D). (Note that if you choose different points, your line may have a slightly different slope or y-intercept, but the answer choices will be far enough apart that you should be able to determine which is the *best* fit to the data.)

25. B   Difficulty: Hard

Category: Passport to Advanced Math / Functions

Getting to the Answer: Transformations that are grouped with the x in a function shift the graph horizontally and, therefore, affect the x-coordinates of points on the graph. Transformations that are not grouped with the x shift the graph vertically and, therefore, affect the y-coordinates of points on the graph. Remember, horizontal shifts are always backward of what they look like. Start with $(x + 3)$. This shifts the graph left 3, so subtract 3 from the x-coordinate of the given point: $(5, 1) \rightarrow (5 - 3, 1) =$

(2, 1). Next, apply the negative in front of f, which is not grouped with the x, so it makes the y-coordinate negative: $(2, 1) \rightarrow (2, -1)$. Finally, $- 2$ is not grouped with x, so subtract 2 from the y-coordinate: $(2, -1 - 2) \rightarrow (2, -3)$, which is (B).

26. C   Difficulty: Hard

Category: Problem Solving and Data Analysis / Rates, Ratios, Proportions, and Percentages

Getting to the Answer: Draw a chart or diagram detailing the various price reductions for each 30 days:

Date	% of Most Recent Price	Resulting Price
Jan 15	100 − 25% = 75%	$1,500 × 0.75 = $1,125
Feb 15	100 − 10% = 90%	$1,125 × 0.9 = $1,012.50
Mar 15	100 − 10% = 90%	$1,012.50 × 0.9 = $911.25

You can stop here because the refrigerator was sold on April 2, which is not 30 days after March 15. The final selling price was $911.25, (C).

27. A   Difficulty: Hard

Category: Additional Topics in Math / Geometry

Getting to the Answer: Organize information as you read the question. Here, you'll definitely want to draw and label a sketch:

The lower level, the vertical distance between levels, and the diagonal elevator track form a 30-60-90 triangle, where the elevator track is the hypotenuse. The vertical distance is opposite the 30-degree angle so it is the shortest leg. The rules for 30-60-90 triangles state that the shortest leg is half the length of the hypotenuse, so the vertical distance between levels is approximately $170 \div 2 = 85$ feet, (A).

28. 1/6 or .166 or .167   **Difficulty:** Easy

Category: Problem Solving and Data Analysis / Statistics and Probability

Getting to the Answer: This question requires concentration, but no complicated calculations. First, you need to identify the rows that contain information about the seating on the 777s, which are the bottom two rows. To find the probability that the seat is a Business Class seat, find the total number of seats in that category (in only the bottom two rows), and divide by the total number of seats on the planes (in only the bottom two rows):

$$P(\text{Business Class}) = \frac{37 + 52}{194 + 37 + 16 + 227 + 52 + 8}$$

$$= \frac{89}{534} = \frac{1}{6} = 0.1\overline{6}$$

Grid in your answer as 1/6 or .166 or .167.

29. 440   **Difficulty:** Medium

Category: Heart of Algebra / Systems of Linear Equations

Getting to the Answer: Translate from English into math to write a system of equations with t = the cost of the tankless heater in dollars and c = the cost of the conventional heater in dollars. First, a tankless heater (t) costs $160 more (+160) than twice as much ($2c$) as the conventional one, or $t = 2c + 160$. Together, a tankless heater (t) and a conventional heater (c) cost $1,000, or $t + c = 1,000$. The system is:

$$\begin{cases} t = 2c + 160 \\ t + c = 1,000 \end{cases}$$

The top equation is already solved for t, so substitute $2c + 160$ into the second equation for t and solve for c:

$$2c + 160 + c = 1,000$$
$$3c + 160 = 1,000$$
$$3c = 840$$
$$c = 280$$

Be careful—that's not the answer! The conventional hot water heater costs $280, so the tankless heater costs $2(280) + 160 = \$720$. This means the tankless heater costs $720 - \$280 = \$440$ more than the conventional heater.

30. 252   **Difficulty:** Medium

Category: Problem Solving and Data Analysis / Rates, Ratios, Proportions, and Percentages

Getting to the Answer: Break the question into steps. First, find how long it took Daniel to spray one lawn, and then use that amount to find how long it took him to spray all the lawns. According to the figure, he started the first house at 9:00 and the sixth house at 10:00, so it took him 1 hour, or 60 minutes, to spray 5 houses. This gives a unit rate of $60 \div 5 = 12$ minutes per house. Count the houses in the figure—there are 21. Multiply the unit rate by the number of houses to get $12 \times 21 = 252$ minutes to spray all the lawns.

31. 4   **Difficulty:** Hard

Category: Problem Solving and Data Analysis / Rates, Ratios, Proportions, and Percentages

Getting to the Answer: This part of the question contains several steps. Think about the units given in the question and what you need to convert so that you can get to the answer. The total acreage of all the lawns in the neighborhood is $21 \times 0.2 = 4.2$ acres. This is equivalent to $4.2 \times 43,560 = 182,952$ square feet. Each gallon of spray covers 2,500 square feet, so divide to find that Daniel needs $182,952 \div 2,500 = 73.1808$ gallons to spray all the lawns. The spray rig holds 20 gallons, so Daniel will need to fill it 4 times. After he fills it the fourth time and finishes all the lawns, there will be some spray left over.

PART SIX

Answers & Explanations

CHAPTER 1

PRACTICE

8. C   Difficulty: Medium
Category: Heart of Algebra / Linear Equations

Getting to the Answer: The Kaplan Strategy for Translating English into Math will work well here. Watch out for extra information that may confuse you. Let a be the average of Test One (92); b, the average of Test Two (77); c, the average of Test Three (what you need to find); and d, the overall test average (84). The average is the sum of the terms divided by the number of terms: $\frac{a + b + c}{3} = d$. Plugging in the values you know yields $\frac{92 + 77 + c}{3} = 84$. Multiply both sides by 3 and then subtract to solve for c, which gives 83. This corresponds to (C).

9. D   Difficulty: Medium
Category: Heart of Algebra / Linear Equations

Getting to the Answer: This is another question suited for the Kaplan Strategy for Translating English into Math. Let b represent the total number of candies in the box. Then write each candy quantity as a fraction of b. Putting the pieces together in an equation gives $\frac{1}{4}b + \frac{1}{6}b + \frac{1}{3}b + 9 = b$. From here, you can find a common denominator, but multiplying through by a common multiple (such as 12) will be easier. Solving for b yields 36, but you're not done yet. Plug 36 back into the expressions for peppermints (12) and chocolates (9), then multiply together to get 108, which is (D).

PERFORM

10. C   Difficulty: Medium
Category: Heart of Algebra / Linear Equations

Getting to the Answer: You know there will be a flat fee of $50, and for text messages you'll be looking for 0.1t. This eliminates D. If you're stuck on the data plan cost, plug in some numbers. For $g = 2$, you wouldn't expect

there to be an additional fee. For $g = 3$, you'd expect to see an $8 charge, and for $g = 4$, you'd expect to see a $16 charge. The only answer choice that reflects this is (C).

11. 1/3   Difficulty: Medium
Category: Heart of Algebra / Linear Equations

Getting to the Answer: Notice that $n - 2$ is in both the equation and the desired expression. Determine the value of $n - 2$ by dividing both sides of $3(n - 2) = 6$ by 3. Now you know that $n - 2 = 2$, so plug 2 into the numerator of the desired expression. To find the value of the denominator, continue simplifying the given equation to find that $n = 4$. Plug 4 into $n + 2$, which leaves $\frac{2}{4 + 2} = \frac{2}{6} = \frac{1}{3}$. Grid in $\frac{1}{3}$ and move on to the next question.

12. B   Difficulty: Medium
Category: Heart of Algebra / Linear Equations

Getting to the Answer: Follow the Kaplan Strategy for Translating English into Math. Assemble equations and set them equal to each other. Let d = Die-Hard Package, p = Personal Package, and v = number of visits. Using the information about each package, you know that $d = 250$ and $p = 130 + 4v$. Now, solve for v:

$$250 = 130 + 4v$$
$$120 = 4v$$
$$30 = v$$

This is an exact match for (B).

ON YOUR OWN

1. D   Difficulty: Easy
Category: Heart of Algebra / Linear Equations

Getting to the Answer: The total bill consists of a flat tax and a percentage of annual income. The flat per capita tax is a one-time fee that does not depend on the taxpayer's income and therefore should not be multiplied by i. This means that 25 is the per capita tax. The other expression in the equation, 0.02i, represents the percentage income tax times the annual income (which the question tells you is i). Therefore, 0.02 must represent the amount of the income tax as a percentage, which is (D).

2. A   Difficulty: Medium

Category: Heart of Algebra / Linear Equations

Getting to the Answer: Start by simplifying the numerators. Don't forget to distribute the negative to both terms inside the parentheses on the right side of the equation:

$$\frac{7(n - 3) + 11}{6} = \frac{18 - (6 + 2n)}{8}$$

$$\frac{7n - 21 + 11}{6} = \frac{18 - 6 - 2n}{8}$$

$$\frac{7n - 10}{6} = \frac{12 - 2n}{8}$$

Next, cross multiply and solve for n using inverse operations:

$$8(7n - 10) = 6(12 - 2n)$$

$$56n - 80 = 72 - 12n$$

$$68n = 152$$

$$n = \frac{152}{68} = \frac{38}{17}$$

This matches (A).

3. C   Difficulty: Medium

Category: Heart of Algebra / Linear Equations

Getting to the Answer: If a linear equation has no solution, the variables cancel out, leaving two numbers that are not equal to each other. Start by simplifying the left side of the equation:

$$36 + 3(4x - 9) = c(2x + 1) + 25$$

$$36 + 12x - 27 = c(2x + 1) + 25$$

The variable term on the left is $12x$. Because the variable terms must cancel, the right side of the equation must also have a $12x$, so it must be that $c = 6$, which is (C).

4. B   Difficulty: Medium

Category: Heart of Algebra / Linear Equations

Getting to the Answer: Use the information in the question to write your own equation, then look for the answer choice that matches. Simplify your equation only if you don't find a match. Start with the cost, not including tax or the environmental impact fee. If Jenna rents a car for d days at a daily rate of $54.95, the untaxed total is $54.95d$.

There is a 6% tax on this amount, so multiply by 1.06 to get $1.06(54.95d)$. The $10 environmental impact fee is *not* taxed, so simply add 10 to your expression. The total cost is $c = 1.06(54.95d) + 10$, which matches (B), so you do not need to simplify.

5. A   Difficulty: Medium

Category: Heart of Algebra / Linear Equations

Getting to the Answer: The answer choices are given in slope-intercept form, so start by finding the slope. To do this, substitute two pairs of values from the table into the slope formula, $m = \dfrac{y_2 - y_1}{x_2 - x_1}$. Keep in mind that the projected number of cans sold *depends* on the price, so the price is the independent variable (x) and the projected number is the dependent variable (y). Using the points (0.75, 10,000) and (1.0, 5,000), the slope is:

$$m = \frac{5,000 - 10,000}{1.00 - 0.75}$$

$$= \frac{-5,000}{0.25}$$

$$= -20,000$$

This means that (A) must be correct because it is the only one that has a slope of $-20,000$. Don't let D fool you—the projected number of cans sold goes *down* as the price goes *up*, so there is an inverse relationship, and the slope must be negative.

6. B   Difficulty: Medium

Category: Heart of Algebra / Linear Equations

Getting to the Answer: The x-axis represents the number of golf balls, so find 1 on the x-axis and trace up to where it meets the graph of the line. The y-value is somewhere between $1 and $2, so the only possible correct answer choice is $1.67, which is (B).

You could also find the unit rate by calculating the slope of the line using two of the points shown on the graph. The graph rises 5 units and runs 3 units from one point to the next, so the slope is $\dfrac{5}{3}$, or 1.67.

7. C   Difficulty: Hard

Category: Heart of Algebra / Linear Equations

Getting to the Answer: The key to answering this question is to determine how many arrows hit each circle.

If there are 12 arrows total and *a* hit the inner circle, the rest, or $12 - a$, must hit the outer circle. Now, write the expression in words: points per inner circle (8) times number of arrows in inner circle (*a*) plus points per outer circle (4) times number of arrows in outer circle ($12 - a$). Next, translate the words into numbers, variables, and operations: $8a + 4(12 - a)$. This is not one of the answer choices, so simplify the expression by distributing the 4 and then combining like terms: $8a + 4(12 - a) = 8a + 48 - 4a = 4a + 48$, so the equation is $p = 4a + 48$. Rearrange the order of the terms on the right side to arrive at (C).

8. D   Difficulty: Hard
Category: Heart of Algebra / Linear Equations

Getting to the Answer: In a real-world scenario, the *y*-intercept of a graph usually represents a flat fee or an initial value. The slope of the line represents a unit rate, such as the cost per pound. The *y*-intercept of the graph is 12, so the flat fee is $12. To find the cost per pound (the unit rate), substitute two points from the graph into the slope formula. Using the points (0, 12) and (2, 17), the unit rate is $\dfrac{17 - 12}{2 - 0} = \dfrac{5}{2} = 2.5$, which means $2.50 per pound will be added to the cost. The total cost to ship a 25-pound box is $12 + 2.50(25) = $12 + $62.50 = $74.50, which is (D).

9. D   Difficulty: Easy
Category: Heart of Algebra / Linear Equations

Getting to the Answer: Quickly examine the numbers in the equation and choose the best strategy to answer the question. Distributing the $\dfrac{2}{3}$ will result in messy calculations, so clear the fraction instead. To do this, multiply both sides of the equation by the reciprocal of $\dfrac{2}{3}$, which is $\dfrac{3}{2}$:

$$\frac{3}{2} \cdot \frac{2}{3}(x - 1) = 12 \cdot \frac{3}{2}$$
$$x - 1 = 18$$
$$x = 19$$

Choice (D) is correct. Note that you could also clear the fraction by multiplying both sides of the equation by the denominator (3) and then using the distributive property, but this is not the most time-efficient strategy.

10. C   Difficulty: Easy
Category: Heart of Algebra / Linear Equations

Getting to the Answer: When writing a linear equation, a flat rate is a constant while a unit rate is always multiplied by the independent variable. You can identify the unit rate by looking for words like *per* or *for each*. Because the amount Sandy gets paid per day, $70, is a flat rate that doesn't depend on the number of tires she sells, it should be the constant in the equation. The clue "for each" tells you to multiply $14 by the number of tires she sells, so the equation is *pay* = 14 × *number of tires* + 70, or $y = 14x + 70$. This matches (C).

11. C   Difficulty: Easy
Category: Heart of Algebra / Linear Equations

Getting to the Answer: It is reasonable to assume that the value of the car is determined by multiplying the depreciation rate by the number of years the car is owned, which is given in the equation as 0.15*x*, and subtracting it from the car's initial value. This means 27,000, which is the constant in the equation, is the value of the car when the number of years is 0, or in other words, the purchase price of the car, choice (C).

12. A   Difficulty: Easy
Category: Heart of Algebra / Linear Equations

Getting to the Answer: Read the axis labels carefully. The *y*-intercept is the point at which $x = 0$, which means the number of rides is 0. The *y*-intercept is (0, 8). This means the cost is $8 before riding any rides, and therefore 8 most likely represents a flat entrance fee, (A).

13. A   Difficulty: Easy
Category: Heart of Algebra / Linear Equations

Getting to the Answer: The slope of the line is the rise over the run from one point to another (always left to right). Put your pencil on the *y*-intercept, (0, 6), and move to the point (3, 1). The line moves down 5 units and to the right 3 units, so the slope is $-\dfrac{5}{3}$, which is (A).

You could also substitute two points, such as (0, 6) and (3, 1), into the slope formula $\left(m = \dfrac{y_2 - y_1}{x_2 - x_1} \right)$ to find the slope of the line.

Answers & Explanations

14. C   Difficulty: Easy
Category: Heart of Algebra / Linear Equations

Getting to the Answer: The graph in (C) does not represent a linear relationship because the slope on the left side of the y-axis is negative (the graph is decreasing) while the slope on the right side of the y-axis is positive (the graph is increasing). The graph of a linear relationship does not change direction. Choice (C) is correct.

15. C   Difficulty: Medium
Category: Heart of Algebra / Linear Equations

Getting to the Answer: When a linear equation is written in the form $y = mx + b$, the variable m represents the slope of the line, and b represents the y-intercept of the line. Quickly scan the answer choices—they involve inequalities, so you'll need to translate them into something that makes more sense to you. Use the fact that "< 0" means negative and "> 0" means positive. Now, look at the graph—the line is increasing (going up from left to right), so the slope is positive ($m > 0$). This means you can eliminate A and B. Finally, look at the y-intercept—it is below the x-axis and is therefore negative ($b < 0$), which means (C) is correct.

16. B   Difficulty: Medium
Category: Heart of Algebra / Linear Equations

Getting to the Answer: Use the graph to identify the y-intercept and the slope of the line. Then write an equation in slope-intercept form, $y = mx + b$. The line crosses the y-axis at (0, 6), so the y-intercept (b) is 6. The line falls vertically 1 unit for every 2 units that it runs to the right, so the slope (m) is $-\dfrac{1}{2}$. The equation of the line is $y = -\dfrac{1}{2}x + 6$, which matches (B).

Resist the temptation to graph each answer choice on your calculator—such a strategy is too time-consuming.

17. C   Difficulty: Medium
Category: Heart of Algebra / Linear Equations

Getting to the Answer: Look for a way to make the math easier, such as clearing the fractions first. To do this, multiply both sides of the equation by 6, then solve for h using inverse operations:

$$6\left[\frac{2}{3}(3h)\right] - 6\left[\frac{5}{2}(h-1)\right] = 6\left[-\frac{1}{3}\left(\frac{3}{2}h\right)\right] + 6[8]$$

$$4(3h) - 15(h-1) = -2\left(\frac{3}{2}h\right) + 48$$

$$12h - 15h + 15 = -3h + 48$$

$$-3h + 15 = -3h + 48$$

$$15 \neq 48$$

Because the variable terms in the equation cancel out, and 15 does not equal 48, the equation has no solution. In other words, there is no value of h that satisfies the equation, so (C) is correct.

18. B   Difficulty: Medium
Category: Heart of Algebra / Linear Equations

Getting to the Answer: Write the equation in words first, then translate from English to math. The total cost, c, is the weight of the watermelon in pounds, p, multiplied by the sale price since the purchase is made on Monday: $\$0.60 \times 80\% = 0.6 \times 0.8 = 0.48$. This gives the first part of the expression: $0.48p$. Now add the cost of four sweet potatoes, $0.79 \times 4 = 3.16$, to get the equation $c = 0.48p + 3.16$, which matches (B).

You could also use the Picking Numbers strategy: pick a number for the weight of the watermelon and calculate how much it would cost (on sale). Then add the cost of four sweet potatoes. Finally, find the equation that gives the same amount.

19. A   Difficulty: Medium
Category: Heart of Algebra / Linear Equations

Getting to the Answer: In this scenario, the total cost is the dependent variable and is calculated by multiplying the per person rate by the number of people attending and then adding the room rental fee. Therefore, the total cost is represented by y. Because the room rental fee and the per person rate are fixed amounts (determined by the hotel), they should be represented by constants in the equation—325 and 15, respectively. The total cost depends on the number of people attending, so the number of people is the independent variable and is represented by x. Choice (A) is correct.

20. B   Difficulty: Medium

Category: Heart of Algebra / Linear Equations

Getting to the Answer: There is not a lot of information to go on here, so start by determining the relationship between the number given in the problem, 3,600 bolts per day, and the number in the equation, 150. Because $3,600 \div 150 = 24$ and there are 24 hours in a day, 150 is the number of bolts the machine can produce in 1 hour. If the machine can produce 150 in 1 hour, then it can produce 150 times x in x hours. This means the equation $y = 150x$ represents the number of bolts the machine can produce in x hours, which is (B).

21. B   Difficulty: Medium

Category: Heart of Algebra / Linear Equations

Getting to the Answer: The slope-intercept form of a linear equation is $y = mx + b$, where m represents the slope. If the slope is 0, that means $m = 0$. Substitute 0 for m and simplify $y = mx + b$:

$$y = (0)x + b$$
$$y = b$$

The only answer that matches this form is (B), $y = 2$. You could also memorize that $x = a$ represents a vertical line with an undefined slope, and $y = b$ represents a horizontal line with a 0 slope.

22. A   Difficulty: Medium

Category: Heart of Algebra / Linear Equations

Getting to the Answer: Quickly skim the answer choices to get the right context. Because the number of bacteria *depends* on the temperature of the room, the temperature would be graphed on the x-axis and the number of bacteria on the y-axis. Add these labels to the graph. Then describe what you see using your labels: as the temperature increases, the number of bacteria also increases. Unfortunately, this is not one of the answer choices, so think of the scenario in terms of the type of relationship between the variables: there is a direct variation between them, or in other words, when one goes up, the other goes up. This can also be stated as when one goes down, the other goes down; when the temperature decreases, the number of bacteria decreases, and (A) is correct. Don't let D fool you—the *change* in the number of bacteria is constant, but the actual number of bacteria is not constant.

23. A   Difficulty: Hard

Category: Heart of Algebra / Linear Equations

Getting to the Answer: There is not a lot of information to go on, so put the equation in slope-intercept form, and see what conclusions you can draw:

$$ax + by = c$$
$$by = -ax + c$$
$$y = -\frac{a}{b}x + \frac{c}{b}$$

The slope $\left(-\dfrac{a}{b}\right)$ is negative, so the line is decreasing (going down) from left to right. This means you can eliminate C and D because those lines are increasing. The y-intercept $\left(\dfrac{c}{b}\right)$ is positive, but this doesn't help because the y-intercepts in A and B are both positive. But don't forget, you are given that $c = b$, so rewrite the y-intercept as $\dfrac{c}{b} = \dfrac{b}{b} = 1$. The y-intercept is 1, so (A) is correct.

24. D   Difficulty: Hard

Category: Heart of Algebra / Linear Equations

Getting to the Answer: The graph is increasing, so the slope must be positive. This means you should put each of the answer choices in slope-intercept form and check the sign of the slope. However, you can eliminate some of the answer choices fairly quickly using the other piece of information—the graph has a negative x-intercept, so when $y = 0$, the resulting value of x is negative. Quickly check each equation. You don't need to find the exact value of x, simply whether it is positive or negative.

Choice A: $4x + 3(0) = 1 \rightarrow 4x = 1$, so x is positive.

Choice B: $-x + 2(0) = -8 \rightarrow -x = -8$, so x is positive.

Choice C: $2x + 3(0) = -9 \rightarrow 2x = -9$, so x is negative.

Choice (D): $3x - 5(0) = -10 \rightarrow 3x = -10$, so x is negative.

Eliminate A and B and write C in slope-intercept form:

$$2x + 3y = -9$$
$$3y = -2x - 9$$
$$y = -\frac{2}{3}x - 3$$

Answers & Explanations

Eliminate choice C because it is decreasing (has a negative slope). Choice (D) must be correct.

25. A   Difficulty: Hard
Category: Heart of Algebra / Linear Equations

Getting to the Answer: Sometimes drawing a diagram is the quickest way to answer a question. Sketch a quick graph of any linear equation. Change the signs of the slope and the y-intercept, then sketch the new graph on the same coordinate plane. Pick a simple equation that you can sketch quickly, like $y = -2x + 3$, and then change the signs of m and b. The new equation is $y = 2x - 3$. Sketch both graphs. The second graph is a perfect reflection of the first graph across the x-axis, which is (A). The graph that follows illustrates this:

You could also graph your equations in a graphing calculator and compare them. If you're not convinced, try another pair of equations.

26. D   Difficulty: Hard
Category: Heart of Algebra / Linear Equations

Getting to the Answer: When solving a linear equation that has infinitely many solutions, the variable terms will all cancel out, leaving a number that is equal to itself. Start by looking for an equation that, when simplified, has the same variable term on the left side of the equation as on the right side. Choice (D) is correct because:

$$8\left(\frac{3}{4}x - 5\right) = -2(20 - 3x)$$
$$6x - 40 = -40 + 6x$$
$$-40 = -40$$

27. A   Difficulty: Hard
Category: Heart of Algebra / Linear Equations

Getting to the Answer: Always pay careful attention to units of measure. The units change from hours to days. The mouse receives one pellet every 2.5 *hours*, which is equivalent to $\frac{24}{2.5}$ pellets per *day*. Over the course of d full days, the mouse will be fed $\frac{24d}{2.5}$ pellets, which is (A).

28. B   Difficulty: Hard
Category: Heart of Algebra / Linear Equations

Getting to the Answer: This question sounds more difficult than it is. Try to match each number or term in the expression with a piece of information given in the question. Start with 2f. You are given that 2 is the number of points earned for fish with a purple dot and that Karla catches f of these fish, so 2f is the total number of points she earns for fish with purple dots. Move on to the second term, $5(8 - f)$. You are given that 5 is the number of points earned for fish with a green dot. If Karla catches f fish with a purple dot, then she must catch (the number of attempts minus f) fish with a green dot. Because the term in parentheses is $8 - f$, Karla must have made a total of 8 attempts. Each attempt costs 50 cents, so she spent $\$0.50(8) = \$4$ playing the game. Choice (B) is correct.

29. D   Difficulty: Medium
Category: Heart of Algebra / Linear Equations

Getting to the Answer: Write an equation in words first, then translate from English to math. Finally, rearrange your equation to find what you're interested in, which is the initial amount. Call the initial amount A. After you've written your equation, solve for A.

Amount now (x) = initial amount (A) minus y plus 6:

$$x = A - y + 6$$
$$x + y - 6 = A$$

This is the same as $y + x - 6$, so (D) is correct.

You could also use Picking Numbers to answer this question.

30. C **Difficulty:** Hard
Category: Heart of Algebra / Linear Equations

Getting to the Answer: The birth rate starts high on the *y*-axis, while the gross domestic product (indicating wealth) starts low on the *x*-axis. At the other end of the graph, the birth rate is lower, while the gross domestic product is higher. This tells you that there is an inverse relationship between birth rate and wealth. In other words, as one variable increases, the other variable decreases. The only answer choice that describes this type of inverse relationship is (C).

31. 14 **Difficulty:** Easy
Category: Heart of Algebra / Linear Equations

Getting to the Answer: Eliminate the fractions to simplify the math. To do this, multiply both sides of the equation by 4, then solve for *y* using inverse operations:

$$4\left[\frac{9}{4}(y-8)\right] = 4\left[\frac{27}{2}\right]$$
$$9(y-8) = 54$$
$$9y - 72 = 54$$
$$9y = 126$$
$$y = 14$$

32. 24 **Difficulty:** Medium
Category: Heart of Algebra / Linear Equations

Getting to the Answer: The place where the line crosses the *y*-axis is the *y*-intercept, or *b* when the equation is written in slope-intercept form ($y = mx + b$), so rewrite the equation in this form:

$$4x - \frac{1}{2}y = -12$$
$$-\frac{1}{2}y = -4x - 12$$
$$-2\left(-\frac{1}{2}y\right) = -2(-4x - 12)$$
$$y = 8x + 24$$

The *y*-intercept is 24.

Because the *y*-intercept of a graph is always of the form (0, *y*), you could also substitute 0 for *x* in the original equation and solve for *y*.

CHAPTER 2

PRACTICE

7. A   Difficulty: Medium
Category: Heart of Algebra / Linear Equations

Getting to the Answer: Use the Kaplan Strategy for Translating English into Math to make sense of the situation. First, define your variables: t for texts and p for pictures are good choices. Breaking apart the question, you know this student sent a total of 75 texts and pictures. You're also told each text costs $0.10 and each picture is $0.15, as well as the fact that the bill is $8.90. You'll have two equations: one relating the number of texts and pictures and a second relating the costs associated with each:

$$t + p = 75$$
$$0.1t + 0.15p = 8.9$$

Multiply the top equation by -0.1 to solve for p using combination:

$$\cancel{-0.1t} - 0.1p = -7.5$$
$$+ \cancel{0.1t} + 0.15p = 8.9$$
$$\overline{0t + 0.05p = 1.4}$$

Divide both sides of the resulting equation by 0.05 and you'll find that $p = 28$. But you're not done yet; you're asked for the difference between the text and picture count. Substitute 28 for p in the first equation and then solve for t to get $t = 47$. Subtracting 28 from 47 yields 19, which is (A).

8. 51   Difficulty: Medium
Category: Heart of Algebra / Linear Equations

Getting to the Answer: Creativity is key to getting the correct answer to this question. Rather than multiplying just one equation by a factor, you'll need to multiply both by a factor to use combination. Which factors do you pick? It depends on which variable you want to eliminate. Suppose you want to eliminate x. The coefficients of the x terms are 2 and 5, so you need to multiply the equations by numbers that will give you -10 and 10 as your new x term coefficients. To do this, multiply the first equation by -5 and the second equation by 2:

$$-5(2x + 5y = 49)$$
$$2(5x + 3y = 94)$$

Add the resulting equations:

$$\cancel{-10x} - 25y = -245$$
$$+ \quad \cancel{10x} + 6y = 188$$
$$\overline{0x - 19y = -57}$$

Solving for y gives you 3. Next, plug 3 back in for y in either equation and solve for x, which equals 17. Multiplying x and y together yields 51, the correct answer.

PERFORM

9. A   Difficulty: Hard
Category: Heart of Algebra / Linear Equations

Getting to the Answer: A system of linear equations that has no solution should describe two parallel lines. This means the coefficients of the variables should be the same (so the slopes of the lines are the same). Only the constant should be different (so the y-intercepts are not the same). The easiest way to make the coefficients the same is to look at the second equation. Clearly, multiplying it by 40 would make the coefficients of x the same: $8x + 40zy = 20$. Now equate the coefficients of y to get $4y = 40zy$. Solve for z, to reveal that $z = \dfrac{1}{10}$, which is (A).

10. 14   Difficulty: Medium
Category: Heart of Algebra / Linear Equations

Getting to the Answer: Be on the lookout for "sets" of equations that aren't really systems that require substitution or combination. Here, notice that there is only one variable in each equation, so you can solve for each variable to find that $x = 17 - 6 = 11$ and $y = 12 - 9 = 3$. Therefore, the value of $x + y$ is $11 + 3 = 14$. Grid in 14 and move on to the next question.

11. C   Difficulty: Medium
Category: Heart of Algebra / Linear Equations

Getting to the Answer: Use the Kaplan Strategy for Translating English into Math to extract what you need.

First, define the variables using letters that make sense. Use *c* for children and *a* for adults. Now break the word problem into shorter phrases: children's tickets sold for $8 each; adult tickets sold for $12 each; 60 people attended the concert; $624 was collected in ticket money. Translating each phrase into a math expression will produce the components needed:

Children's tickets (*c*) cost $8 each $\rightarrow 8c$

Adult tickets (*a*) cost $12 each $\rightarrow 12a$

60 people attended the concert $\rightarrow c + a = 60$

$624 was collected in ticket money $\rightarrow$ Total $ = 624$

Now put the expressions together:

$$c + a = 60$$
$$8c + 12a = 624$$

Solving for the variables using combination or substitution gives $a = 36$ and $c = 24$. Remember, the question asks for the product of the number of children and the number of adults, so the correct answer is $36 \times 24 = 864$, which corresponds to (C).

ON YOUR OWN

1. C   **Difficulty:** Easy

Category: Heart of Algebra / Systems of Linear Equations

Getting to the Answer: Translate English into math. One equation should represent the total *number* of meals ordered, while the other equation should represent the *cost* of the meals.

The number of people who ordered chicken plus the number who ordered vegetarian equals the total number of people, 62, so one equation is $c + v = 62$. This means you can eliminate A. Now write the cost equation: cost per chicken dish (12.75) times number of dishes (*c*) plus cost per vegetarian dish (9.5) times number of dishes (*v*) equals the total bill (725.25). The cost equation should be $12.75c + 9.5v = 725.25$. Together, these two equations form the system in (C).

2. A   **Difficulty:** Easy

Category: Heart of Algebra / Systems of Linear Equations

Getting to the Answer: Quickly compare the two equations. The system is already set up perfectly to solve using elimination, so add the two equations to cancel $-4y$ and $4y$. Then solve the resulting equation for *x*. Remember, the question asks for the *y*-coordinate of the solution, so you will need to substitute *x* back into one of the original equations and solve for *y*:

$$2x - 4y = 14 \qquad 2(5) - 4y = 14$$
$$\underline{5x + 4y = 21} \qquad 10 - 4y = 14$$
$$7x = 35 \qquad\quad -4y = 4$$
$$x = 5 \qquad\qquad y = -1$$

Choice (A) is correct.

3. D   **Difficulty:** Medium

Category: Heart of Algebra / Systems of Linear Equations

Getting to the Answer: Because *x* has a coefficient of 1 in the second equation, solve the system using substitution. First, solve the second equation for *x*. Then substitute the resulting expression for *x* into the first equation and solve for *y*:

$$x = 6y + 10$$
$$2(6y + 10) + 3y = 8 - y$$
$$12y + 20 + 3y = 8 - y$$
$$15y + 20 = 8 - y$$
$$16y = -12$$
$$y = -\frac{3}{4}$$

Next, substitute this value back into $x = 6y + 10$ and simplify:

$$x = 6\left(-\frac{3}{4}\right) + 10$$
$$= -\frac{9}{2} + \frac{20}{2}$$
$$= \frac{11}{2}$$

Finally, subtract $x - y$ to find that (D) is correct:

$$\frac{11}{2} - \left(-\frac{3}{4}\right) = \frac{22}{4} + \frac{3}{4} = \frac{25}{4}$$

4. A   Difficulty: Medium
Category: Heart of Algebra / Systems of Linear Equations

Getting to the Answer: Translate English into math to write a system of equations with r being the cost of the radio in dollars and t equaling the cost of the television in dollars. A television costs $25 less than twice the cost of the radio, or $t = 2r - 25$; together, a radio and a television cost $200, so $r + t = 200$.

The system is:

$$t = 2r - 25$$
$$r + t = 200$$

The top equation is already solved for t, so substitute $2r - 25$ into the second equation for t:

$$r + 2r - 25 = 200$$
$$3r - 25 = 200$$
$$3r = 225$$
$$r = 75$$

The radio costs $75, so the television costs $2(75) - 25 = 150 - 25 = 125. This means the TV costs $125 - $75 = $50 more than the radio, which is (A).

5. C   Difficulty: Medium
Category: Heart of Algebra / Systems of Linear Equations

Getting to the Answer: Translate English into math to write a system of equations, with t being the cost of a turkey burger and w equaling the cost of a bottle of water. The first statement is translated as $2t + w = 3.25 and the second as $3t + w = 4.50. The system is:

$$2t + w = 3.25$$
$$3t + w = 4.50$$

You could solve the system using substitution, but combination is quicker in this question because subtracting the first equation from the second eliminates w and you can solve for t:

$$3t + w = 4.50$$
$$-(2t + w = 3.25)$$
$$t = 1.25$$

Substitute this value for t in the first equation and solve for w:

$$2(1.25) + w = 3.25$$
$$2.5 + w = 3.25$$
$$w = 0.75$$

Two bottles of water would cost $2 \times $0.75 = 1.50, which is (C).

6. A   Difficulty: Hard
Category: Heart of Algebra / Systems of Linear Equations

Getting to the Answer: One way to answer this question is to think about the graphs of the equations. Graphically, a system of linear equations that has no solution indicates two parallel lines or, in other words, two lines that have the same slope. Write each of the equations in slope-intercept form ($y = mx + b$), and set their slopes (m) equal to each other to solve for w.

First equation:

$$3x - 4y = 10$$
$$-4y = -3x + 10$$
$$y = \frac{3}{4}x - \frac{5}{2}$$

Second equation:

$$6x + wy = 16$$
$$wy = -6x + 16$$
$$y = -\frac{6}{w}x + \frac{16}{w}$$

Set the slopes equal:

$$\frac{3}{4} = -\frac{6}{w}$$
$$3w = -24$$
$$w = -8$$

This matches (A).

7. B   Difficulty: Hard
Category: Heart of Algebra / Systems of Linear Equations

Getting to the Answer: A system of linear equations has infinitely many solutions if both lines in the system have the same slope and the same y-intercept (in other words, they are the same line). Write each of the equations in slope-intercept form ($y = mx + b$). Their slopes should be the same. To find c, set the y-intercepts (b) equal to each other and solve. Before rewriting the equations, multiply the first equation by 6 to make it easier to manipulate.

First equation:

$$6 \times \left[\frac{1}{2}x - \frac{2}{3}y = c\right]$$
$$3x - 4y = 6c$$
$$-4y = -3x + 6c$$
$$y = \frac{3}{4}x - \frac{3}{2}c$$

Second equation:

$$6x - 8y = -1$$
$$-8y = -6x - 1$$
$$y = \frac{3}{4}x + \frac{1}{8}$$

Set the y-intercepts equal:

$$-\frac{3}{2}c = \frac{1}{8}$$
$$-24c = 2$$
$$c = -\frac{1}{12}$$

Choice (B) is correct.

8. C   Difficulty: Hard
Category: Heart of Algebra / Systems of Linear Equations

Getting to the Answer: Create a system of two linear equations where t represents tables with 2 chairs and f represents tables with 4 chairs. The first equation should represent the total number of *tables*, each with 2 or 4 chairs, or $t + f = 25$. The second equation should represent the total number of *chairs*. Because t represents tables with 2 chairs and f represents tables with 4 chairs, the second equation should be $2t + 4f = 86$. Now solve the system using substitution. Solve the first equation for either variable, and substitute the result into the second equation:

$$t + f = 25 \rightarrow t = 25 - f$$

$$2(25 - f) + 4f = 86$$
$$50 - 2f + 4f = 86$$
$$2f = 36$$
$$f = 18$$

There are 18 tables with 4 chairs each, (C). This is all the question asks for, so you don't need to find the value of t.

9. C   Difficulty: Easy
Category: Heart of Algebra / Systems of Linear Equations

Getting to the Answer: Graphically, the solution to a system of linear equations is the point where the lines intersect. Jot down the coordinates of the point on the graph where the two lines intersect, $(-1, 2)$. The question asks for the sum of $x + y$, so add the coordinates to get $-1 + 2 = 1$. Choice (C) is correct.

CHAPTER 3

PRACTICE

8. D   Difficulty: Easy

Category: Problem Solving and Data Analysis / Rates, Ratios, Proportions, and Percentages

Getting to the Answer: Miles per gallon is a rate, so use the DIRT equation. Determine the fuel used during each leg of Jack's trip. Plugging in values for the first leg, you get 180 mi = 40 mi/gal × t → t = 4.5 gallons. The second leg: 105 mi = 35 mi/gal × t → t = 3 gallons. Added together, you get 7.5 gallons of fuel used, which matches (D).

9. B   Difficulty: Medium

Category: Problem Solving and Data Analysis / Rates, Ratios, Proportions, and Percentages

Getting to the Answer: Remember to avoid merely adding the percentages together. Find each change individually. You're not given a concrete share count in the question, so assume the client starts with 100. To save a step with each change, calculate the shares left instead of the shares gained or lost. The first change is −25%; the number of shares left is 75% × 100 → 0.75 × 100 = 75. The second change is +10%, which corresponds to 110% × 75 → 1.1 × 75 = 82.5 shares. The final change is +50%, which means there are now 150% × 82.5 → 1.5 × 82.5 = 123.75 shares. The percent change is $\frac{23.75}{100}$ × 100 = 23.75%; rounded to the nearest percent, you get 24%, which is (B).

10. 432   Difficulty: Medium

Category: Problem Solving and Data Analysis / Rates, Ratios, Proportions, and Percentages

Getting to the Answer: Determine the number of times the pattern repeats, and then find the corresponding number of green tiles. The question states that the ratio of green to blue tiles is 5:3 and that the pattern appears once per square foot. There are 12 × 18 or 216 square feet in the mosaic, meaning there are 5 × 216 or 1,080 green tiles and 3 × 216 or 648 blue tiles. Taking the difference gives 1,080 − 648 = 432 more green tiles than blue.

11. 324   Difficulty: Medium

Category: Problem Solving and Data Analysis / Rates, Ratios, Proportions, and Percentages

Getting to the Answer: Use the blue tile count from the previous question to determine the new green tile count. The green tile count changes in this question, so determine that first. The blue tile count stays constant, so you can just multiply 2 × 216 to get 432 green tiles needed with the new pattern. The ratio of red to green tiles should be 3:4; you can use this in conjunction with the new green tile count in a proportion to find the number of red tiles needed: $\frac{\text{red}}{\text{green}} = \frac{3}{4} = \frac{r}{432}$. Use cross multiplication to find that 1,296 = 4r. Solving for r yields 324 red tiles.

PERFORM

12. A   Difficulty: Medium

Category: Problem Solving and Data Analysis / Rates, Ratios, Proportions, and Percentages

Getting to the Answer: Draw a diagram to make sense of the given situation. Your diagram should look similar to what's shown:

The two triangles are similar, which means you can use a proportion to answer the question. First, find the correct height by taking 25% of 40, which is 10, and deducting that from 40 to give 30. Keeping the heights on the left of your proportion and the hypotenuses on the right, you have $\frac{30}{40} = \frac{x}{75}$. Reduce the left side to get $\frac{3}{4} = \frac{x}{75}$, then cross multiply to eliminate the fractions: 225 = 4x. Solving for x yields 56.25. But don't stop yet. The question asks for the difference in escalator length, not the new length. Subtract 56.25 from 75 to get 18.75, which matches (A).

13. 3.5   Difficulty: Easy

Category: Problem Solving and Data Analysis / Rates, Ratios, Proportions, and Percentages

Getting to the Answer: Whenever you're asked for the cost of something per a set measurement, think unit rates. First, determine the price per ounce (a.k.a. the unit rate) for the smaller can: $\frac{\$0.72}{8 \text{ oz}} = \$0.09/\text{oz}$.

Next, do the same for the larger can: $\frac{\$1.10}{20 \text{ oz}} = \$0.055/\text{oz}$.

Take the difference to get $0.035, which is 3.5 cents. Pay careful attention to the way the question is worded—grid in 3.5, not .035 because the question asks how many more cents.

14. 330   Difficulty: Medium

Category: Problem Solving and Data Analysis / Rates, Ratios, Proportions, and Percentages

Getting to the Answer: First, find the price at 40% off using the three-part percent formula: $p = 0.6 \times \$2,200 = \$1,320$. Repeat for the extra 25%: $p' = 0.75 \times \$1,320 = \$990$. Notice we used the difference between 100% and the percent off (instead of the percent off itself) to avoid an extra calculation with each step. Lastly, find the difference between what the first customer paid and what the second customer paid: $1,320 − $990 = $330.

15. 1,318   Difficulty: Hard

Category: Problem Solving and Data Analysis / Rates, Ratios, Proportions, and Percentages

Getting to the Answer: Keep your percentages (and whether each is an increase or decrease) for your math steps straight. For this question, you'll need the prices including tax. Using 1, which is equal to 100%, the price of the home theater system, plus the tax rate instead of the tax rate alone will again save you a calculation in each step. The full price with tax is 1.0635 × $2,200 = $2,339.70. After the two price reductions, the total sale price is 1.03175 × $990 = $1,021.43. The difference in price is $2,339.70 − $1,021.43 = $1,318.27. Rounding to the nearest dollar, you get $1,318.

ON YOUR OWN

1. B   Difficulty: Easy

Category: Problem Solving and Data Analysis / Rates, Ratios, Proportions, and Percentages

Getting to the Answer: To answer a question that says "directly proportional," set two ratios equal to each other and solve for the missing amount. Don't forget—match the units in the numerators and in the denominators on both sides.

Let c equal the number of cars that can safely pass through a light that lasts 24 seconds. Set up the proportion and solve for c, to find that (B) is correct:

$$\frac{9 \text{ cars}}{36 \text{ seconds}} = \frac{c \text{ cars}}{24 \text{ seconds}}$$
$$9(24) = 36(c)$$
$$216 = 36c$$
$$6 = c$$

2. B   Difficulty: Easy

Category: Problem Solving and Data Analysis / Rates, Ratios, Proportions, and Percentages

Getting to the Answer: When ratios involve large numbers, simplify if possible to make the calculations easier.

Let b equal the number of snowblowers produced. Set up a proportion and solve for b. Be sure to match the units in the numerators and in the denominators on both sides:

$$\frac{8 \text{ defective}}{4,000 \text{ produced}} = \frac{18 \text{ defective}}{b \text{ produced}}$$
$$\frac{1}{500} = \frac{18}{b}$$
$$1(b) = 500(18)$$
$$b = 9,000$$

This matches (B).

3. B   Difficulty: Medium

Category: Problem Solving and Data Analysis / Rates, Ratios, Proportions, and Percentages

Getting to the Answer: Pay careful attention to the units. As you read the question, decide how and when you will need to convert units. The answer choices are given in hours and minutes, so start by converting the rate from words per second to words per minute:

$$\frac{5 \text{ words}}{1 \text{ second}} \times \frac{60 \text{ seconds}}{1 \text{ minute}} = \frac{300 \text{ words}}{1 \text{ minute}}$$

Next, find the number of words in a 45-page chapter:

$$\frac{500 \text{ words}}{1 \text{ page}} \times 45 \text{ pages} = 22,500 \text{ words}$$

Finally, let m be the number of minutes it takes Jorge to read the whole chapter. Set up a proportion and solve for m:

$$\frac{300 \text{ words}}{1 \text{ minute}} = \frac{22,500 \text{ words}}{m \text{ minutes}}$$
$$300m = 22,500$$
$$m = 75$$

Because 75 minutes is not an answer choice, convert it to hours and minutes: 75 minutes = 1 hour, 15 minutes, (B).

4. C   Difficulty: Medium

Category: Problem Solving and Data Analysis / Rates, Ratios, Proportions, and Percentages

Getting to the Answer: Find the percent increase using the formula: Percent change = amount of change divided by original amount. Then apply the same percent increase to the amount for 2013. The amount of increase is $30,100 - 15,800 = 14,300$, so the percent increase is $14,300 \div 15,800 = 0.905 = 90.5\%$ over 25 years. If the total percent increase over the next 25 years is the same, the average cost of tuition and fees will be $30,100 \times 1.905 = 57,340.50$, or about \$57,300, which is (C).

5. A   Difficulty: Medium

Category: Problem Solving and Data Analysis / Rates, Ratios, Proportions, and Percentages

Getting to the Answer: Don't let all the technical words in this question overwhelm you. Solve it step-by-step, examining the units as you go. First, use the factor-label method to determine the number of *megabits* the computer can upload in 1 night (8 hours):

$$\frac{2 \text{ megabits}}{1 \text{ second}} \times \frac{60 \text{ seconds}}{1 \text{ minute}} \times \frac{60 \text{ minutes}}{1 \text{ hour}} \times \frac{8 \text{ hours}}{1 \text{ night}}$$
$$= \frac{57,600 \text{ megabits}}{1 \text{ night}}$$

Next, convert this amount to gigabits (because the information about the scans is given in gigabits, not megabits):

$$57,600 \text{ megabits} \times \frac{1 \text{ gigabit}}{1,024 \text{ megabits}} = 56.25 \text{ gigabits}$$

Finally, each scan produces about 3.6 gigabits of data, so divide this number by 3.6 to determine how many scans the computer can upload to the remote server: $56.25 \div 3.6 = 15.625$ scans. You should round this number down to 15, (A), as the computer cannot complete the 16th scan in the time allowed.

6. D   Difficulty: Medium

Category: Problem Solving and Data Analysis / Rates, Ratios, Proportions, and Percentages

Getting to the Answer: You need to find the ratio of milk to water. You're given two ratios: milk to eggs and water to eggs. Both of the given ratios contain eggs, but the egg amounts (2 and 3) are not identical. To directly compare them, find a common multiple (6). Multiply each ratio by the factor that will make the number of eggs equal to 6:

Milk to eggs: $(5:2) \times (3:3) = 15:6$

Water to eggs: $(4:3) \times (2:2) = 8:6$

Now that the number of eggs needed is the same in both ratios, you can merge the two ratios to compare milk to water directly: 15:6:8. Therefore, the proper ratio of milk to water is 15:8, (D).

7. 680   Difficulty: Medium

Category: Problem Solving and Data Analysis / Rates, Ratios, Proportions, and Percentages

Getting to the Answer: Break the questions into steps. First, find how long it took Verona to mulch one flowerbed. Then use that amount to find how long it took her to mulch all the flowerbeds.

According to the figure, she *started* the first house at 8:00 and the fifth house at 9:20, so it took her 1 hour and 20 minutes, or 80 minutes, to mulch 4 flowerbeds (she hadn't mulched the fifth flowerbed yet). This gives a unit rate of $80 \div 4 = 20$ minutes per flowerbed. Count the houses in the figure—there are 34. Multiply the unit rate by the number of houses to get $20 \times 34 = 680$ minutes to mulch all of the flowerbeds.

8. 25   **Difficulty:** Hard

Category: Problem Solving and Data Analysis / Rates, Ratios, Proportions, and Percentages

Getting to the Answer: The total acreage of all the flowerbeds in the community is $34 \times 0.006 = 0.204$ acres. Convert this amount to square feet using the conversion ratio given in the question:

$$0.204 \text{ acres} \times \frac{43,560 \text{ sq ft}}{1 \text{ acre}} = 8,886.24 \text{ sq ft}$$

Each bag of mulch covers 24 square feet, so divide to find that Verona needs $8,886.24 \div 24 = 370.26$, or about 370, bags to mulch all the flowerbeds. The wagon holds 15 bags, so Verona will need to fill it $370 \div 15 = 24.7$, or 25 times.

9. C   **Difficulty:** Easy

Category: Problem Solving and Data Analysis / Rates, Ratios, Proportions, and Percentages

Getting to the Answer: When a question involves several rates, break the situation into separate, manageable pieces and deal with each in turn. Visitors must pay the café a flat $25.00 fee to join regardless of the number of visits. The first 50 visits cost $0.30 each, or $50(\$0.30) = \$15.00$. The remaining $72 - 50 = 22$ visits cost $0.10 each, or $22(\$0.10) = \$2.20$. The total cost for 72 visits is therefore $\$25.00 + \$15.00 + \$2.20 = \$42.20$, which is (C).

10. D   **Difficulty:** Medium

Category: Problem Solving and Data Analysis / Rates, Ratios, Proportions, and Percentages

Getting to the Answer: The total budget can be represented by 100%, so start there. The percent of the budget spent on lunch is $100\% - 40\% - 25\% - 20\% = 15\%$. You're told that the club plans to spend $225 on lunch. Let x be the total amount of the budget in dollars. Then 15% of x is 225, so $0.15x = 225$. Solving this equation for x yields $0.15x = 225 \rightarrow x = 1,500$. The total budget is $1,500. Of this amount, 40% was budgeted for a guest speaker, or $0.4 \times \$1,500 = \$600$. Choice (D) is correct.

11. D   **Difficulty:** Easy

Category: Problem Solving and Data Analysis / Rates, Ratios, Proportions, and Percentages

Getting to the Answer: According to the pie chart, 20% of the beads are blue. The percentage of beads that are not blue is $100\% - 20\% = 80\%$. Now be sure to answer the *right* question. This question asks for the number (not the percent) of beads that are *not* blue, not the number that *are* blue. The number of beads that are not blue is 80% of 120, or $0.8 \times 120 = 96$ beads, (D).

12. C   **Difficulty:** Easy

Category: Problem Solving and Data Analysis / Rates, Ratios, Proportions, and Percentages

Getting to the Answer: Break the question into short steps and solve each step, checking units as you go. First, find the total number of *milliliters* of milk Drew will need for 5 loaves:

$$\frac{180 \text{ mL}}{1 \text{ loaf}} \times 5 \text{ loaves} = 900 \text{ mL}$$

Second, convert the total number of milliliters needed to *cups*:

$$\frac{1 \text{ cup}}{236.588 \text{ mL}} \times 900 \text{ mL} = \frac{900}{236.588} \text{ mL} \approx 3.804$$

Drew will need about 3.8 or $3\frac{8}{10} = 3\frac{4}{5}$ cups of milk, (C).

13. C   **Difficulty:** Medium

Category: Problem Solving and Data Analysis / Rates, Ratios, Proportions, and Percentages

Getting to the Answer: Skim through the first couple of sentences to get the context, and then break the actual question into short steps. First, find the number of businesses that were required to have inspections. There are 2,625 businesses. The ratio of exempt to covered businesses is 5:2, so 5 parts exempt (don't need inspections) plus 2 parts covered (do need inspections) equals a total of 2,625. Write this as $5x + 2x = 2,625$, where x represents one part. Next, simplify and solve the equation to find that $x = 375$. Now multiply this by 2 because the ratio states that 2 parts are covered by OSHA: $375 \times 2 = 750$. Now use that number to find the number of businesses that had violations: 12% of 750 or $0.12 \times 750 = 90$.

Finally, find the number of businesses that did *not* have violations by subtracting 90 from 750 to get 750 − 90 = 660 businesses that did not have to address any OSHA safety issues. Choice (C) is correct.

14. B   Difficulty: Medium

Category: Problem Solving and Data Analysis / Rates, Ratios, Proportions, and Percentages

Getting to the Answer: Start with the smallest possible green light length, 8 seconds. The next length must be at least 25% larger, so multiply by 1.25 to get 10 seconds. This is the next light length. Now multiply 10 by 1.25 to get 12.5 seconds. Then round up to the next whole second (which is not necessarily the nearest second) to meet the last requirement. You must always round *up* because rounding down would make the subsequent length *less* than 25% longer than the one before it. Only (B) works.

15. A   Difficulty: Medium

Category: Problem Solving and Data Analysis / Rates, Ratios, Proportions, and Percentages

Getting to the Answer: Let the units in this question guide you to the solution. The speeds of the cars are given in miles per hour, but the question asks about the number of miles each car can travel in 30 seconds, so convert miles per hour to miles per second and then multiply by 30 seconds:

Consumer car:

$$\frac{120 \text{ mi}}{\text{hr}} \times \frac{1 \text{ hr}}{60 \text{ min}} \times \frac{1 \text{ min}}{60 \text{ sec}} \times 30 \text{ sec} = 1 \text{ mi}$$

Race car:

$$\frac{210 \text{ mi}}{\text{hr}} \times \frac{1 \text{ hr}}{60 \text{ min}} \times \frac{1 \text{ min}}{60 \text{ sec}} \times 30 \text{ sec} = 1.75 \text{ mi}$$

The race car can travel 1.75 − 1 = 0.75 miles farther in 30 seconds, which is the same as $\frac{3}{4}$ miles, (A).

16. D   Difficulty: Hard

Category: Problem Solving and Data Analysis / Rates, Ratios, Proportions, and Percentages

Getting to the Answer: Let h be the number of hours Jared spent using the Internet during the month. The first hour costs k dollars, and the remaining hours ($h − 1$) are charged at the rate of m dollars per hour. Therefore, the total charge for a month is $k + (h − 1)m$. Set this equal to the amount Jared paid and solve for h. Note that you're not going to get a numeric answer because the question doesn't give you the actual rates:

$$k + (h - 1)m = 65.50$$
$$k + hm - m = 65.50$$
$$mh = 65.50 - k + m$$
$$h = \frac{65.50 - k + m}{m}$$

This expression matches (D). Note that you could also use the Picking Numbers strategy to answer this question.

17. C   Difficulty: Hard

Category: Problem Solving and Data Analysis / Rates, Ratios, Proportions, and Percentages

Getting to the Answer: It's easiest to compare two amounts when they are written in the same units, so start by converting the car's pints to quarts and then go from there. The conversion from pints to quarts is straightforward:

$$8 \text{ pt} \times \frac{1 \text{ qt}}{2 \text{ pt}} = 4 \text{ qt}$$

Next, find the amount of zinc in each car using the percent formula: Percent × whole = part. Write the percents as decimals and multiply:

Car: 0.09 × 4 quarts = 0.36 quarts of zinc

Truck: 0.04 × 6 quarts = 0.24 quarts of zinc

Finally, compare the amount in the car to the amount in the truck: $\frac{0.36}{0.24} = 1.5$. The car has 1.5 times as much zinc in the oil pan as the truck, which is (C).

18. C   Difficulty: Hard

Category: Problem Solving and Data Analysis / Rates, Ratios, Proportions, and Percentages

Getting to the Answer: Draw a chart or diagram detailing the various price reductions for each 30 days. Determine the percent change and new price for each date.

Date	% of Most Recent Price	Resulting Price
Jul 15	100 − 40% = 60%	$1,050 × 0.6 = $630
Aug 15	100 − 20% = 80%	$630 × 0.8 = $504
Sep 15	100 − 20% = 80%	$504 × 0.8 = $403.20

Stop here because the item was sold on October 5, which is not 30 days after September 15. The final selling price was $403.20, (C).

19. D   Difficulty: Hard

Category: Problem Solving and Data Analysis / Rates, Ratios, Proportions, and Percentages

Getting to the Answer: This is another question where the units can help you find the answer. Use the number of vehicles owned to find the total number of miles driven to find the total number of gallons of gas used. Then you can write an equation relating the tax rate to the amount of taxes paid. The starting quantity is 1.75 vehicles; to relate this quantity to the tax rate, it must first be converted to gallons of gasoline:

$$1.75 \text{ vehicles} \times \frac{11,340 \text{ miles}}{\text{vehicle}} = 19,845 \text{ miles}$$

$$19,845 \text{ miles} \times \frac{1 \text{ gallon of gas}}{21.4 \text{ miles}} = 927.336 \text{ gallons}$$

$$927.336 \text{ gallons} \times \frac{t}{\text{gallon}} = \$170.63$$

$$927.336t = \$170.63$$

$$t = 0.184$$

The tax rate was 18.4 cents per gallon, (D).

20. B   Difficulty: Hard

Category: Problem Solving and Data Analysis / Rates, Ratios, Proportions, and Percentages

Getting to the Answer: Pay careful attention to the units. You need to convert all of the dimensions to inches, then set up and solve a proportion. There are 12 inches in 1 foot, so the real plane's length is (220 × 12) + 6 = 2,640 + 6 = 2,646 inches; the length of the wingspan on the real plane is 176.5 × 12 = 2,118

inches; the length of the amusement park ride is 36 feet, 9 inches, or 441 inches; the length of the wingspan on the ride is unknown. Set up a proportion. Try writing the proportion in words first:

$$\frac{\text{real wingspan}}{\text{real length}} = \frac{\text{ride wingspan}}{\text{ride length}}$$

$$\frac{2,118}{2,646} = \frac{x}{441}$$

$$441(2,118) = 2,646(x)$$

$$934,038 = 2,646x$$

$$353 = x$$

The ride's wingspan should be 353 inches, which is equal to 29 feet, 5 inches, (B).

21. 42   Difficulty: Medium

Category: Problem Solving and Data Analysis / Rates, Ratios, Proportions, and Percentages

Getting to the Answer: Questions that involve distance, rate, and time can almost always be solved using the formula Distance = rate × time. Use the speed, or rate, of the small passenger plane (200 mph) and its distance from FLL (110 mi) to determine when it arrived. You don't know the time, so call it t:

$$\text{Distance} = \text{rate} \times \text{time}$$

$$110 = 200t$$

$$0.55 = t$$

This means it took 0.55 hours for the plane to arrive. This is less than a full hour, so multiply 0.55 by 60 to find the number of minutes it took: 60 × 0.55 = 33 minutes. Now determine how long it took the cargo plane. It left at 8:00 a.m. and arrived at 9:15 a.m., so it took 1 hour and 15 minutes, or 75 minutes. This means the small passenger plane arrived 75 − 33 = 42 minutes before the cargo plane.

22. 1036 Difficulty: Hard

Category: Problem Solving and Data Analysis / Rates, Ratios, Proportions, and Percentages

Getting to the Answer: To get started, you'll need to find the distance for each part of the trip—the question only tells you the total distance. Then use the formula Distance = rate × time to find how long the plane flew at 300 mph and then how long it flew at 500 mph.

Answers & Explanations

First part of trip:

$$\frac{1}{3} \times 825 \text{ mi} = 275 \text{ mi}$$

$$275 = 300t$$

$$t = \frac{11}{12} \text{ hr, or 55 minutes}$$

Second part of trip:

There are two possible approaches: $\frac{2}{3} \times 825 = 550$ miles OR 825 mi $-$ 275 mi $=$ 550 miles. Now solve for t:

$$550 = 500t$$

$$t = \frac{11}{10} \text{ hr, or 66 minutes}$$

This means the plane flew for a total of $55 + 66 = 121$ minutes. Next, add the time the plane circled overhead: $121 + 35 = 156$. The total trip took 156 minutes (2 hours and 36 minutes), which means the plane landed at $8:00 + 2$ hours $= 10:00 + 36$ minutes $= 10:36$. Enter the answer as 1036.

23. 1500 Difficulty: Easy
Category: Problem Solving and Data Analysis / Rates, Ratios, Proportions, and Percentages

Getting to the Answer: Find the amount of the annual fee for each portfolio, multiply these amounts by 4, and then subtract to find the difference.

Lower-risk portfolio:
$0.035 \times 100,000 = 3,500$
$3,500 \times 4 = 14,000$

Higher-risk portfolio:
$0.0125 \times 250,000 = 3,125$
$3,125 \times 4 = 12,500$

Difference:
$14,000 - 12,500 = 1,500$

24. .12 Difficulty: Hard
Category: Problem Solving and Data Analysis / Rates, Ratios, Proportions, and Percentages

Getting to the Answer: This question requires multiple steps and multiple formulas, so make a plan before you dive in. Percent gain is the same as percent increase, so you'll need that formula:

$$\% \text{ Increase} = \frac{\text{final amount} - \text{original amount}}{\text{original amount}}$$

This tells you that you need the final amount of the higher-risk portfolio, which will depend on the total fee for the lower-risk portfolio. You'll need to use the percent formula (Percent $\times$ whole $=$ part) to determine what whole would be required at 1.25% for the fees to be equal.

The annual fee for the lower-risk portfolio is $0.035 \times 100,000 = 3,500$. Use this amount to find the final amount for the higher-risk portfolio:

$$0.0125 \times w = 3,500$$

$$0.0125w = 3,500$$

$$w = 280,000$$

Now use the percent increase formula:

$$\% \text{ increase} = \frac{280,000 - 250,000}{250,000}$$

$$= \frac{30,000}{250,000}$$

$$= 0.12$$

The percent increase needed is 12%, but be careful—the directions given in the question tell you to enter the number as a decimal, so grid your answer in as .12.

25. 53.6 Difficulty: Medium
Category: Problem Solving and Data Analysis / Rates, Ratios, Proportions, and Percentages

Getting to the Answer: Break the question into short steps: Find the in-store price (no percent off and add sales tax), find the infomercial price as one of the first 250 callers (10% off, then 20% off that amount, with no sales tax), and subtract to find the savings.

With tax, the in-store price would be $160 \times 1.055 =$ $168.80. The infomercial price (including the 10% off) would be $160 \times 90\% = 160 \times 0.9 = 144$. As one of the first 250 callers (with 20% more off), the final price of the item would be $144 \times 80\% = 144 \times 0.8 = 115.20$. Thus, you would save $168.80 - 115.20 = 53.60$. Grid in this amount as 53.6.

26. 126 Difficulty: Medium
Category: Problem Solving and Data Analysis / Rates, Ratios, Proportions, and Percentages

Getting to the Answer: When answering questions that share information, you can often save yourself some time by using amounts you found in the first question to answer the second. You already found that the price for 1 item for the first 250 callers is $115.20. Malik buys 5 items at this price for a total of $115.20 × 5 = $576. You also already found that the price for 1 item *after* the first 250 callers is $144. Malik buys 3 items at this price for a total of $144 × 3 = $432. This means he buys 8 items for a total cost of $576 + $432 = $1,008. To find the average price he paid, divide the total amount ($1,008) by the total number of items (8) to arrive at the answer, $126.

27. 28   Difficulty: Medium
Category: Problem Solving and Data Analysis / Rates, Ratios, Proportions, and Percentages

Getting to the Answer: Use the formula:

$$\text{Percent} = \frac{\text{part}}{\text{whole}} \times 100\%$$

To use the formula, find the part of the mass represented by the oxygen: There is 1 mole of oxygen, and it has a mass of 15.9994 grams. Next, find the whole mass of the mole of acetone: 1 mole oxygen (15.9994 g) + 3 moles carbon (3 × 12.0107 = 36.0321 g) + 6 moles hydrogen (6 × 1.00794 = 6.04764 g) = 15.9994 + 36.0321 + 6.04764 = 58.07914. Now use the formula:

$$\text{Percent} = \frac{15.9994}{58.07914} \times 100\%$$
$$= 0.27548 \times 100\%$$
$$= 27.548\%$$

Before you grid in your answer, make sure you follow the directions—round to the nearest whole percent, which is 28.

28. 48   Difficulty: Hard
Category: Problem Solving and Data Analysis / Rates, Ratios, Proportions, and Percentages

Getting to the Answer: This part of the question contains several steps. Think about the units given in the question and how you can use what you know to find what you need. Be careful—there are lots of calculations that involve decimals, and you shouldn't round until the final answer.

Start with grams of acetone: the chemist starts with 1,800 and uses 871.1871, so there are 1,800 − 871.1871 = 928.8129 grams left. From the previous question, you know that 1 mole of acetone has a mass of 58.07914 grams, so there are 928.8129 ÷ 58.07914 = 15.9922, or about 16 moles of acetone left. Don't grid in this amount because you're not finished yet! The question asks for the number of moles of *carbon*, not acetone. According to the table, each mole of acetone contains 3 moles of carbon, so there are 16 × 3 = 48 moles of carbon left.

29. 1.25   Difficulty: Medium
Category: Problem Solving and Data Analysis / Rates, Ratios, Proportions, and Percentages

Getting to the Answer: Try writing an equation in words first and then translate into math. Let p represent the number of British pounds; 1,512 is the number of British pounds needed, including the 5% fee, to get 1,800 euros. This means 1,512 = 105% times p, or 1,512 = 1.05p. Divide by 1.05 to find that the number of British pounds needed (before the fee) is 1,440. Next, determine the exchange rate by setting up a proportion (e euros to 1 pound equals 1,800 euros to 1,440 pounds):

$$\frac{e \text{ euros}}{1 \text{ pound}} = \frac{1,800 \text{ euros}}{1,440 \text{ pounds}}$$
$$e = 1.25$$

The exchange rate is 1.25 euros to 1 British pound.

30. 1.3   Difficulty: Hard
Category: Problem Solving and Data Analysis / Rates, Ratios, Proportions, and Percentages

Getting to the Answer: From the previous question, you know that Rosslyn lost 1,512 − 1,440 = 72 pounds because of the fee she paid to the bank in France. The question states that she lost a total of 74 pounds, so only 2 of those pounds were because of the increase in the exchange rate. Set up a proportion using what you know so far. Label as much as possible so you can keep track of exactly what is being converted:

$$\frac{e \text{ (new number of euros)}}{1 \text{ pound}} = \frac{65 \text{ euros}}{x \text{ pounds}}$$

There are two variables (e and x) in the equation, so there is not enough information to solve it yet. However, you also know that Rosslyn would have received 2 more pounds (or $x + 2$) at the old exchange rate, which was 1.25. Set up another proportion using this information:

$$\frac{1.25 \text{ euros}}{1 \text{ pound}} = \frac{65 \text{ euros}}{(x + 2) \text{ pounds}}$$

Now, solve for x:

$$\frac{1.25}{1} = \frac{65}{x + 2}$$
$$1.25(x + 2) = 65$$
$$1.25x + 2.5 = 65$$
$$1.25x = 62.5$$
$$x = 50$$

This is *not* the answer. The question asks for the new exchange rate, so substitute 50 back into the first proportion and solve for e:

$$\frac{e}{1} = \frac{65}{50}$$
$$50e = 65$$
$$e = 1.3$$

The new exchange rate is 1.3 euros to 1 British pound.

CHAPTER 4

PRACTICE

8. A   Difficulty: Hard

Category: Passport to Advanced Math / Exponents

Getting to the Answer: The goal here is to solve for the variable e. You start with $\omega_p = \sqrt{\dfrac{ne^2}{m_e \varepsilon_0}}$; begin by squaring both sides to eliminate the radical to get $\omega_p^2 = \dfrac{ne^2}{m_e \varepsilon_0}$.

Isolating e^2 gives $e^2 = \dfrac{w_p^2 m_e \varepsilon_0}{n}$; take the square root of both sides to get $e = \sqrt{\dfrac{w_p^2 m_e \varepsilon_0}{n}}$, which is (A).

9. 5   Difficulty: Medium

Category: Passport to Advanced Math / Exponents

Getting to the Answer: Use polynomial long division to find the remainder:

$$
\begin{array}{r}
6x^2 + 2x + 2 \\
x - 1\overline{)6x^3 - 4x^2 + 0x + 3} \\
\underline{-(6x^3 - 6x^2)} \\
2x^2 + 0x + 3 \\
\underline{-(2x^2 - 2x)} \\
2x + 3 \\
\underline{-(2x - 2)} \\
5
\end{array}
$$

The question asks for the remainder, so the correct answer is 5.

10. B   Difficulty: Medium

Category: Passport to Advanced Math / Exponents

Getting to the Answer: Start by separating the radicals: $\dfrac{\sqrt{3} \times \sqrt{x^2} \times \sqrt{y^3}}{4 \times \sqrt{5} \times \sqrt{x} \times \sqrt{y^3}}$. All the terms are being multiplied, so you can cancel a $\sqrt{x}$ and $\sqrt{y^3}$ to get

$\dfrac{\sqrt{3} \times \sqrt{x}}{4 \times \sqrt{5}}$. Rationalize the denominator, then simplify:

$\dfrac{\sqrt{3} \times \sqrt{x}}{4 \times \sqrt{5}} \times \dfrac{\sqrt{5}}{\sqrt{5}} = \dfrac{\sqrt{3} \times \sqrt{x} \times \sqrt{5}}{4 \times 5} = \dfrac{\sqrt{15x}}{20}$. Choice (B) is correct.

PERFORM

11. C   Difficulty: Medium

Category: Passport to Advanced Math / Exponents

Getting to the Answer: Convert the wavelength from nanometers into meters; using scientific notation will help (150 nm $= 1.5 \times 10^2$ nm) because you can use exponent rules: $1.5 \times 10^2 \text{ nm} \times \dfrac{1 \text{ m}}{1 \times 10^9 \text{ nm}} = \dfrac{1.5 \times 10^2}{10^9}\text{m}$ $= 1.5 \times 10^{-7}$ m. Plug this into the given equation along with the speed of light to get 5×10^8 m/s $= 1.5 \times 10^{-7}$ m $\times v$.

Solving for v gives $v = \dfrac{3 \times 10^8}{1.5 \times 10^{-7}}$ s^{-1}. You'll see that 1.5 divides evenly into 3 and the bases of 10 abide by exponent rules, so $v = 2 \times 10^{15}$ s^{-1}. Choice (C) is correct.

12. A   Difficulty: Hard

Category: Passport to Advanced Math / Exponents

Getting to the Answer: The conjugate of the denominator, $2 + \sqrt{3}$, is $2 - \sqrt{3}$. Multiply the original expression by $\dfrac{2 - \sqrt{3}}{2 - \sqrt{3}}$ to get $\dfrac{2 \quad \sqrt{3}}{2 + \sqrt{3}} \times \dfrac{2 - \sqrt{3}}{2 - \sqrt{3}}$, then distribute carefully. The numerator becomes:

$$(2 - \sqrt{3})(2 - \sqrt{3})$$
$$= 2^2 - 2\sqrt{3} - 2\sqrt{3} + (-\sqrt{3})^2$$
$$= 7 - 4\sqrt{3}$$

Repeat with the denominator:

$$(2 - \sqrt{3})(2 + \sqrt{3})$$
$$= 2^2 + 2\sqrt{3} - 2\sqrt{3} + (-\sqrt{3} \times \sqrt{3})$$
$$= 1$$

The answer is $7 - 4\sqrt{3}$, which is (A).

13. 256 Difficulty: Medium

Category: Passport to Advanced Math / Exponents

Getting to the Answer: If $n^3 = -8$, then $n = -2$. Simplify the given expression via exponent rules and then plug -2 in for n:

$$\frac{(n^2)^3}{\dfrac{1}{n^2}} = \frac{n^6}{\dfrac{1}{n^2}} = n^6 \div \frac{1}{n^2}$$

$$= n^6 \times n^2 = n^8 = (-2)^8 = 256$$

ON YOUR OWN

1. B Difficulty: Easy

Category: Passport to Advanced Math / Exponents

Getting to the Answer: Raising 9 to the 4th and 5th powers is very time-consuming without a calculator. Instead, start by using exponent rules to simplify expressions written in the same base. Then raise any remaining numbers to the resulting powers. The power of 9 is larger in the denominator, so subtract the exponents there. Then simplify further if possible:

$$\frac{9^4 \times 3^2}{9^5} = \frac{3^2}{9^{5-4}} = \frac{9}{9} = 1$$

Choice (B) is correct.

2. D Difficulty: Easy

Category: Passport to Advanced Math / Exponents

Getting to the Answer: Distribute each term in the first factor to each term in the second factor, paying careful attention to the signs:

$$(-x + 4)(x - 5)$$
$$= -x(x - 5) + 4(x - 5)$$
$$= -x^2 + 5x + 4x - 20$$
$$= -x^2 + 9x - 20$$

Don't let B fool you—the question asks for the coefficient of x, not x^2, so the correct answer is (D).

3. C Difficulty: Medium

Category: Passport to Advanced Math / Exponents

Getting to the Answer: First, move the term with the negative exponent from the denominator to the numerator. Don't flip the exponent; just move the whole term and make the exponent positive: $\dfrac{3}{k^{-\frac{2}{5}}} = 3k^{\frac{2}{5}}$.

Now, rewrite the expression as a radical expression using the rule "power over root." The numerator tells you the power of the variable before the root is applied—here, the power of the variable is 2. The denominator tells you the degree of the root—here, it is a 5th root because the denominator is 5. The number 3 is simply being multiplied by the variable, so it should be outside the radical. The result is: $3k^{\frac{2}{5}} = 3\sqrt[5]{k^2}$. Choice (C) is correct.

4. C Difficulty: Medium

Category: Passport to Advanced Math / Exponents

Getting to the Answer: Before you can use the rules of exponents, you need to write the radical as a fraction exponent. Write $\sqrt{x}$ as $x^{\frac{1}{2}}$ and then subtract the exponents because the terms are being divided:

$$\frac{x^{\frac{3}{2}}}{\sqrt{x}} = \frac{x^{\frac{3}{2}}}{x^{\frac{1}{2}}} = x^{\left(\frac{3}{2} - \frac{1}{2}\right)} = x^{\frac{2}{2}} = x$$

This matches (C).

5. B Difficulty: Medium

Category: Passport to Advanced Math / Exponents

Getting to the Answer: A fraction is the same as division, so you can use polynomial long division to simplify the expression:

$$\begin{array}{r}
2x + 3 \\
4x + 1 \overline{\smash{)}8x^2 + 14x + 3} \\
\underline{-(8x^2 + 2x)} \\
12x + 3 \\
\underline{-(12x + 3)} \\
0
\end{array}$$

The simplified expression is $2x + 3$, choice (B). As an alternate method, you could factor the numerator of the expression and cancel common factors:

$$\frac{8x^2 + 14x + 3}{4x + 1} = \frac{(\cancel{4x + 1})(2x + 3)}{\cancel{4x + 1}} = 2x + 3$$

Use whichever method gets you to the correct answer in the shortest amount of time.

6. A   Difficulty: Medium
Category: Passport to Advanced Math / Exponents

Getting to the Answer: Substitute 160 for P and simplify using your calculator. Don't try to enter the entire expression into the calculator all at one time—you're likely to miss a parenthesis somewhere. Instead, divide 160 by 0.02 to get 8,000. Then take the cube root of 8,000 using the cube root function or by raising it to the one-third power. The result is 20, so the wind velocity is 20 miles per hour. Choice (A) is correct.

7. A   Difficulty: Medium
Category: Passport to Advanced Math / Exponents

Getting to the Answer: The goal here is to solve the equation for L. First, divide both sides of the equation by 2π to isolate the radical. Then you'll need to square both sides to remove the radical:

$$t = 2\pi\sqrt{\frac{L}{32}}$$

$$\frac{t}{2\pi} = \sqrt{\frac{L}{32}}$$

$$\left(\frac{t}{2\pi}\right)^2 = \left(\sqrt{\frac{L}{32}}\right)^2$$

$$\frac{t^2}{2^2\pi^2} = \frac{L}{32}$$

$$\frac{32t^2}{4\pi^2} = L$$

$$\frac{8t^2}{\pi^2} = L$$

This matches (A).

8. B   Difficulty: Hard
Category: Passport to Advanced Math / Exponents

Getting to the Answer: Find the volume of each box and then subtract:

Box 1: $V = x(x + 1)(x - 1) = x(x^2 - 1) = x^3 - x$

Box 2: Substitute $2x$ for x in the volume you already found:

$$(2x)^3 - 2x = 2^3x^3 - 2x = 8x^3 - 2x$$

Difference: $(8x^3 - 2x) - (x^3 - x) = 8x^3 - x^3 - 2x + x = 7x^3 - x$, (B).

Alternatively, you could also pick a value for x (e.g., $x = 2$, in which case $y = 2(2) = 4$) to determine the difference in volume and then check the answer choices against your result.

9. D   Difficulty: Easy
Category: Passport to Advanced Math / Exponents

Getting to the Answer: To subtract the expressions, simply combine like terms. Be careful—don't forget to distribute the negative to all the terms of N:

$$M - N = \left(12x^2 + 4x - 7\right) - \left(5x^2 - x + 8\right)$$
$$= 12x^2 + 4x - 7 - 5x^2 + x - 8$$
$$= 12x^2 - 5x^2 + 4x + x - 7 - 8$$
$$= 7x^2 + 5x - 15$$

This matches (D).

10. B   Difficulty: Easy
Category: Passport to Advanced Math / Exponents

Getting to the Answer: When you find the language confusing, try to put it in concrete terms. If you wanted to know how much more 9 was than 7, what would you do? You would subtract $9 - 7 = 2$ more. So you need to subtract these two algebraic expressions to get $(6x + 5) - (6x - 1) = 6x + 5 - 6x + 1 = 6$, which is (B).

11. A   Difficulty: Easy
Category: Passport to Advanced Math / Exponents

Getting to the Answer: When asked to simplify a rational expression, start by finding the greatest common factor that can be divided out of the numerator and the denominator. Factor a 2 from both the numerator and the denominator, and then cancel the $\frac{2}{2}$:

$$\frac{2x + 6y}{10x - 16} = \frac{\cancel{2}(x + 3y)}{\cancel{2}(5x - 8)}$$
$$= \frac{x + 3y}{5x - 8}$$

This matches (A).

Answers & Explanations

12. B   Difficulty: Easy

Category: Passport to Advanced Math / Exponents

Getting to the Answer: First, write the question as a subtraction problem. Pay careful attention to which expression is being subtracted: $\dfrac{4x - 9}{x + 3} - \dfrac{3x + 1}{x + 3}$.

The terms in the expression have the same denominator, $x + 3$, so their numerators can be subtracted. Simply combine like terms and keep the denominator the same. Don't forget to distribute the negative to both $3x$ and 1:

$$\frac{4x - 9}{x + 3} - \frac{3x + 1}{x + 3} = \frac{(4x - 9) - (3x + 1)}{x + 3}$$
$$= \frac{4x - 9 - 3x - 1}{x + 3}$$
$$= \frac{x - 10}{x + 3}$$

This matches (B).

13. C   Difficulty: Hard

Category: Passport to Advanced Math / Exponents

Getting to the Answer: Because this is a no-calculator question, you need to rewrite the exponent in a way that makes it easier to evaluate. Use exponent rules to rewrite $\dfrac{3}{2}$ as a unit fraction raised to a power. Then write the expression in radical form and simplify:

$$9^{\frac{3}{2}} = (9^{\frac{1}{2}})^3$$
$$= (\sqrt{9})^3$$
$$= 3^3$$
$$= 3 \times 3 \times 3$$
$$= 27$$

Choice (C) is correct.

14. C   Difficulty: Hard

Category: Passport to Advanced Math / Exponents

Getting to the Answer: Always pay careful attention to units. In this question, the equation is defined in terms of inches and minutes, but the diameter of the puddle is given in feet.

Substitute the diameter (3 feet = 36 inches) for d in the equation and then solve for m. Before dealing with the

radical, divide both sides of the equation by 1.25:

$$d = 1.25\sqrt{m - 1}$$
$$36 = 1.25\sqrt{m - 1}$$
$$28.8 = \sqrt{m - 1}$$
$$(28.8)^2 = (\sqrt{m - 1})^2$$
$$829.44 = m - 1$$
$$830.44 = m$$

The liquid has been leaking for about 830 minutes, which is (C).

15. D   Difficulty: Medium

Category: Passport to Advanced Math / Exponents

Getting to the Answer: Write the first factor as repeated multiplication, expand it using FOIL, and then multiply by the second factor to find the product. Pay careful attention to signs:

$$(a - b)^2 (a + b)$$
$$= [(a - b)(a - b)](a + b)$$
$$= (a^2 - ab - ab + b^2)(a + b)$$
$$= (a^2 - 2ab + b^2)(a + b)$$
$$= a^2(a + b) - 2ab(a + b) + b^2(a + b)$$
$$= a^3 + a^2b - 2a^2b - 2ab^2 + ab^2 + b^3$$
$$= a^3 - a^2b - ab^2 + b^3$$

This matches (D).

16. C   Difficulty: Hard

Category: Passport to Advanced Math / Exponents

Getting to the Answer: Multiply each term in the first expression by $\dfrac{3}{5}$ and each term in the second expression by $\dfrac{1}{2}$. Then add the two polynomials by combining like terms:

$$\frac{3}{5}A = \frac{3}{5}(25x^2) + \frac{3}{5}(10x) + \frac{3}{5}(-45)$$
$$= 15x^2 + 6x - 27$$

$$\frac{1}{2}B = \frac{1}{2}(-12x^2) - \frac{1}{2}(32x) + \frac{1}{2}(24)$$
$$= -6x^2 - 16x + 12$$

$$\frac{3}{5}A + \frac{1}{2}B = \begin{array}{r} 15x^2 + 6x - 27 \\ +(-6x^2 - 16x + 12) \\ \hline 9x^2 - 10x - 15 \end{array}$$

This matches (C).

17. A   Difficulty: Hard

Category: Passport to Advanced Math / Exponents

Getting to the Answer: This is a great question to choose a value for x and see what happens. Take a peek at the answer choices to see that you'll want to pick a value of x that is a perfect square (so you can take the square root). The question states that $x > 1$, and the next perfect square is 4, so let $x = 4$.

Try (A): $\dfrac{\sqrt{4}}{4} - 1 = \dfrac{2}{4} - 1 = -\dfrac{1}{2}$, which is less than 0, so (A) is most likely correct.

Try B: $\dfrac{4}{\sqrt{4}} = \dfrac{4}{2} = 2$, which is not less than 1, so eliminate B.

Try C: $2\sqrt{4} = 2 \times 2 = 4$, which is equal to *but not less than* 4, so eliminate C.

Try D: $\sqrt{4} + 4 = 2 + 4 = 6$, which is not greater than 4^2, so eliminate D.

Choice (A) is correct.

18. 13   Difficulty: Medium

Category: Passport to Advanced Math / Exponents

Getting to the Answer: Treat the square root as a single quantity until you isolate it on one side of the equation. Then square both sides to get rid of the square root:

$$\frac{18}{\sqrt{x-4}} = 6$$
$$18 = 6(\sqrt{x-4})$$
$$\frac{18}{6} = \sqrt{x-4}$$
$$3 = \sqrt{x-4}$$
$$3^2 = (\sqrt{x-4})^2$$
$$9 = x-4$$
$$13 = x$$

CHAPTER 5

PRACTICE

8. C   **Difficulty:** Medium
Category: Passport to Advanced Math / Functions

Getting to the Answer: Because the slopes of all the answer choices are different, you can use the slope formula to determine which choice is correct. The number of colonies *depends* on the time, so start by writing the information given as ordered pairs in the form (time, number of colonies). Using the ordered pairs (21, 8) and (35, 10), the slope is $m = \dfrac{y_2 - y_1}{x_2 - x_1} = \dfrac{10 - 8}{35 - 21} = \dfrac{2}{14} = \dfrac{1}{7}$.
The only choice with this slope is (C).

9. 2 or 5   **Difficulty:** Easy
Category: Passport to Advanced Math / Functions

Getting to the Answer: The notation $r(x) = 0$ means that the function is crossing the *x*-axis (has a *y*-value of 0), so look for the *x*-intercepts. The function $r(x)$ intersects the *x*-axis at $x = -2$, 2, and 5. You can only grid in a positive answer, so use 2 or 5.

PERFORM

10. C   **Difficulty:** Easy
Category: Passport to Advanced Math / Functions

Getting to the Answer: This is a composition of functions, so start with the innermost set of parentheses, which is $g(1)$. According to the table on the right, $g(1) = 0$; this becomes the input for *f*. Now find $f(0)$; the table on the left states this is equal to 4, which is (C).

11. D   **Difficulty:** Medium
Category: Passport to Advanced Math / Functions

Getting to the Answer: Identifying the type of relationship between *h* and $f(h)$ is key to solving this problem. The $f(h)$ values (shingle counts) are increasing at a variable rate, which rules out a linear function. The increase in $f(h)$ is not significant with each increase in *h*, so an exponential relationship is not likely. A quadratic relationship is a good bet. Start with $f(h) = h^2$. That gives $f(1) = 1^2 = 1$, $f(2) = $

$2^2 = 4$, and $f(3) = 3^2 = 9$. Obviously this doesn't match the pattern, so ask yourself how much more $f(h)$ needs to increase after squaring *h*; you'll see you need to add 11 to h^2 to get the corresponding value of $f(h)$. You'll find that $f(h) = h^2 + 11$ accurately depicts the relationship between *h* and $f(h)$. You're asked for the shingle count for the seventh house, so plug 7 into your function: $f(7) = 7^2 + 11 = 49 + 11 = 60$, which matches (D).

12. A   **Difficulty:** Hard
Category: Passport to Advanced Math / Functions

Getting to the Answer: To determine the transformed graph, pick a point on the original function $f(x) = (x - 4)^2$, for example, (3, 1). To get from $x - 4$ to $x + 2$, 6 units are added; thus, the *x*-coordinate is shifted 6 units left to -3: $(-3, 1)$. The plus 3 outside the parentheses indicates the *y*-coordinate is shifted 3 units up: $(-3, 4)$. The negative in front of the *x* indicates a reflection over the *y*-axis, so the *x*-coordinate is now 3: (3, 4). The new point falls on the graph of (A), the correct answer. You can check your answer by plugging in values for *x* in the $g(x) = (-x + 2)^2 + 3$ function to get other points on the graph: $(-1, 12)$, (0, 7), (1, 4), (2, 3).

ON YOUR OWN

1. D   **Difficulty:** Easy
Category: Passport to Advanced Math / Functions

Getting to the Answer: The domain of a function represents the possible input values. In this function, the input values are represented by *n*, which is the number of eggs laid by the fish over a given period of time. Because there cannot be a negative number of eggs laid or a fraction of an egg laid, the list in (D) is the only one that could represent part of the function's domain.

2. C   **Difficulty:** Easy
Category: Passport to Advanced Math / Functions

Getting to the Answer: The notation '$h(x)$' is read *h* of *x* and represents the range value (output) of the function that corresponds to a given domain value (input). Therefore, $h(5)$ means the output value of the function when 5 is substituted for the input (*x*), and $h(2)$ means the output value of the function when 2 is substituted for the input (*x*). Substitute 5 and 2 into the equation, one at a time, and then subtract the results:

$$h(x) = 3x - 1$$
$$h(5) = 3(5) - 1 = 15 - 1 = 14$$
$$h(2) = 3(2) - 1 = 6 - 1 = 5$$

$$h(5) - h(2) = 14 - 5 = 9$$

Choice (C) is correct. Caution—this is not the same as subtracting $5 - 2$ and then substituting 3 into the function.

3. B   Difficulty: Medium
Category: Passport to Advanced Math / Functions

Getting to the Answer: Compare each answer choice, one at a time, to the graph. Be careful—you're looking for the statement that is *not* true, so cross out true statements as you go. The statement in A is true (and therefore not correct) because at $x = 0$, y is also 0. Move on to B. When x is 2, $q(x)$, or y, is somewhere between 1 and 2, not equal to 4, so this statement is not true, making (B) the correct answer. The statements in C and D are both true because the x- (domain) and y-values (range) are all greater than or equal to 0.

4. D   Difficulty: Medium
Category: Passport to Advanced Math / Functions

Getting to the Answer: In this question, you are given that the value of $f(x)$ is 5, and you are asked for the value of x that produces this result. This means you are solving for x, not substituting for x. Set the function equal to 5 and solve using inverse operations:

$$5 = \frac{2}{5}x - 7$$
$$12 = \frac{2}{5}x$$
$$12(5) = 2x$$
$$60 = 2x$$
$$30 = x$$

5. C   Difficulty: Medium
Category: Passport to Advanced Math / Functions

Getting to the Answer: The question tells you that the function is linear, which means you need to know the slope (rate of change in the height of the solution) and the y-intercept (height of the solution when there are 0 pennies) to pick the correct function.

You already know the height of the solution when there are 0 pennies—it's 5 inches. This means you can eliminate B and D. To determine the rate of change in the height of the solution, write what you know as ordered pairs, and then use the slope formula:

At 0 pennies, the height is 5 inches $\rightarrow$ (0, 5).
At 50 pennies, the height is 8.5 inches $\rightarrow$ (50, 8.5).

The rate of change in the height of the solution is $\frac{8.5 - 5}{50 - 0} = \frac{3.5}{50} = 0.07$. This means the correct function is $h(p) = 0.07p + 5$, which is (C).

6. C   Difficulty: Medium
Category: Passport to Advanced Math / Functions

Getting to the Answer: The notation $(g(h(x))$ indicates a composition of two functions that can be read "g of h of x." It means that the output when x is substituted into $h(x)$ becomes the input for $g(x)$. First, use the $h(x)$ table to find $h(-2)$; you'll see it equals 4. Use this as the domain in the $g(x)$ table to find $g(4)$, which is 2. Choice (C) is correct.

7. A   Difficulty: Hard
Category: Passport to Advanced Math / Functions

Getting to the Answer: Transformations that are grouped with the x in a function shift the graph horizontally and therefore affect the x-coordinates of points on the graph. Transformations that are not grouped with the x shift the graph vertically and, therefore, affect the y-coordinates of points on the graph. Remember, horizontal shifts are always the opposite of what they look like.

Start with $(x + 5)$. This shifts the graph *left* 5 units, so subtract 5 from the x-coordinate of the given point: $(-2, 6) \rightarrow (-2 - 5, 6) = (-7, 6)$. Next, apply the negative in front of R, which makes the y-coordinate negative: $(-7, 6) \rightarrow (-7, -6)$. Finally, the $+ 1$ is not grouped with x, so add 1 to the y-coordinate: $(-7, -6) \rightarrow (-7, -6 + 1) = (-7, -5)$, which is (A).

You could also plot the point on a coordinate plane, perform the transformations (left 5, reflect vertically over the x-axis, and then up 1), and find the resulting point.

8. 5   Difficulty: Medium
Category: Passport to Advanced Math / Functions

Getting to the Answer: Evaluate the function at $t = 20$ and at $t = 10$, and then subtract the results. Make sure you follow the correct order of operations as you simplify:

$$c(20) = -0.05(20)^2 + 2(20) + 2$$
$$= -0.05(400) + 40 + 2$$
$$= -20 + 40 + 2$$
$$= 22$$
$$c(10) = -0.05(10)^2 + 2(10) + 2$$
$$= -0.05(100) + 20 + 2$$
$$= -5 + 20 + 2$$
$$= 17$$

The question asks how many more parts per million are in a patient's bloodstream after 20 hours than after 10 hours, so subtract $22 - 17 = 5$.

9. B **Difficulty:** Easy

Category: Passport to Advanced Math / Functions

Getting to the Answer: If a relationship represents a function, then each input can have only one corresponding output. When a function is presented as a set of ordered pairs, this means that no number in the domain (the first value in an ordered pair) can be repeated. Choice (B) is correct because each input (x-value) has only one output (y-value). All other choices have multiple outputs for a single input.

10. D **Difficulty:** Easy

Category: Passport to Advanced Math / Functions

Getting to the Answer: To determine the domain, look at the x-values. To determine the range, look at the y-values. For the domain, the graph is continuous and has arrows on both sides, so the domain is all real numbers. This means you can eliminate choices A and B. For the range, the function's maximum is located at $(0, 5)$, which means the highest possible value of $f(x)$ is 5. The graph is continuous and opens downward, so the range of the function is $f(x) \leq 5$, making (D) correct.

11. D **Difficulty:** Medium

Category: Passport to Advanced Math / Functions

Getting to the Answer: Skim the answer choices. They are all asking about the sign (positive or negative) of $g(x)$ because $g(x) < 0$ means negative and $g(x) > 0$ means positive. When using function notation, $g(x)$ is the same

as y, so you are trying to decide whether (and when) the y-values of the function are negative or positive. The quickest way to do this is to draw a sketch of the function, such as the one shown here:

From the graph, you can see that part of the line will eventually be below the y-axis (or negative) and part above the y-axis (or positive), so you can eliminate choices A and B. To choose between C and D, you'll need to examine the graph more carefully. There are some values of x that are less than 0 (to the left of the vertical axis) for which the y-values are greater than 0, so C is not true either, which means choice (D) must be correct. For all values of x greater than 0, the y-values are in fact all positive (or $g(x) > 0$).

12. A **Difficulty:** Medium

Category: Passport to Advanced Math / Functions

Getting to the Answer: Graphically, the notation $f(3)$ means the y-value when x is 3. Pay careful attention to which graph is which. It may help to draw dots on the graph. Find $x = 3$ on the x-axis, then mark each function at this x-value on the graph as shown here:

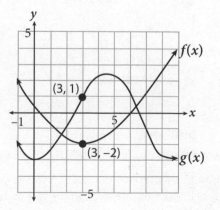

Now read the y-coordinates from the graph and subtract: $f(3)$ is -2 and $g(3)$ is 1, so $f(3) - g(3) = -2 - 1 = -3$, (A).

13. A   Difficulty: Hard

Category: Passport to Advanced Math / Functions

Getting to the Answer: The notation $(f \circ g)(x)$ indicates a composition of two functions that can also be written as $f(g(x))$ and is read "f of g of x." It means that the output when x is substituted into $g(x)$ becomes the input for $f(x)$. Substitute $\frac{1}{4}$ for x in $g(x)$, simplify, and then substitute the result into $f(x)$:

$$g\left(\frac{1}{4}\right) = \sqrt{\frac{1}{4}} + 2.5 = \frac{\sqrt{1}}{\sqrt{4}} + 2.5 = \frac{1}{2} + 2.5 = 3$$

$$f(3) = -4(3) + 1 = -12 + 1 = -11$$

Therefore, $(f \circ g)\left(\frac{1}{4}\right) = -11$, (A).

14. A   Difficulty: Hard

Category: Passport to Advanced Math / Functions

Getting to the Answer: Think about how each transformation affects the graph of $g(x)$, and draw a sketch of $k(x)$ on the same grid. Compare the new graph to each of the answer choices until you find one that is true. The graph of $k(x) = -g(x) - 1$ is a vertical reflection of $g(x)$ over the x-axis that is then shifted down 1 unit. The graph looks like the dashed line here:

Now compare the dashed line to each of the answer choices. The range of $k(x)$ is the set of y-values from lowest to highest (based on the dashed line). The lowest point occurs at the new point B and has a y-value of -5, and the highest value occurs at both ends of the graph and is 1, so the range is $-5 \leq y \leq 1$. This means (A) is correct and you can move on to the next question. Don't waste valuable time checking the other answer choices unless you are not sure about the range. (Choice B: The minimum value of $k(x)$ is -5, not -4. Choice C: The coordinates of point A on $k(x)$ are $(-2, -4)$, not $(2, 0)$. Choice D: The graph of $k(x)$ is decreasing, not increasing, between $x = 0$ and $x = 1$.)

15. D   Difficulty: Hard

Category: Passport to Advanced Math / Functions

Getting to the Answer: When dealing with a composition, the range of the inner function becomes the domain of the outer function, which in turn produces the range of the composition. In the composition $f(g(x))$, the function $g(x) = x^2$ is the inner function. Every value of x, when substituted into this function, will result in a non-negative value (because of the square on x). This means the smallest possible range value of $g(x)$ is 0. Now look at $f(x)$. Substituting large positive values of x in the function will result in large negative numbers. Consequently, substituting the smallest value from the range of g, which is 0, results in the largest range value for the composition, which is $-0 + 5 = 5$. Because $9 > 5$, it is not in the range of $f(g(x))$, making (D) correct.

CHAPTER 6

PRACTICE

8. D **Difficulty:** Medium

Category: Passport to Advanced Math / Quadratics

Getting to the Answer: You'll need to find the y-coordinate of the vertex to discover the maximum height of the projectile. The x-coordinate is given by $h = \dfrac{-b}{2a} = \dfrac{-128}{32} = 4$. Now use that to get the y-coordinate by plugging 4 into the height function:

$$f(4) = -16(4)^2 + 128(4) + 320 = 576$$

Move on to the time it takes for the projectile to hit the ground. You know this will occur when $f(t) = 0$. Plug in and factor to solve:

$$-16t^2 + 128t + 320 = 0$$
$$-16(t^2 - 8t - 20) = 0$$
$$t^2 - 8t - 20 = 0$$
$$(t - 10)(t + 2) = 0$$
$$t = 10 \quad \text{or} \quad t = -2$$

Because you need a positive solution, $t = 10$. Now find the product of 10 and 576 to reveal that (D) must be correct.

9. B **Difficulty:** Medium

Category: Passport to Advanced Math / Quadratics

Getting to the Answer: The y-coordinate will be 0 when the function crosses the x-axis, so plug in points to quickly eliminate A and C. Now FOIL the binomials of the solutions to get a quadratic:

$$f(x) = (x + 2)(x - 5) = x^2 - 3x - 10$$

Calculate the x-coordinate of the vertex of this quadratic: $h = \dfrac{-b}{2a} = \dfrac{3}{2(1)} = \dfrac{3}{2}$. Because (B) and D are in vertex form, simply match to the appropriate function. Recall that form is $f(x) = a(x - h)^2 + k$, so (B) is correct.

PERFORM

10. A **Difficulty:** Easy

Category: Passport to Advanced Math / Quadratics

Getting to the Answer: Rearrange the equation first so you can factor 4 out. From there, divide by 4, then factor as usual:

$$4z^2 + 32z - 81 = -1$$
$$4z^2 + 32z - 80 = 0$$
$$4(z^2 + 8z - 20) = 0$$
$$z^2 + 8z - 20 = 0$$
$$(z + 10)(z - 2) = 0$$

Keep in mind that while z is equal to -10 or 2, the question only asks for the positive value, which is (A). This is very tricky, so read carefully.

11. B **Difficulty:** Hard

Category: Passport to Advanced Math / Quadratics

Getting to the Answer: Because you have variables, you might think to use the Picking Numbers strategy. Unless you coincidentally pick the "right" numbers, you won't actually get an answer choice, but you'll be able to confirm what happens with those numbers. Given the rules of the problem, you might pick $a = -2$ and $b = 3$. Setting up the binomials and performing FOIL, you get:

$$(x + 2)(x - 3) = x^2 - x - 6$$

Unfortunately, this isn't one of the answer choices. What makes this difficult is that when you naturally set up the binomials, you assume the parabola is opening up. If you multiply the entire function by -1, it reflects about the x-axis, but because the solutions are on the x-axis, they will stay the same. The correct answer is (B).

Alternatively, factor each answer choice to determine the solutions of each function. Then see for which function $a < 0$, $b > 0$ and $|b| > |a|$. For choice A, $x = 2$ or -3; $|2|$ is not greater than $|-3|$, so eliminate A. For (B), $x = -2$ or -3; $|3|$ is greater than $|-2|$, so (B) is correct.

12. 0   Difficulty: Easy

Category: Passport to Advanced Math / Quadratics

Getting to the Answer: All the question is really asking you to do is solve for the zeros and subtract them:

$$g(x) = -2x^2 + 16x - 32$$
$$0 = -2x^2 + 16x - 32$$
$$0 = x^2 - 8x + 16$$
$$0 = (x - 4)(x - 4)$$

The quadratic only has one unique solution, 4, so the positive difference between them is actually 0.

13. C   Difficulty: Medium

Category: Passport to Advanced Math / Quadratics

Getting to the Answer: An axis of symmetry splits the parabola in half and travels through the vertex. All you need to do is solve for the *x*-coordinate of the vertex, which can be accomplished using the formula for *h* (the quadratic formula without the square root portion):

$$h = \frac{-b}{2a} = \frac{-4}{2(2)} = \frac{-4}{4} = -1$$

Thus, the answer is (C).

ON YOUR OWN

1. C   Difficulty: Easy

Category: Passport to Advanced Math / Quadratics

Getting to the Answer: Taking the square root is the inverse operation of squaring, and both sides of this equation are already perfect squares, so take their square roots. Then solve the resulting equations. Remember, there will be two equations to solve:

$$(x + 1)^2 = \frac{1}{25}$$
$$\sqrt{(x + 1)^2} = \frac{\sqrt{1}}{\sqrt{25}}$$
$$x + 1 = \pm\frac{1}{5}$$
$$x = -1 \pm \frac{1}{5}$$

Now simplify each equation:

$$x = -1 + \frac{1}{5} = -\frac{5}{5} + \frac{1}{5} = -\frac{4}{5}$$

and

$$x = -1 - \frac{1}{5} = -\frac{5}{5} - \frac{1}{5} = -\frac{6}{5}$$

Choice (C) is correct.

2. B   Difficulty: Easy

Category: Passport to Advanced Math/Quadratics

Getting to the Answer: From the factored form of the equation, you can see that the values of −2 and 7 would make *y* equal 0, so the *x*-intercepts are −2 and 7. This means you can eliminate A and C. From the standard form of the equation, you can see that the *y*-intercept is −14 because $0^2 - 2(0) - 14 = -14$, so (B) is correct.

3. D   Difficulty: Medium

Category: Passport to Advanced Math / Quadratics

Getting to the Answer: Quadratic equations can be written in several forms, each of which reveals something special about the graph. For example, the vertex form of a quadratic equation ($y = a(x - h)^2 + k$) gives the minimum or maximum value of the function (it's *k*), while the standard form ($y = ax^2 + bx + c$) reveals the *y*-intercept (it's *c*). The factored form of a quadratic equation reveals the solutions to the equation, which graphically represent the *x*-intercepts. Choice (D) is the only equation written in factored form and therefore must be correct. You can set each factor equal to 0 and quickly solve to find that the *x*-intercepts of the graph are $x = -\frac{4}{3}$ and $x = 2$, which agree with the graph.

4. B   Difficulty: Medium

Category: Passport to Advanced Math / Quadratics

Getting to the Answer: When finding solutions to a quadratic equation, always start by rewriting the equation to make it equal 0 (unless both sides of the equation are already perfect squares). Then take a peek at the answer choices—if they are all nice numbers, then factoring is probably the quickest method for solving the equation. If the answers include messy fractions or square roots, then using the quadratic formula may be a better choice. To make the equation equal 0, subtract 48 from both sides to get $x^2 + 8x - 48 = 0$. The answer choices are all integers, so factor the equation. Look for two numbers whose product is −48 and whose sum is 8. The two numbers are -4 and 12, so the factors are $(x - 4)$ and $(x + 12)$. Set each factor equal to 0 and solve to find that $x = 4$ and $x = -12$. The question states that $x > 0$, so x must equal 4. Before selecting an answer, don't forget to check that you answered the right question—the question asks for the value of $x - 5$, not just x, so the correct answer is $4 - 5 = -1$, (B).

5. C   Difficulty: Medium

Category: Passport to Advanced Math / Quadratics

Getting to the Answer: Equations that are equivalent have the same solutions, so you are looking for the equation that is simply written in a different form. You could expand each of the equations in the answer choices, but unless you get lucky, this will use up quite a bit of time. The answer choices are written in vertex form, so use the method of completing the square to rewrite the equation given in the question stem. First, subtract the constant, 17, from both sides of the equation. To complete the square on the right-hand side, find $\left(\dfrac{b}{2}\right)^2 = \left(\dfrac{6}{2}\right)^2 = 3^2 = 9$, and add the result to both sides of the equation:

$$y = x^2 + 6x + 17$$
$$y - 17 = x^2 + 6x$$
$$y - 17 + 9 = x^2 + 6x + 9$$
$$y - 8 = x^2 + 6x + 9$$

Next, factor the right-hand side of the equation (which should be a perfect square trinomial), and rewrite it as a square. Finally, solve for y:

$$y - 8 = (x + 3)(x + 3)$$
$$y - 8 = (x + 3)^2$$
$$y = (x + 3)^2 + 8$$

This matches (C).

6. B   Difficulty: Medium

Category: Passport to Advanced Math / Quadratics

Getting to the Answer: Even though one of the equations in this system is not linear, you can still solve the system using substitution. You already know that y is equal to $3x$, so substitute $3x$ for y in the second equation. Don't forget that when you square $3x$, you must square

both the coefficient and the variable:

$$x^2 - y^2 = -288$$
$$x^2 - (3x)^2 = -288$$
$$x^2 - 9x^2 = -288$$
$$-8x^2 = -288$$
$$x^2 = 36$$

The question asks for the value of x^2, not x, so there is no need to take the square root of 36 to find the value of x. Choice (B) is correct.

7. A   Difficulty: Medium

Category: Passport to Advanced Math / Quadratics

Getting to the Answer: The roots of an equation are the same as its solutions. The equation is already written in the form $y = ax^2 + bx + c$ and the coefficients are fairly small, so using the quadratic formula is probably the quickest method. Jot down the values that you'll need: $a = 1$, $b = 8$, and $c = -3$. Then substitute these values into the formula and simplify:

$$x = \frac{-b \pm \sqrt{b^2 - 4ac}}{2a}$$
$$= \frac{-(8) \pm \sqrt{(8)^2 - 4(1)(-3)}}{2(1)}$$
$$= \frac{-8 \pm \sqrt{64 + 12}}{2}$$
$$= \frac{-8 \pm \sqrt{76}}{2}$$

This is not one of the answer choices, which tells you that you'll need to simplify the radical, but before you do, you can eliminate C and D because $\dfrac{-8}{2}$ is -4. To simplify the radical, look for a perfect square that divides into 76 and take its square root:

$$x = \frac{-8 \pm \sqrt{4 \times 19}}{2}$$
$$= \frac{-8 \pm 2\sqrt{19}}{2}$$
$$= -4 \pm \sqrt{19}$$

This matches (A).

8. A   Difficulty: Hard

Category: Passport to Advanced Math / Quadratics

Getting to the Answer: To get a picture of what is going on, you could draw a quick sketch using the information given in the question and what you know about quadratic equations. First, determine the solutions of the equation by thinking about where the x-intercepts, or the zeros, of its graph would be. Because the lead ball is thrown from ground level, the graph would begin at the origin, so one solution is 0. The ball returns to the ground, or has a height of 0 again, at 150 feet, so the other solution is 150. Write the solutions as factors: $x - 0$ and $x - 150$. Then write the equation as the product of the two factors and use the distributive property (or FOIL) to multiply them together: $y = (x - 0)(x - 150) = x(x - 150) = x^2 - 150x$. The general equation is $y = a(x^2 - 150x)$. To find the value of a, use another point that satisfies the equation or, in other words, lies on its graph. Because the graph of a parabola is symmetrical, the ball reaches its maximum height, 45 feet, exactly halfway between the two zeros, 0 and 150, which is 75. Therefore, another point on the graph is (75, 45). Substitute the x- and y-values into the equation and solve for a:

$$y = a(x^2 - 150x)$$
$$45 = a\left(75^2 - 150(75)\right)$$
$$45 = a(5{,}625 - 11{,}250)$$
$$45 = -5{,}625a$$
$$-0.008 = a$$

The equation is $y = -0.008(x^2 - 150x)$ or $y = -0.008x^2 + 1.2x$.

Alternatively, you could evaluate each answer choice to determine for which equation the solution (150, 0) is true: when $x = 150$, does $y = 0$? Or, if you have time, you could graph each equation in your graphing calculator and find the one that has a maximum value of 45. Choice (A) is the only equation for which this is true.

9. B   Difficulty: Medium
Category: Passport to Advanced Math / Quadratics

Getting to the Answer: According to the graph, one x-intercept is to the left of the y-axis, and the other is to the right. This tells you that one value of x is positive, while the other is negative, so you can immediately eliminate choices A and C (both factors have the same sign). To choose between choices (B) and D, find the x-intercepts by setting each factor equal to 0 and solving for x. In choice (B), the x-intercepts are 7 and -3. In choice D, the x-intercepts are 1 and -10. Choice (B) is correct because the

x-intercepts are exactly 10 units apart, while the x-intercepts in choice D are 11 units apart.

10. B   Difficulty: Medium
Category: Passport to Advanced Math / Quadratics

Getting to the Answer: There are no coefficients (numbers) in the equation, so you'll need to think about how the values of a, b, and c affect the graph. You'll also need to recall certain vocabulary. For example, *increasing* means rising from left to right while *decreasing* means falling from left to right, and *zero* is another way of saying x-intercept. Compare each statement to the graph to determine whether it is true, eliminating choices as you go. Remember, you are looking for the statement that is *not* true. The parabola opens downward, so the value of a must be negative, which means you can eliminate A. When a quadratic equation is written in standard form, c is the y-intercept of the parabola. According to the graph, the y-intercept is above the x-axis and is therefore positive, so the statement in (B) is false, making it the correct answer. Move on to the next question. (Choice C is true because the graph rises from left to right until you get to $x = 3$, and then it falls. Choice D is true because the zeros are the same as the x-intercepts, and the graph does intersect the x-axis at -2 and 8.)

11. C   Difficulty: Medium
Category: Passport to Advanced Math / Quadratics

Getting to the Answer: When a quadratic equation is written in vertex form, $y = a(x - h)^2 + k$, the minimum value (or the maximum value if $a < 0$) is given by k, and the axis of symmetry is given by the equation $x = h$. The question states that the minimum of the parabola is -3, so look for an equation where k is -3. You can eliminate choices A and B because k is $+2$ in both equations. The question also states that the axis of symmetry is 2, so h must be 2. Be careful—this is tricky. The equation in choice D is not correct because the vertex form of a parabola has a negative before the h, so $(x + 2)$ actually means $(x - (-2))$, and the axis of symmetry would be -2. This means (C) is correct.

You could also graph each equation in your graphing calculator to see which one matches the criteria given in the question, but this is likely to use up valuable time on Test Day.

12. A   Difficulty: Medium

Category: Passport to Advanced Math / Quadratics

Getting to the Answer: When a quadratic equation is written in vertex form, $y = a(x - h)^2 + k$, the axis of symmetry is given by the equation $x = h$. Don't let the different letters in the equation confuse you. The letter p is simply being used in place of h. Because the h (in the vertex form of a quadratic) has a negative in front of it, the value of h is the opposite sign of the operation performed on h. Here, h (and therefore p) is -5 because $(x - (-5)) = (x + 5)$. So the axis of symmetry is $x = -5$, which is (A).

13. D   Difficulty: Medium

Category: Passport to Advanced Math / Quadratics

Getting to the Answer: Look for an equation that has a maximum value that is less than the one shown in the graph (because Meagan's ball did not go as high). You do not need to graph the equations to determine this. The maximum value shown in the graph is about 31 feet. When a quadratic equation is written in vertex form, $y = a(x - h)^2 + k$, the maximum value is given by k, so check C and D first because they will be the easiest to compare to the graph. In C, k is 35, which is greater than 31 and therefore not correct. In (D), k is 28, which is less than 31 and therefore the correct answer. You do not need to examine the other two equations. Note: If all of the answer choices had been given in standard form, you would have needed to convert each one to vertex form, or you could have substituted the result of finding $\dfrac{-b}{2a}$ into each equation to find the maximum value.

14. A   Difficulty: Hard

Category: Passport to Advanced Math / Quadratics

Getting to the Answer: To answer this question, you need to recall just about everything you've learned about quadratic graphs. The equation is given in vertex form $(y = a(x - h)^2 + k)$, which reveals the vertex (h, k), the direction in which the parabola opens (upward when $a > 0$ and downward when $a < 0$), the axis of symmetry $(x = h)$, and the minimum/maximum value of the function (k).

Start by comparing each answer choice to the equation, $y = -2(x - 6)^2 + 5$. The only choice that you cannot immediately compare is A because vertex form does not

readily reveal the y-intercept, so start with B. Don't forget, you are looking for the statement that is *not* true. Choice B: The axis of symmetry is given by $x = h$, and h is 6, so this statement is true and therefore *not* correct. Choice C: The vertex is given by (h, k), so the vertex is indeed (6, 5) and this choice is not correct. Choice D: The value of a is -2, which indicates that the parabola opens downward, so this choice is also not correct. That means (A) must be the correct answer. To confirm, you could substitute 0 for x in the equation to find the y-intercept:

$$
\begin{aligned}
y &= -2(x - 6)^2 + 5 \\
&= -2(0 - 6)^2 + 5 \\
&= -2(-6)^2 + 5 \\
&= -2(36) + 5 \\
&= -72 + 5 \\
&= -67
\end{aligned}
$$

The y-intercept is $(0, -67)$, not $(0, 5)$, so the statement is false.

15. D   Difficulty: Hard

Category: Passport to Advanced Math / Quadratics

Getting to the Answer: You are not expected to solve each system. Instead, think about it graphically. The solution to a system of equations is the point(s) where their graphs intersect, so graph each pair of equations in your graphing calculator, and look for the ones that intersect at $x = -8$ and $x = -3$. The graphs of the equations in A don't intersect at all, so you can eliminate A right away. The graphs in B and C intersect, but one of the points of intersection for each pair is positive, which means (D) must be correct. The graph looks like the following:

16. 5   Difficulty: Hard

Category: Passport to Advanced Math / Quadratics

Getting to the Answer: Unfortunately, this is a non-calculator question, so you'll need to solve the system using substitution. Substitute the first equation for y into the second. Before you solve for x, multiply the whole equation by 2 to remove the fractions. If you factor along the way, don't forget that you must first set the whole equation equal to 0:

$$x + 1 = \frac{1}{2}x^2 - x - \frac{3}{2}$$

$$2(x + 1) = 2\left(\frac{1}{2}x^2 - x - \frac{3}{2}\right)$$

$$2x + 2 = x^2 - 2x - 3$$

$$0 = x^2 - 4x - 5$$

$$0 = (x + 1)(x - 5)$$

Now set each factor equal to 0 and solve to find that $x = -1$ and $x = 5$. The question only asks for a, which is the x-coordinate of the solution, so you do not need to substitute x back into an equation and solve for y. The two possible values of a are -1 and 5. Because the question specifies that $a > 0$, the answer must be 5.

CHAPTER 7

PRACTICE

7. C   **Difficulty:** Easy

Category: Additional Topics in Math / Geometry

Getting to the Answer: The measures of the interior angles of a triangle must add up to 180, so write an equation that reflects this: $30 + x + (x + 20) = 180$. Simplify the equation to $2x + 50 = 180$, which reduces to $x = 65$. But you're not done yet; this isn't the angle requested. You need an angle that is supplementary to $\angle ACB$. The measure of $\angle ACB$ is $(x + 20)° = (65 + 20)° = 85°$, so the supplementary angle is $180° - 85° = 95°$. This matches (C).

8. 52   **Difficulty:** Medium

Category: Additional Topics in Math / Geometry

Getting to the Answer: First, draw a rectangle to represent the wall space. Next draw another rectangle inside the first to represent the TV. Label the diagram with the information the question provides:

To find the dimensions of the TV, subtract 6 from the length and width of the wall space. Note that many students might erroneously subtract only 3 inches from each dimension, yielding TV dimensions of 25.25∙50. However, the space adds 3 inches on all four sides of the TV, so you should actually subtract 6 inches from the length and width of the wall space. Therefore, the correct TV dimensions are 22.25 × 47.

With the TV dimensions in hand, you can use the Pythagorean theorem to determine the size (a.k.a. the diagonal) of the largest TV that Whitney can fit in this wall space:

$$a^2 + b^2 = c^2$$
$$22.25^2 + 47^2 = c^2$$
$$495.0625 + 2{,}209 = c^2$$
$$2{,}704.0625 = c^2$$
$$52.001 \approx c$$

Grid in 52.

9. 70   **Difficulty:** Medium

Category: Additional Topics in Math / Geometry

Getting to the Answer: The shaded area of the circle is a sector, and x marks a central angle. You're given a vital piece of information about the shaded area: it is $\frac{1}{18}$ of the total circle. This is your area ratio for a circle proportion. You know that a circle contains 360°, so you can find the central angle of the shaded area. Use a variable other than x for this calculation to avoid confusion:

$$\frac{\text{central angle}}{360°} = \frac{\text{sector area}}{\text{circle area}}$$
$$\frac{y}{360} = \frac{1}{18}$$
$$18y = 360$$
$$y = 20$$

The sector marked by A and B has a central angle of 90°. Because $\overline{AD}$ is a diameter, you know this sector combined with the shaded sector and the one marked by x must add up to 180°. That means $x = 180 - 90 - 20 = 70$.

10. D   **Difficulty:** Easy

Category: Additional Topics in Math / Geometry

Getting to the Answer: Pick a pair of manageable numbers to represent the radii when doing your calculations. Suppose the first sphere has a radius of 1 and the second sphere has a radius of 2. That means the volume of the first sphere is $\frac{4}{3}\pi \times 1^3 = \frac{4}{3}\pi$, and the volume of the second sphere is $\frac{4}{3}\pi \times 2^3 = \frac{32}{3}\pi$. The ratio of the volumes is therefore $\frac{4}{3}\pi : \frac{32}{3}\pi$, which simplifies to 1:8, making (D) the correct answer.

You can also use r and $2r$ in your volume calculations: the corresponding volumes of the spheres would be $\frac{4}{3}\pi r^3$ and $\frac{4}{3}\pi(2r)^3 = \frac{32}{3}\pi r^3$. The r^3 and $\frac{4}{3}\pi$ components cancel, leaving 1:8 as the ratio.

PERFORM

11. A   Difficulty: Medium
Category: Additional Topics in Math / Geometry

Getting to the Answer: Although you won't have graph paper on Test Day, drawing a quick sketch is still the quickest path to the correct answer. The coordinates of the vertices are fairly small, so draw a quick grid, plot the vertices of △SNO, and then follow the steps described in the question to determine where △ICE is located. The following coordinate plane shows both:

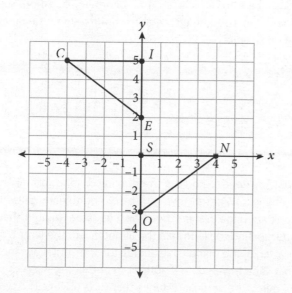

Right away you can see that the y-intercept of the hypotenuse of △ICE is 2, so eliminate B and D. Calculate the slope of the line that forms the hypotenuse: $m = \dfrac{5-2}{-4-0} = -\dfrac{3}{4}$. Choice (A) has the correct equation.

12. D   Difficulty: Medium
Category: Additional Topics in Math / Geometry

Getting to the Answer: The sides of a 30-60-90 triangle are in the ratio $x : x\sqrt{3} : 2x$, so label the triangle accordingly:

The area of a triangle is $A = \dfrac{1}{2}bh$, and you're told that the area of this triangle is $8\sqrt{3}$. Substitute this for A and use the side lengths from the ratio. Then solve for x:

$$8\sqrt{3} = \frac{1}{2}(x)(x\sqrt{3})$$
$$8 = \frac{1}{2}x^2$$
$$16 = x^2$$
$$\pm 4 = x$$

Length must be positive, so the value of x is 4. This matches A, but you're not done yet! You solved for x, which is the length of $\overline{CB}$. The question asks for the length of $\overline{AB}$, which is twice $\overline{CB}$, so the correct answer is 8, which is (D).

13. A   Difficulty: Medium
Category: Additional Topics in Math / Geometry

Getting to the Answer: You can use Picking Numbers, but the math is simple enough that straight algebra will be quicker. First, find the area of the rectangle $A_{\text{rect}} = lw = 5x \cdot 2x = 10x^2$. You're told that $\overline{AB}$ and $\overline{DC}$ are tangent to the circle, so they touch the circle only once, meaning there is no space between the circle and rectangle. Therefore, the circle's diameter equals the width of the rectangle ($2x$), and the radius must be half that, or x. The area of the circle is $A_{\text{circle}} = \pi r^2 = \pi x^2$. This makes the area of the shaded portion $10x^2 - \pi x^2$, which is (A).

14. 44   Difficulty: Hard

Category: Additional Topics in Math / Geometry

Getting to the Answer: Identify familiar 2-D shapes present in the solid that will aid you. The base of the paperweight is a square with a diagonal of length $2\sqrt{2}$ centimeters. The diagonal of a square cuts the square into two 45-45-90 triangles, so each side of the square base is 2 centimeters. The height of the paperweight is 50% larger than this; therefore, it is $1.5 \times 2 = 3$ centimeters high. Plug these values into the volume formula for a right pyramid: $V = \dfrac{1}{3}(2 \times 2) \times 3 = 4$ cubic centimeters. The volume of water in the rectangular box is $2 \times 4 \times 6 = 48$ cubic centimeters. The paperweight displaces 4 cubic centimeters of this water, so the answer is $48 - 4 = 44$.

ON YOUR OWN

1. D   Difficulty: Easy

Category: Additional Topics in Math / Geometry

Getting to the Answer: The sides of a 30-60-90 triangle are in the ratio $x : x\sqrt{3} : 2x$. Don't forget—this ratio is provided for you on the formula page at the beginning of each math section of the PSAT. Because 17 feet is opposite the 30° angle, the hypotenuse will be twice its length, or $17 \times 2 = 34$ feet, (D).

2. C   Difficulty: Medium

Category: Additional Topics in Math / Geometry

Getting to the Answer: First, use the coordinate grid to figure out the dimensions of the triangle. Point B has the same x-coordinate as A and the same y-coordinate as C, so its coordinates are $(-3, -2)$. The length of $\overline{AB}$ is $5 - (-2) = 5 + 2 = 7$, and the length of $\overline{BC}$ is $4 - (-3) = 4 + 3 = 7$.

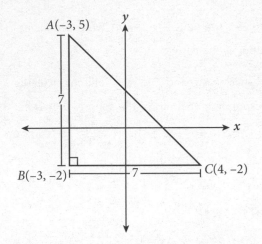

Because the triangle is a right triangle with equal leg lengths, it must be a 45-45-90 triangle, so the measure of angle ACB is 45 degrees, or (C).

3. A   Difficulty: Medium

Category: Additional Topics in Math / Geometry

Getting to the Answer: Many geometry questions require adding lines to the figure given. If you're not sure where to get started on a geometry question, see if you can add a line to make a right triangle or other familiar figure:

First you need to find the straight-line distance from W to Z. Think of $\overline{WZ}$ as the hypotenuse of a right triangle. If you can determine the lengths of the legs of the triangle, then you can find the length of the hypotenuse. The length of one leg of the triangle is 24 miles, the horizontal distance that Gina travels. The length of the other leg is $7 + 3 = 10$ miles, the vertical distance that Gina travels. The two legs of the right triangle are 10 and 24. Now, apply the Pythagorean theorem:

$$\overline{WZ}^2 = 24^2 + 10^2$$
$$= 576 + 100$$
$$= 676$$
$$\overline{WZ} = \sqrt{676} = 26$$

The route shown in the figure is $7 + 24 + 3 = 34$ miles long. The direct route is 26 miles, so if Gina were able to travel from W to Z directly, her trip would be $34 - 26 = 8$ miles shorter, which is (A).

4. D   **Difficulty:** Hard
Category: Additional Topics in Math / Geometry

Getting to the Answer: Recall that the sides of a 30-60-90 triangle are in the ratio $x : x\sqrt{3} : 2x$. Because $\overline{JK} = 2$ and JKM is a 30-60-90 triangle, $\overline{JM} = 2\sqrt{3}$. The question tells you that M is the midpoint of $\overline{JL}$, so $\overline{JL} = 2\left(2\sqrt{3}\right) = 4\sqrt{3}$. The question is asking for $\overline{KL}$, the hypotenuse of JKL, so use the Pythagorean theorem:

$$c^2 = a^2 + b^2$$
$$= 2^2 + \left(4\sqrt{3}\right)^2$$
$$= 4 + 16(3)$$
$$= 4 + 48$$
$$c^2 = 52$$
$$c = \sqrt{52} = \sqrt{4 \times 13} = 2\sqrt{13}$$

This matches (D).

5. B   **Difficulty:** Hard
Category: Additional Topics in Math / Geometry

Getting to the Answer: In a right triangle, one leg is the base, and the other is the height. Use x and $x + 4$ to represent the lengths of these two legs. Use the area formula and set the equation equal to the given area:

$$48 = \frac{1}{2}(x)(x + 4)$$
$$2(48) = 2\left[\frac{1}{2}(x)(x + 4)\right]$$
$$96 = (x)(x + 4)$$
$$96 = x^2 + 4x$$

Now, subtract 96 to make the equation equal 0 and then factor it. The factors are $(x + 12)$ and $(x - 8)$, which means $x = -12$ and $x = 8$. Lengths cannot be negative, so the shorter leg must have a length of 8. This means the longer leg has a length of $8 + 4 = 12$. Now use the Pythagorean theorem to find the length of the hypotenuse:

$$a^2 + b^2 = c^2$$
$$8^2 + 12^2 = c^2$$
$$64 + 144 = c^2$$
$$208 = c^2$$
$$\sqrt{208} = \sqrt{c^2}$$
$$\sqrt{16 \times 13} = c$$
$$4\sqrt{13} = c$$

Choice (B) is correct.

6. D   **Difficulty:** Medium
Category: Additional Topics in Math / Geometry

Getting to the Answer: Corresponding sides of similar triangles are proportional. This means the perimeters of similar triangles are also proportional and in the same proportion as each pair of corresponding side lengths.

Find the perimeter of $\triangle CAT$ and compare it to the perimeter of $\triangle DOG$. $\triangle CAT$ has a perimeter of $7 + 12 + 15 = 34$. The perimeter of $\triangle DOG$ is $\frac{51}{34} = 1.5$ times larger than the perimeter of $\triangle CAT$, so each side length of $\triangle DOG$ must be 1.5 times longer than the corresponding side of $\triangle CAT$. The longest side of $\triangle CAT$ is 15, so the longest side of $\triangle DOG$ is $15 \times 1.5 = 22.5$, which is (D).

7. 81/2 or 40.5   **Difficulty:** Hard
Category: Additional Topics in Math / Geometry

Getting to the Answer: To find the area of a triangle, you need to know the lengths of its base and height. Try drawing a sketch to determine these lengths.

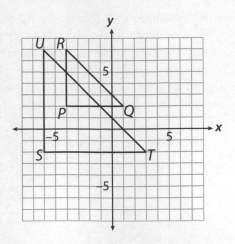

Similar triangles have congruent angles. Based on the sketch, $\triangle PQR$ is a right triangle with leg lengths of 5 and 5, making it a 45-45-90 triangle. Because $\triangle STU$ is similar, it must also be a 45-45-90 triangle. $\overline{ST}$ has length 9, so $\overline{SU}$ must also have length 9. In a right triangle, the legs form the base and the height, so the area of the triangle is $\frac{1}{2}(9)(9) = \frac{1}{2}(81) = 40.5$.

8. 36   **Difficulty:** Hard

Category: Additional Topics in Math / Geometry

Getting to the Answer: There are two right triangles in the diagram—the smaller one that has a base of 3 feet and a height of 4.5 feet (the height of the boy converted to feet) and the larger one that has a base of $3 + 21 = 24$ feet and an unknown height (the height of the pole). The two triangles share one angle (the small angle on the left side), and each has a 90° angle (where the boy and the pole meet the ground), making the third pair of corresponding angles also congruent. This means the triangles are similar by AAA.

Because the triangles are similar, their sides are in proportion. Writing the proportion in words first will help you stay organized:

$$\frac{\text{height of boy}}{\text{distance along ground}} = \frac{\text{height of pole}}{\text{distance along ground}}$$

$$\frac{4.5}{3} = \frac{h}{24}$$

$$4.5(24) = 3h$$

$$108 = 3h$$

$$36 = h$$

The height of the telephone pole is 36 feet.

9. B   **Difficulty:** Easy

Category: Additional Topics in Math / Geometry

Getting to the Answer: Use the relationship $\frac{\text{arc length}}{\text{circumference}} = \frac{\text{central angle}}{360°}$ to answer this question. To help you remember this relationship, just think $\frac{\text{partial distance}}{\text{whole distance}} = \frac{\text{partial angle}}{\text{whole angle}}$.

The unknown in this question is the arc length, so call it a. You need to find the circumference of the circle before you set up the relationship. The question tells you that the radius ($\overline{OC}$) is 9, so use the formula $C = 2\pi r$ to find that the circumference is $2\pi(9) = 18\pi$. The answers are given in terms of π, so don't simplify any further. You also know that the central angle has a measure of 100°, so you're ready to set up and solve the relationship:

$$\frac{\text{arc length}}{\text{circumference}} = \frac{\text{central angle}}{360°}$$

$$\frac{a}{18\pi} = \frac{100}{360}$$

$$360a = 1{,}800\pi$$

$$a = \frac{1{,}800}{360}\pi$$

$$a = 5\pi$$

Choice (B) is correct.

10. A   **Difficulty:** Medium

Category: Additional Topics in Math / Geometry

Getting to the Answer: Add any information you have to the figure. For instance, $\angle ADC$ must be 90 degrees, since it is one corner of a square. This means the shaded sector is equal to $360° \div 90° = \frac{1}{4}$ of the total area of the circle.

Now, find the length of one side of the square. The perimeter of a square is 4 times the length of a side. Because the perimeter of this square is 24, a side of this square has length $24 \div 4 = 6$. One side is equal to the radius of the circle, so the radius is also 6. This means the area of the circle is $\pi(6)^2 = 36\pi$. So, the area of the shaded portion is $36\pi \div 4 = 9\pi$, which is (A).

11. B   Difficulty: Medium
Category: Additional Topics in Math / Geometry

Getting to the Answer: The equation of a circle takes the form $(x - h)^2 + (y - k)^2 = r^2$, where (h, k) is the center of the circle and r is the length of the radius. This means that to find the equation of a circle, you need the radius and the x- and y-coordinates of the center point. Look at the figure—Q and R lie on a diameter of the circle, so the center must lie halfway between them on the x-axis. The diameter of the circle is the length of $\overline{QR}$, or $1.5 - (-2.5)$ $= 4$. Therefore, the radius is 2 and the x-coordinate of the center point is $-2.5 + 2 = -0.5$. This means the center is $(-0.5, 0)$, and the equation of the circle is $(x - (-0.5))^2$ $+ (y - 0)^2 = 2^2$, or $(x + 0.5)^2 + y^2 = 4$. That's choice (B).

12. B   Difficulty: Hard
Category: Additional Topics in Math / Geometry

Getting to the Answer: When the equation of a circle is in the form $(x - h)^2 + (y - k)^2 = r^2$, the r is the radius. To get the equation into this form, complete the square. You already have an x^2 and a y^2 in the given equation and the coefficients of x and y are even, so completing the square is fairly straightforward—there are just a lot of steps. Start by grouping the x's and y's together. Then, take the coefficient of the x term and divide it by 2, square it, and add it to the two terms with x variables. Do the same with the y term. Don't forget to add these amounts to the other side of the equation as well. This creates a perfect square of x terms and y terms, so take the square root of each:

$$x^2 + y^2 + 4x - 12y = 41$$
$$x^2 + 4x + y^2 - 12y = 41$$
$$(x^2 + 4x + 4) + (y^2 - 12y + 36) = 41 + 4 + 36$$
$$(x + 2)^2 + (y - 6)^2 = 81$$

The equation tells you that r^2 is 81, which means that the radius is 9 and the diameter is twice that, or 18. Choice (B) is correct.

13. C   Difficulty: Medium
Category: Additional Topics in Math / Geometry

Getting to the Answer: After it's poured, the volume of the milk in the cylinder will still be the same volume as the rectangular container. The volume of the rectangular container is $4 \times 9 \times 10$, or 360 cubic inches. The volume

of a cylinder equals the area of its base times its height, or $\pi r^2 h$. Because the diameter is 6 inches, the radius, r, is 3 inches.

Now we're ready to set up an equation to solve for h (which is the height of the milk):

Volume of milk $=$ Volume of rectangular container
$$\pi(3)^2 h = 360$$
$$h = \frac{360}{9\pi} = \frac{40}{\pi}$$

This matches (C).

14. B   Difficulty: Easy
Category: Additional Topics in Math / Geometry

Getting to the Answer: Don't forget to refer to the reference page provided for you on Test Day rather than trying to memorize all the area and volume formulas that you might encounter. The volume of a regular pyramid is given by $V = \frac{1}{3}Bh$, where B is the area of the base and h is the height. Here, the base is a square, so write the formula as $V = \frac{1}{3}s^2h$, where s represents the length of one side of the base.

Because you're given the volume and the height of the pyramid, plug them into the formula and solve for s:

$$V = \frac{1}{3}s^2h$$
$$11{,}100 = \frac{1}{3}s^2(37)$$
$$3(11{,}100) = 3\left(\frac{1}{3}s^2(37)\right)$$
$$33{,}300 = 37s^2$$
$$900 = s^2$$
$$\sqrt{900} = s$$
$$30 = s$$

Therefore, the length of one side of the base is 30 meters, or (B).

15. C   Difficulty: Medium
Category: Additional Topics in Math / Geometry

Getting to the Answer: Be careful—the question asks for the volume in *cubic feet*, but the figure shows the dimensions of the building in yards. You must first convert the yards to feet (by multiplying each dimension by 3); then you can find the volume in cubic feet using the formula $V = l \times w \times h$. Write the conversions on the figure so you don't forget.

To find the volume of the building, imagine splitting the figure into two rectangular prisms as shown in the figure:

Then use the volume formula, $V = l \times w \times h$, to find the volume of each prism. The shorter prism on the left has a length of 210 ft − 120 ft = 90 feet, a width of 120 feet, and a height of 150 feet, so the volume of this prism is 90 × 120 × 150 = 1,620,000 cubic feet. The taller prism on the right has a length of 120 feet, a width of 120 feet, and a height of 300 feet, so the volume of this prism is 120 × 120 × 300 = 4,320,000 cubic feet. The total volume of space inside the building is 1,620,000 + 4,320,000 = 5,940,000 cubic feet, which is (C).

16. B   Difficulty: Medium

Category: Additional Topics in Math / Geometry

Getting to the Answer: Find the diameter of each sphere using the volume formula. Be careful—the formula gives the radius, not the diameter, so after you solve for r, be sure to multiply it by 2 to find the diameter. Start with the smaller sphere:

$$V = \frac{4}{3}\pi r^3$$

$$\frac{4}{3}\pi = \frac{4}{3}\pi r^3$$

$$\frac{4}{3} = \frac{4}{3}r^3$$

$$1 = r^3$$

$$1 = r \rightarrow d = 2$$

Now, the large sphere:

$$36\pi = \frac{4}{3}\pi r^3$$

$$36 = \frac{4}{3}r^3$$

$$3(36) = \cancel{3}\left(\frac{4}{\cancel{3}}r^3\right)$$

$$108 = 4r^3$$

$$27 = r^3$$

$$3 = r \rightarrow d = 6$$

Therefore, the diameter of the larger sphere is 6 − 2 = 4 units longer than the smaller sphere, (B).

CHAPTER 8

PRACTICE

Suggested Passage Map notes:

¶1: panda classification controversy

¶2: homologous trait categorization

¶3: analogous trait categorization

7. C   **Difficulty:** Medium
Category: Inference

Getting to the Answer: Review your notes from the second and third paragraphs to determine how these two paragraphs differ. Your notes for the second paragraph should focus on homologous traits; the third paragraph focuses on analogous traits. Choice (C) accurately depicts the difference between the paragraphs.

8. B   **Difficulty:** Easy
Category: Vocab-in-Context

Getting to the Answer: Remember, the author *must* explain unfamiliar terms through context in the passage. In the cited line, the author discusses classifying. When you check your Passage Map, you'll find the word "taxonomists" in the first paragraph in the discussion about classifying pandas. Choice (B) is, therefore, the correct answer.

PERFORM

Suggested Passage Map notes:

¶1: influence of autos in U.S. (purpose)

¶2: manufacturing: U.S. v. Europe, pros v. cons

¶3: pop. dist. impact: examples

¶4: personal impact: examples

9. C   **Difficulty:** Hard
Category: Rhetoric

Getting to the Answer: This is a Rhetoric question in which you are asked to analyze the purpose of part of the passage. Lines 18–22 are part of the author's discussion, in the second paragraph, of changes to the American workplace brought about by the car. The author mentions

the fact that American factories used assembly lines (as opposed to European factories, which did not) in order to emphasize the value that was placed on efficiency, as opposed to workers' pride in the product, in American factories. That's choice (C).

10. C   **Difficulty:** Easy
Category: Inference

Getting to the Answer: Determine the author's reasoning using context. The author uses the key word "unlike" to show contrast. The passage states that railroads brought people together, while cars brought people apart. Choice (C) correctly expresses this idea.

11. C   **Difficulty:** Medium
Category: Vocab-in-Context

Getting to the Answer: On Vocab-in-Context questions, it's often helpful to use a one-word paraphrase as your prediction. The author's purpose is to explain how cars have "greatly" affected American life, so look for a similar word among the answer choices. Choice (C) matches. Choice A is extreme; an "absolute" effect would mean that there are no other influences. Choice B doesn't make sense in context. Choice D is related to a common meaning of "profound," as when an idea is described as profound. It doesn't fit here, however, as "effects" cannot be "thoughtful."

ON YOUR OWN

Suggested Passage Map notes:

¶1: BSW alone; on other's land

¶2: Who am I? must prove membership for land

¶3: In. tradition = not say name; asked by gov official for parents; orphan

¶4: tradition = not speak of dead; unknown family

¶5: proud of name; puzzled by changes/laws; (theme): ? identity

1. B   **Difficulty:** Easy
Category: Global

Getting to the Answer: Predict the main theme and narrative direction of the passage. The author's focus is on Blue-Star Woman and the effect of a changing world on her identity. Only (B) accurately describes the theme of this story.

2. A Difficulty: Medium
Category: Rhetoric

Getting to the Answer: Predict a reason why the author would use the term identified in the question stem. In the lines surrounding the cited phrase, Blue-Star Woman is compared to the ground squirrel, a creature living in nature. The author has chosen this simile to reinforce the connection between Blue-Star Woman and the natural world. Choice (A) is therefore correct.

3. C Difficulty: Medium
Category: Vocab-in-Context

Getting to the Answer: Predict a synonym for the word in question while making sure your selection also makes sense in the context of the passage. Because the landowner's attitude toward Blue-Star Woman's occupation of his land is described as "easy tolerance" (line 7), you can assume that Blue-Star Woman is allowed to stay there. Choice (C), "permission," conveys this idea.

4. D Difficulty: Hard
Category: Vocab-in-Context

Getting to the Answer: Predict a synonym for the word presented in the question stem within the context of the passage; then select the answer choice that most closely matches that synonym. A good prediction would be a word like *thought*. The text of the passage following the word in the question stem ("abstraction") is about Blue-Star Woman's careful consideration of the nature of her identity and proper place in the world. Choice (D) most accurately describes her thoughts. Although she has questions about her identity, C is incorrect because she has certainty about the natural promptings of the "law of heart" (line 17); she says, "I am being. I am Blue-Star Woman. A piece of earth is my birthright" (lines 18–19).

5. B Difficulty: Medium
Category: Inference

Getting to the Answer: Predict the central idea of the selection quoted in the question stem. Analyze the quotation along with its context in the passage to arrive at the correct answer. Throughout the passage, Blue-Star

Woman's name is a symbol of her identity and culture. For example, "Blue-Star Woman was her individual name" (lines 46–47). By stating that her name seems meaningless, the author implies that Blue-Star Woman's culture and customs are also losing their meaning. This is reflected in choice (B).

6. B Difficulty: Medium
Category: Command of Evidence

Getting to the Answer: Answer choices to Command of Evidence questions are listed in the order they appear within the passage. The correct answer to the previous question establishes that Blue-Star Woman's traditional culture and customs are losing their relevance. Choice (B) most clearly supports the idea that Native American customs are losing relevance by confirming that an old custom has since been disregarded.

7. A Difficulty: Medium
Category: Inference

Getting to the Answer: Read the context of the quoted selections to predict the difference between the two types of "laws." In the second paragraph, the formal nature of "the white man's law" (line 15) is contrasted with Blue-Star Woman's more emotional view of what is right. While the government's law requires proof of tribal membership, the "unwritten law of heart" (line 17) grants a person a piece of earth by virtue of her existence, as a "birthright" (line 19). This is reflected in choice (A).

8. B Difficulty: Medium
Category: Inference

Getting to the Answer: Use your Passage Map to find the parts of the passage that mention the government official to develop a full understanding of his relationship with Blue-Star Woman. The author writes that the official persistently asks Blue-Star Woman who her parents are, even though she doesn't know and would have a cultural aversion to telling him if she did. His behavior is best described by choice (B).

9. C Difficulty: Medium
Category: Command of Evidence

Getting to the Answer: The correct answer to a Command of Evidence question is the excerpt that best *supports* the answer to a previous question, not the excerpt that describes the correct answer or itself answers the previous question. The correct answer to the previous question states that the government official "lacks cultural empathy" and is "unable to understand Blue-Star Woman's difficulties." The correct answer will provide evidence for both of these claims. Choice (C) explains why Blue-Star Woman's culture would make her unwilling to tell the government official her parents' names. The government official is unaware of this custom, so he cannot comprehend why Blue-Star Woman would withhold the information.

CHAPTER 9

PRACTICE

Suggested Passage Map notes:

Passage 1

¶1: argue U.S. reform campaigns; why: costly, too long, ads mean

Passage 2

¶1: argue U.S. elections more democratic if: (1) require debate & (2) law = all vote

4. B   **Difficulty:** Easy
Category: Synthesis

Getting to the Answer: Read this question carefully—it's asking what *element* the passages have in common. The answer is going to be more about form than content. This question asks about similarities, and though the authors aren't disputing each other, they each have very different purposes for writing the passages. Making a specific prediction may be difficult, so evaluate answer choices to find an element that both passages utilize. Both mention other countries in support of their arguments. Choice (B) is correct.

5. B   **Difficulty:** Medium
Category: Synthesis

Getting to the Answer: Just because you pick "Yes" or "No" in questions like these doesn't mean you are done. You have to read both remaining answer choices carefully to decide which one supports your answer. Author 1 would likely agree with something that could improve American election campaigns. Eliminate C and D. Author 2 proposes requiring candidates to debate, enabling the voters to consider "candidates' positions on issues" (line 25). Author 1 argues that campaigns should be cheaper, shorter, and friendlier. Predict that a reason for requiring debates within these parameters would be agreeable to author 1. Choice (B) is correct.

6. C   **Difficulty:** Hard
Category: Synthesis

Getting to the Answer: Read the question closely. You're looking for an answer choice that would undermine the

argument. When you examine the infographic, you will notice that there is no information about where the voter turnout is being counted. When you look at the trend, you see that wherever this is, the turnout is trending down. Remember the relevant part of author 2's argument: U.S. national elections would be more democratic if there were mandatory voting. Think about situations that could be true of the graph that would weaken this argument. A prediction that the graph shows voter turnout after voting became mandatory would weaken the argument, because the trend on the graph is a decline in turnout. Choice (C) matches this prediction.

PERFORM

Suggested Passage Map notes:

Passage 1

¶1: invasive definition; problems; snakehead ex.

¶2: actions to contain; U.S. too slow

¶3: (central idea): must work together to fix

Passage 2

¶1: attention on invasive; inv. = problem; exs.; other issues; media role

¶2: lack of evidence; ex.; need data; (central idea): balance

7. B   **Difficulty:** Medium
Category: Synthesis

Getting to the Answer: Think about the central idea of each passage and how they differ. The author of Passage 1 wants groups to work together to make invasive species a "priority" (line 39). While the author of Passage 2 agrees that "containing invasive species is a worthwhile goal" (lines 70–71), the passage concludes that available resources need to be balanced among various problems. Predict that author 2 considers invasive species just one issue to worry about. Choice (B) matches that prediction.

8. D   **Difficulty:** Medium
Category: Synthesis

Getting to the Answer: Sometimes, you won't be able to make a specific prediction. Just keep in mind the central idea of each passage and consider what they have in common. Be careful to avoid answers that reflect the view of only one author. Although the authors differ in their views of which environmental issues are most important, they agree that such issues should be addressed. Therefore, choice (D) is correct.

9. B **Difficulty:** Medium
Category: Synthesis

Getting to the Answer: Pay attention to which passage a question stem cites. This will help you avoid incorrect answer choices. The question stem points you to the part of the infographic you need: the National Invasive Species Council. Checking for trends shows that they spend a good deal of money fighting the problem. Your notes should mention that the author sees some hope for the future if different groups work together (lines 37–44). Predict that the author thinks the organization is one of those groups. Choice (B) matches that prediction.

ON YOUR OWN

Suggested Passage Map notes:

Passage 1

¶1: (central idea): Bio. 2 mission - followed? interest down
¶2: problems; criticisms; result: doubt data

Passage 2

¶1: Bio. 2 failed; (central idea): media relations changed
¶2: lots of publicity; high expectations; turned negative

1. B **Difficulty:** Easy
Category: Vocab-in-Context

Getting to the Answer: Read around the cited word, looking for the context clues to predict a word that could substitute for "exploded." The word "exploded" is used in the context of unwanted numbers of bugs. Predict that the populations grew a lot. Choice (B) matches that prediction.

2. C **Difficulty:** Easy
Category: Command of Evidence

Getting to the Answer: Use your Passage Map to find the author's claim and how the author supports it. In the first paragraph, the author states that serious questions were raised about the project. In the second paragraph, the author details the problems and actions that raised those questions. Choice (C) is correct.

3. A **Difficulty:** Medium
Category: Rhetoric

Getting to the Answer: Make sure to summarize the purpose of the paragraph to identify the connection that builds to the central idea. Review your Passage Map for the second paragraph. It should move from problems to results. This reflects a cause-and-effect relationship, choice (A).

4. B **Difficulty:** Hard
Category: Inference

Getting to the Answer: Use your Passage Map to review author 1's point of view. Author 1 would likely agree that how the project was conducted cast doubt on its results. Only choice (B) fits these parameters.

5. C **Difficulty:** Medium
Category: Vocab-in-Context

Getting to the Answer: Read around the cited word to figure out its meaning in context and make a prediction. Because the press called it "the most exciting scientific project . . ." (lines 64–65), the scientists must have wanted to slow things down and make the project's goals more realistic. Predict *curb* or *lower*. Choice (C) is correct.

6. C **Difficulty:** Medium
Category: Synthesis

Getting to the Answer: Use your Passage Map to find the same topic in Passage 1. Passage 1 specifically states that food and oxygen were two things that were introduced from the outside. The quote from lines 39–41 makes it sound as though the project was self-sufficient. Therefore, the author of Passage 1 would consider the statement misleading. Choice (C) matches.

7. C   **Difficulty:** Medium

Category: Command of Evidence

Getting to the Answer: Check the lines cited in each answer choice and match them against the evidence you found for your prediction for the previous question. Where does the author of Passage 1 mention food and oxygen? Predict: lines 26–30. Choice (C) matches.

8. D   **Difficulty:** Hard

Category: Synthesis

Getting to the Answer: Review your Passage Map, looking for the central idea of each passage. Consider how they differ; this will be your prediction. Passage 1 describes the problems with the project itself, resulting in the questioning of its findings. Passage 2 focuses on press relations. Choice (D) reflects this difference in focus.

9. C   **Difficulty:** Medium

Category: Synthesis

Getting to the Answer: Make sure to follow the Kaplan Method for Infographics: analyze the question, examine the parts and trends of the infographic, and make a prediction. Pay close attention to what this question is asking for: the most *consistently* published experiment. If you misread this question as asking for the research published most often, you will choose B, which is a trap. The most consistently published type of experiment is manipulative experiments; not only is it the only type that was published every year listed on the chart, but also the numbers across years are more similar to each other than those of other categories. Choice (C) is correct.

10. A   **Difficulty:** Hard

Category: Synthesis

Getting to the Answer: Identify the purpose of each passage and then combine those purposes. The purpose of Passage 2 is to show the changing perceptions about the project. Passage 1 provides specific reasons for those changing perceptions. Only choice (A) correctly combines these purposes.

CHAPTER 10

PRACTICE

Suggested Passage Map notes:

¶1: description of sedimentary = water made

¶2: types of sedimentary rocks

¶3: how fossils are created in most common sed. rocks

¶4: use of fossils in science

4. D **Difficulty:** Easy
Category: Global

Getting to the Answer: Summarize the central idea of the passage even when you can't make a specific prediction. It's tough to make a specific prediction before looking at the answer choices, but you do know that the author thinks fossils are great. Choice (D) makes sense; fossils are important because they provide "windows into the past" (lines 9–10) and are a "vital source of information about animals, insects, and plants from long ago" (lines 50–51).

5. D **Difficulty:** Hard
Category: Rhetoric

Getting to the Answer: Beware of details that are true but not relevant to the question at hand. After making this statement, the author asserts that limestone can be formed when lime settles to the bottom of the ocean or when the shells of sea creatures collect. Lines 22–30 support the assertion that limestone is complex because it can be created in a variety of ways. Choice (D) matches this and is, therefore, correct.

6. B **Difficulty:** Easy
Category: Command of Evidence

Getting to the Answer: Whether or not you used specific lines of text to answer the question preceding a Command of Evidence question, start looking for the answer in the general portion of the passage that led you to your previous answer. In answering the previous question, you established that limestone can be created

in different ways by reviewing lines 22–30. Eliminate C because, although it was a part of the general support for the previous question, it isn't the best evidence to support the various ways limestone can be formed. Choice (B) details these different ways and is correct.

PERFORM

Suggested Passage Map notes:

¶1: Norse colonies disappeared; reason unclear

¶2: theory of decline due to massacre; not proven

¶3: new theories due to climate change; study of fly remains to support theory

¶4: economic changes part of Norse decline; trade between other countries bypassed the Norse

¶5: Norse decline due to culture and social problems; Norse did not adapt to needs of environment

7. A **Difficulty:** Medium
Category: Global

Getting to the Answer: After reading a passage, you should be able to predict a general purpose for the passage. Be careful not to make your prediction overly specific. The author discusses the disappearance of a group of Norse settlers and offers a number of explanations for this occurrence; he does not seem to advocate any one explanation over another. Predict that the main purpose is to explain possible reasons for the disappearance. Choice (A) matches this prediction.

8. A **Difficulty:** Medium
Category: Inference

Getting to the Answer: This question requires you to put together details from different parts of the passage. The author writes, "a particularly warm period for Greenland ... occurred between the years 800 c.e. and 1300 c.e." (lines 36–38). The beginning of the passage states that the colony was founded around the year 1000 c.e., right in the middle of the warm period. Choice (A) works. The "mild," warm weather was uncharacteristic of the usually cold, harsh climate.

9. B   **Difficulty:** Medium
Category: Command of Evidence

Getting to the Answer: If you used a line reference to answer the previous question, start by seeing whether that line reference is one of the answer choices. In answering the previous question, you determined that the climate during the initial founding of the Norse settlements was "uncharacteristically mild." This strange, mild weather is detailed in lines 36–38, choice (B).

ON YOUR OWN

Suggested Passage Map notes:

    ¶1: R: keep mind active; feeling her age

    ¶2: R reflecting on past; sees V as lazy

    ¶3: V takes school for granted; R wanted more schooling

    ¶4–11: father refused to let R continue school, R regrets

1. A   **Difficulty:** Medium
Category: Rhetoric

Getting to the Answer: Look for the answer choice that best paraphrases Rosemary's attitude toward aging. The last three sentences of the first paragraph (lines 14–19) explicitly discuss Rosemary's attitude toward old age: "At 87 years of age, she was glad she could still write at all. She had decided long ago that growing old was like slowly turning to stone; you couldn't take anything for granted." This attitude is best summarized by choice (A).

2. D   **Difficulty:** Easy
Category: Detail

Getting to the Answer: When you read the lines around the cited text, you see that the trip, though short, "seemed to take a long while" (line 21) and that Rosemary "often experienced an expanded sense of time" (lines 22–23). Identify the answer choice that describes this explicit meaning. Choice (D) restates this perfectly, because "elastic" means to be able to expand and contract.

3. D   **Difficulty:** Easy
Category: Inference

Getting to the Answer: Reread the section of the passage that describes Rosemary's first day of high school to develop a firm understanding of her memory of that day. The question refers to Rosemary on that "glorious day" (line 65) when she was going to high school. She gets up, puts on her "best dress . . . her heart racing in anticipation" (lines 66–67). This points to choice (D) as the correct answer.

4. C   **Difficulty:** Medium
Category: Command of Evidence

Getting to the Answer: Identify the answer choice that is the best supporting evidence for the idea expressed in the answer to the previous question. The correct answer to the previous question established that Rosemary was eager to start high school and continue her education using lines 64–67. Choice (C) most clearly demonstrates that by describing how she had begged her father for permission to continue her studies.

5. C   **Difficulty:** Hard
Category: Rhetoric

Getting to the Answer: When you see the words "in order to" in a question stem, rephrase that question as a "why" question. For example: Why did the author include Rosemary's thoughts regarding her grandson in lines 38–44? Choice (C) details why the author includes Rosemary's thoughts on her grandson; these musings set the stage for her memories of her own educational frustrations as a child, which is quite different from her perception of Victor's life as easy. While B is tempting, it is presented as a fact; it may be true that Victor does not appreciate how fortunate he is, but you cannot know this for sure, as the passage is filtered through Rosemary's perspective. Choice (C) is correct.

6. C   **Difficulty:** Hard
Category: Command of Evidence

Getting to the Answer: Review how you answered the previous question to answer Command of Evidence questions. Choice (C) continues where the passage cited in the previous question left off. In the lines cited by choice (C), the author makes the juxtaposition between Victor's and Rosemary's experiences more explicit.

7. C   Difficulty: Medium

Category: Vocab-in-Context

Getting to the Answer: Predict a close synonym for the word in question, while making sure your selection also makes sense in context of the passage. The sentence that follows "sturdy" talks about Rosemary's responsibilities as a child. Combined with the overall theme of the passage—Rosemary reflecting on what could have been if she had more schooling—the word "sturdy" demonstrates Rosemary's *capability*. This prediction is an exact match for choice (C).

8. C   Difficulty: Medium

Category: Inference

Getting to the Answer: Reread the cited line to develop a firm grasp of the author's underlying point. Rosemary refers to Victor as a "lazy bones" (line 34) who has been given every advantage by his "doting parents . . . his future appeared bright—if he ever got out of bed, that is" (lines 42–44). Choice (C) summarizes this well.

9. D   Difficulty: Medium

Category: Global

Getting to the Answer: Identify the answer choice that most directly addresses the central theme and narrative direction of the passage. Though Victor is important in this passage, his real role is to awaken thoughts in Rosemary about her past. Most of the passage is about Rosemary and her life. Choice (D) addresses this.

CHAPTER 11

PRACTICE

Suggested Passage Map notes:

¶1: new kind of music

¶2: ragtime history

¶3: American critics dislike ragtime, but the public and Europeans like it

¶3: cont.: ragtime popular all over

¶4: ragtime musicians = natural, untrained

4. C **Difficulty:** Medium
Category: Vocab-in-Context

Getting to the Answer: Remember to avoid common meanings when answering Vocab-in-Context questions. Read the sentence without "intricate," and ask what the author is trying to communicate. Predict: The rhythm had complicated parts. Choice (C) matches.

5. A **Difficulty:** Medium
Category: Connections

Getting to the Answer: The phrase "According to the author" and the relationship clue word "effect" indicate that you should ask how items are related. The question stem cites the result and asks for the cause. Read around the cited lines. Just before, the author lists the elements of the music that produced the "curious effect." This matches choice (A).

6. B **Difficulty:** Hard
Category: Connections

Getting to the Answer: When only one part of a relationship is presented, look for the other part in the answer choices. The question asks about the basis for the author's opinion. Ask why the author thinks that the piano player is "a natural musician" (line 63). Go to the cited line and look for the reasons that the author gives: He used his "ear." Therefore, choice (B) is correct.

PERFORM

Suggested Passage Map notes:

¶1: infants learn language by differentiating sounds

¶2: detect diff. sounds

¶3: ex. of detecting diff. sounds

¶4: capability based on conditions

¶5: cond. 1 = loudness

¶5, cont.: cond. 2 = familiarity

7. D **Difficulty:** Easy
Category: Connections

Getting to the Answer: "Whether . . . whether" indicates that you should look for what needs to happen to produce a specific outcome. Refer to your Passage Map for paragraph 5. This paragraph describes how an infant can tell two voices apart when one of the voices is louder or more familiar. Because *loudness* is not an answer choice, (D) must be correct.

8. D **Difficulty:** Hard
Category: Vocab-in-Context

Getting to the Answer: Be wary of answer choices that sound or look like the word or phrase in question. This question is hard for two reasons. First, the word "predicated" is used infrequently; second, the context you need is in the following paragraph. Your Passage Map notes that, in the fourth paragraph, the author attributes the ability to distinguish sounds to two conditions; in the next paragraph, the author informs you of how each condition affects the results. Predict that the capability is *altered by* the specific conditions. Choice (D) matches this prediction.

9. C **Difficulty:** Medium
Category: Connections

Getting to the Answer: When you see the phrase "which choice best describes," and the question provides both sides of the relationship, look for the answer choice that joins the sides correctly, even if the author doesn't state it directly. Because describing this relationship is describing why the author wrote the passage, check the first and last paragraphs for clues. In the first paragraph, the author suggests that learning the language is important. In the last paragraph, the author asserts that concentrating on a single stream speeds up the process of language acquisition. Choice (C) matches.

10. C **Difficulty:** Medium
Category: Vocab-in-Context

Getting to the Answer: Be careful when a Vocab-in-Context question asks about a phrase that includes a preposition. Make sure your answer uses the correct word and preposition. Read the sentence without "attend to" and ask what the author is trying to communicate. Because the paragraph is about focusing on one specific speaker, predict: *pay attention to*. Choice (C) is correct.

ON YOUR OWN

Suggested Passage Map notes:

¶1: G happy and surprised
¶2: G's book to be published
¶3: pre-pub excitement
¶4: book based on G's hometown
¶5: excited for article about him
¶6: difficult writing process
¶7: owns his process
¶8: article = mixed feelings

1. B **Difficulty:** Medium
Category: Global

Getting to the Answer: You need to develop a firm grasp of the passage as a whole to be able to accurately summarize central ideas and characters; your Passage Map is extremely useful for this type of question. Over the course of the passage, the author describes George experiencing a wide range of emotions, including joy over his recent publication, fear over how people in his hometown will feel, and disappointment over how his story in *Rodney's Magazine* is received. Choice (B) is correct.

2. A **Difficulty:** Medium
Category: Global

Getting to the Answer: Remember that your approach to reading U.S. and World Literature passages should include keeping a running tally of a character's traits. Choice (A) is correct because the main character, George Webber, is hungry for fame and recognition. This is alluded to throughout the passage and is addressed clearly in lines 14–15 ("So . . . knocking at his door").

3. B **Difficulty:** Medium
Category: Detail

Getting to the Answer: Look at your notes for the paragraph that introduces and discusses the subtopic mentioned in the question stem. Once you have a firm grasp on the details, select the answer choice that best summarizes the subtopic. In the fourth paragraph, the author explains that George's new book is a "novel" (line 24) and that it is based on his hometown of Old Catawba (line 26). Choice (B) is correct.

4. C **Difficulty:** Easy
Category: Command of Evidence

Getting to the Answer: The correct answer choice should explicitly address the subtopic discussed in the previous question. Choice (C) is correct because it is in these lines that the author explicitly addresses that George's new book is a novel based on his experiences in his hometown of Old Catawba.

5. A **Difficulty:** Hard
Category: Vocab-in-Context

Getting to the Answer: Pay attention to the author's use of the word in the sentence and the point being made in that section of the passage. In lines 4–8 ("All he could remember . . . broad grin"), the author describes George's transition from confusion to remembrance and then excitement for his recent success at getting his book published. George is described as feeling "incredulity" because he still has trouble believing his good fortune; predict *skepticism*. Choice (A) is correct.

6. C **Difficulty:** Medium
Category: Inference

Getting to the Answer: Develop a firm grasp of the author's intent in the section cited in the question stem. Choose the answer that best describes what is implied by the text. The cited section is located within paragraph 4, which discusses the book's basis in George's hometown. In this section, George seems nervous that people from his hometown "might recognize themselves" (line 36) in characters from his new book and "be offended" (line 36). The reader can infer that the book is closely based on details of real events and people in Old Catawba. The correct answer is choice (C).

7. D   Difficulty: Medium
Category: Detail

Getting to the Answer: Review your notes for the section that discusses George's writing process: paragraph 6. In lines 61–71 ("Already . . . morning"), the author describes George's tumultuous creative periods. It is made explicit that the writing process takes a toll on George's body and mind. Choice (D) is correct.

8. B   Difficulty: Medium
Category: Command of Evidence

Getting to the Answer: The answer to the previous question will not be directly stated in the answer choice to this question. Rather, the correct answer to this question will provide the strongest support for your answer to the previous question. Identify lines 61–71 as the lines that helped you describe George's writing process. These lines are featured in choice (B), which is correct.

9. B   Difficulty: Medium
Category: Vocab-in-Context

Getting to the Answer: Reread the sentence that includes "fury" and predict another word that could be substituted. Your Passage Map notes that paragraph 6 is about George's difficult writing process. Choose a close synonym for "fury" that would describe his "creation" (line 65); *energy* or *intensity* works well. Choice (B) is correct, as agitation is the best synonym of "fury" in this particular context. The definitions of "fury" that imply indignation or animosity are not valid to describe George's creative process.

CHAPTER 12

PRACTICE

Suggested Passage Map notes:

¶1: changed rel. between U.S. press & readers
¶2: some causes = indust. & urban landscape
¶3: result = press influences pop culture

4. A   Difficulty: Medium
Category: Rhetoric

Getting to the Answer: When faced with an EXCEPT question, locate each answer choice within the passage. The answer choice you cannot find is the answer. This question stem references the author's thesis, which you know from your Passage Map is in lines 16–21: "Yet, the formative significance of these periods in the constitution of the American press aside, it was the last few decades of the nineteenth century that produced the most profound change in the relationship between the American press and its readership." If you read this sentence closely, you'll notice that the thesis has to do with how the American press related to its readership—therefore, increased readership, choice (A), is not evidence, but instead part of the original thesis, or claim, itself.

5. D   Difficulty: Hard
Category: Rhetoric

Getting to the Answer: When you see the phrase "in order to," pay attention to how the element in question fits into the overall structure of the passage. The author spends the majority of the passage discussing developments in the history of the newspaper and the causes and effects of those developments. The last sentence, which is what this question is about, discusses how the "advent of radio and television" (lines 63–64) expanded the "social position" (line 62) established by the American press. This statement points beyond the contents of the passage itself, rendering choice (D) correct.

6. B   Difficulty: Medium
Category: Rhetoric

Getting to the Answer: This question stem is rather long and involved. Make sure you take time to figure out what the question is asking before trying to predict an answer. Your Passage Map will indicate that the factors mentioned in the question stem are discussed in the second paragraph. The last sentence of that paragraph reads, "But to look at these two areas of change, one social and the other technological, as separate catalysts is to miss the point; it was their union that created a massive newspaper readership that has only grown over the past century" (lines 40–44). This conclusion supports the idea that the factors worked together, choice (B).

PERFORM

Suggested Passage Map notes:

¶1: amt. of ozone ↓
¶2: chlorine destroys ozone
¶3: 1985 - ozone hole reported
¶4: CFCs deplete ozone
¶5: choose CFC or ozone
¶6: nat. events make prob. worse
¶7: stopping CFC won't completely fix ozone
¶8: sci. working on CFC subst.

7. D   Difficulty: Hard
Category: Rhetoric

Getting to the Answer: Avoid answer choices that go beyond the scope of the passage. Even stopping all CFC production today wouldn't solve the problem, you're told, because CFCs can live for up to 400 years. Choice (D) captures the underlying point here; measures against ozone depletion may take years to have an effect.

8. A   Difficulty: Medium
Category: Rhetoric

Getting to the Answer: Sometimes, you will be given evidence and asked to find what it supports instead of the other way around. In this part of the passage, the author is providing a progress report on ozone depletion in the 1990s. He states that the layer is "depleting faster than expected" (line 53), in addition to natural events "making the problem worse" (lines 55–56). Choice (A) summarizes this idea that the situation is worsening.

9. B   Difficulty: *Medium*
Category: Rhetoric

Getting to the Answer: Use your Passage Map to summarize the purpose of any one paragraph within a passage. The last paragraph focuses on what scientists are doing about the problem, and your Passage Map states that scientists are working on a CFC substitute. Even if things are bad, the author says that "nobody can say that the situation will not improve" (lines 74–75) if people lend a hand. Choice (B) captures this positive note.

ON YOUR OWN

Suggested Passage Map notes:

¶1: human brain flexibility = plasticity

¶2: continues to grow and develop

¶3: can adapt/rewire

1. C   Difficulty: Medium
Category: Global

Getting to the Answer: You must have a firm grasp of the overall passage to understand the author's central idea. If you're uncertain, look at your Passage Map notes for the first and last paragraphs. Predict that the author is emphasizing the brain's plasticity, or flexibility. Choice (C) is correct.

2. A   Difficulty: *Medium*
Category: Detail

Getting to the Answer: When presented with a Detail question, use your Passage Map to locate the section that describes the issue raised by the question stem. Paragraph 2 discusses the brain's growth and development. In lines 26–31 ("The first few . . . synapses"), the author states that three-year-olds have "15,000 synapses per neuron" and that adults have about half of that number. Use this prediction to determine that choice (A) is correct.

3. B   Difficulty: *Easy*
Category: Command of Evidence

Getting to the Answer: The lines cited in the correct answer choice should explicitly address the topic of the previous question. Predict that the best evidence will come from lines 27–31. Choice (B) is correct.

4. B   Difficulty: *Medium*
Category: Vocab-in-Context

Getting to the Answer: The author is describing the brain as "unrivaled" (line 8) and "unique" (line 16). Predict that "sophisticated" most nearly means *complicated* or *elaborate*. Choice (B) is correct.

5. A   Difficulty: *Medium*
Category: Vocab-in-Context

Getting to the Answer: Remember to use the Kaplan Strategy for Vocab-in-Context questions. In this section of the passage, the author explains the significant capacity changes that the human brain can experience, even well into adulthood. Predict that "marked" most nearly means *significant* or *extraordinary*. Choice (A) is correct.

6. D   Difficulty: *Medium*
Category: Inference

Getting to the Answer: Reread around the lines cited in the question stem to determine what can be concluded. In this section, the author describes an experiment that showed that rats in enriched environments developed "heavier, thicker brains with more neurons and synaptic connections" (lines 69–70). The author goes on to say that these results have also been observed in humans. Predict that the results from the experiments show that enriched environments positively impact both rats and humans. Choice (D) is correct.

7. C   Difficulty: *Medium*
Category: Global

Getting to the Answer: Use your Passage Map to locate the appropriate section of the passage. In the second paragraph, the author explains that the brain's ongoing flexibility was guessed by William James (lines 42–46). The author then details how this flexibility was proven in late twentieth-century experiments (lines 49–73). Predict that the brain's flexibility was hypothesized over 100 years ago but only recently proved correct. Choice (C) is correct.

8. B   Difficulty: *Medium*
Category: Command of Evidence

Getting to the Answer: Remember to use Kaplan's Strategy for Command of Evidence questions. In the previous question, lines 42–46 and lines 49–73 were used to describe the various scientific views of brain flexibility over time. The transition between these two sections, "Then, several provocative experiments dramatically complicated conventional thinking about the human brain" (lines 46–48), is an excellent summary of the change in thinking over time. Predict that the best evidence for the answer to the previous question involves lines 42–48. Choice (B) is correct.

9. B **Difficulty:** Medium
Category: Vocab-in-Context

Getting to the Answer: Read around the cited line and word for context to determine the correct answer. The author describes the rats' environment as being "enriched," or enhanced, by more stimuli than the environment of the control group. Predict that "enriched" most nearly means *enhanced*. Choice (B) is correct.

10. D **Difficulty:** Easy
Category: Vocab-in-Context

Getting to the Answer: Make sure to avoid common meanings when answering Vocab-in-Context questions. In this sentence, the author is referring to new stimuli's ability to "mold the brain's . . . architecture" (lines 88–89). Predict that "architecture" most nearly means *structure*. The correct answer is (D).

CHAPTER 13

PRACTICE

3. C **Difficulty:** Hard
Category: Sentence Formation

Getting to the Answer: Make sure introductory modifiers are modifying the correct items. The introductory modifier phrase in this sentence is "During their seasonal migration." However, "there are large numbers migrating" appears after this phrase. As written, this sentence states that the large numbers are migrating, not birds and bats. Even though both (C) and D correct the error, only choice (C) retains the original meaning: that the number of birds and bats migrating is large.

4. B **Difficulty:** Medium
Category: Sentence Formation

Getting to the Answer: Make sure verbs and verb phrases in a sentence are parallel in structure. The underlined word "assessing" does not match the sentence's prior verb: "to allow." "Assessing" should be "to assess," which is choice (B).

5. A **Difficulty:** Medium
Category: Usage

Getting to the Answer: Make sure verbs agree with their subjects in person and number. This sentence is correct as written because the word "data" is the plural form of the singular "datum." Therefore, the plural verb "provide" is necessary. Choice (A) is correct.

PERFORM

6. D **Difficulty:** Medium
Category: Effective Language Use

Getting to the Answer: When you see an underlined portion with no obvious grammatical errors, check to make sure the style and tone are appropriate for the passage. As written, this segment uses the cliché "Life goes on," which is inappropriate in style and tone. Choices B and C also use clichés and overly familiar language, making choice (D) the correct answer.

7. C **Difficulty:** Easy
Category: Usage

Getting to the Answer: Make sure you don't confuse possessive determiners, contractions, and adverbs. "It's" is a contraction for "it is," which makes no sense in the context of the underlined portion, and "their" is plural, but this pronoun refers to "the business," which is singular. The "it's" in the passage should be the possessive form: "its," which matches choice (C).

8. B **Difficulty:** Hard
Category: Usage

Getting to the Answer: Whenever you see the word "it," make sure you know exactly what it is referring to. In this sentence, it's ambiguous what "it" refers to, so replacing the pronoun "it" with the noun it refers to is necessary. It is the "sole proprietorship" that "does not come without its share of disadvantages," so the answer is choice (B).

9. A **Difficulty:** Easy
Category: Usage

Getting to the Answer: When a preposition is underlined, make sure it's used correctly. The word preceding the preposition is "separate." When things are separate, they are separate *from* each other, which means the correct preposition is being used, and the sentence is correct as written, choice (A).

10. D **Difficulty:** Medium
Category: Usage

Getting to the Answer: Use *who* when the pronoun acts as the subject of a sentence and *whom* when the pronoun acts as the object. Always use the objective form when using a pronoun in a prepositional phrase, so "with whom" is grammatically correct. "Who" comes after "with," a preposition, in this sentence. Therefore, "who" should be "whom" so that it's correct as the object of a preposition. Choice (D) is correct.

11. C **Difficulty:** Hard
Category: Sentence Formation

Getting to the Answer: This sentence needs to be separated into two independent clauses, because, as written, it is a run-on sentence. One way to correct a run-on sentence is to separate the two independent clauses with a semicolon. The only answer choice that corrects the run-on is choice (C), which uses a semicolon and a comma after "however."

12. D   Difficulty: Medium
Category: Effective Language Use

Getting to the Answer: Avoid the passive voice whenever possible. The underlined portion is written in the passive voice. Choices B and (D) both correct this issue. However, choice (D) is more succinct and, therefore, the correct answer.

13. D   Difficulty: Medium
Category: Quantitative

Getting to the Answer: Read answer choices to Infographics questions carefully so you don't get caught in a misused-word trap. As written, this sentence claims that partnerships are less lucrative than sole proprietorships. The graph, however, indicates the opposite, as each of the partnership bars soars above the corresponding sole proprietorship bars. You need to find the answer choice that states partnerships are *more* lucrative than sole proprietorships, which is choice (D).

14. D   Difficulty: Medium
Category: Usage

Getting to the Answer: When you see a pronoun underlined, always check to make sure it refers to a clearly identifiable noun. It's unclear what "it" is referring to. The beginning of the sentence mentions the business being sold; therefore, "it" should be "this sale," choice (D).

ON YOUR OWN

1. C   Difficulty: Medium
Category: Effective Language Use

Getting to the Answer: When a phrase is underlined, look for the choice that best conveys the author's intended meaning in the context of both the sentence and paragraph. In this sentence, the author is addressing the perceived need that people had after World War II to move away from crowded, dirty urban centers. Choice (C) is correct because the suburbs were a response to this need.

2. A   Difficulty: Easy
Category: Punctuation

Getting to the Answer: When an underlined section includes punctuation, make sure that the punctuation enhances the reader's understanding of the passage. If the punctuation harms understanding, consider changing it or eliminating it altogether. In this case, the comma included in the underlined section clearly separates an independent and dependent clause. No punctuation at all would create a run-on, and words are not being omitted, so there is no reason to use the ellipsis. The semicolon is used to separate two independent clauses and is incorrect in this context. Because the sentence is correct as written, choice (A) must be correct.

3. B   Difficulty: Easy
Category: Effective Language Use

Getting to the Answer: Look for the clearest, most straightforward wording of the idea underlined in the passage and avoid answers that contain unnecessarily complicated syntax. In the underlined section, the author is simply trying to address the self-sufficiency of the sub-urbs. Choice (B) is correct because it conveys this idea in the clearest manner.

4. C   Difficulty: Hard
Category: Development

Getting to the Answer: The last sentence of a para-graph usually ties the different claims in that paragraph together. In this paragraph, the author introduces the tension between the desire to move away from the city and the need to return to the city for work and leisure. Choice (C) is correct because it effectively expresses that dichotomy.

5. D   Difficulty: Medium
Category: Effective Language Use

Getting to the Answer: When a single word is underlined, make sure it clearly conveys the author's intended meaning in the context of both the sentence and paragraph. The author explains how suburbanites do not want to be too far away from things that can be found in the city. Therefore, it makes sense to describe these things using a positive adjective such as "benefits" rather than using a negative adjective. Choice (D) is correct.

6. A **Difficulty:** Medium
Category: Punctuation

Getting to the Answer: One use of commas, like parentheses, is to set aside unnecessary information. Choice (A) is correct because the clause "while offering a respite from city pollution" needs to be set aside by punctuation. The existing use of commas is the best available option, meaning that no change is necessary.

7. A **Difficulty:** Easy
Category: Usage

Getting to the Answer: When a single verb is underlined, make sure it agrees with its subject in person and number and that the tense makes sense in the context of the sentence and paragraph. Choice (A) is correct because "have" agrees with its subject ("laws") and is the correct tense in the context of the sentence and paragraph.

8. D **Difficulty:** Easy
Category: Effective Language Use

Getting to the Answer: When an underlined portion is grammatically correct, look for words or phrases that differ from the overall tone of the passage. Most of the answer choices for the question depart from the professional tone of the passage. Choice (D) is correct because it maintains the author's meaning and tone.

9. C **Difficulty:** Medium
Category: Effective Language Use

Getting to the Answer: Select the answer choice that clearly conveys the author's position with the most effective syntax. Choice (C) is correct because it clearly and concisely demonstrates the author's opinion. The other answer choices relate the same thing, but with many unnecessary words.

10. B **Difficulty:** Hard
Category: Quantitative

Getting to the Answer: Study the graph to develop a sound understanding of the information it is showing. Choose the answer choice that accurately describes what the graph displays. The graph shows that population growth in primary cities outpaced growth in the suburbs from 2010 to 2011, a reversal of the dominant trend of the previous decade. Choice (B) is correct because it accurately describes the graph's data and draws a reasonable conclusion from it.

11. A **Difficulty:** Hard
Category: Organization

Getting to the Answer: Make sure sentences are presented in the most logical order that suits the passage's clarity and narrative. Choice (A) is correct because the information from the graph serves as logical support to this paragraph's first sentence. The population shift back to primary cities makes sense in the context of growing anti-suburb sentiment.

CHAPTER 14

PRACTICE

5. D   Difficulty: Easy
Category: Usage

Getting to the Answer: The noun closest to an underlined verb may not be the subject of that verb. It is important to read enough of the sentence to identify the subject of the underlined verb. In this sentence, the noun closest to the underlined verb is "Pennsylvania," a singular noun that agrees with "was." Rereading the sentence reveals that "Pennsylvania" is part of a phrase that modifies the actual subject of the sentence, "Canvases." Choice (D) is correct.

6. B   Difficulty: Medium
Category: Usage

Getting to the Answer: The correct preposition can often only be determined in the context of the sentence. This sentence states that the Hudson River School was suited to the task of competing with Europe. The job of the prepositional phrase is to explain how that was accomplished. Choice (B) conveys this precisely.

7. C   Difficulty: Hard
Category: Usage

Getting to the Answer: If you can't identify who or what a pronoun refers to, the pronoun's antecedent is unclear. Because the paragraph mentions only Europe and not Europeans, eliminate D. In the previous sentences, the passage discusses "writers" and their interest in the influence of "wilderness" on their "nationality." Choice (C) is correct.

8. A   Difficulty: Easy
Category: Usage

Getting to the Answer: Look for clues that indicate when some things are being compared. Then, check to make sure that the comparison is logical, parallel, and properly phrased. At the beginning of the sentence, the phrase "Unlike European painters" tells you that the writer is comparing "European painters" to something else. Logically, that something else must also be painters. Choice (A) logically compares painters to painters.

PERFORM

9. C   Difficulty: Easy
Category: Usage

Getting to the Answer: Adjectives in the comparative form compare only two items or people. Use the superlative form to compare three or more items or people. In context, it is clear that many "financial panics" have occurred in U.S. history. As a result, the superlative form must be used when comparing them. Because the superlative of "bad" is "worst," there is no need to add "most" to indicate the comparison. Choice (C) is correct.

10. A   Difficulty: Medium
Category: Usage

Getting to the Answer: When nouns in a sentence relate to each other, they need to agree in number. The sentence discusses "types of gadgets" and gives two examples. Each of the examples must match the plural nouns "types" and "gadgets." Choice (A) makes all the related nouns plural. While D uses the plural forms, it uses an improper connection between the two nouns.

11. B   Difficulty: Hard
Category: Usage

Getting to the Answer: Remember that a pronoun and its antecedent may not be close to each other. The possessive pronoun "its" correctly indicates the owner of the loan as "investors," but does not match in number. Choice (B) correctly uses the plural pronoun "their." Choices C and D are incorrect because they are singular.

12. D   Difficulty: Easy
Category: Usage

Getting to the Answer: Remember that *barely*, *hardly*, and *scarcely* imply a negative; when paired with explicitly negative words, they create a double negative, which is grammatically incorrect. Adding the word "hardly" when the predicate contains "could not" creates a double negative and is incorrect. Choice (D) corrects the error by eliminating "hardly."

13. C   **Difficulty:** Medium

Category: Usage

Getting to the Answer: A pronoun is ambiguous when its antecedent is either missing or unclear. To find the antecedent for the underlined pronoun, read the previous sentence and think about the focus of the passage. Although the previous sentence has more than one possible antecedent, in the context of the passage, choice (C) is the clearest and most relevant.

14. B   **Difficulty:** Medium

Category: Usage

Getting to the Answer: The pronoun "which" may be used only to refer to things or animals. "Who" and "whom" may be used only to refer to people. In this sentence, the pronoun "which" is used incorrectly to refer to "investors," who are people. To determine whether "who" or "whom" is correct, substitute the appropriate third-person pronoun for "who" or "whom," and read the sentence. Choice (B) is correct.

15. D   **Difficulty:** Hard

Category: Usage

Getting to the Answer: Idiom questions often hinge on correct preposition usage. The preposition must convey the correct meaning. Read the sentence carefully to understand the meaning that the preposition must convey. The "pressure" was on the "market," not "on everyone." Choice (D) conveys the sense that the sellers were the source of the pressure.

16. A   **Difficulty:** Medium

Category: Usage

Getting to the Answer: Subjects and verbs must agree in person and number. Singular subjects are paired with singular verbs, and plural subjects are paired with plural verbs. Although many things and people make up a market, the noun is singular and requires a singular verb. Because the market is a thing being spoken about, it takes the third-person verb. The verb "to start" is a regular verb, and its third-person singular form is "starts." Choice (A) provides the third-person singular verb.

ON YOUR OWN

1. A   **Difficulty:** Medium

Category: Effective Language Use

Getting to the Answer: When a single word is underlined, make sure that it is the word that best conveys the author's intended meaning in the context of both the sentence and paragraph. No change is necessary. One of the definitions of "propagate" is "to cause to spread out" over a great area or population. This sense of the word is correct in the context of this sentence and paragraph. Choice (A) is correct.

2. D   **Difficulty:** Medium

Category: Punctuation

Getting to the Answer: When an underlined sentence fragment includes a parenthetical remark, look for the answer that shows the correct way to punctuate that clause. Choice (D) is correct. "Such as murder" is a parenthetical remark because it is not necessary for the sentence to be complete. It is best set aside by two commas.

3. B   **Difficulty:** Easy

Category: Punctuation

Getting to the Answer: An underlined section that includes punctuation requires an assessment of the punctuation. Choose the answer that provides the correct punctuation for the sentence and context. Choice (B) is correct. The sentence cannot be correctly combined with the following sentence using a semicolon, so a question mark is the only appropriate option to follow the word "child."

4. A   **Difficulty:** Medium

Category: Organization

Getting to the Answer: Make sure sentences are presented in the most logical order for the clarity of the passage. Choice (A) is correct, as the current placement is the correct one for this paragraph. Moving sentence 2 before sentence 1 would be confusing for the reader, and moving it later in the paragraph would interfere with the author's transition to the next paragraph.

5. A   Difficulty: Hard
Category: Development

Getting to the Answer: Determine whether the underlined sentence is effective and correct in its current form or whether one of the other options more clearly develops the author's ideas. No change is necessary. The current sentence covers all of the points it needs to in order to address the questions posed in the previous paragraph. It also serves as an introduction to the new paragraph. Choice (A) is correct.

6. C   Difficulty: Medium
Category: Effective Language Use

Getting to the Answer: Pay attention to the construction of the sentence (its syntax). Choose the option that correctly and effectively conveys the author's narrative intent, while also preserving additional points the author is trying to make. Choice (C) is correct because it uses a more effective and clear active voice sentence structure. Choice D is also active voice (unlike choices A and B), but it leaves out the author's additional point about the exchange being "one of the most terrifying conversations in all literature."

7. B   Difficulty: Medium
Category: Effective Language Use

Getting to the Answer: Determine whether the underlined sentence is effective in its current form. Pay attention to word choice and precision of language. In this case, the original sentence is not grammatically incorrect, but there are less wordy options that get the point across clearly. Choice (B) is the best option, as its language is precise and helpful to the overall narrative.

8. D   Difficulty: Medium
Category: Development

Getting to the Answer: For the first sentence of a paragraph, look for the answer choice that embodies the central idea of the paragraph while also serving as an effective connection to, or transition from, the previous paragraph. Choice (D) is correct because it serves as a logical and effective transition from the previous paragraph. Here, the author is shifting from describing the unsavory aspects of fairy tales to explaining a theory for why they evolved to be that way.

9. A   Difficulty: Medium
Category: Effective Language Use

Getting to the Answer: When a single word is underlined, make sure that it is the word that best conveys the author's intended meaning in the context of both the sentence and paragraph. No change is necessary because "fantastic" is the best option for this context; the author is creating a parallel between "realistic" threats in the real world and the unrealistic elements of fairy tales. Choice (A) is correct.

10. B   Difficulty: Medium
Category: Sentence Formation

Getting to the Answer: When an underlined section includes the connection between two sentences, consider whether the two sentences should remain separate. If they should be joined, choose the best option for doing so. Choice (B) is correct because these two sentences need to be combined, and a comma is the correct way to do so in this instance. If kept separate, the second sentence is actually a fragment.

11. C   Difficulty: Medium
Category: Development

Getting to the Answer: The final sentence serves the important dual function of concluding the paragraph and the passage. Choose the option that is true to the author's intent for both. Choice (C) is correct because it effectively states the author's main idea that violence in children's media has been present for centuries in fairy tales. It also connects the main idea of the passage to the main idea of the final paragraph: fairy tales possibly helped children navigate the dangers of real life.

CHAPTER 15

PRACTICE

4. D **Difficulty:** Medium
Category: Punctuation

Getting to the Answer: Make sure to use the correct punctuation to connect independent clauses. "However" cannot join two independent clauses with just a comma. It can join them with a semicolon or start a new sentence, as long as "however" is still followed by a comma. Choice (D) is correct.

5. D **Difficulty:** Medium
Category: Punctuation

Getting to the Answer: Remember to use punctuation to separate nonessential information from the rest of a sentence. In this case, it might be useful information to know what the author says the restorers claimed; however, the sentence still makes logical sense without the information. Only (D) properly sets off the parenthetical (nonrestrictive) phrase.

6. B **Difficulty:** Easy
Category: Punctuation

Getting to the Answer: Make sure you don't confuse possessive determiners, contractions, and adverbs. "It's" is a contraction for "it is," which makes no sense in the context of the underlined portion. "Their" can refer only to people, not objects. The "it's" in the passage should be possessive, which is "its," (B).

7. A **Difficulty:** Medium
Category: Punctuation

Getting to the Answer: Because the underlined portion contains a dash, find the other dash and check whether the information inside the dashes is essential to the logic of the sentence. The information inside the dashes is nonessential, so the underlined portion is correct as written, (A).

PERFORM

8. D **Difficulty:** Medium
Category: Punctuation

Getting to the Answer: When you see an underlined segment featuring a noun followed by "the," make sure the correct punctuation is being used. As written, the sentence to which the underlined segment belongs is a run-on because of the lack of punctuation between the introductory phrase ("Unlike most city museums") and the independent clause that follows ("the design museum displays . . ."). Choice (D) corrects the error by introducing a comma between "museums" and "the."

9. C **Difficulty:** Hard
Category: Punctuation

Getting to the Answer: When a period is underlined, make sure it's being used correctly. The second clause is dependent and, with a period, creates a fragment, so eliminate A. You can eliminate B because a semicolon won't fix the error. Choices C and D are both grammatically correct but have different meanings. Choice D, without the comma, suggests that the "spotlights" were breaking down barriers. When separated with a comma, the phrase modifies the entire preceding clause, which makes (C) correct.

10. D **Difficulty:** Medium
Category: Punctuation

Getting to the Answer: Check whether the sentence makes sense without "however." It does. When "however" is used within a clause, it is nonrestrictive and must be set off by commas. Choice (D) is correct.

11. A **Difficulty:** Hard
Category: Punctuation

Getting to the Answer: Adjectives are single-word modifiers that modify nouns. When two adjectives modify the same noun, they must be separated by either a comma or the conjunction "and." The adjectives "impressive" and "innovative" both modify "products." Choice (A) properly separates the items in the list.

12. C **Difficulty:** Medium
Category: Punctuation

Getting to the Answer: When you encounter two nouns in a row, check to see whether the possessive form is needed. Who or what has "visitors"? The "museum." Is "museum" singular or plural? "A design museum" is singular, so choose the singular possessive. Choice (C) is correct.

13. B **Difficulty:** Medium
Category: Punctuation

Getting to the Answer: When a comma is underlined, check to see whether it can be replaced by a period. The clause before the comma can stand on its own, but the rest of the sentence can't. A quick read indicates that the verb "show" has the same subject as "illustrate," forming a compound predicate with "museums" as the subject. The comma is unnecessary. Choice (B) correctly eliminates the punctuation.

14. D **Difficulty:** Medium
Category: Punctuation

Getting to the Answer: Remember that dashes are used to indicate a hesitation or break in thought. Read the sentence without the verbs. The sentence still makes sense, signaling that the verbs are either nonessential information or an aside. Choice (D) sets the information off with a dash.

15. B **Difficulty:** Easy
Category: Punctuation

Getting to the Answer: With two nouns in a row, check to see whether the possessive is needed. Who or what has "humorous aspects"? The "societies." Is "societies" singular or plural? The author never refers to multiple societies, so choose the singular possessive, which is (B).

ON YOUR OWN

1. D **Difficulty:** Hard
Category: Development

Getting to the Answer: With an underlined "and," make sure to identify what job the conjunction is doing in the

sentence. Because both clauses can stand on their own as sentences, you need to fix the run-on in the best possible way. This question is difficult because choices B, C, and D all correct the grammatical error. Carefully read each answer choice into the sentence. Choice (D) makes the clause dependent, giving information about the professionals' complaints.

2. C **Difficulty:** Medium
Category: Punctuation

Getting to the Answer: When an underlined apostrophe appears with a noun, determine the noun's number. Look for context clues that tell you how many "professions" possess "status." Logically, each profession has its own status. In the previous sentence, the author refers to "groups" that professionals are part of. Choice (C) properly uses the plural possessive form.

3. A **Difficulty:** Hard
Category: Sentence Formation

Getting to the Answer: It might seem like the comma is unnecessarily separating the predicate from the object, but reading around the underlined section shows that the comma closes a nonrestrictive phrase. The underlined portion needs no change, so choice (A) is correct.

4. D **Difficulty:** Hard
Category: Development

Getting to the Answer: Whenever you have the chance to omit the underlined portion, carefully consider what function the underlined portion is performing. As written, the dash correctly sets off the phrase. However, the phrase itself contains information that shifts the focus of the passage. Choice (D) is correct.

5. B **Difficulty:** Medium
Category: Punctuation

Getting to the Answer: When you see a phrase set off by commas, always read the sentence without the phrase. In this case, you need the information enclosed by the commas; without the information, the sentence doesn't make sense. The "aspirants" must be restricted to those whom the author discusses. Choice (B) correctly removes both commas.

6. D   Difficulty: Medium
Category: Development

Getting to the Answer: When a transition is underlined, quickly summarize each paragraph and how the ideas are connected. Paragraph 2 talks about how it used to be, while paragraph 3 discusses how it is now. Things have changed. When things are different, look for the answer that provides contrast, which is choice (D).

7. A   Difficulty: Easy
Category: Usage

Getting to the Answer: "Who" and "whom" refer only to people; "when" refers to time. Only (A) has the pronoun match.

8. B   Difficulty: Hard
Category: Effective Language Use

Getting to the Answer: Check whether a period is the best way to join clauses. The period correctly separates the two sentences, but the change is abrupt. Choice (B) provides a better connection by showing the logical connection between the two clauses.

9. C   Difficulty: Easy
Category: Punctuation

Getting to the Answer: If an underlined comma does not connect two independent clauses, ask what else it is doing. Here, the comma is separating items in a list containing only two elements. There is no need for the comma, so choice (C) is correct.

10. B   Difficulty: Medium
Category: Effective Language Use

Getting to the Answer: Identify the overall tone of the passage. The tone in this passage is formal and informative. The author is careful to explain each idea introduced. The phrase "jumped on the bandwagon" does not fit because it is casual and, while giving a sense of the responses, does not clarify the author's meaning. Choice (B) matches the overall tone and provides a detailed explanation.

11. D   Difficulty: Easy
Category: Effective Language Use

Getting to the Answer: When you can't identify a grammatical error, make sure to check for a stylistic error. In the context of the sentence, "sustain" and "preserve" mean the same thing. Choice (D) eliminates the redundancy error.